What the Bible Is All About

Bible Handbook

New International Version

Henrietta C. Mears

What the Bible Is All About

Bible Handbook

New International Version

Regal

From Gospel Light
Ventura, California, U.S.A.

PUBLISHED BY REGAL BOOKS
FROM GOSPEL LIGHT
VENTURA, CALIFORNIA, U.S.A.
PRINTED IN THE U.S.A.

Regal Books is a ministry of Gospel Light, a Christian publisher dedicated to serving the local church. We believe God's vision for Gospel Light is to provide church leaders with biblical, user-friendly materials that will help them evangelize, disciple and minister to children, youth and families.

It is our prayer that this Regal book will help you discover biblical truth for your own life and help you meet the needs of others. May God richly bless you.

For a free catalog of resources from Regal Books/Gospel Light, please call your Christian supplier or contact us at 1-800-4-GOSPEL *or* www.regalbooks.com.

Cover Design by Robert Williams
Interior Design by Britt Rocchio
Edited by Bayard Taylor and Virginia Woodard

What the Bible Is All About® is a registered trademark of Gospel Light. Any use of this name is prohibited without the express written consent of Gospel Light.

For more information on the life of Henrietta Mears, see *Dream Big: The Henrietta Mears Story* (Ventura, CA: Regal Books, 1990). ISBN 0-8307-1254-2

Library of Congress Cataloging-in-Publication Data
Mears, Henrietta C. (Henrietta Cornelia), 1890-1963
    [What the Bible is all about]
    What the Bible is all about handbook / Henrietta C. Mears.
        p. cm.
Includes index.
Originally published: What the Bible is all about. Ventura, Calif.:
Regal Books, c1999.
    ISBN 0-8307-3085-0 (NIV)
    ISBN 0-8307-3086-9 (KJV)
    1.   Bible—Criticism, interpretation, etc. I. Title
    BS511.3 .M43 2002
    220.6—dc21

14 15 16 17 18 19 20 / 15 14 13 12 11 10

Rights for publishing this book in other languages are contracted by Gospel Light Worldwide, the international nonprofit ministry of Gospel Light. Gospel Light Worldwide also provides publishing and technical assistance to international publishers dedicated to producing Sunday School and Vacation Bible School curricula and books in the languages of the world. For additional information, visit www.gospellightworldwide.org; write to Gospel Light Worldwide, P.O. Box 3875, Ventura, CA 93006; or send an e-mail to info@gospellightworldwide.org.

Contents

Part Two: The New Testament

Part Three: Appendices

Foreword

Dr. Billy Graham

Millions of people today are searching for a reliable voice of authority. The Word of God is the only real authority we have. His Word sheds light on human nature, world problems and human suffering. But beyond that, it clearly reveals the way to God.

The message of the Bible is the message of Jesus Christ who said, "I am the way, the truth, and the life" (John 14:6, *KJV*). It is the story of salvation; the story of your redemption and mine through Christ; the story of life, of peace, of eternity.

Our faith is not dependent upon human knowledge and scientific advance, but upon the unmistakable message of the Word of God.

The Bible has a great tradition and a magnificent heritage. It contains 66 books written over a period of several hundred years by many different men. Yet the message, divinely inspired by the Holy Spirit, is clear throughout. The 66 books become one.

The Bible is old; yet it is ever new. It is the most modern book in the world today. There is a false notion that a book as ancient as the Bible cannot speak to modern needs. People somehow think that in an age of scientific achievement, when knowledge has increased more in the past 25 years than in all preceding centuries put together, this ancient Book is out-of-date. But to all who read and love the Bible, it is relevant for our generation.

It is in the Holy Scriptures that we find the answers to life's ultimate questions: Where did I come from? Why am I here? Where am I going? What is the purpose of my existence?

One of the greatest needs in the Church today is to come back to the Scriptures as the basis of authority, and to study them prayerfully in dependence on the Holy Spirit. When we read God's Word, we fill our hearts with His words, and God is speaking to us.

William Lyon Phelps, called the most beloved professor in America, and one-time president of Yale University, made the oft-quoted statement, "I thoroughly believe in a university education for both men and women; but I believe a knowledge of the Bible without a college course is more valuable than a college course without the Bible."

One of the greatest tragedies today is that, although the Bible is an available, open book, it is a closed book to millions—either because they leave it unread or because they read it without applying its teachings to themselves. No greater tragedy can befall a person or a nation than that of paying lip service to a Bible left unread or to a way of life not followed.

The Bible, the greatest document available for the human race, needs to be opened, read and believed. One survey indicated that only 12 percent of the people who said they believe the Bible actually read it every day; 34 percent read it only once a week, and 42 percent read it only once in a great while.

This book, *What the Bible Is All About*, will help make the reading and study of God's Word interesting, challenging and useful. We commend it to you.

Preface

William T. Greig Jr.
Chairman, Gospel Light

In the early 1950s my wife, Doris, and I were invited to teach the high school class in a small Baptist church in a suburb of Minneapolis, Minnesota. We were newly married and accepted the challenge with some trepidation. We agreed we would do better if we divided the group. I would teach the boys and Doris would teach the girls.

Doris and I both wanted to understand the Bible better. Doris had become a believer in a Billy Graham meeting at a Youth for Christ conference about two years earlier. I was fortunate to have been brought up in a Christian home and had been taught the Word by my parents since childhood. Yet we each hungered to know more of the Word. We also were aware that the kids in Sunday School knew precious little of Bible truth. So we decided to tackle the daunting task of teaching each of our classes through the entire Bible—all sixty-six books—in one year, fifty-two weeks. We secured a high school course then published by Gospel Light called the *Scripture Panorama Series*.

This classic course was authored by Dr. Henrietta C. Mears, founder of Gospel Light. She believed firmly that no young person in her Sunday School should be able to say what a young college man had told her many years before: "If I had to pass a test in the Bible, I would absolutely flunk!" So she wrote this "crash" course for people who knew little if anything about the Bible, but who wanted to know enough to understand the essential message of each of the books as they studied or read devotionally. The central theme of the entire Word of God is His dealings with His people and His provision of salvation through faith in Jesus Christ the Messiah—promised throughout the Old Testament and revealed fully in the New Testament.

Doris and I learned much that year, and so did our classes. It was intense, but rewarding. Nothing of great value is ever accomplished without consistent effort invested on our part. You only get out what you put in. So it was with this course. It was a spiritual growing experience for all, and it helped us both to grow in grace and in our relationship to Jesus Christ and to each other, not to mention our class members.

In the mid-1950s I was challenged by Richard Woike, president of the Christian Business Men's Committee, to read through the Bible every year. He would buy a new Bible each year on his birthday and read through it from Genesis through Revelation in one year. I liked the idea, but got bogged down in Leviticus and Numbers, as many do. So I developed my own plan, which I found particularly rewarding. I began in Genesis, Job and Matthew and read a page or two of each section every day. This took me through the entire Bible in one year. It was rewarding, particularly having this book *What the Bible Is All About* at my side, to answer hard questions and give me perspective about each book.

I decided I wanted more time each day for personal reflection and cross-referencing, so I developed a two-year plan, which also allowed me time to adopt Richard Woike's other discipline: He wrote in the head margin of every page the key message he learned from that page. This Bible reading plan is adapted in the form of bookmarks, included with this volume. You will find them at the back of the book. Keeping a copy of *What the Bible Is All About* on hand as you read through the Bible will give you an unforgettable experience. You will grow both in your knowledge of the Word of God and also in your relationship to the Living Word, the Lord Jesus Christ.

In the early 1960s, a friend in the Billy Graham Association (BGA) headquarters in Minneapolis inquired about creating a book out of the *Scripture Panorama Series* teacher's books. Working together we jointly published *What the Bible Is All*

About. Dr. Graham, who had a close relationship with Henrietta Mears going back to the late 1940s, wrote the foreword. A copy was given by the BGA to each person who responded to Dr. Graham's invitations in crusades, on TV or on radio. Millions of copies were given away through the years.

Dr. Mears believed firmly that the Bible is the authority of the teacher so the teacher should teach directly from an open Bible, though some of us need outlines and personal notes to be more effective. Teachers and class members alike will grow deeper in their knowledge of the truth and their personal relationship to Jesus Christ, the Living Word, as they are taught spiritual truth directly from the Bible by the Holy Spirit. Jesus promised that His Holy Spirit would lead us into all truth (John 17:1).

George Barna tells us that at the close of the twentieth century the vast majority of people, including many Christians, do not believe in absolute truth. According to Barna, 71 percent of all adults say there is no such thing as absolute truth. This is divided into groups: 78 percent among baby busters; 68 percent among born-again Christians; 71 percent among those who attend a mainline Protestant church; 75 percent among those who attend a Catholic church. This book can be used by the Holy Spirit to open His Word to us and teach us God's absolute truth, Jesus Christ.

How to Use This Book

The purpose of this book is to familiarize the reader with the Bible through a general overview. This book contains 52 chapters, spanning from Genesis to Revelation. These chapters can be studied one chapter a week for the year. At the beginning of each chapter is listed a Selected Bible Reading section, suggesting a Scripture reading for each day of the week related to the chapter.

Appendix 2 at the back of the book—"Becoming a Member of God's Family"—explains how to become a Christian and then how to live as a Christian.

"A Glossary of Bible Words" in appendix 3 explains unfamiliar words that may be new to the reader, including a pronunciation guide for many of the words.

Chapter 1

Understanding the Bible

The Bible portrays Jesus Christ, the Savior of the World

Selected Bible Readings

Sunday:	God-Given (2 Timothy 3:10-17)
Monday:	Should Be Treasured (Deuteronomy 11:1-9; Joshua 1:8,9)
Tuesday:	Should Be Kept (Psalm 119:9-18)
Wednesday:	A Lamp (Psalm 119:105-117)
Thursday:	Food (Isaiah 55:1-11; Matthew 4:4)
Friday:	Fulfilled (Luke 24:36-45)
Saturday:	Complete (Revelation 22:8-21)

"Behind and beneath the Bible, above and beyond the Bible, is the God of the Bible."

The Bible is God's written revelation of His will to humanity.

Its central theme is salvation through Jesus Christ.

The Bible contains 66 books, written by 40 authors, covering a period of approximately 1,600 years.

The Old Testament was written mostly in Hebrew (a few short passages in Aramaic). About 100 years (or more) before the Christian Era the entire Old Testament was translated into the Greek language. Remember, our English Bible is a translation from these original languages.

The word "Bible" comes from the Greek word *biblos*, meaning "book."

The word "testament" means "covenant," or agreement. The Old Testament is the covenant God made with people about their salvation before Christ came. The New Testament is the agreement God made with people about their salvation after Christ came.

In the Old Testament we find the covenant of law. In the New Testament we find the covenant of grace that came through Jesus Christ. One led into the other (Galatians 3:17-25).

The Old commences what the New completes.

The Old gathers around Mount Sinai—

The New around Mount Calvary.

The Old is associated with Moses—

The New with Christ (John 1:17).

The authors were kings and princes, poets and philosophers, prophets and statesmen. Some were learned in all the arts of the times and others were unschooled fishermen. Other books soon are out-of-date, but this Book spans the centuries.

Most books must be adapted to age, but old and young alike love this Book.

Most books are provincial and only interest the people in whose language it was written, but not this Book. No one ever stops to think it was written in what are now dead languages.

The Old Testament begins with God (Genesis 1:1).

The New Testament begins with Christ (Matthew 1:1).

From Adam to Abraham we have the history of the human race.

From Abraham to Christ we have the history of the chosen race.

From Christ on we have the history of the Church.

"Most people's knowledge of history is like a string of graduated pearls without the string," said a historian. This statement seems to be especially true of Bible history. Many people know the Bible characters and the principal events, but they are hopelessly lost when they are called upon to connect the stories in order. Anyone who has experienced the thrill of learning to place the individual characters in their right setting as to place and time can realize the difference it makes in the enjoyment of God's Word.

Pick up the "pearls" in the Scriptures and string them into

order from Genesis to Revelation so that you can "think through" the Bible story.

Interesting Facts

Old Testament Books
Law—five
Historical—twelve
Poetical—five
Prophetical—seventeen
   (Major, five; Minor, twelve)

New Testament Books
The New Testament was written to reveal to us the character and teaching of Jesus Christ, the mediator of the New Covenant, by at least eight men, four of whom—Matthew, John, Peter and Paul— were apostles; two—Mark and Luke—were companions of the apostles; and two—James and Jude—were brothers of Jesus. The books were written at various times during the second half of the first century.

The books in the New Testament may be grouped thus:
Gospels—four
History—one
Prophecy—one
Epistles—twenty-one
   (Pauline, thirteen; General, eight)

God, humanity, sin, redemption, justification, sanctification, glorification: In two words—grace, glory. In one word—Jesus.

Christ quotes from twenty-two Old Testament books: in Matthew, nineteen times; in Mark, fifteen times; in Luke, twenty-five; in John, eleven.

The book of Hebrews quotes the Old Testament (quotations or allusions) eighty-five times.

Revelation quotes the Old Testament 245 times.

The *King James Version* contains these interesting elements:
Number of verses—31,102
Number of words—775,693

Longest chapter—Psalm 119
Shortest chapter—Psalm 117
Longest verse—Esther 8:9
Shortest verse—John 11:35
Longest book in the Old Testament—Psalms
Longest book in the New Testament—Luke
Most chapters in the New Testament—Matthew.

Old Testament—Principal Places
The twelve principal places around which the history of the Old Testament is written are:

1. Eden (Genesis 1—3)
2. Ararat (Genesis 8:4)
3. Babel (Genesis 11:1-11)
4. Ur of the Chaldees (Genesis 11:28—12:3)
5. Canaan (with Abraham) (Genesis 12:4-7)
6. Egypt (with Joseph) (Genesis 37—45, esp. 41:41)
7. Sinai (Exodus 19:16—20:21)
8. Wilderness (Numbers 14:26-35)
9. Canaan (with Joshua) (Joshua 1:1-9)
10. Assyria (captivity of Israel) (2 Kings 18:9-12)
11. Babylon (captivity of Judah) (2 Kings 24:11-16)
12. Canaan (return of the exiles) (Ezra 1:1—2:70).

As you build the story of the Bible around these places you see the whole history in chronological order.

Still another way to think through the Bible is by following the great facts in order.

Old Testament—Principal Facts
1. Creation (Genesis 1:1—2:3)
2. Fall of man (Genesis 3)
3. Flood (Genesis 6—9)
4. Babel (Genesis 11:1-9)
5. Call of Abraham (Genesis 11:10—12:3)
6. Descent into Egypt (Genesis 46—47)

7. Exodus (Exodus 7—12)
8. Passover (Exodus 12)
9. Giving of the Law (Exodus 19—24)
10. Wilderness wanderings (Numbers 13—14)
11. Conquest of the Promised Land (Joshua 11)
12. Dark ages of the chosen people (Judges)
13. Anointing of Saul as king (1 Samuel 9:27—10:1)
14. Golden age of Israelites under David and Solomon—united kingdom (2 Samuel 5:4-5; 1 Kings 10:6-8)
15. The divided kingdom—Israel and Judah (1 Kings 12:26-33)
16. The Captivity (2 Kings 17; 25)
17. The Return (Ezra).

New Testament—Principal Facts

1. Early life of Christ (Matthew 1:18—2:23; Luke 1—2)
2. Ministry of Christ (Gospels of Matthew, Mark, Luke and John)
3. Church in Jerusalem (Acts 1—2)
4. Church extending to the Gentiles (Acts 10—11, 13—20)
5. Church in all the world (Romans 10—11,15; Ephesians 2:22-23).

Principal Periods

I. Period of the patriarchs to Moses—Genesis
    A. The godly line—leading events
       1. Creation
       2. Fall
       3. Flood
       4. Dispersion
    B. The chosen family—leading events
       1. Call of Abraham
       2. The descent into Egypt—bondage
II. Period of great leaders: Moses to Saul—Exodus to Samuel
    A. Exodus from Egypt
    B. Wandering in wilderness
    C. Conquest of Canaan
    D. Rule of the Judges
III. Period of the kings: Saul to the captivities—Samuel,

Kings, Chronicles, the prophetical books
- A.   The united kingdom
    1.   Saul
    2.   David
    3.   Solomon
- B.   The divided kingdom
    1.   Judah
    2.   Israel
IV.   Period of foreign rulers: Captivities to Christ—Ezra, Nehemiah, Esther, Prophecies of Daniel and Ezekiel
- A.   Captivity of Israel
- B.   Captivity of Judah
V.   Christ—the Gospels
VI.   The Church—Acts and the Epistles
- A.   In Jerusalem
- B.   Extending to the Gentiles
- C.   In all the world

How to Study the Bible

Remember that in God's Word the foundation of Christianity is laid in the revelation of the one and only true God. God chose a people (the children of Israel) to show forth this truth and to preserve a record of Himself.

1. Look for purpose—God's plan for salvation.

The Bible tells us of the origin of sin and how this curse separated us all from God. We discover how utterly impossible it was for the law to bring to us the salvation we need, for by the deeds of the law could no flesh be justified, for "all have sinned" (Romans 3:20-23). Then we find the promise of a Savior, One who was to come "to seek and to save what was lost" and "give his life as a ransom for many" (Luke 19:10; Matthew 20:28). We see all through the ages one purpose is evident, that of preparing a way for the coming of the Redeemer of the world.

2. Ask the Holy Spirit to guide you.

There is no royal road to learning and certainly there is no royal road to knowledge of the Bible. The Spirit of God will lead us into all truth, to be sure, but God's command is that we do our best to be approved, workmen unashamed (2 Timothy 2:15).

3. Read attentively.

Give to the Bible attention with intention, and intention will necessitate attention. Perhaps there is so little attention in Bible reading today because there is so little intention. We must come to it with a purpose and have a clearly defined object; we must know what we are about.

Many say, "The Bible is so great. I don't know where to begin and don't know how to go on." This is often said quite earnestly and sincerely. It is true that unless we have some method, we shall assuredly lose the very best results, even though we may spend much time with the Book.

G. Campbell Morgan (1863-1945, the well-respected Bible teacher) once stated, "The Bible can be read from Genesis 1 to Revelation 22 at pulpit rate in 78 hours." A lawyer challenged him on that. Morgan told him to go on and try it before he challenged. The lawyer went home and read the Bible in less than 80 hours.

4. Make a reading plan (or use one of the reading plans provided at the back of this book).

Do you want to read through the Bible? Leave 80 hours for it. Schedule that time. How much time can you give each day? How many days a week? This is a highly practical proposition and should be seized by the very busiest. We are all busy and must take time for it. If we are going to know the Bible, we must give time to it and arrange for it. We must adjust our lives so that time is made. Unless we do, we shall never come into any worthy knowledge of the Word; for it is impossible from pulpit ministry to acquire that needful knowledge of the Word. The Bible reveals the will of God so as to lead us into it. Each book has a direct teaching. Find out what it is and conform to it. This is our purpose. We are going to consider a book of the Bible in each chapter of this book.

Now the Bible, although it is a library of books, is also "the Book." It is a story, a grand story that moves on from commencement to finish. Here surely is something that is phenomenal in literature. Suppose, for instance, you were to cover the great fields of knowledge, such as law, history, philosophy, ethics and prophecy, and you were to bring these different subjects all together and bind them up into one book. What, to begin with, would you call the book? Then what unity could one possibly expect to find in such a jumble of subjects? Such an infinite number and variety of themes and styles as are found in the Bible, brought together across not a few generations in the history of the people, but across centuries, makes the likelihood of any unity being present amazingly small. No publisher would risk publishing such a book, and if he or she did, nobody would buy it or read it. That is, however, what is done in the Bible.

Remember, the books of the Bible were given to us by 40 different authors over a period of about 1,600 years. All these are brought together and bound and are called "the Book." We can begin at Genesis and read on through to the end. It is not jarring. We can pass from one style of literature to another as easily as though we were reading a story written by one hand and produced by one life, and indeed we have here a story produced by one Mind (2 Peter 1:21) though not written by one hand.

5. Appreciate the Bible's uniqueness.

Although divine, it is human. The thought is divine, the revelation is divine, the expression of the communication is human. "But men [human element] spoke from God as they were carried along by the Holy Spirit [divine element]" (2 Peter 1:21).

So we have here a book unlike all others. The Book, a divine revelation, a progressive revelation, a revelation of God to humanity communicated through men, moves on smoothly from its beginnings to its great end. Way back in Genesis, we have the beginnings; in Revelation we have endings; and from Exodus to Jude we see how God carried out His purpose. We can't dispense with any part of it.

Bible history takes us back into the unknown past of eternity and its prophecies take us into the otherwise unknown future.

The Old Testament is the foundation; the New Testament is the superstructure. A foundation is of no value unless a building be built upon it. A building is impossible unless there be a foundation. So the Old Testament and New Testament are essential to one another. As Augustine (Saint Augustine, A.D. 354-430, one of the most influential Christians who has ever lived) said:

> The New is in the Old contained,
> The Old is in the New explained.
> The New is in the Old latent,
> The Old is in the New patent.
> The Old Testament and New Testament constitute a
> divine library, one sublime unity, origins in past to issues
> in future, processes between, connecting two eternities.

One Book, One History, One Story

The Bible is one book, one history, one story, His story. Behind 10,000 events stands God, the builder of history, the maker of the ages. Eternity bounds the one side, eternity bounds the other side, and time is in between: Genesis—origins, Revelation—endings, and all the way between, God is working things out. You can go down into the minutest detail everywhere and see that there is one great purpose moving through the ages: the eternal design of the almighty God to redeem a wrecked and ruined world.

The Bible is one book, and you cannot take it in texts and expect to comprehend the magnificence of divine revelation. You must see it in its completeness. God has taken pains to give a progressive revelation and we should take pains to read it from beginning to end. Don't suppose reading little scraps can ever be compensation for doing deep and consecutive work on the Bible itself. We must get back to the Book and then we will not tolerate such work. One would scorn to read any other book, even the lightest novel, in this fashion.

Another way we can study the Bible is by groups—law, history, poetry, major and minor prophets, Gospels, Acts, Epistles and Revelation. Here again we find great unity for "it is written about me in the scroll—I have come to do your will, O God," says Christ (Hebrews 10:7). Everything points to the King!

Each book has a message, and we should endeavor to discover what that message is. Read until you discover the message of the book. For instance, in John it is easy to discover the purpose. It is stated in John 20:31. It is not always given clearly, but the truth may be found.

In one sense we should treat the Bible as we treat any other book. When we get a book from the library we would never treat it as we do the Bible. We would never think of reading just a paragraph, taking some ten minutes, reading a little at night and then reading a little in the morning, and so spending weeks, perhaps months, in reading through the book. No interest could be maintained in any story by such a procedure. Take a love story, for instance; we would naturally begin at the beginning and read right through to the end, unless we turned to the finish to see how the story ended.

Do you come to the Bible with such eagerness? Do you read with that purpose and persistence? The Bible is not a book of texts—it is a story—it is a revelation, to be begun and pursued and ended as we start and continue other books. Don't trifle with the Bible. Don't divide it into short devotional paragraphs and think you have understood its messages. It may be excusable for those who can hardly read to open the Bible and take whatever their eyes light upon as the message of God. Many people do that, but the Bible isn't to be misused in that manner. We must come to it in a common-sense fashion. Believe that every book is about something and read and reread until you find out what that something is.

First we read the Book, not read books about the Book, nor turn to the comments. They will come in good time, perhaps, but give the Book a chance to speak for itself and to make its own impression; to bear its own testimony. As Johnny Cash (country-music singer) is credited with saying: "The Bible sure does throw a lot of light on the commentaries."

Don't wish to put on colored glasses of people's opinions and then read through the interpretation put on it by other minds. Let the Spirit of God Himself teach you. We all have a right to read it for ourselves. "No prophecy of Scripture came about by the prophet's own interpretation" (2 Peter 1:20). Read it seeking for illumination. It is a revelation and He will flash light upon the page as you come humbly.

We have been studying the Bible piecemeal. Now we must turn to reading books as wholes and not tinker with texts. No part of any book will give you the whole message of the book.

The Word of God is alive and every part is necessary to the perfection of the whole. We don't say that every part is equally important. If you were to ask me whether I would give up my finger or my eye, of course I would part with my finger; so it is with the Word of God. All is necessary to make a perfect whole, but some portions are more precious than others. You can't take away the Song of Solomon and have a perfect revelation. No one says the Song of Solomon is comparable with John's Gospel, but both are parts of an organism and that organism is not complete if any part is missing.

The Bible is a whole and we can't tamper with it. For example, to add anything to the book of Revelation or to take anything from it would mar its absolute perfection (Revelation 22:18-19). The canon of Scripture is closed. Other works throw valuable light upon it, but this stands unique, alone, and complete, and these parts all partake of the perfection of the whole.

Read a Book a Week

So we come to these books as complete in themselves, yet bearing in mind their vital relation to what precedes and what succeeds. We should read them one at a time. Read a book in a week. Now don't suppose that this is impossible. It is not. How much time do you spend reading in 24 hours? How much time on newspapers? magazines? How much time do you give to fiction? to other reading? And how much time do you give to television? Now the longest of these books doesn't take longer than some of you devote to reading or watching television in one day.

Some of the larger books in the Old Testament, such as Genesis, Exodus, Deuteronomy and Isaiah, might take some hours to read carefully; and if it is too much, divide them into seven equal parts, but put your reading into strict limits. Don't give yourself time to lose the impression made by the first reading before you get to the second and don't suppose that you can grasp the content and intent of any book at a single reading.

Don't suppose that as you walk down the corridors of a gallery and look at the pictures you have seen the gallery. You see some pictures on the wall, but you don't know what they are about. You must sit in front of a picture and study it.

Christ, the Living Word

The Old Testament is an account of a nation (the Jewish nation). The New Testament is an account of a Man (the Son of man). The nation was founded and nurtured of God in order to bring the Man into the world (Genesis 12:1-3).

God Himself became a man so that we might know what to think of when we think of God (John 1:14; 14:9). His appearance on the earth is the central event of all history. The Old Testament sets the stage for it. The New Testament describes it.

As a man Christ lived the most perfect life ever known. He was kind, tender, gentle, patient and sympathetic. He loved people. He worked marvelous miracles to feed the hungry. Multitudes—weary, pain ridden and heartsick—came to Him, and He gave them rest (Matthew 11:28-30). It is said that if all the deeds of kindness that He did were written, the world could not contain the books (John 21:25).

Then He died—to take away the sin of the world, and to become the Savior of men.

Then He rose from the dead. He is alive today. He is not merely a historical character, but a living Person—the most important fact of history and the most vital force in the world today. And He promises eternal life to all who come to Him.

The whole Bible is built around the story of Christ and His promise of life everlasting to all. It was written only that we might believe and understand, know and love, and follow HIM.

Apart from any theory of inspiration or any theory of how the Bible books came to their present form or how much the text may have suffered in passing through the hands of editors and copyists or what is historical and what may be poetical—assume that the Bible is just what it appears to be. Accept the books as we have them in our Bible as units; study them to know their contents. You will find a unity of thought indicates that one Mind inspired the writing of the whole series of books; that it bears on its face the stamp of its Author; that it is in every sense the WORD OF GOD.

Master the Contents of Each Book

On the following pages you will find a bit of rhyme that will give you a clue to the contents of each book of the Bible.

Old Testament
Pentateuch

    In Genesis the world was made,
     In Exodus the march was told;
    Leviticus contains the law,
     In Numbers are the tribes enrolled;
    In Deuteronomy again
     We're urged to keep God's law alone.
    And these five books of Moses make
     The oldest writings that are known.

Historical Books

    Brave Joshua to Canaan leads,
     In Judges oft the Jews rebel;
    We read of David's name in Ruth,
     And First and Second Samuel;
    In First and Second Kings we read
     How bad the Hebrew state became;
    In First and Second Chronicles,
     Another history of the same.
    In Ezra captive Jews return,
     While Nehemiah builds the wall;
    Queen Esther saves her race from death.
     These books "Historical" we call.

Poetical Books

    In Job we read of patient faith,
     In Psalms are David's songs of praise;
    The Proverbs are to make us wise;

Ecclesiastes next portrays
How vain fleeting earthly pleasures are;
The Song of Solomon is all
About the love of God, and these
Five books "Poetical" we call.
Prophetical Books
Isaiah tells of Christ to come,
While Jeremiah tells of woe,
And in his Lamentations mourns
The Holy City's overthrow.
Ezekiel speaks of mysteries,
While Daniel foretells kings of old;
Hosea calls men to repent;
In Joel, judgments are foretold.
Amos tells of wrath, and Edom
Obadiah is sent to warn,
While Jonah shows how Christ should rise,
And Micah where He should be born;
In Nahum, Nineveh is seen,
In Habakkuk, Chaldea's guilt;
Zephaniah, Judah's sins,
Haggai, the temple's built.
Zechariah tells of Christ,
And Malachi of John, his signs.
The Prophets number seventeen,
And all the books are thirty-nine.

New Testament
Matthew, Mark, Luke and John
Tell of Christ, His life they trace;
Acts shows the Holy Spirit's work;
And Romans how we're saved by grace.
Corinthians instructs the church,
Galatians shows God's grace alone;
Ephesians, how we are "in Christ,"
Philippians, Christ's joys made known.
Colossians portrays Christ exalted.

And Thessalonians tells the end.
In Timothy and Titus both,
    Are rules for pastors to attend.
Philemon pictures charity,
    Thirteen Epistles, penned by Paul.
The Jewish law prefigured Christ;
    And Hebrews clearly shows it all.
James shows that faith by works must live,
    And Peter urges steadfastness,
While John exhorts to Christian love;
    And those who live it, God will bless.
Jude shows the end of evil men,
    While Revelation tells of heaven.
These end the whole New Testament,
    In all, they number twenty-seven.

Part One

The Old Testament

Books of Law
Genesis • Exodus • Leviticus
Numbers • Deuteronomy

Books of History
Joshua • Judges • Ruth • 1 Samuel • 2 Samuel
1 Kings • 2 Kings • 1 Chronicles • 2 Chronicles
Ezra • Nehemiah • Esther

Books of Poetry
Job • Psalms • Proverbs • Ecclesiastes • Song of Solomon

Books of the Major Prophets
Isaiah • Jeremiah • Lamentations • Ezekiel • Daniel

Books of the Minor Prophets
Hosea • Joel • Amos • Obadiah • Jonah
Micah • Nahum • Habakkuk • Zephaniah
Haggai • Zechariah • Malachi

Books of Law
of The Old Testament

**Genesis • Exodus • Leviticus
Numbers • Deuteronomy**

Key Events of the Books of Law

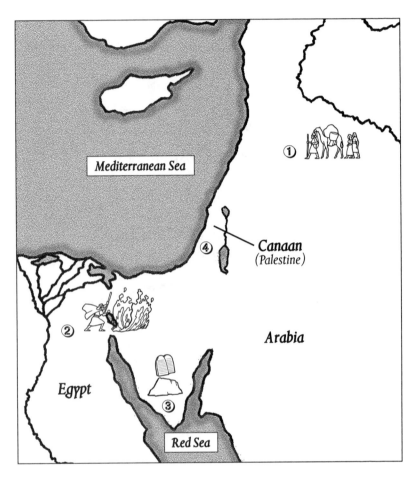

Books of Law: There Is One and Only One True God

The five books of the Law are also called "the Pentateuch," which means "five scrolls." The core of this ancient literature was written by Moses (Luke 24:27; John 5:46). These books describe the creation of the world, God's call to the Hebrews ① to be His special people, their captivity and release ② from Egypt, the law ③ that guided them on their way to the Promised Land ④ and how God blessed the people when they obeyed and disciplined them when they disobeyed.

Chapter 2

Understanding Genesis

Genesis Portrays Jesus Christ, Our Creator God

Selected Bible Readings

Sunday: Creation (Genesis 1:1-5; 26-31; 2:7-22)
Monday: The Fall (Genesis 3:1-24)
Tuesday: The Flood (Genesis 6:1-7; 7:7-24; 8:6-11; 18-22; 9:1-16)
Wednesday: Beginning of Languages (Genesis 11:1-9)
Thursday: The Abrahamic Call and Covenant (Genesis 12:1-9;
13:14-18; 15:1-21; 17:4-8; 22:15-20; 26:1-5; 28:10-15)
Friday: Story of Joseph (Genesis 37:1-36; 42)
Saturday: Jacob's Final Blessing (Genesis 49)

Genesis is the seed plot of the Word of God. The title Genesis, which is Greek, means "origin," and the first word in the Hebrew of Genesis is translated "in the beginning"—words that indicate both the scope and the limits of the book. It tells us the beginning of everything except God. Another thing to notice is that it tells only of beginnings. There is no finality here. Upon its truths all the future revelation of God to people is built up.

Satan appears to have special enmity for the book of Genesis. No wonder the adversary has bent his attacks upon it. It exposes him as the enemy of God and the deceiver of the human race; it foretells his destruction; it depicts his doom (Genesis 3).

Without Genesis our knowledge of a creating God would be pitifully limited; we would be woefully ignorant of the beginnings of our universe.

Genesis is the book of beginnings:

1. the beginning of the world—1:1-25
2. the beginning of the human race—1:26-2:25
3. the beginning of sin in the world—3:1-7
4. the beginning of the promise of redemption—3:8-24
5. the beginning of family life—4:1-15
6. the beginning of civilization—4:16—9:29
7. the beginning of the nations of the world—10,11
8. the beginning of the Hebrew people—12—50.

Adam began with God and fell through disobedience—3:1-24.

Abel began with God by the blood of sacrifice—4:4.

Noah began with God by way of the ark—6:8,14,22.

Abraham began with God when he built altars—12:8.

These all made new beginnings for the race.

Genesis is the record of the beginnings of all these things. No wonder that when people, because of spiritual blindness (Ephesians 4:18), reject God's revelation in this peerless record of beginnings, they worship chance as the creator, beasts as their ancestors and fallen humanity as the flower of natural evolution!

Genesis begins with "God" but ends "in a coffin." This book is a history of human failure. But we find that God meets every failure. He is a glorious Savior. We find that "where sin increased, grace increased all the more" (Romans 5:20).

Genesis gives us at least 2,000 years of record. It is not entirely history; it is a spiritual interpretation of history. In two chapters God flashes on the wall an account of the creation of the world and of humanity. From there on we see the story of redemption. God is bringing lost people back to Himself.

We have noted Satan's reasons for attacking this majestic book. Its authorship by Moses, its scientific accuracy and its literal testimony to human sin as deliberate disobedience to God have all been bitterly assailed. The Word of God, however, definitely declares Genesis to be one of the living oracles delivered to Moses. To its infallible truth and its testimony to the Messiah, our Lord Jesus set His seal (John 5:46-47).

When Genesis goes, a divine Creator, a divine creation, a divinely promised Redeemer and a divinely inspired Bible must also go. Around its sacred pages is the protection of the Holy Spirit of God who inspired its words. If there were more study of Genesis instead of so much argument about it, its truth would be clearer. Many origins are recorded in the first eleven chapters: natural universe, human life, sin, death, redemption, civilization, nations and languages.

The remainder of the book from Genesis 12 delves into the beginnings of the Hebrew people, first in its founding through Abraham, then in its subsequent development and history through the great figures of Isaac, Jacob and Joseph. This great Hebrew nation was founded with a definite purpose that through it the whole world should be blessed.

God promised Abraham, a believer in Him, that his descendants:

1. Should inherit the land of Canaan (Genesis 12:1-3)
2. Should become a great nation
3. Through them all nations should be blessed.

God repeated these promises to Isaac and Jacob (Genesis 26:1-5; 28:13-15).

Seven great names and messages are:

1. Bow with Abel at the cross of the slain lamb.
2. Catch step with Enoch and walk with God.
3. Believe God and launch out with Noah on God's waters.
4. Go forth with Abraham in faith.
5. Dig wells with Isaac and get down to divine resources.
6. Climb ladders with Jacob and see God.
7. Be true like Joseph and live with God.

Won't you make a book of Genesis (beginning) and of new love to your Lord in your own life?

Genesis answers the great questions of the soul:

1. The eternity of God.
2. Where did we come from?
3. Whence came sin?

4. How can sinful people get back to God (Abel's sacrifice)?
5. How can we please God (Abraham's faith)?
6. How can we have power with God and people (Jacob's surrender)?

Three words also might give us the outline of Genesis:

1. Generation—"In the beginning God" (1:1)
2. Degeneration—"Now the serpent" (3:1)
3. Regeneration—"Now the Lord" (12:1, *KJV*).

Genesis is the record of human failure, first in an ideal environment (Eden), then under the rule of conscience (from the Fall to the deluge) and finally under patriarchal rule (Noah to Joseph). In every case of human failure, however, God met human need with marvelous promises of sovereign grace. It is therefore fitting that the Bible's first book should show us the failure of humanity under every condition met by the salvation of God.

Hints of the Messiah:

Remember, Jesus Christ is the center of the Bible. He is somewhere on every page. In Genesis we see Him in type (the foreshadowing of Christian meanings in Old Testament people and events) and prophecy (supernatural knowledge given by God to holy people to reveal truth and to foretell events) in:

1. Seed of woman—3:15
2. The entrance into the ark of safety—7:1,7
3. The offering up of Isaac—22:1-24
4. Jacob's ladder—28:12
5. Judah's scepter—49:10
6. Joseph lifted from pit to throne—37:28; 41:41-44.

The patriarchal period

The period of the patriarchs is the groundwork and basis of all history. It covers the time from Adam to Moses. In consequence of the failures on the part of people during this early period, God called out an individual. He put aside the nations and called a

man, Abraham, who was to become the father of the Hebrew
nation. We enter into this period in Genesis 12.

There are five patriarchal fathers—Abraham, Isaac, Jacob,
Joseph and Job—for the book of Job must be put after the book
of Genesis and before the book of Exodus. Job certainly lived
before Moses and we read of Moses in Exodus 2.

God called out Abraham and made a covenant with him,
known as the Abrahamic Covenant. Be familiar with this
covenant (Genesis 12:1-3). If you are not, the whole study of the
chosen people (in fact, the whole Old Testament) will have little
meaning. God repeated that covenant to Abraham's son, Isaac,
and again to his grandson, Jacob (Genesis 26:1-5; 28:13-15). He
repeated it to no one else.

These three, therefore, are the covenant fathers, and that is
why you read in Scripture "I am the God of your fathers, the God
of Abraham, Isaac and Jacob" (Acts 7:32). He never adds anyone
else. God gave His covenant to these three and it is for them to
communicate it to others. What is the covenant? Read Genesis
12:1-3; 26:1-5; 28:13-15.

From family to nation

A very large portion of the story of Genesis is devoted to
Joseph (Genesis 37—48). Why? Because Joseph is the link between
the family and the nation. Up till the time of Joseph it is a family,
the family of Abraham, Isaac and Jacob. Some seventy souls are
found at the end of the book of Genesis, constituting the family
of Jacob. But still it is a family with which God is dealing. Read
about this family and the blessings Jacob gave to each of his sons
in Genesis 49.

The moment we turn over the page and step into Exodus it is
a nation, not a family. During the long period from the end of
Genesis to the opening of Exodus this nation has developed.
Joseph is the link between the family and the nation.

Joseph is a character presented without fault—not that he had no
faults, but his faults are not recorded. He was a man of flesh and
blood like us. God honored him, for there are at least 130 parallels
between the life of Joseph and the life of Jesus. He is therefore the
messianic patriarch, the patriarch who reflected the Christ Himself.

The Author of Genesis

The age-long Hebrew and Christian position is that Moses, guided by the Spirit of God, wrote Genesis. The book closes approximately three hundred years before Moses was born. Moses could have received his information only by direct revelation from God or from historical records to which he had access that had been handed down from his forefathers. See what Jesus said about Moses (Luke 24:27; John 7:19).

Every year there are being dug up in Egypt and Israel evidences of writing in Moses' day and of the historical truth of what is recorded in the Pentateuch. Moses was educated in the palace of Pharaoh and "was educated in all the wisdom of the Egyptians" (Acts 7:22), which included the literary profession. Moses did make use of writing (Exodus 34:27; Numbers 17:2; Deuteronomy 6:9; 24:1,3; Joshua 8:32).

No doubt the creation story was written long before, maybe by Abraham or Noah, or Enoch, the grandson of Adam (Genesis 4:17). Who knows? Writing was in common use before the days of Abraham. In Ur, as in every important city in Babylonia, the libraries contained thousands of books, dictionaries, grammars, reference works, encyclopedias, works on mathematics, astronomy, geography, religion and politics. No doubt Abraham had received traditions or records from Shem, the son of Noah (Genesis 6:10), about the story of Creation and the Fall of humanity and of the flood. Abraham lived in a society of culture, books and libraries. He no doubt made careful and accurate copies of all that happened to him and of the promises God had made to him. He put it down on clay tablets in the cuneiform writing (the alphabet of the Babylonians) to be handed down in the annals of the nation he was founding.

Creation (Genesis 1—2)

As the book begins we see these words untarnished by the ages, "In the beginning God created the heavens and the earth." In these few simple words we have the Bible declaration of the origin of this material universe. God called all things into being by the word of His power. He spoke and worlds were framed (Hebrews 11:3). Interpretations of the method of God may vary but the truth of the fact remains.

God's creative work was progressive:

1. The world of matter—1:3-19
2. The system of life—1:20-25
3. Humanity, the crown of Creation—1:26-27.

Who was the God mentioned so many times in the first thirty-one verses of Genesis? Read John 1:1 and Hebrews 1:1. Here we see that the One who redeemed us by His precious blood, our Savior, was the Creator of this universe. Someone has said that God the Father is the architect; God the Son, the builder and God the Holy Spirit, the beautifier of the universe. We find the Holy Spirit in Genesis 1:2.

In chapter 1 we have the account of Creation in outline, in chapter 2 part of the same in detail. The detail concerns the creation of humanity, for the Bible is the history of the redemption of humanity.

Know this, God created people in His own image to have fellowship with Himself. But we have cut ourselves off from God by sin. Only when sin is removed can we have fellowship again. This is why Jesus Christ came to this earth: that he might bear "our sins in his body on the tree" (1 Peter 2:24). Read in 1 John 1 how sin keeps us not only from fellowship with God, but also with one another. First John 1:9 tells us what we can do to have a restored fellowship.

The Fall (Genesis 3—4)

Adam and Eve were created in a state of innocence but with the power of choice. They were tested under the most favorable circumstances. They were endowed with clear minds and pure hearts, with the ability to do right. God gave them His own presence and fellowship (Genesis 3:8).

Satan, the author of sin, acting through a serpent, tempted Adam and Eve to doubt God's Word. They yielded to the temptation and failed in the test. Here sin entered the world. Satan still influences people to disobey God. The results of Adam's and Eve's sin are enumerated in Genesis 3. They were separated from God, the ground was cursed and sorrow filled their hearts.

In mercy, God promised One who would redeem us from sin (Genesis 3:15). The offspring of the woman (the virgin-born Jesus) would come to destroy the works of the devil (1 John 3:8).

Immediately after the Fall, people began to offer sacrifices unto the Lord. No doubt these sacrifices were ordered of God. They were for the purpose of keeping before people the fact of their fall and of the coming sacrifice. It would be by the shedding of Jesus' blood that people were to be redeemed from sin and death (Hebrews 9:22).

Two of Adam's sons, Cain and Abel, brought their sacrifices unto the Lord. "Cain brought some of the fruits of the soil as an offering to the Lord. But Abel brought fat portions from some of the firstborn of his flock" (Genesis 4:3,4). Abel's offering was accepted while Cain's was rejected. From our knowledge of the Word, it is quite evident that it was not accepted because any sacrifice brought to the Lord must be done so with proper motivation and through faith and obedience. Cain became angry with his brother Abel and in his wrath killed him.

The first writing began when God put a "mark" or "sign" on Cain (Genesis 4:15). That mark stood for an idea and the people knew what it stood for. Thus "marks," "signs," "pictures," came to be used to record ideas, words, or combinations of words. These pictures were made on pottery or hard clay tablets, painted or engraved. This is the kind of writing found in the lowest levels of the prehistoric cities of Babylonia. The oldest known writings are of pictures on clay tablets.

Long before God gave the law to Moses (Exodus 20), we find several very definite ordinances given in the book of Genesis. At the very beginning God instituted the Sabbath (Genesis 2:1-3) and marriage (Genesis 2:24).

The law of the tithe was evidently observed. Read about Abraham's tithe in Genesis 14:20, and read Jacob's words in

Genesis 28:22. God has evidently made people realize from the very beginning that they were only stewards of all they had.

This civilization before the flood is called the "antediluvian civilization." It perished in the judgment of the flood. It was the civilization started by Cain. It ended in destruction.

The Bible teaches and the archaeologist confirms that the people of the world before the flood were not mere savages. They had attained a considerable degree of civilization. Everything in material civilization is touched on in Genesis 4:16-22. Although not much is known about the antediluvians, yet some places have been discovered that could possibly be from this period. Some relics of their handwork that have been uncovered give evidence of a civilization such as the Bible seems to describe.

In three cities, Ur, Kish and Fara, the layer of silt possibly left by the flood has been found by Professor Woolley (Sir Leonard Woolley, 1880-1960, British field archaeologist, excavated at Ur, Charchemish, Amarna and Alalakh), sent out by the British Museum and Pennsylvania University. Underneath the flood deposit in Ur, layers of rubbish full of stone and flint instruments, colored pottery, seals and burnt brick were found. The same is true of the other two cities.

Turn to Genesis 4:16-22 and see what is mentioned of early civilization in the Scriptures.

1. Herdsmen: "Adah gave birth to Jabal; he was the father of those who live in tents and raise livestock" (4:20).
2. Musicians: "His brother's name was Jubal; he was the father of all who play the harp and flute" (4:21).
3. Artificers and manufacturers: "Zillah also had a son, Tubal-Cain, who forged all kinds of tools out of bronze and iron" (4:22).
4. Builders: "Cain lay with his wife, and she became pregnant and gave birth to Enoch. Cain was then building a city, and he named it after his son Enoch" (4:17).

The civilization founded by Cain may have been equal to that of Greece or Rome, but God's judgment was upon it. Why? (6:5-7).

The Flood (Genesis 5—9)

The account of the flood in the Bible is very plain and straightforward. The story is not told because it is startling or interesting, but because it is an incident in the history of redemption that the Bible relates. Evil had grown rampant. It threatened to destroy everything that was good. Only one righteous man remained, Noah. God sent the flood to restore good upon the earth.

Adam and Eve had yielded to an outward temptation, but now people had yielded to temptation which was within. "The Lord saw how great man's wickedness on the earth had become, and that every inclination of the thoughts of his heart was only evil all the time" (Genesis 6:5). God was going to separate the righteous from the wicked. He was taking the first step toward a chosen nation.

After the Fall, God gave the world a new beginning, but soon the wickedness of people increased until there remained but one righteous man, Noah.

God had been long-suffering in His patience with people. The Holy Spirit had been in conflict with people. Noah had warned them for 120 years while he was building the ark. Even after Noah and his wife and his three sons and their wives—taking with them two of every unclean animal and fourteen of every clean animal—had entered into the ark of safety, there was a respite of seven days before the flood came; but God's mercies were refused and so people had to perish (Genesis 6—7). Noah was saved from the flood by the Ark (a perfect type or Old Testament picture example of Christ, our Ark of safety). When he came out, the first thing he did was to erect an altar and worship God (Genesis 8:20).

Out of the fearful judgment of the earth by the flood, God saved eight people. He gave the purified earth to these people with ample power to govern it (Genesis 9:1-6). He gave them control of every living thing on earth and sea. For the first time God gave people human government. People were to be responsible to govern the world for God. The most solemn responsibility God gave to humans is the taking of a life for a life (Genesis 9:6). God established capital punishment for homicide.

Sir Charles Marston (1867-1946, British field archaeologist, excavator of Jericho) outclasses all the great detectives of modern fiction. He has unearthed thousands of witnesses in stone and pottery to learn the truth concerning the Scriptures. Whenever he wields spade or pen, Sir Charles silences the critics of the Bible. Records of many people who scientists have said never existed have been brought to light; many geographical locations they said were only Bible names have been unearthed.

Marston tells us that the scene of the events recorded in the first chapters of the book of Genesis appears to be laid around the river Euphrates. The surrounding country is called Shinar, or Chaldea, or Mesopotamia. We have known it as Babylonia; today it is called the kingdom of Iraq.

It is a land of deserts through which the Tigris and Euphrates flow down to the Persian Gulf. But the deserts are studded with the ruins of ancient cities, and scored with the channels of old irrigation canals; the silt has submerged all.

Excavations have revealed the ruins of a vast civilization that existed in 5000 B.C. These evidences of an era, until lately almost forgotten, have been left by two great peoples—the Sumerians and the Semites. We do not know the origin of the Sumerians. The Semites take their name from Shem, the eldest son of Noah, and the Hebrew race, from which Abraham sprang, was a branch of this people.

Archaeological discovery in Mesopotamia bares evidence of the flood, both in the cuneiform writings and in the actual flood deposits. The cuneiform libraries seem to have given us ample accounts of, and references to, this catastrophe. A clay prism has also been found on which are inscribed the names of the ten kings who reigned before the flood.

Dr. Langdon (Stephen Herbert Langdon, 1876-1937, American field archaeologist, excavated at Kish near Babylon in the 1920s, sponsored by the University of Oxford and the Field Museum of Chicago) in his expedition found evidences of the flood at Kish near ancient Babylon, and his findings were subsequently published in his book *Excavations at Kish* (1924).

Professor Woolley's discoveries of the deposits were made while excavating Ur of the Chaldees, a good deal farther south, about halfway between Baghdad and the Persian Gulf. The excavations at Kish revealed two distinct flood strata, the one nineteen feet below the other.

Dr. Langdon associates the Ur deposits with the lower level of Kish. He reports that Babylonian and Assyrian scribes frequently refer to the age "before the flood." One king praises himself as one "who loved to read the writings of the age before the flood."

Babel (Genesis 10—11)

After the flood the world was given a new start. But instead of spreading out and repeopling the earth as God had commanded, they built the great tower of Babel in defiance of God. They thought they could establish a worldwide empire that would be independent of God. In judgment God sent a confusion of tongues and scattered them abroad.

The human race was then divided into nations speaking different languages, according to Noah's three sons, Shem, Ham and Japheth. Shem's sons settled in Arabia and to the east; Ham's sons settled in Africa; Japheth's sons settled in Europe.

The great Jewish historian, Josephus, declares that the tower of Babel was built because the people did not want to submit to God.

As we read the story in Genesis 11:1-9, the narrative seems to imply that the people were at cross purposes with God. As a result there was this confusion of tongues and dispersion abroad. A difference in language tends to separate people in more ways than one and to check progress in commerce, in arts and in civilization.

At the tower of Babel, people in their pride tried to glorify themselves, but it is God's purpose that people shall only glorify Him. If you read Genesis 10 and 11, you will find the basis upon which the nations were divided according to the three sons of Noah—Shem, Ham and Japheth. You will also find the reason for the division.

The main body of Noah's descendants seems to have migrated from Armenia, where Noah's family left the ark, back toward the plain of Babylonia where they built the tower.

The Call of Abraham (Genesis 12—38)

In spite of the wickedness of the human heart, God wanted to show His grace. He wanted a chosen people:

1. To whom He might entrust the Holy Scriptures
2. To be His witness to the other nations
3. Through whom the promised Messiah could come.

He called a man named Abram to leave his home in idolatrous Ur of the Chaldees to go to an unknown land where God would make him the father of a mighty nation (Genesis 12:1-3; Hebrews 11:8-19). This begins the history of God's chosen people, Israel.

Wherever Abraham went, he erected an altar to God. God signally honored him by revealing Himself to him. He was called "God's friend" (James 2:23). God made a covenant with him that he should be the father of a great nation and that through him the nations of the earth would be blessed (Genesis 12:1-3). His family became God's special charge. God dealt with them as with no other people. The Jews are always spoken of as God's chosen people.

Through Isaac, Abraham's son, the promises of God were passed down to Jacob, who, despite his many faults, valued God's covenant blessing. He was enthusiastic about God's plan of founding a nation by which the whole world would be blessed. Jacob in his wanderings suffered for his sin, and through chastening came out a great man. His name was changed to Israel, a prince with God (Genesis 32:28). This is the name by which God's chosen people were called—Israelites. His twelve sons became the heads of the twelve tribes of Israel. Read Genesis 49.

Descent into Egypt (Genesis 39—50)

Isaac and Rebecca made the mistake of playing favorites with their two sons. Isaac favored the hunter Esau. Rebecca favored the quiet Jacob. Jacob did the same thing in the treatment of Joseph, which aroused jealousy in the other sons. Joseph is one of the outstanding noble characters of the Old Testament. It was through Joseph that Jacob's family was transplanted into Egypt. Joseph's life is one of the most perfect illustrations in the Bible of God's overruling providence. He was sold as a slave at seventeen. At thirty he became ruler in Egypt; ten years later his father, Jacob, entered Egypt.

After Isaac's death and after Joseph had been sold into Egypt, Jacob and his sons and their children, numbering seventy in all, went down into that land because of a famine. Here they were exalted by the Pharaoh who was reigning at that time. When he learned that they were shepherds, he permitted them to settle in the land of Goshen where they grew in number, wealth and influence.

God knew it was necessary that the Israelites leave Canaan until they had developed national strength so they would take possession of the land of Canaan. God wanted to safeguard them against mingling and intermarrying with the idolatrous peoples then in the land.

Read Jacob's dying words to his twelve sons (Genesis 49). We see here again the promise to Judah of a descendant who is to be the coming ruler. Remember, Christ is called the Lion of the tribe of Judah (Revelation 5:5).

The book of Genesis ends in failure. The last words are in a coffin in Egypt. Death only marks the pathway of sin; the wages of sin is death (Romans 6:23). The people needed a Savior!

Eight names are mentioned in Genesis that we should remember in order: God, Adam, Satan, Noah, Abraham, Isaac, Jacob and Joseph.

Six places are of supreme importance in connection with the history of Genesis—Eden, Ararat, Babel, Ur of the Chaldees, Canaan (Promised Land) and Egypt.

Chapter 3

Understanding Exodus

Exodus Portrays Jesus Christ, Our Passover Lamb

Selected Bible Readings

Sunday: Bondage (Exodus 1:1-22)
Monday: The Call of Moses (Exodus 3—4)
Tuesday: The Plagues (Exodus 7:20—11:10)
Wednesday: The Passover (Exodus 12:1-51)
Thursday: The Law (Exodus 20:1-26)
Friday: The Worship (Exodus 25:1-9; 28:1-14,30-43)
Saturday: Moses' Commission Renewed
(Exodus 33:12—34:17)

Exodus follows Genesis in much the same relation as the New Testament stands to the Old Testament. Genesis tells of humanity's failure under every test and in every condition; Exodus is the thrilling epic of God hastening to the rescue. It tells of the redeeming work of a sovereign God.

Exodus is preeminently the book of redemption in the Old Testament. It begins in the darkness and gloom, yet ends in glory; it commences by telling how God came down in grace to deliver an enslaved people, and ends by declaring how God came down in glory to dwell in the midst of a redeemed people.

Exodus, which is Greek, means "way out." Without Genesis the book of Exodus has no meaning. It begins with the Hebrew word *we*, which means "And" or "Now" *(KJV)*. The story is just continuing. This book, like many other books of the Old Testament, begins with the word "And." This seems to point to the fact that each author was not just recording his own story but only his part of a great drama that began in the events of the past and looked forward to that which would come. Take the five books of Moses—Genesis, Exodus, Leviticus, Numbers and Deuteronomy. Each book is about something and those five things are vitally related to one another.

The Great Hero, Moses

The book gives us the story of Moses, the great hero of God. D. L. Moody (Dwight Lyman Moody, 1832-1899, American evangelist) said that Moses spent

Forty years thinking he was somebody

Forty years learning he was nobody

Forty years discovering what God can do with a nobody. See Hebrews 11:23-29.

The Law

The last half of the book (chaps. 19—40) teaches us that the redeemed must do the will of their Redeemer, consecrating themselves to His service, and submitting to His control. Therefore, the moral law is given, followed by the ceremonial law which was in part provision for the violator of the moral law.

The Tabernacle

God gave the tabernacle as a detailed picture of the Redeemer to come, in His many offices, and as a dwelling place for His visible glory on earth. Its wonderful typology is rich in Christian truth.

The Bondage (Exodus 1:1-22)

As this book opens, three-and-a-half centuries have passed since the closing scene of Genesis. The book of Genesis is a family history. The book of Exodus is a national history. We have no account of what happened during this long period of silence. The patriarch, Abraham, died when Jacob, his grandson, was fifteen years old. Jacob's favorite son Joseph had been sold as a slave into Egypt and had risen to great power and influence. The sons of Jacob had gained great favor because of their brother Joseph. Only seventy people went down into Egypt, but before they left Egypt the people had grown into a nation of 3,000,000.

When Joseph died and a new dynasty came to the throne in

Egypt, the wealth and great numbers of the children of Israel made them objects of suspicion in the eyes of the Egyptians. The pharaohs, wishing to break with them, reduced them to a slavery of the worst sort. This was hard for a people who had lived free, having had every favor upon them. They remembered the promises God had given to Abraham and his descendants, and it made this bondage doubly hard to understand (Genesis 12:1-3ff.).

The story told in the books of Exodus, Leviticus, Numbers and Deuteronomy shows that God did not forget the promise He had made to Abraham—"I will make you into a great nation" (Genesis 12:2).

The family records of Abraham, Isaac and Jacob no doubt had been carried into Egypt, and there became part of Israel's national annals. Through the long years of bondage, they clung to the promise that one day Canaan would be their home.

We will see God coming down to deliver the people from Egypt (Exodus 3:7,8). Now the individuals and families had been organized into a nation. God was going to give them laws with which to govern themselves. He was going to take them back to the land He had promised them.

The Exodus (Exodus 3—4)

Think of the preparation that had to be made for moving so great a host, "six hundred thousand men on foot, besides women and children. Many other people went up with them, as well as large droves of livestock, both flocks and herds" (Exodus 12:37-38).

No doubt it was a well-organized expedition. Moses had appealed to Pharaoh again and again to let the children of Israel go (Exodus 5:1; 7:16). The plagues and the negotiations Moses had to make with Pharaoh must have lasted for nearly a year. This gave the children of Israel more time to gather their things. The plagues taught the children of Israel some great things, besides forcing Pharaoh to let the children of Israel go.

In the construction of any great edifice, a blueprint has to be drawn and a pattern made. Our salvation was designed by God before the foundation of the world (Ephesians 1:4). We find the pattern in the book of Exodus. Exodus is the historical picture of divine grace in the redemption of humanity by God to Himself by Jesus Christ, who is at once our great Apostle (Moses) and High Priest (Aaron) (Hebrews 3:1).

The story of Exodus is repeated in every soul that seeks deliverance from the enmeshing and enervating influence of the world. From this point of view, the book is human, from the first verse to the last. The things that happened were by way of example, and they were written for our admonition (1 Corinthians 10:6-11). We study Exodus in order to see God's way of delivering sinful people, and His gracious purposes in thus rescuing them.

The Passover (Exodus 12—19)

Exodus 12 gives us the thrilling story of the Passover, the clearest Old Testament picture of our individual salvation through faith in the shed blood of our Lord Jesus Christ. In this chapter is the basis for calling Christ the "Lamb of God, Christ our Passover," and the many tender references to His crucifixion as the death of our own Passover Lamb.

"For Christ, our Passover lamb, has been sacrificed" (1 Corinthians 5:7).

As the Passover chapter is the heart of the book, so is the whole book a pattern of our salvation.

The Passover is the prominent feature of Exodus (chap. 12). Perhaps the children of Israel did not know the significance of this feast the night before they left Egypt, but they believed God and obeyed.

God had sent nine plagues on Egypt in order to make Pharaoh willing to let His people go. Almost a year had passed and with each plague there was a hardening of Pharaoh's heart. Finally God said that the firstborn in all Egypt should die. This tenth plague would have fallen on the Israelites, too, had they not killed the paschal lamb and been protected by its blood of redemption (Exodus 12:12,13).

Every person should study the divine order of the Passover as it is given in Exodus 12.

1. "Take a lamb"(Exodus 12:3): see also Hebrews 9:28; Isaiah 53:6; John 19:14; 1 Corinthians 5:7. It was not the spotlessness of the living

lamb that saved them (Hebrews 9:22; 1 John 1:7; Revelation 1:5). It was not Christ's sinless life that saves us, but His death on the cross.

2. "Strike the lintel and the two side posts with the blood" (Exodus 12:22, *KJV*). It is not enough for the lamb to be slain. The blood was sufficient but not efficient unless applied.

Every Israelite head of family had to apply it to his own household; notice over the doorway, not under. What have you done with the blood, the blood of our Passover Lamb who died on Mount Calvary? (Luke 23:33 [*Calvaria* is Latin for "skull"]; see also John 1:12).

The hyssop—a common weed, but obtainable by everyone—is typical of faith. The blood on the lintel is that which saved; not what they thought about it, but what they did with it counted. "When I see the blood, I will pass over you" (Exodus 12:13).

Not blood in the basin but blood applied saves a soul. Not all the blood shed on Calvary's cross can save a soul from death unless it is applied, then—"When I see the blood, I will pass over you."

Not feelings—not personal worthiness, but one thing saved them—"the blood" (Hebrews 9:22).

3. "Eat the lambs" (Exodus 12:7). After the blood was shed and applied to the doorframe, then there was direction for nourishment. So with us: salvation first, then feeding—fellowship, worship, walk and service.

Feeding did not save them, but blood first; then nourishment was possible (John 6:54-58). "My flesh is real food."

4. "Remove the yeast" (Exodus 12:15). "Search me, O God, and...see if there is any offensive way in me" (Psalm 139:23-24). Yeast (or "leaven," *KJV*) is often a type of sin: "Be on your guard against the yeast of the Pharisees and Sadducees" (Matthew 16:6); "Get rid of the old yeast" (1 Corinthians 5:7).

Leaven of unrighteousness must be removed from our lives if we are to eat with God.

5. "Eat the meat...with bitter herbs" (Exodus 12:8). Christ tasted the bitter cup for us and some bitterness we, too, must suffer. "No discipline seems pleasant at the time, but painful" (Hebrews 12:11).

The lamb was to be feasted upon not raw, not unbaked, but as a suffering lamb which had passed through fire. It was to be eaten in haste with nothing remaining. Not a bone was to be broken! Christ's body was broken, but not His bones (Psalm 34:20; John 19:36).

6. "Be dressed and ready to travel" (Exodus 12:11, *CEV*). They ate the food standing, fully dressed, ready to go. All provision was made for the journey. What a contrast that night! Peaceful feasting in the houses of Israel; awful mourning in the houses of Egypt!

We have read here of the Passover. Now comes the Passage. The Passover sealed them. The Passage of the Red Sea steeled them. They left Egypt under the blood, a marked people. They passed through the Red Sea a directed, determined people. God led them out and shut the door behind them!

"When I came out of Egypt" (Exodus 13:8). When did you come out? (Remember, Egypt represents allegiance to the world.)

The Giving of the Law (Exodus 20—24)

In Exodus 20—24 we see the law given, broken and restored. Up till this time in Israel's history all has been grace and mercy. God had heard the cry of their bondage and answered them. God selected a leader and trained him. God defeated their enemies. God fed them and yet they rebelled. Now a new order of things is brought about at Sinai.

The law demands nothing short of perfection. The psalmist says, "The law of the Lord is perfect" (Psalm 19:7; read verses 8-11). Only one Man since it was given has been able to keep it perfectly. Christ not only kept the law, but He also paid the complete penalty for the broken law. Christ suffered that we might be spared (see Hebrews 9:13-15; 10:1-22; 1 Peter 1:18-20).

If we could not keep the law, why was it given? That we might know our exceeding sinfulness. The law did not make us sin, but it showed us that we are sinners. The physician comes and looks at a child and the symptoms reveal that she has measles. He gives her some medicine that makes her break out. The doctor did not make the child have measles, but he proved that measles was there. (Read Galatians 4:4,5; Romans 8:1-4; 3:19-28.)

The law is God's mirror to show us our exceeding sinfulness. "So then, the law is holy, and the commandment is holy, righteous and good" (Romans 7:12).

Two mountain peaks stand in contrast to each other in God's Word.

1. Mount Sinai, with all of its horror thundered forth the law (Exodus 19).
2. Opposite this God places Mount Calvary. Calvary took away all the fire and thunder and made possible a meeting place between God and the sinner.

We each have a choice about how we shall approach God, either by law or by blood (Hebrews 12:18-29).

No provision was made in the law for failure. It is all or nothing—the whole law or a broken thing. One hole in a bowl, one crack in a pitcher, unfits it for its purpose. One flaw in a character mars the perfection God requires under the law.

Laws may be divided into two parts:

1. Laws regarding our attitude toward God.
2. Laws regarding our attitude toward our fellow humans.

We are told that God spoke all these words (Exodus 20:1). God gave the whole testimony and the people assumed the whole responsibility of keeping it. Read what the people said in Exodus 19:8. Why did Israel accept the law rather than cry for mercy? Human pride always makes us think that we can please God by ourselves. Before Israel even received the law or started to keep it, they were dancing around the golden calf, and worshiping a god they had made (Exodus 32:1-10,18).

The Building of the Tabernacle (Exodus 25—40)

Exodus 25—40 gives us one of the richest veins in inspiration's exhaustless mines. We must use our imagination and reason as we enter the holy precincts and gaze upon the significant furniture. God told Moses He wished a sanctuary or holy dwelling place that should point to Christ and tell of His person and work.

The Outer Court:

Herein we see the altar on which the burnt offerings were sacrificed. Remember, Christ is our sin-offering (27:1-8).

The bronze basin was there for the cleansing of the priests before they could enter into the holy place to render their service (30:18).

The Holy Place:

Herein was the golden lampstand (25:31-40), typifying Christ, the Light of the world; and the Bread of the Presence (25:23-30), for Christ is the Bread of life; and the golden altar of incense (30:1-10), symbolizing Christ's intercession for us.

Holy of Holies:

Now if we draw back the beautiful veil (which typifies the body of Christ), we will see the Ark of the Covenant, the symbol of God's presence. Into this holy of holies, the high priest came only once a year to sprinkle the blood of atonement. The book of Hebrews tells us that Christ is not only our High Priest, but that He was also our atonement, and so we can go into the holy of holies (the presence of God) at any time with boldness.

The Tabernacle itself:

The Tabernacle, having the cloud of glory over it, taught the people that God was dwelling in their midst (25:8).

The Tabernacle was the common center and rallying point that could be moved from time to time. Critics say that the account of the Tabernacle and its wonderful structure could not be true. They say that the times were too primitive, but research has given abundant evidence of great skill in such matters long before the Exodus. Fine linen was used in many ways. Fine work in gold has been discovered in the tombs dating back to as early as the twelfth Egyptian dynasty, and Moses lived in the eighteenth dynasty.

> Redemption was not an afterthought with God,
> Ephesians 1:4.
> The Law was broken in the people's hearts
> before it was broken by Moses' hand.
> Over against Sinai is Calvary!
> God's mirror reveals but never cleanses.
> The blood of the Lamb makes us safe;
> our trust in God's Word makes us sure.
> God's plan will never be frustrated.

Chapter 4

Understanding Leviticus

Leviticus Portrays Jesus Christ, Our Sacrifice for Sin

Selected Bible Readings

Sunday:	Burnt Offering (Leviticus 1)
Monday:	The Priests (Leviticus 8)
Tuesday:	Pure Food Laws (Leviticus 11)
Wednesday:	The Day of Atonement (Leviticus 16)
Thursday:	The Feasts of Jehovah (Leviticus 23)
Friday:	God's Pledge (Leviticus 26)
Saturday:	Dedication (Leviticus 27)

"Get right," say the offerings. There are five of them: burnt offering, grain offering, fellowship offering, sin offering and guilt offering.

"Keep right," say the feasts. There are eight of them: Sabbath, Passover, Pentecost, Trumpets, Atonement, Tabernacles, the Sabbath year and Jubilee.

Leviticus is called the Book of Atonement (Leviticus 16:30-34).

God says, "Be holy, because I am holy" (Leviticus 11:44-45; 19:2; 20:7,26).

The book of Leviticus is God's picture book for the children of Israel to help them in their religious training. Every picture pointed forward to the work of Jesus Christ.

The title of Leviticus suggests the subject matter of the book—the Levites and the priests and their service in the Tabernacle. It is also called the Book of Laws.

We remember in the book of Exodus how God gave Moses the

exact instructions about how to build the Tabernacle and about the institution of the priesthood to carry on the service in this holy place.

Like Exodus, Leviticus begins with the Hebrew word *we* ("and"). As this book opens, the children of Israel are still at Mount Sinai. God is continuing to give His instructions for orderly worship in the Tabernacle.

In Genesis, we see humanity ruined.

In Exodus, humanity redeemed.

In Leviticus, humanity worshiping.

Leviticus is a timely book for it insists on keeping the body holy as well as the soul. It teaches that the redeemed ones must be holy because their Redeemer is holy. It gives us not only the key for our spiritual life and its holy walk, but it also surprises us with real lessons in hygiene and sanitation for the care of the body. The Jewish people are wonderful evidence of the result of this latter in their long and vigorous lives.

It is a divine book. The opening verse affords us the clue to the whole, "The Lord called to Moses and spoke to him from the Tent of Meeting." Leviticus is God speaking to us through the Tabernacle and its meaning.

It is a personal book. The second verse intimates this, "When any of you brings an offering to the Lord." Notice, He expects each person to bring his or her own gift. The way is often as important as the gift. Have you an offering for the Lord? Then this book will appeal to you.

Sacrifice and Separation (Leviticus 1:1—6:7)

One of the most important questions in life is "How may an unholy people approach a holy God?"

At the very beginning of the book we see God making provision for His people to approach Him in worship. This book shows redeemed Israel that the way to God is by sacrifice and the walk with God by separation.

Isn't it strange that deep down in every heart there is a sense of guilt and the feeling of a need of doing something to secure pardon or gain the favor of the one wronged? Pagans bring their sacrifice to the altar of their gods, for they realize that they cannot do anything about their sin themselves. They must make atonement for it. The mothers in India used to throw their babies into the river Ganges to appease their gods. The British colonial government tried to put a stop to this, but the practice still continues.

Pagans cannot see beyond their sacrifices. When we look at the sacrifices in this book, we find that they are only types, or symbolic representations that point to the Perfect Sacrifice for sin which was to be made on Calvary.

All the sacrifices in this book point to "the Lamb of God, who takes away the sin of the world" (John 1:29).

Sin may be forgiven, but it must receive its penalty. "The wages of sin is death" (Romans 6:23). Sin keeps us from drawing near to God. He is "too pure to look on evil" (Habakkuk 1:13).

There can be no fellowship between God and the sinner until sin has been dealt with; the only way is sacrifice. "Without the shedding of blood there is no forgiveness" (Hebrews 9:22).

Five offerings are described in Leviticus. God wants us to understand the awful reality of sin, so He asks for a sacrifice each day.

Here is a list of the offerings, with a keyword to identify them. Learn this simple outline to fix in mind the first six chapters of Leviticus.

1. Burnt Offering: "Surrender" of Christ for the world—Leviticus 1
2. Grain Offering: "Service" of Christ in life—Leviticus 2
3. Fellowship Offering: "Serenity" of Christ in life—Leviticus 3
4. Sin Offering: "Substitute" of Christ for sin—Leviticus 4—5:13
5. Guilt Offering: "Satisfaction" by Christ for demands of God—Leviticus 5:14—6:7.

The Burnt Offering—Leviticus 1:

The offerings start with the burnt offering and end with the guilt offering.

The burnt offering is a type of Christ offering Himself without spot to God. There were daily burnt offerings. Christ offered Himself in the sinner's place (Leviticus 1:4).

This was an offering of Dedication. Why first? Because sacrifice comes first. No one begins with God until all has been yielded to God. (See Leviticus 1:3.) This was the most common sacrifice in the ancient Temple.

> Dedication is our part.
> Consecration is God's part.
> We dedicate ourselves to God.
> He consecrates us—to His service.

> Consecrate me now to Thy service Lord,
> By the power of grace divine;
> Let my soul look up with a steadfast hope,
> And my will be lost in Thine.

We sing, "Take my life and let it be consecrated, Lord, to Thee." (This is a burnt offering.)

The Grain Offering—Leviticus 2:

This is the sacrifice of daily devotion.

As the burnt offering typifies Christ in death, so the grain offering typifies Christ in life.

The fine flour speaks of the character of Christ—His perfection in thought, in word, in action.

Let us feed on the perfect grain offering.

We must come to Him first with our whole burnt offering. Then we keep coming with our continual grain offering. It is our very best, our gift of life. Notice, the slain offering must come first.

The Fellowship Offering—Leviticus 3:

Christ is our peace (Ephesians 2:14). He has reconciled all things to Himself "by making peace through his blood, shed on the cross" (Colossians 1:20).

This offering represents fellowship and communion with God. It is an offering of thanksgiving.

The Sin Offering—Leviticus 4—5:

This shows us Christ on the cross in the sinner's place.

In this offering we see an acknowledgment of sin, "When anyone sins...he must bring" (4:2-3). This offering is for expiation. In the other offerings the offerer comes as a worshiper, but here as a convicted sinner. God holds us accountable for our sin. We are like criminals who have been tried, found guilty and sentenced to death.

Though placed last, the sin and guilt offerings are included in all that goes before. The only reason burnt offerings, grain offerings or fellowship offerings can be made is that the blood of pardon has been shed. God has accepted the one offering of His Son, which every lesser offering typified (symbolically represented).

In non-Christian religions, worshipers bring sacrifices to their god; Christians accept the sacrifice from their God.

The Guilt Offering—Leviticus 5:14—6:7:

Christ has even taken care of our sin against others.

The blood of the guilt offering cleanses the conscience and sends the trespasser back to the one he or she has wronged, not only with the principal but with the fifth part added (6:5). The injurer is forgiven and the injured becomes an actual gainer.

It is a grave error to suppose that you are safe and right if you live up to your own conscience. God has scales. We can never comprehend His holiness.

None of these sacrifices forgave sin. They only pointed forward to the true Sacrifice, God's very own Son (Hebrews 10).

Notice that bullocks, oxen, goats, sheep, turtle doves and pigeons were mentioned for sacrifice. The offering was determined by the ability of the one who brought it.

What we bring is our sin; what Christ brings is the offering and the atonement for sin.

The Priest (Leviticus 8—10)

We have been studying the great subject of sacrifice, but no one could bring his or her own sacrifice to God. Each one had to bring it to the priest and he in turn would offer it to God.

God chose one tribe out of the twelve to care for the Tabernacle. This was the tribe of Levi. One family of Levites, Aaron's, should be the priests. The priests had charge of the sacrifices and were supported by the tithes of the people.

The priest offered the prayers and praises and sacrifices of the people to God in their behalf. He stood for them and pleaded their cause.

The burdened Israelites who desired to approach God brought their animals to the court of the Tabernacle. At the altar of burnt offerings they laid their hands on an animal's head to express penitence and consecration. The animal was killed and its blood sprinkled on the altar.

The priest representing the worshiper then came to the laver, in which he washed his hands, thus indicating the clean life that should follow the forgiveness of sins. He entered the holy place, passed by the sacred furnishings, the lampstand, the table of bread, and came to the altar of incenses, where prayer was offered.

One day in the year the high priest passed beyond the veil that separated the holy and the most holy place and stood before the mercy seat, with the blood of the atonement, to intercede for the people.

The priest could not consecrate himself. Moses acted for God in this service. Each priest presented his body a living sacrifice for service, just as Paul wants us to do in Romans 12:1-2.

The priests had charge of the sacrifices. The Levites were their assistants. They took care of the Tabernacle, formed choirs, were guides and instructors in the later Temple.

Notice the opening of Leviticus 10. At the very beginning of the history of the work of the priesthood evidences of failure could be noticed. Nadab and Abihu, two sons of Aaron, offered "strange fire" *(KJV)* before the Lord "contrary to his command. So fire came out from the presence of the Lord and consumed them."

We read in Leviticus 10:3 that Aaron held his peace. He was their father, but he dared not question God. We talk too much before God. We must learn to walk softly in the divine Presence. The other priests were solemnly charged to show no signs of mourning and to abide at their posts.

The priests were the ministers of the sacrifices we have just been studying. Each was a picture of the great sacrifice of Christ for the sin of the world.

Animal sacrifices are no longer necessary because all sacrifices were fulfilled in Christ. Therefore priests are no longer necessary. Christ Himself is the great High Priest for humanity (Hebrews 2:17; 4:15). He is the only Mediator between God and humanity. No one else can come between God and humanity.

Christ is our High Priest and He is at the right hand of the Father today making intercession for us. We approach God by Him and Him alone (Hebrews 10:12; 7:25; John 14:6).

When we see Christ as Sacrifice, we see beauty and completeness.

When we see Christ as Priest, we see His divine perfection. "For we do not have a high priest who is unable to sympathize with our weaknesses, but we have one who has been tempted in every way, just as we are—yet was without sin" (Hebrews 4:15).

As Sacrifice He establishes the relationship of His people with God.

As Priest He maintains that position.

We read of this perfect and eternal priesthood in the book of Hebrews. Heaven, not earth, is the sphere of Christ's priestly ministry. He never appeared in the Temple on earth to offer sacrifice. He went there to preach and teach but not to sacrifice. Except in the sense that all believers are priests (1 Peter 2:5), there is no such thing as a priest on earth. The believer is a spiritual priest. It is not necessary that any child of God go before any person on earth to obtain entrance into the presence of God. Every Christian has the right to enter because he or she knows Jesus Christ. The Lord said, "I am the way" (John 14:6). "Let us then approach the throne of grace with confidence, so that we may receive mercy and find grace to help us in our time of need" (Hebrews 4:16).

The God-appointed priests belonged to the tribe of Levi.

Eight Feasts (Leviticus 23; 25)

As the first part of the book has to do with offerings and the offerers, so the last part of the book deals with feasts and feasters.

Five great festivals are mentioned in Leviticus 23.

The sacrifices spoke of the blood that saved.

The feasts spoke of the food that sustains.

Both are of God.

The sacrifices correspond to the cup of the Lord's Supper that reminds us of Christ's death on the cross whereby we are redeemed. The bread of the Communion witnesses to His life of which we are partakers.

The Feast of the Sabbath—23:1-3:

The Sabbath was given the foremost place. It was a perpetually recurring feast to be obeyed through the whole year on every seventh day. It was a day of worship and rest, celebrating the finished work of God in creation (Genesis 2:2-3). Christians celebrate the first day of the week, the day our Lord arose from the grave (Luke 24:1; Acts 20:7; 1 Corinthians 16:2). Thus we celebrate the finished work of redemption.

The Feasts of the Passover—23:4-5 and Unleavened Bread—23:6-8:

The Passover spoke of redemption and was celebrated every spring at our Easter time. It was the Fourth of July for the children of Israel. They did not celebrate it by fireworks and parades but by a great service of worship to God. All the Israelites who could, made their way to Jerusalem.

Passover lasted one day, but the Feast of Unleavened Bread that immediately followed lasted seven days. With these the year commenced.

The Jewish people were still celebrating this feast when our Lord was on this earth. Read in the Word the times that He went to the Passover feast (Luke 2:41-52; Matthew 26:19; John 13). The Jewish people today continue to celebrate this same feast. They are still looking for their Messiah.

The Feasts of First Fruits—23:9-14 and Pentecost—23:15-22:

The Israelites observed first fruits during the Feast of Unleavened Bread. This feast of the first fruits typified Christ's resurrection and ours (1 Corinthians 15:20). Fifty days later Pentecost was observed. Fifty days after Christ's resurrection, the Holy Spirit descended upon the disciples and the Church was born. Pentecost was the birthday of the Church. The death and resurrection of Christ had to be accomplished before the descent of the Holy Spirit.

The Feast of Trumpets—23:23-25:

This has become the New Year's Day (Rosh Hashanah) of the Jewish people. The children of Israel celebrated it in the fall, in

September or October. This feast points forward to the future gathering of the dispersed people of Israel (Zechariah 14:16).

Day of Atonement—23:26-32:

The Day of Atonement followed the Feast of Trumpets by ten days. This was the most solemen day of the year of God's chosen people. On this day the sins of the nation were confessed. Confession is always the first step toward righteousness. It reveals a right attitude toward sin. It leads to a desire for forgiveness. God says, "If we confess our sins, he is faithful and just and will forgive us our sins and purify us from all unrighteousness" (1 John 1:9).

On this day Jehovah's (Jehovah is a form of the divine name, more properly, "Yahweh") relationship to His people was established—all the nation's sins, failures and weaknesses of the people were atoned for. The blood was shed and the sins of the people were covered so that God could take up His abode in the midst of His people in spite of their uncleanness.

We learn in Leviticus 16 that God was hidden behind a veil in the Tabernacle and the priests and the people were to remain at a distance. Read Leviticus 16:2. The way was not yet made open to approach God. Now "we may approach God with freedom and confidence" (Ephesians 3:12). We can run into God's presence at any time for Christ has made the way possible for us. In the book of Leviticus, God was shut in from humanity and humanity was shut out from God.

The Day of Atonement was the only day in the year when the high priest was permitted to enter the holy of holies. He went in with an offering for the atonement of the sin of the people. Atonement means "cover." This offering "covered" the sins of the people until the great sacrifice on Calvary was made. None of these offerings "took away" those sins. Read Hebrews 10:1-2,11-12.

The Feast of Tabernacles—23:33-36:

This was the last required feast of the year. Also called the Feast of Booths or Ingathering, it commemorated the time when the children of Israel lived in tents during their wilderness journey. It was celebrated in the fall of the year and lasted an entire week. The people lived in booths out-of-doors and heard the reading of the Law.

The Feast of the Passover in the spring and the Feast of Tabernacles in the fall kept before the children of Israel the marvelous way in which they were delivered from Egypt and were sustained in the wilderness. God did not want them to forget the way in which the gods of Egypt were utterly discredited and the great nation of Egypt humbled.

The Feast of Tabernacles recalled to their minds that by their own disobedience they were compelled to wander forty years in the wilderness, but in spite of their unbelief God was faithful in caring for them and in bringing them to their inheritance. These days reminded them of their dependence upon Jehovah and the blessings that would come if they would be obedient to His will.

The Sabbatical Year—25:1-7:

This was the year of meditation and devotion. It was a year-long Sabbath. The purpose and character of the Sabbath was magnified. God impressed it upon the minds of the people. This He did every seven years.

God wanted to impress upon them that the very land was holy unto Him. Thus, "the land he promised them" (Deuteronomy 9:28) became "the holy land" (Zephaniah 2:5). There was quiet over the whole land during these days. All breathed the spirit of rest and meditation. Every day was like the Sabbath, and the minds of the people were kept on the things of the Lord. The Law was read. This time exerted a tremendous influence upon the lives of the people.

The Year of Jubilee—25:8-55:

This was celebrated every fiftieth year. It was inaugurated on the Day of Atonement with the blowing of trumpets. As in the sabbatic year, the land was not cultivated. All slaves of Israelite blood were freed. The blowing of the trumpets that ushered in the year released every bondperson. Jewish historians tell us that the Year of Jubilee was observed at the time of the fall of Judah in 586 B.C. References are made to it in Isaiah 5:7-10; 61:1-2; Ezekiel 7:12-13; 46:16-18.

Another outstanding event was the restoration to the original owner of all land that had in any way been taken away. That is, it was returned to the family to whom it had been assigned in the original distribution. What a wise provision it was from an economic standpoint. But God no doubt had a more far-reaching plan bearing upon the coming of the Messiah. Every tribal and family register must be carefully kept so that the rights of all would be protected. This would apply especially to Judah, the tribe from which the Messiah was to come. From these registers our Lord's natural descent could be exactly traced.

This book is for a redeemed people, showing how God is to be approached and worshiped. The book of Exodus is the book of redemption, but the book of Leviticus tells how the redeemed ones can worship God.

Only through the blood of Christ can we have access to God.

God demands a holiness that Christ alone can give, for we are sharers in his holiness (Hebrews 12:10).

In Genesis we see humanity ruined.

In Exodus, humanity redeemed.

In Leviticus, humanity worshiping.

Seven is a significant number in Leviticus:

Every seventh day was the Sabbath. Every seventh year was a sabbatic year.

Every seven times seven years was followed by a year of Jubilee.

Pentecost was seven weeks after Passover.

In the seventh month were the feasts of trumpets, tabernacles and atonement.

Pentecost lasted seven days. Passover lasted seven days.

This book, like Revelation, is built around a series of seven.

Chapter 5

Understanding Numbers

Numbers Portrays Jesus Christ, Our "Lifted-up One"

Selected Bible Readings

Sunday: The Guiding Cloud (Numbers 9:15-23)
Monday: The Report of the Spies (Numbers 13:16-33)
Tuesday: Israel's Unbelief (Numbers 14:1-45)
Wednesday: Water from the Rock (Numbers 20:1-13)
Thursday: The Brazen Serpent (Numbers 21:1-9)
Friday: Balaam's Feast (Numbers 22:1-41)
Saturday: The Cities of Refuge (Numbers 35:6-34)

The children of Israel were saved to serve. So is every child of God today.

Beware of unbelief! The apostle Paul says to us, "You were running a good race. Who cut in on you and kept you from obeying the truth?" (Galatians 5:7). Unbelief hinders blessing. God tells why we cannot enter into His blessings (Hebrews 3:19).

This book might be called the Wilderness Wandering from Sinai to the border of Canaan, the land of promise, covering about forty years.

Numbers is also called the Book of the March and the Roll Call (Numbers 33:1-2).

It might, too, be called the Book of Murmurings because from beginning to end it is filled with the spirit of rebellion against God. Read what God says about this in Psalm 95:10.

Numbers is indeed the book of the wilderness, recording the

pitiable failure of Israel at Kadesh-barnea, and the consequent wanderings and experiences of the people in the wilderness. It records the pilgrimage, warfare, service and failure of the second generation of the nation after the Exodus from Egypt. This, however, is not all the message of Numbers. The first ten chapters give us the divine legislation; chapters 11—20 tell the story of the nation's failure; but the closing chapters of the book record Israel's return to Jehovah's favor and final victory, even in the wilderness.

While the annals of many powerful nations of that same time are lost to the world, these of a comparative handful of people are preserved. The reason for this is that the Messiah who would redeem the world was to come from this people. This is the reason God was so patient with them. He wanted to preserve them for Himself. In 1 Corinthians 10, we learn that the things that happened to them were "examples" unto us. In other words, their whole history was an "object lesson" to us, illustrating God's dealing with us today.

The key thought is discipline. Numbers is the fourth book of Moses. Someone has said that the order of the books is as follows:

1. In Genesis, we see humanity ruined.
2. In Exodus, humanity redeemed.
3. In Leviticus, humanity worshiping.
4. In Numbers, humanity serving.

This is the order the Law lays down. Only someone who is saved can serve and worship God. Remember, we are saved to serve. We are not saved by good works, but we are "created in Christ Jesus to do good works, which God prepared in advance for us to do" (Ephesians 2:10). The law can bring us up to the land of promise, but only our divine Joshua (Christ) can bring us in. Paul says that the law is the "schoolmaster" *(KJV)* to bring us to Christ (Galatians 3:24). The law cannot save us, for we are saved "not by works, so that no one can boast" (Ephesians 2:9).

Leviticus deals with the believer's worship.

Numbers deals with the believer's walk.

In Leviticus we see the believer's privileges.

In Numbers the wilderness is the drill field.

If you know five names, you will master the story of the book of Numbers.

Moses, the great leader.

Aaron, the high priest, Moses' brother.

Miriam, who was Moses' and Aaron's sister.

Joshua and Caleb, the two spies who dared to believe God, the only men of their generation who lived to enter Canaan.

The geography of the book takes us:

1. From Sinai to Kadesh
2. From Kadesh around back to Kadesh
3. From Kadesh straight to the border of Canaan.

The children of Israel learned:

1. That they must trust God, not people, in the day of crisis (Psalm 37:5). Read Numbers 13:26—14:25.
2. That God would supply all their need according to His riches (Philippians 4:19).
   He gave them food—Numbers 11:6-9
   He gave them meat—Numbers 11:31-33
   He gave them water—Numbers 20:8
   He gave them leaders—Numbers 1:1,3
   He gave them a promised land—Numbers 14:7-8.
3. That they must worship God according to His instructions.

It was God's plan that the children of Israel should go straight into the land He had promised them, the land of Canaan, but the people would not. God said that all those at Kadesh over twenty years old, except Joshua and Caleb, would have to die. A new generation arose during the forty years of wandering, but at the end the nation was about as strong in numbers as the day they left Egypt. (Read Numbers 26.)

Preparation for the Journey (Numbers 1—12)

As the book opens we see the children of Israel in the wilderness of Sinai. The Law had been given, the Tabernacle had been built and the priests had been assigned to their service. Now God was going to prepare the nation for its work. The teachings of this book are very applicable to the Christian life.

Order is heaven's first law. We see God numbering and arranging the tribes (chaps. 1 and 2), choosing and assigning duties to the priests and Levites (chaps. 3 and 4). God is the author of order.

The thought of God numbering His people and gathering them about Himself is most precious to our hearts. He dwelt in the camp. The twelve tribes guarded the Tabernacle of the Lord. The Levites encamped directly around the court, and Moses and Aaron and the priests guarded the entrance whereby God was approached.

The circumference of the camp arranged in this way and facing the Tabernacle is supposed to have been twelve miles. What an imposing sight the camp must have been to the outward eye, in the midst of the desert, with God stretching over them in a cloud by day and fire by night (Numbers 9:15-23). He was their night lamp and their day shade. Their shoes and their clothes did not wear out (Deuteronomy 29:5). Think of 600,000 men, twenty years old and upward, and about 3,000,000 men, women and children in this great camp! But the most glorious thing was that God was in their midst.

In the first chapter, Moses is commanded to take a census. The Lord knows all by name that are His (2 Timothy 2:19; Philippians 4:3). Even the hairs of our head are numbered. How wonderful to know that God cares for each of His children!

For Christians, too, there is a census, for Christ numbers His jewels and knows them who are His. "A scroll of remembrance was written in his presence concerning those who feared the Lord and honored his name" (Malachi 3:16).

In this chapter we find the declaration of their pedigree. Can you trace your genealogy to the risen Lord? Are you sure of your pedigree (John 1:12)?

Here were about three million people on a sterile desert, very little grass, very little water, no visible means of support. How were they to be fed? God was there! How were they to trace their way through a howling wilderness where there was no path? God was there!

God's presence provides everything! What? Are all these three million to be fed on air? Who has charge of the commissary? Where is the baggage? Who is to attend to the clothing? God was there! In faith's arithmetic God is the only figure that counts.

No one had gone before to blaze a trail for the children of Israel. There was not a footprint, not a landmark. It is much like our life as a Christian today. We are passing through a trackless desert—a moral wilderness. There is no trail. We would not know where to walk except for one little sentence from the lips of the Lord, "I am the way" (John 14:6). He will guide us step by step. There is no uncertainty, for He said, "Whoever follows me will never walk in darkness, but will have the light of life" (John 8:12).

God gave His children a cloud to guide them by day and a pillar of fire by night. It is interesting to see how they were guided a step at a time. They did not know when they were to go and when to stop, but the Ark of the Covenant (signifying God's presence) went on before, the pillar of cloud always leading (Numbers 10:33).

Sin crept into this well-ordered camp life. The people began to murmur against God. God sent judgment of fire (Numbers 11:1-3). Then they complained about their food (11:4). It seemed monotonous. They longed for the garlic and onions of Egypt and they wanted fish. As a result of their complaining, God sent them quails for thirty days. They made gluttons of themselves, "But while the meat was still between their teeth and before it could be consumed, the anger of the Lord burned against the people, and he struck them with a severe plague" (Numbers 11:33). Many became ill and died.

Then we read of the sin of Aaron, the high priest, and Miriam, the sister of Moses. God had chosen Moses to be the leader of this great people and Aaron and Miriam were only his assistants. Jealousy crept into their hearts. They wanted more honor. Read of Miriam's terrible punishment. She was smitten with leprosy for seven days (Numbers 12:1-16).

We find the invitation of God's marching host to the people round about them, "Come with us and we will treat you well, for the Lord has promised good things to Israel" (Numbers 10:29). Can we say this, do we say it, to those about us?

The Ark of the Covenant is the Word of God in the midst.

The sound of the silver trumpet is the witness of a faithful prophet.

The pillar of fire and of cloud is the comfort and guidance of the Holy Spirit.

The Tabernacle and its ordinances are for the worship of God in the sanctuary.

Christ "the Apostle and High Priest" of our profession gives significance to it all.

We are just humans making many mistakes and capable of wandering far. God has given us these heavenly attendants and guides. Who does not need them? Who can make progress without them? Invite others to join our band and go with us. We should always be taking others by the hand and inviting them to go with us.

Wilderness Wanderings (Numbers 13—20)

After one year at Mount Sinai, the Israelites journeyed to Kadesh. This is at the southern border of the Promised Land. Afraid to enter, they turned back and wandered in the wilderness to the south and east till that generation died. They did not travel all the time but remained in some places with their flocks and herds grazing on the surrounding hills. When the cloud lifted, they marched. They finally approached Canaan from east of the Dead Sea.

Think of the lost years from Kadesh back to Kadesh because people would not believe God. After two years in the wilderness, the children of Israel could have gone into the land of promise immediately had it not been for the sin of unbelief. They listened to the discouraging words of most of the spies.

When the spies came back and told them about the giants in the land and the high-walled cities, their hearts failed them. They would not listen to Joshua and Caleb who agreed with all that was told, but added, "We should go up and take possession of the land, for we can certainly do it" (Numbers 13:30). But the people would not trust God. They said, "We should choose a leader and go back to Egypt" (Numbers 14:4).

When they refused to enter Canaan, the door was closed to

them. It meant wandering in the wilderness for forty years. God said that He would not allow any of those who were over twenty years old to enter Canaan, except Joshua and Caleb.

At the beginning, the journey from Sinai to Kadesh was a swift and jubilant one! Then came sad doubt and delay. Hesitant Israel was plunged down into the wasting years of wilderness wanderings. Sadly Moses reminded them of it, "Thirty-eight years passed from the time we left Kadesh Barnea until we crossed the Zered Valley. By then, that entire generation of fighting men had perished from the camp, as the Lord had sworn to them" (Deuteronomy 2:14).

Eleven days from the land of promise! But they turned back. They could have made eleven days of progress, but they chose forty years of wandering.

God opens doors that no human can close, and He closes doors that no human can open (Isaiah 22:22; Revelation 3:8).

God opened the door and about three million souls walked out of Egypt; He closed the door when the Egyptians tried to follow.

God took the children of Israel out of Egypt so that He could take them into Canaan, the land of promise. God did not want the children of Israel just to come out of Egypt. He wanted to have them come in to the Promised Land. This they could have done in comparatively a few days; not more than two or three weeks. Remember the spies made the trip and returned within forty days. As we have already seen, their fear disqualified them to take over the land of promise.

Oftentimes our fear keeps us from enjoying all that God wants to give us. We fear what others will say. We fear what might happen if we put our trust completely in Christ.

One of the reports of the spies was that there were giants in the land and that the Israelites were as grasshoppers in their sight (Numbers 13:33).

This record tells the story of many a Christian life and in part the story of every life. Giants of selfishness and greed, far outranking the Anakim (a people the Israelites feared because they were "strong, numerous and tall" [Deuteronomy 2:21]), oppose our advance! But when the returns are all in, the fact remains that there is One with us stronger than they!

Like the ten, we can be pessimists; or like the two, optimists. Like the ten, we can put difficulties between us and God and say we are not able; or like the two, we can put God between the difficulties and ourselves and say we are able!

We start out with high hope in the enthusiasm of our first love. Yonder lies the land of possibilities and achievement. Then the giants appear—giants of opposition from without; giants of fear from within. Our faith fails. We forget God. We compare our difficulties with our own strength rather than committing them to the great arm of God. Then we turn back into the wilderness of half trust, half victory and whole despair.

Numbers 33 is the pitiful logbook of this journey: "They left Hazeroth and camped at Rithmah. They left Rithmah and camped at Rimmon Perez. They left Rimmon Perez and camped at Libnah" etc., to the end of this dismal chapter! Going, going, pitching and departing, but never arriving anywhere. An endless circle of aimless wandering with no success. When we doubt God we find this to be our experience, too. We feel defeated and discouraged. We wander around but never accomplish anything. It is like a swinging door—lots of motion but getting no place.

Before this scene ends we find Israel murmuring again, this time because of the shortage of water. Chapter 20 describes how the people complained bitterly to Moses and Aaron and said they wished they had never been brought out of Egypt. The land was dry and parched and there was no water to drink. Moses and Aaron again went to God. God told Moses to take his rod and speak to the rock before the people, and the rock would give forth water.

Moses' patience was at an end. The people had complained about everything. In a fit of anger he called the people rebels and instead of speaking to the rock he struck it. The water gushed out. Even though Moses disobeyed, God was faithful and kept His promise. That stream may still be flowing. In this district the Turkish army put a pipeline and got their water during World War I. Kadesh-barnea is a beautiful oasis. Ruins of the ancient city of Kadesh are to be found here today.

Is it not sad that even children of God fail under testing? Moses' error was great, yet it showed him to be just like us. Moses put himself up as God—"Listen, you rebels, must we bring you water out of this rock?" (Numbers 20:10). This dishonored Jehovah God. Because Moses smote the rock a second time (see first time, Exodus 17:5,6) instead of speaking to it, he was not permitted to enter the Promised Land. Christ, like the rock, was to be smitten once for our sins (1 Corinthians 10:4). He need not be smitten again.

There are three ways of knowing people, a rabbi in the Talmud says:

In their cups
With their cash
In their wrath.

How true it is that ill behavior at the table discloses bad culture; ill conduct in business reveals the unscrupulous; ill speaking in wrath proclaims the ignoble.

One of the important things we have not covered is an incident in Numbers 17.

Aaron's priesthood had been questioned, so God Himself was to confirm it. Moses gathered twelve staffs, one from the leader of each tribe, and placed them overnight in the Tent of Meeting. God put life into Aaron's alone, causing it to sprout and bud. So we find that all the authors of the religions of the world have died—even Christ died—but only Christ was raised from the dead and exalted to be our High Priest (Hebrews 4:14; 5:4-10).

On to Canaan (Numbers 20—36)

As this scene opens, we discover that all the Israelites who left Egypt had died except Moses, Aaron, Joshua, Caleb, Miriam and the children who were under twenty years of age when the spies entered the land. While they camped in Kadesh, Miriam, Moses' sister, died (20:1) and Aaron, his brother, now over 100 years old, also died (20:28).

Israel was to move on again. They started from Kadesh-barnea, this time with faces set resolutely toward the land of promise. The way was difficult, much harder than before, but faith had been renewed, discipline had done its work and the arm of God went forth conquering and to conquer.

Learn here the lesson of God's second best. He offers the perfect way and we refuse it. It is gone forever. Every male over twenty years of age who refused to go into the land of promise the first time (except Joshua and Caleb who believed God) died in the wilderness. Not one of them entered the land.

But God is kind, and He sets before us another way, a second best; it may even be a third, for His mercy is wonderful. He forgives us seventy times seven. He brings us through, provides for us, never failing in His grace, but, oh, how much we miss and how many burdens we have to bear by not taking the first and the best. How costly this is!

Israel was complaining again, although over and over again God had proven to them that His way is best. Discontent and murmuring seem to have been ingrained habits of the children of Israel. Grumbling is the easiest thing in the world to learn. "No talent, no self-denial, no brains, no character is required to set up the grumbling business," are the words written in a large business office.

What's the use of grumbling? It never makes a heavy burden light. It never subtracts from ills. Instead it always adds to them.

They battled with the Canaanites and became discouraged. Then they grumbled because they had to march around the land of Edom instead of through it. They growled again against God and against Moses because they loathed the manna (Numbers 21:5). They never were content.

This time God sent venomous snakes among the people, which caused suffering and death. After they confessed their sin, Moses prayed for the deliverance of his people. God did not take away the venomous snakes, but told Moses to make a bronze snake and fasten it to a pole so that all could see it. As soon as they looked, they would live. (See Numbers 21:6-9.)

The Bible reveals that the whole human family has felt the ancient Serpent's sting of sin, which means death (1 Corinthians 15:56; Hebrews 2:14-15). The only way people can live is by looking to the One who took upon Himself the likeness of a human and was lifted up on the cross to take the sting of death upon Himself (Philippians 2:7-8). If we look on Him, our Savior, we shall live (John 3:14-15).

Chapter 6

Understanding Deuteronomy

Deuteronomy Portrays Jesus Christ, Our True Prophet

Selected Bible Readings

Sunday: Forward March (Deuteronomy 1:6-46)

Monday: Instructions (Deuteronomy 5:1-33; 6:4-18)

Tuesday: The Messiah, Prophet (Deuteronomy 18:15-22)

Wednesday: God's Covenant (Deuteronomy 30:1-20)

Thursday: The Song of Moses (Deuteronomy 32:1-44)

Friday: God's Blessings (Deuteronomy 33:1-29)

Saturday: The Death of Moses (Deuteronomy 34:1-12)

"Observe to do" is the word of Moses to the people. He wanted them to be "doers of the word, and not hearers only" (James 1:22, *KJV*).

This book shows the blessings of obedience and the curse of disobedience.

Everything depends on obedience—life itself, possession of the Promised Land, victory over foes, prosperity and happiness. We find this book teaching the inflexibility of the law. "Thou shalt" and "thou shalt not" *(KJV)* occur over and over again—"the blessing if you obey" and "the curse if you disobey" (Deuteronomy 11:27-28).

The book of Deuteronomy is a collection of the orations and songs of Moses he gave as his farewell to the children of Israel. These noble orations were given as he stood on the great divide between his earthly and heavenly life. He was looking from the top of Mount Pisgah over a century crammed full of epoch-creating events. Then he turned his gaze upon the future of the people he was about to leave.

The book contains a most interesting and instructive summary of the wilderness history of Israel, and in the last chapter we find an account of Moses himself. Carefully compare Moses' review of the events with the account itself given in Exodus and Numbers. It will be found that Deuteronomy gives the divine rather than the human view. Compare Deuteronomy 1 with Numbers 13,14.

Deuteronomy is a book of remembrance. The name "Deuteronomy" means "second law," which indicates that the law is repeated. Moses did this to remind the people what God had done for them and what they were to do to serve Him when they reached the Promised Land. It omits the things that relate to the priests and Levites and includes the things that the people should know.

This book is the last of the five books of Moses. These five books are often called the "Pentateuch," meaning five books.

Genesis tells of the beginnings of the chosen nation Israel.

Exodus relates the organization of the people into a nation and the giving of the law.

Leviticus tells the way this people were to worship God.

Numbers gives a story of the wanderings of this people.

Deuteronomy relates the final preparation for entering the Promised Land.

Deuteronomy covers only about two months, including the thirty days of mourning for Moses.

Moses delivered his counsels probably within a period of seven days and about a month before the passage of the Jordan River (Deuteronomy 1:1-3).

Moses was the writer but not the author of the Pentateuch. More than five hundred times in these first five books we find expressions such as these: "The Lord spake"; "God said." Who is the divine Author of the Bible? (2 Peter 1:20-21).

The Christian heart always quickens its beat when it comes to Deuteronomy, for this book was a favorite with our Savior. From this book He quoted in His temptation in the wilderness with His adversary the devil. The following passages were His weapons with which He repelled the tempter: Matthew 4:1-11; Luke 4:1-13;

Deuteronomy 8:3; 6:16; 6:13; and 10:20. Thus this book of Deuteronomy, God's book about obedience, Moses' last charge to his people, seems to have about it the peculiar blessing and protection of Christ Himself.

You will come to appreciate the full force and magnetic beauty of Deuteronomy only as you read its pages. Read it through in a single sitting.

Nothing in literature matches the majesty of its eloquence; nothing in the Old Testament has any more powerful appeal for the spiritual life. No book in all the Word of God pictures better the life that is lived according to God's will, and the blessings showered upon the soul who comes into the richness and fullness of spiritual living along the rugged pathway of simple obedience.

Jesus often quoted from Deuteronomy. In fact, it is almost invariably from this book that He quotes. He took Deuteronomy as His code of conduct (Luke 4:4,8,12). He answered the devil in the hour of temptation from its writings.

Why do people pick flaws in the Bible and leave Homer, Virgil, Horace and others alone? Because the Bible reveals people and their wicked hearts. No one wants to be told he or she is a sinner.

If you want a taste of heaven on earth, become familiar with Deuteronomy. Catch step with Moses and march ahead by way of the "Honey Land" (i.e., the Promised Land, Canaan, the "land flowing with milk and honey," Exodus 3:8).

"Brethren," a man once said, "when I get to the gates of heaven, if they shut me out, I'll say, 'Anyhow, I had a good time getting here.'"

Are you having a good time on your way to heaven? God "has blessed us in the heavenly realms with every spiritual blessing in Christ" (Ephesians 1:3), but we must appropriate and possess them by faith.

Moses' First Address: "Looking Back" (Deuteronomy 1—4)

As the book opens we see the children of Israel on the border of the land of Canaan, in a place where eleven days' journey, some forty years before, could have brought them. Yet it had taken them forty years. How slowly they covered the ground! What windings and turnings! How often we have to go over the same ground again and again. We marvel at Israel's slowness. We can rather marvel at our own! We, like they, are kept back by unbelief. We should be ashamed at the time it takes us to learn our lessons! God is such a faithful teacher. He never lets us pass on to another grade until we are ready.

How deplorable is unbelief! God never fails us when we put our trust in Him, but He cannot do many mighty works because of our unbelief (Matthew 13:58).

Several hundred years before, God had promised to Abraham and his "seed" (Hebrew: *zerah*, offspring, descendant[s]) a rich and wondrous land upon whose borders they were standing (Genesis 17:8, *KJV*). Now they were ready to enter in after all the years of anticipation and hope. The closing chapters of Numbers found them camped by the Jordan, waiting to go over into the good promised land itself.

As we shall see, in Deuteronomy God is putting before the children of Israel the conditions of their entering and holding the land. We see all these conditions summed up in one great word: Obedience.

The children of Israel entered the Promised Land under the conditions of the law.

The book of Deuteronomy is one long plea for hearty obedience to God based on two grand motives of love and fear. "And now, O Israel, what does the Lord your God ask of you but to fear the Lord your God, to walk in all his ways, to love him, to serve the Lord your God with all your heart and with all your soul" (Deuteronomy 10:12).

In the first four books of the Pentateuch, God is choosing Israel. Now He is letting Israel choose Him.

Besides Moses, only Caleb and Joshua were left from the generation that had come out of Egypt. All the others were dead. The younger generation who now lived had suffered hardships in the wilderness wanderings and were ready and anxious for conquest! But Moses must rehearse the law to them. He knows his work is finished, for God has told him another will lead them into Canaan (Numbers 20:12).

Moses, the grand old man, was now one hundred and twenty years old. We see him giving his farewell address to the people whom he had led these past forty years.

Moses gives the children of Israel a look back. He recalls the history of Israel and reviews their wanderings. He reminds them of God's faithfulness and urges them to be grateful and obedient. He likens God's care of them to a loving father who cherishes his little ones lest they should be lost in the wilderness or be injured by the heat of the sun. He supplied all their needs; they lacked nothing (Deuteronomy 2:7).

He spoke to his beloved people in the most earnest and eloquent way and appealed to them to serve and obey God. His words still echo down the corridors of time!

Moses' work was done. He had spent the last forty years of his life in delivering his people from the bondage of Egypt, in guiding them through the many dangers that confronted them. He trained them, gave them forms of government, laws, religious institutions and molded them into a nation.

The children of Israel were now at the end of their journey, in the plain east of the Jordan, overlooking the land they had come so far to possess. It lay before them in the glories of the springtime. But the impassable Jordan river rolled between, and walled cities rose up in seemingly impregnable strength. The Israelites were like young graduates leaving high school or college, about to enter upon their life's work.

Moses' Second Address: "Looking Up" (Deuteronomy 5—26)

In Deuteronomy 12:1 we see the key to this section. "These are the decrees and laws you must be careful to follow in the land." Israel was going into a new land and everything would depend on their constant and intelligent obedience to God who was giving them the land. God wanted to teach Israel the love that is the real fulfilling of the law (Romans 13:8-10; Matthew 22:37-40).

Moses now sets forth the law simply and clearly so that it would take a living hold of the people. God says, "You are My people; I love you. I have chosen you; I am in the midst of you. I will protect you. I am only asking you to obey Me for your good" (paraphrased from several passages). He repeatedly reminds them that they are "a people holy to the Lord" (7:6; 14:2,21: 26:19). Because God's people are His, He wants them to walk in the world in the way that befits them, separating themselves from evil (chap. 14). They should show charity toward their fellow humans (chap. 15). They must gather together to worship (chap. 16). (See Hebrews 10:25.)

Today people are careless about church going and worship. This speaks of spiritual decay. God demands discipline. (See Deuteronomy 17.)

In Deuteronomy 18, God tells of the great Prophet, the Lord Jesus Christ. He alone knows the future. In this day, many are turning to enchanters, soothsayers, fortune-tellers, mediums, consulters with familiar spirits and the black art of sorcery. Spiritualism is rampant today! If you want to know what God thinks about the modern seance, look up Isaiah 8:19,20; Leviticus 19:31; 20:6; and study the dark story in 1 Samuel 28 in the light of 1 Chronicles 10:13.

God showed the Israelites that their highest duty was to exhibit the spirit of loving obedience. They were to be thankful, yes, really thankful. They were to be full of joy and gladness. Why shouldn't they be joyful in the best land on earth and with such a God as Jehovah? Surely they ought to be glad and love their God with all their heart.

Moses' heart, however, was burdened because he knew that Israel had a hard heart and the people were self-willed (Deuteronomy 31:24-29). How many children in these days of ours (see their description by Paul in 2 Timothy 3:1-9), should have been put to death, under the solemn command of Deuteronomy 21:18-21?

Note this! Disobedient children who are rebellious toward their parents are an abomination in God's sight.

If we read Deuteronomy 21:22-23 and compare it with John 19:31, we see why Christ was accursed as He hung between heaven and earth on the cross. In Galatians 3:10-13 we read that He is cursed because He was bearing our sin (2 Corinthians 5:21). What effect did this have upon Paul (2 Corinthians 5:14-15)?

Moses' Third Address: "Looking Out" (Deuteronomy 27—33)

We see Moses giving the people some solemn warnings. He first spoke of the blessings the children of Israel could enjoy if they would be obedient. He then told them the results of disobedience. Misfortune would follow them in everything they would undertake—in business, in farming and in health. They would suffer for their disobedience to God.

Deuteronomy 28 is a most remarkable chapter. It traces what Israel might have been through obedience (1-14) and is yet to be in the millennial age to come (see Isaiah 60—62; Zechariah 14:8-21; Jeremiah 31:1-9; Deuteronomy 30:1-10; Romans 11:25-31).

Verses 47-49 could refer to the Roman invasion, A.D. 70, under Titus. This was indeed a bloody page of history!

Verses 63-67 describe the Jewish people today. God spoke this more than 3,000 years ago. Chapter 28 leaves Israel where that nation is today—"scattered" (v. 64).

1. "Scattered"—The Jewish people shall be scattered from one end of the earth to the other. Today, Jewish communities are found throughout the world.
2. "Restless"—only rarely in their history have the Jewish people found complete security (v. 65).
3. "Suspense" and "dread"—Jewish history is full of persecution and tragedies. Think of the way they have been treated in many countries (vv. 65-67). God foretold all this!

Moses spoke to Joshua, his personal attendant throughout the wilderness wandering. He was one of the spies who dared to believe God. He was now eighty years old and Moses committed to him the leadership of this great people! Read his words in Deuteronomy 31:7,8.

The charge that Moses gave to the people and to Joshua was built on one great fact, "The Lord is with you; be strong." If God is present, fear is baseless!

This grand old man, one hundred and twenty years of age, stood a witness to the grace of God. He sang a song for Israel (chap. 32). Moses had celebrated the deliverance of Israel from Egypt with a song (Exodus 15), and now he closed his life's work with another. He wrote a third, which we know as the ninetieth Psalm. Christians have always had a song! And in heaven throughout the ages everyone will sing!

In Deuteronomy 34, after the song and final words of blessing, Moses went up to Mount Nebo's heights (sometimes called Mount Pisgah) and there God showed him the Promised Land toward which his face had so long been set. We know he died there and the Lord buried him. No one knows where. Someone said, "God buried his burial." God buries the workman but carries on the work.

Whether Moses himself wrote Deuteronomy 34 by revelation or whether Joshua added it later is immaterial.

The horde of slaves made into a nation by Moses wept for him thirty days. Had it not been for their perversity they might still have had him with them.

Why do you think Moses' grave was hidden? No doubt it would have become the object of superstitious idolatry.

We read of Moses again in the Gospels. One day Jesus took Peter, James and John and climbed up Mount Hermon to the north of the Sea of Galilee. Then Moses and Elijah appeared and talked with Jesus about His coming death (Matthew 17:1-3).

Books of History

of The Old Testament

Joshua • Judges • Ruth • 1 Samuel
2 Samuel • 1 Kings • 2 Kings
1 Chronicles • 2 Chronicles
Ezra • Nehemiah • Esther

Key Events of the Books of History

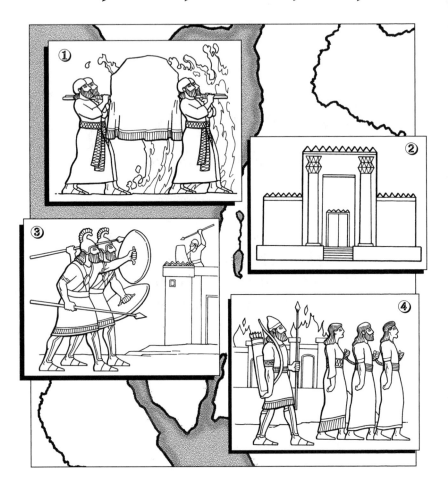

Books of History: The Rise and Fall of the Davidic Kingdom

God brought His chosen people ① into the Promised Land with miracles, military victories and treaties. Then God allowed the Israelites a brief measure of earthly glory ② in the reigns of David and Solomon. To King David, God promised an everlasting kingdom. However, the Davidic dynasty split. Assyrians ③ erased the Northern Kingdom (722 B.C.) and Babylonians ④ conquered the Southern Kingdom (605-586 B.C.). Eventually, the Persians allowed the Jewish people to resettle Judah and rebuild the Jerusalem Temple.

Chapter 7

Understanding Joshua

Joshua Portrays Jesus Christ, Captain of Our Salvation

Selected Bible Readings

Sunday:	Joshua's Commission (Joshua 1—2)
Monday:	Crossing the Jordan (Joshua 3)
Tuesday:	The Fall of Jericho (Joshua 6)
Wednesday:	The Sin of Achan (Joshua 7)
Thursday:	Occupation of the Land (Joshua 11)
Friday:	Caleb's Possession (Joshua 14)
Saturday:	Joshua's Farewell (Joshua 24)

"Take possession of the land the Lord your God is giving you for your own" (Joshua 1:11). It is God's to give! It is ours to possess!

When we open the book of Joshua, we are beginning the second division of the Old Testament, the books of History. No book has more encouragement and wisdom for the soldier of the Cross than this book of Joshua. It is full of spiritual truth.

Joshua is the book of conquest or the battlefield of the Canaan heritage. This book relates the settlement of the children of Israel in Canaan, proving God's faithfulness in keeping His promise with Abraham. What was the promise (Genesis 12:1-3)?

This book bears the name of Joshua, the hero of this great conquest. The name "Joshua" was originally *Hoshea*, meaning salvation, or *Jehoshua*, the Lord's salvation. Joshua is called the servant of Jehovah, one by whom God issued His orders and by whom He accomplished His purposes—God's prime minister.

For all you know, God may have set His heart to appoint you a captain of His army, or to make you a standard-bearer in the legion of His cross. Are you getting ready?

This book goes on where Deuteronomy leaves off. It is a continuation of the history of the chosen people.

The chosen people were led out of bondage by Moses, and led into the Promised Land by Joshua. In this book, Israel not only overcomes the enemy, but also occupies the land God promised them.

Moses passed through the Red Sea.

Moses led Israel from bondage.

Moses gave a vision of faith.

Moses told of an inheritance.

We see anticipation in Deuteronomy.

Joshua completes what Moses began! God never leaves His work unfinished. Remember the great Craftsman always has another tool sharpened and ready for use. Service awaits everyone. You can always honor God best by taking up your task with a strong and resolute heart that trusts God.

The nation that was led out by Moses was led in by Joshua!

Moses was dead, but the march must continue! God's voice was still speaking to Joshua. Yes, God's voice is still speaking today and if we listen we will hear Him speak to us.

The apostle Paul is dead, but the Cross he preached abides. People may perish, but the true Leader, though invisible, is on the field and will never fail!

"Moses is dead!" Then the march must be halted! Without the leader the followers were left forlorn. There was gloom in the camp. Joshua was appalled by the magnitude of his task. To go forward under such conditions would mean failure. But...

Joshua passed over Jordan.

Joshua led Israel into blessing.

Joshua led them into a life of faith.

Joshua led them into possession.

We see realization in Joshua.

When great hearts fail, faint hearts will flee! The poor Israelites were ready to turn back into the desert and dig their graves among the sand dunes where the bones of their fathers were buried. They could not invade this land filled with giants and take their walled cities. The conquest of the land was impossible!

Who talks like that? Not God! A million people may die! No one is indispensable to the God of heaven. The greatest that ever lived is only a servant and when the task is completed, God has another to follow.

To destroy slavery was the great motive that nerved Livingstone (David Livingstone, 1813-73, British missionary and explorer) to his heroic life in Africa. For thirty years he toiled, pushing his way through the jungles more than 30,000 miles to give Christ to the African people and to discover the source of the Nile. He thought discovering the Nile would give him greater credibility when protesting at home against the curse of the African slave trade. But others discovered the source of the Nile; others freed the slaves. He died far away from his countrymen, but together with God and his African friends in the remote African forests. His heroic Christian death touched the hearts of his countrymen as not even his life had done, and Britain determined to finish his work and stop the African slave trade.

So it is in all our work in the world, especially in our Christian service. We are just a part in a mighty whole. Do your little part and do not care if it is not singled out in the completed whole. The waters of the brook are lost in the river.

God had been preparing Joshua for years. He was born in slavery in Egypt, but God led him out and made him a colaborer of Moses. He was always a valiant captain. He was the one that was almost stoned to death because he urged the children of Israel to advance into Canaan forty years earlier (Numbers 14:6-10).

Tomorrow some great judge or merchant or statesman will die. The young man who is ready for that place will find the mantle falling on his shoulders. Success is readiness for opportunity!

Remember as we study this book of Joshua that God gives—people take. This book focuses on overcoming the enemy and occupying the land. God says, "Take it all."

This book seems to fall into two great parts. If you can only remember this much of an outline, you will remember the most important things:

1. Conquest of the Promised Land: chapters 1—12.
2. Occupation of the Promised Land: chapters 13—24.

Mobilization of the Army (Joshua 1—2)

Open your Bible to the text, Joshua 1—2. We find the children of Israel
right on the border of the land of promise, near the banks of the
Jordan. The boundaries of the Promised Land, as given in Joshua 1:4
are: wilderness on the south, the Lebanon mountains on the north,
Euphrates River on the east, and the Mediterranean on the west.

Joshua is the leader of the children of Israel now! We hear God
say, "Moses my servant is dead. Now then, you and all these people, get ready to cross the Jordan River" (Joshua 1:2). Joshua
stands with bowed head and a lonely heart, for his wise counselor and friend has gone. But God said to him, "I will never leave
you nor forsake you....Be strong and courageous. Do not be ter-
rified; do not be discouraged, for the Lord your God will be with
you wherever you go" (Joshua 1:5,9).

Moses had to die before the children of Israel could go into
Canaan. Moses could not even enter Canaan himself, to say nothing
of bringing anyone else in. Israel had to wait until Moses was out of
the way. To the Christian, Moses represents the law. Joshua represents Christ. Christ alone can lead us into the inheritance that is
ours. Paul says, "not by works, so that no one can boast" (Ephesians
2:9). Oh, that all Christians would simply lean on their faithful
Joshua and follow Him only! Christ wants to lead us into what He
has purchased on the cross for us. It takes Moses and Joshua together to present to us typically the finished work of Christ.

We see an anxious crowd of people all waiting to enter the
land they had so long been promised. Can you picture the row
upon row of tents and all the people wondering when Joshua
would say, "Go"? Joshua sent men through the camp to tell them
that in three days they would cross the Jordan, and to be prepared
for the journey (Joshua 1:10-11).

God called Joshua to lead the children of Israel into the
Promised Land. We have the words that must have come to him
in answer to a prayer for help in his great undertaking. "As I was

with Moses, so I will be with you; I will never leave you nor forsake you" (Joshua 1:5). These words are just as true for us.

God says some very important things in this passage:

1. Set your foot down. "I will give you every place where you set your foot, as I promised Moses" (Joshua 1:3).
2. Take it all. "Your territory will extend from the desert to Lebanon, and from the great river, the Euphrates—all the Hittite country—to the Great Sea on the west" (Joshua 1:4). Not until Solomon's day, some five hundred years later, was this fully realized (2 Chronicles 9:26), but it was coming all the time.
3. Be on the move. "Moses my servant is dead. Now then, you and all these people, get ready to cross the Jordan River" (Joshua 1:2).
4. Take the sword. "Do not let this Book of the Law depart from your mouth" (Joshua 1:8).
5. Go in for a full life. "Three days from now you will cross the Jordan here to go in and take possession of the land the Lord your God is giving you for your own" (Joshua 1:11).

The book of law was Joshua's Bible. Our Bible is far more complete and we know more about God's will because Christ has interpreted it for us. Do we meditate upon the Word? Do we turn from it to the right or to the left? Read God's words to Joshua (Joshua 1:7).

Joshua called the officers together and gave them detailed directions. Hear these men speak. "Whatever you have commanded us we will do, and wherever you send us we will go" (Joshua 1:16). They were ready for any service.

We see both Joshua and the people prepared for the journey. Remember, Joshua had been one of the twelve spies who had been sent to Canaan forty years earlier. Now he sends two scouts to bring a report of the land. Read the story of Rahab and the spies in Joshua 2.

Joshua asked them especially to find out the strength of Jericho for this was the first stronghold they would have to attack after crossing the river. The spies aroused suspicion but were saved from death by Rahab who hid them under flax that was spread on the roof of her house. The spies learned from Rahab that all the city was in terror of the Israelites, and they promised they would spare her and her household when the city was taken. Rahab let them down by a rope through the window of her house which was part of the city wall, and they returned to tell Joshua the good news that "all the people are melting in fear because of us" (Joshua 2:24).

Rahab hung a scarlet cord out of her window so that her house might be marked and spared when the city was destroyed. We find this woman's name in the genealogy of Jesus (Matthew 1:5).

The Canaanites, the people of the land, were the descendants of Canaan, the son of Ham. They were a wicked and idolatrous people. God had warned them in the destruction of Sodom and Gomorrah (Genesis 19:24-25), but they had not changed a bit. Now God was going to destroy their power and give their land to the Israelites.

Forward March (Joshua 3—5)

Read Joshua 3—5. Encouraged by the report the spies had brought, the Israelites moved from their encampment at Shittim, six miles from the Jordan, to a spot near the swollen stream. At dawn the officers passed through the camp and ordered all to watch the Ark and follow it at a distance of two thousand cubits (about a thousand yards), "then you will know which way to go, since you have never been this way before." (Joshua 3:4). The great leader, Joshua, instructed the people to sanctify themselves, for on the morrow the Lord would do wonders among them (Joshua 3:5).

The children of Israel had followed the cloud in the wilderness. Now they would follow the Ark of the Covenant, which represented the presence of Jehovah.

The long journey in the desert was over, and the mystery of an unknown country and an unknown life lay before them. The people grew serious. It was the impressiveness of a new experience. Life is always opening new and unexpected things to us. There is no monotony in the life of a Christian.

At the beginning of the Exodus from Egypt there was a crossing of the Red Sea. Now at the close of Exodus, there is a crossing of the Jordan river. Both were most memorable events in the history of the children of Israel. Of all the great host that crossed the Red Sea, only Caleb and Joshua remained of their generation. Why?

It was the time of the overflow of the Jordan, and the people of Jericho must have thought it impossible for the Israelites to cross or they would have been there to oppose them. There were no bridges and only a few fords, and these not passable at this season of the year. The spies had crossed and recrossed by swimming, no doubt. But how could a great host with women and children and baggage cross?

God has a way. He gave the directions for the people to follow. Martin Luther said, "I know not the way He (Christ) leads me, but well do I know my Guide."

Remember how Christ told the man with the withered arm to do what he could not do—yes, to stretch it forth. The man made the attempt to do the impossible and Christ made it possible. The way to stretch forth the crippled arm was to stretch it forth. The way to cross the Jordan was to cross it. Joshua told the priests to take up the Ark and step into the Jordan, when the river was overflowing all its banks. When the soles of their feet touched the waters of the Jordan, they stood on dry ground. And all Israel passed over on dry ground (Joshua 3:9-17). With men this is impossible, but with God all things are possible. God is always doing the impossible. God's biddings are His enablings.

A man once said, "If God tells me to jump through a stone wall, it would be my duty to jump; it would be God's duty to remove the wall!"

What was the Ark? The symbol of the divine Presence. And Christ is the reality of the divine Presence. He says, "Surely I am with you always" (Matthew 28:20).

He goes before us and says, "Follow me," and He sends His Holy Spirit to whisper in our ear and say, "This is the way, walk ye in it." The living Ark of the Covenant is still our guide. He will guide us in the little as well as the great things of life. Yes, "If the Lord delights in a man's way, he makes his steps firm" (Psalm 37:23).

The Bible tells us of the crossing of the river. From the riverbed, "right where the priests stood," the stones were taken and piled up on the other shore as a lasting memorial of the wonders God did for them (Joshua 4:3). No formal prayer is recorded, but memorial stones are set up. The people wanted to perpetuate the memory of their great Deliverer.

The Fall of Jericho (Joshua 6)

Jericho was not far from the Jordan and about a short twenty-minute walk from the encampment of Gilgal. The author has stood on the site of the city of Joshua's conquest whose massive walls have been unearthed. The modern Jericho, or Ericha, as the village is called, is a mile away from the ancient stronghold that was destroyed and rebuilt in the reign of Ahab.

A man, passing by a building that was being torn down, stopped to look at a laborer who was pulling away on a rope fastened to the top of the wall.

"Do you think that you are going to pull that thick wall down that way?" he finally asked in amazement.

Between his tugs the man answered, "It doesn't look that way to me, but I guess the boss knows what he's about."

And the boss did know, for the wall had been undermined, and after an hour of tug after tug the great wall vibrated, swayed and fell down flat.

The walls of Jericho had to come down so that the Israelites might proceed to conquer the Promised Land, for Jericho was the key to southern Canaan. How could this be brought about? To the Israelites God's directions seemed strange, but like that laborer they kept steadily at the part assigned them. They were confident their Leader knew what they did not, and that they would soon enter the city. What was their task? Read Joshua 6.

The procession of priests, Ark, men and trumpets that marched around the city daily were the only visible means for its capture. How futile must such a march have seemed to the people of Jericho, yes, and to the Israelites themselves. But God knew what He would do.

Some would try to explain that the fall of Jericho was no miracle but a simple scientific fact. God knew that a certain vibration would destroy the wall. It was struck in the sound of the trumpet and shout, and the wall fell before the Israelites.

Whether this is the case or not, the miracle remains that the wall fell. God accomplished the destruction with or without "scientific" means. The glory is the Lord's, not Joshua's. When the people obeyed the command of the Lord given by Joshua, they saw God's power.

The fall of Jericho before the blast of Joshua's rams' horns was a miracle so stupendous that the rationalist can but discredit it. The Israelites believed they were following God's plan. The seven trumpets, leading a procession seven days, and seven times on the seventh day, showed the Israelites that this was Jehovah's plan of conquest as directly as an American flag would inform people today that the property over which it waved was under the protection of the United States. God put an invisible band around the foundation of that city wall and tightened it, and when God does that to the foundation of any structure, national or personal—beware!

It is not hard work that is needed; it is the lack of vision that makes us fail (Proverbs 29:18). It is easy to blow a trumpet; a little thing to walk around a wall. The hard thing is to see the good in it. Say, "Lord, one step is enough for me."

No one wants long delays. We love to see things happen. If there must be six days of weary traveling around the walls, the seventh day will come when the walls will fall. God gives us victories through ways that seem utterly foolish to us. (See 1 Corinthians 1:17-29.)

Campaign at Ai (Joshua 7—8)

The capture of Jericho gave the Israelites a chance to enter central Canaan. The next place strategically important was Ai, which commanded the entrance into the valley leading into western Canaan.

As he had done in the case of Jericho, Joshua sent spies to Ai to learn the situation. Made overconfident by their recent success, they gave poor counsel on their return, saying, "Not all the people will have to go up against Ai. Send two or three thousand men to take it and do not weary all the people, for only a few men are there" (Joshua 7:3). The small force was sent up the steep ascent, but when the garrison at Ai sallied forth and attacked them, the Israelites fled without striking a blow. In the disaster all saw the withdrawal of God's guiding hand. They soon learned that they could not trust in their own strength alone. "'Not by might nor by power, but by my Spirit,' says the Lord Almighty" (Zechariah 4:6).

One man's sin caused Israel's defeat. (Israel had become a nation and no one could act alone.) Achan had hidden the wedge of gold. Read the story in Joshua 7. Beware of the wedge of gold (Joshua 7:13)! Achan alone was guilty, yet we read: "Israel has sinned; they have violated my covenant, which I commanded them to keep. They have taken some of the devoted things; they have stolen, they have lied, they have put them with their own possessions" (Joshua 7:11).

No one can sin in total isolation. None of us live exclusively for ourselves. One stricken with chicken pox can infect an entire schoolroom. A few influenza germs can infect a whole nation. The sin of one becomes the sin of the community.

Every sin you commit will hunt you down, find you out and make you pay. Know this, not one sin has been committed on this earth for which the person who committed it did not suffer. You may escape the law of the land. You cannot escape the law of God.

Central Campaign (Joshua 10)

The Israelites went out a second time to Ai. This time they were victors. The taking of Ai shows real military strategy. In working for the Lord there must always be a recognition of the value of the best in human reason, but strategy without obedience is worth nothing. Dwight L. Moody said, "Work as if everything depended upon you, and pray as if everything depended upon God."

The fame of Israel began to spread far and wide. The kings of Canaan formed a league against the oncoming hosts. But we read of the treaty with the Gibeonites who played a trick on the

Israelites. As a result Joshua condemned the Gibeonites to become the "woodcutters and water carriers for the entire community" (Joshua 9:21).

Then Joshua routed the allied army. Read about the hail storm and the prolonged daylight God sent to help His warrior (Joshua 10:10,11,13).

"O sun, stand still over Gibeon" (Joshua 10:12). Ordinary things come to a standstill when God's work is on.

Northern Campaign (Joshua 11)

After all of central and southern Canaan was in Israel's possession, a new confederacy had to be faced and conquered. The northern kings had joined together and tried to break the power of the conquering Israelites. But in divine strength Joshua routed them all. This did not all happen at once. Scripture says that it took a "long time." At last the land rested from war (Joshua 11:23).

Jerusalem is so named here for the first time in the Bible. To think that since then it has become possibly the most famous place in the world! The Crusaders (A.D. 1099-1250) shed rivers of blood trying to capture it. In 1917, General Allenby (Edmond Henry Hynman Allenby, 1861-1936) led a victorious offensive against Turkish armies and walked in with head uncovered, taking this citadel without a shot of cannon being fired! In 1948, Jewish settlers fought for and established Jerusalem as the capital of the modern state of Israel. In 1967, as a result of the Six-Day War, the city was reunited after nearly twenty years of division. It is a city with a great past history and a bright future history. Here Christ will reign when He comes again in power and great glory (Luke 21:27).

We see God judging these wicked people, the Canaanites. Until recently it was supposed that Canaan was at this time a country of semibarbarians. Now we know that as early as 2500 B.C., Canaan was subject to Mesopotamian rulers, whose language and civilization had been adopted there. Next came Egyptian domination; and we know the high culture of Egypt. Many of the Tell-el-Amarna tablets, dating 1350 B.C.—just after the conquest of Canaan by the

Israelites—are letters to the Pharaoh of Egypt, written in the Babylonian language by tributary princes in Canaan. At that period Canaan had already behind it a long civilized past. The country was filled with schools and libraries, with richly furnished palaces, and workshops of artisans. The cities in the coast had their fleets, partly of merchantmen, partly of warships, and an active trade was carried on with all parts of the known world.

Division of the Land (Joshua 13—24)

Joshua was an old man now, about ninety years of age, and he realized that the conquest of the land was by no means complete. There yet remained "very large areas of land to be taken over" (Joshua 13:1). In order that the children of Israel might do this, he divided it among them.

"This is Judah's; this is Asher's; this is Simeon's; and this is Benjamin's," we hear the people saying as the scene opens. They said this even while the Amorites, the Jebusites, and the Hittites were in open possession of the Promised Land (Joshua 13). The division made of the land was the announcement by faith of certain things that under God's guidance they proposed to accomplish. A long struggle followed.

Alas for the dull-eyed people whose aspirations never get a foot in advance of their present achievements. Unless we keep a vision before us and dream dreams, we will never win either materially or spiritually. This is just what the Israelites did. They reached out into a hoped-for but unknown future when they divided great stretches of country that were still in the hands of their foes!

Although all this land was allotted to the various tribes, all of it was not conquered until the time of David. All that was subdued at the time of Joshua was the mountainous land; the cities and the plains were hardly touched.

The strong did not take the best part of the land because they were strong, leaving the fragments for the weak. Neither did the rich purchase the choicest spots, leaving the poor the more undesirable sites. They tried to determine God's will in the matter. God cares about distribution of goods.

Do you see any application of this principle today? God cares about the inequalities of condition of His children. He cares that the weak are thrust aside by the shrewd and strong. There is a will of God concerning all the questions of hours and wages, capital and labor. God is concerned in a more equal division of His blessings in this world when He rules that "every man will sit under his own vine and under his own fig tree" (Micah 4:4).

When the assignment was made by lot no one could be jealous. They met before the Ark of Jehovah, the symbol of His presence.

"Moses...had not granted the Levites an inheritance among the rest" (Joshua 14:3). You remember that this tribe was set apart for the sacred service of the priesthood, therefore the Levites received no land.

The Priesthood (Joshua 14)

Caleb now was eighty-five years old! Joshua and he were alone among the spies because they had dared to trust God! How many spies did Moses send into Canaan? How many of their names do you remember? No doubt these two are the only ones. Two trusted God and these are the only names we know. As a reward for obedience, these were the only ones in their generation who were permitted to enter Canaan.

Caleb asked his friend Joshua for the high and walled cities! He added, "the Lord helping me, I will drive them out just as he said" (Joshua 14:12). He valued his inheritance because of the hard work it offered and the opportunity it gave him for conquering it! Joshua's recognition of his friend, and of his right to a choice possession was quick and generous. He granted him the mountain and blessed his aged friend.

Caleb was old but he gloried in the hardness of the task. One of the teachers of Helen Keller (1880-1968, American author and lecturer who overcame deafness and blindness) said Helen was the happiest person she had ever met even though she was deaf and blind. Her teacher attributed it to her having overcome so much. Caleb was the happiest man in the camp because he had overcome so much and yet had fields to conquer! Horace Mann

(1796-1859, American early champion of state-sponsored public schools) said, "Difficulties are things which show what men are."

The Lord has never promised His children that they will have an easy time serving Him. In fact, Christ said, "In this world you will have trouble" (John 16:33). The promise is not for ease; the promise is for victory. Christ says, "I have overcome the world." We grow in adversity, for we learn to trust the Lord more. Paul said to Timothy, "Endure hardship with us like a good soldier of Christ Jesus" (2 Timothy 2:3).

"General Booth [William Booth, 1829-1912, British evangelist and lover of the poor, founder and first general of the Salvation Army], tell me what has been the secret of your success all the way through," begged Dr. J. Wilbur Chapman (1859-1918, American pioneer of city evangelism).

Slowly General Booth replied, "I will tell you the secret. God has had all there was of me."

Caleb said, "I, however, followed the Lord my God whole-heartedly" (Joshua 14:8).

We might call attention to the fact that the cities of refuge that God planned, spoken of in Numbers 35:6-34 and Deuteronomy 4:41-43 and 19:4-13, are now established (Joshua 20:1-9).

Joshua's Farewell (Joshua 24)

Joshua had become an old man. He knew that he could not live much longer. He wanted to give the people some last words of admonition.

He called first the leaders and then all the people together and urged them to remember the power and faithfulness of God and admonished them to be faithful to Him. "Now fear the Lord and serve him with all faithfulness" (Joshua 24:14). He warned them against apostasy. He said, "then choose for yourselves this day whom you will serve, whether the gods your forefathers served beyond the River, or the gods of the Amorites, in whose land you are living. But as for me and my household, we will serve the Lord" (Joshua 24:15).

It is a good thing to have people make an open confession and commit themselves to a solemn promise. These older men who had made an open confession were true to their promises.

It is a great help for young people to stand and make a public confession of Christ and unite with the church. You have made a definite commitment that gives you something to live up to. See what Paul says about confession, Romans 10:9-10.

The people said that day, "Far be it from us to forsake the Lord to serve other gods!...We too will serve the Lord" (Joshua 24:16-18).

At 110 years of age the grand old man, Joshua, died. The book closes with death. We see three graves. Joshua's, the great leader of Israel; Eleazer's, the priest; and Joseph's, whose bones the children of Israel had carried with them from Egypt and which were now buried in the land of promise.

Here is a great tribute to a great leader, "Israel served the Lord throughout the lifetime of Joshua" (Joshua 24:31).

Canaan, or the Promised Land, was 180 miles long and approximately 40 miles wide. The boundaries were the wilderness on the south, the Lebanon ranges on the north, the Euphrates on the east and the Mediterranean on the west.

It was in the center of mighty civilizations that made ancient history:

Egypt—300 miles to the south
Nineveh—700 miles northeast
Babylon—700 miles east
Persia—1,000 miles east
Greece—800 miles northwest
Rome—1,500 miles northwest.

Do not pray for an easy task. Pray to be stronger!

The greatness of your power is the measure of your surrender. It is not a question of who you are or of what you are, but whether God controls you.

"I...followed the Lord my God wholeheartedly" (Caleb).

Be sure—be sure—be sure your sin will find you out.

God commands a complete out-and-out for him.

Facts do not change; feelings do.

It is not enough to light a fire; you must put fuel on it.

Chapter 8

Understanding Judges and Ruth

Jesus Christ, Our Deliverer Judge; Our Kinsman-Redeemer

Selected Bible Readings

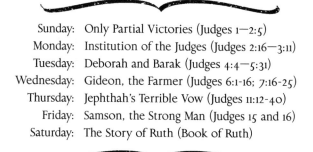

Sunday: Only Partial Victories (Judges 1—2:5)
Monday: Institution of the Judges (Judges 2:16—3:11)
Tuesday: Deborah and Barak (Judges 4:4—5:31)
Wednesday: Gideon, the Farmer (Judges 6:1-16; 7:16-25)
Thursday: Jephthah's Terrible Vow (Judges 11:12-40)
Friday: Samson, the Strong Man (Judges 15 and 16)
Saturday: The Story of Ruth (Book of Ruth)

Someone has called the book of Judges the account of the Dark Ages of the Israelite people. The people forsook God (Judges 2:13) and God forsook the people (Judges 2:23).

Ingersoll (Robert Green Ingersoll, 1833-1899, American orator known as the Great Agnostic) spoke much of "the liberty of man, woman and child." His was a godless liberty. The modern equivalent is "doing our own thing." You see this in the book of Judges.

Judges covers the period after the death of their great leader, Joshua, to the ascension of Saul to the throne of Israel. During this time, the people were ruled by judges whom God raised up to deliver His oppressed people. We read, "In those days Israel had no king" (Judges 17:6). It covers the history of the first 350 years in the land of promise. It gives us a record of great exploits.

It was a new hour in the history of Israel. Remember, Israel had come from a long era of bondage in Egypt to a period of forty years when she lived in tents and wandered in the wilderness. Now the march was over. The nomads were to become settlers in a land of their own. The change was not as easy for them as they expected it to be. The book of Judges is in a way another book of beginnings where we see a new nation adjusting her national life. It is filled with struggle and disasters, but also with the moral courage of a select few.

There is a decided monotony in the description of each successive stage of sin in Israel, but there is an equally remarkable variety in the instruments and methods of deliverance God used. There is something different in the story of each judge.

There are fourteen judges—Othniel, Ehud, Shamgar, Deborah, Gideon, Tola, Jair, Jephthah, Ibzan, Elon, Abdon, Samson, Eli and Samuel. (Abimelech, a petty ruler, was not called of God to judge.)

There were three types of Judges:

1. The warrior-judges as Gideon and Samson
2. Priest-judges as Eli
3. Prophet-judges as Deborah and Samuel.

The chief judges were Deborah, Gideon, Samson and Samuel.

Just how long these judges ruled we do not know, but it is believed about 350 years. The judges were not just one governor after another. They were probably raised up as deliverers on different occasions in different parts of the land, and there could have been overlapping of the time of their rule.

A phrase runs through the last five chapters of the book— "Everyone did as he saw fit" (Judges 17:6; "Every man did that which was right in his own eyes," *KJV*). Mark this phrase every time you find it. We find the people falling away from Jehovah and worshiping the gods of the nations round about them (Judges 2:13). They forgot that God had chosen them for a purpose—to tell the world the truth that there is but one true God. In punishment for their sins God would deliver them into the hand of that nation. Then under the oppression of these new enemies they would cry to God for mercy and He would hear them and send a judge to deliver them. And so the book is full of rebellion, punishment, misery and deliverance. It has a minor key throughout.

The book begins with compromise and ends with confusion. This is what happens in every unsurrendered life!

After reading Judges you may think that the whole of these three or four hundred years was spent in rebellion and sin. But if you read it carefully, you will see that only about one hundred out of these possibly 350 years were spent in disloyalty to God.

One thing we learn in the book of Judges is that a people who spend much of their time in disobedience to God make little progress during their lifetime. The book of Numbers recounts the forty years of wandering in the wilderness, but this book repeats again and again a record of departure from God.

This book is in sharpest contrast to Joshua.

In Joshua	In Judges
Joy	Sobs
Heavenly vision	Earthly in emphasis
Victory	Defeat
Progress	Declension
Faith	Unbelief
Freedom	Servitude

Here is an outline for Judges that is easy to remember. "Seven apostasies, seven servitudes to seven idolatrous and cruel nations, seven deliverances!"

We read of humans' constant failure and God's constant mercy.

Read this book through this week. It can be done in an hour or two. To learn just the great facts of the Bible, however necessary this is, will never satisfy or make Christians real blessings to others. We must know what God is teaching us.

Study carefully the following:

1. The wickedness of the human heart (Judges 2:11-13,17,19; 8:33-35; 10:6; 13:1).

2. God's delight in using the weak things (1 Corinthians 1:26-29). Note the stories of: Ehud, an assassin with a home-

made dagger (Judges 3); Deborah, a woman (Judges 4; see also Judges 9:53); Gideon, from an obscure family in the smallest tribe (Judges 6); Shamgar, a rustic with an ox goad (Judges 3:31); Gideon's little pitcher-armed band (Judges 7); the jaw bone used by Samson (Judges 15:14-19).

3. The Holy Spirit in Judges. Othniel—"The Spirit of the Lord came upon him" (Judges 3:10). Gideon—"The Spirit of the Lord clothed himself with Gideon" (see note on Judges 6:34, *NASB*). Jephthah—"The Spirit of the Lord came upon Jephthah" (Judges 11:29). Samson—"The Spirit of the Lord began to stir him" (Judges 13:25; see also 14:6; 15:14, etc.).

Over the book of Judges as a guide to its spiritual interpretation might be written Zechariah's great words (Zechariah 4:6)—"'Not by might nor by power, but by my Spirit,' says the Lord Almighty."

The critics of the Bible would have the history of God's chosen people start here in these dark days of the judges as a wild, lawless, nomadic people, developing finally into a higher civilization. Just because Israel failed to keep God's law does not mean there was no law. Just as today, because the people of this world disregard the Ten Commandments and put aside the teachings of Christ, it does not prove that these words were never spoken.

Human pride would love to believe that humanity's trend is upward. But God's Word shows us that the natural course is downward.

Israel's Failure (Judges 1:1—3:4)

Joshua had died (Judges 1:1). Much of the Promised Land must be conquered. The first act of the children of Israel was to seek God's will about how they should commence the final conquest. They began well. They consulted God.

God appointed Judah, the kingly tribe (Judges 1:2). The work began in earnest but it ended in weakness. The people did not obey God.

Israel's troubles were due directly to her disobedience to God. They did not exterminate the enemies in the land, but rather worshiped the idols of the peoples and became corrupted in their morals.

The children of Israel went into the land and settled where they wanted and began to raise enough for their living. Soon enemies without would come along, catch the tribe off guard, and take people captive. Their enemies were also traitors within. God had told His people to do away with them.

Chapter 1 is a failure chapter. They did not drive out the enemy as God had commanded. "But Manasseh did not drive out the people of Beth Shan or Taanach or Dor...Nor did Ephraim...Nor did Zebulun ...Nor did Asher...Neither did Naphtali...The Amorites confined the Danites..." (Judges 1:27-36), six nonfulfillments in succession.

Since chapter 1 records a series of disobediences, of course chapter 2 is a chapter of defeat and failure. God gave them up to their own will. God said, "'You shall not make a covenant with the people of this land, but you shall break down their altars.' Yet you have disobeyed me. Why have you done this? Now therefore I tell you that I will not drive them out before you; they will be thorns in your sides and their gods will be a snare to you" (Judges 2:2-3). The children of Israel brought on their own judgment upon themselves and became their own executioners. Several times Israel was on the verge of being exterminated, but thankfully God intervened.

Sometimes we wonder why God didn't remove all the enemies from the Promised Land before He let the children of Israel go in. But God had a definite reason (Judges 3:1-4).

God uses the results of our lack of faith in Him to prove to us our sin and weakness. He does not forget His covenant, but He allows our very weakness, our guilty weakness, to drive us back to Him.

God wanted the chosen people to realize that they were a holy people. They must not mix with the wicked nations about them. They must continually separate themselves. God knew that separation makes a people strong. Christians today must remember that they cannot mix with the world. They must keep close to God and war against sin and unrighteousness. God wants us to be good warriors. Read Ephesians 6:10-18 and see the armor He provides.

And so we see that an uncritical toleration toward a people so utterly corrupt resulted in the undoing of God's chosen people. See the result of this disobedience, Judges 2:20-22.

The Judges (Judges 3:5—16:31)

Here we have a picture of seven failures, seven servitudes and seven deliverances. The Israelites intermarried with the surrounding idolatrous peoples, worshiped at their shrines and practiced their values.

First Oppression, Judges 3:7-11:
      Sin—Idolatry
      Punishment—Eight years
      Deliverer and Judge—Othniel
Second Oppression, Judges 3:12-31:
      Sin—Immorality and idolatry
      Punishment—Eighteen years
      Deliverer and Judge—Ehud and Shamgar
Third Oppression, Judges 4—5:
      Sin—Departed from God
      Punishment—Twenty years
      Deliverer and Judge—Deborah and Barak
Fourth Oppression, Judges 6—8:32:
      Sin—Departed from God
      Punishment—Midianites for seven years
      Deliverer and Judge—Gideon
Fifth Oppression, Judges 8:33—10:5:
      Sin—Departed from God
      Punishment—Civil war, etc.
      Deliverer and Judge—Tola and Jair
Sixth Oppression, Judges 10:6—12:15:
      Sin—Idolatry increased
      Punishment—Philistines and Ammonites, eighteen years
      Deliverer and Judge—Jephthah (and successors)
Seventh Oppression, Judges 13—16:
      Sin—Departed from God
      Punishment—Philistines, forty years
      Deliverer and Judge—Samson

Joshua had no successor. After his death, each tribe acted independently. There was no capital and no fixed government.

There was no unity of action, except in the time of danger when the tribes combined for their own good. When the people sinned against God, their enemies defeated them and ruled them. When in their distress they sought the Lord, He sent great leaders called judges who delivered them.

But this scene is not only filled with servitude; it also records deliverances, for God was always near His people, and when they cried, He answered. God is always brooding over His disobedient children. He promises us that He will never leave us nor forsake us (Hebrews 13:5). We see defeat on our part but deliverance on God's part. "Where sin increased, grace increased all the more" (Romans 5:20).

We see His dealings with His own rebellious people whom He has crowned with His best blessings and upon whom He has lavished His tender love. We find the patience of God and His constant readiness to respond to the least sign of penitence in His people (Judges 3:9,15; 4:3-7; 6:6-12; 10:15-16).

He repeated His mercy again and again although it was never appreciated. If you think on these things it will draw you nearer to this God of mercy and love and grace. Look up, repent and trust God.

We have found that God fulfilled His purpose for Israel by leaving around them in Canaan a circle of strong tribes unlike each other. It is said, "These are the nations the Lord left to test all those Israelites who had not experienced any of the wars in Canaan...They were left to test the Israelites to see whether they would obey the Lord's commands, which he had given their forefathers through Moses" (Judges 3:1,4).

One of the best-known nations whom the Lord used to test Israel was the Philistines, who had settled on the coastal plain. They were a maritime people much like the Danish invaders of Saxon England, sea rovers and pirates, ready for any fray that promised land and gain. In wealth and civilization they no doubt presented a real contrast to the Israelites, and their equipment gave them great advantage in war. Even in the period of the judges there were imposing temples in the Philistine cities. The Israelites feared the Philistines and did not mix freely with them. They only met in war.

First Apostasy (Judges 3:7-11)

We find the Israelites settling among the Syrian nations. They seemed too ready to live at peace with these other nations and to yield not a little for the sake of peace. (Read the few verses 3:5-8 to see what they did.) They intermarried to make their position safer. They traded with the Amorites, Hivites and Perizzites. They determined on boundary lines to make things run smoothly. Next they accepted their neighbors' religion (Judges 3:7) and then their bad customs. But soon the Mesopotamians began to oppress them (Judges 3:8). The Israelites then realized that they had a God from whom they had departed. Israel was a prodigal people. They had left the God whose presence before had assured them victory. For eight years they were under the oppression of these northern nations. Year by year conditions grew worse.

It was from the far south that God sent help in answer to their pitiful cry (Judges 3:9). The deliverer was Othniel, who was Caleb's nephew. No doubt he had had frequent skirmishes with the Arab marauders from the wilderness. "The Spirit of the Lord came upon him, so that he became Israel's judge and went to war" (Judges 3:10). First he prayed, then went out to battle. When we see an army bow in prayer, as the Swiss did at Morat, the Scots at Bannockburn and General MacArthur's troops in the Philippines, we have faith in their spirit and courage for they are feeling their dependence on God!

Othniel's first concern was to put away the idolatry of Israel and teach them the law of the Lord and remind them of their calling as a nation. Soon success and victory was theirs (Judges 3:10-11).

Othniel, the first of the judges, was one of the best. He pointed Israel to a higher level of reverence for God and His plans. Forty years of rest followed.

No one can do real service for his or her country who does not fear God and love righteousness more than country.

Second Apostasy (Judges 3:12-31)

God used different kinds of personalities to deliver His people. Israel's second judge, Ehud, is in marked contrast to Othniel, the judge without reproach.

The long peace the country enjoyed after the Mesopotamian army had been driven out let the people fall into prosperity and to lapse again into spiritual weakness (Judges 3:12). This time the Moabites led the attack. The punishment lasted for eighteen years. Again the people cried to God, and Ehud, with whom Shamgar's name is associated, was the deliverer (Judges 3:15). This Benjamite chose his own method of action and assassinated the Moabite king. His crime is one that stinks in our nostrils. But eighty years of rest for Israel followed (Judges 3:30).

Shamgar, the man of the ox goad, follows in line (Judges 3:31).

Third Apostasy (Judges 4—5)

Now a prophetess arises in Israel (Judges 4:4). She was one of those rare women whose heart burns with enthusiasm when people's hearts are despondent. Many a queen, like England's Elizabeth II, has reigned with honor and wisdom, and often a woman's voice has struck a deep note that has roused nations.

Israel had been oppressed for twenty years (Judges 4:3). The oppression was terrible under Sisera. Again they cried and God heard. This time the story of deliverance is filled with romance and song. Deborah, the daughter of the people, had gained the confidence of the people to such a degree that they had appointed her as judge.

Deborah called Barak to help her. Together they delivered Israel from their oppression. The land had been so filled with Canaanite spoilers that the highways could not be used. War was everywhere, and the Israelites were defenseless and crushed; but God delivered them.

After Jabin, king of Canaan, was defeated and his nine hundred chariots turned into plowshares, we might expect that Israel would at last make a real start to accomplish her true career. The tribes have had their third lesson and should know by now the danger of leaving God. Without God they were as weak as babes.

Will they not now bend themselves to Him? Not yet. Not for more than forty years. The true reformer had not yet come. Deborah's work was not in vain. She was destroying the pagan altars and improving the land. Everywhere they were plowing new ground, building houses and repairing roads. But they were falling into the old habit of friendly association with the Canaanites.

Following deliverance from this servitude the land rested for forty years.

Fourth Apostasy (Judges 6—8:32)

But a fourth apostasy came (Judges 6:1). This time the deliverer was Gideon, a humble farmer. The Midianites had held the Israelites under bondage for seven years. So terrible was it that the people hid themselves in caves and dens and were hunted in the mountains (Judges 6:2). Again they cried unto the Lord. Gideon was called to act as deliverer. He broke down the altar of Baal and restored the worship of God. The story of the conflict is one of the most fascinating in history. Everyone knows the story of Gideon and his band of 300 with their pitchers and horns. Refresh yourself with this story (Judges 7:7-24).

After the great victory over the Midianites, the Israelites sought to make Gideon king. He refused. Gideon was not perfect. We find in the record some things that he should not have done, but he did have faith in Jehovah that God could honor, and He gave his name a place in the Hall of Faith in Hebrews 11.

Archaeological excavations have shown how insecure life and property were in those days. There was no organized defense against the Midianites who made constant raids upon the Israelites. The people took refuge in dens and caves.

Fifth Apostasy (Judges 8:33—10:5)

A fifth time, we see the people falling into the sin of idolatry by worshiping the Baalim almost immediately upon the death of Gideon. The record is: "No sooner had Gideon died than the Israelites again prostituted themselves to the Baals" (Judges 8:33). How often the personal influence of the hero is everything while he is alive, but confusion follows on his death.

Gideon was one of the most successful judges to maintain order, and the country was in quietness forty years. But no sooner was Gideon's funeral over than discord began. There was no rightful ruler to follow. Gideon left many sons, but not one of them could take his place. Abimelech, a son of Gideon, unprincipled and brutal, secured the allegiance of the men at Shechem and usurped the position of king. He ruled three years in tyranny. He was slain by a woman and a period of forty-five years of quietness followed under the judgeship of Tola and Jair.

Those who are busy are those who have moved the world upward!

Sixth Apostasy (Judges 10:6—12:15)

In the sixth apostasy we find the people almost entirely given over to idolatry. Their condition was appalling. God sent judgment this time from the Philistines for eighteen years. At last, sorely distressed, they cried to God. For the first time it is recorded that He refused to hear them and reminded them of how repeatedly He had delivered them (Judges 10:13). The true attitude of Jehovah toward them is found in this statement—"And he could bear Israel's misery no longer" (Judges 10:16).

Deliverance came through Jephthah. The Middle East has consistently produced people of passionate religious fervor. They are both fierce and generous. They rise to great faith, then sink to earthly passions. We have the type in Deborah, David, Elijah and Jephthah. Jephthah's history is full of interest. He was a man of heroic daring and impetuous foolishness. Read the story of his vows and victories, especially the vow he made concerning his only child (Judges 11:30-40). After his great victory, Jephthah judged Israel only six years.

Seventh Apostasy (Judges 13—16)

The seventh apostasy opens with the words, "Again the Israelites did evil in the eyes of the Lord" (Judges 13:1). This time they were disciplined by the Philistines under whose awful oppression they lived for forty years. Here we read the story of Samson. It is a story filled with opportunity and failure. This man was appointed of God before birth, to deliver Israel from the Philistines (Judges 13:5).

In those days, everything was dependent upon physical strength. That was what made a leader great. In this case, God used it to begin the deliverance from the Philistines. Everything should have been in Samson's favor, but he entered into an unholy alliance, which meant his downfall. The final fall occurred at Gaza (Judges 16). Nothing is more pathetic than Samson, blind and bound, grinding in the house of the Philistines, when he ought to have been delivering his nation from them (Judges 16:20,21).

The story ends with Samson and is taken up in 1 Samuel. The remaining chapters, and the book of Ruth, have their chronological place in this period.

The Appendix (Judges 17—21)

These last chapters give us a picture of anarchy and confusion. Israel had forsaken God and now we see the depths into which they have sunk. Read Judges 17:6 and you will find the reason for it all.

First, we find confusion in the religious life of the nation (Judges 17,18).

Second, we find confusion in the moral life of the nation (Judges 19).

Third, we find confusion in the political life (Judges 21).

These events no doubt took place soon after Joshua's death. It gives us a picture of the internal condition of the chosen people. The story of the backsliding of individuals is followed by the backsliding of the nation.

The last chapter proves that the children of Israel had lost the way to God's house, so low had they sunk. We find faithlessness, failure and forfeiture! But God loves His own.

The history of the Church through the ages has been like this with Martin Luther (1483-1546, leader of the Protestant Reformation); John Knox (1513-1572, Scottish Reformer); and John Wesley (1703-1791, founder of the Methodists) as deliverers. The biography of many a Christian in just the common run of life is like this. God opens doors and gives us grace for great tasks. Then we forget Him and begin to have our interests in the world about us. This brings loss and defeat. But God hears our cry of repentance and restores us to favor again.

Understanding Ruth

This delightful story should be read in connection with the first chapters of Judges, as no doubt it gives us an idea of the domestic life of Israel at that period of anarchy. Samuel may have been the author of this book, but no one knows where or when it was written. This book, written on a separate scroll, was read at Pentecost, the harvest festival.

Ruth was the great-grandmother of David. This book establishes the lineage of David, the ancestor of Christ. It tells of the beginning of the Messianic family within the Messianic nation into which, over a thousand years later, the Messiah was to be born.

There are some interesting things to notice in this book. Ruth was a Moabitess. These people were descendants of Lot. They were pagans, worshiping many gods and goddesses. God, in establishing the family that was to produce the world's Savior, chose a beautiful pagan girl, led her to Bethlehem where she met Boaz, her "kinsman redeemer," a relative of Naomi who first made her a family member and then made her his bride. This is God's grace. He adopts the Gentiles into Christ's family. Of course we know that although Ruth was born a pagan, through her first husband, or through Naomi, she learned of the true God.

Boaz was the son of Rahab, the harlot found in Jericho. See Matthew 1:5. So we see that David's great-grandmother was a Moabitess and his great-grandfather was half Canaanite. This is found in the bloodline of the Messiah.

Chapter 9

Understanding First Samuel

First Samuel Portrays Jesus Christ, Our King

Selected Bible Readings

Sunday: Samuel, "Name of God" (1 Samuel 1—3)

Monday: Samuel, the Prophet (1 Samuel 4—7)

Tuesday: Saul, the King (1 Samuel 8—12)

Wednesday: Saul, the Self-Willed (1 Samuel 13—15)

Thursday: David Anointed (1 Samuel 16—18)

Friday: David's Adventures (1 Samuel 19—20; 22; 24)

Saturday: Death of Samuel and Saul (1 Samuel 25—26; 31)

We enter now our study of the king books. Let us look at the six before us:

- 1 Samuel—The people's choice—Saul
- 2 Samuel—God's choice—David
- 1 Kings—Solomon and Israel
- 2 Kings—Israel's kings
- 1 Chronicles—Solomon and the Temple
- 2 Chronicles—The kings and the Temple.

Royal history begins with the book of Samuel. The long period of the rule of the judges ends with Samuel. When Samuel came into power the people were in an awful state. They had practically rejected God, and we hear them clamoring for an earthly king (1 Samuel 8:4-7). This book begins the five-hundred-year period of the kings of Israel (approximately 1050-586 B.C.).

The events recorded in 1 Samuel cover a period of about 115 years from the childhood of Samuel through the turbulent times of Saul to the beginning of the reign of the king whom God chose—David. In the personal lives of these three men this book gives us an exceedingly graphic picture of these times. Samuel was the last of the judges; Saul was the first of the kings. The record brings us up to the time when David is ready permanently to establish the monarchy and God is ready permanently to establish David's throne (Psalm 89).

The book may be divided under the names of three of its chief characters—Samuel (1—7); Saul (8—15); and David (16—31). The history of this book is presented to us in the attractive cloak of biography. Everyone likes a true story.

We all have known and loved the stories recorded in 1 Samuel from the time we were little children. Who does not know the story of the boy Samuel (chap. 3), and David and Goliath (chap. 17), and the friendship of David and Jonathan (chap. 18)?

This book, of course, is named for its most prominent figure, Samuel. Probably he wrote the greater part of it through chapter 24. Nathan and Gad finished it (1 Chronicles 29:29; 1 Samuel 10:25).

Samuel, the King Maker (1 Samuel 1—7)

Samuel—"name of God" is the meaning of his name. This book opens with the record of Hannah, Samuel's mother, praying for a son whom God could use. Samuel, the last of the judges, was God's answer to this prayer. "But Samuel was ministering before the Lord—a boy wearing a linen ephod" (1 Samuel 2:18).

Throughout Samuel's long and useful life he was God's man. He was preeminently a man of prayer. This first book that bears his name is a marvelous study in the place and power of prayer, illustrated from life. He was a child of prayer (1 Samuel 3:1-19); he brought victory to his people through prayer (7:5-10); when the nation wanted a king, Samuel prayed unto the Lord (8:6); intercessory prayer was the keynote of his life (12:19-23).

In the dark and turbulent times of Israel we hear the prayer of faith from the lips of a simple trusting woman, Hannah. She asked God for a son whom she could dedicate to Him for service (1 Samuel 1:9-19).

When Samuel was born, Hannah brought him to the Tabernacle at Shiloh. Although the corruption of the priesthood was appalling, Samuel was protected and grew as a boy in the fear of the Lord (1 Samuel 1:24-28; 2:12-26; 3:1-21).

Eli was both judge and priest at this time. He had ruled for forty years. He was an indulgent father and as a result his two sons, Hophni and Phinehas, also priests, were allowed to act in a most disgraceful manner. As a result there was moral corruption and God warned Eli of the downfall of his house.

Fungus growth in a tree usually is not detected for a long time. Everything seems right outwardly; but when the crash suddenly comes, the state of the tree is seen. Israel had been sinning for a long time. At length the catastrophe came in the disaster recorded at this time (1 Samuel 4).

During the next invasion of their enemies—the Philistines— Israel was defeated, the Ark was taken and Eli's sons were killed. When Eli heard all this, the old man, now ninety-eight years of age, died of the shock (1 Samuel 4).

Read the history of the Philistines' possession of the Ark.

This mention of the Philistines is the first since Judges 13—16. The bondage lasted forty years (Judges 13:1), and seems to have come to a close in the days of Samuel (1 Samuel 7:13-14), about his twentieth year as judge (1 Samuel 7:2). The battle with this enemy probably was fought about four miles northwest of Jerusalem.

The Philistines were Israel's powerful enemies living to the southwest on the coast. Perhaps this renewed action on their part was due to the death of Samson. The battle soon went against Israel. They wondered why God had deserted them. While warring against God they asked God to war for them. Read the account of the revival at Mizpeh (1 Samuel 7).

We cannot win while we war against God! Apart from the immediate causes, rebellion against God is the root reason for tragic wars today. Civilization in general has not been seeking first and always the glory and will of God. The United States has failed to meet this test, as well as all other nations. Civilized nations have failed, as they were bound to do, and they always will fail as long as God is left out.

Though this life is bound to be a fight, it may always be a winning fight if we enlist under the banner of the Captain of our Salvation and make His will our will. "We are more than conquerors" (Romans 8:37).

After Israel's first defeat by the Philistines, did they do right by looking to the Ark of God for protection (1 Samuel 4:3-7,10)?

The Ark of God was a very poor substitute for the God of the Ark. Many people think that when they wear religious symbols or perform religious rituals or give money to charitable causes that they will be safe. They think that these things are a charm, or talisman, to bring them victory. Can you give some illustrations of this?

"Man's extremity is God's opportunity!" Although at the time the loss was terrible, yet God overruled for good. Through Samuel God provided (1) deliverance from the Philistines, (2) preparation for the kingdom, (3) a permanent sanctuary instead of a tabernacle at Shiloh and (4) a better priesthood.

Samuel was the last of the judges, the first of the prophets and the founder of the monarchy. Besides this, he started a school of the prophets, a kind of seminary. The record of this great man's life is beyond reproach. It is hard to find a single mistake that Samuel made.

God always gives us the best we will take, for his mercy endureth forever. We are free human agents. We can choose for ourselves; but we may well tremble at the consequences. We must choose God's best or our own way.

"The Lord continued to appear at Shiloh" (1 Samuel 3:21). God revisited Shiloh! For Shiloh had been left. Read Judges 21:19-21. The place of worship had been turned into a place of feasting and dancing. Shiloh was the location of the house of God from the days of Joshua to Samuel. David moved it to Jerusalem. The Ark was removed by the Philistines in Samuel's childhood and from then on Shiloh ceased to be of great importance (1 Samuel 4:3,11).

What brought about this timely revival? Three things:

1. A praying mother, chapter 1
2. A chastened people, chapter 2
3. A faithful prophet, chapter 3.

We need a praying band of Christians, a people brought to a sense of their need, and a consecrated preacher to bring about revival. Under the Philistine rule, Israel had no definite center of worship. Samuel grew into manhood and assumed the leadership for which he had been born. The first hopeful sign after Israel's long rebellion and defeat was that they had a sense of need. They began to want God. They "lamented after Jehovah." The Jews are going to do this again some day (Zechariah 12:10-11) when Christ "the one they have pierced" returns to this earth and reveals Himself to His own people.

God cannot do much for people who do not feel they need anything. God pities that person. There are those who think they are "all right."

"Well," said Samuel, "if you really mean business, you've got to show me. Do something. Prove it. How? Put away your strange gods" (author's paraphrase of 1 Samuel 7:3). "Put away" might be translated "cut it out." If you mean business, God will mean business. Religion is not just a matter of emotion but also of the will.

It is often easy for us to talk big, but it is another thing to live up to what we say. We often make promises to God that we never keep. How sad that sometimes our lives shout, "Lie!" to what our lips say.

The people began to lament and Samuel took advantage of this and called on them to return to their God and put away their idols. Samuel erected an altar and called it Ebenezer (1 Samuel 7:12). *Ebenezer* means "stone of help." Christ our victory is called "the stone" in both the Old Testament and the New (Psalm 118:22; Matthew 21:42; see also Daniel 2:35).

In just a brief paragraph we find the actual story of Samuel's judgeship. His home was at Ramah. From here he was a circuit rider covering his territory once a year to Bethel, Gilgal and Mizpeh, and overseeing and administering the affairs of the people (1 Samuel 7:15-17). We find missionaries doing this today. They choose some place as home center and then move out through the surrounding country.

Samuel established a school for the prophets at his home in Ramah. This was the beginning of the "order" of the prophets, or seers. When the Ark was taken, the priests were scattered. This is when Samuel retired to his home in Ramah. Through Samuel, God introduced a new way of dealing with Israel. He called prophets through whom He would speak. Through Samuel prophecy became a definite part of the life of Israel. Samuel gathered groups about him called "sons of the prophets." They were found in Shiloh, Gilgal, Bethel, Samaria and Ramah. (See Acts 3:24.)

Samuel's greatest ministry was the organization of the kingdom. The independent tribes were now going to be formed into a nation. In order to survive among other strong nations, Israel must become powerful. They had refused to take God seriously and obey Him as He had commanded them, so He permitted Samuel to find a king for them. The people wanted to be "like all the nations." God wanted them to be unlike the other nations. In Deuteronomy 17:14-20, God had prophesied that Israel should have a king, but He did not want them to become independent of Him.

Saul, the King Chosen (1 Samuel 8—15)

God never intended Israel to have any king but Himself. He would send them great leaders and these in turn would receive their orders directly from Him. But Israel in her falling away had become restless. They wanted a king like the other surrounding nations. We find God granting their request. Here is a great lesson. We either can have God's best or His second best, His directive will or His permissive will.

Saul, their first king, was a failure. He was handsome to look at, he was tall and of a noble mien. He started out splendidly. He proved to be an able military leader. He defeated the enemies about him—the Philistines, the Amalekites and the Ammonites.

Saul was humble at first, but we find him becoming proud and disobedient to God. No man had a greater opportunity than Saul and no man ever was a greater failure. His jealousy of David bordered on insanity.

Inasmuch as Saul was granted to Israel as king in response to Israel's sinful demand for a king, contrary to God's will, did Saul ever really have a chance to "make good" in God's sight? Could he possibly have succeeded under such circumstances? Was he not condemned by God to failure even before he started as king?

We find the answer clearly in God's Word. In 1 Samuel 12:12-15, the prophet of God tells Israel that, although they had demanded their king in defiance of God (v. 12), if both they and their king would fear Jehovah and serve Him, all would be well. Note what follows this word of Samuel (vv. 16-18). Then we see the fact that Israel confesses her sin in asking for a king (v. 19), and Samuel reassures Israel, promising blessing if they serve God.

The only reason any soul is ever rejected by God is that that soul has first rejected God. God takes the initiative in love. "We love because he first loved us" (1 John 4:19). People take the initiative in sin (1 Samuel 15:23).

Note four things in Saul's ordination. It was a:

1. Divine ordination (1 Samuel 9:3-20). He went out with a bridle and came back with a scepter.
2. Prophetic ordination (1 Samuel 10:1). Samuel was his tutor and friend. What an advantage, but it was thrown away. How often we do this today!
3. Spiritual ordination. "The Spirit of God came upon him" (1 Samuel 10:10). He *grieved* this Spirit; then he *quenched* Him. If the Holy Spirit is to remain, He must be loved and obeyed.
4. Popular ordination. "Then the people shouted, 'Long live the king!'" (1 Samuel 10:24).

Saul failed God in several ways:

1. Saul's presumption at God's altar (1 Samuel 13:11-13)
2. Cruelty to his son Jonathan (1 Samuel 14:44)
3. Disobedience in the matter of Amalek (1 Samuel 15:23)
4. His jealousy and hatred of David (1 Samuel 18:29)
5. His sinful appeal to the witch of Endor (1 Samuel 28:7).

Saul waged six campaigns:

1. Against the Ammonites: Beginning of reign; against insurmountable obstacles; army mobilized with great haste; Ammonites completely ruined; Saul's prestige as king strengthened.
2. Against the Philistines: Saul's sin in assuming function of priest; God rejected Saul; bravery of Jonathan and single companion created panic among Philistines; enemy routed.
3. Against the Amalekites: Saul drove enemy into desert; marred success by disobedience; seized valuable property; lied to Samuel; prophet repeated that God had rejected him.
4. Against the Philistines: Saul in constant warfare with Philistines; boy David appeared after his anointing; met Goliath, giant of Philistines; slew him; panic caused; David won distinction.
5. Against David: Blind jealousy drove Saul to seek David's life; David became an outcast; David repeatedly delivered; Saul, David's enemy till his death; David's immortal friendship with Saul's son Jonathan.
6. Against the Philistines: Battlefield plains of Esdraelon; when dark Saul made his visit to the witch of Endor; Samuel called up; defeat and death announced; Israel completely defeated; Saul and three sons slain.

All through the years, Samuel mourned for Saul. When Saul failed, Samuel was faithful in warning him, then in loneliness he mourned over him. Multiplied verses tell the story. (See 1 Samuel 15:35.)

In a battle with the Philistines, Saul and his three sons met death. Here a life so full of promise ended in defeat and failure. Saul had not obeyed God absolutely. For instance, if I should sell one thousand acres of land and would reserve one acre in the center, I would make sure I had the right to go over those one thousand acres to get to mine. One trouble with us is that we reserve a room for Satan in our hearts and he knows he has his right-of-way. This was the trouble with Saul.

Think of the difference between the end of Saul of Tarsus (Paul) and Saul the king! One put God first, the other himself!

God is showing in this book that He must be all in all; that His children have no blessing apart from Him.

The morning of Saul's life was bright, but soon the sky became overcast. Then his sun set in the blackest storm clouds. Follow carefully his rise, his reign and his ruin.

David, the King Proven (1 Samuel 16—31)

As the third division of the book opens we see Samuel mourning for Saul. God rebukes him and tells him to arise and anoint the new king (1 Samuel 16:1).

David, "the apple of God's eye," was one of the greatest characters of all times. He made great contributions to the history of Israel both spiritually and nationally.

In this book we see David as a shepherd lad, a minstrel, an armor bearer, a captain, the king's son-in-law, a writer of psalms and a fugitive. He was anointed three times and was to be the founder of the royal line of which the King of kings came.

David, Jesse's son and the great-grandson of Ruth and Boaz, was born in Bethlehem. He was the youngest of eight sons. When David was only eighteen, God told Samuel to anoint him king to succeed Saul. As a boy he tended his father's sheep, and we read of his brave deeds in defending them from wild beasts.

As a harpist, David's fame reached the king. Saul's melancholy caused David to be called into the court to play. One of the most charming stories of real love in friendship is found between David and Jonathan, Saul's son.

When David was promoted to a high command in the army, his great success roused the jealousy of Saul who determined to kill him. He made five attacks on David's life (1 Samuel 19:10,15,20-21,23-24). But God preserved David. "If God is for us, who can be against us?" (Romans 8:31). David was delivered from all these dangers. Read David's words in Psalm 59. Read Psalm 37.

These were trying days for the young man David who had been appointed to the kingly office. It was natural that he should go to Samuel for protection. All this was training for the one whom God was preparing for the throne. He not only learned how to handle men, but also how to handle himself. He became independent and courageous. He learned, too, in those trying days, to trust God, not men. He always awaited God's time.

He was an outcast for no wrong that he had done but because of the insane jealousy of Saul. David grew under his trials and afflictions. Instead of letting Saul's hatred harden his heart, he returned love for hate.

He learned to be a warrior during those days, too. He was to become the head of a great nation, and God was training him for active service.

Finally David took refuge in flight. During this time Samuel died. Twice was Saul's life in David's hand but both times he spared Saul. Feeling that he should perish one day by the hand of Saul, he took refuge among the Philistines. Psalm 56 was written then. After Saul and his sons were killed by the Philistines David's exile ended.

The closing chapter of our book is draped in black. It gives the closing picture of one of the most disastrous failures. Saul died on the field of battle by his own hand. Advantages and opportunities in youth never guarantee success in manhood. One must keep true to God. Saul's undoing was not so much disobedience, as half-hearted obedience (1 Samuel 15). He was a victim of human pride and jealousy.

Chapter 10

Understanding Second Samuel

Second Samuel Portrays Jesus Christ, Our King

Selected Bible Readings

Sunday:	David Mourns for Jonathan and Saul (2 Samuel 1:1-27)
Monday:	David, King of Judah (2 Samuel 2:1-32; 3:1)
Tuesday:	David, King of All Israel (2 Samuel 5:1-25)
Wednesday:	David's House Established (2 Samuel 7:1-29)
Thursday:	David's Sin (2 Samuel 11:1-27)
Friday:	David's Repentance (2 Samuel 12:1-23; Psalm 51)
Saturday:	David Numbers the People (2 Samuel 24:1-17)

We must not only crown Christ as King of our lives, but we must also set Him on His rightful throne.

The book of 1 Samuel records the failure of the people's king, Saul. Second Samuel describes the enthronement of God's king, David, and the establishment of the "House of David" through which the Messiah, Jesus Christ, should later come. When Christ comes again, He will sit upon the throne of David (Isaiah 9:7; Luke 1:32).

The book of 2 Samuel is occupied with the story of David as king (2 Samuel 5:3). It does not tell the whole story, for it begins with 1 Samuel and runs into 1 Kings. First Chronicles deals with it from another standpoint.

The contents of this book will be easier to remember if we

study it as a biography. David now occupies the field of view. He comes into his own. Let us begin with 1 Samuel 16, David's preparation and discipline.

These were the testing days. David was

1. Called from the sheepfold (1 Samuel 16:11-13)
2. Given victory over Goliath (1 Samuel 17)
3. Persecuted by Saul (1 Samuel 18 to the end).

The children of Israel had clamored for a king. God first gave them one after their own heart, Saul. Then He gave them one after His own heart, David.

This is the substance of 2 Samuel:

1. David was made king over Judah, 2 Samuel 1—4
2. David was made king over all Israel, 2 Samuel 5—24.

Notice the blessedness of the life that recognizes the "Lord's anointed," and puts the true King on the throne of the heart. Such a life is sheltered. "Thou wast he that leddest out and broughtest in Israel" (2 Samuel 5:2).

Such a life is nurtured. "You will shepherd my people Israel" (2 Samuel 5:2; see also Psalm 23:1-2).

Such a life is victorious, with Christ's own victory. "and you will become their ruler" (2 Samuel 5:2).

Jesus says, "Follow me." If we obey, it means He will shield us and shepherd us and make our victory sure!

If we read 2 Samuel 7:18-22; 8:14-15, we find David at his very best, when he was at the height of his prosperity. It shows what he had become and what he might have continued to be if only he had remained faithful to God.

David was a man after God's own heart—not because of boasted perfection, but because of confessed imperfections. He hid himself in God. Read what God tells us to do when we sin, 1 John 1:9.

The story of David the shepherd is found in 1 Samuel 16 and 17; then we see him as a prince in the court, 1 Samuel 18—20; and finally an exile in chapters 21—31.

No one found anywhere in God's Word is so versatile. He is David, the shepherd boy, the court musician, the soldier, the true friend, the outcast captain, the king, the great general, the loving father, the poet, the sinner, the brokenhearted old man, but always the lover of God. We find him as a sort of Robin Hood of the Bible. We love the stories of his daring courage, his encounter with lions and bears and the giant.

He was a man of wonderful personal power and charm. Can you find, as you read this book, the record that portrays the following qualities that stand out so clearly?

1. Faithfulness
2. Modesty
3. Patience
4. Courage
5. Bigheartedness
6. Trustfulness
7. Penitence

It would be well to compare Saul and David and roughly measure their stature one against the other. Both were kings of Israel. Both reigned about the same length of time, forty years. Both had the loyal support of the people, and both had the promise of God's power to back them. Yet Saul was a failure and David was a success. Saul's name is a blot on Israel's history, and David's name is honored today both by Jew and Gentile.

What is the reason for the differences? It is well for us to find out, for these same factors may work in your life and mine, and we may deliberately choose the forces that shall carry us on either course.

Saul had a brilliant start and for a while made good. But with success came pride. (Read Proverbs 16:18.) Thirty-five years of his reign were spent in insecurity and failure. He had lost hold upon God. He finally died a suicide in a lost battle and left his kingdom at war with its neighbors and divided in its loyalty (1 Samuel 31).

The immediate link between the last chapter and this ought to be reviewed. After David had spared Saul (1 Samuel 26), he realized that his life was in danger, but he made the great mistake of associating himself with the Philistines instead of quietly trusting God (1 Samuel 27). Meanwhile, the closing scenes and final tragedy of Saul's life took place (1 Samuel 28—31). David's lament about Saul's death showed his attitude. Everything was clear now for David to fulfill the divine purpose and become king of Israel.

Now 2 Samuel draws our attention. Really there is no division between the first and second books. Originally, the two books were one, covering the period from the beginning of Samuel's life to the end of David's. But 2 Samuel is occupied wholly with David.

There is no parallel account to that in 2 Samuel 2 of David's succession to the kingdom of Judah, but 1 Chronicles 11 and 12 give a vivid picture of the men of Israel as they came to make David king over the whole land. Saul was the people's choice; David was God's choice.

After the results of Gilboa when both Saul the king and Jonathan his beloved friend lay dead, David naturally desired to know what was to be the next step. So David sought guidance of God (2 Samuel 2:1). David did not ask about being a king, but only about the place where he should go. The nation of Israel needed a leader and the divine answer was that he should go up to the city of Hebron (v. 3).

Hebron was one of the most ancient cities (Numbers 13:22). It was in existence in Abraham's day. When Canaan was conquered it became the possession of Caleb and was one of the cities of refuge (Joshua 14:13-15; 21:11-13). This was David's capital for the first seven years of his reign. This made it still more important. It was fifteen miles south of Jerusalem, in the center of Judah, and a strong place. It was especially suitable as a capital of the new kingdom, with the Philistines on the one side and the followers of Saul on the other.

David seemed every inch a king when he spared the life of Saul. He was willing to wait for God to tell him that he would surely prevail (1 Samuel 26). He was on the heights. David's training seemed complete.

The devil would rather throw a man when he is on the heights; he falls farther and harder. He threw David. For David now passed into one of the worst periods of his life and stayed there for almost a year and a half (1 Samuel 27:1). David fell from a mountain peak of spiritual victory and privilege to a black valley of defeat and he deliberately chose to stay there, weak and discouraged, for a long time. (Yet the instant he turned to God, God gave him a sweeping victory over his enemies. When he asked God's guidance, God directed him to Hebron where he was promptly made king.)

David's faith had collapsed. Without God's counsel he left the country of God's people, went to live in the land of the enemy, hopelessly certain of dying at Saul's hand unless he would escape. He joined Achish, king of Gath, who gave him Ziklag in which to live (1 Samuel 27:1-7).

David lied to Achish to win his favor, saying that he had raided the people of Judah when he had not. David met calamity. At last he flung himself upon God. "But David found strength in the Lord his God" (1 Samuel 30:6). He asked God what to do. God answered and under His guidance David had a real victory (1 Samuel 30).

Notice what happened at almost exactly the same time in the lives of Saul and David. Saul, an unrepentant sinner, went down to death, dragging his family and his country with him (1 Samuel 31:3-7). David, a repentant sinner, is given a glorious victory over the enemy and many are saved with him (1 Samuel 30:17-20). We are all sinners of one kind or another. Which ending do we want for our lives?

Read David's sorrowful lament over Saul and Jonathan, 2 Samuel 1:17-27.

How did Saul meet his death? (1 Samuel 31:4).

Why is suicide wrong?

Can it ever be justified?

What motive prompts suicide?

Who fell in the same battle with Saul? (1 Samuel 31:2).

What was David's attitude when he heard of their deaths?

Might one not expect him to have been glad for Saul's death?

Still in Ziklag in the enemy's country, David asked God just what he should do, but not whether he was to be king (2 Samuel 2:1). He obeyed God and returned to Hebron where the men of Judah made him their king. Study the facts of 2 Samuel 2:8 to 4:12. Amid fighting and civil war and intrigue, David does not lift a finger to secure the kingdom of Israel. The opposition steadily weakens itself and his cause steadily grows stronger. Seven and one-half years after ascending Judah's throne, David was made king of Israel.

Why are we assured of David's success when he is made king? Saul chose the way of self; David chose God's way. Because of this, God calls him "a man after his own heart" (compare with 1 Samuel 13:14). Notice after Saul's death David made no effort to seize the kingdom by force. After Judah claimed him as king, it was seven and one-half years before Israel crowned him. David knew that it was God's plan that he should be king of Israel, but he was willing to wait.

Some people grow under responsibility; others swell. We learn from Saul's failure that the surrendered life is the only secure and truly successful life.

David's Rise—Supremacy and Rule (2 Samuel 1—10)

As this book opens, we find David just returning to Ziklag after his great victory over the Amalekites. He had come back weary in body, but refreshed in spirit because of his great success. No doubt he was wondering what had been the outcome of that great battle at Mount Gilboa. His dearest friend, Jonathan, and King Saul, were in that battle.

David was not kept in suspense long. An Amalekite from the camp of Israel came running that great distance to tell David of the disaster. Because he claimed to have killed Saul, the Lord's anointed, David dealt severely with him. (Read 2 Samuel 1:1-16.)

David's age was now thirty (2 Samuel 5:4), and never did a man at that age, or any age, act in a nobler way. His generous heart not only forgot all that Saul had done, but remembered all that was favorable in Saul's character. Recall some of the things Saul had done against David.

How beautiful is this spirit of forgiveness! See that spirit when men nailed Christ to the cross (Luke 23:34) and when men stoned the martyr Stephen to death (Acts 7:60). David wrote a song for this occasion called "The Song of the Bow." It is filled with extreme tenderness when it speaks of his beloved friend (2 Samuel 1:19-27).

The death of Saul did not end David's troubles. He had formed an alliance with Achish. He had gone as near to the position of a traitor to his country as he could without actually fighting against it.

His own tribe, Judah, was by far the friendliest. They knew better how cruelly Saul had hunted him down. This is why he had thrown himself into the hands of Achish.

David inquired of God where he should set up his kingdom, and God told him in Hebron. No sooner had David gone up to the city, than the men of Judah came and anointed him king over the house of Judah. Although it was not all that God had promised David, it was a large installment, for Judah was the royal tribe.

David's start was slow and discouraging. But David had faith in God. He was patient and was willing to wait for God to lead. He was humble before God and the people. He was humble in his success, and when he sinned he genuinely repented. David's was a great career. He used every talent God gave him for the glory of his Creator and built up the people of God's choice. He brought Israel to the height of her glory, extending her boundaries from the Mediterranean to the Euphrates by conquest of battle. He left a rich heritage to his race—a heritage that included power, wealth, honor and songs and psalms. But above all, he left an example of loyalty to God.

Will we not all adopt David's plan of life? He started right! He began with God. He committed every plan into His keeping (Psalm 37:5). David never forgot that God was supreme. When he sinned, he bowed in penitence and sorrow, and God forgave him.

The men of Judah who came to meet David were probably the elders of his own tribe. They came to elect him as king, and although he had been anointed privately by Samuel to indicate that God had chosen him, it was natural and necessary to repeat the anointing in public as the outward and visible inauguration of his reign.

Remember Saul was anointed privately, too (1 Samuel 10:1). Anointing with oil meant a divine appointment. Saul was set apart for the service of king. He was given the right to rule the people.

However, David's kingship was not acknowledged by all of the people. Abner, the captain of Saul's army, at once took steps to appoint Saul's son to take his place.

The earnest efforts of David to ward off strife and bring the people together in recognizing him as king were all in vain. The spirit of Saul, which was so antagonistic to David, was perpetuated in Abner who was determined to center the kingdom of Israel around the house of Saul, not of David (2 Samuel 2:8-10).

The people did not consult Jehovah (a form of the divine name, more properly, Yahweh), but merely tried to stem the popular tide in David's direction.

Civil war followed, but finally everything turned to David and he was made king of all Israel. The monarchy in Israel was never an absolute autocracy (1 Samuel 10:25; 1 Kings 12:3).

In the prime of his life, thirty years of age, David entered upon his complete inheritance. This was the task God intended him to do. He reigned forty years in all, including seven and one-half years in Hebron over Judah and thirty-three years in Jerusalem over the whole land. The fortress of Jerusalem was still in the hands of the Jebusites but was captured early in David's reign (2 Samuel 5:6-10).

One of the great results of David's kingship was the unity of the whole nation under him as leader. He brought the various conflicting elements into one group. We find a united people under a young leader united to God. The Israelites needed only to have kept on following David's leading down the years to have gone on from greatness to greatness. They had only to follow David's greater Son to have gone on from glory to glory!

David trusted God with all his heart and leaned not to his own understanding. He acknowledged God in all his ways and God did direct his path (Proverbs 3:6). How did David obtain guidance? By asking for it. Just how God gave the answer we are not told. God has assured us that if we ask He will answer (1 John 5:14-15; Jeremiah 33:3). God never breaks His word. We have to make decisions almost every hour of our lives. Shall I continue this course in my life? Shall my vacation be spent at home, traveling, at rest? Would we take false steps if He made the decisions for us? Could we fail?

"The war between the house of Saul and the house of David lasted a long time. David grew stronger and stronger, while the house of Saul grew weaker and weaker" (2 Samuel 3:1). The cause of its weakness was that God was against it.

After seven and one-half years of opposition, David finally won the heart of all Israel by his justice and great spirit. He was left now without a rival. Representatives of all the tribes came to Hebron to anoint him king of the whole nation (2 Samuel 5).

From the anointing of David as king at Hebron, we go with him to the field of battle.

The first thing that engaged David was the capture of Jerusalem, the stronghold of Zion. Since the days of Joshua, Jerusalem alone had defied the attack of Israel. It was an impregnable fortress. David thought it was best suited to be his nation's capital. This became the residence of David and the capital of his kingdom.

What is the city of greatest importance as far as God is concerned? The record of how it came for the first time completely into the possession of God's people is given in 2 Samuel 5:6-9; 1 Chronicles 11:4-8.

After David had established the capital at Jerusalem, he wished to bring the Ark of God into the new ruling center. He realized the people's need of God. But we are not told that he consulted God. A real tragedy followed. What was it? (See 2 Samuel 6:1-19.) What do you know of God's directions for carrying the Ark?

It is not what we think, but what God says that is important. Uzzah's human opinion was that it was all right to take hold of the Ark to keep it from falling. He was sincere, but it was directly contrary to what God said. He died. We can always know what God has said if we are willing to pay the price of knowing by studying His Word and trusting what He says (John 7:17).

What was the greatest thing David did for his people?

He captured Jerusalem, built it bigger and stronger, conquered the Philistines and unified the people. But all this would be of little use without putting God at the center. This is really what gave the nation unity and power. Neither a nation nor an individual can be great without Christ in its heart.

All the events in David's reign that followed the capture of Jerusalem may be summed up in these words, "And David became more and more powerful, because the Lord Almighty was with

him" (1 Chronicles 11:9). God had been getting David ready for this
reign. Training is difficult. It is good to bear the yoke in youth.
Many a great person can testify to this.

The first concern of David when he settled in Jerusalem was
bringing up the Ark of the testimony. His attempt to place the Ark
in Mount Zion failed through want of due reverence on the part
of those carrying it, but after three months it was duly placed in
the Tabernacle. (Read the story in 2 Samuel 6.)

David was an active man. He was fond of work. His wars with
outside nations had ceased. Now he sought to find what he could
do to improve and beautify his kingdom. He compared the elegance of his own palace with the Tabernacle where Jehovah
dwelt. He thought this difference ought not to be. He called
Nathan the prophet and consulted him about building a temple
for Jehovah. At first it seemed as though God would let him do
this, but God had a different purpose for David. Read what God
told Nathan to tell David (2 Samuel 7:4-17).

David's spirit is again revealed in his submission to God's plan
for him. God allowed him to gather materials for his son to use
to build the temple.

God's servants do not think it a misfortune that the Lord
thwarts their plans and desires. A real servant learns what God's
will is and yields the will to the Master's!

Don't pass over the sweet story of David's treatment of crippled young Mephibosheth when he found Mephibosheth was his
best friend's son (2 Samuel 9).

David was powerful in every art of war, although his heart was
inclined to peace. Chapter 10 recounts some perilous undertak-
ings. This story gives the closing account of David's rise to power
and prepares for the terrible story of his fall.

Under David's rule, Israel reached its high-water mark. It has
been called Israel's golden age. No idol worship and no worldly
functions occurred when "the sweet singer of Israel," the "shepherd boy of Bethlehem," commanded the ship of state. His merchant caravans crossed the deserts and his routes went from the
Nile to the Tigris and Euphrates, and Israel prospered in those days.
When Israel was right with God, she was invincible against all odds.

David's Fall (2 Samuel 11—20)

We wish the life of David could have ended before chapter 11 was written. The golden era has passed away and what is left is a checkered tale of sin and punishment. In all of God's Word no chapter is more tragic or more full of warning for the child of God. It tells the story of David's fall. It is like an eclipse of the sun. His sins of adultery and virtual murder were a terrible blot on David's life. He became a broken man. God forgave him but the Word says, "The sword will never depart from your house" (2 Samuel 12:10). He reaped just what he had sown. We see the harvest in his own house and in the nation.

Look over the steps in David's fall. You will find the steps downward in rapid succession.

First, he was idle (2 Samuel 11:1-2). It was the time for a king to go to war, but he was not there. He remained in Jerusalem in the place of temptation. At evening time he arose from his bed and walked on the roof of his house. He was in that idle, listless mood that opens one to temptation. He saw the beautiful Bathsheba and he wanted her. His first sin was in the fact that he saw. Don't look on evil. Ask God to keep your eyes. Refuse the admission of sin into your mind. If David had nipped the temptation in the bud he would have saved himself a world of agony and awful sin. Instead of driving it out of his mind, he cherished it.

Next, "David sent someone to find out about her" (2 Samuel 11:3). He makes inquiry about this woman and then he took her (v. 4). He brings her to his house. He forgets what is due to the faithful soldier whose wife she is.

But the next step is far worse—his sin against Uriah, one of the bravest of his soldiers. He must get rid of him. He makes Joab his confidant in sin, his partner in murder.

This sin was the more terrible because it was committed by the head of the nation. This man had been signally favored by God. He was no longer a young man. He had passed through many experiences. Then, too, the excellent service of Uriah entitled him to rewards, not death.

Why do you suppose this tragic story is given in the Bible? It bears the character of a beacon, warning the mariner against some of the most perilous rocks that are to be found in the sea of life. Never neglect watching and praying. An hour's sleep left Samson at the mercy of Delilah. Don't fool with one sin even in thought. The door may be opened to a dangerous brood. It doesn't take a whole box of matches to start a fire. One will do it!

A year later the prophet Nathan visited David and charged him with his sin. We can imagine the anguish of David's heart that year. We read of David's sincere repentance (Psalm 51). God told David that his child should die because of his sin. See how David accepted this punishment (2 Samuel 12:13-32). When the child died, David arose and worshiped God.

"A living sorrow is worse than a dead one," says a proverb. The death of his child was a grievous sorrow to David, but the living sorrow he endured through his beloved son Absalom we cannot imagine. The rebellion of this young man is full of tragedy. Absalom was a handsome young man, but he was treacherous. He weaned away his father's subjects by treachery. He sat at the city gate and told the farmers what he would do if he were their ruler. When men bowed in honor, he kissed their hands. He drove a beautiful chariot drawn by prancing horses. He became a favorite.

Through a spy system, he stole the kingdom from his father. When David left Jerusalem, Absalom gathered his army in Hebron and marched triumphantly into the city. Finally David prepared for battle with Absalom. During the fray, Absalom was caught by his long hair in the trees of the forest.

Absalom was heartless and cruel. David suffered alike in the day of Absalom's victory and in the dark hour of his defeat and slaying. Read his lament over Absalom when he heard the news of his death (2 Samuel 18:19—19:4).

David's Last Days (2 Samuel 20—24)

After the rebellion was crushed, King David returned to his kingdom. New officers were installed and reconstruction began on every hand. We see David's sin in numbering the people, because

God had not told him to. The land was punished with a three-day pestilence.

He gathered great provisions for building the Temple and directed his son Solomon to build it. David was only seventy years old when he died.

David was a mighty king and warrior. He ranked with Abraham, Moses and Paul. His great spirit is revealed to us in the psalms that he wrote. But he sinned. The story does not end here, because he repented. Read the great confession in Psalm 51.

This is the "man after God's heart." We need to understand David's life to understand and use the Psalms. We must know, too, why Christ was called the "Son of David" (Acts 13:22-23). David stands halfway between Abraham and Christ.

David had his faults. He did much that was very wrong, but he kept his nation from going into idolatry. Although his private sins were grievous, he stood like a rock for Jehovah. He sinned, but he repented and gave God a chance to forgive and cleanse him. He illustrates the conflict Paul describes in Romans 7. He was a great saint even though he was a great sinner.

David took a chaotic nation and established a dynasty that was to last to the time of the captivity, a period of more than 450 years. There never was a greater warrior or statesman than David. He made Israel the dominant power of western Asia.

The last verses of 2 Samuel 24:18-25 tell of King David's buying Araunah's threshing floor. He erected an altar there. This has special significance, for on this site the great Temple of Solomon was later built. On this sacred spot today stands the Dome of the Rock, one of the most important Islamic mosques in the world. It is a most galling thing to the Jews to have this sacred ground in the hands of the Muslims.

Do not pray for an easy task. Pray to be stronger! The greatness of your spiritual power is the measure of your surrender. It is not a question of who you are, or of what you are, but whether God controls you.

Consider, what constitutes a missionary call? How does God call men and women today?

The angel of Jehovah generally comes when you are busy (Judges 6:11-12).

- Saul was out hunting the livestock.
- David was tending sheep.
- The disciples were fishing.
- Deborah was an Ephramite housewife.
- Martin Luther was a busy pastor and professor.
- George Washington (1732-1799), the first president of the United States, was a farmer-surveyor.
- Abraham Lincoln (1809-1865), the sixteenth president of the United States, was a country lawyer.
- Frances Willard (1839-1898), the social reformer and temperance leader, was a schoolteacher.
- Dwight L. Moody was a shoe salesman.
- William Carey (1761-1834), the founder of modern missions and missionary to India, was a cobbler.

You say, "Those people outside the Bible never saw an angel!" How do you know they didn't? God speaks to men and women in many different ways and surprises us as much as He surprised the young Hebrew farmer, Gideon.

Chapter 11

Understanding Kings and Chronicles

Kings and Chronicles Portrays Jesus Christ as King

Selected Bible Readings

Sunday: Building and Dedicating the Temple
(1 Kings 6:1-14; 8:22-53)

Monday: Solomon's Glorious Reign (1 Kings 10:1-29)

Tuesday: The Kingdom Divided (1 Kings 12:1-33)

Wednesday: The Prophet Elijah (1 Kings 17:1—18:46)

Thursday: Elijah and Elisha (2 Kings 2:1-22)

Friday: The Captivity of Israel (The Northern Kingdom)
(2 Kings 17:7-23)

Saturday: The Captivity of Judah (The Southern Kingdom)
(2 Kings 25:1-21)

Understanding Kings

If we reject God, He will reject us. If we obey God, He will bless us. "In those days the Lord began to reduce the size of Israel" (2 Kings 10:32).

In the original Hebrew in which these books were written, 1 and 2 Kings formed one book, 1 and 2 Samuel another, and 1 and 2 Chronicles a third. When they were translated into the Greek language, they were divided by the translators because the Greek required one third more space than the Hebrew and the scrolls on which they were written were limited in length.

The book of Kings was written while the first Temple was standing. First and 2 Kings are just a continuation of the books of Samuel. As their name suggests, they record the events of the reign of Solomon and then of the succeeding kings of Judah and Israel. They cover a period of 400 years and tell the story of the growth and then decay of the kingdom. We see the kingdom divided. We see both Israel and Judah led into captivity. The Southern Kingdom (Judah) had twenty kings, and the Northern Kingdom (Israel) had nineteen kings.

These are two of the most important books of history in the world. Every day expeditions are digging up the records of history about which nothing has been written outside the books of the Kings. At first they may seem dry to you, but the lives of the kings, and the stories in these books prove that:

1. "God does not show favoritism" (Acts 10:34; "is no respecter of persons," *KJV*).
2. When our all is on the altar, God never keeps us waiting for the fire (1 Kings 18:38). What is the spiritual meaning of this?
3. The final captivity was because of disobedience to God. It was prophesied before (Deuteronomy 28:49). What has God said about the individual who forgets Him?

Kings begin with King David and end with the king of Babylon.

Kings open with the building of the Temple and end with the burning of the Temple.

Kings open with David's first successor to the throne of his kingdom, Solomon, and end with David's last successor, Jehoiachin, released from captivity by the king of Babylon.

Remember these books of Kings cover practically the whole rule of the kings over God's chosen people. During Solomon's reign, the kingdom reached the height of its grandeur. With the death of Solomon, the kingship really ceased to be the medium through which God governed His people. The period of the prophets is introduced at this time by the great Elijah. First Kings ends with the story of this prophet. Second Kings centers around Elisha. The decline of the kingdoms is given until we see both Israel and Judah led into captivity.

The Splendid Reign of Solomon (1 Kings 1—10)

As the scene opens, we find that "King David was old and well advanced in years." He was prematurely aged for he was only seventy. His son Solomon was but nineteen. Because of David's feebleness we find a rebellion started against him. Adonijah's attempt to get his father's throne was natural because he was the oldest surviving son (2 Samuel 3:4). This rebellion called for prompt action, which Nathan the prophet took. David saw that Solomon was the most fit to succeed him. Solomon was God's choice (1 Chronicles 22:9; 1 Kings 2:15). It was clear that the choice of Solomon was popular (1 Kings 1:39-40). Adonijah soon saw that opposition was useless. Because of this rebellion, Solomon was crowned before David's death (1 Kings 1:30,39,53).

Solomon received his religious training from Nathan the prophet. This wise prophet loved Solomon and gave him the name Jedidiah, "the Lord's darling" (2 Samuel 12:25). Solomon's reign began in a blaze of glory. It was splendor without surrender. And as with Saul, Solomon's life ended in an anticlimax.

"His heart was not fully devoted to the Lord his God, as the heart of David his father had been" (1 Kings 11:4). Remember, God wants our hearts!

Yet Solomon was a magnificent king; his throne was the grandest the world had ever seen and his life was filled with happenings of marvelous significance. His kingdom of 60,000 square miles was ten times as great as that which his father had inherited.

Solomon Was a Great and Good Man
1. His rearing was under the religious and wise Nathan.
2. His kingship was clear. All the city rang with the glad cry, "Solomon has taken his seat on the royal throne" (1 Kings 1:46).
3. His charge from his father was full of promise (1 Kings 2:1-9).
4. His choice of wisdom from God was a divine choice (1 Kings 3).
5. His cabinet was greater than any king of Israel ever had (1 Kings 4).

6. His lifework was building the Temple. Several million dollars was expended in erecting it. Its service of dedication has gone down on record because of its sublimity.
7. The kingdom he established realized at last, after 400 years, the broad dimensions outlined to Joshua (Joshua 1:4).
8. The wealth and glory of Solomon's reign fairly took the breath of the Queen of Sheba. "There was no more spirit [breath] in her" (1 Kings 10:5, *KJV*).
9. His beauty of person is hinted in Psalm 45.
10. His ardent affection is seen in the song that bears his name (Song of Solomon).

Solomon was a great and glorious king, but we soon find the note of decline.

Solomon the Weak and Erring One

1. Unlike his father, David, Solomon dealt cruelly with his brother Adonijah (1 Kings 2:24-25).
2. Like Saul, his heart was lifted up in pride (1 Kings 10:18-29).
3. Led by his heathen wives, he fell into idolatry (1 Kings 11). "Do not be yoked together with unbelievers" (2 Corinthians 6:14).

Solomon did not display spiritual wisdom. The book of Ecclesiastes, with its note of despair, is a confession of it. He did not have a heart at peace with God.

After David's final words of admonition to his son to be absolutely loyal to Jehovah, the king died, having reigned for forty years.

When the young Princess Victoria learned early one morning that she had become Queen of England, the first thing she did was to ask the Archbishop of Canterbury to pray for her. The Archbishop and Lord Chamberlain knelt down together and prayed that grace, strength and wisdom might be given to her throughout her reign. Governing is a serious business. Solomon realized its seriousness as a young man, and began his reign with prayer.

God appeared to Solomon in a dream early in his reign and asked him to make a choice of anything that he might wish. The young king's wise choice revealed his feeling of inability to do all that was put upon him. What was his request of the Lord? God gave him the wisdom for which he asked. What is God's promise to us (James 1:5)? "Ask for whatever you want me to give you" (1 Kings 3:5). This is the high privilege of each one of us. Each of our lives tell what we have asked for. What is your choice?

The youth had not been swept off his feet by his father's praise when David twice called him a wise man (1 Kings 2:6-9). Solomon asked for a "discerning heart." Have we a heart that listens to the Spirit's voice?

Solomon was the wisest man the world ever saw until the coming of Him who could say of Himself, "and now one greater than Solomon is here" (Matthew 12:42). All the earth acknowledged Solomon, but when the One greater than Solomon came His own received Him not (John 1:11). That is tragedy. But have you received Him?

First Solomon organized his leaders. He gathered around him a wise company of officers of state, each having his own department for which he was responsible. This led to days of tremendous prosperity in the kingdom.

The greatest undertaking of Solomon's reign was building the Temple. This was what his father, David, had longed to do. The immense foundation of great hewn stones upon which Solomon's Temple was built remains till this day under the Dome of the Rock. One stone alone is thirty-eight feet, nine inches long. The huge stones, the fragrant cedar wood and copper-covered dome gave it unusual splendor.

The Temple site was a historic spot. On Mount Moriah, Abraham offered up Isaac (Genesis 22:2). We saw how David secured Araunah's threshing floor and here today the Dome of the Rock stands, the sacred spot of the Muslims.

The Israelites used to have to make pilgrimages to the Temple to meet God. But now we know a wonderful truth that our bodies are the temples of God (1 Corinthians 3:16; 6:19). Is your body a real temple? God wishes to live in you, but He cannot if you are defiled with sin.

Three earthly temples are mentioned in Scripture. The first is Solomon's, which was destroyed by the Babylonians about 587 B.C. (2 Kings 25:8-9). The second was Zerubbabel's (Ezra 5:2; 6:15-18). This was not comparable in elegance to Solomon's. The third was

Herod's temple, an expansion of Zerubbabel's, erected on a grander scale in 20 B.C. and completed in A.D. 64. This temple was destroyed by Titus in A.D. 70. The Dome of the Rock now stands on this site.

The Glory of Solomon's Reign

Read 1 Kings 9:1-28 and 10:14-29 to find the possible, not to say the probable, dangers to Solomon in all this wonderful glory. Note his high position, his great wisdom, his countless riches. It is hard not to forget God in the hour of such prosperity. We think only of our possessions. It was this very glory that led to Solomon's downfall.

Because of Solomon's backsliding, God raised up enemies to vex him. In the book of Ecclesiastes, Solomon describes the futility of his life at this time.

The Queen of Sheba witnessed Solomon's reign at its zenith and saw the fulfillment of David's prayer for his son, offered about a year before his death.

Solomon's reputation probably had spread through the voyages of his navy (1 Kings 9:21-28). The fame of Solomon was associated with Jehovah. His fame concerning the name of the Lord was the thing that interested her Majesty, the Queen of Sheba. She was impressed by (1) Solomon himself, with his wisdom and wealth, 1 Kings 10:1,7; (2) his servants, verse 8; and (3) his God, verse 9.

The Kingdom Torn Asunder (1 Kings 11—16)

Solomon reigned forty years, the second great period of the complete kingdom (1 Kings 11). At first all went well, but later there was serious trouble. Note that Saul, David and Solomon each reigned forty years (Acts 13:21; 2 Samuel 5:4; 1 Kings 11:42).

Taxes under Solomon's reign had weighed the people down. Luxury and idolatry had broken down their morale. The kingdom now was to be divided. A rise to such prosperity and power as Solomon enjoyed had its dangers. It cost money and meant increased taxation, which grew into burdens that were unbearable and that bred the seeds of unrest and revolution.

Solomon set up a great establishment in Jerusalem. He built his famous Temple, bringing in foreign workmen and materials to do it, and then he built himself a palace that dazzled his own subjects and his foreign visitors.

During this time there was much corruption, and under all these burdens the people grew restless and rebellious.

Consider the events leading up to the division. For years there had been jealousy between the Northern Kingdom (Israel) and the Southern Kingdom (Judah). The cause for the jealousy went back 300 years and was a result mainly of the jealousy between the tribes of Ephraim and Judah. Note the blessings Jacob gave to Ephraim (Genesis 48:17-22; 49:22-26). And from the time of Joshua, who was of that tribe, Ephraim took a leading place. The transfer of authority to Judah came under David, who was of the tribe of Judah. All this tribal jealousy was intensified by the hardships felt by the people through Solomon's high-handed actions. His demands created oppression and his unfaithfulness to God demanded judgment (1 Kings 11:26-43; 12:4).

When Solomon's son, Rehoboam, threatened to levy heavier burdens upon the people, his unwise headstrong action added fuel to a fire that had been gathering and burning for nearly 300 years, from the time of the judges.

The revolt of the ten tribes immediately followed (1 Kings 12:16), though the two tribes of Judah and Benjamin remained loyal (1 Kings 12:17). This tension led to the appointment of Jeroboam as king of the northern section (v. 20).

The Secret of Decline

A new name of great importance appears in the pages of this story: Jeroboam. This young man of low origin had risen to notice because of faithful service and deeds done. The prophet Ahijah made a startling revelation to Jeroboam. Using a Middle-Eastern symbolic gesture, he took off his new coat and tore it into twelve strips and then he said to Jeroboam, "Take ten pieces for yourself, for this is what the Lord, the God of Israel, says: 'See, I am going to tear the kingdom out of Solomon's hand and give you ten tribes'" (1 Kings 11:31).

The kingdom was divided. The judgment was upon Solomon for his long years of luxury and pride and power. Every ruler should look ahead and see toward what rocks he may be steering his kingdom, and whether or not he is heading toward the day when his power shall be taken out of his hand.

Have we not seen men in our day, rising to great wealth and power in which they had piled up millions, stripped to nothing and fleeing from outraged justice?

Things do not happen by accident. There is a cause at the root of every revolution. The event may come as suddenly as an explosion, or as the eruption of a volcano, but somewhere secret causes were at work undermining the structure. The French Revolution had its roots down under centuries of oppression.

Religious apostasy had been gnawing like a deadly worm at the root of Israel's life. One day the tree fell. Nothing destroys a nation like religious decline. Take the sun out of the sky and there will be no grass or flowers or orchards. Take God out of our nation and there will be no homes or schools or social life.

Sin Brings Division
Though they didn't know it, the people were carrying out the divine purpose (1 Kings 12:15; 11:29-33). God could not overlook the disobedience of Solomon to His clearest commands.

The kingdom of God's chosen people was divided. It has been divided for almost 3,000 years. It was divided through sin. We see this kingdom go to pieces and finally into captivity (2 Kings 17 and 25). It is part of the gospel, the good news, that those two great sections of divided Israel are going to be united again on this earth at Christ's return in glory. (Read the wonderful passages in Isaiah 11:10-13; Ezekiel 37:15-28.)

The Ministry of Elijah
(1 Kings 17—22; 2 Kings 1:1—2:2)

Elijah was a bolt of fire God let loose upon wicked Ahab and idolatrous Israel. He flashed across the page of history as sudden and terrible as a flash of lightning. Elijah, the Tishbite, who was of the inhabitants of Gilead, is his brief biography by which he was introduced. His name Elijah means "Jehovah is my God." It fit him perfectly. He was the most outstanding of the prophets. Follow his sudden appearance, his undaunted courage, his zeal, the heights of his triumph on Mount Carmel, the depths of his despondence, the glorious rapture into heaven in the whirlwind, his reappearance on the Mount of Transfiguration (see Matthew 17:1-8).

He was a striking character from the highlands of Gilead. His long thick hair hung over a cloak of sheepskin. Jehovah sent him to do away with the awful worship of Baal during the reign of Ahab who had married the wicked foreign princess, Jezebel. Suddenly emerging from the desert and standing before the corrupt king in the splendor of his court, the stern prophet boldly said, "As the Lord, the God of Israel, lives, whom I serve, there will be neither dew nor rain in the next few years except at my word" (1 Kings 17:1). He was given power to shut up the heavens so there would be no rain for three and a half years. He called down fire from heaven before the prophets of Baal at Mount Carmel. He was the evangelist of his day, thundering out warnings to this idolatrous people. The events in this great career will intrigue you. Read them carefully.

The Ministry of Elisha (2 Kings 1—9)

Elisha succeeded Elijah. He was beneficent in contrast to the fiery Elijah. Elijah trained Elisha as his successor. Elisha's ministry lasted fifty years. Most of his miracles were deeds of kindness and mercy. Elisha had a great influence upon the kings of the day, and although he did not approve of what they did, he was always coming to their rescue.

Elijah and Elisha are in marked contrast to each other:

Elijah, the prophet of judgment, law, severity.

Elisha, the prophet of grace, love, tenderness.

Baal worship was introduced by the wicked Jezebel, and after thirty years was exterminated by Elijah, Elisha and Jehu.

The Corruption of Israel (2 Kings 1—17)

Jeroboam, the ruler of the Northern Kingdom, Israel, made Shechem his capital. It seemed the natural place because it was in the center of the land.

It was the custom, according to the law, to go up to Jerusalem regularly to worship (Deuteronomy 12:11,14; 16:6,15-16; 1 Samuel 1:3,7). Jeroboam was afraid to have his ten tribes journey to Jerusalem, the capital of Rehoboam's kingdom, to worship God; so he made two golden calves and placed them in convenient spots—Bethel (Genesis 28:11-19) in the south, and Dan (Judges 18:29-30) in the northern end of the kingdom, so the people would not have to go to Jerusalem.

More than twenty times he is described as "Jeroboam, the son of Nebat, who caused Israel to sin." Beware of man-made religion. We must worship where and how God tells us!

God says, "Let us not give up meeting together, as some are in the habit of doing" (Hebrews 10:25). God knows we need fellowship in worship to keep the spiritual coals alive, but we hear people say constantly that they can worship better alone in the woods or by the sea. Learn now to do what God asks you to do. Remember, a request from a king is a command!

After 200 years, the people were carried into captivity by the king of Assyria in 722 B.C. (2 Kings 17). Many of God's prophets had warned Israel of captivity, but they would not turn from their idolatry to Jehovah.

The Assyrians were great and cruel warriors. They built their kingdom on their pillage from other countries. Their practices were horrible. They skinned men alive, cut out their tongues, put out their eyes, dismembered their bodies and then made mounds of the skulls of men to instill fear! For 300 years Assyria was a world empire.

The Captivity of Judah (2 Kings 13—25)

The Southern Kingdom tried to conquer the Northern Kingdom. For eighty years there was continuous war between them. But these wars failed. Then there was a period of eighty years of peace between these two kingdoms following the marriage of the son of Jehoshaphat (southern king) to the daughter of Ahab (northern king). Finally there was a period of fifty years when the kingdoms intermittently warred with each other until the captivity.

In the Southern Kingdom, there was only one dynasty (Davidic) from King Rehoboam to Zedekiah. The great prophets of that day were Nathan, Isaiah, Micah, Jeremiah, Joel and Zephaniah.

About 136 years after the Northern Kingdom had been taken into captivity by Assyria, the Southern Kingdom was taken captive by Nebuchadnezzar, king of Babylon. Jerusalem was destroyed, the Temple burned and the princes led away. The people had forgotten God and refused to listen to the warnings of the prophets. God wanted His people to learn the lesson of obedience and dependence upon Him.

In 1 Kings we see the kingdom of Israel, filled with pride and arrogance, falling apart. In 2 Kings, sinning yet more, Israel goes into captivity. Surely the way of the transgressor is hard. The history of the Jews is a record of God's dealings with disobedient children. In all His punishment, He is kind and merciful for He loves them still.

The secret of the downfall of the Jewish people is found in 2 Kings 3:2: "He did evil in the eyes of the Lord." Be loyal and true to God. It does not pay to do evil.

The moving figures and powerful factors of those days were the prophets Elijah and Elisha. Elijah was the strength of Israel. Jezebel and Ahab had frightened the people into submission. But Elijah stood. Read 1 Kings 17:1, where he said, "As the Lord God of Israel liveth, before whom I stand" *(KJV)*. And there he stood for God, like a rock, in the face of all the weakness of Israel. We ask today, "Where now is the Lord, the God of Elijah?" (2 Kings 2:14). Would that we might see some of this old-time power.

Elijah was the champion of the Most High. He brought God to the people. He was the pastor-evangelist of Israel's day.

There is a great difference between the fall of Israel and Judah. Israel was scattered throughout the nations for an indefinite period, but God specified the length of Judah's captivity to seventy years. Judah was to return to Jerusalem, which she did later. The Messiah was to come out of Judah and God was preparing the way for Him to come there and not to Babylon or Assyria.

God was using even the rulers of foreign nations to work out His plan. Cyrus, king of Persia, for example, was going to issue a decree that would allow the Jews to return to their homeland.

Look up the following questions:

1. What was Solomon's greatest work? Describe it.
2. What books of the Bible did Solomon write?
3. Why was the kingdom divided after Solomon's death?
4. Describe the kings of Israel. How did this kingdom end? Who were her conquerors? (Know this.) Who were Israel's prophets?
5. Describe the kings of Judah. Who took Judah captive and where was she taken?

Understanding First Chronicles

The History of Judah
Through such books as the Chronicles we get the history of the Jewish nation. Through this nation our Lord came to earth. God chose this people for the fulfillment of His great promises and purposes. He is still their God (Romans 11:1) and He has His purposes yet to be fulfilled in them. In the light of this truth, books such as the Chronicles take on new meaning and power.

Understanding Second Chronicles

A Book of Revivals!
Great revivals under:

1. Asa—2 Chronicles 15
2. Jehoshaphat—2 Chronicles 20
3. Joash—2 Chronicles 23—24
4. Hezekiah—2 Chronicles 29—31
5. Josiah—2 Chronicles 35.

Jesus Christ is portrayed as King in the books of Kings and Chronicles.

Chapter 12

Understanding Ezra and Nehemiah

Ezra and Nehemiah Portray Jesus Christ, Our Restorer

Selected Bible Readings

Sunday: Jews Return to Jerusalem (Ezra 1—3)
Monday: Discouragement and Joy (Ezra 4—6)
Tuesday: Ezra's Expedition (Ezra 7—10)
Wednesday: Nehemiah Rebuilds the Wall (Nehemiah 1—3)
Thursday: Overcoming Opposition (Nehemiah 4—6)
Friday: Nehemiah Rebuilds the Morals (Nehemiah 7—9)
Saturday: Reforming Through Religion (Nehemiah 11—13)

Understanding Ezra

Again we find that Ezra and Nehemiah were one book in the Hebrew Bible, as were the two books of Samuel and Kings. These books tell the story of the return of God's chosen people after the exile. They give the record of one of the most important events in Jewish history—the return from exile in Babylon.

The time covered by these two books is about 100 years.

Both books begin at Persia and end at Jerusalem.

Both center around the man of God who wrote them.

Both stories begin with a Persian king's decree.

Both tell of building as their chief theme.

Both books contain a long prayer of humiliation and confession in the ninth chapter.

Both end with the purification of the people.

Ezra 7:10—Ezra's keynote

Nehemiah 6:3—Nehemiah's keynote

The purposes of God may sometimes seem delayed, but they are never abandoned. "Remember the instruction you gave your servant Moses," prayed Nehemiah (Nehemiah 1:8). The books of Ezra and Nehemiah tell the story of how God remembered and how He brought back His people from exile. Jeremiah 29:10-13 tells us of this remembrance.

During the captivity, the prophets Jeremiah and Ezekiel told the Jews of their restoration and predicted that they would return to their own land and rebuild Jerusalem. Jeremiah, the prophet, told them this would happen at the end of seventy years. "When seventy years are completed for Babylon, I will come to you and fulfill my gracious promise to bring you back to this place" (Jeremiah 29:10). Remember that the books of Kings ended with the story of the captivity of first the Northern Kingdom of Israel and then the Southern Kingdom of Judah.

Daniel was carried away captive to Babylon at the time of the captivity of Judah. The last incident in the book of Daniel was the story of Daniel in the lions' den (Daniel 6:16-24). This happened about ten years before Cyrus became king over Babylon. Daniel was an old man when these events took place.

Rebuilding the national life of the Jewish people covered 100 years.

Two periods of time are very important.

1. Twenty years (537-517 B.C.) from the first year of Cyrus to the sixth year of Darius when the people under Zerubbabel, the governor, and Joshua, the priest, rebuilt the Temple. For this period, read Ezra 1—6; Zechariah and Haggai; the genealogies of 1 Chronicles 1:1—9:44; the last two verses of 2 Chronicles; Psalms 126; 137; and the reference to Cyrus in Isaiah 44:23 to 45:8.

2. Twenty-five years (458-433 B.C.) when Nehemiah, the governor, and Ezra, the priest, rebuilt the wall of Jerusalem and restored the city. Malachi was the prophet of this day.

Ezra gives the record of both of these periods.

Nehemiah tells of the second period, building the walls.

The book of Ezra has both a backward and a forward look.

The backward look: We find a second exodus for captive Israel. The first exodus was out of Egypt. This second exodus was from Babylon. This time Ezra is leader in the place of Moses. He, like Moses, is an inspired writer and leader. Both men were great organizers, lawgivers and teachers raised up to fulfill God's gracious purpose and bring captive Israel out of bondage. Both of these great leaders dealt with Israel in a strong and merciful way.

The forward look: In history, it is like the landing of our pilgrim fathers on a bleak and hostile shore. They came in timid, struggling relays back to Jerusalem. But God gave them a foothold. It was His city and it is His city still. He will again bring back His own; He will raise up Zion out of ruins.

The ten Northern tribes (the Northern Kingdom) were taken captive first by Assyria (2 Kings 17), then the two Southern tribes (Benjamin and Judah, the Southern Kingdom) by Babylon (2 Kings 25). They were restored to their own land under the Persian Empire. The Babylonians had been conquered by the Medes and Persians. The ten northern tribes who were carried away to Assyria never returned.

In 537 B.C. the first Jews returned to Jerusalem from Babylon.

In 516 B.C. the Temple was restored.

In 479 B.C. Esther became queen of Persia. (She was wife of Xerxes.)

In 458 B.C. Ezra led second expedition from Babylon.

In 445 B.C. Nehemiah rebuilt the wall of Jerusalem.

Return and Rebuilding of the Temple (Ezra 1—6)

As the book opens (Ezra 1:1-6), we find Cyrus, king of Persia, making a proclamation throughout his kingdom permitting the Jews who were captives in his kingdom to return to Jerusalem.

Two hundred years before, God had prophesied that He would do this. He named Cyrus as the one He would use. The record of this remarkable prophecy, which calls a king by his name 200 years before his time, is found in Isaiah 44:28; 45:1-4. No doubt this proclamation of Cyrus was made in part due to the fact that he saw these words of Isaiah.

Daniel's influence in the court was very powerful. He had been the Disraeli of the court in Babylon. He was one of the princes carried away by Nebuchadnezzar to his court. Now he was an old man.

At Cyrus's first call (537 B.C.), (Ezra 1:1-4) no more than 50,000 Jews availed themselves of the opportunity of returning to Jerusalem under Zerubbabel. Notice from this time the Israelites are called Jews because most of them were of the tribe of Judah and the name Jews comes from Judah.

Cyrus gave back to Zerubbabel the golden vessels Nebuchadnezzar had taken from the Temple in Jerusalem (Ezra 1:5-11). They started back over 700 miles of barren desert from Babylon to Jerusalem.

At the time of the captivity seventy years before, only the higher classes were taken into Babylon. The rest were left in their own land to suffer (Jeremiah 24:5-8; 44:15). Now everyone did not return; only the earnest and pious Jews went back. It was a time of real sifting among the people. Most of them after seventy years had built homes and established themselves and were content to remain in Babylon. They did not care to face the dangers and hardships of returning across the desert and arriving in a city that had been destroyed.

How like the Jews of today when thousands are returning again to Israel from all over the world! Many of those who have prospered in other lands do not care to go back to make a new start in Jerusalem.

Although the leaders were from the tribe of Judah, no doubt there were representatives from the whole of Israel. Only those who loved God were ready to make the attempt. Many of the Jews had been born in Babylon during the seventy years. These were not considered captives, but exiles.

Everything is taken care of when God is in charge. Not only money for rebuilding the Temple in Jerusalem, but also traveling expenses and all other needs were provided by God at Cyrus's direction (Ezra 1:4,6). Someone has said that God used Babylon as the safety deposit vault for the silver and gold vessels of the Temple.

The names of those who returned are given in chapter 2. They laid the foundation of the Temple the first thing upon returning. It was a time of great rejoicing. It is interesting to notice that before they built homes for themselves they first thought of a house for the Lord. They did not build the Temple first, but the altar (Ezra 3:2).

The place where sin must be dealt with must come first in every life. The heart must be right if God is to bless. The altar was the center of the Jew's religion, the Cross the center of the Christian faith.

Read about the hindrances to the work (Ezra 4:1-22). Hindrances to all real work for God are to be expected. The Church must not have the help of the world.

The opposition disheartened them. They needed Haggai's message. Refer to the book of Haggai. Haggai and Zechariah, the prophets, encouraged the people from within the ranks (Ezra 4:23—5:17), and within four years the Temple was complete and dedicated (Ezra 6).

Zerubbabel's Temple was very plain and simple. It was not the sumptuous edifice that Solomon's was. In fact, it was in such contrast to the elegance of the first Temple that the old men who had seen Solomon's Temple wept aloud. But it was God's house and so the people thanked God and took courage.

Return and Reformation Under Ezra (Ezra 7—10)

Ezra appears in person in the seventh chapter (458 B.C.). At least sixty years after the Jews had first returned to Jerusalem, he led a second expedition from Babylon to reinforce the struggling colonists in Judah. Ezra received a commission from Artaxerxes the king (Ezra 7:11—8:14) who half-blindly aided in accomplishing God's plans for His people. Read Ezra 7:25 and find how impressed the king was with Ezra's love of God's Word. Oh, that we might live in such a way that others would learn to have respect for God's Book!

This contingent under Ezra consisted of 1,700 Jews. It took them four months to make the journey, and it was financed by King Artaxerxes (Ezra 7:12-26). Thirteen years later this same king authorized Nehemiah to build the walls of Jerusalem (Nehemiah 2). Cyrus, Darius and Artaxerxes, the three Persian kings, were very friendly to the Jews.

Tradition tells us that Ezra was the founder of the synagogue worship that arose in the days of the captivity. Because the Temple had been destroyed and the people were scattered, they needed some place to worship God. Each Jewish community had its place of worship and instruction. After the Jews returned to their homeland, the synagogues were started at home as well as in other lands where they were scattered.

The Old Testament history closes about 100 years after the Jews returned from their captivity. Alexander the Great (336-325 B.C.) broke the Persian hold and world power passed from Persia to Greece. Alexander showed consideration to the Jews, as we find in history.

Ezra the Scribe

Of Ezra it is said he "had devoted himself to the study and observance of the Law of the Lord, and to teaching its decrees and laws in Israel" (Ezra 7:10). His name means "help." He belongs to the great triumvirate of the Old Testament law (Moses, Samuel, Ezra). He wrote and worked to keep the record intact and to hold Israel, God's chosen people, to her divinely appointed mission. We are indebted to Ezra for the literary and ecclesiastical renaissance of that day. According to tradition, he did a work in forming the Scripture canon for which he was appointed of God. Tradition makes him the president of a council of 120 men who formed the Old Testament canon.

In addition to Ezra's outstanding ministry of the Word, he probably wrote portions of 1 and 2 Chronicles, and Psalm 119, which is a wonderful poem about the Word of God. As we have said, he instituted the synagogue worship that is the parent of our own form of worship, and assisted by the great synagogue of which he was president, settled the canon of Old Testament Scripture. Under Ezra we see the great revival of Bible study.

Ezra was the Thomas Jefferson of his time, laying the constitutional foundations for the future. To him we are indebted for codifying Israel's laws and the formation of her Scripture canon.

When Ezra returned to Jerusalem, he found things even worse than he had expected. Although the people had not returned to idolatry, they had intermarried with the people of the land and had done everything the pagans had taught them (Ezra 9:1-4). The princes and rulers were the worst offenders. Ezra rent his garments and literally pulled out his hair in grief! Read Ezra's touching prayer and confession (9:5-15).

As Ezra was praying and weeping before God, a great congregation assembled. What happened? (Read Ezra 10:1-44.) The people who had gathered about him through the long hours of the day came to a consciousness of the greatness of their sin as they saw how it affected Ezra. Finally one of their number spoke and acknowledged the sin. At once Ezra led them into a sacred covenant with God. Read what God says about confession of sin (1 John 1:9).

Nehemiah's Prayer

Now turn to Nehemiah 9 and you will find the prayer of Nehemiah. Prayer is the most important privilege of a Christian. Nehemiah's prayer began where Ezra's ended—with utter surrender to God. (Compare Nehemiah 9:1-2 with Ezra 9:15; 10:1.)

God had definitely promised to bring the Jews back after seventy years in Babylon (Jeremiah 25:11-12; 29:10). We read in the very first verse of Ezra that it was to fulfill this word that "the Lord moved the heart of Cyrus king of Persia" to proclaim the restoration. (Look this up!) But it is through prayer that God wishes to have His will brought to pass. The restoration was wholly undeserved by Israel, but purposed in "God's heart of mercy."

See the results of this restoration of God's people to their land again:

First, through the rebuilding of the Temple, God opened the door of fellowship with Himself. Through the seventy years of suffering, they were ready to return and build and wait until He, the true Servant, should come.

Second, He renewed His promise of a coming Redeemer. It was prophesied that the Redeemer would be associated with Judah (Genesis 49:10; Isaiah 11:12, 40:9; Jeremiah 23:5-6; Micah 5:2).

Third, to make ready for the "fulness of the time" when Christ should come, as spoken of by Paul in Galatians 4:4 *(KJV).*

Understanding Nehemiah

Repairing the City's Wall (Nehemiah 1—7)

Nehemiah was the cupbearer at the court of King Artaxerxes. This was a position of high honor. But in this position of familiarity with the king, he had not forgotten his people. The news brought to him about Jerusalem made him very sad. This sadness could not be wholly hidden and the king detected it. The Jews had been back home for almost a hundred years, but had made no attempt to build Jerusalem beyond the restoration of the Temple, because their enemies made it almost impossible.

Artaxerxes' stepmother was Esther, the Jewess, who no doubt was still alive. It may have been that Nehemiah received his appointment through her influence. He was loyal enough to his people to leave the luxury of a king's court and go back to rebuild Jerusalem, the capital of his homeland. The king gave consent. We find even today Jews everywhere long to see Jerusalem flourish, and they turn their faces there as their homeland.

When Nehemiah reached Jerusalem in 445 B.C., Ezra had been there for thirteen years. Ezra was a priest and had been teaching the people the Word of God. But Nehemiah was a civil governor. He had come with the authority of the king of Persia to build the walls of Jerusalem. After he had been there only three days, he went up and viewed the walls at night. When he saw their dilapidated condition, he encouraged the people to begin building immediately. The work was accomplished in fifty-two days by assigning a portion of the wall to each family. Their attitude was expressed in the sentence, "The people worked with all their heart" (Nehemiah 4:6). Nehemiah was a real engineer.

First the Samaritans, the enemies of the Jews, derided them. They hindered their work so that the Jews had to keep watch night and day. Their derision turned to anger and Nehemiah divided the men into two groups, one keeping watch while the other worked.

Then opposition rose within the ranks. Some of the Jews became tired and complained that there was so much rubbish that the walls could not be built. All this rubble had to be removed in a thick canvas pad on the carrier's back; there were, of course, no wheelbarrows nor cars to convey the material. Then, the complaint arose that the rich were demanding usury that the poor were unable to pay.

Again the enemies tried by craft to bring Nehemiah away from his building, but Nehemiah only prayed and again he foiled his enemy. The Persian kings were ever the friends of the Jews.

Nehemiah gave the city of Jerusalem into the charge of his brother Hanani (Nehemiah 7:1-4). When he took a census (7:5-73), the whole number was 42,360 besides 7,337 servants and 245 singing men and women.

Repairing the People's Morals (Nehemiah 8—13)

All the people gathered in the street before the water gate in the city of Jerusalem and requested Ezra the scribe to bring out the book of the Law of Moses. He stood upon a pulpit of wood and read and explained the Law to the people (Nehemiah 8:1-13). This public reading brought true repentance to the people and a great revival broke out. When Josiah found the book of the Law, a great reformation started. When Martin Luther read the Bible, the Protestant Reformation began. We need to have the Word read today!

Their captivity in Babylon cured the Jewish people of idolatry. Remember, up to that time, in spite of all the warnings of the prophets, the people would worship the idols of the peoples around them. But from the days of the captivity to the present (about 2,500 years) the Jewish people have never been guilty of this sin. The Jews had intermarried with the idolatrous neighbors and this was the reason for their sin. Intermarriage of Christians with those who do not believe is a dangerous thing today. Paul says, "Do not be yoked together with unbelievers" (2 Corinthians 6:14).

Remember, Nehemiah left a life of ease and luxury and security for a life of toil and danger and heartbreaks. He was a reformer!

And no one appreciates the man who tries to reform him.

Nehemiah was a man of prayer. We do not find a blot on his character. He was fearless and courageous.

The important thing in the study of the Bible is to find how Jesus Christ is portrayed in each book.

THE BIBLE portrays Jesus Christ as the Savior of the World.
GENESIS portrays Jesus Christ as our Creator-God.
EXODUS portrays Jesus Christ as our Passover Lamb.
LEVITICUS portrays Jesus Christ as our Sacrifice for Sin.
NUMBERS portrays Jesus Christ as our "Lifted-Up One."
DEUTERONOMY portrays Jesus Christ as our true Prophet.
JOSHUA portrays Jesus Christ as Captain of our salvation.
JUDGES portrays Jesus Christ as our Deliverer-Judge.
RUTH portrays Jesus Christ as our Kinsman-Redeemer.
FIRST AND SECOND SAMUEL portray Jesus Christ as our King.
KINGS AND CHRONICLES portray Jesus Christ as our King.
EZRA AND NEHEMIAH portray Jesus Christ as our Restorer.

Time Line
Genesis to Nehemiah

—to 2000 B.C.   **GENESIS 1—11**
Period: The world before Abram (Creation—Sin—Flood—Babel)
People: Adam—Eve—Cain—Seth—Noah—Shem—Ham—Japheth

2000-1700 B.C.   **GENESIS 12—50**
Period: Age of the patriarchs (Call of Abraham— Migration to Egypt—Growth of Israel)
People: Abraham—Isaac—Jacob—Joseph

1700-1450 B.C.   **EXODUS—DEUTERONOMY**
Period: Oppression in Egypt (The Exodus—The Law—Worship—Wilderness)
People: Moses—Miriam—Aaron—Joshua

1450-1100 B.C.   **JOSHUA—1 SAMUEL 7**
Period: Conquest of Canaan and time of the Judges (Invasion of Canaan—Bondage and deliverance)
People: Joshua—Caleb—Othniel—Ehud—Shamgar—Deborah—Barak—Gideon—Jephthah—Samson—Eli—Samuel

1100-600 B.C.   **1 SAMUEL 8—2 CHRONICLES**
Period: Monarchy—united, divided, declining (Kingdom established—Temple built—Kingdom divided—Destruction of Samaria—Discovery of the Law—Destruction of Jerusalem)
People: Saul—David—Solomon—Jeroboam—Rehoboam—Ahab—Asa—Jehu—Elijah—Elisha—Jehoshaphat—Joab—Amaziah—Jeroboam II—Hoshea—Uzziah—Jotham—Ahaz—Hezekiah—Manasseh—Josiah—Jehoiakim—Zedekiah

500-400 B.C.   **EZRA—NEHEMIAH**
Period: Return from the Exile (Decree of Cyrus—Close of Old Testament History)
People: Zerubbabel—Ezra—Nehemiah

Chapter 13

A Quick Look at the Old Testament

Genesis Through Nehemiah

Outline of Old Testament History

I.   Period of Patriarchs: Adam to Moses (Genesis)
II. Period of great leaders: Moses to Saul (Exodus to 1 Samuel)
III. Period of Kings: Saul to the Babylonian Captivity (Samuel, Kings, Chronicles, prophetical books)
IV. Period of Foreign Kings: Captivity to coming of Christ (Ezra, Nehemiah, Esther, Ezekiel, Daniel)

I. Period of Patriarchs: Adam to Moses

Bible account found in book of Genesis. We find in this period: (1) God's chosen men; (2) God's chosen family; (3) God's chosen people—the tribes of Israel.

1. *God's chosen men:* In the beginning we find no nations. God chose men who made Him known, but the earth became more and more wicked (Genesis 6:5). The chosen men were:
    Adam, created in God's image
    Seth, his godly son
    Enoch, who walked with God
    Noah, who built the ark
    Shem (Noah's son) and his descendants.

The important events during this time were:
      Creation (Genesis 1—2)
      Fall (Genesis 3)
      Flood (Genesis 6—8)
      Babel and the Dispersion (Genesis 11).

Four great nations were established as a result:
      Egypt in North Africa
      Canaan on the Mediterranean
      Babylonia between the Tigris and Euphrates Rivers
      Assyria, north of Babylonia.

2. *God's chosen family:* The race had failed (Genesis 6:5) so God limited His promises to a single family. He called Abraham to become the father of this nation.

The important events are:
      Abraham called (Genesis 12:1—25:11)
      Jacob chosen (Genesis 25:19—36:43)
      Joseph cherished (Genesis 45—46).

3. *God's chosen people:* Twelve tribes became a nation.

II. Period of Great Leaders: Moses to Saul

Bible account found in Exodus to 1 Samuel. We find in this period:

1. The Exodus (Exodus)
2. The wilderness wandering (Exodus, Leviticus, Numbers, Deuteronomy)
3. Conquest of Canaan (Joshua)
4. The rule of the judges (Judges).

III. Period of Kings: Saul to the Babylonian Captivity

Bible account given in Samuel, Kings, Chronicles and the Prophets. Tribal life developed into national life. We find in this period:

1. The United Kingdom—Saul, David, Solomon
2. The divided kingdom
      Kings of Israel—Northern Kingdom

Kings of Judah—Southern Kingdom
The fall of the Northern Kingdom
The fall of the Southern Kingdom.

IV. Period of Foreign Kings: Captivity to Christ

Bible account in Ezra, Nehemiah, Esther, Ezekiel and Daniel. God was preparing the land, the people and the world for the coming Christ. We find in this period:

Restoration under Persian kings

Review the books of the Bible by stating how Christ is portrayed in each one.

Survey Quiz

Who Are the Following?

1. THIS man (a) was never born; (b) never had a birthday; (c) owned a great estate; (d) was perfect physically; (e) was a great zoologist, gave every animal a name.
    (Adam)

2. THIS man (a) was father of the oldest man in the world; (b) lived a godly life in one of the most wicked generations in the world; (c) was the only man in 3,000 years who did not die; (d) walked into heaven.
    (Enoch)

3. THIS man (a) was radiant with righteousness in the midst of moral darkness, and saved his family of seven by his faith in God; (b) was a great ship builder, but built a huge ship on a desert, miles from the sea; (c) never had to launch his ship into the sea—the sea came to it and lifted it to the top of a mountain; (d) gathered the greatest collection of animals the world has ever known; (e) had sons who were the fathers of the nations of the world.
    (Noah)

4. THIS man was akin to a covered wagon pioneer: (a) he

left a great city of culture at God's request and traveled across a trackless desert; (b) he left a beautiful home and lived in a tent for 100 years; (c) he was called "a friend of God"; (d) he was the father of a great nation; (e) his son was born after he was a hundred years old; (f) angels visited him.

(Abraham)

5. THIS man (a) and his young friend believed God when no one else would; (b) was a great general; (c) did not have to build a bridge to transport his army into the land that he wanted to conquer; (d) used trumpets instead of bombers and priests instead of trained soldiers to destroy a city.

    (Joshua)

6. THIS man (a) was an adopted child; (b) lived amidst the wealth of the day; (c) enjoyed unlimited education; (d) in spite of this, chose to identify himself with the poor people from whom he came rather than with the rulers with whom he lived; (e) was forced to live in a desert for forty years; (f) was chosen as the leader of three million people and led them out from under the bondage of the strongest ruler of his day without firing a shot; (g) made slaves become rich overnight; (h) was the meekest man on earth and yet he lost his temper; (i) talked with God; (j) died an unknown death; (k) was buried by no man.

    (Moses)

Did You Know This?

Between chapters 6 and 7 of Ezra, three great world battles (Salamis, Thermopylae and Marathon) were fought; and two great world leaders (Confucius and Buddha) died! Time elapsed: fifty-eight years! (516-458 B.C.)

In the Old Testament, Esther (which takes place in previously named period) follows Nehemiah; in history, the events in Esther occur thirty years before Nehemiah!

The purposes of God are sometimes delayed; but never abandoned!

Chapter 14

Understanding Esther

Esther Portrays Jesus Christ, Our Advocate

Selected Bible Readings

Sunday:	Rejection of Vashti (Esther 1)
Monday:	Crowning of Esther (Esther 2)
Tuesday:	Plotting of Haman (Esther 3—4)
Wednesday:	Venture of Esther (Esther 5)
Thursday:	Mordecai Exalted (Esther 6)
Friday:	Esther's Feast (Esther 7—8)
Saturday:	Deliverance of the Jews (Esther 9—10)

You have heard of the great Xerxes, king of Persia, the Ahasuerus of the book of Esther, of his famous expedition against Greece, and how the Greeks defeated his tremendous fleet at the battle of Salamis in 480 B.C. Historians tell us that this was one of the world's most important battles. From parallel passages in Herodotus, we find that the feast described in the first chapter of Esther was the occasion for planning the campaign against Greece (third year of his reign). Esther replaced Vashti in the seventh year of his reign (Esther 2:16) when Xerxes was seeking comfort after his disastrous defeat.

In the midst of this famous chapter in world history occurs the beautiful and charming Bible story of Esther. Although God's name is not mentioned in the book of Esther, every page is full of God, who hides Himself behind every word.

Matthew Henry, (1662-1714, British Presbyterian minister and famous Bible commentator), says, "If the name of God is not here, His finger is." Dr. Pierson (Arthur Tappan Pierson, 1837-1911, American editor, lecturer, biographer, missionary statesman and pastor), calls it, "The Romance of Providence." God has a part in all the events of human life.

Although Yuri Gagarin (1934-68, Soviet cosmonaut), the first man to travel in space, scoffed that he did not see God in outer space, the world today cannot get rid of God; neither could Israel. He has never let His people go in the past and He will never let them go in the future. He followed them in their captivity into Babylon. When the prophets were silent and the Temple closed, God was still standing guard. When the kings of earth feasted and forgot, God remembered, and with His hand He wrote their doom or moved their hand to work His glory.

This book opens with a feast of the world's prince—Ahasuerus; it closes with the feast of God's prince—Mordecai. For a while Haman is exalted; at last, Mordecai. As you read this story, note the upsets in human history and the final triumph of God's chosen people.

Esther is like Joseph and David. God had each one hidden away for His purpose. When the day came, He brought them to the front to work out His plan. God hid Joseph away in a dungeon in Egypt, but when He was ready, He placed him in the position of prime minister of that country. God always has someone in reserve to fulfill His purposes. Sometimes it is a man like Joseph, or Moses. Sometimes it is a woman like Hannah, or Esther or Mary. Recall men in history such as Martin Luther and Abraham Lincoln and Billy Graham whom God seems to have prepared and kept for the hour.

Esther stands out as God's chosen one. She is a sweet and winsome person. She has come to the kingdom for just "such a time as this" (Esther 4:14). We see her taking her life in her hand. As she goes in for her people's sake unto the king, she says, "and if I perish, I perish" (Esther 4:16).

Two beautiful girls join hands in behalf of God's people. They are Ruth and Esther. Ruth becomes the ancestress of the Deliverer of Israel and Esther saves the people so that the Deliverer might come. God carefully protected this nation through the centuries for the purpose of blessing the whole world. They could not be wiped out before they brought the Savior into the world. This was not according to God's plans. Therefore God kept this nation according to His promise to Abraham.

In what period this story was written and who was its author are unknown. In point of time, it is placed between chapters six and seven of the book of Ezra. Comparatively few, not more than 50,000, of the captive Jews had returned from Babylon under the edict of Cyrus. Many were born in Babylon and had established themselves in business there and were not inclined to cross the desert and begin all over again in the land of their fathers. If they had all returned to Jerusalem, the book of Esther would not have been written.

The book of Esther is named for a Jewish orphan who became a Persian queen. This book and Ruth are the only books in the Bible that bear the names of women. The name "Esther" means "star."

Someone has said that all the events of this book center around three feasts:

1. Feast of King Ahasuerus (Esther 1—2)
2. Feast of Esther (Esther 7)
3. Feast of Purim (Esther 9).

Rejection of Vashti (Esther 1)

The great feast to which Vashti refused to come, as has been learned from the inscriptions, was held to consider the expedition against Greece, for which Xerxes spent four years in preparation. King Ahasuerus of the story was Xerxes, the famous Persian monarch (485-465 B.C.).

As this book opens, the king was entertaining all the nobles and princes of his kingdom in the royal palace at Shushan. The banquet was planned on a colossal scale. It lasted 180 days (Esther 1:4). The men were feasting in the gorgeous palace gardens and the women were entertained by the beautiful Queen Vashti in her private apartment.

Shushan was the winter residence of the Persian kings. Remember, Nehemiah was in the palace in Shushan (Nehemiah 1:1).

In 1852, its site was identified by Loftus (William Kennett Loftus, 1821?-1858, British archaeologist, geologist and traveler), and in 1884 a Frenchman named Dieulafoy (Marcel, dates unknown, architectural archaeologist) and his wife, Jeanne Rachel Dieulafoy, (1851-??, descriptive writer and novelist) continued the excavation. They definitely located the places mentioned in the book of Esther—the "inner court," the "outer court," the "king's gate," the "palace garden." He even found a die, or *pur*, which they used to cast lots.

When the king and princes were in the midst of their drunken revelry, the king called for Vashti so that he could show off her beauty. Of course, no Persian woman would permit this. It was an affront to her womanhood. Drunkenness had outraged the most sacred rules of Oriental etiquette. The seclusion of the harem was to be violated for the amusement of the dissolute king and his boon companions. Vashti refused. This made the king a laughingstock. To defend himself, he deposed the queen. (See Esther 1:12-22.)

Remember, modesty is the crown jewel of womanhood. Never be false to your pure ideals. Men are bound to protect this crown jewel in womanhood. Modesty seldom rises in a breast that is not enriched by nobler virtues.

Crowning of Esther (Esther 2)

The minute Ahasuerus saw Esther, he made her his queen. The little Jewish orphan girl, raised by her cousin Mordecai, was lifted to the Persian throne. According to the Roman historian, Herodotus (485-425 B.C.), at this time the Persian Empire comprised more than half the then-known world.

Between chapters 1 and 2, Ahasuerus made his historic attack on Greece with an army of five million men, suffering a terrible defeat in the famous battles of Thermopylae and Salamis (480 B.C.).

Two years later, Xerxes (Ahasuerus) married Esther. She was his queen for thirteen years. Esther, no doubt, lived for many years into the reign of her stepson, Artaxerxes. Under this king, Nehemiah rebuilt Jerusalem. Esther's marriage to Xerxes gave the Jews prestige at this court and made it possible for Nehemiah to rebuild Jerusalem. (See Nehemiah 2:1-8.)

The great palace of Xerxes at Persepolis, where Esther no doubt spent much of her time, has been excavated. The description of it, even in its ruin, is magnificent. The city itself was destroyed by fire by Alexander the Great in 331 B.C. It has been buried in the sands of the desert ever since. In 1930, the Oriental Institute of Chicago received permission from the Persian government to excavate and restore the palace as completely as possible.

To make the story of this Jewish girl more real and interesting, let us give you a little description of this palace. The foundation of the palace was a platform fifty feet high and covered an area of two and a half acres. Underneath was a vast sewer system miles in length through which one may walk today. The walls of the palace were covered with the most magnificent carvings and reliefs and sculptures. Two large rooms in the Louvre display these treasures. When the rubbish was finally cleared away, they found these carvings preserved, as fresh and beautiful as they were when Queen Esther walked through the corridors and looked upon them.

The second chapter describes the scene in this palace. Richly colored awnings were stretched across from marble pillars to silver rods, shading the exalted guests as they reclined on gold and silver seats while they feasted gluttonously and drank heavily day after day (Esther 1:5-8).

There was a grand audience hall where men came from the four corners of the earth to pay their honor to the great king, Esther's husband. The giant columns still rise in their grandeur, speaking of the former glory of the palace. This was the place to which Esther was brought as queen.

Note: Here, parenthetically, occurs the story of Mordecai's saving the king's life. This account figures prominently later in the book (Esther 2:21-23).

Plotting of Haman (Esther 3—4)

We see a form casting a shadow across the picture. This scene is one of sorrow and mourning. In Esther 3—5 we read of the ascendancy of a man by the name of Haman. He was a wicked man whose day of triumph was short and whose joy endured but for a moment. (See Job 20:4-5.) We see him becoming the chief minister of the king.

Haman was the Judas of Israel. He was a wicked monster in the life of God's chosen people. During the reading of the book of Esther in a Jewish synagogue at the Feast of Purim, the congregation may be found taking part in a chorus at every mention of the name of Haman, "May his name be blotted out," while boys pound stones and bits of wood on which his hated name is written.

When Haman appears in the book of Esther, he had just been exalted to the highest position under the king of Persia (Esther 3:1). The high honor turned his head. He swelled with vanity and was bitterly humiliated when Mordecai, who was sitting at the gate, did not do homage to him as to the king (Esther 3:2).

Inflated with pride, he could not endure the indifference of any subject. The little fault of Mordecai was magnified into a capital offense. Mordecai, a Jew, could not give divine honor to a man! Haman became so enraged that he wanted to have a wholesale massacre of all the Jews in the kingdom (Esther 3:6). To determine the day his enemies should be destroyed, he cast lots, which fell on the thirteenth day of March, just ten months away (Esther 3:7). Haman tried to prove to the king that all the Jews were disloyal subjects. He offered to pay the king a bribe of millions of dollars (Esther 3:9). The king signed a royal decree that meant that every Jewish man, woman and child should be killed and all their property should be taken. Compare this treatment with that used by the Nazi regime.

Imagine the fasting and praying and the weeping in sackcloth that took place among the Jews (Esther 4:1-3).

Queen Esther saw it all and inquired of Mordecai what it meant. He gave her a copy of the king's decree that told the sad story. Then he added, "And who knows but that you have come to royal position for such a time as this?" (Esther 4:14).

It would do well for all of us to pause and ask ourselves this same question. Why has God allowed me to live at this particular hour? To do what is right may mean that we must jeopardize our lives. Then we must face the issue and answer with this young queen, "And if I perish, I perish."

Venture of Esther (Esther 5)

Queen Esther answers the challenge of Mordecai. She who had been placed in the palace on flowery beds of ease had not succumbed to the luxury of her surroundings. She chose a course at terrible danger to herself for the sake of her oppressed people, the Jews.

There is one thing to do always. Do what is right and leave the rest to God. God prepares people for emergencies. Failure is not sin; faithlessness is. There is a time to act. "There is a tide in the affairs of men which taken at the flood leads on to fortune." Act when God speaks.

The beauty of Esther was that she was not spoiled by her great elevation. Though she became the queen of a great king, she did not forget the kind porter who raised her from childhood. Once she accepted her dreaded task, she proceeded to carry it out with courage. It was a daring act for her to enter unsummoned in the presence of the king. Who could tell what this fickle monarch would do? Think what he had done to Vashti!

When she had been received by the king, she used her resources. She knew the king's weakness for good living so she invited him to a banquet. Read what happened that night when the king could not sleep (Esther 6:1-11). How was Haman trapped (Esther 6:6)? At the second banquet Esther pleaded for her own life. She had Haman on the spot.

The king granted Esther's wish. Haman was hung on the very scaffold he had prepared for Mordecai, and Mordecai was elevated to the place of honor next to the king.

As you study God's Word, you will find that through the ages Satan has ever tried to destroy, first, God's people, the Jews, then the Church, and even Christ Himself. But God has thwarted his plans. Even "the gates of hell shall not prevail" *(KJV)* against His Church (see Matthew 16:18). God will triumph! Christ has won the victory!

Deliverance of the Jews (Esther 6—10)

The book of Esther closes with the account of establishing the Feast of Purim and lifting Mordecai to the place made vacant by Haman

(Esther 10:3). The Jewish porter became the second man, just under the king of Persia. The Feast of Purim was to be celebrated annually. It is always inspired by the dramatic story of Esther.

The Feast of Purim, celebrated even today, sets the seal upon the accuracy of the story. The feast does not celebrate the downfall of Haman so much as the deliverance of the people.

This feast celebrates a deliverance of the Jewish people from a fearful danger. It was a Thanksgiving Day for the chosen people. Although they had forsaken God, He had spared them. Deliverance seems to be the keynote of Jewish history. God has always delivered this nation from danger and servitude. Even yet, God will deliver His people in the hour of their trouble.

This book of Esther is an important link in a chain of events that tell of reestablishing the Hebrew nation in their own land in preparation of the coming of the Messiah into the world. The Jewish people had escaped extermination. It was God's purpose that they should be preserved to bring forth the Savior of the world.

The character of Ahasuerus illustrates how unlimited power often is crushed and dissolved beneath the weight of its own immensity. Those who are exalted to the pedestal of a god are made dizzy by their own altitude.

King Ahasuerus (the Xerxes of the historian Herodotus) was punished with childishness. This silly monarch decorated a tree with the jewelry of a prince in reward for its fruitfulness. He flogged and chained the Hellespont as a punishment for its tempestuousness. Such actions are akin to insanity.

Character Study of Esther

Esther is a sweet and attractive character:
Beautiful and modest—Esther 2:15
Winsome—Esther 2:9-17; 5:1-3
Obedient—Esther 2:10
Humble—Esther 4:16
Courageous—Esther 7:6
Loyal and constant—Esther 2:22; 8:1-2; 7:3-4.

There is always one thing to do—do what is right and leave the rest with God.

"I will go to the king, even though it is against the law. And if I perish, I perish" (Esther 4:16).

God meets emergencies with human lives He has redeemed and prepared.

"And who knows but that you have come to royal position for such a time as this?" (Esther 4:14).

Prayer moves the hand that moves the world. A devoted woman moved a determined monarch.

"Surely the wrath of man shall praise thee" (Psalm 76:10, *KJV*).

Those who walk in holy sincerity with Christ may walk in holy security among humanity.

God's pioneers leave all—to gain all.

Books of Poetry
of The Old Testament

Job • Psalms • Proverbs
Ecclesiastes • Song of Solomon

Key Events of the Books of Poetry

Books of Poetry: The Heart of Wisdom and Worship

Biblical poetry teaches that true worship and wisdom can only come from appropriate fear and affection for God. Coming in the form of a cosmic struggle between the Lord and His angelic enemies (Job) ① , the full range of emotions in verse (Psalms) ② , a father's and mother's wisdom sayings to their son (Proverbs), musings about the human condition (Ecclesiastes) ③ , and the love song of a bride and groom (Song of Songs), the books of poetry also teach us how to anticipate a hopeful end to history through the coming of the Messiah.

Chapter 15

Understanding Job

Job Portrays Jesus Christ, My Redeemer

Selected Bible Readings

We have finished reading the historical books of the Old Testament—Joshua through Esther. Now we open the books of poetry—Job, Psalms, Proverbs, Ecclesiastes and Song of Solomon. These books tell of the experiences of the heart.

Job's key word is "tested." "But he knows the way that I take; when he has tested me, I shall come forth as gold" (Job 23:10).

Trials and suffering are for our education and training. The athlete is not put under strict discipline for punishment, but merely to make him ready for the race. Christ is ever preparing us for the race that is set before us (Hebrews 12:1-2).

Job is no doubt one of the most wonderful poems ever written. Tennyson (Alfred Tennyson, also known as Lord Tennyson, 1809-92, English poet) called it "the greatest poem, whether of ancient or modern literature." The scene in this amazing book takes place in the patriarchal days. For all we know this book may be one of the most ancient pieces of finished literature in existence. It is one of the oldest, if not the oldest, books in the Bible. The Word of God settles the fact that Job was a real person. God speaks through the prophet Ezekiel and says, "even if these three men—Noah, Daniel and Job—were in it, they could save only themselves by their righteousness" (Ezekiel 14:14; see also 14:20). If you doubt Job's existence, you will have to refute Noah and Daniel.

It is fitting that the oldest book should deal with the oldest problems. Among these is, Why do godly people suffer? This is the theme of the book. People have always asked why God permits good people to suffer. Haven't you wondered yourself why some good person has to die of an awful disease or has to be confined to a bed of pain? The drama of Job offers a solution to these problems. We believe it gives God's answer.

It is easy to become confused about this problem of suffering. Remember, the disciples of Christ thought that suffering was the result of sin in a life (John 9:2). The book of Job gives an entirely different reason for the suffering of Job. In this case, Job was being honored by God. It was the truth that God could trust Job to remain faithful to God in spite of everything. How wonderful it would be if you and I learned to thank God in all that happens to us.

This book should first be read as a narrative. The story of Job is a simple one. It opens with a scene in heaven and then tells of Job's fall from prosperity to poverty. This is followed by the great discussion between Job and his four friends: Eliphaz, the religious dogmatist, much like an ancient Pharisee; Bildad, who sought to comfort Job with worn-out platitudes; and Zophar, who thought he had a corner on all religious wisdom. Then comes Elihu, the impetuous youth. Finally, the climax is reached when God speaks. Job answers, at last in a humble spirit, and the problem is solved. This is the story of the book.

Next, we should study the problem of the book. It may be stated, Why do the righteous suffer? We find:

1. The shallow view of Satan—that the children of God love and serve Him because it pays in riches and honor (Job 1:1—2:8). Satan said that Job's godliness was selfishness,

that he served God for profit, that when prosperity ended he would be no more godly. He received permission to test Job (Job 2:6). Satan added, "Who wouldn't serve God for a handsome income of so many thousand a year? Watch him when his prosperity ends."

2. The scarcely less false view of Eliphaz, Bildad and Zophar (who agreed for the most part) that the unrighteous suffer because of their sins and the righteous are rewarded. Hence they reasoned that Job must have sinned, and this suffering was his punishment. Job was a great sufferer; therefore he must have been a great sinner. They said, "Who, being innocent, has ever perished?" (Job 4:7). But Job knew that his heart was true to God, and he could not accept the accusation of his friends. He showed them that their conclusion was false and that the wicked often prospered in the world (Job 24:6).

3. Elihu had a far more just answer of the problem, but his eloquent discourse was marred by conceit. He defended God and saw in affliction the chastisement of a loving Father. But this did not explain the reason of suffering to Job. Elihu argued that suffering was God's discipline to bring His sons back into fellowship with Himself. He believed that suffering was sent to keep us from sinning.

4. Jehovah explained to Job (by revealing Himself to him) that when men see God something always happens. The godly are allowed to suffer that they may see themselves first. Read Isaiah 6:1-5; Genesis 17:1-3; Daniel 10:4-8. When we come to the end of ourselves, God can lift us up. Job was a good man, but self-righteous. Read Job 29:1-25 and you will find the personal pronouns "I," "my" and "me" fifty-two times. It reminds one of Romans 7.

God has a wise purpose in all of our suffering. God wants to show His manifold wisdom (Ephesians 3:10). He wants the trial of our faith to work patience. He wants to bring out the gold as by fire. He wants to reveal real character. Furthermore, we have an unseen cloud of witnesses gathered in the great stadium of heaven to watch us in the conflict (Hebrews 12:1-2).

How little did Job realize that so much hung on his steadfast-ness and trust in God when he said, "Though he slay me, yet will I hope in him" (Job 13:15). I wonder if we realize today the issues that hang upon our faithfulness to God. If God could only find more of us who would trust Him, how much we might encour-age others to trust!

The problem of suffering has had much light thrown upon it from the New Testament—especially from the cross of Christ. Here we see the world's most righteous Man, the world's greatest Sufferer. We know now that the righteous suffer with the wicked today because of sin that fills the world with misery. We know there are natural consequences of sin, for the godly as well as the sinner. We have already noted that chastening is sometimes for training and correction. There is a suffering Christians must endure for Christ's sake and the gospel's.

The book of Job is a commentary on 1 Corinthians 11:31-32; Hebrews 12:7-11; Luke 22:31-32; 1 Corinthians 5:5. The chief subject of the book of Job is the riddle of all times: Why do the righteous suf-fer? But it deals with a wide scope of knowledge—the power of Satan, telling of his might and the limit of his authority; the fact of the Resurrection; and why a person should serve God.

The book of Job tells us much about human suffering. Job's friends, as thousands do today, made the mistake of thinking that all suffering was God's way of punishing sin. They asked, "Who, being innocent, has ever perished?" (Job 4:7).

Do you know of any good person today who is suffering? Of course you do. One of the greatest saints I ever knew was blind; another was so poor that we, as children, carried things to him to eat and saved our money to buy clothes for him. We gave material things to him, but he gave spiritual blessings to us.

God allowed Stephen to be stoned (Acts 7:59) and Paul to have a thorn in his flesh to buffet him (2 Corinthians). Even Jesus knew suffering.

Job's friends concluded that Job must have sinned greatly to account for such exceptional suffering. Let us find out what God proved.

What was Job's attitude toward God? He first had access to God through the blood of the sacrifice (Job 1:5). Then he walked with God in integrity of heart and life.

Job had a conscience right toward God. He knew his heart was true and so he could accept the accusations of his friends. He finally could show them that their conclusion was wrong and that the wicked often prosper in this world (Job 24:6).

God trusted Job; therefore He assigned to him this great problem of suffering. Because He loved Job He allowed him to be chastened, for "because the Lord disciplines those he loves" (Hebrews 12:6). When Job was in the midst of his anguish, he realized it is only the gold that is worth putting into the fire. Anything else would be consumed. James said, "Consider it pure joy, my brothers, whenever you face trials of many kinds, because you know that the testing of your faith develops perseverance" (James 1:2-3).

When Job was prosperous and upright and benevolent, he was in danger of becoming self-confident, and could easily forget that he only held his power and place in this world as a steward of God. God does not give us great gifts just to please ourselves. The Westminster Confession tells us that the chief end of man is to glorify God. "For even Christ did not please himself" (Romans 15:3). He came to glorify the Father.

God dealt with Job:

1. He was broken (Job 16:12,14; 17:11).
2. He was melted (Job 23:10).
3. He was softened so he could say, "The hand of God hath touched me" (Job 19:21, *KJV*). "God maketh my heart soft" (Job 23:16, *KJV*).

Do you ever sing, "Spirit of the Living God, fall fresh on me. Melt me, mold me, fill me, use me"? Do you know what it might mean for you? This is what happened to Job.

Job never really saw himself until he saw God. This is true of every life. See how it affected Isaiah when he, as a young man, saw God (Isaiah 6:1-9).

Job was all ready to reason with God, as many do today, about His dealings with him. He could not understand Him. A vision of God Himself completed the work in Job and brought him to the dust.

Listen to God speak of Job, "Will the one who contends with the Almighty correct him?" (Job 40:2). Think of trying to correct the God of this universe! The wisdom of people is only foolishness with God. Hear Job's answer. "I am unworthy—how can I reply to you? I put my hand over my mouth" (Job 40:4).

God kept dealing with Job till he came to the very end of himself! Hear him speak again, "Surely I spoke of things I did not understand, things too wonderful for me to know...My ears had heard of you but now my eyes have seen you. Therefore I despise myself and repent in dust and ashes" (Job 42:3-6).

We find Job a chastened, softened servant. God turned the tide and his prosperity was given back to him doubled—twice as many sheep and oxen, asses and camels! He rejoiced again in his sons and daughters, just the same number as before.

Job no longer asked a question but made a statement. "I know that my Redeemer lives, and that in the end he will stand upon the earth. And after my skin has been destroyed, yet in my flesh I will see God" (Job 19:25-26).

Job's vision of a future life, that had been uncertain before, was clear now. We had heard him asking a question multitudes have asked, "If a man dies, will he live again?" (Job 14:14). Paul answered this question in the great resurrection chapter of the Bible, 1 Corinthians 15. Jesus answered it in His statement, "He who believes in me will live, even though he dies" (John 11:25).

What a wonderful vision of the future life we have in these words! What a prophecy of the coming of the Savior!

Job was "blameless and upright, a man who fears God and shuns evil" (Job 1:8).

1. He was "blameless"—complete, all-round.
2. He was "upright"—Hebrew word means "straight."
3. He "feared God"—this is the beginning of wisdom.
4. He "shunned evil"—this is his moral conduct.

Job was right with man and with God, and remember it was God who said this. God added, "There is no one on earth like him" (Job 1:8). What an honor God gave to Job to use these words to describe him!

As the book opens, we see Job surrounded by wealth, family, position and friends. Let us watch this man whom God said was perfect! We see this man visited by Satan. A swift succession of calamities followed. Remember, these things did not come because of anything wrong in this man Job. All Job's friends thought the reason for his trouble lay in himself. But God made it very plain in the opening of the book that this was not true.

Watch this man stripped of his wealth and reduced to poverty! His children are taken! Health is gone! Then he loses the confidence of his wife! Finally his friends go!

Satan and the Saint (Job 1:6—2:10)

In Job 1:6, the "sons of God" (Hebrew: *bene ha-elohim*) presented themselves before the Lord. These "sons of God" were angelic beings, the messengers of God. The mystery is that Satan was among them. He was angelic, but he had fallen. There was no hint that he was out of place or that he had forced himself into the audience chamber.

In contrast to the Almighty, we have the figure of the adversary, or Satan. Let us stop and study this person for a while. Satan as the adversary is depicted with great clearness, representing a real being, not an imaginary one. We cannot help but contrast the Satan of the book of Job with the grotesque, gigantic, awful figure depicted by the poets. The Bible tells us that Satan comes as "an angel of light" to deceive and to tempt (2 Corinthians 11:14).

Our strange idea of the devil is derived from Dante's (Dante Alighieri, 1265-1321, Italian poet and philosopher) *Divine Comedy*. In part one, *The Inferno*, Dante attempted to paint a picture of this monster of hell. In Dante's depiction, Satan's enormous size is matched by his hideousness. We also find a portrayal of Satan in Milton's (John Milton, 1608-1674, British poet) *Paradise Lost* and *Paradise Regained*. Milton's description of Satan is magnificent, but his regal archfiend has no kinship with the Satan of the book of Job. Neither is Goethe's (Johann Wolfgang von Goethe, 1749-1832,

German poet, dramatist and scientist) Mephistopheles in *Faust* the true picture, although, no doubt, Goethe's picture of a cynical devil, gaily damning a mind, is based on the book of Job.

Satan could bring up the hosts of Sabeans and Chaldeans and have them carry away the oxen and asses and camels of Job (Job 1:13-17). He could slay the sheep by lightning, and cause the wind to kill Job's children, and even smite Job himself with boils. Remember, he is "the prince of the power of the air" (Ephesians 2:2, *KJV*).

Know this besides! Satan has great power, but there are limits to his might. Satan is mighty, but God is Almighty! He can break through only where God allows (Job 1:10). What a comfort it is to know that no calamity can come to us that the Father does not allow. He who has "shut up the sea behind doors" and said, "This far you may come and no farther; here is where your proud waves halt" (Job 38:8,11), will never let us be tempted beyond what [we] can bear (1 Corinthians 10:13).

Remember, Satan is so held by the Almighty that he can only strike where he is given permission (Job 1:12).

1. Job tore his robe (Job 1:20). It is worthwhile for us to learn that we are meant to feel grief. Sorrow has its use in our lives. We are told "do not make light of the Lord's discipline" but be "trained by it" (Hebrews 12:5,11).

    "Jesus wept" (John 11:35)! Christ does not destroy our natural emotions. Jesus told the women of Jerusalem to weep for themselves and for their children (Luke 23:28).

2. Job recognized that loss and sorrow are the laws of life. We have to learn that all possessions are transient. We are losing something every moment. We cannot stop and weep about everything that is taken from us. We have to learn a hard lesson—that we can live on in spite of all our losses. Begin to learn while you are young that nothing is necessary but Christ.

Only pure gold can stand the fire. All dross is burned up. God, the great metallurgist of heaven, puts us in the fire, but He watches and tries us Himself. He trusts no other. When the fire has burned long enough to destroy the impurities, He pulls us out.

God speaks to Satan, "Where have you come from?" What a tragedy in the answer! "From roaming through the earth and going back and forth in it" (Job 1:7). Remember, this reveals the "endless restlessness of evil." "Be self-controlled and alert. Your enemy the devil prowls around like a roaring lion looking for someone to devour" (1 Peter 5:8).

God speaks again, "Have you considered my servant Job?" (Job 1:8).

What do you think God meant by "considering" Job? It is a strong word, as if he had been watching his every act. "Have you been trying to find a flaw?"

Satan says, "Does Job fear God for nothing?" He seems to imply—"I'm trying to find out why this fellow is so perfect. There is a reason." "Have you not put a hedge around him and his household and everything he has?" That was the truth, of course. Then he added, "You have blessed the work of his hands." This was true also. "So that his flocks and herds are spread throughout the land." Yes, all this was correct (Job 1:9-10).

But Satan went on, "But stretch out your hand and strike everything he has, and he will surely curse you to your face" (Job 1:11). Satan's charge against Job was that a man only serves God for what he can get out of it. Really Job is not so much on trial here as God. It is less a question of Job's loyalty than it is one of God's power. Is God able "to guard what I have entrusted to him for that day" (2 Timothy 1:12)?

This same thing is being said today! Some say that ministers are preaching the gospel only for what they can get out of it; that poor non-Christians in other lands are turning to Christ only because it gives them food and shelter.

So God says, "All right, try it out! Take everything away from Job and see what happens!" (Author's paraphrase.)

Do you see that the real conflict here was between God and Satan? God was proving the truth about His statement of Job's integrity in following Him.

When the trials came, Job did not understand the meaning of all his suffering. He knew it was not because he had sinned, as his friends said. He wondered what God was doing. We will not always understand what God is working out on the battleground of our hearts. But know this: there is a reason and value to everything God allows and that "in all things God works for the good of those who love him, who have been called according to his purpose" (Romans 8:28).

Job proved that Satan's statement concerning God's children was a lie, that is, that they only serve Him for what they can get out of it.

Don't always try to find the reason for your trials and experiences. Sometimes we will have to wait for the answer. We wonder why God takes a Borden of Yale (the title of Mrs. Howard Taylor's book about William Whiting Borden [1887-1913]) when he is only a young man at the threshold of a life of service, and allows an old, drunken, apparently good-for-nothing to live.

We will never find the answer to all of God's dealings. We may be honest and sincere as far as it goes, as were Job's friends, but God's ways are past finding out. God never allowed the devil to prove that God blundered when He made humans by suggesting that they only serve God for what they can get out of Him.

Do not be surprised to find hypocrites in every congregation of God's children. Satan comes to do mischief to saints. He distracts our attention. He sets us to criticizing. He sows dissension in the congregation. He excites the pride of preachers and singers, of givers and those who publicly pray. He chills our spirit and freezes our prayers. Yes, when the Word is being sown, the fowls of the air come to pluck it away (see Matthew 13:3-23).

Remember, you can never walk before God and try to lead a godly life without Satan coming in to walk with you—accusing you, finding fault and vexing you.

What Kind of a Man Was Job?

He was a "perfect" (blameless) man (Job 1:1)
He was a prosperous man (Job 1:2-4)
He was a praying man (Job 1:5)
He was a popular man (Job 29:21,25)
He was a proven man (Job 42:10,12).

Job and His Friends (Job 2:11—37:24)

Get acquainted with Job's friends. Let us introduce you to them. First there is courtly Eliphaz, then argumentative Bildad, and blunt Zophar, and the youthful Elihu.

This is a familiar scene. Everyone has a reason to offer as an explanation for his experiences and problems. Job's four friends came. Do you know Job was rich in friends? Generally when a man loses his wealth and position and health, he has no friends left.

There are things we can say in favor of these men, although their words of "comfort" were anything but that. The first is that they came at all. They were friends who stuck through adversity. When all the multitude of acquaintances had forgotten Job, they came.

You notice they kept still for seven days. This is good! They seemed to be trying to find out the reason for all of Job's troubles before they spoke. Someone has said that instead of talking about Job, they came and talked with him.

They all had a reason; they wished to tell Job why they thought he was suffering as he did. They all agreed he must have sinned miserably to have caused this suffering.

Eliphaz backs his argument by a dream (Job 4:1—5:27); Bildad, by some old proverbs (Job 8); Zophar, by experience and reason (Job 11). Elihu came nearest the truth when he argued that suffering was God's discipline to bring the soul back into fellowship with God; but it was not the whole truth.

God called Job "perfect and upright." His friends were wrong in charging him with sin as the only possible cause of his calamities.

Wretched Comforters

The chief question returns: Why does God permit the righteous to suffer? Job cries out from the ashes, "I cannot understand it. It doesn't seem right."

Job's wife, looking on discouraged, says, "Something is wrong. Your religion is a failure. Curse God and die" (author's paraphrase of Job 2:9). This means nothing other than, "say good-bye to God." It is the voice of despair.

Eliphaz adds, shaking his head, "God never makes a mistake.

What have you done to bring this on yourself?"

Bildad says, "God is just. Confess your sin."

Zophar next speaks, "God is all-wise. He knows man."

Elihu, God's man, says the wisest thing, "God is good; look up, and trust Him, for He is God."

The Righteous Comforter

Jehovah now is heard from the whirlwind: "Brace yourself like a man; I will question you, and you shall answer me" (Job 40:7).

Now Job speaks himself: "I know that you can do all things; no plan of yours can be thwarted" (Job 42:2). Then comes the great confession, "My ears had heard of you but now my eyes have seen you. Therefore I despise myself and repent in dust and ashes" (Job 42:5-6).

This is the victory of submissive faith. When we bow to God's will, we find God's way. Stoop to conquer. Bend to obey. This is the lesson of Job.

The philosophy of Job's friends was wrong. Job was glad to see them and he could pour out his troubles to them, but they did not understand him.

Job even lost his friends! He had tried to explain, but he was misunderstood. Only God understands!

Jehovah and Job (Job 38—42)

The scene begins with God gloriously revealing Himself. In a series of approximately sixty questions, God is saying, in effect, "Who can do all these things but Myself?" God is thus revealed to Job, and Job to himself.

As so often is true with us, when Job came into the presence of God, he forgot the speech he thought he would make (Job 40:4-5)! There was no arguing with God. Finally, Job went flat down on his face, repenting in "dust and ashes" (Job 42:6). This is the only place to learn God's lessons—on your face, with your mouth shut!

Jehovah explains to Job (by revealing Himself to him) that when men see God something always happens. The godly are allowed to suffer that they may see themselves. Read Isaiah 6:1-5. When Isaiah saw himself as he really was, he fell on his face undone and cried out, "I am a man of unclean lips."

Did you ever think you looked all right until some friend dropped in to invite you to go some place with him? When you saw how immaculate your friend looked, you immediately realized how you needed a good grooming. So often this is true in the presence of Christ. The very immaculateness of His Person makes us feel sinful. Measure your life by His life and you will feel as Job did.

In Job 42 we find:

1. A Consciousness of God (v. 5)
2. A Collapse of Job (v. 6)
3. A Commission to serve (v. 7).

As you read the chapter, you see that Job enjoyed a double portion of prosperity from the hand of God. God allows His children to suffer in order to reveal character, to set forth an object lesson and to bring to light some hidden sin. In Job's case, that hidden sin was self-righteousness.

This book well illustrates the text of Romans 8:28. How wonderful to hear of the patience of Job and to have seen that the end of the Lord is pity and mercy. A morning of joy always follows the night of sorrow.

Job found God in his trouble. Many know God as a Creator and believe in His greatness, but they do not really know God. The more we understand His ways the more we will love Him and put our trust in Him.

Job is rich:

1. In philosophy: Ancient as the book is, it is filled with a divine record of human philosophy, and blind gropings of human wisdom. Human reason has never been able to go beyond Job's friends in explaining the great mysteries of human experience on natural grounds. (See 1 Corinthians 2:14 and Colossians 2:8.)

2. In gems of spiritual truth: Be sure to read the following references: Job 1:21; 5:17; 13:15; 14:14; 16:21; 19:23-27; 23:10; 26:7-14; 28:12-28; 42:1-6. These are some of the most frequently quoted and best-loved passages in the Bible.

Chapter 16

Understanding Psalms

Psalms Portrays Jesus Christ, Our All in All

Selected Bible Readings

Sunday: Psalms of Law (Psalms 1; 19)
Monday: Psalms of Creation (Psalms 29; 104)
Tuesday: Psalms of Judgment (Psalms 52; 53)
Wednesday: Psalms of Christ (Psalms 22; 40; 41)
Thursday: Psalms of Life (Psalms 3; 31)
Friday: Psalms of the Heart (Psalms 37; 42)
Saturday: Psalms of God (Psalms 90; 139)

"Come, let us sing for joy to the Lord; let us shout aloud to the Rock of our salvation" (Psalm 95:1). Here we take this view of the Psalms in panorama. The sights that catch and hold our attention are so numerous that they defy exhaustive treatment in one short chapter.

"Ascribe to the Lord the glory due to his name; worship the Lord in the splendor of his holiness" (Psalm 29:2). This is the key verse to the book of Psalms. The door into the temple of praise and prayer is open. Go in with the psalmist to rest and pray. It is a real privilege to go apart during the rush of earthly things.

No doubt Psalms is the best-loved book in the Old Testament. Someone has called it the solid gold of Christian experience. Slip in wherever you will and you will find a treasure. Every Psalm is a direct expression of the soul's consciousness of God. With which Psalms are you familiar? Pause a moment to think.

The Hebrew title of this book is "Praise," or the "Book of Praises," which indicates that the main contents of the book are praise, prayer and worship. The name "Psalms" comes from the Greek. We find that the early Christian fathers called it the "Psalter."

The Psalms is the national hymnbook of Israel. It contains 150 poems to be set to music for worship. Worship is the central idea. The Psalms magnify and praise the Lord, exalt His attributes, His names, His Word and His goodness. Every human experience is related to Him.

We see the life of the believer pictured in all its experiences of joy and sorrow, victory and failure.

The Psalms are full of Christ. They describe the whole program of His suffering and death. Let us look and see!

We have Christ's own warrant for looking for Him in the Psalms. He said, "Everything must be fulfilled that is written about me in the Law of Moses, the Prophets and the Psalms" (Luke 24:44).

His prophetic office is found in Psalm 22:22.

His priestly office in Psalms 40:6,8; 22; 49; 110.

His kingly office in Psalms 2; 21; 45; 72.

His sufferings in Psalms 22 and 69.

His resurrection in Psalm 16.

Another extremely useful classification of the Psalms may be made according to the subjects of the individual psalms:

Instruction 1; 19; 39

Praise 8; 29; 93; 100

Thanksgiving 30; 65; 103; 107; 116

Penitence 6; 32; 38; 51; 102; 130; 143

Trust 3; 27; 31; 46; 56; 62; 86

Distress 4; 13; 55; 64; 88

Aspiration 42; 63; 80; 84; 137

History 78; 105; 106

Prophecy (Psalms of the Messiah) 2; 16; 22; 24; 40; 45; 68; 69; 72; 97; 110; 118.

We speak of the Psalms as the Psalms of David. He has been considered the principal writer. He gives the keynote and his voice rises highest in the sacred choir. But there were other authors besides him. Seventy-three of the 150 Psalms are assigned to him; fifty are anonymous. Psalm 90 is written by Moses. Two are written by Solomon—Psalms 72 and 127. Besides these, Asaph, David's choir leader, the sons of Korah, a family of official musicians, and Jeduthun wrote some. But let us not be too engrossed in finding who penned them. Let us rather read and enjoy these grand expressions of praise. They are of God for you. Sing them and make them your own. Catch David's note and spirit. He wrote marching songs, prayer songs, rally songs, hilltop songs, confession songs. Sing as you march. Keep step with David and David's Lord all the way.

Many quotations from this book are found in the New Testament. At least twenty of these directly refer to Christ and His life and death.

Man (Psalms 1—41)

1. Man blessed (Psalm 1)
2. Man fallen from his high position and at enmity with God (Psalms 2; 14)
3. Man restored by his blessed Redeemer, the Man Christ Jesus (Psalms 16—41).

In this section we have a collection by David of the psalms that tell of the state of man—his blessedness, fall and recovery. Psalm 1 tells us of the road to success. Everyone wants to prosper. No one wishes to fail. The psalmist says that everyone may prosper. Think of it! It will be well for every young person to master the rules for success laid down here.

Things Not to Do

1. Refuse to walk in the counsel of the ungodly; do not take their advice or follow the pattern of their lives.
2. Refuse to stand in the way of sinners. Standing is even a lower step. When you stand in sin, it shows that you have been brought under the spell of evil.
3. Refuse to sit—to take the scorner's seat is to take the

most despicable place possible. The scorner sits idly watching the struggles of others and cares not that many are losing the fight. You ask the scorner, "Isn't there great need in this world?" "I suppose," the scorner answers, but just sits and plays the cynic. The scorner is sure "that every minister, missionary or Christian worker is either a fool or a hypocrite."

Things to Do

1. Read the Bible.
2. Delight in it.
3. Meditate upon it.

The more you read the Word, the more you want to. As one great Christian leader has said, "The gospel feeds you, then it makes you hungry." It never grows stale. You cannot read it too often or too much.

Things That Result

When the Christian has followed the don'ts and do's, what is the result? Three things (Psalm 1):

"Planted"—"He is like a tree planted by streams of water"—the settled and steadfast life in a luxuriant soil;

"Purposive"—"which yields its fruit in season"—the productive life;

"Prosperous"—"and whose leaf does not wither"—the abiding, happy life.

Other Psalms in this group that show the final blessings of man because of the glorious work of the Man Christ Jesus are Psalms 22; 23; 24.

Psalm 22 tells of the Good Shepherd giving His life for His sheep. We see the cross and hear the cries of our dying Savior. As you read this Psalm, you will recognize the facts.

Psalm 23 tells of the great Shepherd keeping His sheep. We read, "The Lord is my shepherd, I shall not be in want." He promises to guide and provide and keep me.

Psalm 24 tells of the chief Shepherd in His glory rewarding His sheep. He is my King and He is coming to reign in power and great glory.

Psalm 22 gives a picture of Calvary. We see the crucifixion portrayed here more clearly than in any other part of the Old Testament. The Psalm opens with the cry of our Lord in the darkest hour of His life; "My God, my God, why have you forsaken me?" It closes with, "for he has done it." The original Hebrew means, "It is finished"—the last cry of the Savior (John 19:30).

Psalm 22:6 says, "But I am a worm and not a man, scorned by men and despised by the people." This tells us of the offense of the Cross!

Read and compare these verses:

Psalm 22:1 . . . . .Matthew 27:46
Psalm 22:6-7 . . . . . .Luke 23:35-36
Psalm 22:6-8 . . . . . .Matthew 27:39,41,43
Psalm 22:12-13 . . . . .Matthew 27:36,44
Psalm 22:28 . . . . . . .1 Corinthians 15:23-24

"I am poured out like water, and all my bones are out of joint. My heart has turned to wax; it has melted away within me" (Psalm 22:14). This depicts excessive perspiration because of physical torture. It also means the breaking of Jesus' heart.

He tells us why His heart was broken. "Scorn has broken my heart" (Psalm 69:20). In John 19:34-35, we read that "one of the soldiers pierced Jesus' side with a spear, bringing a sudden flow of blood and water. The man who saw it has given testimony, and his testimony is true. He knows that he tells the truth, and he testifies so that you also may believe."

Jesus died of a broken heart. He bore the reproach and shame for others. Bearing our sins hid Him from His Father's face; this is what broke His heart. Death by a broken heart is very rare. It is caused by intense agony of suffering.

"My tongue sticks to the roof of my mouth" (Psalm 22:15). This verse describes intense thirst. The account in the New Testament said, "Knowing that all was now completed, and so that the Scripture would be fulfilled, Jesus said, 'I am thirsty.'" Yes, Psalm 69:21 says, "They put gall in my food and gave me vinegar for my thirst." Read John 19:28-29.

"They have pierced my hands and my feet" (Psalm 22:16). Crucifixion! The Roman method of death by crucifixion is described here. The Jewish law did not know of this method. These words give the description of death by crucifixion—hands and feet nailed to the cross—bones of hands, arms, shoulders out of joint as a result of hanging from the cross, straining bone and muscle.

"They divide my garments among them and cast lots for my clothing" (Psalm 22:18). Even the act of the soldiers is described here. See Matthew 27:35.

Israel (Psalms 42—72)

1. Her Ruin (Psalms 42—49)
2. Her Redeemer (Psalms 50—60)
3. Her Redemption (Psalms 61—72).

Here in this section we find additional Psalms compiled for use in the Temple. It opens with "a cry" from the depth of oppression—Psalms 42—49. It ends with the King reigning over the redeemed nation. "He will rule from sea to sea and from the River to the ends of the earth" (Psalm 72:8). Read this glorious Psalm.

Several Psalms speak of penitence, but the chief is Psalm 51. It is a psalm of David. If you turn to 2 Samuel 11 and 12, you will find the story of David's sin. When you read this, notice three things David said. When Nathan the prophet was telling David the story of the despicable fellow who took the only lamb belonging to the poor man, we hear him say to David: "You are the man!" David did not try to dodge the issue but said, "I have sinned against the Lord." Then Nathan reassured him, saying, "The Lord has taken away your sin." (2 Samuel 12:7,13).

We think it strange when we read that David was "a man after his [God's] own heart." When we compare what other kings would have done under the same circumstances, we are not so surprised. But David confessed and said, "I have sinned against the Lord" (2 Samuel 12:13). That is what sin is—breaking God's law.

Notice in Psalm 51:4 these words, "Against you, you only, have

I sinned and done what is evil in your sight." This psalm is a prayer of contrition and confession. David cries for mercy from a God whom he knows is merciful and full of loving kindness.

We learn from this psalm that we must confess our sin to God (1 John 1:9) and that God is just to forgive. Whenever we are sincere in our confession to God, He will cleanse our sin.

The Sanctuary (Psalms 73—89)

In the psalms of this third section we see the sanctuary mentioned or referred to in almost every one.

We see God's counsels in relation to the sanctuary. The sanctuary is seen from its ruin to its restoration in the fullness of blessing.

The Earth (Psalms 90—106)

Blessing needed (Psalms 90—94)
Blessing anticipated (Psalms 95—100)
Blessing enjoyed (Psalms 101—106).

The first of this group of psalms was written during the wanderings in the wilderness. The psalms are not arranged in chronological order.

Read the opening verses of Psalms 90 and 91 together. "Lord, you have been our dwelling place throughout all generations...He who dwells in the shelter of the Most High will rest in the shadow of the Almighty." If God is our dwelling place on this earth, we shall live in confidence, sheltered by the Almighty. Christ says, "If you remain in me and my words remain in you, ask whatever you wish, and it will be given you" (John 15:7). The secret of a godly life is remaining or "abiding" *(KJV)* in the Almighty. When the devil tempted Him (using Psalm 91:12), the Lord answered by quoting from Deuteronomy 6:16 (see Matthew 4:7). Christ was victorious because He lived in the "dwelling place" described by these two psalms. We are told that there is a point of perfect calm at the center of a cyclone. There may be raging storms, snares, pestilences, terror by night, darkness and destruction, but when the soul is abiding under the shadow of the Almighty, it is safe.

If you wish to praise the Lord for His goodness, read Psalm 103. It is full of worship, adoration, praise and thanksgiving. This is great exercise for the soul.

The Word of God (Psalms 107—150)

All the teaching in the psalms is grouped around the Word of God. This section opens with Psalm 107, which gives the key: "He sent forth his word and healed them" (v. 20).

Psalm 119 is the great psalm of the whole book. It extols the Word of God, which is the great revelation of the heart and mind of the Lord. This book is "more desirable than gold, yes, than much fine gold; sweeter also than honey and the drippings of the honeycomb" (Psalm 19:10, *NASB*). Almost every verse speaks of God's Word or law or precepts or statutes.

Value God's Word:

1. It blesses little children—Matthew 19:14.
2. It strengthens young men—1 John 2:14.
3. It sanctifies and cleanses all who read it—Ephesians 5:26.
4. It protects the widows—Exodus 22:22-23.
5. It honors the aged—Leviticus 19:32.
6. It offers eternal life to everyone—John 3:36.

Praise is the highest duty that any creature can discharge. Man's chief end is to glorify God. There is no heaven either here or in the world to come for people who do not praise God. If you do not enter into the spirit and worship of heaven, the spirit and joy of heaven cannot enter you!

The Psalms begin with the word "blessed." This word is multiplied in this book. The book seems to be built around this first word. There is not one "woe" in the entire book of Psalms.

How can we make the Psalms our own in experience?

Why do you like the Psalms?

What Psalms can you quote?

Probably no other book has so largely influenced the turning points in people's lives, given expression to their deepest experiences and woven itself into every fiber of their character as the book of Psalms.

The Position of the Book

Hold your Bible in your hand and turn to the middle of the book. Most often you will open to the Psalms. Not merely is this true physically. There is a deeper truth. The Psalms are central also in human experience.

This book is used by Hebrew and Christian alike even in our day. The Psalms were for use in the Temple, for which many were prepared. They were written for the heart to worship God out under the open heavens or in the pit of despair or in a cave of hiding. When you find yourself in deep need, you can always find a psalm that expresses your inmost feeling. Or, if you have an abounding joy, the words are there for you, too.

It is the book for all who are in need, the sick and suffering, the poor and needy, the prisoner and exile, the person in danger, the persecuted. It is a book for the sinner, telling him or her of God's great mercy and forgiveness. It is a book for the child of God, leading him or her into new experiences with the Lord. It tells of God's law in its perfection and pronounces blessings upon the one who will keep it.

Chapter 17

Understanding Proverbs, Ecclesiastes, Song of Songs

*Jesus Christ, Our Wisdom; the End of All Living;
the Lover of Our Souls*

Selected Bible Readings

Sunday: Get Wisdom (Proverbs 1—4)
Monday: To Sons (Proverbs 5—7)
Tuesday: Good and Bad (Proverbs 15—17)
Wednesday: Wise Words (Proverbs 20; 22; 31)
Thursday: All Is Vanity (Ecclesiastes 1—3)
Friday: Only God Satisfies (Ecclesiastes 11—12)
Saturday: Joyful Communion
(Song of Songs 1:1-7; 2:1-7)

Understanding Proverbs

"Blessed is the man who finds wisdom, the man who gains understanding" (Proverbs 3:13).

The books classed as poetical are Job, Psalms, Proverbs, Ecclesiastes and Song of Songs. These are not "poetical" in the sense that they are fanciful or unreal, but in form only. There is no meter or rhyme, but rather a thought rhyme expressed in parallelism—repeating the same thought in different words.

In Psalms we find Christians on their knees.

In Proverbs we find Christians on their feet.
The Psalms are for the Christian's devotions.
The Proverbs are for the Christian's walk.
The Psalms are for the closet of prayer.
The Proverbs are for the business place, home and playground.
We find in Proverbs that godliness is practical. Every relationship in life is mentioned. We find our duty to God, to our neighbors, the duty of parents and children, our obligations as citizens.

The Jewish people likened Proverbs to the outer court of the Temple; Ecclesiastes to the holy place; the Song of Songs to the holy of holies. Remember that the altar of burnt offering and the laver of cleansing were in the outer court. If we come to the book of Proverbs with a cleansed and surrendered heart and mind, we will get most out of the book.

The book of Proverbs takes us out in the court of the congregation where the people are. Here they live their daily lives, and jostle each other in the highways of life. This is a book for everyday instruction. It deals with the practical affairs of life. The author, Solomon, wrote more wisely than he lived. Solomon wrote 400 years before the seven wise men of Greece (Bias of Priene, Chilon of Sparta, Cleobulus of Lindus, Periander of Corinth, Pittacus of Mitylene, Solon of Athens and Thales of Miletus). The wise give heed to the commands of God and obey them. The foolish ignore God's will. This book divides people into two classes—wise and foolish.

Notice how the book opens—"The proverbs of Solomon." Solomon was a great king, famous for his wisdom and riches. He wrote 3,000 proverbs, 1,005 songs (1 Kings 4:31-32). Solomon was peculiarly qualified to write this book. God had given Solomon "wisdom and very great insight, and a breadth of understanding as measureless as the sand on the seashore" (1 Kings 4:29). Solomon was a philosopher; he was a scientist of no mean ability. He was an architect of a Temple that was one of the wonders of the world, and then, too, he was a king.

That Solomon was the author of this book implies no more than that he took the lead in gathering these sayings already current among the people, given by the Holy Spirit through the centuries, and put them into the orderly arrangement we have today. See what

Solomon said about this in Ecclesiastes 12:9, where it is recorded—"He pondered and searched out and set in order many proverbs."

Someone has said that they were a collection of maxims, woven into a didactic poem around a general topic, wisdom.

Several names are given in the book regarding authorship:

Solomon—Proverbs 1:1; 25:1

The wise—Proverbs 22:17

Men of Hezekiah—Proverbs 25:1

Agur—Proverbs 30:1

King Lemuel and his mother—Proverbs 31:1.

This book is filled with words of wisdom. There is one terse saying after another. People have tried to add to them and failed. A brilliant lawyer tried it once. He thought he could write a few before breakfast. He came away from his task humbled and baffled and glorying in the marvelous wisdom of God.

Proverbs is divided into three sections:

1. Counsel for young men—Proverbs 1—10
2. Counsel for all men—Proverbs 11—20
3. Counsel for kings and rulers—Proverbs 21—31.

The book closes with one of the most beautiful chapters in the Word (Proverbs 31). This is a chapter about women's rights. "Give her the reward she has earned, and let her works bring her praise at the city gate" (v. 31). Wherever Christ goes, womanhood is lifted up. In non-Christian countries, where Christ is not known, woman is rarely more than a chattel or slave. In Christian lands, woman is equal to man.

This book presents a system of conduct and life. You cannot find any agnosticism here. The existence of God is assumed. Be wise and find God's way for your life! This book is to provide rules for the righteous life.

The real power and beauty in this book lie hidden in the true meaning of the word "wisdom." It is evident that this word means more than an excellent attribute. It is found that the wisdom of Proverbs is embodied in the Incarnate Word of the New Testament. Christ found Himself in this book (Luke 24:27).

Wisdom is represented as dwelling with God from all eternity. "I was appointed from eternity, from the beginning, before the world began....I was there when he set the heavens in place, when he marked out the horizon on the face of the deep...when he marked out the foundations of the earth. Then I was the craftsman at his side" (Proverbs 8:23-30). Jesus was the Designer of the universe. Compare these with John 1:1-2; Hebrews 1:2; Colossians 1:15-16; 2:3.

When you read the book of Proverbs, put "Christ" in place of "wisdom" in the verse. (See 1 Corinthians 1:30.) You will see a wonderful power in this book. "We know also that the Son of God has come and has given us understanding, so that we may know him who is true" (1 John 5:20).

The purpose of the book of Proverbs is stated clearly at the beginning. See Proverbs 1:2-4. We find that the first of all duties is the fear of God (Proverbs 1:7). "Receive the instruction of wisdom, justice, and judgment, and equity" (Proverbs 1:3, *KJV*). This is the true college of spirit education of the self, "for giving prudence to the simple, knowledge and discretion to the young" (Proverbs 1:4). Plain common sense is needed in life. Don't be a fool!

God wants to give us of His wisdom—the wisdom that created heavens and earth, that we might use it in all of life (James 1:5). This would put an end to all the confusion and evil in this world, wouldn't it? Human wisdom can never solve life's problems. Only God knows the ways of people. "The fear of the Lord is the beginning of wisdom" (Proverbs 9:10; Psalm 111:10).

Counsel for Young Men (Proverbs 1—10)
"Wise Up!"—worship is the first step to wisdom (1:7).

"Walk Straight!"—the straight and narrow has the lowest accident rate (2:20).

"Directions"—ask God about everything: He knows every road (3:6).

"Watch Your Step!"—every step helps mold character; step well (4:26).

"God's Black List"—pride, lies, murder, deceit, mischief, betrayal, discord (6:17-19).

"A Bad Woman"—read carefully Proverbs 7:15-27.

"Riches"—rubies of wisdom command highest prices on the market of character values (8:11).

"More Fun"—nothing you ought not to do is ever more fun. Wait till you see what results (9:17-18).

"Wanted! Silence"—wordy men seldom are wise men (10:19).

This whole book is extremely practical. It would be well for us all to give it closer study for our guidance in daily life. "In all your ways acknowledge him, and he will make your paths straight" (Proverbs 3:6). This is the Lord's rule for our feet. The way of evil—"Avoid it, do not travel on it; turn from it and go on your way" (Proverbs 4:15). This is God's "Stop! Look! Listen!"

The fear of the Lord spoken of here is not a fear of fright, but a fear of a son who is afraid he might grieve his father's love. It is the fear coming from love, the fear of displeasing the Lord, that leads to godliness. We shall not begin to be wise until our lives are in right relation with Christ, the fount of all wisdom. "Wisdom is supreme; therefore get wisdom. Though it cost all you have, get understanding" (Proverbs 4:7).

God wants to give us instruction "for giving prudence to the simple, knowledge and discretion to the young" (Proverbs 1:4). Don't be a fool. God wants you to have plain common sense. The most uncommon thing in the world today is common sense.

In Proverbs 4:23-26, we find that the whole body is included:

"Guard your heart."—verse 23.

"Put away perversity from your mouth"—verse 24.

"Let your eyes look straight ahead"—verse 25.

"Make level paths for your feet"—verse 26.

The duty of parents to chastise their children is enforced and is based upon God's chastening of His children (Proverbs 3:11,12). One of the signs of the last wicked days upon the earth is given by Paul as "disobedient to their parents" (2 Timothy 3:2). What happened to Eli and his boys because he allowed his sons to sin?

The young are warned against the influence of bad companions, against impurity and intemperance, against anger, strifes and quarrels. (See Proverbs 1:10-19; 4:14-19; 19; also chapters 3; 10; 13; 15; 16; 18.)

There are many sins of the tongue. We use it too freely. We lie and are deceitful in dealings with others. Much is said about guarding the tongue, for in the tongue is the power of life and death. (See Proverbs 12:22; 18:21.)

As we read this book, we find the author pleading with us to shun evil companions, pride, envy, intemperance, sins of the tongue and idleness. This would be impossible to do unless we had Christ, the Wisdom of God, within us.

Read about pride and its consequences in Proverbs 8; 11; 16; 19. See Proverbs 16:18. The Lord wants us always to be humble before Him and not to esteem ourselves better than others. Every truly great person is humble.

Counsel for All Men (Proverbs 11—20)

"False Economy"—a gift is never lost; only what is selfishly kept impoverishes (11:24).

"Fools"—you cannot convince a fool of his folly; only a wise man will accept a rebuke for foolhardiness (12:15).

"Lying"—righteousness and lying are enemies; to a wicked man they are synonymous (13:5).

"A gentle answer turns away wrath"—two people ought not to get angry at the same time (15:1).

"Clean Sin"—a man deep in wickedness will invent "pretty names for sin" (Charles Haddon Spurgeon, 1834-92, British, Baptist preacher) (16:2).

"To Win Friends"—a friendly man will have friends; being a relative does not ensure being a friend (18:24).

"Drink Up!"—When you decide for strong drink, don't be surprised when it decides against you (20:1).

"People curse the man who hoards grain" (Proverbs 11:26). This reveals the sin of the grain speculator. It is a warning to the speculators of our day.

"The righteous man leads a blameless life; blessed are his children after him" (Proverbs 20:7). The Douai (Catholic) version of the Bible says: "He leaves behind him blessed children." This is a good man's legacy to the world. Godly parents are a blessing to children (Proverbs 20:7) and should instruct them in the right way (Proverbs 22:6).

There has never been a time when men did as well as they knew how. However imperfect their instructions, they have never lived up to them. The last thing a man could complain of is a lack of good advice.

Who has heart trouble? Who has woe? Sorrow? Contentions? (Read Proverbs 20; 23; 31.) In Scripture drunkenness is roundly condemned with other severe sins: "Do you not know that the wicked will not inherit the kingdom of God? Do not be deceived: Neither the sexually immoral nor idolaters nor adulterers nor male prostitutes nor homosexual offenders nor thieves nor the greedy nor drunkards nor slanderers nor swindlers will inherit the kingdom of God" (1 Corinthians 6:9-10). The words in Proverbs are "like apples of gold in settings of silver" (Proverbs 25:11). Study the picture, but do not miss the apples of gold depicted here.

Proverbs is an intensely practical book, exposing a series of traps that would ensnare us. "There is no wisdom, no insight, no plan that can succeed against the Lord" (Proverbs 21:30). At last we see God's will and God's way! Hasten it, O Lord!

Counsel for Kings and Rulers (Proverbs 21—31)

"Self-Control"—a guarded mouth makes for a serene soul (21:23).

"Reputation"—choose a good name rather than great riches. Your name goes on; your wealth stops at death (22:1).

"Soberness"—red wine is colorful but calamitous (23:31).

"Counsel"—the sober judgment of a sane thinking group is more reliable than your own opinion (24:6).

"Women"—better solitude on top of the house than sojourning in the house with a nagging woman (25:24).

"Gossip"—fire goes out when fuel gives out; scandal stops when mouths are stopped (26:20).

"Tomorrow"—there is never a tomorrow, only today. Get it done now, for now soon becomes then (27:1).

"Understanding"—rank does not guarantee an understanding heart (28:16).

"Bribes"—seek justice and our land shall stand; accept bribes and it will fall (29:4).

"Security"—a trust in God is the only safe soul armor (30:5).

Understanding Ecclesiastes

Jesus is the beginning of all in Proverbs.

He is the end of all in Ecclesiastes, the *summum bonum* of life.

Wisdom in Proverbs is piety.

Wisdom in Ecclesiastes is prudence and sagacity.

Ecclesiastes is the soul's autobiography or the book of experience.

"Vanity" *(KJV)* or "meaningless" *(NIV)* is the key word. See Ecclesiastes 2:11.

You do not have to go outside the Bible to find the merely human philosophy of life. God has given us in the book of Ecclesiastes the record of all that human thinking and natural religion has ever been able to discover concerning the meaning and goal of life. The arguments in the book, therefore, are not God's arguments, but God's record of people's arguments. This explains why such passages as 1:15; 2:24; 3:3-4,8,11,19-20; 8:15 are at positive variance with the rest of the Bible.

The writer is Solomon, and the book is a dramatic autobiography of his experience and reflections while he was out of fellowship with God. Solomon may have been wise, but he did not follow his own wisdom. Ecclesiastes has its origin in his tragic sin of forsaking God and seeking satisfaction in philosophy and science "under the sun," that is, based only upon speculation and thought. The inference of the book that "all was vanity and vexation of spirit" *(KJV)*, or "meaningless, a chasing after the wind" *(NIV)* is inevitable. The message of Ecclesiastes is that, apart from God, life is full of weariness and disappointment.

The problem that faced Solomon was how he could find happiness and satisfaction apart from God (Ecclesiastes 1:1-3). He sought satisfaction in science (1:4-11), but could get no answer. He sought it in philosophy (1:12-18), but in vain; he found pleasure (2:1-11), mirth (v. 1), drinking (v. 3), building (v. 4), possession (vv. 5-7), wealth and music (v. 8); but they were all empty.

He tried materialism (2:12-26), fatalism (3:1-15) and deism (3:1—4:16), but these likewise were vain. Natural religion (5:1-8), wealth (5:9—6:12) and even morality (7:1—12:12) proved equally fruitless.

The conclusion is found in Ecclesiastes 12:13 and is the best thing possible to people under the law. It is interesting to notice the place of youth in the argument (11:9—12:1). We must begin young to know God if we are to find life worth living.

Remember, Ecclesiastes only shows us the best that people can do apart from God's gospel of grace.

The name "Ecclesiastes" means "preacher." This is so named because it contains the meditations and sermons of the wise man, Solomon.

Confession (Ecclesiastes 1—7)

The great question, "Is life worth living?" is presented. Solomon has tested it to the full. No man could better do it or better tell it— and the answer he gives is not reassuring for the life that now is.

Try wisdom (Ecclesiastes 1)! What better thing is there in all the world? Solomon declared, "I applied myself to the understanding of wisdom." Yet even here he was forced to cry out, "Chasing after the wind. For with much wisdom comes much sorrow; the more knowledge, the more grief" (vv. 17-18). This is always true of mere earthly wisdom. But "The fear of the Lord is the beginning of wisdom" (Psalm 111:10).

Try pleasure (Ecclesiastes 2)! "I thought in my heart, 'Come now, I will test you with pleasure to find out what is good.' But that also proved to be meaningless" (v. 1). This is his deliberate conclusion. God made us all to be joyful. He has given us a thousand avenues of enjoyment. Let us not sacrifice true happiness for questionable pleasure. Always make your recreation a re-creation.

Philosophy has failed, says the preacher, so let merriment be tried. Music, dance, wine (not to excess), the funny story, the clever repartee: these are now cultivated. On television, *Monday Night Football* will outdraw *Masterpiece Theatre* every time. Clowns are now welcomed to the court, where only grave philosophy had been. The halls of the palace resounded with laughter and gaiety. Yet after a while all this palled on the king's taste. He even goes so far as to say that laughter is foolish (vv. 1-2). Cheerfulness is admirable. A hearty laugh in its place is delightful, but the person who is always giggling is a bore.

Try architecture (2:4)! Now he becomes practical. He attends to great works of state. Aqueducts, pools, palaces and other public buildings occupy his thoughts. Now the court fools are frowned upon and great architects are welcomed to the palace. But the excitement incident to building soon fades away.

Try gardening (2:5-6)! Vineyards, gardens, orchards, rare flowers, tropical plants are all the rage. Jerusalem and the vicinity bloom like the Garden of Eden. Soon it is like a new toy for a child that pleases for a while but is soon tossed away.

Try cattle breeding and art collecting (2:7 and 8)! Then the king tries cattle breeding, art collecting and even becomes an amateur musician (v. 8, *KJV*; *NIV* says the king acquired a harem). Choruses and orchestras gather in the royal palace. But even though "music hath charms," it is powerless to charm with permanent happiness.

Try just living the weary round of life—with discretion (Ecclesiastes 3)! But again, "What benefit or gain is there?" (See verse 9; compare with 1:3; 2:11; 5:11,16; 6:11.) Vanity of vanities!

Try the stoic's philosophy (Ecclesiastes 4)! Surely this also is meaningless. He wails, "vanity and vexation of spirit" (v. 16, *KJV*)!

Try ritualism—formal religion (chap. 5)! Be sure that "when you make a vow to God, do not delay in fulfilling it" (v. 4). This, too, is meaningless.

Try wealth (chap. 6)! Solomon had it. He was a man to whom God had given "wealth, possessions and honor...But God does not enable him to enjoy them, and a stranger enjoys them instead. This is meaningless, a grievous evil" (v. 2). Many agree with Solomon in the emptiness of pleasures, but they think money is the supreme goal in life. Jesus told us to seek first the kingdom of God and His righteousness and all these things would be added (Matthew 6:33).

Try reputation (chap. 7)! "A good name is better than fine perfume, and the day of death better than the day of birth" (v. 1). It doesn't last long in this world. People are soon forgotten when they die. Vanity still!

Admonition (Ecclesiastes 8—12)

Now comes a turning point. Ecclesiastes 8:12 says, "I know that it will go better with God-fearing men, who are reverent before

God." The full meaning of this is found in the last chapter—"Fear God and keep his commandments, for this is the whole duty of man" (Ecclesiastes 12:13).

The "Preacher," as he is called, has been looking out and back and around. Now he looks up and he sees God and is satisfied.

The phrase "under the sun" (1:3) is found twenty-eight times in this little book. The "under-the-sun-life" is hardly worth living; but above the sun, and in the heavenlies that Paul describes, it is glorious (Ephesians 1).

Dr. Pierson (Arthur Tappan Pierson, 1837-1911, American editor, lecturer, biographer, missionary statesman and pastor) well said, "The key to Ecclesiastes is that a man is too big for this world." We find in this book that we can never find satisfaction and happiness in this world. True happiness apart from Christ is impossible. We find dissatisfaction among the poor and rich alike, among the ignorant and learned, among people and kings.

Ecclesiastes closes with a call to the young! Lay the foundations early. "Remember your Creator in the days of your youth" (Ecclesiastes 12:1). This book is given as a danger sign so that we may be spared having to learn the bitterness of life by finding the cisterns we have sought to be empty. The greatest proportion of men and women who are living to serve God have chosen Him in childhood.

Understanding Song of Songs

The Song of Songs has been called the Christian's love song. Key text is Song of Songs 6:3.

This is a song of love in marriage in Middle Eastern language and imagery. The characters in the song are Solomon, the Shulamite maid and the daughters of Jerusalem. The love of Solomon and the maid illustrates the love between Jehovah and His people. This is seen in many passages in the Bible. Moreover, Solomon as a lover was a type of Christ (see Ephesians 5). Personal love to Christ is the greatest need of the Church today. The knowledge of sin forgiven and of Christ's redeeming work has drawn us to Him.

Books of the Major Prophets

of The Old Testament

**Isaiah • Jeremiah • Lamentations
Ezekiel • Daniel**

Key Events of the Books of the Major Prophets

Books of the Major Prophets: God Is the Sovereign of History

The major prophets wrote from the eighth to the sixth centuries before Christ, as nations were rising and falling ① around Israel, and idolatry ② and injustice were endemic in Israel. The major prophets teach us that God has a plan for history and that through the coming Messiah He will eventually subdue all His enemies under His feet and bring peace ③ to the Earth. The major prophets also vividly teach us that God is deeply concerned with moral integrity and justice in our daily lives.

Chapter 18

Understanding Isaiah

Isaiah Portrays Jesus Christ, the Messiah

Selected Bible Readings

Sunday:	God's Case Against Judah (Isaiah 1:1-18)
Monday:	Isaiah's Commission (Isaiah 6:1-13)
Tuesday:	Christ—Israel's Hope (Isaiah 7:10-16; 9:1-21)
Wednesday:	The Coming Kingdom (Isaiah 11:1-16)
Thursday:	A Great God (Isaiah 40:1-31)
Friday:	Christ Our Substitute (Isaiah 53:1-12)
Saturday:	A Glorious Salvation (Isaiah 55:1-13)

The keynote of Isaiah is "salvation." Isaiah's name means "Jehovah saves."

Introduction to the Prophetical Books

The poetical books belong to the golden age of the nation.

The prophetical books belong to the dark ages of God's chosen people.

The prophets were men whom God raised up during the dark days of Israel's history. They were the evangelists of the day, the religious patriots of the hour. Read what God says about them in 2 Kings 17:13: "The Lord warned Israel and Judah through all his prophets and seers: 'Turn from your evil ways. Observe my commands and decrees, in accordance with the entire Law that I commanded your fathers to obey and that I delivered to you through my servants the prophets.'" We read everywhere in the New Testament that God spoke through the prophets. The period of the prophets in Israel covered 500 years from the tenth to the fifth century B.C. Then the voices of the prophets were silenced until John the Baptist. These prophets spoke fearlessly to kings and people alike of their sins and failures.

The office of prophet was instituted in Samuel's time. When the kingdom was divided and Judah and Israel were established as separate monarchies, the great prophets appeared. There were four major and twelve minor prophets.

There are seventeen prophetical books in the Old Testament (including Lamentations). They are subdivided into major and minor prophets. This classification is made not because of their importance, but because of their length.

The captivities of Israel (the Northern Kingdom) and of Judah (the Southern Kingdom) are largely the theme of the Old Testament prophets. The record of these is found in 2 Kings 17:1-23; 24:11—25:21. These are called the Assyrian and Babylonian captivities. Some of the prophets served before the exile, some during and some afterwards. These are called pre-exilic, exilic, and post-exilic prophets.

The prophets before the exile (or pre-exilic prophets) in chronological order of their writings were: Obadiah, Joel, Jonah, Amos, Hosea, Isaiah, Micah, Nahum, Habakkuk, Zephaniah and Jeremiah.

The pre-exilic prophets to Israel were Jonah, Amos and Hosea. The pre-exilic prophets to Judah were Obadiah, Joel, Isaiah, Micah, Nahum, Habakkuk, Zephaniah and Jeremiah.

The prophets during the exile (or captivity in Babylon) were Ezekiel and Daniel. They prophesied to all the Israelites. Jeremiah's lifetime also extended into this period. Those who prophesied after the exile were Haggai, Zechariah and Malachi.

Prophets according to intended hearers:

Three to Israel—Amos, Hosea, Ezekiel

Two to Nineveh—Jonah, Nahum

One to Babylon—Daniel

One to Edom—Obadiah

Nine to Judah—Joel, Isaiah, Micah, Jeremiah, Habakkuk, Zephaniah, Haggai, Zechariah, Malachi.

The Prophets—Their Message

The prophet's chief duty was to deal with the moral and religious life of his own people during his day. The prophet was never sent while the nation was walking in obedience to God. All the writings are rebukes because of the bad condition that existed at that very time. Nothing was general about the prophet's denunciations.

The prophet was always an Israelite. He not only spoke of judgment that would come to pass to the people because of their sin, but he was also a foreteller of future events. The events of which he spoke mainly concerned the nation of Israel. Other peoples were mentioned only as they came in contact with Israel.

Let us note some of the prophecies of the future that are recounted. Keep these in mind as you study their writings.

1. The dispersion and captivity of God's chosen people: Everywhere the prophet tells that the Jews are to be scattered among the nations of the world.
2. The coming of the Messiah: Religious Jews were and are still looking for their Messiah.
3. The restoration of the chosen people to their own land under the coming Messiah, David's greater Son: Jewish people are returning from the four corners of the earth to dwell in their own Promised Land. Almost all Jewish people have a longing in their hearts to be a part of Israel as a nation. Now this is possible!
4. The reign of the Messiah over the whole earth: Even though we see the collapse of God's people in the Old Testament—first Israel, then Judah being led into captivity—nevertheless, God revealed that the ending of His nation did not end His plans for His people. There is yet to be a glorious future when the Prince of Peace shall reign over His people and sway His scepter "from sea to sea and from the River to the ends of the earth" (Psalm 72:8).

When you read the Gospels, you constantly find phrases such as, "so was fulfilled what the Lord had said" and "to fulfill what was spoken through the prophet." We find in examining these passages that God fulfills prophecy literally. Learn to interpret the meaning of the words of the prophets in a literal, natural way. Do not force a spiritual interpretation and read out all the real meaning. There are figurative passages, of course. But you will find that as soon as you determine the meaning of the figure that that, too, will have its literal fulfillment. This method makes the study of the prophets a simple one.

The Prophets—Their Character

The prophets were fearless men. They denounced the sins of their day. They called people away from idols back to God. It is true that the prophets were concerned about the moral and political corruption of the nation, but the fact that the people were worshiping idols was their greatest concern. The nation had a wrong attitude toward God. Christ gave us a succinct statement of what our attitude should be: "Love the Lord your God with all your heart and with all your soul and with all your strength and with all your mind" (Luke 10:27). God knows that what someone's attitude is toward God will affect that person's whole moral life. Creed always determines conduct. This is true not only of individuals, but also of nations. The adage "it makes no difference what a man believes" is completely refuted in the prophets.

The prophets exposed the cold formalism of their religion. They constantly reminded the people that Jehovah was the only true God. They pointed men to the law. They were statesmen of the highest order. They were prophets in that they came to tell forth what God said. They were not only forth-tellers but also fore-tellers.

So important is prophecy in God's Word that it occupies about one third of the whole Bible. Prophecy is God's revelation of His plans to His children.

G. Campbell Morgan says that there were three elements in the message of the prophets:

1. A message to their own age—directly from God
2. A message of predicted future events

(a) The failure of God's chosen people and God's judgment upon them and the nations around them

(b) The coming of the Messiah and His rejection and final glory

(c) The Messianic Kingdom ultimately to be established on the earth

3. A living message to our own age—eternal principles of right and wrong.

The Spirit of God spoke by the prophets: "as he said through his holy prophets of long ago" (Luke 1:70). Read 2 Peter 1:21; Jeremiah 1:9; Ezekiel 2:7 to find how the message was given.

Read what Christ said of the prophets (Luke 24:25-27).

The prophecies concerning Christ Himself are so definite that it gives great assurance to us that the Bible is the Word of God.

Understanding Isaiah

God puts a telescope before the eyes of the prophets and lets them look far into the future. Especially do we find this spirit of expectation in Isaiah. We hear the prophet cry, "He is coming!" Isaiah was a man of vision. Read the opening words: "The vision concerning Judah and Jerusalem that Isaiah son of Amoz saw" (Isaiah 1:1).

Isaiah was a man who certainly spoke boldly to his own time, but as a prophet he spoke of the future as well; hence he is the prophet for all times. We sit at his feet today, and following his index finger as it points into the future, we hear him say, "Lo, your King!"

This great statesman was the prophet of the Southern Kingdom of Judah. He lived at the time that the Northern Kingdom of Israel was destroyed by Assyria. Isaiah was the one whose voice saved the kingdom of Judah during these trying hours.

It is interesting to note that this is also the time of Romulus and Remus and the founding of Rome. The traditional date of the building of Rome is 753 B.C., just a few years after the birth of the prophet Isaiah. About this time Sparta and Athens in Greece were founded.

The prophets were the most unpopular men in their day, for they dealt with the moral and religious conditions of the hour! Generally conditions were bad. Prophets were sent when the nation was out of step with God—when they were walking in disobedience. The words the prophets used to rebuke or exhort the people were very pointed. They were for the very people to whom they addressed themselves. Truth is seldom popular with the sinner.

Let us find the scriptural definition of a prophet. Look in Deuteronomy 18:18: "I will raise up for them a prophet like you [Moses] from among their brothers; I will put my words in his mouth, and he will tell them everything I command him." Also verse 19: "If anyone does not listen to my words that the prophet speaks in my name, I myself will call him to account."

Although the prophets spoke to their own age, as we have already noted, they were ever looking forward to future events. Besides this, we find abiding principles stated for all times. They foretold the failure of the chosen people and the coming of the Messiah. Each showed how God was to bring to pass His purposes through the Messiah. We see today how most religious leaders have failed to recognize Jesus as the promised Messiah. "He came to that which was his own, but his own did not receive him" (John 1:11). The Messiah came to establish His kingdom, but the religious leaders rejected Him. However, His kingdom will yet be established over the whole earth (John 19:15).

Isaiah told of the judgment that must fall on Judah because she would not fulfill her mission in the world. But through the whole book we find the ultimate triumph of God's plan through His appointed Servant, the Lord Jesus Christ, who would bring in final victory through suffering and death (Isaiah 53).

Two Emphases

This book of Isaiah is written with two distinct emphases. Because of this, some Bible scholars believe that there was more than one author. This need not be the case. It is the work of one man with two messages. In the first of the book Isaiah pictured

Israel. In the last of the book, the prophet beheld Jesus bearing our load of sin, and he told the story; then he beheld Christ exalted and glorified and shouted of his vision from the housetop. It is the same prophet all the time but suiting his language to the theme at hand.

The only way to understand Isaiah is to understand the prophet's Christ. It is far more important that we be familiar with the truths of the book than the theories of its authorship. Don't let anyone interpret the book for you who does not know its author.

The divisions of Isaiah are an interesting coincidence. Isaiah is a miniature Bible in structure. This book has sixty-six chapters, just as the Bible has sixty-six books. There are two great divisions, just as there are in the Bible, with thirty-nine chapters in the first (like the Old Testament) and twenty-seven chapters in the second (like the New Testament).

The Old Testament opens with God's case against humans because of their sin. Isaiah opens the same way (Isaiah 1:18). The first section closes with the prophecy of the coming King of Righteousness and the redemption of Israel (chaps. 34—35), just as the prophets close the Old Testament with the prediction of His coming kingdom. The second part of Isaiah (beginning with chapter 40) opens with the "voice of him that crieth in the wilderness" (Isaiah 40:3, *KJV*), and is concerned with the person and work of Jesus Christ. The New Testament opens in exact accord with this. John the Baptist, the forerunner of Jesus, is announced as "the voice of one crying in the wilderness" (John 1:6,23, *KJV*). The book of Isaiah ends with the vision of new heavens and a new earth in which righteousness perfectly dwells (Isaiah 62:1-2; 65:17; 66:22). The New Testament closes with this same view in Revelation 21. This striking similarity between Isaiah and Revelation is unforgettable when once mastered.

Isaiah is like a jewel case; and the fifty-third chapter is the jewel. This has a central position in the group of the chapters to which it belongs. As you see, it is located in the second division of the book or the last twenty-seven chapters. In the very middle of this precious group of twenty-seven chapters lies chapter

53. This is the chapter that tells of the Savior who "took up our infirmities and carried our sorrows." Chapter 53 is a wonderful one to store in your memory. Each verse is a nugget of golden truth. This is the chapter that pictures Christ, our suffering Redeemer.

Two Comings of Christ

We see Christ in this book and hear the prophet crying, "He is coming!" and "He is coming again!" He is coming as Savior, pictured in chapter 53, in humiliation as our sin-bearer. He is coming again in power and great glory, pictured in chapter 34.

As we look through the telescope, we see two mountain peaks with a valley between. One is called Calvary; on its hilltop is a cross. But as we look farther we see another peak. It is radiant with the light of a crown! This hill is Olivet, where Christ will return. The eye of the ancient seer went farther than the sufferings of Calvary; his eye caught the kingdom and the glory that should follow!

Isaiah speaks of Christ's death when he says, "Though your sins are like scarlet, they shall be as white as snow; though they are red as crimson, they shall be like wool" (1:18). Again, "He was despised and rejected by men" (53:3). This speaks of the first time when He came unto His own, and His own received Him not. When He will come again we shall hear, "Arise, shine, for your light has come, and the glory of the Lord rises upon you" (60:1). Then he tells us of His coming kingdom. "In the last days..." (2:2-5).

The life of Christ is portrayed in Isaiah:

Birth—7:14; 9:6
Family—11:1
Anointing—11:2
Character—11:3-4
Simplicity of life—7:15
Gentleness—42:1-4
Death—Chap. 53
Resurrection—25:8
Glorious reign—11:3-16; 32.

Isaiah the Prophet

Isaiah was a man of royal blood. He was a young aristocrat from a princely line. He was brought up in the court and had high standing with the people of Jerusalem. He not only was a prophet, but he also married a prophetess (8:3,18). His training was of the best. After his labor of sixty years, tradition tells us that he died a martyr in the reign of Manasseh at the age of 120.

Isaiah was a special messenger to Judah. Look over 2 Kings 15-20 and note the moral and political rottenness of Judah and Israel, and the danger from the surrounding Gentile nations. Assyria was strong and aggressive, striving for world power. Egypt was on the south, and Judah and Israel lay on the road between these two enemies. Both Assyria and Egypt aimed at a world empire. Therefore the Holy Land became the battleground of the ages.

Isaiah did not fail in his ministry. He laid bare the sins of his people and called them to repent and turn to God. "Come back to God," he cried. But his chief theme was the coming One. It was Jesus. He saw Christ's near first coming and His faraway second coming, but in all he saw Christ.

Johannes Kepler (1571-1630, German astronomer, discovered the three laws of planetary motion), in failing to bring the heavenly bodies into satisfactory adjustment with one center, at last conceived of the ellipse with two foci and everything fell into harmony. So when in our reverent study of God's Word we catch the dual center of Christ on the cross and Christ on the throne, then the Word shines clear and we begin to see what the prophet saw, the world's Redeemer, coming first in humiliation, then again in power and great glory.

Four words to Judah:

Rebellion—"Ah, sinful nation" (1:2-4,10-15,21-23)

Retribution—"You will be devoured" (1:5-8,15,20,28)

Repentance—"If you are willing and obedient" (1:16-19,27)

Restoration—"Zion will be redeemed" (1:9,18,24-31).

Judah thought that in keeping up all outward observances in their religious service all would be well. Isaiah denounced their hypocrisy (1:15). He told them of forgiveness if they would repent, but promised them a sword if they continued in their rebellion against God.

Because of their sin and their forsaking God, Judah was facing judgment (1:1-31; 2:6—3:26). Yet there is a glorious future for Judah when Christ comes again. Jerusalem is to be the capital of the coming Kingdom (2:1-5; 4).

God's truths of redemption go beyond our reason, but they do not insult our reason; they rather appeal to it. To worship aright in the presence of God we must be right in the presence of people.

Under Uzziah and Jotham (Isaiah 1—6)

Read Isaiah 1:1 and you will discover that Isaiah was prophet during the reigns of Uzziah, Jotham, Ahaz and Hezekiah. During this time, the statesman prophet preached in Jerusalem.

Now turn to Isaiah 6:1-13 and you see that Isaiah received his real commission in the year King Uzziah died. No doubt he had written chapters 1-5 before this time. Uzziah's long reign of fifty-two years was so glorious during the greater part; however, it ended in gloom. For the last four years of his life Uzziah was a leper. He was shut off from all the business of state, and the kingdom was under the regency of his son Jotham. The early chapters of Isaiah fit the situation perfectly.

When Isaiah preached that God was about to abandon Judah, it may have seemed too cruel, but the Lord is infinitely more concerned with the purity of His people than with their prosperity.

Uzziah was a leper and Jotham was regent (2 Kings 15:5). "Azariah" is another name for "Uzziah." Uzziah's reign did not directly affect Isaiah's prophecy.

Jotham, Uzziah's successor, is only mentioned twice in the book (Isaiah 1:1; 7:1). It does not seem that Isaiah was active during his reign. It is with the reign of the next two kings, Ahaz and Hezekiah, that Isaiah's prophecy deals.

Ahaz reigned sixteen years and Hezekiah reigned twenty-nine years. Ahaz was a wicked king, and more, he was an idolater. Hezekiah was for the most part a good king and he did much to remove idolatry from the people.

Isaiah's Message

Isaiah warned Judah of her folly and rebellion (1:2-9). They separated themselves from God by the sins of greed, foreign alliances and idolatry (2:6-9). God called them a fruitless vine. God had tried patience, then punishment; now they must be destroyed by foreign kings.

God called Isaiah just as He called Moses, Joshua, Gideon or Paul. Isaiah's commission came at the tragic death of the grand old King Uzziah (6:1). His call was a never-to-be-forgotten experience. It taught him his own unworthiness and gave him his real commission to a sinning, needy world calling out for help. It came to him in the form of a "vision." For years Isaiah preached and told of doom and deliverance. Hardship and peril awaited him, but God gave him a victorious strength. He was the man of the hour. Let us look at the steps leading from the opening of the vision to his final commission.

Secret of Isaiah's Life

This experience of Isaiah's should be every disciple's experience. The secret of all Isaiah's power lay in this vision in the Temple, "I saw the Lord!"

Conviction—"Woe to me!...I am ruined!" was the cry brought on by the sense of sinfulness before God's holiness (6:5).

Confession—"A man of unclean lips." A broken heart and a contrite heart is precious to the Lord (6:5).

Cleansing—"Your guilt is taken away and your sin atoned for." After confession, a flying seraph (an angel) cleansed his lips with a hot coal from off the altar (6:7).

Consecration—"Here am I. Send me!" (6:8).

Commission—Go, God's command (see 6:9).

Under Ahaz (Isaiah 7—14)

"And it came to pass in the days of Ahaz" (Isaiah 7:1). Ahaz was utterly bad. He was an open idolater. For this sin God allowed Rezin, king of Syria, and Pekah, king of Israel, to invade his kingdom. Isaiah had been silent under Jotham but this invasion brings him to the front in his ministry. "Then the Lord said to Isaiah,

'Go out...to meet Ahaz'" (7:3). He appealed to him to put his trust in God for help rather than call in Tiglath-Pileser from Nineveh.

God sent the prophet to encourage Ahaz. Besides predicting the Assyrian invasion in Isaiah 8, the prophet saw an end to all of Israel's troubles through the birth of the Christ child who shall rule over the kingdom of David in righteousness forever and forever. He gave Ahaz a "sign" that Judah was not to perish—the prophecy of Immanuel, the virgin's Son, Jesus Christ. "Therefore the Lord himself will give you a sign: The virgin will be with child and will give birth to a son, and will call him Immanuel" (7:14). Read these important words in Isaiah 7:10-16. Ahaz refused the evidence upon which his faith might have been established. He pursued his own plans with Assyria, and that nation on which they now leaned was to become the means of their punishment (7:17-20).

Then followed the sentence of doom upon king and land (8:6-22). With nations, this is God's policy: doom for idolatry.

In Isaiah 9:6-7 we find another great prophecy concerning Christ. "For to us a child is born, to us a son is given, and the government will be on his shoulders. And he will be called Wonderful Counselor, Mighty God, Everlasting Father, Prince of Peace. Of the increase of his government and peace there will be no end. He will reign on David's throne and over his kingdom, establishing and upholding it with justice and righteousness from that time on and forever. The zeal of the Lord Almighty will accomplish this." The Son to be given, the child to be born, was to sit on David's throne. Remember the "throne of David" is as real as the "throne of the Caesars." Yes, Christ will sit on the throne of David. Hear the angel's words to Mary: "He will be great and will be called the Son of the Most High. The Lord God will give him the throne of his father David, and he will reign over the house of Jacob forever; his kingdom will never end" (Luke 1:32-33).

We find present woe and future glory strangely mixed in Isaiah 10. But in Isaiah 11 we see the picture of the glory of the future kingdom Christ is coming to establish on this earth. Some day He is coming to Jerusalem to sit upon the throne of David and peace shall cover the earth "as the waters cover the sea" (11:9).

In this kingdom, the people will worship the Lord Jehovah.

The prophet says, "Sing to the Lord, for he has done glorious things" (Isaiah 12:5).

In Isaiah 13 we see great Babylon's doom. She was to carry Judah away captive, but the prophet sees her destruction. God is keeping His promise to Abraham. "I will bless those who bless you, and whoever curses you I will curse; and all peoples on earth will be blessed through you" (Genesis 12:3). God always brings a curse on any nation that afflicts Israel. You can follow this truth through history. God often allows nations to punish Israel for her national sins, but retribution is inevitable (Deuteronomy 30:5-7; Isaiah 14:1-2; Joel 3:1-8).

Read every word of Isaiah 11 and 12, which gives a picture of this coming King and kingdom.

1. The King Himself—11:1
2. His anointing—11:2
3. His righteous reign—11:3-5
4. His glorious Kingdom—11:6-9
5. His gathering together of His people from the four corners of the earth—11:10-16
6. His kingdom worship—12:1-6.

When it was my privilege to drive out to old Babylon and look over the ruins of that once magnificent city and see the absolute devastation, I thought of Isaiah's prophecy concerning this city found in Isaiah 13:19-22. God said, "Babylon, the jewel of kingdoms, the glory of the Babylonians' pride, will be overthrown by God like Sodom and Gomorrah. She will never be inhabited or lived in through all generations; no Arab will pitch his tent there, no shepherd will rest his flocks there. But desert creatures will lie there, jackals will fill her houses; there the owls will dwell, and there the wild goats will leap about. Hyenas will howl in her strongholds, jackals in her luxurious palaces. Her time is at hand, and her days will not be prolonged."

This is true today. Not even the tent of an Arab is pitched there. Only bats and owls make their home in its ruins. Not a shepherd is seen on the plains. There is only desolation. Yes, God's Word is true!

In Isaiah 14:28 we read that King Ahaz died. But Isaiah warns the people that his death must not be hailed as the end of their burdens. Even worse oppressors than Ahaz were yet to come (14:28-32).

Under Hezekiah (Isaiah 15—39)

The reign of Hezekiah occupied one of the most important periods in all of Israel's history. Hezekiah was a godly king. The Assyrian armies, like a dark storm cloud, were threatening the northern frontiers. Before Hezekiah had completed his sixth year, Samaria had fallen beneath this invader. This success only whetted the Assyrian appetite for further conquest. Eight years later Judah was invaded. The first invasion was by Sargon and the second by his son, Sennacherib. Assyrian history tells us this. The critical year in Hezekiah's reign was the fourteenth (Isaiah 36:1). It was then we have the Assyrian invasion, the king's mortal sickness and his recovery, and the final withdrawal of Assyrians from the land. (This covered a period of about four years).

These stony-hearted Assyrian warriors came year after year, blazing with steel and banners. The watchmen on the walls of Jerusalem could see them advance by the smoke of the burning towns and cities.

King Hezekiah stripped the Temple of its treasures and took the gold from its doors and pillars in order that he might send them 300 talents of silver and 30 talents of gold to buy them off (2 Kings 18:13-16). In desperation, help from Egypt was sought. But nothing availed in face of the fury of these Assyrians.

Finally the Assyrians built their campfires around the city of Jerusalem and demanded its surrender. Read the intensely dramatic account of the parleyings between the Assyrian general and the chiefs of Jerusalem.

See the account of the swift and terrible disaster that fell upon the Assyrians as they were slain by a mysterious visitation in their camp (Isaiah 37:36-38).

Isaiah denounced the alliance with Egypt and said it was relying "on horses" and trusting "in the multitude of their chariots and in the great strength of their horsemen, but do not look to the Holy One of Israel" (31:1).

Is it not true that we today have put our trust in the "horses and chariots" of war's machinery? Have we not multiplied our horses and chariots beyond the wildest dreams of Egypt and Babylon? We have hitched all the forces of nature to our chariots. We have armored tanks, jet airplanes, battleships, aircraft carriers and nuclear submarines. We have added nuclear missiles and ICBMs. War has been turned into a hideous prospect of devastation and death.

We need to hear the prophet say today, "Woe to those who go down to Egypt for help, who rely on horses, who trust in the multitude of their chariots" (31:1). How great need there is today for those who will "trust in the name of the Lord our God" (Psalm 20:7), who know the "saving power of his right hand" (Psalm 20:6)!

History reveals a graveyard of the nations that have gone down to death through their own moral rottenness. Egypt, Babylon and Rome are memorable examples of this.

God wants us to recognize Him in national affairs. He calls His people to "Return to him you have so greatly revolted against" (Isaiah 31:6). As a people, we must get right with God before we can get right with other nations.

The kingdoms of Judah and Israel had become so weakened by idolatry and corruption that the enemies swept down upon them from the north like a wolf on the fold. First, Israel rolled in the dust under the tramp of the terrible Assyrian hosts (722 B.C.), and then Judah fell with the Babylonians thundering at her gate and breaking down her walls (586 B.C.). Both kingdoms ended and her people were carried into captivity. Isaiah lived and prophesied in Jerusalem during the Assyrian invasion of the north.

Isaiah spent his life trying to get Judah to become acquainted with God and His Word. He wanted them to trust wholly in God's guidance. Isn't this a worthy aim for any minister today?

Glorious Future—Restoration! (Isaiah 40—66)

This part of the book, chapters 40—66, is called the "Book of Consolation" because Isaiah tells in glowing terms not only of the restoration of Judah, but also of the coming of Jehovah's "Servant" to be the Messiah King.

The restoration is assured, for they must return to their own land to prepare the way for the coming Messiah, the Servant of Jehovah, who is to redeem His people.

Isaiah 53 gives us a perfect picture of our suffering Redeemer. "Surely he took up our infirmities and carried our sorrows" (v. 4). "We all, like sheep, have gone astray...and the Lord has laid on him the iniquity of us all" (v. 6). He was the substitute for the sinner.

Can you repeat verse 5 and say, "But he was pierced for [my] transgressions, he was crushed for [my] iniquities; the punishment that brought [my] peace was upon him, and by his wounds [I am] healed"? Accepting this great fact makes you a child of God. He was wounded, bruised, pierced—not for His own sins, but for ours. He bore on His own body the sins of the world.

Isaiah 60—66 tells of the coming Kingdom—the future glory of Israel. God's goodness to redeemed Israel is seen in chapters 61 and 62. He promises an era of prosperity in chapters 63—65.

Chapter 19

Understanding Jeremiah and Lamentations

Jeremiah and Lamentations Portray Jesus Christ,
the Righteous Branch

Selected Bible Readings

Sunday: Jeremiah Warns Judah (Jeremiah 1:1-10; 2:1-13; 3:12,22-23; 4:14-19; 6:1-30)

Monday: A Rebuke (Jeremiah 7:1-15; 9:1-16; 17:5-18)

Tuesday: The Potter (Jeremiah 18:1-17)

Wednesday: The Faithless Shepherds (Jeremiah 23:1-40)

Thursday: Repentance and Restoration (Jeremiah 24-25)

Friday: Israel's Last Days (Jeremiah 30:18—31:40)

Saturday: The Overthrow of Judah (Jeremiah 52:1-34)
Comfort to the Sorrowing (Lamentations 1—5)

Understanding Jeremiah

Here is the story of a diffident, sensitive lad who was called from the obscurity of his native town to assume, at a critical hour in the nation's life, the overwhelming responsibilities of a prophet. Jeremiah came from the village of Anathoth some three miles from Jerusalem. This gave him the advantages of the Holy City. His father, Hilkiah, was a priest. (Some think that this was "Hilkiah the priest" in 2 Kings 22, who brought the book of the Law to the notice of king Josiah, which started the great revival in the kingdom.) He inherited the traditions of an illustrious ancestry. His early life was, no doubt, molded by strong religious influences. God had something better for Jeremiah than to spend his life as a priest serving at the altars. God appointed this young man to be a prophet of the Lord in this most trying hour in the history of the chosen people.

God often chooses unlikely instruments to do His work. He chose the sensitive, shrinking Jeremiah for what seemed a hopeless mission, with the words: "'Do not say, "I am only a child." You must go to everyone I send you to and say whatever I command you. Do not be afraid of them, for I am with you and will rescue you,' declares the Lord" (Jeremiah 1:7-8). This is what a prophet is—one that "tells forth" what God says. Although many prophets told of future events, it is not necessary that they do so to be a prophet.

Jeremiah, unlike many of the prophets, has much to say concerning himself. He tells us that he was a priest by birth (1:1). He was called by the Lord to be a prophet at an early age (1:6). He pleaded, first, his youth (only twenty-one), second, inexperience, and third, his lack of eloquence (1:6) as reasons for not accepting the call. Are these not just the excuses that youth make today for not obeying Christ?

Jeremiah was assured that Jehovah ordained him to this work before his birth (1:5). God tells us in Ephesians 2:10 that we were created unto good works before God even laid the foundation of the world. God has a plan for each one of our lives. (Read Jeremiah 1:1-8.) He was not allowed to marry, for God had a special mission for him in life (16:1-2). Jeremiah prophesied during the time when Israel had been taken into captivity and Judah was in her declining days.

Soon after Josiah's death, the kingdom of Judah hastened to its end. Judah was reduced to practical vassalage to Egypt at the battle of Carchemish. About twelve years later Nebuchadnezzar, king of Babylon, took Jerusalem and began deporting all the princes and men of station, which ended in the complete captivity of Judah eleven years after. A few of the poorest were left in the land. Jeremiah kept on with his ministry among them until they went into Egypt. He followed them into Egypt and the last we hear of him he was still rebuking his people. There are conflicting traditions concerning his death.

Tertullian says that the Jews in Egypt stoned him to death. According to the rabbis, he escaped to Babylon and died there.

He was called to be a prophet in the thirteenth year of the reign of King Josiah (1:2). No doubt his early ministry, and that of the prophet Zephaniah, were among the influences that led to the reforms under the young King Josiah. Jeremiah prophesied for more than forty years. He began his ministry sixty years after the death of Isaiah, the great evangelical prophet.

Jeremiah was contemporary with the prophetess Huldah, and with Habakkuk, Zephaniah, Ezekiel and Daniel, and perhaps even Nahum.

Jeremiah's message was never a popular one. At one time he barely escaped with his life (26:7-16). At another time his enemies beat him and put him in prison. Men have always treated God's witnesses thus.

It is almost impossible to outline this book chronologically. Some of the first messages are found later in the book and some of the last messages are first. He wrote on a great roll. No doubt he had given his messages many times to the people and had repeated them often before he began to write. His faithful scribe, Baruch, wrote them down. After he had written one of his discourses, some other message given years before might come to his mind and he would record it, possibly without dating it. He would fill up his parchment as he unrolled it. Later on, when he wished to write down another incident, or record another message, he would have to begin on the roll where he left off, whether it fitted in chronologically or not. This is important to remember.

Analysis of Jeremiah

Because the book of Jeremiah is not arranged chronologically, a division of the book is difficult. The analysis is more moral than structural.

Jeremiah prophesies concerning:

1. Judah—captivity; restoration
2. Cities—Jerusalem; Babylon; Damascus

3. Gentile nations—Egypt; Philistia; Moab; Ammon; Edom; Elam; Babylon
4. Messiah.

Jeremiah uses many symbols given him by Jehovah in teaching the people. On one occasion he wore a rotted girdle; another time he put a yoke on his neck, like an ox; again, he broke a bottle in the presence of the ruler; he bought a field and buried the deed. The interpretation is given in the text.

Here is a list of object lessons found in the book:

The almond rod—1:11-12
The boiling caldron—1:13-14
The marred girdle—13:1-11
The full bottle—13:12-14
The drought—14:1-12
The potter's vessel—18:1-6
The broken bottle—19:1-2
Two baskets of figs—24:1-10
Bonds and bars—27:1-12
Buying a field—32:6-15
The hidden stones—43:9-13
Book sunk in the Euphrates—51:59-64.

Christ is pictured in Jeremiah as:

Fountain of Living Waters—2:13
Great Physician—8:22
Good Shepherd—31:10; 23:4
The Righteous Branch—23:5
David the King—30:9
The Redeemer—50:34
Lord our Righteousness—23:6.

Jeremiah was the ninth of the prophets. He prophesied to the Southern Kingdom of Judah, before the exile and during the trying days of the captivity. He saw five kings upon the throne of Judah: Josiah, Jehoahaz, Jehoiakim, Jehoiachin and Zedekiah. He was to Josiah what Isaiah had been to Hezekiah. (Read 2 Kings 21:1-25 to find the history of Jeremiah's time.)

There were three great events in Jeremiah's life:

1. Battle of Megiddo (609 B.C.), between Judah and Pharaoh-Necho of Egypt in which good King Josiah was killed.

2. Battle of Carchemish (605 B.C.) about four years later, during Jehoiakim's reign. He had become a vassal of Egypt. In this battle, the Egyptians were defeated by Babylon under Nebuchadnezzar. The first deportation of Jews followed.

3. Capture of Jerusalem by Nebuchadnezzar (587-6 B.C.), destruction of city and temple, and exile of greater part of those who were left to Babylon.

There was a great contest for world supremacy in the day of Jeremiah. Assyria had been in the place of leadership for 300 years. Now she was growing weak; Babylon was ascending in power. Egypt, too, was striving for supremacy. In 607 B.C. Assyria was defeated by Babylon. In 605 B.C. Egypt was crushed in the battle of Carchemish, and Babylon became the world's master. In the few years that followed, she invaded Jerusalem and took the Jews captive. False prophets swarmed the city of Jerusalem in these days. They flattered the king and prophesied to him whatever they thought he wanted to hear.

Call and Commission of Jeremiah (Jeremiah 1)

This unique tragedy opens in the little village of Anathoth. At twenty-one, Jeremiah was becoming aware that God had ordained him before his birth to be a prophet (Jeremiah 1:5). God has a plan for the life of every person. Some see clearly how their lives are to be used. Many learn to wait upon God and trust Him for the outcome. These latter cannot understand the ways of the Lord, but they believe His promises. Jeremiah must have been one of these. He must have wondered what God had planned for him. But because he let the Lord have His way, his life affected all of Israel.

We hear Jeremiah speak, "'Ah, Sovereign Lord,' I said, 'I do not know how to speak; I am only a child'" [like a young man] (1:6). He protests and shrinks from the task God gave him and begs to be excused. Notice Jeremiah's reluctance to undertake the task.

A prophet is simply God's messenger boy delivering not his own ideas, but conveying to the last detail God's thoughts. (Compare Jeremiah's call with Moses' call, Exodus 4:10-12.) God had called Jeremiah to be a prophet and he entered bravely upon the task, but now he is overwhelmed at the thought of hurting anyone. He would rather live at peace with them.

Jeremiah is saying, in effect, "I have not yet reached the years of maturity," for in Middle Eastern society a young man has no role to play until he is of age. (Read Matthew 11:25.) His prophetic message would not be received. Would not his career be cut short by those he provoked? Would they not try to kill him?

The young man is only too conscious of his inexperience and he almost makes the great refusal. But God knows how to overcome his hesitancy. He made the young Jeremiah conscious of a divine call. He made him see that the work to which he was commissioned was not his own.

The path of duty is the path of safety! While Jeremiah is pondering, a hand touches his mouth and we hear a voice saying, "Now, I have put my words in your mouth" (Jeremiah 1:9). No longer could he complain of inability to speak. God promises to put the message into the mouth of His prophets. (See what Christ said to His disciples in Matthew 10:20.) Then Jeremiah heard the voice add, "See, today I appoint you over nations and kingdoms to uproot and tear down, to destroy and overthrow, to build and to plant" (Jeremiah 1:10).

Secret of National Power
What God asks us to do He fits us for, and what He fits us for He asks us to do. That was quite a position for just a poor country preacher.

The church and the minister who have answered God's call today are still in a place of power. They need no other weapons than the promise of God, and they really control the building and the breaking, the planting and the plucking of the community.

Jeremiah's commission was worldwide, including not only his own country, but also all nations and kingdoms of Egypt, Ammon, Moab, Tyre and Sidon. His commission was to root out and to pull down, to destroy and to throw down. He must root out the idolatry and pride, but he must finally "build and plant." Jeremiah was to go only to those persons or peoples to whom the Lord sent him. And he was to say only what the Lord commanded him to say. This must be true of us also if we are to be true workers together with God.

Jeremiah's Reluctance

Jeremiah, like men today, was engaged in the Lord's work because God said he must. He had heard the "Thou shalt" of heaven. Although at first the cost may be great, the gain in after years cannot be estimated. Jeremiah was shrinking and offered every excuse for his unfitness, but the task was forced upon him. "You must go" (Jeremiah 1:7). He hated the limelight. He loved the simple life. He wanted to live in the country, but the Lord had work for him in the cities. Jeremiah had to choose between his desires and God's will.

Because he was forced into the task that was so distasteful to him, in later years he cried, "Alas, my mother, that you gave me birth, a man with whom the whole land strives and contends!" (Jeremiah 15:10). God told Jeremiah, "Do not be afraid of them, for I am with you and will rescue you" (1:8). He was not a public speaker, and he shrank from bearing such an unwelcome message to so undisciplined a people. How often he must have thought of that promise of God when he was haled before princes and rulers. We like to carry good news, but to bear bad is always hard. We are afraid of the faces of people. When they register pleasure, we feel safe. When they show disgust, we melt before them.

The Touch of God's Hand

"Then the Lord reached out his hand" (Jeremiah 1:9). Compare this story of Jeremiah's call with that of Isaiah's (Isaiah 6:7). Paul says that prophecy is a spiritual gift (1 Corinthians 14:1). The touch of God's hand was a tangible pledge for Jeremiah that God was with him. He could not get away from it.

The Word of the Lord is a power that carries out His will and accomplishes what He wishes (Isaiah 55:11; Hebrews 4:12). Against this power nothing can stand. It is a hammer that breaks rocks into pieces (Jeremiah 23:29). God's Word shows its power in two ways—in destruction and in construction. We see this in God's words to Jeremiah. If people accept God's Word it will give life; if they reject it, it will bring condemnation (John 3:36).

Before the Fall of Jerusalem (Jeremiah 2—38)

The prophecies of Jeremiah before the fall of Jerusalem were made in this order (long silences divide these):
Prophecies in the reign of Josiah—2:1—12:17
Prophecies in the reign of Jehoiakim—13:1—20:18; 25:1—27:11
Prophecies in the reign of Zedekiah—21:1—24:10; 27:12—39:18.

Reign of Josiah

"During the reign of King Josiah, the Lord said to me" (Jeremiah 3:6). The first twelve chapters cover the prophecy of this period.

Jeremiah 2—6: These chapters tell of Judah's sin and give God's call to repentance. Judgments are predicted.

Jeremiah 7—9: Again we read of threatenings. We see the prophet's grief.

Jeremiah 10—12: Here we see idolatry and disobedience continued. The Lord's disappointment in His people is shown.

In the early years of his ministry, during the reign of Josiah, Jeremiah's message for the most part was a warning to Judah and a call to her to repent (Jeremiah 3:6,12-13,22-23). He spared nothing in exposing the moral rottenness of the people (7:1-26). He warned them of coming judgments if they would not return to God. He especially told them of the danger from the north (4:6). He said that the avengers would come like a raging lion from the thicket (4:7). They would sweep over the land with chariots like the whirlwind and with horses swifter than eagles, spread terror before them and leave ruin in their train (4:13).

In chapter 26, we see Jeremiah taking a stand on the same spot as in Jeremiah 7. On this occasion he nearly lost his life. The address in chapter 7 was probably given during the reign of Josiah himself.

It is probable that for some time after his call Jeremiah continued to reside in Anathoth, but before long he was compelled to leave the home of his birth and take up his residence in Jerusalem. The men of his hometown had made a conspiracy to put him to death (11:18-23). The disloyalty of his neighbors, and especially his own relatives, came as a painful shock to the unsuspecting prophet. But Jehovah told him that this was only the beginning of his troubles and it was a time of preparation for still greater trials in the days to come (12:5-6). Jeremiah's chief enemies were the priests and the prophets (26:7-8). They had a large following among the people. It is sad to notice that the principal opposition to the message of God came from the professedly religious people. It was the same in our Lord's case, and it is often the same today. Remember that the Pharisees and Sadducees always were taking counsel how they might kill Jesus. Jesus tells us that today if we live godly lives we will suffer persecution. Many people hate God and they will hate His children.

We do not know much of Jeremiah's work during the later years of Josiah's reign. No doubt he was in great sympathy with this young reformer, but he realized that his work did not go deep enough. In the death of the good King Josiah, at the battle of Megiddo, Judah suffered a calamity from which she never recovered. In this battle Judah made a noble attempt to withstand the Egyptian army advancing against Assyria under Pharaoh-Necho.

King Josiah was succeeded by his younger brother Jehoahaz whom "the people of the land" placed on the throne instead of the older brother Eliakim. But Jehoahaz was allowed to reign for only three months. He was deposed by Necho and carried off in chains to Egypt, where he died. Necho now virtually was overlord of Judah. He appointed Jehoiakim to be ruler.

Reign of Jehoiakim

Dr. Graham Scroggie (William Graham Scroggie, 1877-1958, American theologian and author) says that prophecies in Jehoiakim's reign recount the events in this order:

Jeremiah chapters 26; 46—49; 25; 36:1-8; 45; 36:9-32; 14; 15; 16; 17; 18:1—19:13; 19:14—20:1; 35; 22:1—23:8; 23:9-40; 13.

In substance, Jeremiah predicted the judgment of the nations and Judah. He reproved the false prophets. He foretold the Babylonian captivity. He suffered for his message.

It was a sad day for Judah when Jehoiakim ascended to power. It was a bad day for Jeremiah, too. Read what God said to Jeremiah at the beginning of Jehoiakim's reign (Jeremiah 26:1-7). Jehoiakim was a bad ruler. He was proud, selfish, covetous and vindictive. He weighed the land down with taxes to meet the demands of his Egyptian conqueror (2 Kings 23:35). He was indifferent to the suffering of his people. He devoted most of his time to enlarging and adorning his palace and carried out his costly schemes with incredible meanness.

Jehoiakim reigned eleven years, and after his death his son, a youth of eighteen, came to the throne. But Jehoiachin's reign was short (about three months and ten days) because Nebuchadnezzar's army soon appeared at the gates of Jerusalem; and after a three-month siege the city was captured. He took with him many of the princes and the flower of the people to Babylon. Among them was Jehoiachin and the queen-mother. None were left, "only the poorest people of the land" (2 Kings 24:14).

It was then that Jeremiah first mentioned the seventy years' captivity (Jeremiah 25:1-14). God told them just how long they must remain in exile (Daniel 9:2).

Jeremiah did not hesitate to denounce even the king in his shameless wrongdoing. In Jeremiah 22:13-19, we see him verbally putting Jehoiakim in stocks and then releasing the lash of a righteous scorn, predicting that he would die without being mourned and would be buried with the burial of an ass.

The reformation under Josiah only touched the surface. The work was abandoned after his death and the nation, in Jehoiakim's reign, fell back into the worst form of idolatry.

Jeremiah's mission was to endeavor to turn his people back to God. During the reign of Josiah, he began to prophesy the dreadful calamity threatening them from the north (4:6) if they would not return to God. Jeremiah told Judah that her salvation was still possible, but each year her sin grew worse and her doom more certain.

Standing in the Temple, Jeremiah told the people that the Temple would be destroyed and Jerusalem itself would become a desolation. Jeremiah's hearers were shocked (26:7-9). They called his words blasphemy.

They said, "This man should be sentenced to death because he has prophesied against this city" (26:11). The Jewish people always remembered that they were the chosen people of God. God had given them privileges, hence they concluded that God would not proceed to do such things as Jeremiah had said He would do against the people whom He had chosen (Amos 3:2). God had consecrated the Temple as an abode for His name, therefore the people thought He would not let it be destroyed by enemies. This is quite false. Let us not entertain this spirit ourselves. We think we are God's children, therefore He must forgive us, He must make us win in battle and put our enemies to rout.

Jeremiah was charged with being unpatriotic. The cry then would have been "Un-Judaistic!" as today it is "Un-American!" For his opponents it was, "My country, right or wrong." For Jeremiah it was, "God's will in my country" (Jeremiah 26:12-15). It is not so much a question of what we think is right as it is that we learn what God considers to be the best for us and our country. God said to Jeremiah, "Do not be afraid of them, for I am with you" (1:8). We may have to endure ostracism and ridicule for Christ's sake, but His promise is sufficient.

The priests and prophets, aided by the people, laid hold on Jeremiah and threatened him with death. But Jeremiah was delivered from the hand of his enemies (26:15-24).

The fourth year of Jehoiakim was one to be remembered because in this year Jeremiah first put his prophecies in writing on a roll (36:1-2). Baruch, his intimate friend who was such a comfort to him through his trials, took down the prophet's words.

We next see the prophet in a dimly lighted dungeon. What happened? The rulers had bound him so they would no longer be troubled by the word of the Lord. But the Lord told Jeremiah to write the words down. There he was, with his loyal friend Baruch at his side busily writing the words on the roll as the prophet spoke them. "So Jeremiah called Baruch son of Neriah, and while

Jeremiah dictated all the words the Lord had spoken to him, Baruch wrote them on the scroll. Then Jeremiah told Baruch, 'I am restricted; I cannot go to the Lord's temple. So you go to the house of the Lord on a day of fasting and read to the people from the scroll the words of the Lord that you wrote as I dictated'" (36:4-6).

What Baruch was to read were the words of the Lord. He read them in the Temple (36:6,8).

Investigating Committee

The Royal Investigating Committee immediately sent for Baruch and commanded him to read the roll again (36:14-15). They decided the roll must be brought to the king. "We must report all these words to the king" (36:16). Knowing full well the character of this ruler, they advised Jeremiah and Baruch to go into hiding before the roll was read in the royal presence (36:19).

They asked Baruch, "'Tell us, how did you come to write all this? Did Jeremiah dictate it?' 'Yes,' Baruch replied, 'he dictated all these words to me, and I wrote them in ink on the scroll'" (36:17-18). Then the princes wanted the king to see it.

The scene changes. We are no longer in the dark dungeon but in the winter palace of Jehoiakim, surrounded by all the luxury of an Eastern court. The king is sitting before his hearth. A fire is burning. Jehudi is reading the roll of Jeremiah. All are listening intently. When three or four columns had been read, Jehoiakim could stand no more. With penknife and angry hands he cut the roll to pieces and threw it into the fire. The very act of Jehoiakim seemed to symbolize the doom of the city, the Temple and all the people of Judah. They had heard God's Word and rejected it (36:20-26).

Of course, Jehoiakim gave the order to seize Jeremiah and Baruch but God "had hidden them" (36:26). How often God does this for His children. He hides us under His wings and in the hollow of His hand far from harm.

Now the Lord commanded Jeremiah to take another roll, and to write "So Jeremiah took another scroll and gave it to the scribe Baruch son of Neriah, and as Jeremiah dictated, Baruch wrote....And many similar words were added to them" (36:32).

Jeremiah stood in the Temple gate and spoke boldly for righteousness and God. He uttered a series of accusations against Judah and warnings of God's inevitable judgment of sin. But he always made an appeal to turn back to God and receive forgiveness. We see him standing in the gate, hurling thunderbolts into the faces of the false worshipers, but always holding up the pardon of God.

Jeremiah's was a moral battle, and a moral battle is harder to fight and keep fighting.

After the Fall of Jerusalem (Jeremiah 39—52)

In the fourth year of Jehoiakim's reign, Nebuchadnezzar invaded Judah (605 B.C.), and it was then that Daniel and his companions were carried away to Babylon and Jehoiakim himself was put into chains.

Nebuchadnezzar placed Zedekiah, Jehoiakim's brother, on the throne in place of Jehoiachin. Only the poor were left in Jerusalem now. Jeremiah likens them to bad, worthless figs, in contrast to those who had gone who were good figs (chap. 24). The picked men of the nation were carried away. Remember that Daniel afterward became prime minister of Babylon. The men who were left were so weak and degenerate that the prophet could see nothing but doom for Jerusalem.

Zedekiah was disposed to be friendly to Jeremiah, but he was a weak man and had no courage to make decisions of his own. He was like clay in the hands of the princes who surrounded his throne. The remnant of men who were left were not qualified to govern. They had taken the places of the real nobility of the nation, but they were in great contrast to those who had been carried into captivity.

Jeremiah incurred the displeasure of the prophets who had gone to Babylon because, in a letter to the exiles, he directly opposed their prediction of an early return from captivity (29:1-14). Neither did the prophets in Jerusalem like it because they thought that soon they could throw off the yoke of Nebuchadnezzar. Zedekiah's advisers were in favor of throwing off the Babylonian yoke and looking to Egypt for help, but Jeremiah kept insisting that the Chaldeans would certainly capture the city (37:3-10). Finally, Zedekiah broke his covenant with the king of Babylon. Nebuchadnezzar swiftly marched against Jerusalem and the final siege began.

As the siege proceeded, the hostility of Jeremiah's enemies became more intense. They charged him with desertion and thrust him into prison. They even petitioned the king to put him to death (38:4). Weakling that he was, Zedekiah gave Jeremiah over into the hands of the princes. Then for some reason they shrank from killing him. But they chose a worse thing for Jeremiah; they lowered him with cords into a miry dungeon, and left him to die of starvation and exposure. But God was with him and raised up a friend to deliver him. An Ethiopian, Ebed-melech, heard of Jeremiah's plight and made his way to the king. Gaining permission, he rushed to the dungeon and lowered a quantity of "old rags and worn-out clothes" for the prophet to put under his armpits beneath the cords, for Jeremiah had "sank down into the mud" and the work of getting him out would mean a great strain (38:6-13).

After Jeremiah's deliverance, Zedekiah, driven by fear, visited Jeremiah to find out what was in store for him. Jeremiah could only promise him doom for the city. Jeremiah still insisted that the king should surrender to Nebuchadnezzar, but Zedekiah was afraid of the princes (38:14-28).

After eighteen months of siege, Jerusalem was taken (587 B.C.). Zedekiah's sons were put to death before his eyes, and afterward he himself was blinded and carried in chains to Babylon (39:1-7). Jeremiah was given the choice of going to Babylon where freedom and honor awaited him, but he chose to cast his lot with the remnant left in the land (39:11-12; 40:1-16).

We can see how close Jeremiah was to the affairs of Judah during her captivity. He had seen the condition of Judah's decline after Josiah's good reign till the day of Zedekiah. He saw the people carried away captive and witnessed the destruction of Jerusalem and the Temple.

We find in chapter 24 one of the first discourses of Jeremiah in Zedekiah's reign. Jeremiah urged Judah to submit to Babylon in accordance with God's will, but without effect (21:1-10). Jeremiah never ceased urging this submission to Babylon, so much so that his enemies accused him of being a traitor. King Nebuchadnezzar of Babylon regarded his stand and made him an offer of any honor he would accept, besides saving his life (39:11-12).

At the same time Jeremiah was crying out against Babylon for her heinous crime in destroying God's children, he told them Babylon would be demolished and would be in ruins forever (51:37-43). This is literally true of this wonder city of the ancient world. Read again Isaiah 13:17-22 along with Jeremiah 51:37-43.

By the time of Christ, Babylon's power had gone, and in the first century A.D. it was mostly in ruins. Its bricks have been used in building Baghdad and repairing canals. For centuries it has lain in heaps of desolate mounds. Only beasts of the desert inhabit it. This is a remarkable fulfillment of prophecy. When this writer stood and looked over its ruins, it was hard to believe that once this was a city of wonder and beauty, filled with luxury and gross extravagance, unsurpassed in the history of the world, for today it is only a heap of fallen bricks.

In 605 B.C. the first deportation of the Jews to Babylon occurred. During this year Jeremiah was ordered to write the predictions he had made and to have them read to the people.

These predictions are scattered throughout chapters 24—49 and concern the future of the Jews, the Babylonian captivity and the coming Messiah.

Teachers may wish to know the order of the prophecies during Zedekiah's reign. Dr. William Graham Scroggie is our authority in this: chapters 24; 27; 28; 29; 49:34; 51:1; 21; 34; 37; 38; 39:15-18; 32; 33; 30; 31; 39:1-14.

Predictions

1. Concerning God's future dealings with Judah (Jeremiah 23; 31)
2. Conquest of land by Nebuchadnezzar, king of Babylon (Jeremiah 20:4)
3. Judah's exile or captivity in Babylon and return after seventy years (Jeremiah 25 and 26)
4. Concerning the Messiah (Jeremiah 23:6; 30:4-11; 33:14-26)

5. Israel will be scattered among all the kingdoms of the earth (Jeremiah 24)
6. Final recovery of Israel (Jeremiah 23:1-40; 32:37-41; Ezekiel 37:21-22).

Jeremiah got his messages to the people by speaking to them as they thronged to the feasts. Often he did symbolic things to attract their attention. When he was shut up in prison, he dictated his messages to Baruch, the scribe, who wrote them down and read them to the people. The roll of Jeremiah that Jehoiakim burned no doubt took Jeremiah and Baruch about one and one-half years to prepare. Writing in those days was not like it is now. It was a long and laborious task.

In the days when David's throne was tottering and Judah was going into captivity, the prophet announced the coming Christ, King of the house of David, a righteous Branch. "In his days Judah will be saved and Israel will live in safety. This is the name by which he will be called: the Lord Our Righteousness" (Jeremiah 23:6).

Judah's future redemption through Christ is given in chapters 30; 31. The Jews are scattered today, but God is bringing them back (30:10-11; 31:10).

Jeremiah 23 is dear to the Jews, God's chosen people, and dear to the heart of God. It tells of the future of Judah, redeemed through the work of their Messiah. Jesus, the Good Shepherd, is promised (vv. 1,3). He will gather His sheep from every corner of the earth and they will return to their own country, the Promised Land. This will take place when the King shall come and sit upon the throne of David (v. 5).

Judah's History in a Word

"Chosen"—Jeremiah prophesied to God's chosen people Judah before their exile into Babylon.

"Captured"—He warned them of their captivity if they would not listen to Jehovah.

"Carried Away"—They sinned until God allowed them to be carried away by Nebuchadnezzar into Babylon. God tells them they must remain captive seventy years (Jeremiah 25:1-14; Daniel 9:2).

"Coming Messiah"—But God will not allow His children to remain scattered through the nations of the world forever. Someday the Jews will be gathered to their own land and the good Shepherd will appear (Jeremiah 33:14-17).

Finally those left in Jerusalem all fled to Egypt in spite of God's warning against it (Jeremiah 43). They asked Jeremiah to pray for guidance, but when it was given they refused to obey it. The prophet and Baruch were compelled to accompany them. Even in Egypt we find the prophet carrying out his commission. He prophesies the conquest of Egypt by Nebuchadnezzar (43:8-13). The Jews who dwelt in the Nile valley were practicing idolatry and Jeremiah warned them against this wickedness. When they refused to listen to his warning, and went on worshiping these other gods, Jeremiah told them the judgment of God would fall (44:26-28).

This is the last we hear of Jeremiah. How long he lived in Egypt afterward we know not. Other prophets had at least occasional successes to cheer their hearts in the midst of difficulties, but Jeremiah seemed to be fighting a losing battle to the very end. Disaster, failure and hostility were rewards for his work. He preached to deaf ears and seemed to reap only hate in return for his love for his people. In life he seemed to accomplish little. He was brokenhearted. But God has given us a record that makes him one of the greatest of all prophets.

Jeremiah's life was one of deepening gloom. He had to watch the people and city he loved fall from sin to sin. And all the time he had no hope that things might change. How deeply he felt all this can be seen in his Lamentations. Hudson Taylor (James Hudson Taylor, 1832-1905, British missionary to China and founder of China Inland Mission) one time wrote, "God delights to trust a trustworthy child with a trial." How God must have trusted Jeremiah! We have seen the bitter opposition he had to meet. Now we have to watch the hatred of his enemies reaching a climax in a savage demand for his death. "This man should be put to death." This came from the princes (38:4).

Being confined in the court of the guard attached to the royal palace, Jeremiah had opportunities to talk to the soldiers on duty as well as to the citizens who came along (37:21). To every one he declared the Word of the Lord (37:6-10). That message was that it was foolish to resist the Chaldeans. It would only result in destruction. This was so galling to national pride that the princes named in Jeremiah 38:1 resolved to kill Jeremiah. Yet King Zedekiah was convinced that Jeremiah was right.

Of course Jeremiah discouraged ("weakened the hands of") the soldiers and people (38:4, *KJV*). The people were convinced that resistance was useless because God had said that Jerusalem would be captured and burned by the Chaldeans. People and soldiers were unwilling to sacrifice their lives any longer in defending the city.

We find, in chapters 40—44, prophecies given by Jeremiah after the fall of Jerusalem.

1. To the remnant in Judah—40:1—43:3
2. To the remnant in Egypt—43:4—44:30.

A bit of history recorded in chapter 52 gives the facts about the captivity of Judah.

Jeremiah and His Times

The prophecy of Jeremiah comes out of the turmoil in Judah preceding and during the Babylonian captivity like the song of a lark on the battlefield of Flanders. It is like a beautiful symphony of sorrow, God's oratorio of tears and consolation as His great heart of love weeps over the people He is chastening. The message of the book deals with the certainty of God's judgment because of sin, yet the tenderness and eternity of His boundless love. The prophecies are not chronological, but each prophecy is bound up with the history of the times, under the five kings Josiah, Jehoahaz, Jehoiakim, Jehoiachin, Zedekiah, and finally with the captivity. Jeremiah is concerned with backsliding. Judah had forsaken the Lord, and through Jeremiah God sent warnings of impending judgments, beseeching His people to return to His commandments.

Jeremiah was God's prophet, speaking God's words. Read of his marvelous call, Jeremiah 1:4-10. Many times Jeremiah cries, "This is what the Lord, the Lord Almighty says." In Jeremiah 22:29 he adds, "O land, land, land, hear the word of the Lord!" The book abounds in golden passages: 6:16; 9:23-24; 10:10-13; 17:7-8; 18:1-6; 20:9; 22:29; 23:5-6. The golden chapters are 31 and 33. It is hard to find words in any language of more touching beauty.

Christ appears in Jeremiah. He is wonderfully pictured in 23:5-6. His future kingdom is lavishly described in chapters 31 and 33. The whole book is a series of messages, each of which was spoken to fit the need of the moment. Therefore these messages are like "apples of gold in settings of silver" (Proverbs 25:11), and when we apply them to ourselves we discover that they meet our needs just as they met the needs of Jehovah's wandering people.

Understanding Lamentations

Here is another of the Bible's exquisite books of poetry. It is commonly attributed to Jeremiah. Five beautiful, distinct poems are bound together in the book. It is not all sorrow. Above the clouds of the poet's weeping over the sins of his people, God's sun is shining. In Lamentations 3:22-27, the light breaks through to throw a shining rainbow across the murky sky. God's grace always shines above the clouds of sin (see Romans 5:20), and it will always shine in the heart that is trusting in God through faith in the Lord Jesus Christ who gives "to bestow on them a crown of beauty instead of ashes, the oil of gladness instead of mourning, and a garment of praise instead of a spirit of despair" (Isaiah 61:3).

Chapter 20

Understanding Ezekiel

Ezekiel Portrays Jesus Christ, the Son of Man

Selected Bible Readings

Sunday: The Prophet's Call (Ezekiel 2:1—3:9)
Monday: The Prophet a Watchman (Ezekiel 3:10-27)
Tuesday: Israel Shall Be Saved
            (Ezekiel 11:14-21; 28:25-26)
Wednesday: Israel's Sins (Ezekiel 22:3-31)
Thursday: Israel's Future (Ezekiel 34:1-31)
Friday: Israel's Restoration (Ezekiel 36:1-38)
Saturday: Vision of the Dry Bones (Ezekiel 37:1-14)

Ezekiel, the faithful preacher to the exiles in Babylon, is the author of this book.

Jeremiah, the great prophet whom we have just finished studying, was the last of the prophets in Jerusalem before the exile. His ministry was still going on when the end came. Recall the story. The young prophet Ezekiel was already at work among the exiles in Babylon. God had prepared a witness to the people in their captivity. God needed a voice to warn the people and to remind them of the reason all these calamities had befallen them. For twenty-two years Ezekiel dealt with the discouraged captives to whom God had sent him.

"The word of the Lord came to me" (Ezekiel 24:15). This phrase occurs forty-nine times in Ezekiel. God's greatest communications can only be made by his servants whose own hearts have been broken. The instrument in God's hands must personally be ready to share in suffering with others. Jesus' body was broken for us.

Ezekiel is for the Jewish people today. It tells them that God will fulfill His sure promises. Their land, their city, their Temple will be restored to them. It reveals God's plan for them.

Ezekiel is for the Christian today. It is a book of the times, for God's time is always revealed by His dealing with the Jews. Israel is beginning to return to her land and divine history is being made. The nation now exists officially. When the Jews move we know God is getting ready to act.

You find little of Ezekiel in the Gospels or Epistles. But look in Revelation. Ezekiel and John seem to lock arms across the centuries, and looking into the future they see the unfolding of a new heaven and a new earth. Ezekiel, the prophet, peering forward with rapt gaze, half whispering, says, "Above the expanse over their heads was what looked like a throne of sapphire, and high above on the throne was a figure like that of a man" (Ezekiel 1:26). And John, a little nearer, revealing God's vision to him, says in clearer tones these thrilling words, "At once I was in the Spirit, and there before me was a throne in heaven with someone sitting on it. And the one who sat there had the appearance of jasper and carnelian. A rainbow, resembling an emerald, encircled the throne" (Revelation 4:2-3).

Like Jeremiah, Ezekiel was not only a prophet, but he was a priest as well. He was a prophet during the captivity. When he was twenty-five years old, he was carried captive to Babylon in 597 B.C. with the upper class of people, eleven years before the destruction of Jerusalem. This means that for eleven years 10,000 exiles were living in a concentration camp in Babylon while Jeremiah and the folks at home tried to carry on in Jerusalem. For five years the captives had no preacher. Then Ezekiel began to serve them. He immediately tried to remove their false hopes of an early return to Judah. He tried to prepare them for the news of the tragic destruction of their beloved Jerusalem. He lived at the same time as Daniel and Jeremiah. Jeremiah remained among the Jews in Jerusalem. Ezekiel lived with the exiles in Babylon, and Daniel lived in the court of the rulers in Babylon.

Daniel and a few other Jewish boys had been brought to Babylon in 606 B.C. Ezekiel came nine years later. Ezekiel found that Daniel had attained a high position in the palace of Nebuchadnezzar, although he was only a youth. No doubt Daniel helped ease the lot of the captives because of his station. No doubt Ezekiel and Daniel were both young men about the same age. Jeremiah was older. He had been prophesying for about thirty years in Jerusalem when Ezekiel was taken away. No doubt Ezekiel had been Jeremiah's pupil while he was in the Holy City, and we find him preaching to the captives in Babylon the same things Jeremiah had preached. He told them of their sin and their certain judgment. He reiterated their folly in relying on Egypt.

Ezekiel's Day

The Northern Kingdom of Israel had been taken captive 120 years before by the king of Assyria (722 B.C.). Then God brought judgment upon the Southern Kingdom of Judah. Nebuchadnezzar had come to Jerusalem and carried away ten thousand of the chief men of the Southern Kingdom and some of the royal seed, including Daniel and Ezekiel (2 Chronicles 36:6-7; Daniel 1:1-3; 2 Kings 24:14-16). The people of Israel had been living in constant trouble. It took Nebuchadnezzar twenty years to completely destroy Jerusalem. He could have done it sooner, but he wanted tribute money. Then, too, Daniel was his court favorite and he may have been influenced by his young prime minister. He was finally forced to devastate Jerusalem because the city persisted in allying herself with Egypt. It was a tragic hour for Jerusalem when her walls were laid flat, her houses burned, the Temple destroyed and her people dragged away as captives.

God had told of Judah's captivity by Babylon more than 100 years before it happened (Isaiah 39:6; Micah 4:10). The seventy years of its duration was foretold by Jeremiah (Jeremiah 25:11-12). It is interesting to notice that God told them the exact time of their exile. But the captivity did not bring the people of Judah back to God. This judgment of God only seemed to drive the people into greater wickedness. They worshiped idols and set up shrines in the hills and defiled the sanctuary of Jehovah (Ezekiel 5:11). Ezekiel began his prophecies to them.

Ezekiel's Babylonian home was by the Chebar River. It was a ship canal that branched off from the Euphrates above Babylon, the most beautiful city of the world, filled with palaces, gardens, temples and bridges, making it an outstanding showplace of the East. Chebar was probably one of many canals we know the Babylonian monarchs had dug. Ezekiel was among the captives digging the canal. Tradition tells us that the little village of Kifil was the town where Ezekiel lived, died and was buried. Tel-abib, where a colony of captive Jews dwelt, was near at hand. Ezekiel lived with these. He was fifty miles from Babylon. No doubt he often visited Daniel in the palace. The Jewish people presented a pitiable picture—no temple, national life gone, little opportunity for business. To such an audience Ezekiel devoted the best years of his life.

Ezekiel has a style and method of preaching all his own. He uses symbols, as in the mimic siege of Jerusalem (chap. 4), visions (chap. 8), parables (chap. 17), poems (chap. 19), proverbs (12:22-23; 18:2) and prophecies (6; 20; 40—48).

Ezekiel is an artist. He paints strange pictures for us. They are mystifying and full of terror and sometimes hard to decipher. They glow with life and action. He talks of sin and punishment, of repentance and blessing.

God told Ezekiel to go to the people in captivity. He was a captive ministering to captives. We must get alongside people to help them. This was our Lord's way. God tells Ezekiel to speak "whether they listen or fail to listen" (3:11). Ezekiel's responsibility was to deliver God's message. The results were not in his hands.

Soon after Ezekiel was born, a great reformation of popular worship and social life was aroused. This was caused by the inspiration of the book of Deuteronomy, which had just been published (621 B.C.). But the reformation was only superficial. The religious decline was crowned by political disaster and Jerusalem was taken after an eighteen-month siege amid horrors untold. The Temple, on which such a passion of love had been lavished, was reduced to ashes and the people deported to Babylon.

The Glory of God

The "glory of God" seems to be the key phrase to Ezekiel. It occurs twelve times in the first eleven chapters. Then it does not occur again until chapter 43. The "glory of the Lord" was grieved away from the Temple at Jerusalem by the idolatry of the people. God says, "Because you have defiled my sanctuary with all your vile images and detestable practices, I myself will withdraw my favor; I will not look on you with pity or spare you" (Ezekiel 5:11). In Ezekiel 8, we see Ezekiel in a vision transported to Jerusalem and he sees four kinds of idolatry that were practiced in the courts of the Lord's house, even worshiping the sun, with their backs to the sanctuary while their faces were to the East. We see "the glory of the Lord" gradually grieved away from the inner sanctuary by the sin of idolatry, and the brightness filled the court. Then it departed to the threshold and rested over the cherubim. As the cherubim rose from the earth, "the glory of the Lord" abode above their pinions and mounted with them, forsaking the city and removing to the mountains (chap. 10).

Young Christians, this is just what can happen to us. We can grieve the Holy Spirit and resist Him until He is quenched and our heart becomes like a ruined temple bereft of its glory (see Ephesians 4:30 and 1 Thessalonians 5:19). There are so many blighted Christian lives from which the radiance has gone through disobedience.

We grieve the Spirit when we do not allow ourselves time to read the Word or pray. We limit the Spirit when we refuse to be clean vessels through which He can work. We resist Him by allowing idols to be in our hearts. Remember, your body is the temple of the Holy Spirit (see 1 Corinthians 6:19). Does His presence glow in your life?

In the Old Testament, the glory of God refers to the light that shone between the cherubim in the holy of holies as the evidence of the presence of God. Ezekiel opens with this heavenly glory in the vision (chap. 1). The book ends with earthly glory (chaps. 40—48). Ezekiel's visions given in between tell of the departing of this glory (9:3). First it left the cherubim for the threshold of God's house (10:4), thence to the east gate (10:18-19), and finally clear away from the Temple and city to the Mount of Olives (11:22-23). Thus gradually, reluctantly, majestically, the glory of the Lord left the Temple and Holy City. Then captivity came.

This was Ezekiel's message to the nation. Their captivity was a result of their sin, and before they could hope for return to their land they must return to their Lord. This message reaches its climax in the impassioned cry of Ezekiel 18:30-32.

God's judgment on sin is certain and severe. His redemption is equally certain when it is welcomed by the human heart. Ezekiel's message closes with the promise of future glory. Ezekiel 37 is the great classic of Israel's hope. The closing vision of the Temple is equally significant. The glory of the Lord returns (43:2-6) and fills the house of the Lord (44:4).

Ezekiel's prophecy is intensely practical for nation and church. As Israel's captivity was the result of sin, so we must remember that sin is a reproach to any people. A nation's troubles are the result of national apostasy from God.

The same is true of the Church of Christ. The glory of the Lord left the house of the Lord because of the sins of God's people. It is also true of individual Christian experience. God's blessing returns to His people when His people return to Him.

Ezekiel and the Captivity

It seems God called Ezekiel that He might explain and justify His action in allowing His children to be taken into captivity. They had been wicked and stiff-necked; they were guilty of unspeakable sin and abomination. When other nations did what Israel had done, God wiped them out. But all of God's dealings with Israel were for correction. They should say, "I know, O Lord, that your laws are righteous, and in faithfulness you have afflicted me" (Psalm 119:75). He was punishing His children for their sin and was teaching them great lessons. He said a remnant would survive. "They shall know that I am God" was His purpose. After the captivity, the Jews were cured from polytheistic worshiping of the gods of the surrounding peoples. They had insisted upon it before, in spite of the warnings of God, but after they came out of

Babylon, the names of other gods were banished from their lips.

God set Jeremiah to be a tower of strength in the land of Judah. In the same way He set Ezekiel to be a tower among his own captive people by the river Chebar, in the land of the Chaldeans. He told Ezekiel that "I will make your forehead like the hardest stone, harder than flint" (Ezekiel 3:9). Strength characterized the ministry of the prophet whose name means "God will strengthen."

Ezekiel—A Home Missionary

Ezekiel was sent to his own people. It is sometimes easier to go as a missionary to another culture like China or India than to speak to the members of your own household or your own friends.

Perhaps God is speaking to us as He spoke to Ezekiel—"You are not being sent to a people of obscure speech and difficult language, but to the house of Israel. Go now to your countrymen in exile and speak to them. Say to them, 'This is what the Sovereign Lord says,' whether they listen or fail to listen" (3:5,11). It was difficult to speak to false prophets, elders, shepherds and princes, but God commanded it.

Ezekiel—A Watchman

God told Ezekiel to be a watchman. He told the prophet not to fear the people but give them warning, and that if he did not do it, He would require their blood at his hands (chaps. 3 and 33). These chapters state plainly our personal responsibility in giving out the gospel message. Paul was so faithful in doing this that he could say, "I am innocent of the blood of all men" (Acts 20:26).

Ezekiel—The Sign

To be God's sign to the people, Ezekiel underwent the loss of all personal interests. He stood ready to do anything God asked of him in order to demonstrate the plan of God for His people, and God asked some extraordinary things of him. He shut himself up in his house (Ezekiel 3:24). He was placed in weird positions (4:4-8). He ate his food by weight (4:10). He sacrificed personal appearance (5:1), smote with hand or struck with foot (6:11), and even moved personal and domestic goods out of his house to show the removal of Israel into captivity (12:2-7). God may never ask these of us, but He may ask us to do things that cross our wills and desires. Will He find us as obedient as Ezekiel? Christ seeks for such—"I looked for a man among them who would build up the wall and stand before me in the gap on behalf of the land so that I would not have to destroy it, but I found none" (22:30).

In Ezekiel 25—32, we hear pronouncements of doom on surrounding nations. We remember Isaiah gave warnings in chapters 13—23. Jeremiah gave warnings in chapters 46—51. Each mentioned different nations. Ezekiel warned Ammon, Moab, Edom, Philistia, Tyre, Sidon and Egypt.

The remarkable thing about these prophecies is that they were given at a time when these cities and nations were strong and powerful. Each one has passed into a state of utter desolation, as Babylon, or has been put into a place of insignificance among world powers. Many of the specific prophecies have already been fulfilled to the most minute detail. "Righteousness exalts a nation, but sin is a disgrace to any people" (Proverbs 14:34).

Visions of Ezekiel

Ezekiel is a prophet of visions. The key text of the book shows this: "While I was among the exiles by the Kebar River, the heavens were opened and I saw visions of God" (Ezekiel 1:1). It is urgent that you scan all these visions before you enter into further detailed study.

Vision of the Cherubim (1:1—3:13)
In this vision, "four living creatures" appear, having unusual faces, but each with the general appearance of a man. The main purpose of the vision is twofold—to commission Ezekiel for service, and to impress upon him the need for assimilating the words God spoke to him and giving them to the people. Note "the scroll" he ate in his vision (3:1). The unswerving obedience to God's will of the creatures symbolized the obedience expected of Ezekiel. Their movement as a single unit is the picture of God's will perfectly executed. Ezekiel and Revelation are often alike in symbolism. The

"figure like that of a man" upon the throne (1:26) is the Son of God. The "appearance of a rainbow in the clouds on a rainy day" spoke of the covenant God made with Noah (1:28). The "fire" (1:4,13,27) bespoke God's Spirit. In Revelation, all these appear. Christ figures prominently in all the symbolism.

Vision of Glory and Godlessness (8:1—11:25)

Before the siege of Jerusalem, Ezekiel is given an extended vision that shows the people's abominations in defiling the sanctuary, and the contrasting glory of God. "Abominations" occur all the way through the section. "Glory" stands in sharp contrast. God was trying to show why Israel was to be led into captivity (8:17-18).

Vision of the Burning Vine (15:1-8)

The vine becomes a symbol of Judah, and the burning of a useless vine that bears no fruit is the destruction of the people of God. The abominations of Jerusalem are so great as to warrant the most severe punishment. This vision of doom is followed by the parable of the unfaithful wife. Israel was Jehovah's "bride" who had forsaken God to go whoring after other gods. Love of idols, rather than the love of God, caused Israel's downfall (chap. 16).

Vision of Dry Bones (37:1-18)

In this vision, Ezekiel sees a great valley filled with dry bones, said to be the "whole house of Israel" (37:11). The main lesson of the vision is the restoration of God's people. He takes them from among the heathen and gathers them out of all countries through which, as bones without flesh, they have been scattered. It is a picture also of the power of God to raise those who have not only been scattered, but also dead in sins. This "new birth" was explained to Nicodemus. God promises it here to Israel. They are to be brought forth, filled with God's Spirit and brought to their land.

Parables and Signs in Ezekiel

Parables and signs, as well as visions, abound in Ezekiel. The more outstanding ones command great interest. (1) The parable of the two eagles (chap. 17) reveals the king of Babylon (v. 12) and the king of Egypt. The "top" of the cedar (v. 3) corresponds to Jehoiachin carried captive to Babylon. The "seed of your land" was Zedekiah (v. 5). The "tender sprig" (v. 22) Jehovah will plant is the Messiah, the future King of David's line through whom all nations will learn to know God. Jeremiah also tells of the "highest branch" (23:5-6; see also Isaiah 11:1; Zechariah 3:8; Isaiah 53). For "the mountain of the Lord," see 17:22; 20:40; Micah 4:1-2; Isaiah 2:2-3. (2) Chapters 20—23 include several parables, prominent among which is that of the two sisters Aholah and Aholibah. They represent Israel's and Judah's deterioration into idolatry. (3) The parable of the boiling caldron (chap. 24) symbolizes the holocaust in Jerusalem at the hands of the invading Babylonians. Much fuel, hot fire, boiled flesh and burnt bones show the intensity of the siege (vv. 5,10). (4) Two sticks—one Judah, the other Israel—are shown as ultimately reunited under the Shepherd King of God's people—Christ (37:24). This is one of the important "signs."

Predictions Before the Siege of Jerusalem— Against Judah (Ezekiel 1—24)

As the book opens we see Ezekiel, a young man of about 30, captive, yet being commissioned by God for a great service.

Like the prophets generally, Ezekiel entered upon his ministry only after he had a vision and a call from God. Read of Jeremiah's call in Jeremiah 1:4-10. Turn to Isaiah 6 and review the facts of Isaiah's commission. Ezekiel opens with the description of the experiences of the prophet when he was called.

The pivot of the book is the destruction of Jerusalem:

1. Pre-siege (1—24)—Ezekiel began six years before the destruction of Jerusalem with his prophecies and kept predicting its certainty until it occurred.
2. Siege (25—32)—After that his prophecies deal with Judah's enemies and the overthrow of these heathen nations.
3. Post-siege (33—48)—Finally the restoration and reestablishment of Judah is pictured.

Ezekiel gives us a very dramatic picture of his vision and call to service. The Holy Being who appeared to him could go everywhere. He was all powerful, could see everything and could rule the entire universe by His mighty hand.

The vision he saw was unusually complicated and elaborate. Notice how many times Ezekiel uses the words "appearance" and "likeness." He knows he is trying to describe things impossible to picture.

The prophet saw a fiery cloud approaching. From out of the glow were four living creatures, suggested by the cherubim of the Temple. (See 1 Kings 6:23-28; Genesis 3:24; Psalm 18:10.) Each had four wings and four faces: that of a man, a lion, an ox and an eagle, symbolizing intelligence, dignity, strength and speed. They faced east, west, north and south, suggesting that all parts of the universe are open to the gaze of God. The wings showed that no spot was inaccessible to divine power. There were eyes in the wheels—wheels so equipped cannot miss their way. We see a symbol of the omnipotence (all power), omnipresence (all presence) and omniscience (all knowledge) of God.

The mysterious whir of the mighty wings was followed by an equally mysterious silence. The wings dropped. The chariots stopped. Above the heads of the creatures was a crystal floor on which rested a sapphire throne, and on the throne almighty God Himself, a figure of supernatural brilliance and glory. The terror of divine majesty was softened by the sight of a lovely rainbow around the throne. Little wonder that when Ezekiel saw this vision he fell prostrate. The vision was to destroy all self-confidence the prophet might have.

The Call

Following the vision, the awful silence was broken by the Almighty upon the throne. The prophet was receiving his call. God told the prostrate prophet to rise and accept his commission for service. God wants more than inactive submission. He wants loving service. God called Ezekiel "son of man." One hundred times this phrase is used. Ezekiel was called to declare the message of God—a message of doom to the people. (Read Ezekiel 2:1-10.) This doom was justified by their rebellion. Ezekiel had every temptation to "rebel," but he went without flinching to speak the word.

The prophet's authority is suggested by the symbolic swallowing of a scroll. He must make the message his own. He must eat it (Ezekiel 3:3). Bitter as its contents were to his mouth, they were sweet as honey, for it is sweet to do the will of God and to be trusted with tasks for Him.

Then Ezekiel heard the whir of the wings and the roar of the wheels when the glory of Jehovah rose from the place and the chariot departed, leaving the prophet in a state of bitterness and heat of spirit. In this mood he found his way to Tel-abib, a colony of his fellow exiles, and remained for a week in a state of utter stupefaction.

The Watchman

At the end of the week he received another message from God. This time it was more explicit. He was called to be a watchman. "I have made you a watchman...give them warning from me....[if] you do not warn him...I will hold you accountable for his blood. But if you do warn the wicked man...but you will have saved yourself" (Ezekiel 3:17-19).

God places a great responsibility on His watchmen. How can we be so careless in the light of such words as these? How can we go to sleep and fail to warn others of their sins? Let us answer this challenge and heed this warning.

Ezekiel 33:7 says, "I have made you a watchman."

As a watchman, Ezekiel must warn individual people of the coming catastrophe he so clearly sees. It is not enough to warn the crowd. He must deal with individuals, good or bad, who compose the crowd and tell them to turn from their evil ways.

God impressed Ezekiel with individual responsibility. Each one must repent. Each one must hear the Word. How true this is today of every person. Each one must accept Christ personally. No one can do it for another. "Yet to all who received him, to those who believed in his name, he gave the right to become children of God" (John 1:12; see also John 3:16; 5:24; 3:36).

Four Symbols of Coming Doom of Jerusalem

1. The siege of Jerusalem—4:1-3. Ezekiel cannot speak, but he is a prophet still and he can preach, if not by word, by symbol (Ezekiel 3:22-27).
2. The exile—its duration—4:4-8. This section is curious. Remember Ezekiel was a sign. He lay upon his side to symbolize the years of punishment the Jews were to suffer in exile—a day for a year.
3. The hardships of the exiles—4:9-17. The horrors of famine due to siege are symbolized here by the prophet's food and drink, carefully measured out—about one-half pound of food a day and a pint of water.
4. The fate of the besieged—5:1-17. This last symbol, the knife and razor, is the most terrible of them all. It suggests the completeness of the destruction.

All of these visions and symbols reveal the method of Ezekiel's prophecy. This is the method used in Daniel and Revelation.

The prophet was shown the way the people profaned the Temple of Jehovah. This justified to the new generation the national punishment (8:1—11:12).

The prophet pled that Jehovah spare a remnant and Jehovah promised to be a "little sanctuary" to them in the land of their exile. He promised to restore them finally (11:13-21).

The next chapters reveal the past sins of both Samaria and Jerusalem, and the punishment and instructions in righteousness for the elders of Israel (11:22—24:27). God says, "I will give them an undivided heart and put a new spirit in them....They will be my people, and I will be their God" (11:19-20). God wants a religious experience of the heart. God will give His people a new spirit (18:31; 36:26).

Predictions During the Siege of Jerusalem—Judgment Against Judah's Enemies (Ezekiel 25—32)

Ezekiel's gloomy predictions are completed (Ezekiel 1—24). With the news of the fall of Jerusalem he immediately begins to prophesy about the future restoration of Israel. God often reveals a bright picture of Israel's future against the backdrop of divine judgment (chaps. 33—48). But before Israel is restored to her land, those who are her enemies must be put out of the way. So at this point we hear of the future doom of these foreign powers. First we hear of her near neighbors who have insulted and harassed her, and then of the more distant and more powerful ones. God pronounces His judgment upon Ammon, Moab, Tyre, Sidon and Egypt for their sins against Israel. All of these powers were ancient enemies of Israel. They dated back before the days of the monarchy. From Israel's petty neighbors with their petty spite, Ezekiel turns to the great empires of Tyre and Egypt. They, too, must go. In a passage of great literary power, Ezekiel describes the brilliance of Tyre, the extent of her commerce, the pity and terror inspired by her fall.

Ezekiel 29—32 tells of the collapse of Egypt. The mighty Nebuchadnezzar with his terrible army will deal a crushing blow and Egypt will be devastated.

Predictions After the Siege of Jerusalem— Judah's Restoration (Ezekiel 33—48)

We can now look into the future and see the final restoration and glory of Israel. God will gather together His scattered people. God says over and over, "I will, I will."

Shepherds of Israel had proven faithless to the people, the flock had been scattered; but now Jehovah will set up a Shepherd, "my servant David" (Ezekiel 34:23-24). This, no doubt, refers to the Davidic covenant and to the seed of David, the Messiah. Look up this series of passages: 2 Samuel 7:16; Psalm 89:20-36; Isaiah 7:13-14; 9:6-7; 11:1-12; Jeremiah 23:2-7; Ezekiel 37:21-28; Hosea 3:4-5; Luke 1:30-33; Acts 2:29-31; 15:14-17. All this reveals that the future blessing of Israel will come with the Messiah, David's Son. When the Jews rejected Jesus they did not thwart God's plan or defeat His purpose, for in Acts we read that He was raised from the dead to sit on David's throne, and He will return for that purpose (Acts 2:30).

The restoration Ezekiel tells about does not refer to the feeble remnant that returned to Jerusalem after the seventy years of captivity (see Ezra and Nehemiah), for it is a restoration from all nations (Ezekiel 36:24).

Ezekiel sees a vision of all this. There is a valley of dry bones (37:1-14). The "bones" are the Jews who shall be alive at the restoration of the nation. The "graves" are the nations where they are dwelling but "buried." God first will bring them into their own land. Then they will be converted—a nation shall be born in a day. The Spirit will give them life. The revival of national life is possible! It is not beyond the power of God. Even dry bones, without sinew and flesh, are made to live. The Holy Spirit can bring life. This truth is seen everywhere when the Spirit comes with His quickening power (see Genesis 2:7; Revelation 11:11). Israel shall multiply as they return to their own land. This restoration of Israel will be a national one. They shall look on Him whom they have pierced and mourn because of Him. And a nation shall be born in a day (see Zechariah 12:10; John 19:37; Romans 11:26). The resurrection in this chapter is not of the individual Jew, but of the whole nation.

Ezekiel 38 opens with the doom of "Gog, of the land of Magog, the chief prince of Meshech and Tubal." The reference is to the Northern (European) powers, perhaps headed up by Russia. (Read these passages in connection with Zechariah 14:1-9; 12:1-4; Matthew 24:14-30; Revelation 14:14-20; 19:17-21.) Before the curtain falls we read the description of the kingdom during the coming millennial age. This is what the thousand-year reign of Christ on earth is called when He shall sit upon the throne of David, in Jerusalem (Revelation 20:6). All the prophets tell us what a glorious day this will be for both Jew and Gentile. We read of the Temple, the worship and the final possession of the land promised to Abraham and to his seed according to the covenant God gave to him (see Genesis 12:1-3; 13:14-15; 15:18; 17:3-8) and of the many nations that will know that God alone is Lord of all (Ezekiel 38:23).

Golden Truth About the Golden Age

Back here in the Old Testament, while the Jews were in what seemed hopeless captivity, God declares constantly that He will restore the Jews to their own land, set up the throne and the kingdom of David through David's greater Son. With His reign will come such earthly and spiritual blessings as have not been known since the world began. This is the golden truth about the golden age that is coming to pass here on this earth (Ezekiel 34:22-31).

Gabriel's prophecy at Jesus' birth in Luke 1:30-33 will be literally fulfilled through David's Son, the Lord Jesus Christ. This promise of a Messianic King and Kingdom must be carefully distinguished from our Lord's spiritual rule over hearts and lives. The words of Gabriel to Mary still wait complete, literal fulfillment (see Ezekiel 34:23-24; 37:24; 1 Kings 14:8; Jeremiah 30:9).

The appearance of the Messiah will usher in a glorious future. God will make a covenant of peace (Leviticus 26:6; Jeremiah 31:31; Ezekiel 37:26). Wonderful blessings are promised to His people. They will be assured of absolute protection from idolatrous nations, the evil beasts of Ezekiel 34:25, because they are possessed by none other than God Himself (34:31).

Chapter 21

Understanding Daniel

Daniel Portrays Jesus Christ, the Striking Stone

Selected Bible Readings

Sunday:	Daniel the Captive (Daniel 1—2)
Monday:	Nebuchadnezzar, the Proud King (Daniel 3—4)
Tuesday:	Belshazzar's Reign (Daniel 5; 7—8)
Wednesday:	Darius's Reign (Daniel 6—9)
Thursday:	God's Glory (Daniel 10)
Friday:	The Conflict of Kings (Daniel 11)
Saturday:	Daniel's Last Message (Daniel 12)

"Young men without any physical defect, handsome, showing aptitude for every kind of learning, well informed, quick to understand, and qualified to serve in the king's palace" (Daniel 1:4)—these are some of the men with whom this book deals. They were skilled in God's wisdom as opposed to human wisdom. They had an understanding of God's revelation that unlocks the mysteries of human science. They had ability in them such as God gives to live the overcoming life!

Chief among these princely young men was the incomparable Daniel. He stands in God's Word as the man who dared to keep a clean heart and body (1:8), and the man therefore whom God chose as a channel for His message to the Gentile nations of the world. A large part of this book is concerned with the thrilling personal life of this peerless captive prince of Judah.

Daniel was in the palace at Babylon the same time Ezekiel was toiling in a slave gang. If Daniel's was the easier life in many of its material aspects, it may also be considered by far the more perilous.

Ezekiel's work during these dreary exile years was to proclaim to his people God's truth and to explain the real meaning of the miseries that had befallen them. Daniel's task was to share in the actual government of Babylon.

Daniel has been called the prophet of dreams. God revealed to him His secrets. "During the night the mystery was revealed to Daniel in a vision" (2:19). Daniel, like Ezekiel, looks far into the future. He is quoted most in Revelation. One cannot understand the great signs of Revelation without looking at their meaning in Daniel.

Daniel belonged to a family of high rank. He was taken captive to Babylon during the first invasion by Nebuchadnezzar (died 562 B.C., king of Babylonia 605-562 B.C.) at about the age of sixteen. Ezekiel was taken captive eight years later during the second invasion. Daniel lived to be over ninety years of age. He saw the Babylonian kingdom fall (539 B.C.) and the Medo-Persian empire established. He held high positions under kings Nebuchadnezzar, Belshazzar, Darius (550-486 B.C., king of Persia from 522-486 B.C.) and Cyrus (585-529 B.C., called "the Great").

Daniel's whole life from the time of his captivity was spent in the great and glamorous city of Babylon, the ancient Hollywood. He spent sixty-nine years in a vile court. There he lived a life without blame and well favored. Ezekiel 14:14-20; 28:3 refer to him as a model of righteousness.

Although Daniel was a captive, he rose to be prime minister of Babylon. The wonderful thing is that he always remained true to Jehovah God.

Daniel—Book of Devotions

This book is packed with heart-touching devotional passages for the personal Christian life:

The surrendered life—1:1-21
Light amidst darkness—2:20-22
Triumph through trial—3:17-25
The reward of service—5:17

Prayer and confidence in God—6:10-24
Confession of sin—9:3-19
The wisdom of soul winning—12:3.

"Daniel was among the great on this earth." The historical portions of his own book hint it. Ezekiel, nearest to him in his own day and therefore knowing him best, ranks him as one of the world's triumvirate of virtue—Noah, Daniel and Job (Ezekiel 14:14).

Daniel was also great in heaven. God broke the silence of the skies twice over to cry out, "Daniel, you who are highly esteemed" (Daniel 10:11,19). Furthermore, no position, no matter how difficult, found him without trust in God. God is able, in all temptations, to keep us from falling (Jude 24) unless we have deliberately placed ourselves, with Peter, at the fire of the enemy.

"God honored Daniel in his prayers." Marvelous in power that they were, God sent a special embassy of angels from the throne with the thrilling words, "I have come in response to [your words]" (Daniel 10:12). God exhibited His power in a remarkable way in Daniel's life and Daniel never introduced himself or his own actions except as illustrations of that power.

"Daniel was the companion of kings." He was a leader of men. He was a pioneer in reform. He started the first Society of Total Abstinence (Daniel 1:12). Daniel was, like Joseph, God's candle shining in pagan darkness. He was chief statesman in the first empire of the world, chief adviser of a great monarch and a great protector of his own people. God gave him favor and love in the sight of the court official, Ashpenaz. Even proud Nebuchadnezzar seemed to have had real affection for Daniel.

The feelings of Darius toward Daniel are revealed when he finds that a trap has been set for him. He was "greatly distressed; he was determined to rescue Daniel and made every effort until sundown to save him" (6:14).

No doubt Cyrus was greatly influenced by the aged statesman. Daniel may have shown him the prophecy Isaiah had written concerning him 100 years before he was born. This made Cyrus issue the decree for rebuilding the Temple at Jerusalem (2 Chronicles 36:22-23; Ezra 1).

In the book Daniel wrote, we see him preeminently as a prophet of God. He drew back the curtain and unveiled, as no one had ever done before, the hidden things of the future. Indeed, we are seeing more and more that his great prophecies are only history written before it occurred. The book of Daniel is one of the world's great annals in anticipation.

This book reveals the power of God and His universal sovereignty. God's power is contrasted with world power.

God the Keeper—Daniel 1: God's power in keeping Daniel and his companions. They were given understanding and wisdom above all the wise men of Babylon.

God the Revealer of Secrets—Daniel 2: God's power in revealing the dream of Nebuchadnezzar to Daniel. None of the wise men of Babylon could do this.

God the Deliverer—Daniel 3: God's power in delivering Daniel's three companions from the fiery furnace. These young men stood up alone, against a nation, with the calm assurance that God would deliver them, yet adding, "But if he does not, we want you to know, O king, that we will not serve your gods, or worship the image of gold you have set up" (v. 18). This occurred after they had been in Babylon about twenty years, and God was demonstrating in this most dramatic way His power over all the gods of this country.

God the Potentate—Daniel 4: God's power in dealing with the mighty Babylonian monarch, Nebuchadnezzar. God struck him while the proud king was boasting of his power as he was strolling on the roof of his magnificent palace. He was driven from his kingdom to dwell among beasts—victim of a strange form of insanity.

God the Judge—Daniel 5: God's power is shown in the awful judgment revealed to Belshazzar, son of Nabonidus, by the handwriting on the wall. That night the king was slain by the Persian army and his city taken.

God the All Powerful—Daniel 6: God's power revealed in the deliverance of Daniel from the lions' den. Remember, Daniel was an old man. When he was a young man of about twenty he was honored by the highest office in the whole empire. Now at ninety he was thrown into the den of lions. It seems that even the lions honored him.

God used the times of captivity to reveal His power among the nations of the world. When the chosen people were captives in Egypt, He worked miracles and wonders by the hand of Moses and showed, not only to the Israelites, but also to the Egyptians, that the Lord God is Almighty.

Now, during the Babylonian captivity, God uses this as a special occasion to manifest His power. We find these great world monarchs confessing that He is the living God, the Most High, the King of heaven. He visits His children even in exile and shows them again that He is mighty to save.

Unlike the other prophets, Daniel deals more fully with the Gentile nations than with his own Jewish nation. The other prophets only mention the Gentiles as incidental to something concerning Israel. But Daniel gives us the history of the Gentile powers from Babylon to the end. The prophecies are considered among the most remarkable in the whole Scriptures.

The Book of Daniel is divided into two great sections:

(1) historical—narration, chapters 1—6
(2) prophetic—revelation, chapters 7—12.

Reign of Nebuchadnezzar (Daniel 1—4)

This scene opens upon a little company of four young men, Daniel, Hananiah, Mishael and Azariah (also called Shadrach, Meshach, Abednego). They had been taken captive from Jerusalem by Nebuchadnezzar and carried away to his palace in Babylon. Daniel was only about sixteen years old, Nebuchadnezzar a little older. He came to the throne about the time Daniel was taken captive into Babylon, and was the most powerful and distinguished king of the Babylonian empire. Daniel's career was marked by its extent in time and its greatness in accomplishment.

Daniel was carried to Babylon during the first deportation of the captives. He gained a high position in the kingdom and was influential through the seventy years of his captivity. He saw his captive brothers return to Jerusalem under the decree of Cyrus. He saw world-ruling Babylon pass away and a new empire arise. Even at the age of ninety he received a position of high distinction in the court of Persia.

Daniel and his friends lived in an atmosphere of loose morals and low standards even though they were in a palace. Yet we read that they kept themselves apart from the evil of that court—true to God in a day when everything was against them. Evils much like those of today were rampant everywhere in the courts of royalty.

Observe that these brave youths stood with Daniel when they faced their first temptation in the court of the Babylonian king: "Daniel resolved not to defile himself with the royal food and wine, and he asked the chief official for permission not to defile himself this way" (Daniel 1:8). To young men like these God could tell His secrets and demonstrate His power. Remember, "The Lord confides in those who fear him" (Psalm 25:14).

These youths met every emergency and were victors. We will find them in three difficult positions:

1. In the court of a powerful emperor
2. In the fiery furnace
3. In the den of lions.

In this first scene we find them in the luxurious royal court. The youths were brought very quickly face to face with a serious practical difficulty. This was a real test for these chaps. As favored ones, they had been put into one of the apartments in the palace and given many of the delicacies of the king's table. They were to be trained in state affairs and equipped for high positions. It was hard indeed to refuse the king's meat and ask for a simpler fare. It would look as if they had no choice in the matter. Many of us would have argued that way. They asked to be able to prove that their faces would be satisfactory. And God gave them favor in the eyes of their companions. Remember, we ought always to obey God rather than people. The king's meat had probably been offered to idols (see Exodus 34:15; 1 Corinthians 10:20), and the flesh food would have been killed with the blood left in the animal, which was unclean (see Leviticus 3:17; 7:26).

There was nothing priggish about Daniel. It was something to make a man like Ashpenaz love him. Notice how loyal his companions were to him. This is a fine trait. Success did not turn Daniel's head. He was a man to whom, early in his career, men turned.

We are told that God gave these young men knowledge and

skill in all learning and wisdom; and Daniel had understanding in all visions and dreams. This was God's reward. God's power is shown through His dealing with Daniel and his three companions in all the wisdom and understanding He gave them.

There was a stir in the palace. Nebuchadnezzar had dreamed a dream and not one of the wise men of the kingdom could tell him what it was. A decree had been sent forth that all the wise men should be slain, and Daniel and his friends were sought. But Daniel was not afraid. God would tell him the dream and give him the meaning of it.

Daniel called his prayer partners (Daniel 2:17) and they presented their problem before God. "During the night the mystery was revealed to Daniel in a vision" (Daniel 2:19). God never disappoints faith.

The Dream of World Empires

Nebuchadnezzar's dream and the interpretation teach us some interesting things about the history of the world from that time till the end of this age. This period the Bible calls "the times of the Gentiles" (Luke 21:24; Romans 11:25) because God has put aside His own people, the Jews, for a time and has turned over the government of the world to the Gentiles.

Daniel 2 has been called the ABC of prophecy. It stretches out before us the most complete picture in all the Scriptures of what is to come to pass—the future.

God revealed His plan of the future to King Nebuchadnezzar in a dream (2:29). After Nebuchadnezzar had dreamed, he forgot! But it worried him. No one could tell him his dream but one who knew "the God of heaven." (Master the outline of history given in this second chapter.)

Picture a great image. The head was of gold, its breast and arms of silver, the belly and thighs of brass, and its legs of iron, with its feet and toes of iron and clay. Then a Rock cut out without hands struck the image and broke it to pieces; and the Rock became a great mountain and filled the whole earth. (This Rock was no other than Jesus Christ.)

God first reveals the Gentile powers. Four great empires were to succeed one another in the government of the world from Nebuchadnezzar to the end. God says, "You are that head of gold" (Daniel 2:38).

The breast and arms of silver represented the Medo-Persian empire, which overthrew Babylon and became its successor. Its power began with Cyrus under whom the Jews returned to Jerusalem (see Ezra 1:1-2).

Then the belly and thighs of brass represented Greece, which overturned the Medo-Persians. It pictures the Grecian rule "over the whole earth" (Daniel 2:39) under Alexander the Great (356-323 B.C.). The legs of iron represent Rome.

Daniel's Historical Summary

Daniel tells us what each metal represents. Daniel 2:38 says that the head of gold is Babylon. In Daniel 8:20 we find that the Medo-Persians are to follow. Then in Daniel 8:21 it states that Greece is to follow Persia. Daniel 9:26 indicates a fourth world power. From then on we find an ever-dividing kingdom and a government ever weakened in its power and represented by toes of iron and clay that cannot hold together. More is said of the fourth Gentile government than of the others. Maybe it is because it is the last. There will be a division into many kingdoms, as the toes. Deterioration is represented by the feet and toes being part iron and part clay, which cannot hold together. This last government will be the weakest. It will not be completely unified, and will finally end in chaos.

Kingdom of Christ

In the "Rock" cut out without hands we see the kingdom of Christ, whose kingdom shall never be destroyed, bringing to an end all the other kingdoms. Christ will come and set up a kingdom that will last forever (Daniel 2:44-45). If you wish an interesting study, see what the Word says about the "Rock" or "Stone" (Psalm 118:22; Isaiah 8:14; 28:16; Zechariah 3:9).

Remember, at the time Nebuchadnezzar dreamed his dream the Persian kingdom did not exist. It was merely a Babylonian satrapy. It would have seemed impossible that a strong Grecian empire would rise. Only wandering tribes inhabited the Hellenic states. The city of Rome was only a little town on the banks of the Tiber. Yet God told Daniel what would come to pass.

Notice that the metals in the image deteriorate in value—gold, silver, brass and iron. This reveals the weakening in the power of each succeeding empire. Finally we will find a condition of iron mixed with brittle clay, suggesting unions attempted between incompatible partners. Name the forms of government that exist today. Do these resemble the toes of clay, "brittle" and not holding together (Daniel 2:42)?

Many ask, "When will this Rock break the iron, the bronze, the clay, the silver and the gold to pieces?" We know not the day nor hour, but the King is coming with power and great glory with all His holy angels to establish His kingdom.

The great King Nebuchadnezzar fell on his face and worshiped Daniel, and declared that his God was the God of all gods (see Daniel 2:46-47). But we find as we go on in the story that this wonderful revelation of God had little real effect upon Nebuchadnezzar. It did not bring him to his knees before God.

The Fiery Furnace

As the curtain is pulled back again we face a very tense moment (Daniel 3). Nebuchadnezzar had set up a golden image on the plain of Dura and had commanded all peoples to fall down and worship it. If any refused, he should be cast into a fiery furnace.

But three in the throng refused to obey the king. Yes, here they are again after twenty years, Shadrach, Meshach and Abednego. Spies reported their disobedience. These three knew what God had said: "You shall not make for yourself an idol...You shall not bow down to them or worship them" (Exodus 20:4-5). They were fearless in the presence of this eastern despot.

The story of the fiery furnace is a familiar one. What was the wonderful thing about that scene? Yes, the Son of God was with them. What effect did this have on Nebuchadnezzar? He was filled with great admiration for the miraculous power of the God of these men. But still he does not bow to worship God in humility. He calls Jehovah "their own God" (Daniel 3:28). Remember, God wants us to say, "My Lord, and my God." Christ said, "When ye pray, say, our Father" (Luke 11:2, *KJV*). This scene demonstrated in a most dramatic way, before the dignitaries of the far-flung empire, the power of the Most High God. Erecting an image will be repeated by the beast, the Antichrist, last head of Gentile world dominion (Revelation 13:11-15; 19:20).

The King Dreams Again

This time the king has another dream (Daniel 4:4-27). Job 33:14-17 says: "For God does speak—now one way, now another—though man may not perceive it. In a dream, in a vision of the night, when deep sleep falls on men as they slumber in their beds, he may speak in their ears and terrify them with warnings, to turn man from wrongdoing and keep him from pride."

God has spoken often to men in dreams to reveal His will when the Bible was not open to them. God spoke to Nebuchadnezzar once and gave him the image representing the Gentile kingdoms and showed him his doom. But the king did not repent. Then God spoke to him again from the fiery furnace where He revealed His power to him. But still Nebuchadnezzar's proud heart felt no repentance.

Now we find God speaking to Nebuchadnezzar for the third time in the dream of the great tree that was cut down (Daniel 4:4-27). This was a warning to Nebuchadnezzar of his coming madness. God was trying to bring this proud king to the end of himself. But a year later we see him a madman, his mind gone. He fancied himself a beast (4:28-34). All this because he had set himself up as a rival against almighty God. Hear him say, "Is not this the great Babylon I have built as the royal residence, by my mighty power and for the glory of my majesty?" (4:30).

Through his insanity, Nebuchadnezzar's eyes were opened and his conscience was touched. He confessed to the greatness of God and bore his testimony to the goodness of God (4:34). He learned that man is not the architect of his own fortune.

Reign of Belshazzar (Daniel 5; 7—8)

The following outline may help you know who Belshazzar was and where he came from:

Nebuchadnezzar—reigned to 562 B.C.

Merodach—dissolute son of Nebuchadnezzar reigned two years.

Neriglissar—brother-in-law of Merodach and his murderer, followed with a four-year reign. No successor.

Nabonidus—son of Nebuchadnezzar's second wife ascends throne in 556 B.C. Other name "Labyretus."

Belshazzar—son of Nabonidus, co-regent with him. Medes, imprisoning Nabonidus, press on to capture reveling Belshazzar and Babylon.

As chapter 5 opens, we see a great banquet hall with a thousand lords sitting about the tables. It was "ladies' night." All the king's sweethearts were there besides the thousand lords. Often the presence of ladies seems to inspire a man to do something spectacular. So as an extra feature, Belshazzar sent for the sacred golden and silver vessels his grandfather Nebuchadnezzar had stripped from the Temple in Jerusalem. He showed them just how little he regarded the God of Israel. As the people looked, behold, golden and silver vessels adorned the tables! They had been taken out of the "temple of God" in Jerusalem. The last prince of Babylon, Belshazzar, drank wine to the idols in these sacred vessels.

God shows His power in the awful handwriting on the wall. Daniel was called in to explain the meaning. The prophet fearlessly condemned this foolish and sensual young king. Read the details of the divine interruption in Daniel 5.

A bad reign came to a sudden end. "That very night Belshazzar, king of the Babylonians, was slain" (Daniel 5:30). We are not told how in the Scriptures, but we learn from historians Xenophon and Herodotus and Berosus the strange story of the fall of the great city.

Many of the tablets from Babylon tell us that the Persian army took Babylon without a battle. Four months later Cyrus entered the city. Darius probably received the kingdom from Cyrus as his vice-regent over some part of it.

During the first year of Belshazzar's reign, Daniel had a vision of four wild beasts, which symbolized the four kingdoms pictured in Nebuchadnezzar's dream (Daniel 7). Picturing them as beasts gives us a hint about the moral character of these empires, for they are represented by ferocious wild beasts. How history's wars reveal the true heart of nations!

In Nebuchadnezzar's dream-image, we have a human view of the magnificence of these kingdoms. In Daniel's dream we have God's view of the same. See who Daniel says these four beasts are in Daniel 7:17-23. The first—Babylon—was like a lion with eagle's wings. Jeremiah likened Nebuchadnezzar both to the lion and eagle (Jeremiah 49:19-22). Persia was the bear, the cruel animal who delights to kill for the sake of killing. The third was a leopard or panther, a beast of prey. His four wings portray swiftness. Here we see the rapid marches of Alexander's army and his insatiable love of conquest. In thirteen short years he had conquered the world. The fourth beast was different from all the rest. He was "terrifying and frightening and very powerful. It had large iron teeth" (Daniel 7:7).

This vision of the four beasts covers the same ground as the great image of Daniel 2. Compare them carefully.

The "little horn" coming up among the ten is the Antichrist yet to come. We see him represented in Revelation as the beast coming up out of the sea (see Revelation 13:1 and Daniel 7:15-25). The saints will be oppressed by Antichrist, the last world ruler before Christ comes. The rule of dictators is beginning to hint at the extent of the power and authority possible to this last great dictator, the Antichrist. This period terminates the great tribulation (see Revelation 5—18). This is the period during which the judgments of God are to come upon the earth for the rejection of Jesus Christ.

Two years later, in Daniel 8, we have another vision of the ram and the he-goat. Belshazzar was still on the throne. This vision includes only two of the four kingdoms, Persia and Greece (Daniel 8:20-21).

The kingdom of Medo-Persia is overthrown by the king of Greece. It contains the prophecy of the division of the latter kingdom on the death of Alexander between his four generals. Daniel had this vision at Shushan, the capital of Persia, where seventy years later the events recorded in Esther took place.

Reign of Darius (Daniel 6; 9)

One of the most difficult questions in the Old Testament is the identity of Darius the Mede (Daniel 5:31). He must have been someone appointed by Cyrus, and the statement that he "took over the kingdom" confirms this. Some think he was the father or grandfather of Cyrus, known otherwise as Astyages; and thus allowed to act as king until his death. Others think he was a commander in the army of Cyrus, named Gobryas, and the difference between this and Darius in the original would be slight.

Twenty-three years after the death of Nebuchadnezzar, his great city, Babylon, fell into the hands of the Medes.

Even under these new rulers Daniel was in a place of power. The jealousy of the other officials was aroused by the preference given to Daniel, and a plot to destroy him was quickly formed. "The administrators and the satraps tried to find grounds for charges against Daniel" (Daniel 6:4). Of course they did. He "okayed" all their tax receipts and they soon found that Daniel would not allow any graft. They had always "knocked down taxes." If Daniel didn't let them "get by," how were they going to get along with the high cost of living in Babylon? So Daniel had trouble because he would not stand in with the political crowd.

They used his religion to set their trap, with the very same result as always when men are fools enough to try to trip the Lord's faithful children (see 1 Peter 3:12-13; Deuteronomy 9:3). Remember there is always access to God through prayer in Christ. We may speak not just three times a day, but whenever the need arises. The Lord Jesus invites us to pray. (Read again John 14:13-15.)

All unconsciously the king was induced to pass the decree solely for Daniel's destruction. Just imagine, if you can, a David, an Alexander, a Caesar, a Peter the Great, a Napoleon, a Queen Victoria, or any other strong ruler letting a cabal of his court trick him into sacrificing a favorite if he or she did not want to! Signing that law without finding out what was back of it was inexcusable. When he found the trap he had walked into, he should have broken the promise. "A bad promise is better broken than kept."

The envy of these men no doubt was due to Daniel's ability and his Jewish blood. This spirit of anti-Semitism is in fulfillment of God's prophecies that the Jewish people would be hated. It continues rampant even in modern times.

Daniel's conduct in face of danger was quite deliberate. He knew he had to deny his religion or be prepared to die for it. There was nothing different in his actions. He prayed as was his custom. His example would influence the other Jews. By drawing attention to himself he might reduce the danger for others. Daniel's faith during this ordeal was glorious and just what we would expect from a man ripened in years with God.

The officials knew that the king would not lift a finger against Daniel, so they had to trap the king. What was their bait? Notice the subtle appeal to the king's pride.

The law of Medes and Persians was unchangeable. (See Esther 1:19; 8:8.) The king saw that he had been deceived, and realizing the injustice of putting Daniel to death, did his best to avoid carrying out the law.

Contrast the edict of Darius before and after Daniel's deliverance from the den of lions (Daniel 6:26-27). Over the vast realm a proclamation went, declaring the power and greatness of Daniel's God. This scene closes with Daniel's prospering during the reign of Darius, and also on to the reign of Cyrus.

Daniel was thrown into the den of lions, but he fell into the hands of the living God. The world cannot breed a lion that God cannot tame. Shutting lions' mouths of difficulty and temptation is God's specialty.

Notice that Daniel prayed with thanksgiving (Daniel 6:10; see also Philippians 4:6-7). When Daniel found out that the writing was signed, he did not fall down in terror and agony, but he praised God. "Commit your way to the Lord; trust in him and he will do this" (Psalm 37:5).

Reign of Cyrus (Daniel 10—12)

During the reign of Cyrus the decree was sent out for the captives to return and rebuild the walls of Jerusalem (Ezra 1:2-4). Daniel, now nearly ninety years old, was too aged to return. No doubt he was needed among the exiles in Babylon. Daniel had outlived all the friends and companions of his youth. Now he saw the Israelites gathering in the streets of Babylon and the aged man watched the last caravan leave the west gate of the city to return to Jerusalem. Daniel was concerned about his people. We will see how he was comforted in his perplexity. In Daniel 10 we see the vision of the glory of God.

The Last Days
In Daniel 11 we find the vision that concerns the near future of the kingdom in which Daniel was so great a personage. Three kings were yet to come in the Medo-Persian empire. Then Alexander, the mighty king of Greece, would appear (11:2-3). His empire would be divided among his four generals as had already been predicted. The course of affairs is followed down to Antiochus Epiphanes, the "little horn" of Daniel 8. His desecration of the sanctuary is again mentioned (12:11).

Beginning with Daniel 11:36, we see the description of the final "little horn" of Daniel 7.

The great tribulation follows. How is it described in Daniel 12:1? This is a time of unparalleled trouble. Our Lord spoke of it in Matthew 24:21. What does He say? Mention is made of two resurrections (Daniel 12:2). These two will be 1,000 years apart. (See Revelation 20:1-6.) The first is the resurrection of the saints at Christ's coming to life everlasting. This is followed by 1,000 years, called the millennium. Then the resurrection of the wicked to shame everlasting. "Multitudes who sleep in the dust of the earth will awake: some to everlasting life, others to shame and everlasting contempt" (Daniel 12:2). Those now that "turn many to righteousness" are given significant rewards, showing us the necessity of diligence in soul winning during our wait for Christ's return (12:3).

Daniel's Prophecy of Seventy "Weeks"

"Seventy 'sevens' are decreed for your people and your holy city to finish transgression, to put an end to sin, to atone for wickedness, to bring in everlasting righteousness, to seal up vision and prophecy and to anoint the most holy.

Know and understand this: From the issuing of the decree to restore and rebuild Jerusalem until the Anointed

One, the ruler, comes, there will be seven 'sevens,' and sixty-two 'sevens.' It will be rebuilt with streets and a trench, but in times of trouble.

After the sixty-two 'sevens,' the Anointed One will be cut off and will have nothing. The people of the ruler who will come will destroy the city and the sanctuary. The end will come like a flood: War will continue until the end, and desolations have been decreed.

He will confirm a covenant with many for one 'seven.' In the middle of the 'seven' he will put an end to sacrifice and offering. And on a wing [of the temple] he will set up an abomination that causes desolation, until the end that is decreed is poured out on him" (Daniel 9:24-27).

"Seventy sevens" (Hebrew: *shabu'im shibim)* is translated "seventy weeks" in the *KJV*, a poor English equivalent. The term probably means seventy periods of seven years. If there are seventy seven-year periods, this is 70×7, or 490 years.

Scripture divides these seventy sevens into three divisions (Daniel 9:24-27) with a parenthetic time lapse for the present "Gentile rule."

The first "seven weeks"—forty-nine years-began at the command to build and restore Jerusalem under Ezra and Nehemiah.

The second "sixty-two weeks"—434 years-began at the building of the wall of Jerusalem, and continues to the Crucifixion. Christ is "cut off and will have nothing" (Daniel 9:25-26). At this point, after 483 years, the clock of Israel's national life stops.

("Gentile rule"—an unknown number of years, intervenes after the sixty-ninth week. We are in this period now, awaiting the coming of Christ.)

The last, or "seventieth week"—seven years-not yet begun, are years during which God deals with Israel exclusively. Beginning after the coming of Christ, Antichrist takes power, makes covenant with the Jews, breaks the covenant after half the week is up. This ushers in the time of trouble of Daniel 12:1—the Great Tribulation of Revelation. When will the seventieth week begin?

Books of the
Minor Prophets
of The Old Testament

Hosea • Joel • Amos • Obadiah • Jonah
Micah • Nahum • Habakkuk • Zephaniah
Haggai • Zechariah • Malachi

Key Events of the Books of the Minor Prophets

Books of the Minor Prophets: A Future Hope

By the time most of the minor prophets were writing ① (the seventh to the fifth centuries before Christ), the promise God had made to David of an everlasting kingdom was already at least 300 years old. These prophets foresaw tremendous destruction ② and sorrow for God's chosen people and for nations that would not humble themselves before God. Even so, they had faith that God would make good on His promises and send a Deliverer ③ for His people and for those nations who would bow before Him.

Chapter 22

Understanding
Hosea, Joel, Amos

*Jesus Christ, Healer of the Backslider;
Restorer; Heavenly Husbandman*

Selected Bible Readings

Sunday:	Israel's Willful Ignorance (Hosea 4)
Monday:	Israel's Glorious Future (Hosea 3; 14)
Tuesday:	Punishment and Blessing (Joel 2)
Wednesday:	The Restoration of Israel (Joel 3)
Thursday:	Personal Admonitions (Amos 3:1-7; 4:6-12)
Friday:	The Prophet's Intercession (Amos 7:1-17; 8:1-7)
Saturday:	Future Kingdom Blessings (Amos 9:1-15)

Understanding Hosea

With the study of Hosea's prophecy we enter upon twelve books known as the minor prophets. Remember the difference between the major and minor prophets is not a matter of importance, but of the amount of material written.

Hosea was sent to the ten northern tribes called Israel. He prophesied in the reign of Jeroboam II of Israel. He lived in this Northern Kingdom when the splendors of Jeroboam's brilliant reign of forty-one years were beginning to fade into the black midnight of Israel's captivity. He prophesied during the eighth century B.C. This was a stirring time in the world's history. Rome and Carthage were both founded around this period. Phoenician sea traffic founded the latter great city. The big Phoenician west-bound ships made their terminus Tarshish, a Phoenician colony in southern Spain. But during the time of Hosea they ran north-ward to the tin mines of Cornwall.

Another important fact in this period was the religious refor-mation Siddartha Gautama (563-483 B.C.) introduced in India, which gave birth to Buddhism. It was a time of commotion and change. It presented many things akin to those of the sixteenth century after Christ.

Hosea's contemporaries were Amos, Isaiah and Micah. He has been called the Jeremiah of the Northern Kingdom. Remember, Jeremiah prophesied to Judah. In Hosea, Israel means the ten tribes that formed the Northern Kingdom. Judah means the tribes of Judah and Benjamin that formed the Southern Kingdom. Hosea was not trained in a seminary (school of the prophets), but he was a layman called by God to give the distinct message to Israel that God loved them.

Israel's Unfaithfulness (Hosea 1—3)

The hero of this book, Hosea, is one of the greatest lovers in all literature. We find his love so strong that even the worst actions of an unfaithful wife could not kill it. Read Hosea 1:1 for a bit of the personal history of the prophet. We hear God speaking His first words to Hosea Himself (1:2). The people had given no heed to Amos. Hosea knew that the country was due for a downfall, but they were not disposed to listen to him.

Turn to 2 Kings 15—17 and read the page of history that covers the period of the prophet. As we have already stated, it was a very unsettled time. Sin was rampant. The golden age of Jeroboam II was passing and a dark cloud hung over Israel. On the death of Jeroboam, six kings followed in quick succession. Within twenty years, four were assassinated. About the middle of Hosea's ministry, a large part of the nation was carried away by the Assyrians. At the end of Hosea's life, the kingdom of Israel came to an end with the fall of Samaria. The prophet lived to see his prophecies fulfilled.

We know little about Hosea other than that he had a very sad home life. The book pictures this man as gentle, frank and affectionate. He had a deep loving nature that made him attached to his home.

A Strange Love Story

As chapter 1 opens, we see a young man marrying a girl unworthy of him. He loved her truly. God told him to do something that would have been very repulsive to him. What was it (Hosea 1:2-3)? It was a severe test. But as in the case of Isaiah, he was to be a sign for Israel.

Hosea is told to marry a woman worthless in character, in fact, a harlot. God was using this for a sign to His people of how they remained the object of Jehovah's love in spite of their sinfulness. This all seems very strange to us. But God was making this picture of His redeeming grace. Grace is unmerited favor. Here we see Israel so undeserving of Jehovah's love, yet still He is lavishing it upon them. God has not chosen the righteous but sinners. "But God demonstrates his own love for us in this: While we were still sinners, Christ died for us" (Romans 5:8). God's dealings with Israel picture His dealings with us now. "These things happened to them as examples and were written down as warnings for us, on whom the fulfillment of the ages has come" (1 Corinthians 10:11).

Hosea obeyed God and married Gomer (Hosea 1:3). His name was hers. Home, reputation, God's favor, comfort, were Gomer's. All that he had he gave her. In return, Hosea's name, domestic reputation, love, were all sacrificed on the altar of a shameful and worthless woman. How like our Lord Jesus this is! He not only came to us while we were yet in sin, but He also died the death of shame on Calvary for us that all He had might be ours. (See Titus 2:14.)

Gomer ran away from home and left her young husband, Hosea, with two little sons and a daughter to care for. Lured away by the sin about her, she fell into the moral cesspool of the day and finally was carried off a slave. Through it all, Hosea was true to her. Still loving her, he tried everything to win her back to a happy family life. But she would not. What a sad picture of a person's stubbornness! What a wonderful picture of God's love!

Just as Hosea was married to an unfaithful bride, Gomer, so

God was married to unfaithful Israel. This experience of Hosea helped him to understand God's heart of love as He yearned over wayward Israel to come home to Him. No doubt there were tears in his voice, for there was tragedy in his life. He had thrown himself wholly into his mission.

"Who best can suffer, Best can do" (John Milton, 1608-1674).

God's Bride

God frequently uses marriage to symbolize His relation to Israel. "As a bridegroom rejoices over his bride, so will your God rejoice over you" (Isaiah 62:5). "For I am your husband" (Jeremiah 3:14). Israel is Jehovah's bride while the Church is the Lamb's bride. God said of Israel, "I will betroth you to me forever" (Hosea 2:19). God had been true to His bride, the Jews. He had loved them and protected them and lavished every gift upon them. But they left God and went after other gods. They disobeyed His laws. Like Hosea's wife, they had broken their marriage vows and had fallen into slavery, sin and shame. Israel, like Gomer, had forgotten who had given her past blessings in abundance. (See Hosea 2:8.)

In his book *Whatever Became of Sin?*, Karl Menninger, the famed psychiatrist, defines sin in a rather penetrating manner as "a refusal of the love of others." Most important of all, sin is a refusal of the love of God (see Psalm 51:4).

There are differing interpretations of this part of the book of Hosea. Some believe that Hosea was told by God to marry a sinful woman, which he did; others, that God told Hosea to marry a woman who did not go into sin until after the marriage; still others, that this experience of Hosea's was only a vision, not an actual experience. In any case, the undefeatable love of a true husband, to whom God likens Himself, is shown; and Israel's strange, sad, persistent backsliding is revealed.

Backsliding a Historical Fact

But why should Israel's backsliding seem strange to us? Isn't it exactly what we all know about by personal experience? The history of people has been a history of backsliding, and will continue to be so.

Creation of people (Genesis 1:28): People started at the top but soon they were moving toward the bottom.

Fall of people: People went steadily downhill from the expulsion from Eden (Genesis 3:23) to the time of the flood.

Human government (Genesis 8:20): People went downhill until they tried to ignore God in exalting themselves (11:4) and the judgment of the confusion of tongues fell upon them.

Promise to Abraham (Genesis 12:1): Israel, God's chosen people, went down until they found themselves at the bottom of the hill in bondage in Egypt.

Mosaic Law given (Exodus 19:8): Israel, during its entire national history, had its ups and downs. Hosea's day pictures it.

The Word shows us that until the end, people will sin, will break God's heart of love; but a wonderful and patient God has endured this through the centuries.

In Hosea 3:4, the present state of the Jewish people is described. Read it! Read it! Ever since the destruction of Jerusalem by Titus (A.D. 70), the Jewish people have answered the description given here by Hosea. They have been a nation of wanderers over the face of the earth, going from nation to nation, and city to city. They are scattered, despised and often hated people. (See Deuteronomy 28:63-65.) But notice what is happening to them today. Hosea 3:5 describes the Jewish people's glorious future. King, prince, sacrifice, image, ephod and teraphim all are then restored in Christ.

Israel's National Sin and Chastisement (Hosea 4—10)

Here we hear a voice from the north where Israel dwelt (Hosea 4:1). Two hundred years before, the ten tribes had seceded from Judah and set up an independent kingdom called Israel. They began immediately worshiping idols. God had sent Elijah, then Elisha, to warn them, but in vain. They refused to return to God. Now we hear a new voice. It is Hosea! "Come, let us return to the Lord" (Hosea 6:1) is the much-needed cry of the prophet. His message is: Return to God and He will return to you.

Hosea, whose name means "salvation," was poet laureate to the king. But he was more than that. He was God's voice to the people. They did not care to hear his message, for his appeal was to a backslidden nation in behalf of a God grieved by His children's sins. It is well to remember that the names of Israel and Ephraim are closely associated with sin and backsliding. Both names are used thirty-seven times in this book. "I know all about Ephraim; Israel is not hidden from me. Ephraim, you have now turned to prostitution; Israel is corrupt" (5:3).

It is not more liberty we need today, but more loyalty. Do not give God ready-made plans for Him to bless. Do not make your plans and then come to Him for approval. Let Him make the plans. Israel had foolishly made their own decisions. The people had become stiff-necked. God will not do anything with a rebellious spirit and a defiant will.

God's Word is a mirror. What is a mirror really for? Is it to see how well you look? No! I believe it is to see the flaws—to see what is wrong so you may correct it. "How can a young man keep his way pure? By living according to your word" (Psalm 119:9). "Hear the word of the Lord, you Israelites, because the Lord has a charge to bring against you who live in the land" (Hosea 4:1).

Israel's blacklist of sin:
   No faithfulness, no love, no acknowledgment of God—4:1
   Prostitution, drunkenness—4:11
   Murder—5:2
   Deceit, thievery, banditry—7:1
   Cheating and defrauding—12:7.

God's figures for sin:
   An adulterous wife—3:1
   A patron of prostitutes and a drunkard—4:11
   A stubborn ("backsliding," *KJV*) heifer—4:16
   Marauders/robbers—6:9
   Adulterers—7:4
   Hot as an oven—7:7
   A cake not turned (half-baked)—7:8
   Like an easily deceived dove—7:11
   Like a faulty bow—7:16

Swallowed up—8:8
A worthless thing—8:8
A wild donkey—8:9.

Israel's Hope (Hosea 11—14)

Light breaks over these last chapters. They give us a picture of Israel's ultimate blessings in the future kingdom. We get a glimpse into God's heart of love when He, as a father, says, "When Israel was a child, I loved him, and out of Egypt I called my son" (Hosea 11:1).

God's Choice

As God looked over the vast and glittering expanse of empire, He did not choose Israel for His people because they were the greatest or richest of the nations of the world (Deuteronomy 7:6-8). He rather chose a weak, unattractive slave child to be the object of His love and care and blessings (Hosea 11:1).

There lay Babylon in all her glory. She was then a strong and mighty nation and gave great promise of a powerful future. To the south was the glory of Egypt, wrapped in the rich and jeweled web of centuries we are just now unwrapping. Even today our eyes are dazzled as we look on their splendors. The Hittites, to the north, had a culture and power, and the ships of the Phoenicians were plowing the seas. But God did not choose these. He chose a slave child in Egypt who was making bricks without straw in his awful bondage, upon whom He could lavish His love and blessing (Exodus 3).

We can never understand God's choices. He chooses the weak things of the world to confound the things that are mighty. (See 1 Corinthians 1:27.) Whenever people love God, it is because He loved them first (1 John 4:19).

Israel's Sin

But Israel, the child who had been outwardly adopted in history at the time of the Exodus from Egypt, began to grow persistently disobedient and rebellious. The more the prophets warned the people, the farther they went away from God. They showed no gratitude to God for all the blessings of their land. But in their freedom they forgot God and fell into sin and idolatry and were plunging into captivity (Hosea 11:2). Israel finished her training in the slave markets of Assyria and Babylon. (Read Hosea 4:6-7.)

God has been good to us and set His love upon us and has sent us prophets and teachers and put us in the midst of resources and luxury. But the more they warn us the more we are prone to turn away, and the greater our education and learning the more sufficient we become unto ourselves. Nations today are educating themselves away from God. So did Israel. God taught Israel that when people refuse light, the light is withdrawn. (See Hosea 5:6.)

We must understand God's attitude toward sin. He says, "The wages of sin is death" (Romans 6:23). "Do not be deceived: God cannot be mocked. A man reaps what he sows" (Galatians 6:7).

God reveals to His children through Hosea that knowledge always creates responsibility. This truth is taught also by the apostle Peter. He says, "It would have been better for them not to have known the way of righteousness, than to have known it and then to turn their backs on the sacred command that was passed on to them" (2 Peter 2:21). It is a dangerous thing to play with God's grace.

The Grace of God

We find grace abounding in the Old Testament as well as in the New.

Jehovah says to Israel here, "I led them with cords of human kindness, with ties of love" (Hosea 11:4). Christ drew us with cords of a man when He became man and died for us. "But I, when I am lifted up from the earth, will draw all men to myself" (John 12:32).

God has agonized over His rebellious people and will not give them up. His mercy is kindled and He says, "I will heal their waywardness and love them freely" (Hosea 14:4). "But where sin increased, grace increased all the more" (Romans 5:20).

God has threatened Israel with His wrath, but now God offers her grace. God appeals to Israel to return and repent (Hosea 14:1-3). Then He gives her a promised blessing (14:4-8).

In Hosea 1:11, God tells Israel that one day Judah and Israel shall be gathered and have one head. They are looking for this Messiah to come who will be their ruler. God again promises this in Hosea 3. Read Hosea 9:17 to see the condition of the Jewish people today—"wanderers among the nations." God will do more than forgive their backsliding; He will cure them and remove the cause.

Hosea 14 is the best chapter in the Bible for backsliders. Read the wonderful words of the Lord to backsliding Israel in Hosea 14:4. "I will heal their waywardness and love them freely." God's great heart is bursting with love, but our sins keep Him from telling us all that is there. As with Israel, you may know the joy of barriers broken down and love poured out. "I will be like the dew to Israel; he will blossom like a lily" (14:5). The dew speaks of the presence of the Holy Spirit. See how God pictures His abiding joy in His people after they are healed.

Understanding Joel

Joel is considered by some to be one of the earliest of all the prophets whose writings have come down to us. He possibly would have known both Elijah and Elisha in his youth.

His personal history is stated in one verse, "The word of the Lord that came to Joel son of Pethuel" (Joel 1:1). His name means "Jehovah is my God." His ministry was to Judah. Remember, Hosea prophesied to Israel.

Joel has been called the prophet of "religious revival." He knew that revival must follow repentance. "A rent heart is followed by a rent veil and heaven." He tried to bring his people to this place. We will find access to the throne of grace and know the presence of the Holy Spirit when we truly repent.

The land of Israel had just suffered a terrible plague of locusts that had devoured every green thing, leaving only desolation. Joel believed that this had been a judgment sent by God because of the sin of His people. He was the first to prophesy the outpouring of the Holy Spirit upon all flesh (2:28). Joel appears just a little before Hosea, only he speaks to the Southern Kingdom of Judah, while Hosea speaks to the northern tribes. His message is to us all today.

The Plague—The Warning (Joel 1)

Appalling famine, caused by an awful plague of locusts, followed
by a prolonged drought, devastated the land. People and flocks
were dying for lack of food and water.

Using the judgment of a plague of locusts he called his people
of Judah to repentance. He wanted to spare them from greater
judgments at the hands of hostile armies. The locust was a type
and forerunner of the devastation they would bring.

Graphically, he described the plague, calling the old men to
confirm the fact that there had never been one like it before (Joel
1:2). Drunkards felt the effect of it, for the vines had been
destroyed (1:5). Priests had no meat-offering, nor drink-offering
of wine to offer (1:9). Cattle and sheep cried in the fields (1:20).
Joel urged the people to call a fast (1:13). Then he continued to
describe the plague.

Joel called the people to consider the cause of the calamity.
They must mourn with true penitence if they wished to be spared
further judgment (2:12-17). Desperate, they were ready to listen to
anyone who could explain their plight. It was a great hour for the
preacher, for now, in their extremity, people would turn to God.

The Fast—The Promise (Joel 2)

The blast of the ram's horn calling an assembly for a great fast
opens this chapter (Joel 2:1). Everyone is there—old and young
alike. Even brides and bridegrooms on their wedding day attend
(2:16). The priests come in black sackcloth, and bow to the ground
and cry to God within the sanctuary. "Rend your heart and not
your garments. Return to the Lord your God, for he is gracious
and compassionate" (2:13). It was an event to bring the people
back to God.

The locusts had made an Eden into a desolate wilderness (2:3).
For one who has not seen it, an army of locusts is an incredible
thing. They fill the air and darken the sun like an eclipse (2:2).
They spread for miles over the land. Armies of "soldiers" with
leaders in front advance, destroying everything that is green. In

a few minutes every leaf and blade is destroyed. Others following strip the bark from the trees (1:6-7). The people dig trenches and kindle fires and beat and burn to death heaps of insects, but the effort is utterly useless. A land that has been devastated by locusts takes years to recover (1:17-20). Their flight is heard for miles, much like a roaring fire (2:5). The land over which they pass looks as if it had been fire swept (2:3). After the country is stripped they go into cities and, like mailed horsemen, they march into houses and consume everything that can be consumed (2:4,7-9). God's promise, "I will repay you for the years the locusts have eaten" (2:25), becomes more graphic in the mind when one sees the desolation wrought by the consuming insects.

The Promise of Pentecost

The prophet assures the people that God will indeed send both temporal mercies (Joel 2:18-27) and spiritual blessings (2:28-32). Yes, and God will send deliverance from the sky! "And afterward, I will pour out my Spirit on all people. Your sons and daughters will prophesy, your old men will dream dreams, your young men will see visions. Even on my servants, both men and women, I will pour out my Spirit in those days" (2:28-29). Here is the prophecy of Pentecost.

Spiritual deliverance is the great central promise of the book of Joel. Other prophets have foretold details concerning the Lord's life on earth, and even His future reign. To Joel was committed the privilege of telling that He would pour out His Spirit upon all flesh. He tells us that the blessing will flow forth from Jerusalem (2:32; 3:18). This prophecy we are definitely told was fulfilled at Pentecost. Peter said, "No, this is what was spoken by the prophet Joel" (Acts 2:16). Read all of Acts 2.

There is a lesson for us today. The Church is in a desolate condition. It has been laid waste by many spiritual foes, well described in Joel 1:4. There are famine and drought on all sides. The call goes to Christians today to go into the dust before the Lord in the true repentance of heart. This repentance must begin with ministers and elders. If we will return unto the Lord, He will fulfill His promise to us by His outpouring of the Holy Spirit and then "I will repay you for the years the locusts have eaten" (Joel 2:25). This great outpouring on Israel is future (Ezekiel 36:23-33). The great need in pulpit and pew today is the power of the Holy Spirit.

The Day of the Lord

"The day of the Lord," spoken of five times in this short book, refers to judgment. It tells of a series of judgments—the present locusts, the armies of invasion that were about to come as a scourge of God upon the land, and the final day of the Lord described in the third chapter of Joel. "The day of the Lord" is the period of time from the return of the Lord in glory until the new heavens and the new earth (See Isaiah 2:17-20; 3:7-18; 4:1-2; 13:6-9; Jeremiah 46:10; Malachi 4:5; 1 Corinthians 5:5; 1 Thessalonians 5:2; 2 Thessalonians 2:2; 2 Peter 3:10). "The day of the Lord" is at least one thousand years in length. (Read Revelation 20:4.)

The Blessing—The Future (Joel 3)

Enemies—Overthrown—3:1-15
Jerusalem—Delivered—3:16-17
Land—Blessed—3:18
Judah—Restored—3:19-21

Only God could have told Joel of the return of the Jews from captivity. Joel not only saw the return from Babylon, but also the last regathering of the Jews from among the Gentile nations. He also tells of the judgment of the nations after the battle of Armageddon (3:2-7). (Read Matthew 25:32 and Revelation 19:17-21.) The people's day of decision is over. God's hour of destiny has arrived.

After Israel is restored and the nations of the earth are judged (Joel 3:1-2) then will the everlasting kingdom be set up (3:20). Once again the Holy Land, the land of promise, will be the center of power and the gathering place of the nations for judgment. Christ will return to establish His rule as sovereign. God will dwell in Zion (3:17).

Understanding Amos

Amos was from Tekoa, a small town about twelve miles south of Jerusalem. He was not a prophet nor the son of a prophet (Amos 7:14). He was not a priest nor a member of the prophets school. He was a sheepherder and dresser of the sycamore trees. He must have been educated, for his book shows literary skill. Perhaps he traveled extensively selling his wool. The places he mentions may have been scenes of his visits.

In Amos, we find one of many instances in the Bible of God calling a man when he was occupied in his daily work (1:1). God called him, shepherd's crook in hand, and sent him forth to gather his straying people. Remember, David was caring for his sheep and Gideon was at the threshing floor when they received their commissions.

On the wild uplands of Judah, beyond Tekoa, Amos received his training as a prophet straight from the hand of God. His beautiful writing abounds with illustrations from his mountain home. Like David, he had gazed on the stars and looked beyond to their Creator. He was not a courtier like Isaiah, nor a priest like Jeremiah, but just an ordinary working man. Though a native of Judah, he prophesied in and about Israel.

Amos was not the only prophet of his day. God had sent a great galaxy of messengers to save His people from the destruction they were inevitably facing. No doubt, as a boy Amos had known Jonah and possibly Elisha. Hosea was his coworker. These men surely knew each other well. Maybe they had gone on evangelistic campaigns together. When Amos's work was coming to a close, Isaiah and Micah appeared. These men, when boys, might have heard Amos preach on one of his tours. These younger prophets would have received much from this champion of Jehovah.

Amos prophesied while Uzziah was on the throne of Judah and Jeroboam II was king of Israel. This was a time of great prosperity. The old boundaries of the kingdom of David were gained back. Money poured in and armies were victorious. Amos and Hosea were prophets to Israel (Northern Kingdom) and Isaiah and Micah to the Southern Kingdom of Judah.

Under these two kings mentioned, the two kingdoms reached the summit of their prosperity (2 Chronicles 26 and 2 Kings 14:25). Assyria had not yet risen as a conquering world power. The idea of the approaching doom of their kingdoms seemed utterly improbable to Israel. They were enjoying a period of peace. The surrounding nations were not strong enough to give them trouble. (See Amos 6:1-13.) All they thought of was pleasure and having a good time (2:6-8; 5:11-12; 6:4-6). God tried to arouse His people to a sense of their danger, hence He sent two witnesses, Hosea and Amos.

Amos feared God so much that he feared no one else at all. A modern student of Amos says, "Amos proclaimed a message so far ahead of his time that most of the human race, and a large part of all Christendom have not yet caught up with it." The herdsman of Tekoa's daring words date back some 800 years before our Lord.

Such courage was no more heeded in Israel's time than it is today. Of course, we will find among the evils Amos denounced some of the very same that prevail in our day. Here you find his voice raised against intemperance, in a far larger sense than merely excessive use of wine. Were he speaking primarily to our day, he would raise his voice in thundering tones against this abuse that has increased practices of intemperance unknown and undreamed of by the luxurious lives of Israel. But the secret of all such sin is revealed in Amos's words, because the children of Israel have rejected the law of Jehovah and have not kept His statutes.

The law of our beloved country will be kept when we learn to keep the law of God. The law of God is fulfilled in love.

Amos was humble—in not hiding his station in life.

Amos was wise—in not preaching over the heads of the people.

Amos was clever—in catching people's fancy by judging their enemies first.

Amos was fearless—in not tickling the ear but telling the truth.

Amos was faithful—"Thus saith the Lord" was his message.

This raw young herdsman, Amos, had a certain rugged frankness about him that was refreshing. He always hit straight from the shoulder (1:2). He didn't fail to tell even King Jeroboam II what he should do. God wanted someone to bear His message courageously, and Amos did not fail Him. Israel needed a prophet who would tear the scales from their eyes and let them know the sure consequences of their idolatry, and Amos fearlessly set them forth. God abhors sin. The horrible cruelty of sin must be punished.

Jeroboam had brought Israel to the zenith of her power. The kingdom was flourishing and was at peace with her enemies. About the most unpopular man would be a "calamity howler," and Amos knew that is what they would call him if he delivered God's message. David before Goliath could not have been more courageous than Amos before Jeroboam, the idolater who caused Israel to commit sin (1 Kings 14:13; 15:26). Hear him in some of his unique figures of speech.

"The archer will not stand his ground" (2:15), Amos prophesied. Jeroboam's stalwart archers were accustomed to press forward upon the enemy. They never gave in. What foolishness to talk of the unerring archers of Israel failing to stand anywhere at anytime!

"The fleet-footed soldier will not get away" Amos went on. What? Shall Israel's fleet-footed runners be using their speed to run away from battle? Has this insolent prophet gone crazy?

"And the horseman will not save his life" thunders the messenger. There were no horsemen in all the world like Jeroboam's invincible cavalry.

But the climax is reached in these words of Amos: "This is what the Lord says: 'As a shepherd saves from the lion's mouth only two leg bones or a piece of an ear, so will the Israelites be saved, those who sit in Samaria on the edge of their beds and in Damascus on their couches'" (3:12). This sounded like mockery! The idea of powerful Israel being likened to a poor sheep—or rather the fragments of a poor eaten sheep!

Yet this is what came to pass! In less than fifty years, Israel was utterly destroyed, and the pitiful remnant of her people was not even as the leg of a sheep taken from the jaw of the devourer. Such is the picture of God's abhorrence of sin.

To every question about why great empires have fallen, the answer is sin. The secret of a great person's undoing is sin. Let Amos help you see sin in its true light.

If a ship at sea follows a wrong course, what happens? Yes, some sort of trouble, and wreckage in the end. But what of a captain that follows a wrong course knowingly? Something is wrong with his mind. No wonder prophets like Amos spoke plainly in warning people about the wrong course of sin.

Judgment Against Nations (Amos 1—2)

This simple country preacher left his home in Judah and traveled twenty-two miles to Bethel in the Northern Kingdom to preach to the kingdom of Israel. Why did God send him to Bethel? Surely Jerusalem needed his ministry. But God wanted the kingdom of Israel to have a strong word of warning. Bethel was the religious capital of the Northern Kingdom. Idolatry was there. They had substituted calf worship for Jehovah. The people felt no need of preaching. (See 1 Kings 12:25-33.)

Amos started his preaching to the assembled crowds at Bethel, for it was a sacred feast day, by proclaiming the Lord's judgment upon six neighboring nations—Damascus (Syria), Gaza (Philistia), Tyre (Phoenicia), Edom, Ammon and Moab. Then he came nearer home and pronounced judgment against Judah (Amos 2:4), and against Israel itself (2:6) and finally the whole nation (3:12). Amos's approach was clever. We are always willing to hear of our enemy's doom. Our own is harder to swallow, but we are forced to take it with our enemy.

When the people doubted his authority, Amos gave a series of seven questions to show that the Lord revealed His secret to him. Therefore he must prophesy (3:3-8).

Amos denounced the sin of Israel more graphically than Hosea (chap. 2). He spoke of their careless ease and luxury, their oppression of the poor, the lying and cheating, and worse than all, their hypocrisy in worship. The Lord grieved over His people not heeding His warnings. "'Yet you have not returned to me,' declares the Lord" (4:6). Then the invitation, "Seek me and live" (5:4).

The book opens with judgments on the nations surrounding Israel:

Damascus was threatened because it had invaded Israel (Amos 1:3; 2 Kings 10:32-33)

Gaza and Tyre for conspiracy with Edom in its invasion of

Judah (Amos 1:6,9; 2 Chronicles 21:16-17; 28:18)

Edom for continuing hostility (Amos 1:11; compare Obadiah 10-12)

Ammon for attacking Gilead (Amos 1:13)

Moab for pagan practices (Amos 2:1; 2 Kings 3:27)

Judah for neglect of God's law (Amos 2:4; 2 Chronicles 3—19; 2 Kings 25:9)

Israel for her unrighteousness (Amos 2:6; 2 Kings 17:17-23).

The nations of the world, no matter how powerful they may be, cannot withstand the judgments of God. God sets up kingdoms and brings them down. The mighty power of the Pharaohs has come to naught. Napoleon thought he could rule the world but he languished in Saint Helena. The Kaiser thought he could act independently of God and he was soon brought low. In World War II, there were tyrants who thought they could stamp out God's chosen people and set themselves up as rulers of the earth, but hinderers of God's ultimate plan are always brought low (Psalm 2).

Judgment Against Israel (Amos 3—6)

Amos was called to tell of certain punishment (Amos 3). If people will reject the repeated warning of God, they must be punished (chap. 5).

Amos told the people of Israel they were greedy, unjust, unclean and profane (2:6-12), and that they defended and excused themselves on the ground that they were God's chosen people (3:2). He reminded them that this made their sin the greater. The Israelites looked at their relationship to God differently. They saw it as merely an outward and formal thing. They boasted that they were the chosen nation and no real evil could befall them. We see many professing Christians today in the same danger. They imagine their salvation is secured by their being members of a church. They are conferring a favor upon God and He cannot condemn them. (Read Amos 5:21,23-24.)

The first of God's punishments concerns the sins of six of the heathen nations that surround Israel. Then the prophet passes on to Judah and Israel. The sin of Judah had been her contempt of God's law, expressed in her idolatry. Only during the exile was

Judah freed of this sin. The punishment of Judah was fulfilled in the destruction of Jerusalem by Nebuchadnezzar (2:5).

Amos condemned Israel. Israel was a chosen nation. She knew God's law. Therefore her sin was the greater. Amos told the people about their injustice in the administration of the law. They "sell the righteous for silver, and the needy for a pair of sandals" (2:6). He enumerated their evil oppression. They had forgotten righteousness. The rich were cruel and they longed to see the poor oppressed. Even among Christians today we find wealth often counts more than character. Nothing is more dangerous in the Church than influence and power given to those who have wealth but no Christian scruples.

Amos called the women of his day "cows of Bashan" because they only cared for luxury and worldly pleasures (4:1). This is the prophet's picture of the cruel, heartless, brainless women—a herd of cows, who are heavy, heedless animals treading on all in their way as they seek to gratify their appetites.

Even the religious sacrifices and feasts of the people became an abomination. God said, "I hate...your religious feasts" (5:21). When they made their pilgrimages from Gilgal to Bethel, they only sinned the more, for it was merely an outward form mixed with idolatry (5:4-6). God demands conduct worthy of Himself, not just empty sacrifices. Amos called attention to how God sent drought, plagues and earthquakes. Still they did not repent.

God always warns before a punishment, yes, and offers a way of escape. God denounces sin, but He offers a remedy for sin. Israel's rejection of repeated warnings should lead her to prepare for God's judgment (chap. 5). If Israel had sought the Lord, the "day of the Lord" spoken of in Amos 5:20 would not have overtaken her. She did not seek Him and Assyrian fighters ushered in that day.

Amos tells of Israel's coming judgment in five visions:

1. The devouring locusts—7:1-3. In the first vision, the prophet sees green fields, and, "This is what the Sovereign Lord showed me: He was preparing swarms of locusts after the king's share had been harvested and just as the second crop was coming up. When they had

stripped the land clean, I cried out, 'Sovereign Lord, forgive! How can Jacob survive? He is so small!' So the Lord relented. 'This will not happen,' the Lord said."

2. The consuming fire—7:4-6. In this vision, fire so terrible as to consume the waters and the land is seen. Amos prays: "'Sovereign Lord, I beg you, stop! How can Jacob survive? He is so small!' So the Lord relented. 'This will not happen either,' the Sovereign Lord said."

3. The searching plumb line—7:7-11. In this vision, Amos sees God measuring the city for destruction. The measuring revealed how far out of line Israel was. This time Amos has not the heart even to pray. Israel's judgment was certain—"I will spare them no longer."

4. The basket of ripe fruit—8:1-14. The Lord says, "The time is ripe for my people Israel; I will spare them no longer." The basket revealed the sad truth that Israel, like a basket of overripe fruit, looked fine, outwardly, but was rotting at the heart. The guilty nation was "ripe" for judgment.

5. The Lord at the altar—9:1-10. The last vision shows God standing upon the altar, bidding Amos to break the doorposts and shower the fragments over the people's heads. All the worshipers are to be scattered and slain by the sword. This speaks of final dispersion. The visions end with judgment, but God closes the book with a bright outlook.

Visions Regarding the Future (Amos 7—9)

We do not know how long Amos preached in Bethel, but we know that throngs heard his fearless message. When he spoke of the doom of the surrounding nations, the people were drawn to him and they cheered him to the last echo.

Then Amaziah, the priest of Bethel, could not stand up against Amos's preaching. So, backed by the king, the priest rebuked Amos. Listen to the report he sent to the king: "Amos is raising a conspiracy against you in the very heart of Israel. The land cannot bear all his words. For this is what Amos is saying: 'Jeroboam will die by the sword, and Israel will surely go into exile, away from their native land'" (Amos 7:10-11). Amaziah told Amos to go back and mind his own business.

Amos was silenced by the false prophet. He was driven from Israel. Freedom of speech was not given the true prophet of God. Neither Elijah nor Amos was safe in Israel. When Amos found that Israel would not hear him, he returned to Judah and put his writings in a book so all the people could read and understand it.

Amos, as do most of the prophets, tells us of a bright future for God's chosen people. The whole land will once more be a kingdom under the house of David (9:11-12). The Tabernacle of David, now torn down, shall be rebuilt (Acts 15:16-17). Israel shall be restored to her land and prosper. A happy people shall dwell in a happy land.

Always keep in mind that the Jewish people who have been scattered over the face of the world are being gathered back to their land of promise. National prosperity will again flourish. Jerusalem shall be the capital of a mighty kingdom. Converted Israel shall be God's witnesses (9:13-15).

People need such dealing as Amos gives at times when sin abounds. We get to be too tender and gentle with the common sins of the people. We forget how to denounce; we lose the power of righteous indignation.

Not so with Amos, plumb line prophet that he was. The crooked wall always hates the straight line. So people hated Amos. They will hate us if we speak out. Nevertheless, learn to speak, no matter what it costs. Recall here the Man with the scourge of small cords purging the Temple (John 2:13-16).

Repentance is not just an easy or jaunty turning to God and saying, "I'm sorry." Not even the truest repentance can remit sin. Redemption is costly. Christ has paid the price. Salvation is the establishment of a personal relationship between the individual person and God. Nothing can take the place of that. (See John 1:12.)

Chapter 23

Understanding Obadiah, Jonah, Micah

*Jesus Christ Our Savior; Our Resurrection and Life;
Witness Against Rebellious Nations*

Selected Bible Readings

Sunday:	Doom and Deliverance (Obadiah 1—21)
Monday:	A Fish Story (Jonah 1—2)
Tuesday:	An Obedient Prophet (Jonah 3—4)
Wednesday:	A Message to the People (Micah 1—2)
Thursday:	A Message to the Rulers (Micah 3—4)
Friday:	The Birth and Rejection of the King (Micah 5)
Saturday:	A Message to the Chosen People (Micah 6—7)

Understanding Obadiah

Petra is one of the wonders of the world. It was a city unique of its kind among the works of humans. It perched like an "eagle's nest" (Obadiah 4) amid inaccessible mountain fastnesses. Its only approach was through a deep rock cleft more than a mile long with massive cliffs more than 700 feet high rising on either side. The city was able to withstand any invasion. We are told that its temples numbered a thousand. They were cut out of the pink rock on the side of the massive cliffs. The dwellings were mostly caves hewn out of the soft red sandstone (Obadiah 3,6) and placed where you can hardly believe it possible for a human foot to climb.

South of the Dead Sea and on the western border of the Arabian plateau lies a range of precipitous red sandstone heights known as Mount Seir. Here Esau settled after he sold his birthright to his brother Jacob. Having driven out the Horites (see Genesis 14:5-6), he occupied the whole of the mountain. Read Deuteronomy 2:12. These Horites are first spoken of in the time of Abraham (Genesis 14:5-6). Sela, or Petra, "Rock," was their capital. Today it is called "the silent city of the forgotten past."

The descendants of Esau were called Edomites. They would go out on raiding expeditions and then retreat to their impregnable fortress where they kept alive in their hearts a bitter enmity toward the Jews, which began with Jacob and Esau. They never failed in helping any army who attacked the Jews. During the period of the Maccabees, they became bitter enemies of the Jews. And in the time of Christ, through Herod they obtained control of Judea. They disappear from the pages of history after the destruction of Jerusalem by Titus in A.D. 70.

This book is the shortest in the Old Testament. It contains only twenty-one verses, but it includes two important themes—the doom of the proud and rebellious and the deliverance of the meek and humble.

It is directly spoken to Edom and Zion and represents Esau and Jacob, the two sons of Isaac. But it appeals to us all with our two natures—the earthly represented by Esau on one side, so proud and bold, and the spiritual by Jacob, chosen and set apart by God. The story of the bitter family feud that takes us back to the days of the two brothers, Jacob and Esau, unfolds before us.

The Doom of Eden (Obadiah 1—16)

Of the prophet who wrote this book we know nothing. His contemporary was Jeremiah. We find the occasion of this prophecy as we read it in Obadiah 11—"On the day you stood aloof while strangers carried off his wealth and foreigners entered his gates and cast lots for Jerusalem, you were like one of them." No doubt, it was the awful day when Nebuchadnezzar took Jerusalem and reduced it to a desolate heap. The Edomites had helped the marauders by catching the fleeing Israelites, treating them with cruelty and selling them as slaves.

This prophecy was written because of this confederacy against Jerusalem in which Edom took the part of the enemy (Obadiah 7—14). Against this people, the prophecy of the unknown prophet Obadiah, "a worshiper of Jehovah," was directed. Edom looked on while Jerusalem was being plundered. They seemed to manifest fiendish delights in the calamity that overtook its inhabitants.

We read the denunciation of the selfish, indifferent and presently hostile spirit of nearby Edom! She, holding the attitude of Esau, remained aloof and allowed Jerusalem to be despoiled. She even became party in the destruction and went in for her part of the spoils.

God had commanded Israel, "Do not abhor an Edomite, for he is your brother" (Deuteronomy 23:7). But Edom had shown an implacable hatred to Israel from the time Israel was refused a passage through Edom on the way to Canaan (Numbers 20:14-21) to the day of the destruction of Jerusalem by the Chaldeans, when Edom cried, "Tear it down," they cried, "tear it down to its foundations" (Psalm 137:7).

Because of the pride and cruel hatred of Edom, her utter destruction was decreed (Obadiah 3—4,10). Nothing could save the guilty nation. The people were driven from their rocky home five years after the destruction of Jerusalem when Nebuchadnezzar, passing down the valley of Arabah that formed the military road to Egypt, crushed the Edomites. They lost their existence as a nation about 150 B.C., and their name perished with the capture of Jerusalem by the Romans. "As you have done, it will be done to you" (Obadiah 15).

Zion's Deliverance (Obadiah 17—21)

The book closes with the promise of deliverance for Zion. "But on Mount Zion will be deliverance; it will be holy, and the house of Jacob will possess its inheritance" (Obadiah 17). The first step in the future reestablishment of the Jewish nation is the recovery of what was previously their own.

God's chosen people had just been carried into captivity by Nebuchadnezzar; the holy land was deserted; and God had told Edom of her doom. Jeremiah gave this same prophecy in chapter 49. Both Jeremiah and Obadiah had probably said these things many times. Five years later Edom fell before the same Babylon she had helped. She would be as though she had never been, swallowed up forever. This was the prophecy against Edom. But Israel shall rise again from her present fall. She will possess not only her own land, but also Philistia and Edom. She will finally rejoice in the holy reign of the promised Messiah. God's chosen people, the Jews, shall possess their possessions, and among the dearest to them is their Holy Land. Obadiah, as the other prophets, predicts the coming of the day of the Lord and the establishment of Messiah's kingdom. Remember, a Christian, too, is an heir of promises to be fulfilled when Christ comes. The believer possesses all things in Christ. (Read 2 Corinthians 6:10.)

God's judgment on Edom as Israel's notable enemy should warn nations today that God has not cast off His people and nations that oppress them will surely bring down His judgments (Genesis 12:3).

Understanding Jonah

Jonah was a native of Gath-hepher, a town about an hour's distance from Nazareth. Jewish legend tells us that he was the son of the widow of Sarepta whom Elijah brought to life. Whether this is true or not we do not know, but he probably was a disciple of the great Elisha and succeeded him as a prophet.

Jonah lived in the reign of Jeroboam II and aided him in making the Northern Kingdom of Israel very powerful and prosperous. (See 2 Kings 14:25.) Jonah was a famous statesman.

For the past half century, we have been living in an age that has created a certain attitude toward the book of Jonah. It is impossible to open the book and take a reading from it anywhere without people's thoughts centering upon a fish! People have been so busy with tape lines trying to find the dimensions of the fish's belly that they seem to have had no time to plumb the depths of the teaching of the book. Be sure to read through this short book. Many stumble over this book. Few know it.

God is in this book. He is taking care of His prophet. God is working. Find the statement four times concerning Him.

God prepared:

A great fish—1:17

A gourd—4:6

A worm—4:7

A vehement east wind—4:8.

Jonah is the test book of the Bible. It challenges our faith. Our attitude toward Jonah reveals our attitude toward God and His Word. Is the story of Jonah mere naturalism or supernaturalism? Right here we stand or fall.

Jesus Christ Himself made the book of Jonah important. When He was asked for a sign to prove His claims, He gave the people only the sign of the prophet Jonah (Matthew 12:38-40).

Two events are of great importance in Jonah. One is the great fish swallowing Jonah and the other the possibility of such a large heathen city as Nineveh being converted by an obscure foreign missionary in just a few days. See what Jesus said in Matthew 12:41.

An Obstinate Prophet (Jonah 1—2)

As the book opens, God is speaking to Jonah, giving him his commission. "Go to the great city of Nineveh and preach against it, because its wickedness has come up before me" (Jonah 1:2).

God is very definite with His orders. He told Jonah to arise and go. "But Jonah ran away from the Lord and headed for Tarshish. He went down to Joppa" (1:3). He said no to God. Why did he flee? Read Jonah 4:2. Jonah knew that Assyria was Israel's dreaded enemy. Just at this period in history Assyria seems to have been somewhat weakened in power. It was then that God told him to go to the capital of that hostile country and pronounce judgment against it for its great wickedness. Jonah fears that Nineveh may repent and be spared impending doom. If Assyria falls, Jonah's own beloved Israel may escape judgment at Assyria's hands. Jonah has the spirit of a national hero. He decides to sacrifice himself in order to save his people, but his heroism is sadly misguided.

Nineveh was one of the greatest cities of the world, situated on the east bank of the Tigris, 400 miles from the Mediterranean. It was the capital of Assyria (Genesis 10:11-12). The stronghold of the city was about thirty miles long and ten miles wide. It was marvelous in appearance. Five walls and three moats (canals) surrounded it. The walls were 100 feet high and allowed four chariots to be driven abreast. The palaces were great and beautiful with the finest of gardens. Fifteen gates guarded by colossal lions and bulls opened into the city. Seventy halls were decorated magnificently in alabaster and sculpture. The temple in the city was in the form of a great pyramid that glittered in the sun. The city was as great in wickedness as it was in wealth and power. Intellectual attainments were almost incredible.

As soon as Jonah fled, God began to act. "Then the Lord sent a great wind on the sea, and such a violent storm arose that the ship threatened to break up" (1:4). God loved Jonah too much to let him prosper. Failure never relieves us of responsibility to serve.

Read events that took place before Jonah was thrown into the sea (1:3-15). Jonah was cast into the sea, but he was gripped by the hand of God (1:17). God's way is best. If we don't accept it, He forces strange things upon us.

The story of Jonah 2 tells us how Jonah came to the end of himself. After much praying, he confessed that he could do nothing by himself. "Salvation comes from the Lord" (2:9). Then God could afford to set him at liberty (2:10).

An Obedient People (Jonah 3—4)

God gave Jonah another chance to be of service. "Then the word of the Lord came to Jonah a second time" (3:1). How foolish he was to make the Lord repeat His call! How much better to obey at once!

God said again, "Go to the great city of Nineveh and proclaim to it the message I give you" (Jonah 3:2).

It was not easy for Jonah to go through the streets and cry, "Forty more days and Nineveh will be overturned" (3:4). There was no mercy in his message. There was no tear in the prophet's voice. He was obeying God, but his heart was unchanged (4:1-3). The common people of Nineveh repented first. Then the nobles followed. This is always true. Revival starts among the people. Think of a city like Chicago repenting and turning to God in one day because of the preaching of a modern prophet. It would be a miracle of the ages. But this is what happened when Jonah preached in his day.

Obedient but Perplexed

Look at him sulking as he sits out on the hill on the east side of the city under a gourd that God provided for a shadow over his head, waiting to see what God would do (Jonah 4:6).

The book ends abruptly! But we must notice two things in this book. First, Jonah is a type of Christ in His death, burial and resurrection. "For as Jonah was three days and three nights in the belly of a huge fish, so the Son of Man will be three days and three nights in the heart of the earth" (Matthew 12:40). Second, Jonah is also a type of Israel—disobedient to God, swallowed by the nations of the world, who will yet give her up when Christ comes. Then shall Israel be witnesses of God everywhere.

No doubt, two things hindered Jonah when God told him to go to Nineveh—his pride of self and his scorn of the rest of the world. God took this out of him in the fish's belly.

Jonah, Type of Israel

Jonah was called to a world mission. So was Israel.

Jonah refused to fulfill his mission by obeying God. So did Israel.

Jonah was punished by being cast into the sea, Israel by being scattered among the nations.

Jonah was preserved. So was Israel.

Jonah repented and was cast out of the fish and restored to life. Israel shall be cast out by all the nations and restored to her former position.

Jonah, obedient to God, goes on his mission. Israel in obedience shall become a witness to all the earth.

Jonah was blessed in that Nineveh was brought to salvation. Israel shall be blessed in the conversion of the whole world.

Understanding Micah

Micah was a country preacher who lived in the days of Isaiah and Hosea. His home was about twenty miles south of Jerusalem in the town of Moresheth on the Philistine border. He was preaching there the same time Isaiah was preaching in Jerusalem and Hosea in Israel. Micah was a prophet of the common people and country life; Isaiah preached to the court in the city of Jerusalem. Micah knew his fellow country people well. Read what he says his real equipment is. "But as for me, I am filled with power, with the Spirit of the Lord, and with justice and might, to declare to Jacob his transgression, to Israel his sin" (Micah 3:8).

Micah prophesied concerning Samaria, the capital of Israel, and Jerusalem, the capital of Judah, but the burden of his prophecy was for Judah. The times in which he lived were difficult. Oppression was present within the walls and foes were coming from without. The condition was the same both in the kingdom of Judah and in the kingdom of Israel. The kings Jotham, Ahaz and Hezekiah reigned during Micah's day.

The prophet denounced the social sins of his day (2:2). Micah felt keenly these social evils. He saw the unfair treatment of the poor by the rich. He felt that these sins cried up to heaven. No class was free from corrupting influences; princes, priests and people alike were all affected (2:2,8-9,11; 3:1-3,5,11). Micah makes them all smart under the lash. Micah wanted the people to know that every cruel act to one's fellow citizen was an insult to God. God is offended by the conduct of the people and the rulers. In spite of the state of things, the people tried to carry on their religious observances. Micah shows the uselessness of all this (6:7-8).

The Northern Kingdom of Israel was taken into captivity during Micah's lifetime. Israel would not heed the warning of the prophets. Judah did and was spared for 150 years. Micah knew that national sins would lead to national downfall. "Righteousness exalts a nation, but sin is a disgrace to any people" (Proverbs 14:34).

The book of Micah seems to be divided into three parts, each beginning with, "Hear ye" (Micah 1:2; 3:1; 6:1). And each closes with a promise.

1. A promise of deliverance—2:12-13
2. A promise to overthrow the enemies in the land—5:10,15
3. A fulfillment of promise to Abraham—7:20.

Catalogue of national sins:
    Idolatry—1:7; 6:16
    Covetousness—2:2
    Oppression—2:2
    Violence—2:2; 3:10; 6:12; 7:2
    Encouraging false prophets—2:6,11
    Corruption of princes—3:1-3
    Corruption of prophets—3:5-7
    Corruption of priests—3:11
    Bribery—3:9,11; 7:3
    Dishonesty—6:10-11.
Passages concerning Christ:
    Birthplace named—5:2
    Christ as King—2:12-13
    Christ reigning in righteousness over the whole earth—4:1,7.
Micah is quoted on three occasions:

1. By the elders of Judah—Jeremiah 26:18 quoting Micah 3:12.
2. By magi coming to Jerusalem—Matthew 2:5-6 quoting Micah 5:2.
3. By Jesus when sending out the Twelve—Matthew 10:35-36 quoting Micah 7:6.

See also Isaiah 2:2-4; 41:15; Ezekiel 22:27; Zephaniah 3:19.
God's government:
    Jerusalem, capital of Christ's kingdom—4:1-2
    Universal, extent of Christ's kingdom—4:2
    Peace, keynote of Christ's kingdom—4:3
    Prosperity, blessing of Christ's kingdom—4:4
    Righteousness, basis of Christ's kingdom—4:5; 4:2.
    The word "remnant" is used often by the prophets. What does it mean? "Remnant" means the small part of the nation that God always preserves for Himself. (See Micah 2:12; 4:7; 5:3,7-8; 7:18.)

A Message to the People
Concerning Israel's Sin
(Micah 1—2)

As the book opens we hear the cry, "Hear, O peoples, all of you, listen, O earth and all who are in it, that the Sovereign Lord may witness against you" (Micah 1:2).

God is not asleep. He knows the sad condition of His people. He will sit in judgment upon His people. Yes, the Lord was coming to call Israel to judgment because of her wrongs. Samaria and Jerusalem were pronounced guilty before the great Judge of the universe. Captivity and exile were their fate. God rebuked them for social injustice, unfaithfulness, dishonesty and idolatry. What were their sins (2:1-11; 1:6-9)?

Micah told them that Samaria, the capital of Israel, would fall (1:6-7). A similar judgment would come upon Judah. Judah's sin is described as an incurable wound. Some kinds of disease are cured only by destruction. All Judah's people shall be taken captive, for God finds incurable oppression, violence and injustice. Notice the towns of Judah mentioned in the last verses of chapter 1. Look at a good Bible atlas and you will see that they all surround the prophet's hometown.

The idolatry of Israel spread rapidly to Jerusalem and the strong city of Lachish (1:13). This awful spread of idolatry, and all its terrible evils, to Judah under King Ahaz, Micah especially denounced. The oppression of the poor (2:2), and women and little children being driven from their homes (2:9) were also rebuked by the prophet. The sins of the people are stated in blunt frankness in Micah 2:1-11. God will bring suffering and shame upon them for their unscrupulous use of power.

More and more we are realizing the social value of the gospel of the Lord Jesus Christ. Wherever this gospel goes, we find conditions bettered and a brotherhood that is based on sonship. Heart worship of God always results in practical demonstrations of changed lives. Missionaries all bear witness of this in a most wonderful way.

A Message to the Rulers
Concerning the Coming Christ
(Micah 3—5)

"Listen, you leaders of Jacob, you rulers of the house of Israel" (Micah 3:1). What does God say of them? Read Micah 3:1-4. God likens their covetousness and self-aggrandizement, even at the price of blood, to cannibalism. The leaders are devouring the poor, defenseless people (3:2,3).

The nation was ready to collapse and the princes and priests were responsible for it. God denounces the sin of the rulers (3:9), the bribery among the judges (3:11), false weights and balances. God describes these men in Micah 3:5. "As for the prophets who lead my people astray, if one feeds them, they proclaim 'peace.'"

Micah, brokenhearted, tells of God's judgment upon Judah for her sins. Jerusalem and its Temple will be destroyed (3:12; 7:13). The people of Judah will be taken captive to Babylon (4:10). But he seems to hasten over words of judgment, and to linger over the message of God's love and mercy. God will bring His people back from captivity (4:1-8; 7:11; 14-17). Micah was a prophet of hope. He always looked beyond doom and punishment to the day of glory when Christ Himself shall reign, when peace shall cover the earth. God gives the promise. The Messiah will come. He will be born in Bethlehem (4:8; 5:2-4).

Then Israel will be gathered from the nations into which she has been scattered (4:6). Oh, that the Prince of Peace might come soon and make all these things come to pass. We pray with John on the isle of Patmos, "Amen. Come, Lord Jesus" (Revelation 22:20).

Little Bethlehem, smallest among the towns of Judah, shall be signally honored by the birth of God's Messiah, Jesus Christ, our Lord. His victories shall not be won by might nor by power but by His Spirit. He comes as a little babe to bring salvation to a world so in need of a Redeemer. This 700-year-old prophecy from Micah 5:2-5, together with the star, led the wise men to Jerusalem to seek the new King.

A Message to the Chosen People Concerning God's Argument (Micah 6—7)

"Hear, O mountains, the Lord's accusation; listen, you everlasting foundations of the earth. For the Lord has a case against his people; he is lodging a charge against Israel" (Micah 6:2). God is pictured as one bringing a lawsuit against His people.

They had ignored God. He told them to remember how good He had been to them and how He had kept His covenant with them (6:3).

The people, conscience smitten, asked how they could please God. Frantically they asked if burnt offerings would do (6:6-7).

Men and women are always trying to get back into the good graces of God with some outward religious service or some worldly rather than spiritual things. But remember, "the sacrifices of God are a broken spirit; a broken and contrite heart, O God, you will not despise" (Psalm 51:17). God wants righteous conduct and a real personal experience of Him in each life. Because of unrighteous conduct, the people had to suffer unbelievable consequences. God is a righteous Judge (Micah 1:3,5; 3:12). What does the apostle Paul tell us to do in return for God's mercies? (Read Romans 12:1-2.) The best way to get back into God's graces is to accept God's grace.

Simple Essentials of Real Religion

The Old Testament gives us a definition of religion. What does God require of you? (Read Micah 6:8.)

How does this compare with people's present-day definitions of "religion"?

"Act justly"—good ethics in all of life.

"Love mercy"—consideration for others, when justice has not been done.

"Walk humbly with your God"—personal experience with God.
Paul would call this "the mind of Christ." "Your attitude should

be the same as that of Christ Jesus" (Philippians 2:5). If our religion is only a great creed, grand cathedrals and elaborate rituals, then we have nothing. All must be filled with the mind of Christ. We must "worship in spirit and in truth" (John 4:24). Christ wants us to have more than a beautiful creed even if it is spiritual and true. He wants this spirit of Christ to be lived out through our daily lives and to be exhibited in all our conduct, in our homes and in our businesses. Can our religion stand this test?

It is interesting that when Christ summed up the same matter (Matthew 23:23), He used the words "justice," "mercy" and "faithfulness." He thus equated "faith with walking humbly with our God," an apt comparison.

Chapter 24

Understanding Nahum, Habakkuk, Zephaniah

*Jesus Christ, a Stronghold in the Day of Trouble;
the God of My Salvation; a Jealous Lord*

Selected Bible Readings

Sunday:	The Judge and the Verdict (Nahum 1)
Monday:	The Execution (Nahum 2—3)
Tuesday:	Habakkuk's Complaint (Habakkuk 1)
Wednesday:	God's Reply (Habakkuk 2)
Thursday:	Habakkuk's Song (Habakkuk 3)
Friday:	Coming Judgments (Zephaniah 1—2)
Saturday:	The Kingdom Blessings (Zephaniah 3)

Understanding Nahum

Nahum, the writer of this book, was a native of Elkosh. In Assyria, near the ruins of Nineveh, the natives point to a tomb as Nahum's. But most authorities think that this Elkosh was in Galilee. Today Elkosh lies in ruins.

In name and in message, "Nahum" means "comfort" for Judah. "The Lord is good, a refuge in times of trouble. He cares for those who trust in him" (Nahum 1:7). Deliverance for Judah, and destruction for her enemy Assyria, was God's great theme for His people. That "Capernaum," where Christ the Comforter wrought so many works, means "village of Nahum" (comfort) is noteworthy. Nearby is the town where he was born, Elkosh.

Nahum was probably a native of Galilee and lived at the time of good King Hezekiah and the great prophet Isaiah. No doubt, when the cruel Assyrians invaded his country and carried away the ten tribes of Israel, he escaped into the Southern Kingdom of Judah. He probably took up his residence in Jerusalem where he later witnessed the siege of that city of Sennacherib, which ended with the miraculous destruction of the Assyrian host. Remember 185,000 perished in one night, as 2 Kings 19:35 records. It may be that Nahum 1:2 refers to this. Shortly after this event, Nahum wrote his book.

The theme of this book is the destruction of Nineveh, the city Jonah warned. Nineveh is a culprit and God is sending Nahum to declare His righteous judgment upon her. In the judgment of Nineveh, God is judging a sinning world. Nahum was written about 150 years after the revival of Jonah's day when the city of Nineveh was brought to repentance in "dust and ashes." Mercy unheeded finally brings judgment.

No doubt the Ninevites were sincere then, but it did not last. They were again guilty of the very sins of which they had repented. Nineveh, the glory of the Assyrians, had come to a complete and deliberate defiance of the living God. The people were not just backsliders! They deliberately rejected the God they had accepted (2 Kings 18:25,30,35; 19:10-13).

God sent Nahum to predict the final doom and complete overthrow of Nineveh and her empire. This empire had been built up by violence. The Assyrians were great warriors. They were out on raiding expeditions continually. They built their state on the loot of other people. They did everything to inspire terror. They said they did this in obedience to their god, Asshur. God was going to doom Nineveh to perish in a violent and extraordinary way. Read of her beastlike violence and cruelty (Nahum 2:11-12).

Assyria had enjoyed a brilliant epoch of three hundred years in which she was a world empire. Nineveh was the capital of this mighty empire. In 722 B.C., she destroyed Israel and threatened Judah, but God was going to see that Assyria's doom was final. The message of Nahum shows what God can do with a wicked and rebellious people. He will utterly destroy them.

The doom of the city was delayed some 150 years after Jonah preached, but it fell at last. Nahum's prophecy was not a call to repentance, but the statement of certain and final doom. Read Nahum 1:9; also 3:18-19. Her name should be utterly cut off (1:14). God would dig her grave.

The Judge (Nahum 1:1-7)

In Nahum 1, we see God the holy Judge on the bench of the court of heaven judging the wicked city of Nineveh. The case is presented. This God is a just God, therefore He must avenge all crimes.

There is a two-fold revelation of the character of this Judge of all the world. We find a sublime and powerful statement of those attributes of God that constitute the basis of all His actions toward people. This lesson gives us an excellent opportunity of presenting the attributes of God.

Study the prophet's vision of God in Nahum 1:2-7. Find the words that are used of Him. As Judge, God:

1. Is jealous
2. Is avenging
3. Is filled with wrath at evildoers
4. Maintains wrath against His enemies
5. Is great in power
6. Will not leave the guilty unpunished
7. Is indignant.

As Father, He is:

1. Slow to anger
2. Good
3. A stronghold in the day of trouble
4. Knowing them that trust Him.

The first eight words of the vision are awe inspiring, "The Lord is a jealous and avenging God." To think of a God like this makes us examine ourselves. We will find that there is no righteousness in us. How this thought drives us into the loving arms of a Savior who is our "covering for sin" and clothes us with the robes of His righteousness.

Notice God did not bring judgment on Assyria in hot haste. He had been patient for a long time. He is "slow to anger," but God sent ruin. He is a God of absolute justice. He is the Lord, the Lord God, merciful and gracious, long-suffering and forgiving iniquity, yet He will by no means clear the guilty. Jonah dwelt on the first side of God's character, love (Jonah 4:2). Nahum brings out the second, the holiness of God that must deal with sin in judgment (Nahum 1:2,6). This holy Judge is "just and the one who justifies those who have faith in Jesus" (Romans 3:26) because His holy law has been vindicated in the cross of Christ.

The Verdict (Nahum 1:8-14)

Nahum 1:8-14 states the battle-and-destruction sentence upon corrupt Nineveh. She has been weighed in the balance and found wanting.

Look at the Verdict of Nineveh:

1. Condemned to utter destruction—1:8-9
2. Captured while defenders were drunk—1:10
3. Name blotted out—1:14
4. God to dig her grave—1:14.

We cannot read this without being struck by the solemnity of it all. Nahum told of this destruction as prophecy. We look at it today as history. Yes, the Judge has brought everything to pass. Today the traveler finds this great city Nineveh of the past still lying in ruins.

This book gives us the picture of the wrath of God. Read the second verse again: "The Lord is a jealous and avenging God; the Lord takes vengeance and is filled with wrath. The Lord takes vengeance on his foes and maintains his wrath against his enemies." This is a picture of God acting in wrath. It is not pleasant to be reminded that God is a God of anger as well as a God of love. But remember both attributes are His. He is a holy God. He hates sin. He will bring judgment upon it.

The Execution (Nahum 2—3)

Read what God says in these short chapters. We find a picture of Nineveh's siege, fall and desolation. All God can do with a rebellious and defiant nation is to destroy it.

The picture of the siege and fall of Nineveh and the desolation that followed are described with graphic eloquence in Nahum 2—3. God would make an end of her with an overrunning flood, her name would be utterly cut off and He would dig her grave. Mustering the armies around Nineveh, and marshaling the forces within the city are pictured in such a way that the prophet makes his hearers see all the horrid sights of the tragic scene.

Outside the walls, the Medes have gathered. Shields are brilliantly painted. Robes are of purple. Terrible spears glitter in the sun. Knives on their chariot wheels flash in the light. Inside the city, pandemonium reigns! Too late, the king tries to rally his drunken nobles to defend the beloved city. But the Tigris has caused a flood that has washed away most of the wall that had seemed to them an impregnable bulwark. This aided their enemies. The queen is taken captive, and her maidens, like a flock of doves, moan around her.

The cries of the Medes are heard as they shout to one another, "Plunder the silver! Plunder the gold! The supply is endless, the wealth from all its treasures!" (2:9). The city is looted while the people stand with their knees smiting together for fear. Nineveh shall no longer terrify the nations because God has made an end of her. This will happen to all wicked nations of the earth.

The Medes and Babylonians completely destroyed Nineveh in 612 B.C. It occurred at the zenith of her power. According to Nahum's prophecy, it came true—a sudden rise of the Tigris, carrying away a great part of the wall, assisted the attacking army of the Medes and Babylonians in its overthrow (Nahum 2:6). The city was partly destroyed by fire (Nahum 3:13,15).

So deep and effectively did God dig Nineveh's grave that every trace of its existence disappeared for ages and its site was not known. When Alexander the Great (Alexander III, 356-323 B.C., conqueror of the Persian Empire, and one of the greatest military genuises of all times) fought the battle of Arbela nearby in 331 B.C., he did not even know there had ever been a city there. When Xenophon (430?-355? B.C., Greek historian, soldier and essayist) and his army of 10,000 passed by 200 years later, he thought the mounds were the ruins of some Parthian city. When Napoleon (Napoleon I, 1769-1821, emperor of the French, one of the greatest military commanders of all time) encamped near its site, he, too, was not aware of it.

This city had one denunciation more, given a few years later by Zephaniah (Zephaniah 2:13). In 612 B.C., the whole was fulfilled. So complete was the destruction that all traces of the Assyrian Empire disappeared. Many scholars used to think the references to Nineveh in the Bible were only mythical. It seemed that no such city ever existed. In 1845, Layard (Sir Austen Henry Layard, 1817-94, British author, diplomat, archeologist and excavator of Nineveh) confirmed the suspicions of the Englishman Claudius James Rich (1787-1820, British traveler, linguist and author) who in 1820 thought the mounds across the Tigris from Mosul were the ruins of Nineveh. The ruins of the magnificent palaces of the Assyrian kings, and thousands of inscriptions were unearthed, which give to us the story of Assyria as the Assyrians wrote it themselves. And so the magnificent capital of the wealthiest and most splendid city in the world of its day has been discovered and the Bible account has been confirmed.

Sowing and Reaping

As Nineveh sowed, so must she reap. This is God's law. Nineveh had fortified herself so that nothing could harm her. With walls 100 feet high and wide enough for four chariots to go abreast, a circumference of 80 miles, and adorned by hundreds of towers, she sat complacently. A moat 140 feet wide and 60 feet deep surrounded the vast walls. But Nineveh reckoned without Jehovah. What are bricks and mortar to God! The mighty empire that Shalmaneser, Sargon and Sennacherib had built up, the Lord threw down with a stroke. The inventions of civilization are powerless against heaven's artillery.

Nineveh is a type of all nations that turn their backs on God. In our day, proud civilizations are staking everything upon the strength of people power and machines and there is a terrible disregard of God. We find that Nineveh was overthrown because of her sin (Nahum 3:1-7) and that her great wealth and strength were not sufficient to save her (3:8-19). Oftentimes nations depend upon might and power to survive. They forget that it is "'not by might nor by power, but by my Spirit,' says the Lord Almighty" (Zechariah 4:6). The person or nation that deliberately and finally rejects God, deliberately and finally and fatally elects doom. Beware of this!

Hear Peter's words of warning spoken hundreds of years later—"The Lord is not slow in keeping his promise, as some understand slowness. He is patient with you, not wanting anyone to perish, but everyone to come to repentance. But the day of the Lord will come like a thief. The heavens will disappear with a roar; the elements will be destroyed by fire, and the earth and everything in it will be laid bare" (2 Peter 3:9-10).

Understanding Habakkuk

Watch and see—Habakkuk 1
Stand and see—Habakkuk 2
Kneel and see—Habakkuk 3

We know little about this prophet of faith except that he asked questions and received answers. He, like many people today, could not reconcile his belief in a good and righteous God with the facts of life as he saw them. He was troubled with an eternal "Why?" Even today, people of faith find themselves bewildered at many things that are going on round about them. We ask, "Why does God allow such awful crimes to go unchecked? Why doesn't God stop people in their mad rush if He is all powerful?"

The question, Why do the wicked prosper? is discussed. It seems to contain a complaint to God that He should destroy His own nation for her wickedness by a nation even much more wicked (Habakkuk 1:13). We even see the prophet complaining of the lack of justice in God's management of the world. Why is God silent in times of disaster (1:13)?

Habakkuk, in all his difficulties, went to God in prayer and
waited patiently for His answer (2:1). He went onto the watchtower and listened to God. G. Campbell Morgan says that when
Habakkuk looked at his circumstances he was perplexed (1:3), but
when he waited for God and listened to Him, he sang (3:18-19).

Habakkuk was a prophet (1:1), but we find something else of
interest about him. He was one of the Levitical choristers in the
temple (3:19), or helped in arranging the services.

We learn much about him as a thinker and a man of faith from
his own words. He was a contemporary with Jeremiah at home
and with Daniel in Babylon.

The world empire of Assyria had fallen just as Nahum had prophesied. Egypt and Babylon had then contended for the place of
power. At the battle of Carchemish, 605 B.C., in which King Josiah
was killed, the Babylonians were conquerors and the great kingdoms of the Babylonians and Chaldeans were united under
Nebuchadnezzar. Habakkuk knew only too well that Judah must
fall before this great rising power. But one question arose in his
mind and troubled him greatly. Why should any nation as wicked
as Babylon conquer a nation like Judah, which was less evil? It
seemed to him that it was just a matter of evil triumphing over evil.
What good could come of this? God had to show him His ultimate
plan. Judah needed punishment. God was using Babylon to correct
Judah, but Babylon's turn would come. Babylon would be utterly
blotted out. As for God's people, there was yet to be a glorious
future and a kingdom where Jehovah Himself would prevail.

This book seems to be a dialogue between Jehovah and the
prophet. Two conversations are recorded and the book closes
with a hymn and doxology, which reveal that all the questions
have been answered and there is a new confidence in God.

Habakkuk's Complaint (Habakkuk 1)

This scene opens with the cry of a man who has a problem he
cannot solve. "How long, O Lord, must I call for help, but you do
not listen? Or cry out to you, 'Violence!' but you do not save"
(Habakkuk 1:2)!

Habakkuk was confused and bewildered. It seemed to him that God was doing nothing to straighten out the conditions in the world. He had lived during the days of the great reformation under good King Josiah. He had seen Assyria fading in power and Babylon, under Nebuchadnezzar, rising to a place of supremacy. The world about him was in an upheaval. Violence abounded and God was doing nothing about it.

But worse, he saw his own land, Judah, full of lawlessness and tyranny. The righteous were oppressed (1:4,13). The people were living in open sin. They were worshiping idols (2:18-19). They were oppressing the poor. Habakkuk knew that the day was dark. He knew that this sin was leading to an invasion of Jerusalem by a strong enemy.

Habakkuk asked his question of God. He did not call a committee or form a society to solve the problem of the day. He went straight to Jehovah and stated his problem. Then God answered, "Look at the nations and watch—and be utterly amazed. For I am going to do something in your days that you would not believe, even if you were told" (1:5). God told Habakkuk that He was not indifferent to His people. He wanted Habakkuk to look beyond the present. He was already working. God called the Chaldeans to the work of punishing Judah. They were a cruel scourge that swept over the land to destroy it (1:5-11).

God's answer horrified Habakkuk. He could not understand how God would allow such awful means to bring about punishing His people, Judah. How could He use such a cruel scourge? How was it possible for God to use such an enemy to punish His own people when He Himself is so pure and holy? Listen to Habakkuk's challenge to God to defend His actions (1:13).

The nations have always been God's object lessons, illustrating His moral laws (1:12).

God's Reply (Habakkuk 2)

As this scene opens, we see Habakkuk facing the great moment of his life. Watch him as he climbs up on the watchtower to wait for God. He expects God to answer him (Habakkuk 2:1).

Everything lies in ruins around the prophet. Chaldea is coming up to destroy what is left. There is only One to whom he can turn, so he waits expectantly for God. God gives an answer. Read God's answer in Habakkuk 2:2-20. God admits the wickedness of the Chaldeans, but declares that they will destroy themselves finally by their own evil. Pride and cruelty always bring destruction. People sometimes have to wait to know what the final outcome will be. God sometimes takes ages to show His plans. "With the Lord a day is like a thousand years, and a thousand years are like a day" (2 Peter 3:8). God's testing always reveals what people are. He burns out the dross. It may seem that the Chaldeans are prospering for a time, but they are doomed. "The righteous will live by his faith" (Habakkuk 2:4) is the heart of the book.

Five "woes" are mentioned in Habakkuk 2. Find what they are. Remember evil will perish. Only righteousness will remain before God.

Habakkuk's Song (Habakkuk 3)

Habakkuk is the prophet who sang in the night. Listen to the magnificent melody with which his prophecy closes—"Though the fig tree does not bud and there are no grapes on the vines, though the olive crop fails and the fields produce no food, though there are no sheep in the pen and no cattle in the stalls, yet I will rejoice in the Lord, I will be joyful in God my Savior" (3:17-18). This ode was set to music and sung at the public worship by the Jews.

After a sincere prayer (3:1-16), God's glory appears. God always responds to the cry for help from His people. Habakkuk realizes that God is in control of this universe and that He is working out His own purpose in His own time. Habakkuk learns that he can trust implicitly in God. He realizes that he can see only a small part of God's plan at one time. One must wait for God to reveal His entire program. One must know God's way is best.

God cannot always give us a satisfactory answer, because our finite minds cannot grasp the thoughts of the infinite. His thoughts are high above our thoughts, and His ways above our ways (Isaiah 55:9), but we can trust God, always! "In all things

God works for the good of those who love him, who have been called according to his purpose" (Romans 8:28).

Remember, God does not promise that He will unravel every problem, but He does assure us that we can put our trust absolutely in Him. (Read Psalm 37:5 and 2 Timothy 1:12.)

One of the texts in Habakkuk has great significance in the history of the Reformation. Do you know the story of the young monk Martin Luther (1483-1546, a Catholic priest and leader of the Reformation in Germany) who rose to his feet as he was crawling up the steps of the Scala Sancta in Rome? He remembered these words, "The just shall live by his faith" (Habakkuk 2:4, *KJV*). Not by works! This started him on his great crusade that brought about the Reformation.

Find where Habakkuk 2:4 is quoted in the New Testament: Romans 1:17; Galatians 3:11; Hebrews 10:38. Mark them.

Understanding Zephaniah

Little is known of Zephaniah, the writer of this book. Two facts of his personal history appear in the first verse of the prophecy. We learn that very likely he was a prince of the royal house of Judah, being a descendant of Hezekiah. He was in a position to denounce the sins of the princes for he himself was an aristocrat. He lived in the reign of good King Josiah. His name means "hidden of Jehovah."

Zephaniah began his ministry as a prophet in the early days of the reign of Josiah (641-610 B.C.). Fifty years had elapsed since the prophecy of Nahum. Three of Hezekiah's descendants had succeeded him (2 Kings 20—21). Two wicked and idol-worshiping kings had preceded Josiah on the throne and the land was overrun with evil practices of every kind. Social injustice and moral corruption were rampant on every hand. The rich had amassed great fortunes by grinding the faces of the poor. The condition was as bad as it could be when King Josiah, only sixteen years of age, undertook to promote a religious revival. He became one of the most beloved of the kings of Judah. He took a hatchet and hewed down the altars and images. How the words of Zephaniah must have encouraged the reformers!

Zephaniah depicts God as both loving and severe. Zephaniah 1:2 and 3:17 gives us these two characteristics.

Zephaniah foretold the doom of Nineveh (2:13). Who else had prophesied her doom? This came to pass in 612 B.C.

We hear Zephaniah denouncing the various forms of idolatry—Baal and Malcham or Molech all being condemned (1:1—2:3). This idol worship was destroyed during Josiah's reign. No doubt Zephaniah was mainly responsible for the revival under Josiah. He was the pioneer in this reform movement. Tradition tells us that Jeremiah was his colleague.

As you start reading this book, you are appalled at its contents. There is nothing but denunciations, dire threats and wrath. Cowper (William Cowper, 1731-1800, British poet and hymn writer) says that punishment and chastisement is "the graver countenance of love." "Because the Lord disciplines those he loves, and he punishes everyone he accepts as a son" (Hebrews 12:6). We see in all of this a proof of God's love. The book begins with sorrow, but ends with singing. The first of the book is full of sadness and gloom, but the last contains one of the sweetest songs of love in the Old Testament.

Zephaniah showed that:

1. A faithful remnant would be delivered from captivity.
2. The Gentile nations shall be converted.
3. One day people could worship God anywhere, not only in Jerusalem (2:11; see John 4:21).

God is searching out the people. "At that time I will search Jerusalem with lamps and punish those who are complacent, who are like wine left on its dregs, who think, 'The Lord will do nothing, either good or bad'" (Zephaniah 1:12).

Judah Searched (Zephaniah 1)

Jehovah is in the midst of the land for judgment (Zephaniah 3:5 and 1:17). He first searches Judah and pronounces doom on all those who are worshiping idols. The land must be freed from idolatry. Jehovah cannot allow such abomination to remain. We see the rulers are denounced, as is every class of sinner (1:7-13):

1. The idol worshipers—1:4-5
2. Those who swear by God one time and at another time by Molech—1:5
3. Those who turned back from the Lord—1:6.

Upon all these shall God bring a blast of fire. It shall strike the whole earth, but especially the inhabitants of Jerusalem. The "day of the Lord" is a day of dread. He calls the people to tremble at God's presence. He is "in the midst" of the land to judge her.

The "day of the Lord" is mentioned seven times in the prophecy. Almost without exception, when "day" is used in Scripture it means a period of time. If a number is used before it, such as forty days, three days, then it is a day of twenty-four hours. But when "day" is used alone, such as the day of the Puritan or Lincoln's day, you mean the time in which they lived. So when the Word says, "the day of the Lord" it means a time of the Lord's special working. To the Jews of Zephaniah's day, it meant the time when God would deal with His people in punishment and captivity. The future day of the Lord is the period of the great tribulation and the millennium. (See Revelation 6:1-17.) Judah was taught that "the day of the Lord" was coming when there would be a special reckoning.

The Nations Searched (Zephaniah 2)

After the prophet calls the people to seek God, hoping that "perhaps you will be sheltered on the day of the Lord's anger" (Zephaniah 2:1-3), he declares that nothing can save the nation from doom but real repentance. "Seek the Lord....Seek righteousness, seek humility" is his admonition. Then he turns to the five heathen nations, Philistia, Moab, Ammon, Ethiopia and Assyria. They shall be visited with the wrath of God because of their pride and scorn toward the Lord's people (2:10). The desolation of Nineveh is described in wonderfully accurate terms (2:13-15). These began to be accomplished in the conquests of Nebuchadnezzar.

The judgment on Israel's local enemies is literally fulfilled (2:4-15). The judgment on Israel's enemies over this wide world is yet to be fulfilled. Read God's Word in Zephaniah 3:8; 2:10-11. God says the idols of their enemies shall be broken up, and the Gentiles shall worship God, every one in his own country (2:11). Instead of all having to make a pilgrimage to Jerusalem, they may worship God anywhere.

The Jews taught that Jerusalem was the place of worship. The Samaritans declared that Mount Gerizim ought to be the religious center, but Zephaniah taught that spiritual worship did not depend upon a place, but on the Presence of God. People have always tried to establish sacred places and shrines. Rome and Mecca have long been "holy" spots, among hundreds of other places. People have undergone every hardship to worship at these shrines. In India, thousands make the pilgrimage to Benares, the Hindus most sacred spot, to worship and to bathe in the Ganges, and to carry back with them its sacred water.

Israel Restored (Zephaniah 3)

The prophet concludes with the most wonderful promises of Israel's future restoration and of the happy state of the purified people of God in the latter days (Zephaniah 3). The redeemed remnant will return cleansed, humbled, trusting and rejoicing with their offerings to Zion. They will be established in their land with God "in their midst" (3:15,17, *KJV*). Zion then shall be a delight among nations and a blessing to the whole earth as was foretold in the promise God made originally with Abraham (Genesis 12:1-3).

The rejoicing of Zephaniah 3:14-20 must refer to something besides the day when the remnant will return after the captivity of Babylon. Judah's worst judgment followed that return. She has seen little but misery ever since. Neither did anything like this occur at Christ's first coming. It must refer to the day when the Lord Himself shall sit on the throne of David, when His people shall be gathered from the four corners of the earth (3:19). This prophecy shall be blessedly fulfilled in the Kingdom age when Christ comes to this earth to reign in power and great glory.

Chapter 25

Understanding Haggai, Zechariah, Malachi

*Jesus Christ, the Desire of All Nations;
the Righteous Branch; Sun of Righteousness*

Selected Bible Readings

Sunday:	Haggai's Message (Haggai 1—2)
Monday:	Visions (Zechariah 1—6)
Tuesday:	Fasts (Zechariah 7—8)
Wednesday:	Restoration of Judah and Israel (Zechariah 9—11)
Thursday:	The Messiah (Zechariah 12—14)
Friday:	Sins of Priests and People (Malachi 1—2)
Saturday:	Message of Hope (Malachi 3—4)

Note: The greater number of Old Testament prophets spoke before the captivity. During the captivity in Babylon, Ezekiel and Daniel prophesied. After the return from Babylonian exile, Haggai, Zechariah and Malachi prophesied. This makes it easy to remember. Of the sixteen prophets, just two prophesied during the exile, three after, eleven before.

Haggai, Zechariah and Malachi are the last of the prophetic books. They prophesied to the Jews after they returned to Jerusalem. Nebuchadnezzar had captured Jerusalem and completely destroyed the Temple. This, however, did not bring the Jews to national repentance. In reading Ezra, we find that when

Cyrus, king of Persia, issued a decree permitting all the captives to return to Jerusalem and to rebuild their Temple, only about 50,000 returned. Most of these were priests and Levites and the poorer among the people. Although the Jews increased in power and in numbers, they never established their political independence. They were a subject people under Gentile rulers from this time on.

Before Haggai's time, the Jews had returned to their own land under Zerubbabel and began to build the Temple (Nehemiah 12). But their enthusiasm soon waned. They made no progress beyond laying the foundation. The Samaritans and their enemy neighbors were determined that Jerusalem should not be rebuilt. This meant that the work lay unfinished for fifteen years. During these years, each person became interested in building a private house. It was then that Haggai arose and gave his message. He encouraged the people to build the Temple again. This time it was finished in four years. It seemed incredible that God's people should have waited so long to do the very thing they came back to do.

Understanding Haggai

We know little of Haggai except that he worked with Zechariah during the days following the exile. He prophesied two months before Zechariah. Zechariah prophesied for three years and Haggai prophesied for four months.

Haggai is the first voice to be heard after the exile. His name means "my feast." His book is a collection of four brief messages written between August and December.

Each message is specifically dated. These dates, rather than places and characters, dominate the scenes. These were given in "the second year of Darius," 520 B.C. Confucius, the Chinese philosopher, was flourishing in China at this time. The book is dominated by one central purpose: Haggai is determined to persuade the people to rebuild the Temple. It is no easy task to move a discouraged nation to rise up and build a temple. But he did it.

A Message of Rebuke (Haggai 1:1-11)

A poor handful of people returned to Jerusalem from Babylon where they had lived in captivity. With a colossal task before them of rebuilding the Temple and restoring the worship of Jehovah, the Jews labored under the same old sins—idolatry and intermarrying with idolatrous neighbors. They were few in number, poor, harassed by enemies and worse, they had lost the inner strength that comes from a joy in the Lord. (Read Nehemiah 8:10.)

Because of all this, the work dragged and the people lost heart and became selfish. Neglecting the Lord's house, they had become more interested in building homes for themselves than for God (Haggai 1:4). God would not allow this to go on and so He sent punishment as a result. Poor crops, droughts, scanty trade, misery and turmoil made their spirits fail (1:6). They were working and slaving, but finding no real joy (1:6,9-11).

We see the effect of Haggai's challenge. His stern call to duty proved to be a good tonic. Zerubbabel, the governor of Jerusalem, Joshua, the high priest, and the people arose and began the work of rebuilding the Temple (1:12-15). How did God respond to their repentance (1:13)?

God sometimes allows hardships because of our indifference to Him. Crops failed and business was depressed because of the sin of the Jews. But God wants us to keep up the Church. Without churches, sin and vice will grow. When people forget to love God, they forget to love their fellow citizens, too. We should beautify God's house. (See 2 Samuel 7:2.) We are not to live in fine homes and allow the church building to be in ruins.

A Message of Courage (Haggai 2:1-9)

Note: How long after the first message was this one given (Haggai 1:1; 2:1)? For the history of this period read Ezra 3:8-13.

As the people were building, a new discouragement seized them. The older ones, remembering the splendor of the Temple of Solomon, were greatly disappointed in this new Temple. It did not measure up in any way, they thought. How inferior in size and costliness of the stones! How much smaller in extent was the foundation itself! How limited were their means! And besides, this second Temple would not have the things that made the first one so glorious—the Ark, the Shekinah and all that went with the service of the high priest. These pessimists dampened the enthusiasm of the builders.

But Haggai came with a word of cheer that God was to pour His resources into that new building. The living God was to be in the midst of this new Temple. "'I will shake all nations, and the desired of all nations will come, and I will fill this house with glory,' says the Lord Almighty" (2:7). "'The glory of this present house will be greater than the glory of the former house,' says the Lord Almighty. 'And in this place I will grant peace,' declares the Lord Almighty" (2:9). What a comfort this must have been to the Jews in their exile.

A Message of Assurance (Haggai 2:10-23)

This message of cleansing and blessing was delivered three months after the Temple was started. By the use of questions and answers, Haggai showed the people their impurity. He made them realize their sinfulness. He showed them that the reason their prayers were not answered was that they had put off so long completing the Temple. They had spoiled all that they had done because of their guilt. If they would renew their zeal, they would find God would bless them. Haggai heard their complaints of seeing no visible signs of blessings, although they had been working for three full months. Haggai showed them that the land had been rendered useless by their neglect, but God was working and it would be different now. "From this day on I will bless you" (2:18-19). God has begun even before we begin.

Understanding Zechariah

Zechariah is a book of the future. It is a book of revelation of the Old Testament.

The Chosen People and the Temple (Zechariah 1—8)

We now find Judah still a remnant, Jerusalem far from restored, the Gentile nations at ease round about her (Zechariah 1:14-16). Zechariah, a young prophet who had stood alongside the aged Haggai, strengthened the children of Israel as they built the Temple and warned them not to disappoint God as their fathers had done. He pictured God's love and care for His people. He quickened their hopes by painting in glowing colors the time of perpetual blessing that was coming to Israel in the far-off ages.

Zechariah, like Haggai, was a prophet to the remnant of the Jews who returned from Babylon after the seventy years of captivity. The Jews, once a powerful nation as God had planned them to be, were now a pitiful and insignificant remnant, dwelling in their Promised Land only because of the courtesy of a foreign ruler. Both Haggai and Zechariah tried to tell the people that it would not always be so. One day the Messiah would come and God's chosen people would rise into power.

Zechariah was the prophet of restoration and glory. Born in Babylon, he was priest as well as prophet. Zechariah, whose name means "Jehovah remembers," prophesied for three years. The glorious future rather than the sad present was his message. He was a poet; Haggai, on the other hand, was a plain, practical preacher.

Zechariah's keen enthusiasm for rebuilding the Temple kept the people at the task of finishing the work. Serious crop failures and business depression among the Jewish people had made them so discouraged that only Haggai's blunt and consistent hammering kept at the work. They needed a new voice. Zechariah's was that one. He threw himself into the work of helping his great friend Haggai.

Zechariah does not condemn the people, but presents in glowing pictures the presence of God to strengthen and help. He especially encourages the governor, Zerubbabel, who was conscious of his own weakness. Hear what Zechariah says, "'Not by

might nor by power, but by my Spirit,' says the Lord Almighty"
(Zechariah 4:6-10). He promised that the mountains of difficulty
would be removed. How marvelously this truth was fulfilled at
Pentecost when God filled people with His power.

Zechariah foretells the Savior more than any other prophet
except Isaiah:

Christ the Branch—3:8
Christ my Servant—3:8
Christ's entry in Jerusalem on a colt—9:9
Christ the good Shepherd—9:16; 11:11
Christ the stricken Shepherd—13:7
Christ betrayed for thirty pieces of silver—11:12-13
Christ's hands pierced—12:10
Christ's people saved—12:10; 13:1
Christ wounded in the house of His friends—13:6
Christ's coming on the Mount of Olives—14:3-8.

He who ascended from the Mount of Olives shall so come in
the same way as He left. Read Acts 1:11.

Christ's coming and coronation—Zechariah 14.

Two Searchlights

Someone has said to read the visions of this book aright you must
get two lights upon them—the light of the Cross and of the
crown. Otherwise you will find these pictures of Zechariah to be
without perspective or background. The prophet, looking far into
the future, saw the Messiah of the days to come as one Person,
but in two aspects. First, he saw Him in humiliation and suffering, and again, in majesty and great glory.

The Jewish person who does not believe that Jesus is Messiah
ignores the Christ of the cross. The Christian, too, often ignores
the Christ of the crown. Both are wrong!

Zechariah seems to let the glory of Christ glow in all his teaching and preaching.

Of the Minor Prophets, Zechariah alone majors in visions—1:1-6.
"During the night I had a vision" (v. 8).

The *angelic horseman*—1:7-17: here is a picture of Israel today,
outcast but not forgotten by God.

The *horns and craftsmen*—1:18-21: the overthrow of Israel by her enemies is foreseen.

The *measuring line*—2:1-13: the coming prosperity of Jerusalem is seen. The city, walled in by the presence of God, is great in extent and blessed by His favor.

Joshua, the high priest—3:1-10: filthy garments clothing the priest and representing Israel's sin are removed, replaced and the Branch, Christ, introduced.

The golden lampstand—4:1-14: Israel is shown as God's future light bearer. Olive trees, anointed of God, speak of Zerubbabel the ruler, and Joshua the priest.

The flying scroll—5:1-4: wicked governments receive God's curse in this unique picture.

The measuring basket—5:5-11: Borne away on divine wings, wickedness is removed.

The four chariots—6:1-8: "Administrative forces of righteousness" (G. Campbell Morgan).

The Coronation Scene

The visions are followed by a symbolic act of crowning the high priest (6:9-11). Gold and silver brought from Babylon was wrought into a crown and placed on the head of Joshua the high priest. By this act, the two great offices of priest and king are united. This is a type of Christ the King who will sit on His throne of glory as a priest when He returns to earth to set up His millennial kingdom.

Two years later, we find a committee from Bethel waiting on Zechariah to ask him if the national fasts should be kept (chaps. 7—8). The Jews themselves had instituted these fasts. They had been used to fasting on their great anniversary days. Zechariah warned them against cold formalism in their religious observances. He urges them to change their fasts into feasts of joy and be practical in their righteousness. God says, "To obey is better than sacrifice, and to heed is better than the fat of rams" (1 Samuel 15:22).

Fasting is only profitable as an outward sign of an inward confession of sin. Merely refraining from eating will never bring a blessing. God wants a humble and contrite heart.

The Messiah and the Kingdom (Zechariah 9—14)

These chapters are full of promises of the coming Messiah and a worldwide kingdom. The prophet no longer pictures a city rebuilt on its old foundations, but a glorious city whose wall is the Lord. It is not armed for war, but is a city filled with peace, for the Prince of Peace reigns. He shall come the first time as the lowly One, riding upon a colt, the foal of a donkey (Zechariah 9:9).

But we see this lowly One becoming a mighty Sovereign (14:8-11). The Messiah in all His glory and might shall put all the enemies under His feet and He shall establish His kingdom in Jerusalem and sit upon the throne of David. "His rule will extend from sea to sea and from the River to the ends of the earth" (9:10).

If we would follow these chapters more closely, we would discover victory over all the enemies of Israel. Chapter 11 reveals the Shepherd who would seek to save Israel, but is rejected. He is sold for thirty pieces of silver, the price of a slave. This all foreshadowed Christ and His betrayal by Judas. Chapter 12 gives us the prophecy of the siege of Jerusalem by the Antichrist and his armies in the last days. Then we see the repentance of the Jews (v. 12) when they shall see Him whom they have pierced. The fountain shall be opened to the house of David for sin and uncleanness (13:1). Then the return of the Messiah upon the Mount of Olives, which shall cleave asunder by an earthquake (14:4), reminds us of the day when He left the earth at that same spot with the promise of His return (Acts 1:11). Finally He shall be King over the whole earth and all people shall be holy unto Him (Zechariah 14:9-20).

The blessings of the kingdom of Christ:

1. The extent of His kingdom—14:9
2. Abundant rain—10:1
3. Outpouring of the Spirit on Israel—12:10
4. Revelation of the "pierced" Messiah—12:10
5. Changes in Jerusalem—14:4-5,10-11
6. Kingdom set up on earth—14:9-15
7. Jerusalem center of worship—14:16-17.

Understanding Malachi

We have now come to the last book in the Old Testament. It sums up much of the history of the Old Testament. Martin Luther called John 3:16 "the little gospel." In the same way, we might speak of Malachi as the "little Old Testament." Malachi is the bridge between the Old and New Testaments. To show this, read Malachi 3:1. Who is "my messenger"? Read John 1:23 and Luke 3:3-4. A silence of 400 years lies between the voice of Malachi and the voice of one crying in the wilderness, "Prepare ye the way of the Lord."

The Old Testament closes with the word "curse." The New Testament closes with blessing—"The grace of the Lord Jesus be with God's people. Amen."

By this time, a hundred years or more had passed since the Jews had returned to Jerusalem after the captivity in Babylon. Malachi is the last prophet to speak to Israel in her own land. Israel here means all the remnant of Israel and Judah that returned after the exile. The first enthusiasm after the return from Babylon had spent itself. Following a period of revival (Nehemiah 10:28-39), the people had become cold religiously and lax morally.

The prophet Malachi came as a reformer, but he encourages while he rebukes. He dealt with a people perplexed, with spirits failing, whose faith in God seemed to be in danger of collapse. If they had not already become hostile to Jehovah, they were in real danger of becoming skeptical.

"Malachi" means "my messenger" (that is, of the Lord). Like the forerunner John the Baptist, of whom he prophesies, he was but a voice.

The Sins of the Priests (Malachi 1:1—2:9)

The skeptical attitude aroused among the people showed itself in religious coldness and social laxity. This is always true. The priests became irreverent and neglectful. Read Malachi 1:6,11-12. God said, "'Where is the honor due me?'...'Where is the respect due me?' says the Lord Almighty. 'It is you, O priests, who show contempt for my name.'" The prophet rebukes these careless priests for offering worthless animals in sacrifice to God that they would not offer to the governor. They stood in marked contrast to God's ideal for the priesthood. They had completely lost sight of their high calling and deserved the ignominy heaped upon them. They refused to work except for money. God's condemnation begins with the leaders (2:1-9). As long as the priests were openly unfit, what could be expected from the people at large? This resulted in a carelessness among God's people in keeping themselves separate from the heathen nations. Mixed marriages with women of outside tribes became common. Some men had not hesitated to divorce their Israelitish wives to make this possible (2:10-16).

The Sins of the People (Malachi 2:10—3:18)

What would you think of a person who deliberately held something before his eyes and then complained that he could see nothing? What would you suggest might quickly solve the difficulty? Well, this is just what Malachi had to do. The people of Israel declared that Jehovah did not love them as He said (Malachi 1:2). They could not see that His love had been of any special advantage to them.

Another result of the people's laxity of loyalty to God was in the growing prevalence of social sin (3:5). Malachi 3:7 reveals the religious indifference and skepticism of the people.

Sins Malachi rebuked:

Spiritless routine worship—1:6-8

Evil associations—2:10-12

Questioning Jehovah's justice—2:17—3:6

Robbing God—3:7-12

Impatience in waiting—3:17—4:3.

Are any of these your sins, too? Suppose we do find some of these sins in our daily lives, what are we to do? Confess them to Jehovah. Israel was troubled about the result of her confession. Malachi had to encourage the people by assuring them of Jehovah's wonderful love and giving the beautiful promise of Malachi 3:7. Turn to it and mark it in your Bible.

The children of Israel could depend on Jehovah to forgive. It was this same picture of the Father Jesus gave when He told of the prodigal's return. The father, seeing the boy while yet a great way off, ran out to meet him. This is ever God's attitude.

The Jewish people had been cured of idolatry, but they had grown careless and indifferent about many things. They had neglected the house of God. The priests had become lax. They were bringing inferior sacrifices to the Temple. They had robbed God of their tithes and offerings. They fell into social sins. They had become so selfish and covetous that Malachi dared boldly to challenge them with these words, "Will a man rob God?" (3:8).

The key that opens God's big blessing windows is your recognition of His ownership by giving back to Him a proper share of the money or the property He permits you to acquire. "Bring the whole tithe into the storehouse" (Malachi 3:10). The tenth (or tithe) is the outward recognition that everything belongs to God. We are to bring Him our whole selves—body, soul and spirit. Then He will accept us and open the windows of heaven to pour out His blessings.

Coming Things (Malachi 3—4)

Why does God permit such things? This attitude of the people was probably because of the feeling that the glowing promises of Haggai and Zechariah and of the other prophets had not been realized. They said that Jehovah did not seem to distinguish between good and bad people (Malachi 2:17). He blesses all alike, and evil people often flourish at the expense of their fellow citizens (3:14-15). What's the use of being good? Is this not one of the standing complaints of those who think they are good? They say, "What is God doing that He permits such things?" The answer to such a complaint is that Jehovah does care. He showed this to them by saying that one day He will send His messenger (John the Baptist) to prepare His way, then He will come in person "suddenly" and sit in judgment and separate the evil from the good (3:1). His judgment will be searching and effective "like a refiner's fire or a launderer's soap" (3:2-3). When God really gets ready to act, what will He do? The action will be final (3:1-3).

We find the burden of God's message by Malachi to His people stated in the second verse of the book, "'I have loved you,' says the Lord." What a message to a people who had sinned as Israel had and had spurned the love of Jehovah God. God is always sending His messenger before Him to prepare His way (3:1). He wants all His children to honor and adore Him. He longs to have us obey and worship Him. But who can stand the day of His appearing? And who can endure His purifying fire (3:2)? God's messenger will be a witness revealing our cruelty, our lies, our injustices, our double-dealing. This can be said of us today just as much as of the Jews of old. Jehovah's representative comes and finds us robbing Him of His due (3:2-5). Yet, Jehovah God is unchanging. He never forgets His promises of undying love and everlasting mercy.

Oh, how we need God's Malachi today to be sent before Him to prepare His way so that God's people may honor and adore Him. Malachi cries, "Back to God's house! Back to God's Word! Back to God's work! Back to God's grace!"

Each one may be like Malachi, a herald of the Christ whose coming we now await. Each one who loves and looks for Him may help prepare His way by the very manner of living and work.

Think of the needs of this day, the needs of the Church and the world. Is not formalism a just charge today against our churches—an outward observance without a wholehearted love? Are not we, too, offering gifts that cost nothing? Are we not robbing God in the matter of tithes?

Amid all the hypocrisy of the day, there were those in the Jewish community (a remnant) who still feared God and remained faithful. If we turn to Malachi 3:16 we will find this. Malachi longed to develop a strong body of enthusiastic believers who could influence his people's future. It is interesting to note that God bent His ear to hear His people speak about Him (3:16).

Close by reading aloud Malachi's solemn declaration concerning the second advent of Christ for which we wait, Malachi 3:16—4:3. Yes, the Sun of Righteousness will come with healing in His wings.

Chapter 26

A Quick Look at the Old Testament

Esther Through Malachi

Themes and Lessons

Esther

Theme: Jesus Christ is portrayed as our Advocate.
Outstanding Lesson: God will deliver His children!

Job

Theme: Jesus Christ is portrayed as our Redeemer.
Outstanding Lesson: Why do the righteous suffer?

Psalms

Theme: Jesus Christ is portrayed as our All in all.
Outstanding Lesson: Praise God!

Proverbs

Theme: Jesus Christ is portrayed as our Wisdom.
Outstanding Lesson: Get wisdom!

Ecclesiastes

Theme: Jesus Christ is portrayed as the End of all living.
Outstanding Lesson: Try wisdom!

Song of Solomon
Theme: Jesus Christ is portrayed as the Lover of our souls.
Outstanding Lesson: Love God!

Isaiah
Theme: Jesus Christ is portrayed as the Messiah.
Outstanding Lesson: Salvation is of God!

Jeremiah
Theme: Jesus Christ is portrayed as the Righteous Branch.
Outstanding Lesson: Go and tell!

Lamentations
Theme: Jesus Christ is portrayed as the Righteous Branch.
Outstanding Lesson: God's grace always shines!

Ezekiel
Theme: Jesus Christ is portrayed as the Son of man.
Outstanding Lesson: Judgment and restoration!

Daniel
Theme: Jesus Christ is portrayed as the Striking Stone.
Outstanding Lesson: God is sovereign!

Hosea
Theme: Jesus Christ is portrayed as the Healer of the backslider.
Outstanding Lesson: Return unto God!

Joel
Theme: Jesus Christ is portrayed as the Restorer.
Outstanding Lesson: Repent, for "the day of the Lord" is coming.

Amos
Theme: Jesus Christ is portrayed as the Heavenly Husbandman.
Outstanding Lesson: Prepare to meet your God!

Obadiah

Theme: Jesus Christ is portrayed as our Saviour.
Outstanding Lesson: Possess your possessions!

Jonah

Theme: Jesus Christ is portrayed as our Resurrection and Life.
Outstanding Lesson: Arise and go!

Micah

Theme: Jesus Christ is portrayed as a Witness against rebellious nations.
Outstanding Lesson: Hear Him!

Nahum

Theme: Jesus Christ is portrayed as a Stronghold in the day of trouble.
Outstanding Lesson: Beware, the Lord avenges!

Habakkuk

Theme: Jesus Christ is portrayed as the God of our salvation.
Outstanding Lesson: Live by faith!

Zephaniah

Theme: Jesus Christ is portrayed as a Jealous Lord.
Outstanding Lesson: God is mighty to save!

Haggai

Theme: Jesus Christ is portrayed as the Desire of all nations.
Outstanding Lesson: Build for God!

Zechariah

Theme: Jesus Christ is portrayed as the Righteous Branch.
Outstanding Lesson: Turn to Him!

Malachi

Theme: Jesus Christ is portrayed as the Sun of Righteousness.
Outstanding Lesson: Repent and return!

Four Hundred Years of Silence

By the time Old Testament history ended, a remnant of the Jewish exiles, chiefly of the tribe of Judah, had returned from Babylonia to the land under Zerubbabel, and about eighty years later another company had returned with Ezra. They were living peaceably in their own land with the Temple rebuilt and religious ceremonies set up.

The last three books of history in the Old Testament—Ezra, Nehemiah and Esther—give us the story of this time. They cover 100 years following the decree of Cyrus the king, allowing the Jewish people to return to their land (536-432 B.C.). (Read Ezra 1:1-4.)

From Nehemiah to the beginning of New Testament times, 400 years passed by. During this period, no biblical prophet spoke or wrote. In fact, it is called the "period of silence." As we come to the year when Jesus was born, it is important that we know some of the things that happened from the days of Nehemiah and Malachi to that time.

The Septuagint

Before Alexander the Great died, he divided his empire—which stretched from Greece to India—among his four generals, for he had no heirs to his throne. Egypt and all of the eastern Mediterranean, including Judah, went to his general Ptolemy. Great numbers of Jews at this time settled in Egypt, as well as other centers of culture, spreading everywhere the knowledge of their God and their hope of a Messiah.

During this time, about 285 B.C., the Old Testament began to be translated into Greek. This version of the Scriptures is called the *Septuagint*, meaning "seventy," because seventy noted Hebrew scholars did this great work. You will find it referred to by Roman numerals LXX.

The Jewish People Persecuted

Now the Syrian kingdom arose. In the conflicts between Syria and Egypt, Antiochus Epiphanes, king of Syria, seized Judea. He began a bitter persecution of the Jewish people. The Jews were forbidden by Antiochus Epiphanes to worship in the Temple and were compelled to eat the flesh of swine, which God through Moses had forbidden (Leviticus 11:1-8). Many courageously refused and a period of martyrdom began.

The cruelties of this terrible king, Antiochus Epiphanes, brought about the revolt of the Maccabees under the leadership of Mattathias. Aroused by the patriotism and religious ardor of Mattathias, a group of patriotic freedom fighters gathered about him and began an insurrection that spread rapidly. When he died, his son Judas took his place. In an attempt to crush this rebellion under the Maccabees, Antiochus was defeated in three deadly conflicts. The cause of Judas had seemed hopeless because his followers were untrained and without equipment, and they were opposed by the trained soldiers of a powerful king. But this band of ragged but loyal Jewish patriots, inspired by an undying faith in God, came out victorious!

The Roman Tribute

In 63 B.C., Rome gained possession of Judea, preparing the way and the time for Jesus to be born. The Jews had some political liberty, but were required to pay a yearly tax to the Roman government.

Part Two
The New Testament

The Gospels
Matthew • Mark • Luke • John

History
Acts

Letters of Paul
Romans • 1 Corinthians • 2 Corinthians • Galatians • Ephesians
Philippians • Colossians • 1 Thessalonians • 2 Thessalonians
1 Timothy • 2 Timothy • Titus • Philemon

General Letters
Hebrews • James • 1 Peter • 2 Peter
1, 2 and 3 John • Jude

Prophecy
Revelation

The Gospels
of The New Testament

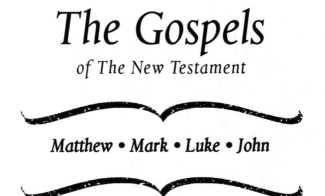

Matthew • Mark • Luke • John

Key Events of the Gospels

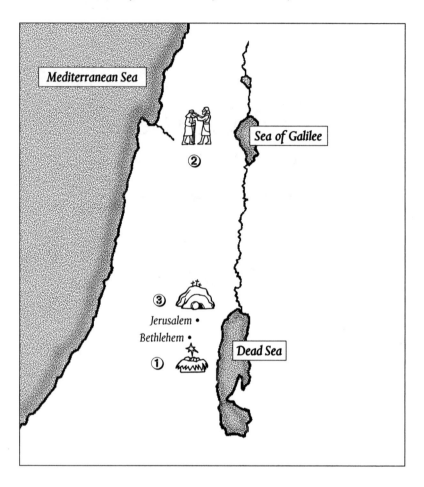

The Gospels: The Person of Jesus Christ

The Gospels record the ① birth, life, miracles, healing ministry ② , teachings, death and resurrection ③ of Jesus Christ. Each Gospel has a slightly different purpose and audience, but together they give us an amazingly clear picture of who Jesus Christ was in His earthly ministry, and they invite us to believe in the Savior of the world (John 4:42) who conquered sin, Satan and death on the cross.

Chapter 27

Understanding the Gospels

The Gospels Portray Jesus Christ, Our Savior and Lord

Selected Bible Readings

Sunday: The King Christ Jesus (Matthew 2:1-12; 21:1-11)
Monday: The Servant Christ Jesus (Mark 10:35-45; 2:1-22)
Tuesday: The Man Christ Jesus (Luke 4:1-13; John 19:4-13)
Wednesday: The God-Man (John 1:1-18; 3:1-16)
Thursday: Our Redeemer, Jesus Christ (John 19:16-42)
Friday: The Master, Jesus Christ (Matthew 4:18-25)
Saturday: Our Master, Jesus Christ (John 21:1-17)

Dr. Van Dyke (Henry Van Dyke, 1852-1933, Presbyterian minister and professor of English literature at Princeton) said, "If four witnesses should appear before a judge to give an account of a certain event, and each should tell exactly the same story in the same words, the judge would probably conclude, not that their testimony was exceptionally valuable, but that the only event which was certain beyond a doubt was that they had agreed to tell the same story. But if each man had told what he had seen, as he had seen it, then the evidence would be credible. And when we read the four Gospels, is not that exactly what we find? The four men tell the same story each in his own way."

The word "gospel" is derived from the two Anglo-Saxon words "God," meaning "good," and "spell," meaning "tidings" or "history."

The four writers of the Gospels are called "evangelists," from a Greek word meaning "bringer of good tidings." The first three Gospels, Matthew, Mark and Luke, are called the "Synoptic Gospels" because, unlike John, they give a synopsis of Christ's life. The word "synopsis" is derived from the two Greek words meaning "a view together, a collective view." So these three Gospels may be viewed together.

The Synoptic Gospels are striking in their similarities. They are equally striking in their differences. The Synoptics narrate Christ's ministry chiefly in Galilee; but John's Gospel stands in a class by itself. He tells of Christ's ministry in Judea. The Synoptics narrate His miracles, parables and addresses to the multitudes; John presents His deeper and more abstract discourses, His conversations and prayers. The three portray Christ in action; John portrays Him in meditation and communion.

He is here! The promised One has come! The One whom all the prophets have foretold, Jesus Christ, the Lord.

Every prophet in the Old Testament assured God's chosen people again and again that a Messiah should come who would be the King of the Jews. They therefore looked forward with passionate longing and patriotism to the coming of that King in pomp and power.

Expect to find in the Gospels "the one Moses wrote about in the Law, and about whom the prophets also wrote—Jesus" (John 1:45). But know that you will find Him infinitely more beautiful in person than any prophet's vision of Him.

We read in Isaiah 7:14: "Therefore the Lord himself will give you a sign: The virgin will be with child and will give birth to a son, and will call him Immanuel" (the name Immanuel means "God with us"). This is just the One the evangelists tell us about. The Gospels present Jesus in our midst. John says, "The Word became flesh and made his dwelling among us" (John 1:14). Think of God coming down to live with people! It seems the Gospels are the center of the whole Bible. All that the prophets have said leads us to our Lord's earthly life and work, and all that follows in the Epistles proceeds from them. The Gospels are the source.

The Gospels tell us WHEN and HOW Christ came.

The Epistles tell us WHY and FOR WHAT Christ came.

Notice where the four Gospels are placed. They stand at the close of the Old Testament and before the Epistles.

Dr. William H. Griffith Thomas (1861-1924, American New Testament scholar) suggests that we remember four words to help us link together the whole of God's revelation.

Preparation—In the Old Testament, God makes ready for the coming of the Messiah.

Manifestation—In the four Gospels, Christ enters the world, dies for the world and founds His Church.

Appropriation—In the Acts and Epistles, the ways are revealed in which the Lord Jesus was received, appropriated and applied in individual lives.

Consummation—In the book of Revelation, the outcome of God's perfect plan through Christ is revealed.

What Is the Gospel?

"Gospel" means "good news." The good news concerning Jesus, the Son of God, is given to us by four writers—Matthew, Mark, Luke and John—although there is but one gospel, the glad story of salvation through Jesus Christ our Lord. The word "gospel" is never used in the New Testament of a book. It always means "good news." When we speak of the Gospel of Luke, we ought to understand that it means the good news of Jesus Christ as recorded by Luke. Nevertheless, from the earliest times the term "Gospel" has been applied to each of the four narratives that record the life of Christ.

No doubt, originally the good news was oral. Men went from one place to another telling the glad story by word of mouth. After a while, a written record was necessary. More than one attempted this, with no success. See what Luke says in Luke 1:1-4:

> Many have undertaken to draw up an account of the things that have been fulfilled among us, just as they were handed down to us by those who from the first were eyewitnesses and servants of the word. Therefore, since I myself have carefully investigated everything from the beginning,

it seemed good also to me to write an orderly account for
you, most excellent Theophilus, so that you may know the
certainty of the things you have been taught.

There is but one gospel with four presentations. Four pictures
of one Christ are given. The combined gospel records set forth a
Personality rather than present a connected story of a life.

Why Four Gospels?

As everyone knows, there are four Gospels, but the question at
once arises, Why four? Why wouldn't one straightforward, continuous narrative have been enough? Would not this have been
simpler and clearer? Might this not have saved us from some of the
difficulties that have arisen in what some have said are conflicting
accounts?

The answer seems plain: Because one or two would not have
given us a sufficient portrayal of the life of Christ. There are four
distinct offices of Christ portrayed in the Gospels. He is presented as: King in Matthew, Servant in Mark, Son of Man in Luke, Son
of God in John.

It is true that each of the four Gospels has much in common
with the others. Each deals with Christ's earthly ministry, His
death and resurrection, His teachings and miracles, but each
Gospel has its differences. At once we see that each of the writers is trying to present a different picture of our one Lord.

Matthew deliberately adds to his account what Mark omits.
There is a lack of completeness about His life history in any one
of the four Gospels. Hear what John says in 21:25: "Jesus did many
other things as well. If every one of them were written down, I
suppose that even the whole world would not have room for the
books that would be written."

There are deliberate gaps that none of the evangelists profess-
es to fill in. For instance, all omit any account of the eighteen
years of Christ's life between the ages of twelve and thirty.
Although each Gospel is complete in itself, each is very selective;
only a few of His miracles are described and only a portion of His

teachings are given. Each evangelist has recorded that which is relevant and pertinent to his particular theme.

In the National Gallery in London, there are three representations on a single canvas of Charles I. In one, his head is turned to the right; in another, to the left; and in the center we find the full-face view. This is the story of this production. Van Dyck (Anthony Van Dyck, 1599-1641, the Flemish painter) painted them for Bernini (Giovanni Lorenzo Bernini, 1598-1680), the Roman sculptor, that he might by their help make a bust of the king. By combining the impressions so received, Bernini would be better able to produce a "speaking" likeness. One view would not have been enough.

It may be true that the Gospels were intended to serve the very purpose of these portraits. Each presents a different aspect of our Lord's life on earth. Together we have the complete picture. He was a King, but He was the Perfect Servant, too. He was the Son of Man, but we must not forget He was the Son of God.

There are four Gospels with one Christ, four accounts with one purpose, and four sketches of one Person.

Jesus in the Four Gospels

Master this outline and you will be familiar with the contents of the Gospels for life.

King—Matthew presents Jesus as King. It was written primarily for the Jew, for He is the Son of David. His royal genealogy is given in chapter 1. In chapters 5—7, in the Sermon on the Mount, we have the manifesto of the King, containing the laws of His kingdom.

Servant—Mark depicts Jesus as Servant, written to the Romans, there is no genealogy. Why? People are not interested in the genealogy of a servant. More miracles are found here than in any other Gospel. Romans cared little for words; far more for deeds.

Man—Luke sets forth Jesus as the perfect Man. It was written to the Greeks; His genealogy goes back to Adam, the first man, instead of to Abraham. As a perfect Man, He is seen much in prayer and with angels ministering to Him.

God—John portrays Jesus as the Son of God. Written to all who will believe, with the purpose of leading people to Christ (John 20:31), everything in this Gospel illustrates and demonstrates His divine relationship. The opening verse carries us back to "the beginning."

Dr. W. H. Griffith Thomas gives the pictures of the Gospels in this way:

> Matthew is concerned with the coming of a *Promised Savior.*
> Mark is concerned with the life of a *Powerful Savior.*
> Luke is concerned with the grace of a *Perfect Savior.*
> John is concerned with the possession of a *Personal Savior.*

Let us present another answer to the question, Why four Gospels? Scripture answers much for us. Many believe Scripture uses numbers with precision, accuracy and real meaning: seven is the perfect number; three is the number of the Godhead; forty is the number of testing. Four is the number of the earth. Look at a few illustrations. There are four points of the compass, north, east, south and west. There are four seasons of the year, spring, summer, autumn and winter. In the parable of the Sower, our Lord divided the field into four kinds of soil. Later He said, "The field is the world" (Matthew 13:38). If four is the earth number, how fitting that the Holy Spirit should have given us four Gospels in which to depict the earthly ministry of the heavenly One.

When we draw nearer, we see then good reason for four Gospels. Christ is the one glorious theme of them all, but each of the writers is absorbed with some special feature in Christ's character and office. Each evangelist takes some office and develops it with convincing power. Unfolding this particular view of the work of Christ stamps the design on each book.

Let us pause to say this: All the Gospels are bound up with the promises of the Messiah in the Old Testament. We cannot explain the Gospels apart from the great Messianic prophecies in the Old Testament.

The prophets have portrayed a magnificent picture of the Messiah. They have told of His offices, mission, birth, suffering, death, resurrection and glory. Let us consider the names and titles the prophets have bestowed upon Him.

He is called the King: Psalm 72; Isaiah 9:6-7; 32:1; Jeremiah 23:5; Zechariah 9:9; 14:9. These passages, among many others, tell of the kingly office of the Messiah. The prophets tell much of His kingdom and its extent, and of Christ's ultimate triumph.

He is called the Servant of Jehovah: Isaiah 42:1-7; 52:13-15; 53.

He is called the Man, the Son of Man: Genesis 3:15; 22:18; Isaiah 7:14-16; 9:6.

He is called God: Isaiah 9:6; 40:3-5; 47:4; Jeremiah 23:6. As these four, Jesus is set forth in the Gospels.

Types of People Then and Now

Christ was going to be presented to widely different types of people who made up the world. Each group of people was capable of appreciating one particular kind of presentation more than another.

Jewish people—The four groups of people in Jesus' day represent four types of people today. For example, the Jewish people had special training. They were steeped in the Old Testament Scripture and the prophets. Matthew writes the story of Jesus' life on earth especially for these people. If Jewish people were to be impressed with Jesus, they would need to be taught by one who understood their customs and way of thinking. Jewish people needed to know that this Jesus came to fulfill the prophecies of the Old Testament. Over and over again we read in Matthew, "And so was fulfilled what the Lord had said through the prophet."

We have the same type of people today. They revel in prophecies fulfilled and unfulfilled. They seek to know what the prophets have spoken, and how it is brought to pass.

Romans—Next came the Romans, masters of the world at that

time. Mark writes especially for Romans. The Romans knew nothing about Old Testament Scripture. They were not interested in prophecy being fulfilled. But they were vitally concerned about a remarkable Leader who had appeared in Judea. He had claimed more than ordinary authority and had possessed extra-ordinary powers. They wanted to hear more about this Jesus—what sort of a person He really was, what He had said and what He had done.

The Romans liked Mark's straightforward message. The word "and" is used in Mark 1,375 times (in the *KJV*). It moves on in a beauty and force all its own. Mark's Gospel is filled with deeds, not words. Clearly it is the Gospel of the Ministry of Christ.

The Romans of Jesus' day were like average businesspeople of today. They are not concerned at first about the genealogy of a king, but with a God "who is able," a God who can meet a person's every need. Mark is the business person's Gospel.

Greeks—Then there is Luke, the Greek doctor, who wrote to his own countrymen, who were lovers of beauty, poetry and culture. The Greeks lived in a world of large ideas. Their tastes were fastidious. The Gospel of Luke tells of the birth and childhood of Jesus. It gives the inspired songs connected with the life of Christ. We find the salutation of Elizabeth when Mary visited her (Luke 1:42-45). We hear the song of the virgin mother (Luke 1:46-55). Even Zacharias burst into praise when speech was restored to him (Luke 1:68-79). At the Savior's birth, a chorus of angel voices ring out (Luke 2:13-14), and then the shepherd's song of praise to God in Luke 2:20 is heard.

The Greek of Jesus' day was like the student and idealist today who is seeking after truth, for he or she believes that truth is the means to happiness.

All people—John's gospel is written to all people everywhere that they might believe that Jesus is the Christ. Christ is portrayed as the Son of God. This Gospel is filled with extraordinary claims that attest His divine character and mission.

The "all people" of John's day were like the masses today who need Christ. They include the "whosoever" who will believe on the Lord Jesus because they have a sense of need and want to receive the gift of eternal life through Jesus Christ the Lord.

Keys to the Gospels

Front-Door Keys

God has hung the key to the Gospel of Matthew right over the entrance. The book opens thus: "A record of the genealogy of Jesus Christ the son of David, the son of Abraham" (Matthew 1:1). This shows His covenant position as the Son of Abraham (see Genesis 12:1-3; Galatians 3:16), and His royal position as Son of David.

Matthew is presenting Christ as King; he gives the royal genealogy in the first seventeen verses. A king is not chosen by popular ballot, but by birth.

Turn now to Mark. See how this book opens. No genealogy is given. The reason is that Jesus is portrayed as a Servant, and no one is interested in the pedigree of a servant.

Turn to Luke. Is a genealogy given? See Luke 3:23. Matthew traces Christ's line back to Abraham and David to show He was a Jew and of the royal line. Luke traces His line back to Adam. Christ is presented as the ideal Man. He was of the line of Adam.

Turn to John. How does this book open? No genealogy, but "In the beginning was the Word, and the Word was with God, and the Word was God." Christ is portrayed as God in John.

Back-Door Keys

Now let us see how the Gospels close. Turn to Matthew 28:18-20. Hear the King commanding and commissioning His disciples. The Messiah is still on earth, for it is on earth and not in heaven that the Son of David shall reign in glory. "'All authority in heaven and on earth has been given to me. Therefore go and make disciples of all nations, baptizing them in the name of the Father and of the Son and of the Holy Spirit, and teaching them to obey everything I have commanded you. And surely I am with you always, to the very end of the age.'"

Now look at the close of Mark. It is very significant and appropriate. "Then the disciples went out and preached everywhere, and the Lord worked with them and confirmed his word by the signs that accompanied it" (16:20). Jesus, the Servant, is pictured as still laboring with His disciples.

Luke ends in a different way. Jesus, the perfect Man, is ascending to the Father. Notice what Luke says in 24:51: "While he was blessing them, he left them and was taken up into heaven."

The closing verse of John is significant: "Jesus did many other things as well. If every one of them were written down, I suppose that even the whole world would not have room for the books that would be written" (21:25). Truly, "No one ever spoke the way this man does" (7:46)! for He was the very Son of God.

Chapter 28

Understanding Matthew

Matthew Portrays Jesus Christ, the Promised Messiah

Selected Bible Readings

Sunday: The King Born (Matthew 1:18—2:23)
Monday: The King Begins Work (Matthew 4:1-25)
Tuesday: The Kings States Kingdom Laws (Matthew 5:1-17,41-48; 6:19-34)
Wednesday: The King and His Followers (Matthew 10:1-33)
Thursday: The Kingdom Mysteries (Matthew 13:1-52)
Friday: The King Offers Himself as King (Matthew 21:1-11)
Saturday: The King Will Return (Matthew 25:14-16)

Matthew has a special object in his Gospel to show the Jews that Jesus is the long-expected Messiah, the Son of David, and that His life fulfilled the Old Testament prophecies. The purpose is given in the first verse. Matthew is "A record of the genealogy of Jesus Christ the son of David, the son of Abraham." This statement links Christ with two of the great covenants God made with David and Abraham. God's covenant with David consisted of the promise of a King to sit upon his throne forever (2 Samuel 7:8-13). God's covenant with Abraham promised that through him should all families of the earth be blessed (Genesis 12:3). David's son was a King. Abraham's son was a Sacrifice. Matthew opens with the birth of a King and closes with the offering of a Sacrifice.

From the beginning, Jesus is associated with the Jewish nation. Matthew used wisdom in not alienating the Jews who might read the story. He is convincing them that this One fulfilled every prophecy spoken concerning their promised Messiah. He quotes freely from the Old Testament more than any of the other evangelists. Twenty-nine such quotations are given. Thirteen times he says that this or that event took place "to fulfill what the Lord had said through the prophet" (Matthew 1:22).

Matthew links us up with the Old Testament. On every page he is trying to connect the Gospel with the prophets and show that all of their teaching is being fulfilled in the person and kingdom of Jesus Christ.

It is difficult for us to appreciate how great the transition is from the old to the new. It seemed to the Jews that they must give up their tradition and orthodoxy and accept another creed. Matthew, in his Gospel, and Paul, especially in Galatians, show the Jewish believers in Jesus that they were not giving up their old faith, but rather were only giving up types and shadows for the real substance.

Matthew was well acquainted with Jewish history and customs. He speaks of farming and fishing and the housekeeping of his people in the seven parables in chapter 13. He knew this intimate record would strike responsive chords in the hearts of the Jewish people.

As you read Matthew, get a clear and comprehensive view of the entire Gospel. Keep in mind the Messianic character of this Gospel. Note the balance between Jesus' ministry and teaching. We find the genealogy of the King; His birth in Bethlehem, the city of David, according to Micah's prophecy (Micah 5:2); the coming of the forerunner, John the Baptist, as Malachi predicted (Malachi 3:1); the ministry of the King; His rejection by Israel; and the promise of His coming again in power and glory.

The author is no doubt a Jewish believer in Jesus (Matthew 9:9; 10:3). Matthew, whose name means "gift of the Lord," was a tax collector at Capernaum under the Roman law when Jesus chose him as one of the twelve disciples. His name is found in all the lists of the twelve, though Mark and Luke give his other name, Levi. The only word the author speaks about himself is that he was a "publican" *(KJV)*, which was then a term of reproach, as the term "politician" so often denotes today. The other evangelists tell about the great feast he gave Jesus, and record the significant fact that he left all and followed Him. No doubt he was a man of means.

Matthew breaks the silence of 400 years between Malachi's prophecy and the announcement of the birth of Jesus. Israel was under the domination of the Roman Empire. No man of "the house of David" had been allowed to sit upon the throne for 600 years.

Herod was not the king of Israel, but a governor of Judea, appointed by the Emperor of Rome. The man who really had the throne-rights of the house of David was Joseph, the carpenter, who became the husband of Mary. See the genealogy of Joseph in Matthew 1, and notice especially one name, Jechonias (Jeconiah), in verse 11. If Joseph had been Jesus' father according to the flesh, He could never have occupied the throne, for God's Word barred the way. There had been a curse on this royal line since the days of Jeconiah. In Jeremiah 22:30 we read, "This is what the Lord says: 'Record this man as if childless, a man who will not prosper in his lifetime, for none of his offspring will prosper, none will sit on the throne of David or rule anymore in Judah.'" Joseph was in the line of this curse. Hence, if Christ had been Joseph's son, He could not have sat on David's throne.

But we find another genealogy in Luke 3. This is Mary's line back to David through Nathan, not Jeconiah (Luke 3:31). There was no curse on this line. To Mary, God said, "Do not be afraid, Mary, you have found favor with God. You will be with child and give birth to a son, and you are to give him the name Jesus. He will be great and will be called the Son of the Most High. The Lord God will give him the throne of his father David, and he will reign over the house of Jacob forever; his kingdom will never end" (Luke 1:30-33).

Now the silence is broken and the coming of the Messiah declared.

The book of Matthew follows after the Old Testament and is the beginning of the New. It is the connecting link between the books. It is written for the Jews and it is fittingly placed. It takes for granted that the course of events is known to its readers. The Old Testament had closed with the chosen nation looking for their long-promised King, their Messiah. Matthew's Gospel shows that Jesus was that King. It is the Gospel of fulfillment.

Matthew presents the Lord Jesus in a distinctly Jewish relationship. Only in this one of the four Gospels do we find a record of the Messiah's declaration, "I was sent only to the lost sheep of Israel" (Matthew 15:24). What did His own people do with Him? (See John 1:11.)

In numerical position, the book of Matthew is the fortieth in the canon. Thirty-nine books in the Old Testament, then Matthew. Forty is always a number of testing or probation in Scripture. Jesus was tempted of the devil forty days; Israel was in the wilderness forty years; David was king forty years; Moses was in a palace forty years, then on the back side of a desert for forty years. What other instances of this number forty do you remember in Scripture? Look it up in your concordance.

In this fortieth book of the Bible, Israel is in the place of probation and testing by the presence of the Messiah in her midst. Christ is presented as King to the Jews, but most of the religious leaders rejected Him not only as their Messiah, but also as their Savior (Matthew 16:21).

Coming of the King *(Matthew 1:1—2:23)*

Jesus would have made it into any book of notables. Matthew is the Gospel of the Messiah, God's anointed One. The main purpose of the Spirit in this book is to show that Jesus of Nazareth is the predicted Messiah, the Deliverer of whom Moses and the prophets wrote. "whose origins are from of old, from ancient times" (Micah 5:2). He is the child that was to be born, the Son given, of whom Isaiah speaks who shall be called "Wonderful Counselor, Mighty God, Everlasting Father, Prince of Peace" (Isaiah 9:6).

The maps of the world and the calendars of time tell of Christ's birthplace and birthday. Jesus was born in Bethlehem of Judea (Micah 5:2; Matthew 2:1), in the days of Herod the king. We know this place and this king. We don't have to build the story out of the imagination. We are given names and dates. Christianity is a historical religion. The Gospel does not begin with, "Once upon a time," but starts with "Bethlehem in Judea." The town is there, so we can know the very place where Jesus was born.

The time is definite, "in the days of Herod the king." History knows Herod. There is nothing mythical about this monster of iniquity.

These statements are facts and no critic or unbeliever can doubt them. The Gospel narrative sets its record in the solid foundation of history. We are not building our faith on a myth, but substantial fact. This thing was not done in a corner, but in the broad daylight, and it is not afraid of the geographer's map and the historian's pen.

The story of the birth of Jesus in Matthew differs from the record in Luke. They complement each other. While there is much untold, God has told us all we need to know. Jesus' earthly life began in a stable. His cradle was a manger. His family and associates were humble folk. He came as a helpless babe. How human was our Lord! But Jesus was heralded by an archangel, welcomed by an angel choir and worshiped by earth's wisest philosophers! How divine was our Lord!

Most young people, when they begin reading Matthew with its "begats" *(KJV)* and Luke 3:23-38 with its "the son of's," wonder what these are all about. We ought to realize that if they were included in Scripture, they were put there for a purpose. We want to look in this lesson at these two genealogies.

A genealogy is "the history of the descent of an individual or family from an ancestor" (Webster). There are two genealogies of Christ: Matthew 1:1-17 and Luke 3:23-38. They are not alike, and the reason is that each traces the descent of Christ for different purposes.

Matthew traces Jesus' line back to Abraham and David to show that He was a Jew (coming from David). Luke traces Jesus' line back to Adam to show that He belonged to the human race.

Matthew shows Jesus as of royal descent, the King, the Messiah, the Lion of the tribe of Judah, the promised Ruler of Israel. Luke shows Jesus as of human lineage, the ideal Man, born of woman.

You will find that these pictures of Jesus are kept all through each Gospel—Matthew portraying Him as Messiah, Luke as Man.

Why are we concerned about these genealogies? Because they give us the key to the whole life of Christ. They show us from the very start that He was not just another man, but that He was descended from a royal family, and there was a king's blood in His veins. If He were not a King, He could not claim the ruler-ship of our lives. If He were not a Man, He could not know "our sorrows" and "be acquainted with our griefs."

Go through Matthew and follow this trail of the King:

A King's name—"They will call him Immanuel" (1:23).

A King's position—"For out of you will come a ruler who will be the shepherd of my people Israel" (2:6).

A King's announcement—"Prepare the way for the Lord, make straight paths for him" (3:3).

A King's coronation—"This is my Son, whom I love; with him I am well pleased" (3:17).

A King's due respect—"Worship the Lord your God, and serve him only" (4:10).

A King's proclamation—"and he began to teach them" (5:2). "He taught as one who had authority" (7:29).

A King's loyalty—"He who is not with me is against me, and he who does not gather with me scatters" (12:30).

A King's enemies—"From that time on Jesus began to explain to his disciples that he must go to Jerusalem and suffer many things at the hands of the elders, chief priests and teachers of the law" (16:21).

A King's love—"The Son of Man did not come to be served, but to serve, and to give his life as a ransom for many" (20:28).

A King's glory—"When the Son of Man comes...Then the King will say...'Come, you who are blessed by my Father; take your inheritance'" (25:31,34).

A King's sacrifice—"When they had crucified him...they placed the written charge against him: THIS IS JESUS, THE KING OF THE JEWS" (27:35,37).

A King's victory—"He is not here; he has risen, just as he said" (28:6).

Matthew alone tells of the visit of the wise men from the East. These were Persian magi, scholars, students of the stars. They came to worship and honor a King. These wise men did not come inquir-ing. "Where is He that is born the Savior of the world?" but,

"Where is the one who has been born king of the Jews?" (2:2).

Mark, Luke and John are silent about the wise men because they are not recording the birth of a king. The holy, sacred star had halted over a manger in Bethlehem to tell of Christ's birth. The whole world at this time was expecting the advent of some great One. "Where is the one who has been born king of the Jews?" was the question on every lip. With all the prophecies that had been made to Israel, neither the world nor Israel could be criticized for expecting a King who would rule the earth from David's throne (Jeremiah 23:3-6; 30:8-10; 33:14-16,25-26; Ezekiel 37:21; Isaiah 9:7; Hosea 3:4-5).

The priests knew where Christ was to be born, but they did not know Christ when He was born.

The wise men were led to a Person, not a creed.

The adoration of the wise men foreshadowed Christ's universal dominion. Some day "every knee should bow...and every tongue confess that Jesus Christ is Lord, to the glory of God the Father" (Philippians 2:10-11). "He will rule from sea to sea and from the River to the ends of the earth" (Psalm 72:8).

Paul tells us in Galatians 4:4-5, "When the time had fully come, God sent his Son, born of a woman, born under law, to redeem those under law, that we might receive the full rights of sons." Jesus came to be the world's Savior.

The birth of Jesus was followed by twelve years of silence until His visit with the doctors in Jerusalem. Then silence shut Him in again, with only the word "carpenter" (Matthew 13:55; Mark 6:3) to throw any light upon the next eighteen years, and let us know what He was doing. Jesus took thirty years of preparation for three years of ministry.

Proclamation of the Kingdom (Matthew 3:1—16:20)

John the Baptist had another name. As the prophet Isaiah began to unfold the real message of his book—the coming of the Messiah, Servant of Jehovah—he introduced a character known simply as a "voice." "A voice of one calling: 'In the desert prepare the way for the Lord; make straight in the wilderness a highway for our God'" (Isaiah 40:3). This "voice," although unnamed here, is to be the herald of Jesus Christ. His two functions—that of voice and that of messenger (Malachi 3:1)—are all that the Old Testament tells us of John the Baptist. But it is much. It is indeed wonderful not only that Christ should have been foretold all through the Scriptures, but that His forerunner, John the Baptist, also is described.

In Matthew we hear the "voice": "Repent, for the kingdom of heaven is near. This is he who was spoken of through the prophet Isaiah: 'A voice of one calling in the desert, "Prepare the way for the Lord, make straight paths for him"'" (Matthew 3:2-3).

The King must be announced! It was the duty of this herald to go before the King, as a Roman officer before his ruler, and command that the roads be repaired over which his Master would travel. John the Baptist did this. He showed that the spiritual roads of the lives of men and women and nations were full of the chuckholes of sin and sharp turns of iniquity, and needed rebuilding and straightening.

We see the King stepping from His personal and private life into His public ministry (Matthew 4). He is facing a crisis. Satan met Him. After the benediction the Father had put upon Him at His baptism when He said, "This is my Son, whom I love; with him I am well pleased" (Matthew 3:17). Jesus comes forth to carry out the plans for which He came into the world. He was led into the wilderness to face the first major conflict of His public ministry.

Notice that Satan offered Jesus a shortcut to that universal Kingdom He had come to gain through the long and painful way of the cross; but Christ came to be a Savior first, then a King. How strong is the temptation to take a shortcut to our ambitions! Jesus stood victor, His shield undented and untarnished. He went forth to conquer all other temptations until His final victory and ascension to heaven as Lord of all. (See 1 Corinthians 10:13.)

The Kingdom Laws

Every kingdom has laws and standards to exercise authority over its subjects. The kingdom of heaven is no exception. Jesus declared that He came not to destroy the law, but to fulfill it. The old law was good in its day. Moses and the prophets were far in advance of their time. They were pioneers. Jesus did not destroy this old law, but He treated it as rudimentary and not as perfect and final.

Jesus says any reform that starts on the outside and works in is beginning at the wrong end. Christ starts on the inside and works out. The only way of getting a good life is first getting a good heart.

From the lofty pulpit of a mountain, Jesus preached the sermon that contains the laws of His kingdom (Matthew 5—7). Read through these chapters and refresh your memory about this most wonderful of Jesus' discourses. It is filled with teaching. After more than 2,000 years, this Sermon on the Mount has lost none of its majesty or power. The teachings of this sermon overtop all human teachings. The world has not yet caught up with its simplest ideals and requirements.

Many a person who is not a Christian claims that the Sermon on the Mount is his religion. How little the person understands the depth of its meaning. It is important that we do not simply praise this rule as a wonderful theory, but that we actually practice it in our own lives. If we let this rule operate in our lives, it will change all our personal relations, heal our social wounds, solve every dispute between nations, yes, set the whole world in order. The root of this law is kindness. It is true, if human society would have its standards as theirs, the world would be set in order. One day filled with kindness would be a bit of heaven. Love would reign instead of lawlessness. Christ shows us that sin lies not just in committing the act, but in the motive behind it as well. (See Matthew 5:21-22,27-28.) No one can expect forgiveness who does not forgive (6:12,14-15). Has anyone yet ever fathomed the depth of Matthew 7:12? It is easy to read; it is hard to do.

Jesus preached that the kingdom of heaven is "near" ("at hand," *KJV*). He set forth the condition for entrance, its laws, its privileges and rewards. The Sermon on the Mount sets forth the constitution of the Kingdom. Fourteen times the King says, "I tell you." Mark them in your Bible. This will reveal Jesus' authority as He deals with the law of Moses. People must not only keep the law outwardly, but in spirit as well. Notice the effect upon the people. "When Jesus had finished saying these things, the crowds were amazed at his teaching, because he taught as one who had authority, and not as their teachers of the law" (Matthew 7:28-29).

The King's Power
We find the King worked amazing special miracles (Matthew 8—9). He met human needs. There are twelve astonishing miracles in these two chapters. What are they? After Jesus had performed the miracles in chapter 12, "All the people were astonished and said, 'Could this be the Son of David?'" (12:23).

The critical scribes now thrust themselves into the scene and passed their hostile judgment on the actions of Jesus (9:3).

The kingdom was proclaimed "at hand" because the King Himself was there.

The King's Cabinet
Jesus not only preached Himself, but He also gathered others around Him. It was necessary to organize His kingdom, to put it on a wider and more permanent basis. A king must have subjects. He would reflect His light through human instruments. He says, "You are the light of the world" (5:14). Jesus still has a great message for the world and He needs us to carry it. Spiritual ideas cannot stalk alone through the world and be of any value. They must be clothed with men and women and institutions who will serve as hearts and brains, hands and feet to carry them out. This is what Jesus was doing. He was calling men and women into His companionship to train them to carry on His work.

Where did Jesus find His helpers? Not in the Temple among the doctors or priests, nor in the colleges of Jerusalem. He found them on the seashore mending their nets. Jesus did not call many mighty or noble, but rather chose the foolish things of the world to confound the wise (1 Corinthians 1:27).

A list of the disciples is given in Matthew 10:2-4. This is probably the most important catalogue of names in the world. These men were given a work to do that would make winning battles and founding empires seem of small consequence. We find their great message was the kingdom of heaven. "As you go, preach this message: 'The kingdom of heaven is near'" (10:7). Their tremendous mission was to start it.

Note some of the warnings and instructions for the disciples Jesus stated in Matthew 10. What were they? If these requirements of discipleship hold true today, could you call yourself a disciple? Consider Christ's words thoughtfully in Matthew 10:32-33.

The Kingdom of Heaven

The word "kingdom" occurs some fifty-five times in Matthew, for this is the Gospel of the King. The expression "kingdom of heaven" is found thirty-five times here and nowhere else in the Gospels. Of the fifteen parables recorded in Matthew, all but three begin, "The kingdom of heaven is like..."

Jewish people understood the term "kingdom of heaven." Neither Jesus nor John defined it. At Sinai, God said to Israel, "You will be for me a kingdom of priests and a holy nation" (Exodus 19:6). Israel at first was a theocracy. God was their King; they formed His kingdom. The prophets had referred to the Messianic kingdom again and again.

Jesus likened the kingdom of heaven to (Matthew 13):

• The sower
• The weeds
• A mustard seed
• A net
• Yeast in the dough
• A hidden treasure
• A pearl of great value.

These parables, called "the mysteries of the kingdom of heaven" (13:11), describe what the result of the presence of the gospel of Christ in the world will be during this present age until the time of His return when He will gather the harvest (13:40-43). We see no bright picture of a converted world. Weeds shall be mixed with the wheat, good fish and bad, yeast in the loaf. (Yeast, or leaven, is often a symbol of sin. The Spirit never uses yeast as a type of anything good. Look this up in your concordance and determine this for yourself.) Then there is an abnormal growth of the mustard seed that admits "birds of the air" to lodge in its branches. This is Christendom. Only Christ can determine what is good and what is bad, and at the harvest He will divide. If we are to have a kingdom on this earth, with the laws which Christ set down, then we must have the King. Some day Christ will come in power and great glory and establish His throne on this earth. We will have peace when the Prince of Peace reigns!

Rejection of the King
(Matthew 16:21—20:34)

The sad story reads that Christ "came to that which was his own, but his own did not receive him" (John 1:11). The gospel of the kingdom was first preached to those who should have been most prepared, the children of Israel. And although many came to believe in Jesus as Messiah, as a whole the people rejected their King. From Matthew 12 on we see much controversy among the leaders concerning Jesus.

Jesus announced that the kingdom should be taken away from the Jewish people and given to another nation. "Therefore I tell you that the kingdom of God will be taken away from you and given to a people who will produce its fruit" (Matthew 21:43). The announcement offended the rulers, and "they looked for a way to arrest him" (21:46).

Our Lord told Nicodemus the requirement for entrance into the kingdom of heaven (John 3:3-7,16). "Whoever" will believe may enjoy its privileges and blessings. The kingdom is for the Gentile as well as the Jew.

Why did the Jewish leaders and many of the people refuse the Kingdom? The world today is longing intensely for the golden age. A millennium of peace and rest is the great desire of diplomats and rulers. But they want it in their own way and on their own terms. They desire to bring it about by their own efforts. They have no longing for a millennium brought about by the personal return of the Lord Jesus Christ. It was just so with the people in the days of John the Baptist.

Have you put Christ on the throne of your life? Have you the peace you long for? Have you accepted Christ's terms for your life?

The Church Promised

We find Jesus with His disciples up north in Caesarea Philippi, apparently with the object of having a private interview with them in which He would disclose a great truth (Matthew 16).

Only in Matthew's Gospel is the Church named. When the kingdom was rejected we find a change in the teachings of Jesus. He began to talk about the Church instead of the Kingdom (16:18). "Church" comes from the word *ecclesia*, which means "called out ones." Because all would not believe on Him, Christ said He was calling out anyone, Jew or Gentile, to belong to His Church, which is His body. He began to build a new edifice, a new body of people, which would include both Jews and Gentiles (Ephesians 2:14-18).

Life's Most Important Question

When they were far away from the busy scene in which they lived, Jesus asked His disciples the question: "Who do people say the Son of Man is?" (Matthew 16:13).

This is the important question today! First asked by an obscure Galilean in that far-off solitude, it has come thundering down through the centuries and has become the mightiest question in the world today. What do you think of Christ? What we think determines what we do and are. The ideas we hold about industry, wealth, government, morals and religion mold society and alter lives. So what we think of Christ is the master force in the world today and more than anything else influences our lives and thought.

The disciples gave the answers others were giving. The answers then were as varied as they are now. All agreed that Jesus was an extraordinary person, at least a prophet or a person who had an element of the supernatural. People's opinions of Christ are high. The answer that Jesus was a myth, a dupe or an impostor is no longer tolerated.

Jesus now turned the general question into the sharp personal inquiry. "But whom say ye that I am?" Ask yourself this question. Important as the general question is, far more important to each one of us is this personal question. No one can escape it. A neutral answer is impossible. He is either God or an impostor.

Life's Most Important Answer

"You are the Christ, the Son of the living God!" exclaimed the impulsive, fervent Peter. It grasps Christ as the Messiah, the fulfillment of the prophecies of the old Hebrew prophets. This confession is great because it exalts Christ as the Son of God and lifts Him above humanity and crowns Him with deity. From now on He reveals to this handful of disciples new truths about His teachings. He said to Peter and the disciples after this answer concerning who He was, "on this rock I will build my church." This is what Christ was going to do—build a Church of which He Himself was to be the chief cornerstone (Ephesians 2:20). This Church was born on Pentecost (Acts 2).

For the first time, the fateful shadow of the Cross fell across the path of the disciples. From this time on, Jesus began to draw back the curtain that veiled the future and to show His disciples the things that would come to pass. He saw His path running to Jerusalem into the awful hatred of the priests and Pharisees and then on to the terrible cross, but He saw the glory of the resurrection morning (Matthew 16:21).

Jesus did not reveal these things until His disciples were ready to bear it. God often in His mercy hides the future from us.

Triumph of the King (Matthew 21:1—28:20)

On the morning of Palm Sunday, there was a stir in Bethany and along the road leading to Jerusalem. It was understood that Jesus was to enter the city that day. The people were gathering in crowds. A colt was procured and the disciples, having thrown their robes over it, placed Jesus upon it, and the procession started. This little parade could not have been compared in magnificence with many a procession that has attended the coronation of a king or the inauguration of a president; but it meant much more for the world. Jesus for the first time permitted a public recognition and celebration of His rights as Messiah-King. The end was approaching with awful swiftness and He must offer Himself as Messiah, even if only to be rejected.

In their enthusiasm, the people tore off branches from the

palm and olive trees and carpeted the highway, while shouts rang through the air. They believed in Jesus, and with all their warm Middle Eastern enthusiasm were not ashamed of their King. In answer to the crowds who asked, "Who is this?" they boldly answered, "This is the prophet, Jesus, from Nazareth of Galilee." It took courage to say that in Jerusalem. Jesus was not entering the city as a triumphant conqueror as the Romans had done. No sword was in His hand. Over Him floated no bloodstained banner. His mission was salvation!

In the evening the crowds dispersed, and Jesus quietly returned to Bethany. Apparently nothing in the way of making Jesus King had been accomplished. His kingdom came not with observation or pageantry. His hour had not yet come. Christ must be Savior first, then come again as King of kings and Lord of lords.

Christ's authority was brought into question as He went into the Temple and ordered the merchants out, overturning their tables and telling them that they had made the house of God a den of thieves. A bitter controversy followed. "Then the Pharisees went out and laid plans to trap him in his words" (Matthew 22:15). He bade farewell to Jerusalem until He would come again to sit on David's throne.

The Future of the Kingdom

When Jesus delivered His Mount Olivet discourse, He foretold the condition of the world after His ascension until He comes back in glory to judge the nations according to their treatment of "His brothers," the Jewish people (Matthew 25:31-46). This is not the judgment of the Great White Throne, which is the judgment of the wicked dead. Neither is it the judgment seat of Christ (2 Corinthians 5:10), which is the judgment of saints according to their works. It is the judgment of Gentile nations concerning their attitude toward God's people.

Much of Jesus' discourse in Matthew 24 and 25 is devoted to Christ's second coming. He exhorts us to be ready in the parables of the faithful servant (24:45-51), the ten virgins (25:1-13) and of the talents (25:14-30).

The Death and Resurrection of the King

We have been passing through some of the highlights in the life of Jesus; now we step into the shadows as we enter Gethsemane. We see the Son of Abraham, the Sacrifice, dying that all the nations of the earth might be blessed by Him. Jesus was slain because He claimed to be the King of Israel. He was raised from the dead because He was the King (Acts 2:30-36). Although a large number of disciples believed in Jesus and followed Him, the opposition of the religious leaders was bitter and they determined to put Him to death. On the grounds of blasphemy, and of claiming to be the King of the Jews, thus making Himself the enemy of the Roman emperor, Jesus was delivered up by Pilate to be crucified.

Matthew is not alone in his record of the terrible circumstances of the Savior's passion; but he makes us feel that in the mock array—the crown of thorns, the sceptre, the title over the cross—we have a witness, though it be only scorn, to the kingly claim.

After hanging on the cruel tree for six hours, the Savior died, not from physical suffering alone but of a broken heart, for He bore the sins of the whole world. We hear His triumphant cry, "It is finished!" He paid the debt of sin and became the world's Redeemer!

Redemption Cost a Great Price!

The mode of the Messiah's death had been foreshadowed by various types and symbols in the Old Testament. The brazen serpent in the wilderness signified that He was to be lifted up; the lamb upon the temple altar that His blood must be shed. His hands and His feet were to be pierced; He was to be wounded and tormented; His ears were to be filled with revilings; upon His robe were lots to be cast and vinegar was to be given Him to drink. All of these incidents at the Messiah's death had been foretold in Jewish prophecy. But this is not all of the redemption story. Jesus was put in Joseph's tomb, and on the third day He arose, as He had said. This is the supreme test of His kingship. People thought He was dead and His kingdom had failed. By His resurrection,

Christ assured His disciples that the King still lived and that one day He will come back to establish His kingdom on earth.

The ascension of Jesus is not recorded in Matthew. The curtain falls with the Messiah still on earth, for it is on earth that the Son of David is yet to reign in glory. The last time the Jews saw Christ He was on the Mount of Olives. The next time they see Him He will be on the Mount of Olives! (See Zechariah 14:4; Acts 1:11.)

A Worldwide Commission

Jesus announced His program and a crisis hour was struck in history. The climax is found in His great commission: "'All authority in heaven and on earth has been given to me. Therefore go and make disciples of all nations, baptizing them in the name of the Father and of the Son and of the Holy Spirit, and teaching them to obey everything I have commanded you. And surely I am with you always, to the very end of the age'" (Matthew 28:18-20).

On what mission were they sent? To overrun the world with armies and make people submit under the sword? No, but to "make disciples of all nations."

From the mountaintop of His ascension, His disciples started forth on this mission, radiating from that center, and they have gone on until they have everywhere reached the rim of the world. Christian faith is no national or racial religion. It knows no bounds of mountain or sea, but it envelops the globe.

Chapter 29

Understanding Mark

Mark Portrays Jesus Christ, the Servant of God

Selected Bible Readings

Sunday:	The Servant's Coming and Testing (Mark 1:1-20)
Monday:	The Servant Working (Mark 2:1—3:25)
Tuesday:	The Servant Speaking (Mark 4:1—6:13)
Wednesday:	The Servant's Miracles (Mark 6:32—8:26)
Thursday:	The Servant's Revelation (Mark 8:27—10:34)
Friday:	The Servant's Rejection (Mark 11:1—12:44)
Saturday:	The Servant's Death and Triumph (Mark 14:1—16:20)

John, whose surname was Mark, is the writer of the Gospel of Mark (Acts 12:12,25). He was the son of Mary, and cousin of Barnabas (Colossians 4:10), and likely a native of Jerusalem. He accompanied Paul and Barnabas to Antioch, and was the cause of a serious disagreement between them (Acts 12:25; 13:5). Then he left them, probably on account of hardships (Acts 13:13). Finally he became a great help to Paul (Colossians 4:10-11; 2 Timothy 4:11). It is believed that the disciples met in the Upper Room of Mark's mother's house in Jerusalem. Peter was the means of Mark's conversion, and affectionately speaks of him as "my son" (1 Peter 5:13). We see the influence of the teaching of Peter in this Gospel.

If we turn to Mark 10:45, we can quite easily determine Mark's object in writing his Gospel. "For even the Son of Man did not come to be served, but to serve, and to give his life as a ransom for many." Unlike Matthew, Mark was not trying to prove certain statements and prophecies concerning Jesus. His only object in writing was to tell clearly certain facts about Jesus, His deeds more especially than His words. That Jesus is the Son of God he proves, not by declaring how He came to earth, but by showing what He accomplished during His brief career on this earth, how His coming changed the world.

There is a general agreement that Mark's Gospel was written for Roman readers. The Roman culture contrasted in many ways with the Jewish. The Romans highly valued strong common sense. Their religion had to be practical. They had no interest in tracing beliefs back into the past. Legal genealogies and fulfillments of prophecy would leave them cold. Arguing fine points of Scripture interpretation held no interest for them. They might have said, "I know nothing of your Scriptures, and care nothing for your peculiar notions; but I should be glad to hear a plain story of the life this man Jesus lived. Tell me what He did. Let me see Him just as He was."

Mark differs widely from Matthew in both character and scope. Mark's Gospel is the shortest of them all.

Matthew has twenty-eight chapters, abounds in parables and portrays Christ as the Son of David with kingly dignity and authority (Matthew 28:18).

Mark has sixteen chapters, and gives four parables. Mark portrays Christ as the humble but perfect Servant of Jehovah. We find the angels ministering unto Him.

General Characteristics of This Gospel

The skill of an artist may lie in what he or she leaves out. An amateur crowds everything in. In strict harmony with Mark's central purpose of emphasizing Jesus as the Servant are the omissions.

There is nothing about the virgin birth. No reference to His birth is made in the whole Gospel. This is significant. No one is interested in the pedigree of a servant.

There is no visit of wise men. A servant does not receive homage.

No account of Jesus as the boy in the Temple is given. In this practical age, as in the age of Jesus, people demand a Christ who can do things. They are not interested in Jesus the boy, but Christ the man who is able and willing to accomplish today what He did of old.

There is no Sermon on the Mount. Matthew devotes three whole chapters to this sermon, which sets forth the laws of the Kingdom and describes the character of its subjects. Mark presents Christ as a perfect "Workman"; a servant has no Kingdom and frames no laws.

No quotations from the prophets are imparted. Mark's one direct quotation from the prophets is found in Mark 1:2. Matthew quotes on every page.

No divine titles are used. Jesus is never owned as King in Mark, except in derision. Matthew says, "They will call him Immanuel"—"God with us." Not so in Mark. Mark calls Him "Teacher" ("Master," *KJV*)—other evangelists call Him "Lord."

Matthew 8:25 says, "Lord, save us! We're going to drown!" Mark 4:38 says, "Teacher, don't you care if we drown?"

There is no statement that His work was finished at His death. In John 19:30 He said, "It is finished." This is not found in Mark. It is not for a servant to say when his work is done.

There is no introduction in Mark. The other Gospels have lengthy openings, but there is none in Mark. The opening verse says, "Gospel of Jesus Christ." Mark adds, "Son of God," to guard His divine glory. How different this is from Matthew, where we found the Gospel of the Kingdom.

The word "gospel" is used twelve times in Matthew, Mark, Luke and John together, and eight of those times are in Mark. Yes, the Servant is to bear good news!

Another term is the Greek word *eutheos*, which is translated with terms such as "immediately," "at once," "as soon as," and "without delay." In all, this word is found no less than forty times in Mark's Gospel. This is a servant's word.

In the *KJV*, if you glance at the word that opens twelve out of sixteen chapters, you will see the little word "and." His service was one complete, perfect whole, with no pause or breaks in it. His service was continuous. We slacken, but not our Lord.

One of the first things that impresses us as we look at Mark's Gospel is its brevity. It is much shorter than any of the other

Gospels. Very little is found here that is not found in the others. It moves off with precision.

Matthew records fourteen parables. Mark only four—the sower, the seed growing secretly (peculiar to Mark), the mustard seed and the wicked husbandmen. Not only do you find omission in number, but also in type. There is nothing about the householder, or the marriage of the king's son or talents.

Miracles have a leading place in Mark, as parables have in Matthew. A servant works; a king speaks. Mark describes more of Jesus' miracles than he records Christ's parables. Twenty miracles are given in Mark in detail.

The Servant Prepared (Mark 1:1-13)

The book of Mark skips over the first thirty years of Jesus' life, but these years were all needful for His human preparation for His life's work. He grew in sympathy with daily toil. He wrestled, like Jacob, with life's problems. He fought many battles in the arena of His heart. He meditated upon the needs of His nation till His heart burned within Him.

Preparation in life is needed. Jesus' life illustrated this. The foundations of the lighthouse are necessary, though unseen beneath the surface. The coral colony builds the foundations for an island and its tropical growth. The plant sends its roots into the dark soil before it can bring forth the flower and leaf. Look at the forty years Moses spent in the desert before he entered upon his great work; the long period of Elijah's youth before he appeared before King Ahab; the youth of Amos spent on a farm; John the Baptist's thirty years of training. So with Jesus! He spent thirty years in obscurity in Nazareth before He appeared for the three years of public ministry. Getting ready for our life's work is of tremendous importance. Don't chafe if Christ uses time in preparing you for life.

Preparation by John the Forerunner
This Gospel begins with John the Baptist making ready for the coming of the Messiah. John's coming was in fulfillment of a

Messianic prophecy, "I will send my messenger ahead of you, who will prepare your way" (Mark 1:2). This quotation refers to Malachi 3:1 and Isaiah 40:3. Isaiah says the messenger is known simply as "a voice." "A voice of one calling: 'In the desert prepare the way for the Lord; make straight in the wilderness a highway for our God'" (Isaiah 40:3). It is this "voice" that is to be the herald of Jesus Christ.

We see this strange man who appears on the scene in an almost sensational way. "John wore clothing made of camel's hair, with a leather belt around his waist, and he ate locusts and wild honey" (Mark 1:6).

There is a lesson here for us. God does not always choose the kind of person we would select. He often picks "the foolish things of the world to shame the wise...the weak things of the world to shame the strong" (1 Corinthians 1:27). No doubt, if we were to select a herald for Christ, we would choose one of high birth, university trained, a person of wide reputation. This person would have to be eloquent and a fearless champion of great causes. Not so with God. Graduated from no outstanding school, of humble birth, little known, dressed like a desert hermit, John the Baptist was approved of God (Matthew 11:11).

John's message was as startling as his appearance. He went before his Monarch as any Roman officer would go before his, demanding that the road be repaired and the highway reconstructed. "Prepare the way for the Lord, make straight paths for him." A true revival is always a revival of righteousness.

Preparation by Baptism

John and Jesus met one day. John recognized immediately that this Man was not a subject for the baptism of repentance that he was preaching. There was in this face a purity and majesty that smote John's heart with a sense of his own unworthiness. He was the Son of God. John hesitated, and said, "I need to be baptized by you, and do you come to me?" (Matthew 3:14).

Jesus was baptized with John's baptism in obedience to an appointed ordinance. "Let it be so now; it is proper for us to do this to fulfill all righteousness" (Matthew 3:15). He set a seal of approval on John's message and work, and acknowledged him as the true forerunner of Christ. The baptism by John was ordained of God and therefore was binding on all those who acknowledged God and meant to keep His commandments.

Christ was the standard and example of righteousness. He would fulfill every duty He required of others (1 Corinthians 10:13).

Preparation by Receiving the Holy Spirit

"As Jesus was coming up out of the water, he saw heaven being torn open and the Spirit descending on him like a dove" (Mark 1:10). The Spirit descended not only in the manner of a dove, but also in the bodily shape of a dove (Luke 3:22). This was a symbol. The coming of the Spirit Himself was a reality. Every event in Jesus' life had significance. In any service for God, the Spirit always prepares the life by giving power and equipment. He is God's great agent for spiritual warfare.

Because Jesus went down into the baptismal water of obedience to God, He could come up under an opened sky with the Holy Spirit descending upon Him, and hear the voice of His Father declaring Him to be His beloved Son.

Jesus came up out of that water a new Man into a new world. His relationship to His Father and His mission were proclaimed.

Preparation by a Divine Call

"A voice came from heaven" (Mark 1:11). God endorsed Jesus and His mission, and showed to the Jewish nation that He was the Messiah. "God anointed Jesus of Nazareth with the Holy Spirit and power, and...he went around doing good and healing all who were under the power of the devil, because God was with him" (Acts 10:38). This has been called "Mark's Gospel in a nutshell." Later we hear this same Voice at His transfiguration. "This is my Son, whom I love. Listen to him!" (Mark 9:7).

Preparation by Testing

Baptism and temptation are here crowded together. Hardly had the voice from heaven died away than we hear a whisper from hell. Out of the baptismal benediction of the Father, Jesus stepped into a desperate struggle with the devil.

Mark says, "At once the Spirit sent him out into the desert," which shows how quickly the Spirit moves (Mark 1:12). "At once" indicated continuity, showing that temptation was as much a part of the preparation of the Servant for His work as His baptism. Suffering and trial are as much God's plan as thrills and triumphs. Jesus was "led" to be tempted. It was no accident or evil fate, but a divine appointment. Temptation has its place in this world. We could never develop without it. There is nothing wrong in being tempted. The wrong begins when we begin to consent to it. We are not to run into temptation of our own accord. Jesus did not go of Himself, but was led of the Spirit. We will find that the path of duty often takes us through temptations, but "No temptation has seized you except what is common to man. And God is faithful; he will not let you be tempted beyond what you can bear. But when you are tempted, he will also provide a way out so that you can stand up under it" (1 Corinthians 10:13). He always makes a way of escape! This subject is of great importance. Be sure you understand it.

The Servant Working (Mark 1:14—8:30)

There is a continuous, unbroken service of the Servant recorded in this Gospel. We read, "And He did this, and He said that." He must teach people; they were in darkness. He must cheer people; they were without hope. He must heal people; they were sick and suffering. He must free people because they were under the power of Satan. He must pardon and cleanse people because they were sinful.

We see Jesus preaching by the seashore and selecting four of the fishermen to become His first disciples to learn under His guidance how to become "fishers of men." Who were they? (See Mark 1:16-20.) They were to turn all the practical knowledge and skill they exercised in the art of catching fish into the work of catching men and women. What disciple was called in Mark 2?

It is interesting to note that Jesus never called any person from idleness. He called busy and successful people to follow him. Everyone can turn a business into a channel of service for Christ. How was Christ's call received? "At once they left their nets and followed him" (Mark 1:18). Too often there is lost time between our call and our coming; our doing lags far behind our duty.

Jesus is introduced at once as "anointed with power," and as fully engaged in His work. You will find no long discourses in these next chapters, but many mighty deeds. Demons were cast out (1:21-28); fever banished (1:29-31); different diseases healed (1:32-34); lepers made whole (1:40-45); paralytic man made to walk (2:1-12); withered hand cured (3:1-5); multitudes healed (3:6-12); storm at sea quelled (4:35-41); maniac's mind restored (5:1-15); woman's hemorrhage of blood stopped (5:21-34); Jairus's daughter brought back to life (5:35-43); five thousand fed (6:32-44); the sea was made His sidewalk (6:45-51); all that touched Him were made whole (6:53-56); deaf and dumb heard and spoke (7:31-37); four thousand fed (8:1-9); blind man healed (8:22-26).

The action is rapid, and events appear to be happening before our very eyes. His descriptions are abrupt and outspoken, but Mark preserves many things for us that would otherwise have been lost. It is only in the Gospel of Mark that we are told Jesus was a carpenter (Mark 6:3).

Mark tells us that He "took one by the hand," and little children "in his arms." Mark tells us that Jesus was "grieved"; that He "sighed," He "wondered." He "loved," He was "angry." He was "touched with the feelings of our infirmities."

Let us spend the Sabbath with Jesus that is recorded in Mark 1:21-34, going with Him to church, listening to His preaching, watching Him when interrupted by a maniac, casting out the unclean spirit and making the healing a powerful aid to His teaching. Then, after service let us go with Him to Peter's house and see Him heal Peter's wife's mother of a severe fever; and then let us spend the Sabbath afternoon in quiet rest and friendly conversation. Toward evening we shall look out in the beautiful twilight and see men and women coming toward the house, bringing great numbers of people, sick with every kind of disease, and watch them as Jesus lays His tender hands upon them and heals them. The lame jump from their stretchers and leap for joy; the blind open their eyes and see their Healer; lines of suffering are turned to an expression of unbelievable happiness as others are delivered from their painful diseases.

Mark records a wonderful statement concerning the Sabbath. "The Sabbath was made for man, not man for the Sabbath" (2:27). This great saying of Jesus is the central principle of Sabbath observance. The Sabbath is not made to annoy humankind, to confine them, to impoverish them, but to enrich and bless them! Try spending one Lord's day as Jesus did. I believe you will like it, and the Lord will be pleased.

Christ answers the question of Sabbath keeping with a practical illustration (Mark 3:1-5). His conclusion is that whatever deed is really helpful to people is proper for the Sabbath and is in perfect harmony with God's design of the day. He illustrated this truth with this miracle of healing. Seven of Jesus' recorded miracles were performed on the Sabbath. The Sabbath was "made." It is God's gift to people.

The Servant at Work
The miracles of Jesus were proofs of His mission from God. They showed that He was the promised Redeemer and King, the One we all need. Because Jesus was God, miracles were as natural to Him as acts of will are to us! Through His miracles, Jesus inspired faith in many of those who saw and heard Him.

The Servant is always found "working." "As long as it is day, we must do the work of him who sent me. Night is coming, when no one can work," are His words (John 9:4). Read this memorandum of the full days of our Lord's ministry. How empty our own lives will seem in comparison!

The Servant at Prayer
The morning following the great Sabbath day of preaching and healing, in which we followed Jesus, He arose very early and went out of the city to a lonely place and prayed (Mark 1:35). His work was growing rapidly, and Jesus needed heavenly communion. The seeming answer was a larger work, the entrance upon His first

Galilean tour of healing and preaching (Mark 1:37-39). Only one healing event of this tour, which lasted several days, is recorded—that of a leper whose disease was incurable (Mark 1:40-45).

If the Son of God needed to pray before He undertook His work, how much more should we pray. Perhaps if we lack success in life, it is because we fail at this point. We have not because we ask not (see James 4:2).

The Servant Forgives Sin

"A few days later...the people heard that he had come home" (Mark 2:1). It is remarkable how rapidly news spread in the East, without newspapers, television, telephones or radios. But in another part of the city a paralytic man had heard of this new Prophet and His gospel of healing. His four friends brought him to Jesus and let him down into the presence of the Teacher. We find in this healing the test and proof of Jesus' power not only as a physician of the body, but also as a healer of the soul. "Who can forgive sins but God alone?" (Mark 2:7). Sins are against God and, therefore, He only can forgive. Jesus said, "'But that you may know that the Son of Man has authority on earth to forgive sins....' He said to the paralytic, 'I tell you, get up, take your mat and go home'" (Mark 2:10-11).

God endorsed Jesus' claim to be the Messiah in this miracle. The man arose, took up his bed, and went forth before them all, a living witness to Jesus' power over sin, a visible illustration of the work Jesus came to do. Jesus came to give His life a ransom for many that He might forgive people their sins. "All have sinned," and all need a Savior (Romans 3:23).

We find the account of choosing the twelve apostles in Mark 3:13-21. Notice the fourteenth verse. It tells why Jesus chose these men, "that they might be with him." Mark it in your Bible. This is what Jesus wants of His disciples today—that they will take time to be in His presence and commune with Him. In John 15:15, He says, "I no longer call you servants...I have called you friends."

As you turn to Mark 4, notice once again that the opening word is "And" *(KJV)*. "And he began again to teach" *(KJV)* as on former occasions (4:1). What a wonderful teacher is Jesus!

The parable of the sower sets forth the hindrances to the Gospel that dwell in the hearts of the hearers (4:3-20).

Everyone should master these parables of the Kingdom in chapter 4. They were a special teaching instrument of Christ. The interpretation of the sower is given in Mark 4:13-20. Jesus used this method of instruction because of the growing hostility to Him and His message. He was surrounded by enemies who tried to catch Him in His words, but no one could object to a simple story. Besides, stories are remembered by the dullest of hearers.

A parable is an analogy. It assumes a likeness between heavenly and earthly things. "Parable" comes from the Greek word meaning "beside" and "to throw." A parable, then, is a form of teaching in which one thing is thrown beside another to make a comparison.

Besides the parable of the sower, our Lord spoke other parables as recorded by Mark:

1. The parable of the lamp—4:21-25
2. The parable of the sprouting seed—4:26-29
3. The parable of the mustard seed—4:30-33.

After interpreting the parables, Jesus took a ship to escape the crowd. On the way, as the weary Teacher fell asleep, a violent storm arose on the Sea of Galilee. About to perish, the frantic disciples awoke Jesus. At a word from His lips, the sea became calm. He had power over the elements (Mark 4:35-41).

Mark 5 begins again with "And" *(KJV)*. Jesus is still working. What does He do now? Read parallel accounts in Matthew 8:28-34; Luke 8:26-39. Compare this miracle with other recorded cures of demoniacs, in Matthew 9:32-33; Mark 1:23-26; Matthew 17:14-18; Luke 9:38-42.

The miracle recorded in Mark 5, like all others, tested the character of people. It took them off their guard and disclosed their true natures. Notice the contrast in the way people receive the work of Christ.

Some shun the Savior. "Those tending the pigs ran off." Others were afraid (vv. 14-15) and "began to plead with Jesus to leave their region" (v. 17). Doubtless there were other herds of swine, and they feared the loss of them. What a true picture of the attitude of many toward Christ! There is some gainful business they do not want to give up. There is some sin that lies close to the heart. For these reasons people thrust away Christ.

Some seek the Savior. The healed man begged Him not to depart out of his coast, but "to go with him." It is so with people today. People either ask Jesus to "depart" because they want to keep their sin, or they ask that He might remain "with" them because they want to lose their sin. Do you want to keep or lose your sin?

"And" starts another episode in Jesus' miracles (5:21, *KJV*). After healing the demoniac, Jesus returned to Capernaum. He heals a woman long sick, and "while Jesus was still speaking" (5:35) He was called upon to raise a child already lying in death, Jairus's daughter.

Jesus started out on a third preaching tour of Galilee (chap. 6). He sent forth the twelve disciples, two by two, on independent missions (6:7-13). Matthew 10 records the instructions they received. As they preached, Herod heard them and we read of his uneasy conscience, thinking that the man he had murdered was back to haunt him (Mark 6:14-29). How much people recklessly give away for passing pleasures. For a glass of wine, a moment of passion, a little more money, a position of empty honor, they give away half—yes, all the kingdom of their souls, their health, home, friendships, peace, happiness and eternal life. Like Esau, they sell their birthright for a mess of pottage. Like Judas, they sell their Savior for thirty bits of metal.

After the apostles were trained, Jesus sent them out on an extensive missionary tour among the villages of Galilee (Mark 6:12-13). On returning they "gathered around Jesus" (6:30), probably at their regular rendezvous, Capernaum. They reported upon their sermons, the number of conversions and the miracles that were wrought. No Christian work can be carried on long without frequent talks with Christ. We need His sympathy, approval, guidance and strength.

We must hasten if we would follow this mighty Servant, this Workman of God. Jesus had gone apart in a desert to rest awhile (6:31), but the multitudes followed Him. Feeding the 5,000 follows without an interval (6:32-44). This is one of the most important miracles. Evidently it made a special impression upon the writers of the Gospels, as it is the only one of the thirty-five miracles that is recorded by all four. Review it carefully. Notice Jesus served in an orderly way.

What miracles are next (6:45-52 and 53-56)? Follow Jesus in what He does and says (7:1-23; 7:24-30; 7:31-37; 8:1-9; 8:22-26).

Peter's confession of faith should be mastered by everyone—Mark 8:29. Jesus does not tell His disciples who He is. He waits until they tell Him. When He asked, "Who do you say I am?" the climax of His ministry was reached. He was testing the aim of all His training of the chosen twelve. Peter's answer gave Him the assurance that His goal had been attained.

What did the Pharisees think of Jesus? Already they had agreed to put Him to death.

What did the multitude think of Him? Already they were deserting Him.

What did the disciples think of Him? Peter gives the answer.

What do you think of Christ?

The Servant Rejected (Mark 8:31—15:47)

Even before Mark sets forth Christ's direct claim to be King of the Kingdom, he reveals the way the King is to be received. His is a pathway of suffering and rejection. Jesus said, "The Son of Man must suffer many things" (Mark 8:31). The evangelists write it down in plain language that He was to be rejected by the rulers of Israel, and killed, and was to rise again the third day.

Jesus tells His disciples that He is to be rejected by the elders, chief priests and scribes (8:31).

He is to be delivered by treachery (9:31).

He is to be put to death by the Romans (10:32-45).

He is to rise again the third day (9:31).

Jesus, nevertheless, claimed the kingdom by presenting Himself at Jerusalem as the Heir of David, according to the prophecy of Zechariah 9:9 (Mark 11:1-11).

How did the people accept this King? At first they welcomed

Him because they hoped He might deliver them from the yoke of Rome and free them from the poverty they were enduring. But when He entered the Temple and showed that His mission was a spiritual one, He was hated by the religious leaders with a satanic hatred that led to the plot to put Him to death (14:1).

The World's Greatest Sin

The greatest sin of this age, as of every age, is the rejection of Jesus Christ. Yet, remember that everyone who has heard the Gospel must either accept the Lord as Savior or trample Him underfoot. The people of Jesus' day made their choice and the people of our day must make theirs.

This wonderful Presence that shines forth in the Gospels, this vision of God in the flesh—are you to look and then pass on as though you had but seen a work of art? This Voice that sounds throughout the centuries, are you to listen as though it were just the voice of a gifted orator? What is Jesus to you? A name? or your Master? If you cannot answer the question as Peter did, will you sign this covenant, worded by Dr. R. A. Torrey (Reuben Archer Torrey, 1856-1928, American evangelist and educator)?

> I promise to examine carefully the evidence that the Bible is God's book, and Jesus Christ is God's Son and man's Savior; and if I find reason to believe that this book is true and He is man's Savior, I will accept Him and confess Him before men, and undertake to follow Him.
>
> (Signed) ————————————————————

After Christ's public ministry, described in Mark 10:46—11:26, we read of His last conflict with the Jewish authorities and of His triumph over the leaders (11:27—12:44).

Jesus sought to persuade the Jews to receive Him as the Messiah (11:15—12:44). It was a busy Tuesday, occupied from morning till night in one great and powerful effort to induce the Jewish nation to acknowledge Him, and thus become that glorious nation, blessing the world, for which it had been set apart.

In the beautiful Temple courts, the simple Galilean met the

religious authorities, arrayed in all the pomp of their official regalia. There is a sharp and prolonged controversy on a puzzling question.

The scribes and chief priests ask Him, "'By what authority are you doing these things?' they asked. 'And who gave you authority to do this?'" (11:28).

The Pharisees and Herodians try to catch Him in His words, "Is it right to pay taxes to Caesar or not?" (12:14).

The Sadducees, who say there is no resurrection, ask Him, "At the resurrection whose wife will she be, since the seven were married to her?" (12:23).

The scribes ask Him, "Of all the commandments, which is the most important?" (12:28).

After Jesus answered them all, "from then on no one dared ask him any more questions" (12:34).

It would seem that He could not escape treason to the Roman government in answering them, but He came out unscathed. Hour by hour Jesus met the attack.

All the way through, the perfect Servant of God was dogged by His enemies. The enemy is not dead! God's servants today are called to tread a similar path. Jesus silenced His enemies, but their hearts would not yield. Then He exposed all their hypocritical practices in words that fell like bombs. He tried to break through their walls of prejudice and cause them to repent before it was too late, but all seemed to be in vain.

Before He goes to the cross, Jesus reveals the future to His troubled disciples in the Olivet discourse (Mark 13). He tells them of the end of this age, and of the great tribulation, and climaxes it with the promise of His return in power and glory.

The plotting of the chief priests, how they might take Him by craft and put Him to death, and the anointing of His body in preparation for burial (v. 8) opens chapter 14. Then the ever sad story of His betrayal at the hand of His own disciple (14:10-11), the celebration of the Passover and the institution of the Lord's Supper all are crowded into twenty-five short verses. Adding insult to injury, we read of Peter's denial of his Lord (Mark 14:26-31,66-71).

Isaiah's great message is that the Son of God shall become the

Servant of God in order that He might die to redeem the world. Mark records how the sufferings of Jesus in Gethsemane and on Calvary fulfilled the prophecies of Isaiah (Isaiah 53).

Jesus was sold for thirty pieces of silver, the price of a slave. He was executed as only slaves were! Yes, Christ was the suffering Servant and died for me! He bore my sins in His own body on the tree.

No reference is made by Mark that in the garden He had the right to summon twelve legions of angels if He so willed. No promise of the Kingdom is given to the dying thief on the cross. These claims are made by a King (in Matthew), but they are not mentioned by a Servant.

The Servant Exalted (Mark 16:1-20)

After the Servant had given His life a ransom for many, He arose from the dead. We read again the Great Commission (Mark 16:15), also recorded in Matthew 28:19-20. Compare the two. In Mark we do not hear a King say, "All authority in heaven and on earth has been given to me," as in Matthew. In Mark we see in Jesus' words that His disciples are to take His place, and He will serve in and through them. He is yet the Worker, though risen (16:20). The command rings with urgency of service. Not a corner of the world is to be left unvisited; not a soul to be left out!

Finally He was received into heaven to sit on the right hand of God (16:19). He who had taken upon Himself the form of a servant is now highly exalted (Philippians 2:7-9). He is in the place of power, ever making intercession for us. He is our Advocate.

But Christ is with us. The Servant is always working in us and through us. We are laborers together with Him (1 Corinthians 3:9). He is still "working with [us]" (Mark 16:20). Let us, being redeemed, follow our Pattern and go forth to serve also!

"Therefore, my dear brothers, stand firm. Let nothing move you. Always give yourselves fully to the work of the Lord, because you know that your labor in the Lord is not in vain" (1 Corinthians 15:58).

Chapter 30

Understanding Luke

Luke Portrays Jesus Christ, the Son of Man

Selected Bible Readings

Sunday: The Man "Made Like unto His Brethren"
(Luke 1:1—3:38)

Monday: The Man "Tempted Like as We Are" (Luke 4:1—8:3)

Tuesday: The Man "Touched with...Our Infirmities"
(Luke 8:4—12:48)

Wednesday: The Man "About My Father's Business"
(Luke 12:49—16:31)

Thursday: The Man "Never Man Spake Like This Man"
(Luke 17:1—19:27)

Friday: The Man, Our Kinsman-Redeemer
(Luke 19:28—23:56)

Saturday: The Man in Resurrection Glory (Luke 24:1-53)

The writer of this third Gospel was Dr. Luke, Paul's companion (Acts 16:10-24; 2 Timothy 4:11; Colossians 4:14). He was a native of Syria and apparently was not a Jew, for Colossians 4:14 places him with the other Gentile Christians. If this is true, he was the only Gentile writer of the New Testament books.

It is easily seen that Luke was an educated man and a keen observer. We learn from Acts 1:1 that the Acts was written by the author of this third Gospel.

Luke's Gospel was written for the Greeks. Besides the Jews and the Romans, the Greeks were another people who had been preparing for Christ's coming. They differed from the other two in many particulars. They possessed a wider culture, loved beauty, rhetoric and philosophy. Luke, an educated Greek himself, would be well fitted for this task. Luke presents Jesus as the ideal of perfect manliness.

Notice that inspiration does not destroy individuality. In the introduction, verses 1-4, the human element is seen in connection with God's revelation. Luke addressed his Gospel to a man named Theophilus. It is thought he was an influential Christian layman in Greece.

Matthew presents Christ as King, to the Jews.

Mark presents Him as the Servant of Jehovah, to the Romans.

Luke presents Him as the perfect Man, to the Greeks.

This is the Gospel for the sinner. It brings out Christ's compassionate love in becoming man to save man.

In Luke, we see God manifest in the flesh. Luke deals with the humanity of our Lord. He reveals the Savior as a man with all His sympathies, feelings and growing powers—a Savior suited to all. In this Gospel, we see the God of glory coming down to our level, entering into our conditions and being subject to our circumstances.

Luke's Gospel is the Gospel of Christ's manhood. This we must know, however; although He mingles with men, He is in sharp contrast to them. He was the solitary God-Man. There was as great a difference between Christ as the Son of Man and we the sons of men, as Christ as Son of God and we the sons of God. The difference is not merely relative, but absolute. Make this fact plain. Read the words of the angel to Mary: "So the holy one to be born" (Luke 1:35) refers to our Lord's humanity. It is in contrast to ours. Our human nature is unclean (Isaiah 64:6), but the Son of God, when He became incarnate, was "holy." Adam in his unfallen estate was innocent, but Christ was "holy."

In keeping with the theme of his Gospel, Dr. Luke has given us the fullest particulars concerning the miraculous birth of Jesus. We are grateful that our chief testimony concerning this fact should come from a physician. Christ, the Creator of this universe, entered this world like any other person. It is a mystery of mysteries, but enough facts are given to let us see that the predictions are true.

Luke alone tells the story of the visit of the shepherds (2:8-20).

We learn from this Gospel that as a boy, Jesus developed naturally (2:40,52). As a child, He was subject to Joseph and Mary (2:51). There was no record of unhealthy or supernatural growth. Only Luke tells of Jesus' visit to the Temple when He was twelve years old.

As a man He toiled with His hands; wept over the city; "kneeled in prayer," and "knew agony in suffering." All is strikingly human. Five out of six of the miracles were miracles of healing. Luke alone tells of healing Malchus's ear (Luke 22:51).

Luke is the Gospel for the outcast on earth. It is Luke who tells of the good Samaritan (10:33), the publican (18:13), and the prodigal (15:11-24), of Zacchaeus (19:2) and the thief on the cross (23:43). He is the writer who has most to say for womanhood (chaps. 1 and 2). Luke records Jesus' compassion for the woman of Nain, and the depths of His mercy to the woman who was a sinner. His regard for women and children is shown in 7:46; 8:3; 8:42; 9:38; 10:38-42; 11:27; 23:27.

Luke alone tells us: when our Lord beheld the city of Jerusalem He wept over it; of the bloody sweat in Gethsemane; of the Lord showing mercy to the dying thief on the cross. Luke alone mentions the walk with the two to Emmaus. He also tells of Jesus leading His disciples out as far as Bethany, and that as He lifted up His hands and blessed them, He was parted from them.

Luke is a poetic book. It opens with a song, "Glory to God!" It closes with a song, "Praising God." The world has been singing ever since. Thank God for such a Gospel! It preserves the precious gems of Christian hymnology:

The Magnificat—Mary's hymn of rejoicing (1:46-55)

Song of Zacharias (1:68-79)

Song of the angels (2:8-14).

Luke speaks more of the prayers of our Lord than any other Gospel writer. Prayer is the expression of human dependence on God. Why is there so much working and activity in the Church and yet so little result in positive conversions to God? Why so much running hither and thither and so few brought to Christ? The answer is simple: There is not enough private prayer. The cause of Christ does not need less working, but more praying.

The hardest thing the Early Church had to learn was that the Gentiles would have full and free admission into the Kingdom and into the Church. Simeon taught this. Read Luke 2:32. Christ sent the seventy disciples not to the lost sheep of the house of Israel alone, as Matthew says, who wrote especially for the Jews, but "to every town and place" (Luke 10:1). All of Jesus' ministry over the eastern side of Jordan was to the Gentiles.

The Preparation of the Son of Man (Luke 1:1—4:13)

The opening of this beautiful book is significant. A Man is to be described, and the writer, Luke, will draw his good friend Theophilus into it. He tells him of his own personal knowledge of his subject—"since I myself have carefully investigated everything from the beginning." He seems to bring something warmly human into his task of presenting the Man Christ Jesus.

The opening chapter is characteristic, too. John, as befits his theme, begins, "In the beginning was the Word, and the Word was with God, and the Word was God." His tone throughout is not of this world. But Luke, so different, begins like a simple story touching people with, "In the time of Herod king of Judea there was a priest." As the story progresses, we are introduced to human sympathies and relationships that none of the other Gospels tells us. We learn all about the circumstances that accompanied the birth and childhood of the holy Babe, and about the one who was sent as His forerunner. The birth of John the Baptist (1:57-80); the angels' song to the shepherds (2:8-20); the circumcision (2:21); the presentation in the Temple (2:22-38); and then the story of the boy Jesus, twelve years of age (2:41-52), are all recorded here.

In chapter 2, Luke notes that "In those days Caesar Augustus issued a decree that a census should be taken of the entire Roman world" (2:1). Then comes a fact that we would never find in Matthew, that Joseph and Mary "went to [Joseph's] own town to register" (2:3). Luke is not showing here One who has claims to rule, but One who is coming down in humility to be involved fully in human affairs.

God brings to pass what the prophets had spoken. Micah said that Bethlehem was to be the birthplace of Jesus (Micah 5:2-5) for He was of the family of David. But Mary lived in Nazareth, a town 100 miles away. God saw to it that Imperial Rome sent forth a decree to compel Mary and Joseph to go to Bethlehem just as the Child was to be born. Isn't it wonderful how God uses the decree of a pagan monarch to bring to pass His prophecies! God still moves the hand of rulers to do His bidding.

Now look on! We hear the message of the angels to the watching shepherds, but we do not find the kings of the East asking for One "who is born King." The angel tells the poor shepherds, "I bring you good news of great joy that will be for all the people. Today in the town of David a Savior (not a King) has been born to you" (Luke 2:10-12).

Why did the Father allow His blessed Son, now incarnate in the flesh, to be born in this lowly place? Luke is the only one of the four evangelists who touches this point concerning His humanity.

Boyhood Days

"The child grew...and the grace of God was upon him" (Luke 2:40). When He was twelve years old, He went up with His parents to Jerusalem to the feast, as every Jewish boy did at that age. "The boy Jesus stayed behind in Jerusalem, but they were unaware of it" (v. 43). How characteristic of a boy this is! He was found sitting in the midst of the doctors, both hearing them, and asking them questions (2:46). How intensely human this is! Yet we read, "Everyone who heard him was amazed at his understanding and his answers" (2:47). Luke says that He was filled with wisdom. Side by side with the human, He was always more than a man. We find Jesus' first words here: "Didn't you know I had to be in my Father's house?" (2:49) Here we find the first self-witness to His deity.

Again we read, "Then he went down to Nazareth with them and was obedient to them"—these earthly parents (2:51). "And Jesus grew in wisdom and stature, and in favor with God and

men" (2:52). All of these things are peculiar to Jesus as man, and
Luke alone records them. It is important that we notice Jesus was
a "favorite" in Nazareth. It is not a sign that we are in the grace
of God when we are out of favor with others.

Eighteen years of silence followed. We read of John the Baptist,
preaching "a baptism of repentance for the forgiveness of sins"
(3:3). Then Jesus came to be baptized. Only Luke tells us, "When all
the people were being baptized, Jesus was baptized too. And as he
was praying, heaven was opened" (3:21). He is linked with "all the
people." He came down to the level of humans. Matthew and Luke
record the baptism of Jesus, but John omits it, for Christ is viewed
as the only begotten Son of God. Here only do we read of the age
at which our Lord entered His public ministry (3:23).

Genealogy

The genealogy of Jesus in Luke is given at the time of His baptism,
and not at His birth (Luke 3:23). There are noticeable differences
between the genealogy in Luke and that found in Matthew 1. In
Matthew we have the royal genealogy of the Son of David through
Joseph. Here it is His strictly personal genealogy through Mary. There
it is His legal line of descent through Joseph; here it is His lineal
descent through Mary. There His genealogy is traced forward from
Abraham; here it is followed backward to Adam. Each is significant!
Matthew is showing Jesus' relation to the Jewish people, hence he
goes back no further than to Abraham, father of the Jewish nation.
But here in Luke is His connection with the human race; hence His
genealogy is traced back to Adam, the father of the human family.

In Luke our Lord's line is traced back to Adam, and is, no
doubt, His mother's line. Notice in Luke 3:23 it does not say Jesus
was the son of Joseph. What are the words? "So it was thought."
In Matthew 1:16, where Joseph's genealogy is given, we find Joseph
was the son of Jacob. Here it says he was the son of Heli. He
could not be the son of two men by natural generation. But
notice this carefully—the record does not state that Heli begat
Joseph, so it is supposed that Joseph was the son by law (or son-
in-law) of Heli. Heli is believed to have been the father of Mary.

The Davidic genealogy goes through Nathan, not Solomon.

This too is important. The Messiah must be David's son and heir, "as to his human nature...a descendant of David" (2 Samuel 7:12-13; Romans 1:3; Acts 2:30-31). He must be a literal flesh and blood descendant. Hence Mary must be a member of David's house as well as Joseph (Luke 1:32).

"Jesus, full of the Holy Spirit, returned from the Jordan and was led by the Spirit in the desert, where for forty days he was tempted by the devil" (4:1-2). Only here do we learn that the Savior was "full of the Holy Spirit" as He returned from His baptism. Then follows the account of His temptation. We may also notice that Luke is the only one to tell us that "Jesus returned to Galilee in the power of the Spirit" (4:14), showing that the old Serpent had utterly failed to break the fellowship of the Son of Man on earth with His Father in heaven.

As Jesus came forth from the fire of testing in the unabated "power of the Spirit," so can we. Only as we are filled with His Spirit can we overcome temptation with the power of the Spirit.

The purpose of the temptation was not to discover whether or not Jesus would yield to Satan, but to demonstrate that He could not; to show forth the fact that there was nothing in Him to which Satan could appeal (see John 14:30). Christ could be tried and proven. The more you crush a rose, the more its fragrance is recognized. So the more the devil assaults Christ, the more will His perfections be revealed.

The Ministry of the Son of Man (Luke 4:14—19:48)

Scan through Luke from chapter 4:14, and find the events in Jesus' life as they are recorded in succession.

His ministry around Galilee is recorded in 4:14 to 9:50:

Ministry in Nazareth, His hometown—4:16-30
Preaching in Capernaum—4:31-44
Call of Peter, James and John—5:1-11
Call of Matthew—5:27-39
The Pharisees—6:1-11
The Twelve Apostles chosen—6:12-16

Disciples taught—6:17-49
Miracles—7:1-17
Discourses of the Teacher—7:18-50
Parables—8:4-18
Real relatives—8:19-21
The sea calmed—8:22-25
The maniac healed—8:26-40
The woman made whole—8:41-48
Jairus's daughter restored—8:49-56
The Twelve commissioned—9:1-10
Five thousand fed—9:10-17
Peter's confession—9:18-21
The Transfiguration—9:27-36
A lunatic healed—9:37-43.

Jesus' ministry in Judea is recorded in 9:51—19:27:
The seventy commissioned—10:1-24
The question of the lawyer—10:25-37
Jesus' friends, Martha and Mary—10:38-42
Disciples taught to pray—11:1-13
Seeking signs—11:14-36
The Pharisees denounced—12:1-12
The sin of greed—12:13-59
Repentance—13:1-9
The Kingdom of heaven—13:18-30
Jesus talks on hospitality—14:1-24
Jesus talks on self-denial—14:25-35
The Savior and the lost—15:1-32
The unjust steward—16:1-30
On His way to Jerusalem—16:31—19:27.

Jesus' Jerusalem ministry is found in Luke 19:28—24:53:
Triumphal entry—19:28-38
Rulers question Jesus' authority—20:1—21:4
Future things—21:5-38
Jesus' last Passover—22:1-38
Jesus betrayed—22:39-53
Tried before the high priest—22:54-71
Tried before Pilate—23:1-26

Crucifixion—23:27-49
Burial—23:50-56
Resurrection—24:1-48
Ascension—24:49-53.

This list is not complete, of course, but it gives a bird's-eye view of the busy life of the Son of Man on earth. The key word of His ministry is "compassion."

Following the temptation, Jesus "went to Nazareth, where he had been brought up, and on the Sabbath day he went into the synagogue, as was his custom. And he stood up to read" (Luke 4:16). He went to the place where He had been "brought up." Bringing up is an important thing in life. We find that Jesus was accustomed to going to the synagogue on the Sabbath day. He had been reared in a godly home.

Jesus here stated that God had anointed Him to preach deliverance to the captives, and bring good tidings to the poor and brokenhearted (4:18-19). He selected a text from Isaiah 61:2, which announced the object of His whole mission on earth. He was commissioned and sent of God, and divinely qualified for His work. He is our Kinsman-Redeemer. He was made like us that He might deliver us. He became man that He might bring man close to God.

At this very early point in Jesus' ministry, we see those of His own hometown determining to kill Him (Luke 4:28-30). They said, "Isn't this Joseph's son?" This is the first hint of His coming rejection. He proclaimed Himself to be the Messiah (4:21). They were angered that He should hint that their Messiah would also be sent to the Gentiles (4:24-30). They believed God's grace was to be confined only to their own kind of people, and so they were ready to kill Him. He refused to work miracles for them because of their unbelief. They attempted to cast Him down the brow of the hill, but He escaped and went to Capernaum (4:29-31). (By comparing Luke 4:16 with Matthew 13:54, it would seem that He made another visit to Nazareth some months later, but with no success.)

A World Gospel

The Jewish people hated the Gentiles for their treatment of them when they were captives in Babylon. They regarded them with contempt. They considered them unclean and enemies of God. Luke pictures Jesus as tearing down these barriers between Jew and Gentile, making repentance and faith the only condition of admission to the Kingdom. "And repentance and forgiveness of sins will be preached in his name to all nations, beginning at Jerusalem" (Luke 24:47). The gospel of Jesus Christ is not just one of the religions of the world. It is the living truth of God, adapted to all nations and to all classes. Read Romans 1:16.

As the Son of Man, Christ is looking at the needs of the Gentiles as He is looking at the needs of all people. In Luke 6, which in substance is the same as the Sermon on the Mount in Matthew, we find simple broad moral teachings, suited to the needs and wants of all people. He condenses what Matthew puts into chapters 5 through 7 into a few verses, Luke 6:20-49. He makes no reference to "the law and the prophets," as in Matthew's Gospel.

Jesus spoke choice words here to His disciples. The Beatitudes are a picture of the Christian. "Blessed are" each one of them begins. It is not what you are striving to be, but what you are in Christ that brings you joy. The Beatitudes are a picture of Christ. They are the picture of the face of Jesus Himself, not boastingly, but truly describing the perfect Christian.

Disciples Commissioned

When the Twelve are commissioned (Luke 9), a broader field of ministry begins. In Matthew we hear the Lord saying, "Do not go among the Gentiles or enter any town of the Samaritans. Go rather to the lost sheep of Israel" (Matthew 10:5-6). Luke omits this and says, "he sent them out to preach the kingdom of God and to heal the sick....So they set out...preaching the gospel and healing people everywhere" (Luke 9:2,6).

Wherever this Man Christ Jesus went, a whole multitude followed Him and "tried to touch him, because power was coming from him and healing them all" (6:19). He gave of Himself. Our service must be of this kind.

We find Jesus' power over disease and death (7:1-17); we find Him the sinner's friend. He had come "to seek and to save what was lost" (19:10). He is called "a friend of tax collectors and 'sinners'" (7:34).

Jesus Christ, the Teacher

The scholars—Jesus was a teacher. His disciples were taught and trained to carry on His message (Luke 6:12-16).

The school—Matriculation in this school is guarded. Requisites are demanded. Yet, on the other hand, entrance is easy. There is no barrier of age, sex, race or color. (Read Luke 14:25-33.)

Entrance requirement—"And anyone who does not carry his cross and follow me cannot be my disciple" (14:27). "Any of you who does not give up everything he has cannot be my disciple" (14:33).

Examinations—Jesus knows the ability and weakness of each student in His school. His examinations are not the same for everyone. He gives individual tests. It is easy to follow Jesus' tests with Peter. In Luke 5, He is testing Peter on obedience (5:5). In Luke 9:18, Jesus sprang an examination upon this impetuous fellow, and Peter gave a startling answer (9:18-20).

Rules to be observed—Right relationship with the Teacher must be maintained at all times. Many think that just because they have at one time entered into a relationship with the great Teacher, this is all that is necessary. But this is false. There must be a constant study of His Word, a laboratory time of prayer (11:1-4), a gymnasium of spiritual exercise (9:59; 5:27).

A practice school—Jesus not only taught them, but He also made them try out the great facts He presented (Luke 10:1-12,28,36-37; 11:35; 12:8-9; 14:25-33; 18:18-26).

The course—The course included a study of the Kingdom and the King (Luke 7:28; 8:1; 9:2,11,62; 13:20-21; 12:32; 19:12,15; 22:29; 13:28-29; 17:20; 18:29).

The Suffering of the Son of Man
(Luke 20:1—23:56)

Jesus is sitting with His disciples around the table, celebrating the feast of the Passover. At this time, He institutes what we call the Lord's Supper. Listen to His words: "This is my body given for you...the new covenant in my blood, which is poured out for you" (Luke 22:19-20). This is different from the account in Matthew and Mark. They say, "My blood...which is poured out for many" (Matthew 26:28; Mark 14:24). His love is expressed in such a personal way in Luke. The evangelist adds: "Do this in remembrance of me" (22:19).

See the sad record of events in connection with His death. We find the disciples arguing over which one of them would be counted greatest in the Kingdom (Luke 22:24-27). We follow Peter from that moment and we read a lamentable story—one that ends in denial of his Lord and Master (22:54-62).

Look into the Garden of Gethsemane. Jesus is praying, and "as it were" *(KJV)* great drops of blood were on that holy brow (22:44). Luke tells us that the angels came to minister to Him, the Son of Man (22:43). Matthew and Mark omit the mention of the ministering angels.

In the shadow of the garden, a band of soldiers were approaching; leading them was Judas (22:47). He stepped up to kiss Jesus. Why, yes, he was a disciple. But the Scriptures had said that Jesus would be betrayed by a friend and sold for thirty pieces of silver (Luke 22:47-62; Psalm 41:9; Zechariah 11:12).

Worst of all, His friends deserted Him. Peter denied Him, and all forsook Him and fled except John the beloved. Luke alone tells us that Jesus looked on Peter, the denier, and broke his heart with that look of love.

We follow Jesus into Pilate's hall; then before Herod (Luke 23:1-12). We follow along the Via Dolorosa ("way of suffering") to the Cross (23:27-38). Only Luke gives the name "Calvary," which is the Latin name for "Golgotha" ("place of a skull"). Luke omits much that Matthew and Mark record, but he alone gives the prayer (23:13-46).

There were three crosses on Calvary's hill. On one of them was a thief, dying for his crimes. Luke tells us this story, too (23:39-45). The way this thief was saved is the way every sinner must be saved. He believed on the Lamb of God who died on the cross that day to pay the penalty of sin.

The scene closes with the Son of Man crying with a loud voice, "Father, into your hands I commit my spirit" (23:46). The centurion, in keeping with this Gospel, bears this witness, "Surely this was a righteous man" (23:47).

The Victory of the Son of Man
(Luke 24:1-53)

We turn with great relief from the sorrow and death of the Cross, the darkness and gloom of the tomb, to the brightness and glory of the resurrection morning.

Luke gives us a part of the scene the others leave untold. It is the story of the walk to Emmaus.

He shows these disciples that Jesus, as their resurrected Lord, is just the same loving, understanding friend He had been before His death. After Jesus' walk and conversation with them, these disciples urged Him to come in and spend the night with them. He revealed who He was when He lifted up those hands that had been pierced on the cross and broke the bread. Then they knew Him, but He vanished out of their sight. On returning to Jerusalem, they found abundant proof of His resurrection. He proved to them that He was a real man with flesh and bones. All these details belong to the Gospel of Luke.

No less than eleven appearances of Jesus are recorded, following His resurrection—not only to individuals, but also to companies and crowds. First, to the women, to Mary, and then to the others (Mark 16; John 20:14); then to Peter alone (Luke 24:34); then to two men walking to Emmaus (Luke 24:13); to ten apostles in Jerusalem (Thomas being absent; John 20:19); and subsequently to the eleven remaining disciples (John 20:26,29); yet later to seven men at the sea of Tiberias (John 21:1). Yet again to the whole number of the apostles on a mountain in Galilee (Matthew 28:16); and afterward to 500 brethren at once (1 Corinthians 15:6). Then to James (1 Corinthians 15:7); and finally to the little group on the Mount of Olives at His ascension (Luke 24:51).

Three times, we are told, His disciples touched Him after He arose (Matthew 28:9; Luke 24:39; John 20:27). He ate with them, too (Luke 24:42; John 21:12-13).

As Jesus put out His hand to bless them, "he...was taken up into heaven" (Luke 24:51).

He is no longer a local Christ, confined to Jerusalem, but He is a universal Christ. He could say to His disciples who mourned for Him, thinking when gone He could be no more with them, "And surely I am with you always" (Matthew 28:20). How different was the hope and joy of those chosen followers from their despair and shame at the Crucifixion! They return to Jerusalem with great joy.

Chapter 31

Understanding John

John Portrays Jesus Christ, the Son of God

Selected Bible Readings

Sunday:	Christ Became Flesh (John 1:1-51)
Monday:	Christ So Loved (John 3:1-36)
Tuesday:	Christ Satisfies (John 4:1-54)
Wednesday:	Christ, the Bread of Life (John 6:1-59)
Thursday:	Christ, the Light of the World (John 9:1-41)
Friday:	Christ, Our Shepherd (John 10:1-39)
Saturday:	Christ Promises the Comforter (John 14:1-31)

The author indicates the purpose of this book in the opening eighteen verses, the prologue, and states it very plainly in John 20:31.

John wrote to prove that Jesus was the Christ, the promised Messiah (for the Jews), and the Son of God (for the Gentiles), and to lead believers into a life of divine friendship with Him. The key word is "believe." We find this word ninety-eight times in this book.

The theme of John's Gospel is the deity of Jesus Christ. More here than anywhere else His divine Sonship is set forth. In this Gospel, we are shown that the Babe of Bethlehem was none other than "the One and Only, who came from the Father" (1:14). There are abundant evidences and proofs. Although "all things were made" by Him (1:3), although "in him was life" (1:4), yet He "became flesh and made his dwelling among us" (1:14). No person can see God; therefore, Christ came to declare Him.

No genealogy is recorded—neither His legal lineage through Joseph (as given by Matthew), nor His personal descent through Mary (as given by Luke).

No account of His birth—because He was "in the beginning."

Nothing about His boyhood.

Nothing about His temptation. Jesus rather is presented as Christ the Lord, not the One tempted in all points just as we are.

No transfiguration.

No appointing of His disciples.

No parables.

No account of the Ascension.

No Great Commission.

Yet only here is He called "the Word"

The Creator

The only begotten of the Father

The Lamb of God

The revelation of the great "I AM" (Exodus 3:14).

The author was John, "son of thunder," "the disciple whom Jesus loved." His father was Zebedee, a fisherman in good circumstances; his mother was Salome, a devout follower of the Lord who may have been a sister of Mary, the mother of Jesus (Mark 15:40; John 19:25). His brother was James. His position was probably somewhat better than that of the ordinary fisherman.

John may have been about twenty-five years of age when Jesus called him. He had been a follower of John the Baptist. In the reign of the Roman Emperor Domitian, John the Disciple was banished to Patmos, but afterward he returned to Ephesus and became the pastor of that wonderful church. He lived in that city to an extreme old age, the last of the twelve apostles. During this time, he wrote his Gospel concerning the deity of the Christ, coeternal with the Father.

John wrote nearly a generation after the other evangelists, somewhere between A.D. 80 and 100, at the end of the first century when all the New Testament was complete except for his own writings. The life and work of Jesus were well known at this time. The gospel had been preached; Paul and Peter had suffered martyrdom and all the apostles had died; Jerusalem had been destroyed by the Roman legions under Titus, A.D. 70.

All the Synoptic Gospels, Matthew, Mark and Luke, were written before A.D. 70, the fateful year of the overthrow of Jerusalem. Already false teachers had arisen, denying that Jesus Christ was the Son of God, come in the flesh. John, therefore, wrote emphasizing those facts, and gave the witnesses and recorded the words and works of Jesus that reveal His divine power and glory.

John is more elevated in tone and more exalted in view than the other Gospels. In each of the first three Gospels, Christ is viewed in human relationship with an earthly people, but in John we find spiritual relationships with a heavenly people.

In Matthew and Luke, "Son of David" and "Son of Man" link Christ to the earth. In John, "Son of God" connects Him with the Father in heaven.

As in Luke, divine care was taken to guard our Lord's perfection in His humanity; so in John, His deity is guarded. In these days of widespread departure from the truth, the deity of Christ Jesus must be emphasized.

In John, Jesus is shown dwelling with God before ever a creature was formed (John 1:1-2). He is denominated as "the glory of the One and Only" (1:14). "This is the Son of God" (1:34ff.).

Thirty-five times He speaks of God as "my Father."

Twenty-five times He says, "Verily, verily" *(KJV)*—speaking with authority.

Besides His own affirmation, six different witnesses avow His deity.

Jesus' Deity Revealed

In every chapter we see Jesus' deity:

In Nathanael's confession, "You are the Son of God"—1:49

In the miracle of Cana, He "thus revealed his glory"—2:11

In His word to Nicodemus, He said He was "his one and only Son" (the "only begotten Son," *KJV*)—3:16

In His conversation with the woman of Samaria He stated: "I who speak to you am he" [the Messiah]—4:26

To the impotent man, He disclosed that "the voice of the Son of God" will call the dead to life—5:25

In the bread chapter, He admits that "I am the bread of life"—6:35

In the water of life chapter He proclaims, "If anyone is thirsty, let him come to me and drink"—7:37

To the unbelieving Jews He disclosed, "Before Abraham was born, I am!"—8:58

The blind man was told, "You have now seen [the Son of Man]; in fact, he is the one speaking with you"; Jesus' unique claim to being the Son of God—9:37

Jesus stated, "I and the Father are one"—10:30

Martha's declaration, "You are the Christ, the Son of God"—11:27

To the Greeks, "But I, when I am lifted up from the earth, will draw all men to myself"—12:32

At the supper He said, "You call me 'Teacher' and 'Lord,' and rightly so, for that is what I am"—13:13

In His statement, "Trust in God; trust also in me"—14:1

Likening us to branches on a vine He says, "Apart from me you can do nothing"—15:5

In promising the Holy Spirit He says, "I will send him to you"—16:7

In this prayer chapter He says, "Glorify your Son"—17:1

In His trial He states, "You are right in saying I am a king"—18:37

In His atonement He had the right to say, "It is finished"—19:30

In his confession Thomas the doubter exclaimed, "My Lord and my God!"—20:28

In demanding obedience, "You must follow me"—21:22.

Seven Witnesses

The book of John was written that people might believe that Jesus Christ was God. John brings seven witnesses to the stand to prove this fact. Here they are. Turn to the Scripture and hear each one making his or her own statement.

What do you say, John the Baptist? "This is the Son of God"—1:34.

What is your conclusion, Nathanael? "You are the Son of God"—1:49.

What do you know, Peter? "You are the Holy One of God"—6:69.

What do you think, Martha? "You are the Christ, the Son of God"—11:27.

What is your verdict, Thomas? "My Lord and my God"—20:28.

What is your statement, John? "Jesus is the Christ, the Son of God"—20:31.

What do you say of yourself, Christ? "I am God's Son"—10:36.

Seven Miracles

Besides the seven witnesses in John, we find seven signs or miracles that prove He is God. "For no one could perform the miraculous signs you are doing if God were not with him," were Nicodemus's words (John 3:2).

Look over these signs as they occur throughout the book.

Turning water into wine—2:1-11

Healing the nobleman's son—4:46-54

Healing the man at Bethesda—5:1-47

Feeding the 5,000—6:1-14

Walking on the water—6:15-21

Healing the blind man—9:1-41

Raising of Lazarus—11:1-57.

Seven "I AM's"

There is another proof of His deity running through John. He reveals His God-nature in the "I AM's" of this book. He says:

"I AM the bread of life"—6:35

"I AM the light of the world"—8:12

"Before Abraham was born, I AM"—8:58

"I AM the good shepherd"—10:11

"I AM the resurrection and the life"—11:25

"I AM the way and the truth and the life"—14:6

"I AM the true vine"—15:1.

John, only, records the triumphant shout, "It is finished!" The finished work of salvation is accomplished only by the Son of God (19:30).

John says that he wrote his Gospel that people might believe that Jesus was the Christ. This part is especially for the Jews, to lead them into a personal belief in the historical Jesus "as the

Messiah," who came in fulfillment of all the Old Testament prophecies.

In John, Christ the Messiah is revealed. "Messiah" means "anointed One, who comes as divine King."

Nathanael says, "Rabbi, you are the Son of God; you are the King of Israel" (1:49).

To the woman at the well, Jesus declared Himself to be the long-expected Messiah (4:26).

To Pilate, Jesus testified that He was King.

There are various ways of remembering the contents of the book of John. We will state several. One gives us the human's estimate of the Son of God.

What individuals thought about Christ, chapters 1—5

What Christ said about Himself, chapters 6—10

What crowds thought of Christ, chapters 11—20.

Three Keys

Dr. S. D. Gordon (Samuel Dickey Gordon, 1859-1936, American author and international lecturer for the YMCA and author of the "Quiet Talk" series published by Fleming H. Revell Co.) suggested: "There are three keys that unlock John's Gospel."

Back door key—John 20:31: This key unlocks the whole of the book. It states the purpose of the Gospel.

Side door key—John 16:28: At the side, a bit toward the back we find a second key. At the Last Supper with His disciples, Jesus reveals this truth to them: "I came from the Father and entered the world; now I am leaving the world and going back to the Father." His constant thought was that He used to be with the Father. He came down to earth on an errand and stayed for thirty-three years. He would go back again to His Father.

Front door key—John 1:12: This key hangs right at the very front, outside, low down, within every child's reach. "Yet to all who received him, to those who believed in his name, he gave the right to become children of God."

This is the great key—the chief key to the whole house. Its use permits the front door to be flung wide open. Anyone who believes may enter.

The Great Prologue (John 1:1-18)

We open the book of John with this question in mind—"What do you think of Christ?" (See Matthew 22:42). Is He only the world's greatest teacher or is He actually God? Was He one of the prophets or is He the world's Savior whose coming was foretold by the prophets?

All that John is to discuss in his book he crowds into these first eighteen verses.

Let us study this Gospel with John's purpose clearly in mind. Read it over again, John 20:31. Let us see how the plan is developed and how the purpose is shown as we read the book.

The Son of God

John begins his wonderful record with Jesus the Christ, before His incarnation. God did not send His Son into the world in order that He might become His Son, for He IS the eternal Son.

Comparing the first verses of John with the other three Gospels we see how differently it opens, how exalted is its theme. Omitting the birth of Jesus, the Son of Man, John begins, "In the beginning." Read John 1:1-18 carefully. It opens like the book of Genesis. Jesus is portrayed as the Son of God.

Our Lord had no beginning. He was in the beginning. He is eternal. Christ was before all things, therefore Jesus is no part of creation—He IS the Creator (Colossians 1:16; Hebrews 1:2).

"The Word was with God." He is the Second Person of the Triune God (God the Father, God the Son, God the Holy Spirit). He is called "The Word." He came to declare God, to tell about God. As words utter thoughts, so Christ utters God. Words reveal the heart and mind; so Christ expresses, manifests and shows God. Jesus said to Philip, "If you really knew me, you would know my Father as well" (John 14:7).

Then comes the wonderful announcement that "through him all things were made; without him nothing was made that has been made. In him was life, and that life was the light of men" (1:3-4). Yes, "The Word became flesh and made his dwelling among us" (1:14). The full claims of Christ are given here: Truly

God, Light of Life. Declarer of God the Father, Baptizer with the Holy Spirit.

The Son of Man

John does not open at the manger in Bethlehem, but before all worlds were formed: "In the beginning." Jesus was the Son of God before He became flesh and dwelt among us. "In the beginning was the Word." How like Genesis this book opens!

Christ became what He was not previously—a man. But Christ did not cease to be God. He was God-Man. He lived in a tabernacle of flesh here in this world for thirty-three years. Incarnation comes from two Latin words, *in* and *caro* meaning "flesh." So Christ was God in the flesh.

People had sinned and lost the image of God, so Christ "the image of the invisible God" (Colossians 1:15) came to dwell in people. No person could see God; therefore the only begotten Son who was "in the bosom of the Father" (John 1:18, *KJV*) came to declare Him to us.

Even the witness of John the Baptist is different in John's Gospel. In Matthew he tells of the "coming Kingdom." In Luke he preaches repentance. In John, the Baptist is a witness to the Light that all men might believe (1:7). He points to "the Lamb of God" (1:32-36). These are all characteristics of this Gospel.

Jesus is God Himself in human form, coming to earth. Jesus is the Witness of the Father to humans. Jesus knew the Father. He lived with Him from the beginning. He came down to tell what He knew. He wanted humans to know the Father as He knew Him.

He told by His words, His deeds, His character, His love, but most of all by His dying on the cross and His rising the third day. All this was a declaring, a witnessing, a telling.

How was Christ the Word received? Read John 1:11: "He came to that which was his own, but his own did not receive him." He presented Himself as Messiah and King to His people, but He was rejected. All through the book we see Jesus dividing the crowds. As He comes out and speaks the truth, the crowds listen. Some believe and some reject. Tragedy indeed! But not all rejected Him. John presents the results of faith.

All of this prologue deals with Christ before His incarnation. God did not send Christ into the world that He might become His Son. Christ is the eternal Son. He is the eternal Word. Jesus is none other than the Jehovah of the Old Testament, "God manifested in the flesh." In Luke we see Christ going down to people's needs; in John we see Him drawing people up to Himself (12:32).

Remember, John is writing to prove that Jesus is the Son of God.

The Way of Salvation

What we must do for salvation: (John 1:12):

What to do: Believe and receive.

Result: You become a child of God.

What not to count on for salvation:

Sometimes the way to better understand what a thing is, is to find out what it is not. In John 1:13, John tells us what salvation is not: being born "of natural descent...of human decision or a husband's will." All of these things are what people are counting on today for eternal life. The "new birth" makes us "children of God."

"Not of natural descent"—heredity; how much we depend on good birth!

"Nor of human decision"—culture and education; it is not what we know but Whom we believe that saves us.

"Nor of the will of man" *(KJV)*—prestige or influence.

"But of God"—by the power of the Holy Spirit of God. God comes down and redeems us, if we will only believe and receive Him as Savior and Lord.

Public Ministry (John 1:19—12:50)

When John the Baptist stepped on the scene, the great drama of John's Gospel began. "Among those born of women there has not risen anyone greater than John the Baptist," Jesus declared (Matthew 11:11; Luke 7:28). John was the forerunner of the Messiah. In this Gospel, the Baptist is not described. He merely bears his witness that Jesus is the Messiah (1:18-34).

A delegation of priests and Levites were sent to ask John who he claimed to be. He told them he was not the Messiah; he was not even Elijah or any other prophet Moses spoke of, but merely "the voice of one crying in the wilderness, Make straight the way of the Lord."

The next day, on seeing Jesus, John points to Him and says, "Look, the Lamb of God!"

Then John the Baptist indicates that he knew Jesus was the Messiah because he saw the "Spirit come down from heaven as a dove and remain on him" (1:32). So John adds, "I have seen and I testify that this is the Son of God" (1:34).

Jesus Gives Signs

Jesus' disciples were convinced of His deity by His first miracle, turning water into wine. He spoke and it was so. This was one of the big factors that brought faith into the hearts of the disciples. This was the first "sign" to prove He was the Messiah (2:11).

There was only one place where Jesus could start His ministry— in Jerusalem, the capital city. Just before the Passover, the Lord entered the Temple, and taking a scourge of cords as a badge of His authority, He cleansed the sanctuary, which He declared was His Father's house. By this act, He claimed to be the very Son of God.

When the rulers asked for a sign to prove His authority after Jesus cleansed the Temple and drove out the money changers, Jesus said, "Destroy this temple, and I will raise it again in three days." The rulers were shocked, for it had taken forty-six years to build this edifice. "But the temple he had spoken of was his body," John explains (2:19-22). The supreme proof of Christ's deity is the resurrection.

Jesus gave to Nicodemus the wonderful teachings about eternal life and His love (3:16) and the new birth (3:6). Nicodemus was a moral, upright man; yet Christ said to him, "You must be born again" (3:7). If Jesus had said this to the woman of Samaria, Nicodemus would have agreed with Him. She was not a Jew and could not expect anything on the grounds that she had been born a Samaritan. But Nicodemus was a Jew by birth and he had a right to expect something on this basis. But it was to him Jesus spoke, "You must be born again" in order to enter the kingdom of heaven. Have you been born again?

Like the Jewish people of his day, Nicodemus knew God's law, but nothing of God's love. He was a moral man. He recognized Jesus as a Teacher, but he did not know Him as a Savior. This is just what the world does today. It puts Jesus at the head of the list of the teachers of the world, but does not worship Him as very God.

Jesus revealed to one woman the truth of His Messiahship. This story gives us Christ's estimate of a single soul. He brought this immoral woman face-to-face with Himself and showed her what kind of a life she was leading. Her loose view of marriage is not unlike the view taken today by many people. Christ did not condemn her or pass judgment upon her, but He did reveal to her that He is the only One who could meet her needs. Christ revealed the wonderful truth to her that He is the water of life. He alone can satisfy. The wells of the world bring no satisfaction. People are trying everything, but they still are unhappy and restless. Did the woman believe Christ? What did she do? Her actions spoke louder than any words could have done. She went back and by her simple testimony brought a whole town to Christ (4:1-42).

In healing the son of the nobleman, Jesus gives another sign of His deity. During His interview with the centurion, Jesus brought him to an open confession of Christ as Lord—yes, and his whole household joining with him (4:46-54).

The miracle of feeding 5,000 was an acted parable. Jesus Himself was the Bread from heaven. He wanted to tell them, that to all who put their trust in Him will He give satisfaction and joy (6:35).

The people wanted to make Christ their King because He could feed them. How like people today! They long for someone who can give them food and clothing. But Christ would not be King on their grounds. He dismissed the excited multitude and departed into a mountain. The people were disappointed that He would not be a political leader, and so they "turned back and no longer followed him" (6:66).

The people were divided because of Jesus (7:40-44). We find unbelief was developing into actual hostility, but in His true followers faith was growing. Some people said, "He is a good man." Others said, "Not so." We must say one or the other today, when facing Christ's claims. Either He is God or an impostor. There is no middle ground.

The healing of the blind man led Jesus to reveal to this fellow who He was. When "they cast him out" because of his confession of Christ, Jesus gave a great discourse on the Good Shepherd (chap. 10). See the opposite results produced by His words in 10:19-21. Notice the accusations of blasphemy they made of Christ when He said, "'I and the Father are one.' Again the Jews picked up stones to stone him" (10:30-31). What happened in the face of all this criticism and opposition (10:42)?

The raising of Lazarus is the final "sign" of John's Gospel. The other Gospel records give the raising of Jairus's daughter and the son of the widow of Nain. But in this case Lazarus had been dead four days. In reality, would it be any harder for God to raise one than the other? Nevertheless, it had a profound effect on the leaders (11:47-48). The great claim Jesus made for Himself to Martha is recorded here, "I am the resurrection and the life. He who believes in me will live, even though he dies; and whoever lives and believes in me will never die. Do you believe this?" (11:25-26).

This scene closes with Jesus' triumphant entry into Jerusalem. His public ministry had come to an end. It is recorded that many of the chief Jewish leaders believed on Him, without making an open confession.

Jesus' Startling Claims

Claims to be equal with God: Calls God "my Father" (5:17). The Jews knew what He meant. He made Himself equal with God, they said. They knew that He claimed God as His Father in a sense in which He is not the Father of any other person.

Claims to be light of the world: "I am the light of the world. Whoever follows me will never walk in darkness, but will have the light of life" (8:12).

Claims to be eternal with God: "'I tell you the truth,' Jesus answered, 'before Abraham was born, I am!'" (John 8:58). This claim of eternity with God was unmistakable. He was either the Son of God or a deceiver. Indeed, He uses the "I AM" of God's personal name, equating Himself with the Father (Exodus 3:14). No wonder the Jews "picked up stones to stone him" (John 8:59).

Private Ministry (John 13—17)

Here we leave the multitude behind and follow Jesus as He lived the last week of His life on earth before His crucifixion. We call it Passion Week.

Sunday—the triumphant entry into Jerusalem
Monday—the cleansing of the Temple
Tuesday—the conflicts in the Temple
Evening—the discourse on the Mount of Olives
Thursday—preparation for the Passover
Evening—the Last Supper with His disciples.

The Last Evening Together

Last words are always important. Jesus is leaving His disciples and is giving them His last instructions. This passage, John 13 to 17, is called the holy of holies of the Scriptures. Prayerfully read it all at one sitting.

Jesus divided the Jewish people—some believed Him, others had rejected Him completely. Now He gathered His own around Him in an Upper Room, and told them many secrets before He departed from them. He wanted to comfort His disciples for He knew how hard it would be for them when He was gone. They would be sheep without a shepherd.

It is wonderful that Jesus should have selected and loved men like these. They seem to be a collection of nobodies with the exception of Peter and John. But they were "His own," and He loved them. One of Jesus' specialties is to make somebodies out of nobodies. This is what He did with His first group of followers, and this is what He has continued to do down through the centuries.

What a picture we have in John 13:1-11! Jesus, the Son of God, girded with a towel, a basin of water in His blessed hands, is washing His disciples' feet! He wanted us to serve in the same spirit. He taught us that greatness is always measured by service. There is no loving others without living for others (vv. 16-17). Christ said, "The greatest among you will be your servant" (Matthew 23:11). The biggest merchant in the city is the one who serves the greatest public.

Jesus foretells His betrayal by Judas (13:18-30), and Judas goes out into the night. It was night in Judas's heart, too. Fellowship brings light. Sin brings darkness. What a pitiable picture Judas is! His opportunities of knowing Jesus were unsurpassed, but he rejected the Lord. This is what unbelief can do. Belief means life; unbelief means death.

After announcing His going, the Lord gives His disciples "a new commandment," that they love one another. "A new command I give you: Love one another. As I have loved you, so you must love one another. By this all men will know that you are my disciples, if you love one another" (13:34-35). Discipleship is tested not by the creed you recite, not by the hymns you sing, not by the ritual you observe, but by the fact that you love one another. The measure in which Christians love one another is the measure in which the world believes in them or their Christ. It is the final test of discipleship. He mentions this "new commandment" again in John 15:12.

Christ's Answer for a Life Beyond

"I am going there to prepare...I will come back and take you to be with me" (14:2,3). This is Jesus' cure for heart trouble—faith in God. We see there is no break between the thirteenth and fourteenth chapters. Jesus goes right on with His discourse. How many hearts have been put to rest and how many eyes have been dried by these words in John 14!

Jesus had spoken of His Father, but now He speaks of the other Person of the Godhead, the Holy Spirit. If He (Christ) is to go away, He will send the Comforter and He will abide with them. This is a wonderful promise for the child of God! Jesus repeats the promise in chapter 15 and again in 16. Look them up (15:26; chap. 16). Few know of this Presence in their lives. It is by His power that we live. Never call the Holy Spirit "it." He is a Person. He is One of three Persons in the Triune God (the Trinity).

"Peace I leave with you; my peace I give you" (14:27). This is Christ's legacy to us. The only peace we can enjoy in this world is His peace.

Jesus reveals the real secret of the Christian life to His disciples in John 15. "Remain ("Abide," *KJV*) in Christ." He is the source of life. Abide in Christ as the branch abides in the vine. The branch cannot sever itself and join itself whenever it will to the trunk. It must abide if it will bear fruit. This is the picture of our lives in Christ. Live and walk in Christ and you will bear fruit. If you are not abiding in Christ, the fruit will soon disappear.

After He ended His talk with the eleven disciples, Jesus spoke to the Father. The disciples listened to His loving and solemn words. How thrilled they must have been as He told the Father how much He loved them and how He cared for them! He mentioned everything about Himself that He had taught them. He would keep them (17:11); He would sanctify them (17:17); He would make them one (17:21); and finally, He would let all His children share in His glory some day (17:24).

If you would know the beauty and depth of these wonderful words, kneel and let the Son of God lead in prayer as you read aloud this seventeenth chapter of John.

Let us look at the teaching about the Holy Spirit as given by John:

1. *The Incoming Spirit* (3:5): This is the commencement of the Christian life, the new birth by the Spirit. We are born by the Spirit into the family of God.
2. *The Indwelling Spirit* (4:14): He fills us with His presence and brings us joy.
3. *The Overflowing Spirit* (7:38-39): "Streams of living water will flow from within him"—not just little streams of blessing, but rivers—Mississippis and Amazons if the Holy Spirit dwells within us.
4. *The Witnessing Spirit* (14—16): He speaks through us. This is the particular task of the Christian through the Holy Spirit—to testify of Christ.

Suffering and Death (John 18—19)

Immediately following His prayer, Jesus went into the Garden of Gethsemane, knowing all things that should come upon Him. The change from the scene in the Upper Room (chaps. 13—17 to chapter 18) is like going from warmth to cold, from light to darkness. Only two hours had passed since Judas left the supper table. Now we see him betraying his best Friend. Remember, Judas was not forced to betray his Lord—he personally chose to betray Christ, and this treacherous act fulfilled prophecy. God did not cause Judas to sin, but Judas's betrayal was prophesied because it was going to happen. No one ever had to sin to carry out any of God's plan.

"The hour" had come! The mission of our Lord on earth was ended. The greatest work of Christ remained to be done. He was to die that He might glorify the Father and save the sinful world. He came to give His life a ransom for many. Christ came into the world by manger and left it by the door of the cross.

Jesus was now ready to give them the real sign of His authority in answer to the question in chapter 2: "'What miraculous sign can you show us to prove your authority to do all this?' Jesus answered them, 'Destroy this temple, and I will raise it again in three days'" (2:18-19).

We see Jesus, always poised, always gentle. He knew His hour had come. He was not surprised when He heard the soldiers approach. He stepped forward to meet them. The men retreated and fell before the majesty of His look.

Follow Him, bound as a captive, to the hall of the high priest. Jesus was the One in command of the situation all through this terrible drama. He went forth (18:4), a voluntary sacrifice. He deliberately tasted death for every person.

Almost as sad as Judas was Peter, the deserter in the hour of need, denying three times that he had any connection with his best Friend! This is a lesson for us—overconfidence. Poor Peter is to be pitied, for he really loved the Master.

Peter did not know that the supreme trial of his life would come in the question of a servant maid. It is so often thus. We lock and bolt the main door, but the thief breaks into a tiny window we had not thought of. We would die at the stake, but deny Christ in our speech.

All the disciples but John deserted Jesus in the hour of His greatest need. (Peter denied Jesus, but he stayed close by.) In that fleeing nine is James of the "inner circle," Nathanael the guile-less, and Andrew the personal worker. Yet, here they were, run-ning pell-mell down the road together, away from their Friend. A sorry sight! Wait! Don't start blaming them. Suppose you look up and see where you are. Are you following Jesus closely? Remember, majorities are not always right. Be sure you are right! Can Christ count on you?

Jesus has come to the supreme, crowning act of His life on earth. It was not a crisis, but a climax. He came to earth to "give his life a ransom for many."

Finally the make-believe trials are over. It is morning at last, and yet it seems like night. It is the world's blackest hour. The courtyard is deserted. The fire at which Peter warmed himself is only gray ashes. The soldiers' jeers and Herod's sneers and Pilate's vacillation are over.

The brief interval between Peter's denial and Jesus' climbing the hill to Golgotha was crowded with incidents. The night trial before Caiaphas and the Sanhedrin probably preceded the last denial of Peter. Then came the awful treatment up to the morn-ing session of the Sanhedrin.

Often the cruel scourging of the Romans was so severe that prisoners died under the torturing blows. The crown of thorns that was thrust upon His holy brow was only another act of cruel torture. When He comes again He will bring many crowns (Revelation 19:12).

Finally Pilate led Him forth and said, "Here is the man!" (John 19:5). What a sight! To see the Creator of this universe, the Light and Life of the world, the holy One treated so! But Satan ener-gized the religious rulers, and they cried, "Crucify! Crucify!...he claimed to be the Son of God" (19:6-7).

At the Cross, we have hate's record at its worst and love's record at its best. People so hated that they put Christ to death. God so loved that He gave people life.

Our religion is one of four letters instead of two. Other reli-gions say, "Do." Our religion says, "Done." Our Savior has done all on the cross. He bore our sins and when He gave up His life He said, "It is finished!" This was the shout of a conqueror. He had finished human's redemption. Nothing was left for people to do. Has the work been done in your heart?

Jesus was crucified on Golgotha, "place of a skull." He is crucified there today—in people's minds. They crucify Him afresh and put Him to an open shame. Salvation is costly. "Christ died for our sins" (1 Corinthians 15:3). It cost Him His life.

Victory over Death (John 20—21)

We have a Savior who is victorious over death. He "ever liveth."

On the third day, the tomb was empty! The grave clothes were all in order. Jesus had risen from the dead, but not as others had done. When Lazarus came forth, he was bound in his grave clothes. He came out in his natural body; he was not "a spirit" (Luke 24:39). But when Jesus came forth, His natural body was changed to a spiritual body. The changed body came right out of its linen wrappings and left them, as the butterfly leaves the chrysalis shell. Read what John says in 20:6-8.

Jesus' appearances, eleven in all after His resurrection, helped His disciples to believe that He was God. Read the confession of the sixth witness, Thomas the doubter (John 20:28). Jesus wanted every doubt to be removed from each one of His disciples. They must carry out His Great Commission and bear the Gospel into all the world (John 20:21).

Jesus gave the disciple who denied Him thrice, Peter, an opportunity of confessing Him thrice. He restored him to full privileges of service again. Christ only wants those who love Him to serve Him. If you love Him you must serve Him. No one who loves Christ can help but serve.

What are Jesus' last words in this Gospel? "You must follow me." This is His word to each one of us. May we all follow Him in loving obedience "till He come"!

"This Gospel opens with Christ in the bosom of the Father, and closes with John in the bosom of Christ"—A. J. Gordon (Adoniram Judson Gordon, 1846-1895, American pastor, missionary executive and educator).

History

of The New Testament

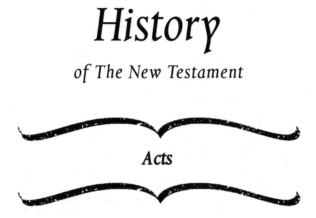

Acts

Key Events of Acts

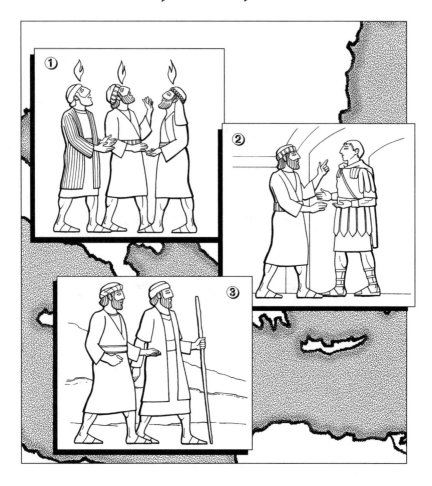

History: The Holy Spirit and the Beginning of the Church

The Holy Spirit comes with power ① at Pentecost, just as Jesus promised. Soon thousands of Jewish people believed that Jesus was in fact the Messiah, the "coming One" God had promised through the Law and prophets. After a few years of growth, the Jewish church decided that Gentiles ② can be full participants in salvation without having to submit to the Mosaic laws. This momentous decision enabled thousands of Gentiles from around the Mediterranean to freely come to Christ, thanks to missionary bands led by people such as Paul the apostle and Barnabas ③ .

Chapter 32

Understanding Acts

Acts Portrays Jesus Christ, the Living Lord

Selected Bible Readings

Sunday:	First Church in Jerusalem (Acts 1:1—4:37)
Monday:	Witnessing in Jerusalem (Acts 5:1—8:3)
Tuesday:	Witnessing in Judea and Samaria (Acts 8:4—12:25)
Wednesday:	Paul Establishes the Churches (First Tour) (Acts 13:1—15:35)
Thursday:	Paul Revisits the Churches (Second Tour) (Acts 15:36—18:21)
Friday:	Paul Encourages the Churches (Third Tour) (Acts 18:22—25:9)
Saturday:	Paul Sent to Rome (Acts 25:10—28:31)

Luke, in his Gospel, shows what Christ began to do on earth; Acts shows what He continued to do by the Holy Spirit.

The ascension of our Lord is the closing scene in Luke. It is the opening fact in Acts (Luke 24:49-51; Acts 1:10-11).

Gospels and Acts

The Gospels set forth the Son of Man, who came to die for our sins. Acts shows the coming of the Son of God in the power of the Holy Spirit.

The Gospels set forth what Christ began to do. Acts shows what He continued to do by the Holy Spirit, through His disciples.

The Gospels tell of the crucified and risen Savior. Acts portrays

Him as the ascended and exalted Lord and Leader.

In the Gospels we hear Christ's teachings. In Acts we see the effect of His teachings on the acts of the apostles.

Acts is not a record of the acts of the apostles, as no extensive accounts are given of any apostles except Peter and Paul. It records the acts of the Holy Spirit through the apostles. His name is mentioned about seventy times. Look for some work of the Holy Spirit in every chapter of this book.

The word "witness" is used more than thirty times.

"You will be my witnesses" (1:8) is the heart of the book of Acts. Salvation comes to this world through Christ alone (Acts 4:12), hence people must know Him. Christ's plan includes us. Are you witnessing for Christ? If not, why not? It is true that Christ alone can save the world, but Christ cannot save this world alone. If you have no witness for Christ, look into your heart. "For out of the overflow of the heart the mouth speaks" (Matthew 12:34).

Christ told His disciples that He would send the Spirit, and "he will testify about me. And you also must testify, for you have been with me from the beginning" (John 15:26-27). This promise of Christ's was fulfilled on the Day of Pentecost when He poured forth the Holy Spirit upon the disciples (Acts 2:16-17,33), and from that moment, as they bore witness to the Savior, the Holy Spirit bore witness at the same time in the hearts of their hearers, and multitudes were brought to the Lord.

It is a wonderful thing to know that when the Spirit prompts you to speak to someone about Christ, He has been working in that heart and making it ready to receive your witness. There is a perfect example of this in Acts 8 where Philip was sent to speak to the Ethiopian. Read this ever-thrilling story!

What was the result of the first sermon on the Day of Pentecost (Acts 2)?

In each widening circle of influence, we find a marked out-pouring of the Holy Spirit. Isn't it amazing that in one generation the apostles had moved out in every direction and had preached in every nation of the then known world (Colossians 1:23)?

The infant church was slow to realize what was the extent of their commission. They confined their preaching to Jerusalem until persecution drove them out. The blood of Stephen, the first Christian martyr, proved to be the seed of the growing church.

The book opens with the preaching of the gospel in Jerusalem, the metropolis of the Jewish nation. It closes with the gospel in Rome, the true metropolis of world power.

Although we call this book the Acts of the Apostles, we find that it is for the most part the acts of the Holy Spirit working through Peter and Paul and their companions.

In Acts 1 through 12, we find Peter witnessing primarily to the Jews. Peter says, "Repent" (Acts 2:36-38).

In Acts 13—28, we find Paul witnessing primarily to the Gentiles. He says, "Believe" (Acts 16:30-31).

There are two natural divisions in Acts. In 1—12 Peter says to the Jews, "Repent." Why? Because they needed a definite change of mind about the Messiah. In 13—28 Paul says, "Believe." Why? Because the Gentiles needed not to change their minds concerning the Messiah; they needed to believe on Him.

The book tells of the extension of the gospel to the Gentiles. All through the Old Testament we find God dealing with the Jewish people. In the New Testament, we find Him working among all nations.

No doubt Acts is the best guidebook to missions that has ever been written. We find in it the motive for missions. The believers' one aim was to bring people to a saving knowledge of Jesus Christ. He was their one theme, and the Word of God their one weapon.

We find the first church pursuing a definite program in carrying out its plans. They chose some great radiating center of population for a base from which the influence of their work might spread to the surrounding area.

The disciples were simple, straightforward and successful. They depended entirely upon the power of God, through His Spirit. They moved with a zeal that could not be quenched, and a courage that was unflinching.

Power for Witnessing (Acts 1—2)

What a wonderful forty days after the resurrection of Jesus the disciples spent with the Lord before His ascension! How anxious they were to hear His last words of instruction! He "spoke about the kingdom of God" (1:3). It was then that Jesus "gave this command: 'Do not leave Jerusalem, but wait for the gift my Father promised, which you have heard me speak about'" (1:4).

The first twenty-six verses of the first chapter are introductory to the rest of the book. They tell of:

The Great Commission—1:6-8

The Ascension—1:2,9,11

The promise of Christ's return—1:10-11.

The disciples still were not satisfied regarding the time when Christ would set up His kingdom on earth. They still expected a Kingdom that would give them political independence and establish them in a place of leadership in the world (1:6). What was Jesus' answer (1:7)?

One day when Jesus "led them out to the vicinity of Bethany, he lifted up his hands and blessed them" (Luke 24:50). He told them their power was not to be political but spiritual. Listen to His words (Acts 1:8).

At the ascension of Christ, our Lord went "out of sight," but stayed with the people in a far more real way. After He had spoken, His last words to His disciples (1:8), He was taken up "and a cloud hid him from their sight" (1:9). Think of so great an event told in such few words! The Father took His Son back to glory.

Christ Shall Return

"This same Jesus...will come back in the same way you have seen him go into heaven" (Acts 1:11). How will His "coming" be, as spoken of here? Will it be merely at death? Is it merely as He comes to dwell in our hearts? No. The promise is that He shall come "in the same way." If this is so, we should examine how He went. Then we shall know how He will come back. See the Scriptures. It will be:

Personal—1 Thessalonians 4:16

Visible—Revelation 1:7

Bodily—Matthew 24:30

Local—Luke 24:50.

Picture the disciples as they returned from the Mount of Olives to Jerusalem. They went into "an upper room." It might have been the very same room where Jesus had eaten the Last Supper with them (Luke 22:12). They "all joined together constantly in prayer" for ten days (1:13-14). Jesus had told them to stay in Jerusalem until they should receive power from on high (Luke 24:49). Even though they had been three years in training with the Lord, they needed the presence of the Holy Spirit, whom Jesus said He would send to empower them. They had proved to be a weak group in themselves.

Christ had told them not to depart from Jerusalem, but to wait there. It would have been natural for them to flee from that place where their Lord had been crucified and to go back to Galilee. But Christ said, "Tarry ye in the city of Jerusalem" *(KJV)* because it was the center of widest influence. We cannot always choose our place of service.

Next in importance to the coming of the Lord Jesus Christ to this earth is the coming of the Holy Spirit. The Church was born on that Day of Pentecost. Become familiar with this account given in Acts 2:1-13. Pentecost was one of the most popular of the feasts, and Jerusalem would be crowded with pilgrims from everywhere. It was fifty days after the Crucifixion. From this time Pentecost was not to be a Jewish feast, but the dawn of a new day, the birthday of the Church of Christ.

The scene opens with the disciples assembled together, with their hearts fixed on Christ, waiting for His promise to be fulfilled. The Holy Spirit Himself descended that day. Luke does not say there was a wind, but sound was a symbol, as were the "tongues of fire" (2:3). The violent wind (2:2) represented heavenly power. The luminous tongues conveyed the symbol of fire, and tongues expressed power to witness. See the results of this advent in Acts 2:6,12. Fire is a symbol of divine presence. It illumines; it purifies.

The Holy Spirit at Pentecost

The Spirit fell on them (Acts 2:1-3). The Spirit came in them (2:4). The Spirit worked through them (2:41-47).

They were filled with the Holy Spirit and thus endowed for special service. They not only were enabled to preach in power, but also could speak in the different tongues represented that day at Jerusalem (2:2-4). Was speaking in new languages a jargon not understood by anyone, or were those present able to understand and benefit (2:6)?

The wonderful thing about Pentecost was not the "blowing of a violent wind," or the "tongues of fire," but the disciples being filled with the Holy Spirit that they might be witnesses to all people. If we do not have the desire to tell others of Christ, it is evident that we do not know the fullness of the Holy Spirit.

Do not think that at this Pentecost the Holy Spirit came for the first time to the world. All through the Old Testament we see an account of how He had been guiding people and giving them strength. Now the Spirit was to use a new instrument, the Church, which was born on that very day.

They were "amazed and perplexed" (2:12). People by nature are unbelieving. Is it not a great exhibition of God's grace when people come to believe God truly and really accept His word?

Some mocked. "They have had too much wine" (2:13). People always try to explain away the miracles of God on natural grounds. But rationalism can never give a reasonable explanation of anything that is divine. Also it was only nine in the morning, and no Jew could touch wine till then. Read Peter's defense against this false charge in Acts 2:14-21.

Peter's Sermon

The theme of this first sermon in Acts was that Jesus is the Messiah, as shown by His resurrection.

Peter is the outstanding figure in the first twelve chapters of Acts. The real power of the Holy Spirit was shown when Peter, the humble fisherman, rose to speak and 3,000 souls were saved! How can we account for cowardly Peter's boldness as he stood that day to preach before a multitude on the streets of Jerusalem? What was the secret of Peter's ministry?

It is a serious thing to charge men with murder; yet Peter did just this (2:36). Will he get away with it? Will he be stoned? The last verses in chapter 2 answer the question (2:37-47).

What a Church was this First Church of Jerusalem, organized with a membership of 3,000 on the Day of Pentecost! What glorious days followed, in "teaching" and "fellowship," and "signs and wonders," and, above all, salvation! "And the Lord added to their number daily those who were being saved" (2:47). This is the real objective of the Church. Are we seeing it today in our churches?

Just as marvelous as the gift of tongues was the daily life of this first church. It is not surprising that they found "favor of all the people," and that additions were made "daily."

These first Christians were "regular Christians":

Regular in church going—"All the believers were together"

Regular in church giving—Acts 2:44-45

Regular in church's mission—Acts 2:46-47.

Witnessing in Jerusalem (Acts 3:1—8:3)

Chapter 3 opens at the Beautiful Gate of the Temple. Peter healed an incurable cripple, lame from birth, who had been carried daily to this place to beg for his living. The miracle attracted the notice of the Jewish leaders and resulted in the first real opposition to the Church.

When a great crowd had gathered around the lame man who had been so miraculously healed, Peter took advantage of the circumstances to preach his second recorded sermon. He did not spare his countrymen. Again he told them that Christ, whom they had crucified, was the long-promised Messiah. So powerful were the words of Peter and John that a total of 5,000 men now turned to this Christ!

The leaders were aroused because the apostles taught the people that this Jesus, whom they had crucified, had risen from the dead, and would appear again (4:2). They commanded the apostles not to preach; but opposition made the Church thrive. Opposition should never be a matter of amazement, not even a matter of surprise to any Christian. The work of the Spirit is always a signal for Satan to work. Whenever the Spirit comes to bless, the adversary comes to curse. But martyrdom is an aid to the Church, and whenever the truth is faithfully preached, fruit will be brought forth. (See 4:3-4.)

As soon as Peter and John were released by the rulers, they sought their friends and reported their experiences and united in prayer and praise. The Church must expect opposition, but in all circumstances we can find courage and help in God. "The place where they were meeting was shaken. And they were all filled with the Holy Spirit and spoke the word of God boldly" (4:31).

We find that this kind of preaching brought unity in the Church. They were of one heart and of one soul (4:32). They went out "to testify to the resurrection of the Lord Jesus" (v. 33). Let us tell it out! Dying people need it; the day demands it!

People were not compelled to part with their personal possessions. It was not expected of them. If they brought what they had, it was a purely voluntary act. Sharing property was voluntary, not obligatory; individual, not general; confined to Jerusalem; temporary; limited to believers.

The Church became so unselfish that many sold all they had and gave it to the apostles to distribute "as he had need" (2:45). But even this act of love and generosity was open to abuse and deception. Barnabas's liberality was an illustration of the spirit of love. Ananias and Sapphira were an illustration of deception in that they deceived themselves and the apostles as well. But the Holy Spirit revealed the truth about it all. Ananias and Sapphira wanted glory without paying the price. They wanted honor without honesty. They were punished with instant death, for, while claiming to give all to God, they had kept back part (5:4-5).

As Christians, we claim to give all to Christ. Complete surrender is the condition He sets down for discipleship. "Give up everything" and "follow me" is His condition (see Luke 14:33). Do we hold back anything from Christ? Are we hypocrites in our testimony?

The power in the apostles' story was in the fact that their lives fitted in with the life of their risen Christ. "You've got to show me," is the attitude of the world today. Those early Christians did show the world. Do you show by your life and conduct that you are a Christian?

When signs and wonders were wrought among the people, the crowds came to see. When the Holy Spirit was in the midst, the people saw the power of God. The same is true today. When churches present Christ in His winsomeness and the Holy Spirit in His power, the people will come. Christ draws all.

Miracles commonly result in converts. Look in this book of Acts. When the miracle of tongues appeared, the people thronged to the place (Acts 2). When Peter healed the man at the Gate Beautiful, "all the people were astonished and came running to them in the place called Solomon's Colonnade" (3:11). When the miracle of judgment came upon Ananias and Sapphira, "More and more men and women believed in the Lord and were added to their number" (5:14). So we will find instances all through the book.

Thousands of articles have been written about how to put people to work in the churches. There will be plenty of service in the church when we give place to the Holy Spirit. The Spirit-filled church will be a serving church.

"Then the high priest and all his associates...arrested the apostles and put them in the public jail" (5:17-18). Again we see that the wonderful work of the apostles aroused the opposition of the Sanhedrin (a court of seventy religious rulers). A few unlearned fishermen had risen up to teach, and multitudes were listening and following after them; hence the religious leaders were disturbed. Even though the apostles were beaten with rods and prohibited to preach, we find them rejoicing that they were counted worthy to suffer shame for His name! "Day after day, in the temple courts and from house to house, they never stopped teaching and proclaiming the good news that Jesus is the Christ" (Acts 5:42). We find their boldest words in this statement: "We must obey God rather than men!" (5:29). Is this the conviction of your life?

Let us have the spirit of these apostles! Let us not be discouraged when opponents multiply.

A meeting of the Church was called, and seven members elected as deacons (6:1-7). There were two offices in the Church now. One was to "serve tables," to attend to the benevolence and to care for the needy. The other office was to devote itself to preaching and prayer.

The first two deacons named were Stephen and Philip (6:5). These two men were mighty in their influence over the Church, perhaps more than any besides Peter and Paul.

The opposition was centered around Stephen. Read the experiences as recorded in Acts 6 and 7. Stephen was just a layman, but he was one of the first deacons. He is described as a man "full of God's grace and power" (6:8). We have a record of only one day of his life—the last. What an account it is! It is not the length of time we live that counts, but how we live. Someone has said, "A Christian is always on duty." This means that every minute of our lives is important and under God's direction.

Stephen was just a layman. Like thousands of other laymen since his time he "did great wonders" because he was "full of faith and power" *(KJV)*.

The layman Stephen's life and death had an incalculable effect upon the history of the world in his influence upon Saul of Tarsus. Who can tell what your life may do in its influence upon some friend?

The leaders in the synagogue "could not stand up against his wisdom or the Spirit by whom he spoke" (6:10). Their anger flared into murderous hatred. Stephen was the first martyr of the Christian Church. To Stephen's death we may trace, without doubt, one of the most outstanding impressions made by the followers of Christ on Saul (see Acts 22:20).

Witnessing in Judea and Samaria (Acts 8:4—12:25)

The disciples had been witnesses in Jerusalem, but Jesus had told them they must go into Judea and Samaria.

If you were quite sure that you would lose your life by remaining in your own hometown, but would be safe in some nearby village, do you think you would go to that village? This is the very problem that faced the Early Church in Jerusalem. There were religious leaders there who thought they were doing God's will when they tried to wipe out the new sect by killing and imprisoning Jewish believers in Jesus, followers of the way (9:2). Paul said: "I too was convinced that I ought to do all that was possible to oppose the name of Jesus of Nazareth" (Acts 26:9).

Paul really began his work of spreading the gospel then, but he did not know it. Read Acts 8:3. He was stamping out what he considered to be a heretical and dangerous group. Instead, he was spreading it. Just laugh when you see anyone opposing the gospel. Persecution almost always has spread the gospel like wind spreads fire. This has been true all down through the centuries since our Lord lived on the earth.

See what kind of a Church this Early Church was. "Those who had been scattered preached the word wherever they went" (8:4).

This is the reason the gospel spread at first. What commission did the disciples have? "Go into all the world and preach the good news to all creation" (Mark 16:15). How many did Jesus train for His work? Just twelve, and one of them forsook Him.

Well, here were the rest of the Twelve, sitting down at Jerusalem and "all the world" needing the gospel. Saul's persecution, like the confusion of tongues at the tower of Babel, scattered the Christians throughout the world. Cowardice did not prompt them to flee, for every place we find them preaching the gospel.

Philip, the Evangelist
Philip (not the apostle), one of the seven who had been chosen as a deacon (Acts 6:5), was an evangelist. He had settled in Samaria as a result of the persecution. Jesus had said, "You shall be my witnesses...in Samaria." Philip preached Christ. Multitudes were following him in his evangelistic campaign. But God called him to leave his successful work and "Go south to the road—the desert road—that goes down from Jerusalem to Gaza" (8:26). Philip obeyed and left, and on the way he met an Ethiopian. "By chance," you say? When you are in the will of God, things do not just happen. No friend crosses your path by accident. No joy or sorrow comes into your life except by God's permission.

This story raises the question about which brings the larger results—preaching to people in great numbers or telling people individually about the Lord. Some people think that winning just one person at a time to Christ would be a slow process, but listen to this!

Today (1953) there are more than 230 million people in the United States (301 million in 2007). Suppose you were the only Christian among these 230 million today. You win one soul of the 230 million today. Then tomorrow you two win one soul each, for Christ. On the following day each one of you four do the same; next day the eight of you win one apiece. Here is a startling fact. If each of these Christians and the newly won Christians were to win one soul a day to Christ, how long would it take to win 230 million? Just less than one month from the day the first one began! Wouldn't it be a good thing for your class to form a G. O. Club? Each one Get One. This is Christ's method of soul winning.

Philip's convert no doubt preached the gospel in Africa. There is nothing to show that Africa previously had any knowledge of the Son of God. The gospel was on its way to the "uttermost part of the earth."

Saul

At Stephen's death, we have the first mention of Saul. Stephen's martyrdom seemed to have inflamed this persecutor of the Church. Saul was struggling with an aroused conscience. He knew he was in the wrong, but he would not give up. This is why Jesus told him in his vision that "It is hard for you to kick against the goads" (Acts 26:14).

Saul made havoc of the Church! The more moral and intelligent a person is, the more harm that person can do when controlled by Satan.

The story of Saul's conversion is one of the most thrilling accounts in history. Become familiar with this great story. He was a man "breathing out murderous threats against the Lord's disciples" (9:1). Then we find him preaching "in the synagogues that Jesus is the Son of God" (9:20).

At every step of his three great missionary journeys, Paul made known Christ's will with unmistakable clarity. There is no doubt that Paul holds the most important place of any man in the New Testament. He was converted and made an apostle by Christ Himself. It was to him that Christ gave first-hand revelations of truth, and to him Christ committed the doctrine of the Church. To what people was Paul especially sent? He was the apostle to the Gentiles, as Peter had been to the Jews.

Peter

What had Peter done since Pentecost? It is not only what a person believes, but what the person is doing about it that counts. Christ had told Peter that he was to be a witness. Peter helped start the first Church, worked miracles and baptized thousands. His work had been among the Jewish people.

We find Peter now in the house of Simon the tanner (10:5-6). God was going to show Peter that the gospel was for the Gentiles as well as the Jews (Acts 10:9-16). The high wall of religious difference between Jew and Gentile must be broken down. Peter was the man God used to start leveling it. Christ was building a Church and He wanted both Jews and Gentiles to be the living stones of which it is to be formed (Ephesians 2:20-22).

At Pentecost, Peter had used the "keys of the kingdom" (see Matthew 16:18-19) entrusted to him to open the door of the gospel to the Jews. While Paul was in Tarsus, Peter in the house of Cornelius put the key into the lock of the door that had barred the Gentiles, and opened it (Acts 10:1-48). Read this account. What about race prejudice today? Do you think that what God told Peter to do was easy (10:14-16)? What is the Church doing today?

Witnessing in Earth's Uttermost Parts (Acts 13—28)

The death of Stephen was only the beginning of great persecution of the believers in Jesus, most of whom were Jewish. How did they ever get to Antioch? (Acts 11:19-21). Someone has called the Church in the early days "A Tale of Two Cities"—Jerusalem and Antioch.

Up through Acts 12, we have seen the beginning of the Church, with Peter as its leader, in Jerusalem. From Acts 13 through 28, we are going to see Paul and the Church at Antioch. Antioch is the new base of operations. All the wonderful missionary journeys of

Paul started from here, not from Jerusalem. It became the new center of the Church for carrying out Jesus' commission.

The Jewish believers in Jesus who had been compelled to leave Jerusalem because of persecution were naturally thrown in with all the Gentiles. They could not help but talk about that which interested them most. The power of the Lord was so manifest that a great crowd joined the Church (11:21).

It was here in this church that a new name was given to Christ's disciples. They were first called "Christians" at Antioch (11:26).

It is interesting to note here that the Church had lost track of Paul. They did not care what had become of him, but Barnabas looked him up (11:25). He had kept track of him all these years. If it had not been for Barnabas, Paul might have remained in obscurity all his life! Think of what the world would have missed had Paul not been discovered! Many a person is waiting to be discovered for God.

Beginning of Foreign Missions

Do we realize that we Americans might have been pagans living in spiritual darkness and superstition, were it not for the early Christian missionaries' travels to Europe? Thomas went to India, others went to Syria, Arabia and so on. Wouldn't you think that Americans, above every people, ought to believe in missions? Think of what our condition might have been today if missionaries had not brought Christ to us.

We see Paul and Barnabas, the first foreign missionaries, starting westward from Antioch (Acts 13:2-3). The greatest enterprise in the world is foreign missions, and this is the very start of this great movement. The whole idea began just the way it should, at a prayer meeting.

While Paul and Barnabas were preaching the gospel and suffering all kinds of persecution and hardship, many at home in Jerusalem were stirring up the most troublesome question the Church had ever faced. It was this: "Must a Gentile become a Jew, accepting Jewish laws and ceremonies, in order to be saved?" (15:1). Paul and Barnabas had said nothing about the law of Moses. They had stated: "Believe in the Lord Jesus, and you will be saved" (16:31). The law doesn't save anyone.

Luke now joined the missionary party (16:10). The first convert in Europe was not a famous scholar or some mighty ruler, but a businesswoman, Lydia, a seller of purple dyed garments.

In Philippi, we find Paul and Silas in prison. Why do we find men like these locked behind iron bars? Read Acts 16:16-24. The second Christian in Europe was very different from the first. Lydia was converted in a prayer meeting, but it took an earthquake to arouse the next convert—a jailer. The jailer's question is one of the most important questions in all the world (16:30).

Paul's experiences in the greatest cities of his day are crowded with interest. He founded a church at Thessalonica (17:4).

In famous Athens, Paul preached his immortal sermon on Mars Hill. This is one of the great scenes in history. What effect did it have on those listeners (Acts 17:32)?

Paul was not only giving a wonderful message to the Athenians when he preached that day, but he was also speaking to you and to me. Paul tells us that God is near. He seems so far away to some that they do not even try to reach Him, yet God hears our faintest whisper if we speak to Him.

Paul left Athens and arrived at Corinth, very much discouraged. We do not know whether he was successful in starting a church in Athens, but in Corinth, one of the most wicked cities of the ancient world, he founded a church and remained there eighteen months to establish the people in the faith (18:8). Here Paul found Aquila and his wife, Priscilla, who afterward became his loyal friends.

After an absence of three or four years, Paul returned to Antioch by way of Ephesus. In Antioch he reported his entrance into Europe.

Paul's Third Missionary Tour

Now we find Paul spending three years in one of the greatest cities of his day. Next to Rome, Ephesus was perhaps the world's largest and most cosmopolitan city. Multitudes of Jews and Gentiles of Asia heard the gospel preached. Ephesus was notorious for its luxury and licentiousness, and for the worship of the goddess Diana. The years Paul spent here are so crowded with interesting details that it is hard to choose the most important. Enthusiastic converts burned their books on "the black art," magic, and threw away their silver idols. There was a great bonfire in Ephesus. It almost seems as though we can see the flames burning to this day. It represented burning their old lives. Paul has taught us that every idol must be torn down from its place in our hearts and the Lord alone must occupy the throne. Is there anything in our lives that calls for a bonfire? Don't be afraid of bringing yourself face-to-face with your own inner self.

Such blessings as these could not last long without opposition. If we read on to the end of the chapter, we will see the results of Paul's work. The silversmiths stirred up a riot, and the apostles were rescued from danger only by the help of the city officials.

As Paul traveled, he kept writing his wonderful letters. We read them today with great profit and interest. From Ephesus, Paul sent his First Epistle to the Corinthians (1 Corinthians 16:8). During this third journey, Paul wrote 2 Corinthians, Galatians and Romans.

Paul's Farewell

Paul's last missionary journey must have been a heartbreaking experience. He had to say farewell at every place. He knew it was a final farewell. Read Acts 20:37-38. They all wept and "embraced him and kissed him," the Middle Eastern expression of sorrow, knowing they would never see him again. Think of this sad experience repeated a dozen times over. Probably no man, except David, has ever inspired such intense personal love in so many hearts.

Sailing out of the harbor of Ephesus, Paul bids his friends a last farewell. He is headed for Jerusalem, and from now on he is seen as "the prisoner of the Lord." Paul makes his last visit to Jerusalem, and here one of those swiftly formed mobs that gather so quickly in the excitable East rushes against the apostle and binds him, declaring he is teaching the Jewish people to forsake Moses. No doubt he recalls the fact that outside that city he himself, twenty-six years before, had assisted in the murder of Stephen. Finding that Paul is a Roman citizen, the chief captain promises to give him a fair trial. Paul makes his defense before the Roman governor Felix at Caesarea. After two years' imprisonment, Paul is tried a second time before the new governor, Festus, and appeals from him to Caesar himself, the emperor (21:27—26:32).

After a most exciting voyage, in which his ship was wrecked in a terrific storm off the coast of Malta, Paul arrived in Rome. Here he was kept a prisoner in his own hired house for two years. Even in prison the great preacher and evangelist led the servants in Nero's own palace to Christ. Service for the Master can brighten life's darkest hours. When we seek to lift others' burdens, we lighten our own (27:1—28:24).

During his imprisonment, Paul wrote many of his Epistles— Philemon, Colossians, Ephesians and Philippians. It was probably during a second imprisonment in a dungeon in Rome, expecting at any hour to be beheaded, that he wrote his second Epistle to Timothy.

Finally, (according to tradition) the beloved apostle was condemned and beheaded. His heroic soul was released and the feeble body buried in the catacombs.

Paul changed the Early Church from a sect within Judaism to a worldwide influence. He tried to break down the barriers between Jew and Gentile and between slave and free.

Acts is the only unfinished book in the Bible. Notice how abruptly it closes! How else could it close? How could there be a complete account of a Person's lifework as long as He lives? Our risen and ascended Lord still lives. From the center, Christ, the lines are seen proceeding in every direction, but the "uttermost part of the earth" is not yet reached. The book is evidently a fragment. The gospel of Christ moves on! You are still living the Acts.

Letters of Paul

of The New Testament

Romans • 1 Corinthians • 2 Corinthians
Galatians • Ephesians • Philippians
Colossians • 1 Thessalonians
2 Thessalonians • 1 Timothy • 2 Timothy
Titus • Philemon

Key Events of the Letters of Paul

Christ is over all and in all, has all authority in heaven and earth.
Colossians 1

Christ is head of His Church, saves by grace through faith, not works.
Ephesians 1; 2

Christ is coming back soon.
1, 2 Thessalonians

Letters of Paul: The Church Is the Body of Christ!

The apostle Paul vigorously pursued relationships with the churches he established on his three missionary journeys through the letters (Epistles) he wrote. These letters instruct us that: Christ is over all and in all; Christ has all authority in heaven and earth; Christ is the Head of His Church; Christ saves us by grace through faith, not by works of the law; through Christ's sacrifice on the cross we are reconciled to God and to one another; and Christ is coming back soon!

Chapter 33

Understanding Romans

Romans Portrays Jesus Christ, Our Righteousness

Selected Bible Readings

Sunday: What We Are by Nature (Romans 1:1—3:20)
Monday: How to Become a Christian (Romans 3:21—5:21)
Tuesday: How to Live a Christian Life (Romans 6:1-23)
Wednesday: A Struggle (Romans 7:1-25)
Thursday: The Life of Victory (Romans 8:1-39)
Friday: The Jews Set Aside (Romans 9:30—11:12)
Saturday: The Christian's Service (Romans 12:1-21)

We now begin a study of the Epistles (letters) in the New Testament. Thirteen of the twenty-one were written by Paul, hence they are called the Pauline Epistles. He wrote his letters to the churches at Thessalonica, Galatia, Corinth and Rome during his missionary journeys. While he was a prisoner in Rome he wrote his letters to the church at Ephesus, one to the Colossians, one to Philemon and one to the Philippians. After his imprisonment, he wrote two letters to Timothy and one to Titus.

Paul was born at Tarsus, "circumcised on the eighth day, of the people of Israel, of the tribe of Benjamin, a Hebrew of Hebrews; in regard to the law, a Pharisee" (Philippians 3:5). His teacher was Gamaliel, the great teacher of the Pharisees. Like all Hebrew boys, he learned a trade—he was a tentmaker. At Jerusalem, he was present at the stoning of Stephen, the first Christian martyr. No doubt this scene made a tremendous impression upon the young Saul. On the way to Damascus, on a mission of persecution of the Christians, the young Pharisee had a head-on collision with Jesus Christ! After his miraculous conversion, he was baptized and received his commission to preach the gospel. He spent three years in Arabia in study and preparation.

After laboring for three years in Tarsus and one year in Antioch, directed by the Holy Spirit, Paul became the great missionary to the Gentiles. On his three missionary journeys, he founded many churches and wrote his Epistles. The combination of Roman citizenship, Greek education and Hebrew religion wonderfully qualified him for his great work, but you will find that he trusted alone in the grace and apostleship he received directly from Jesus Christ (Romans 1:5).

After a life filled with sacrifice and suffering, he sealed his testimony with his own life's blood. Tradition says he was beheaded at Rome, and his body buried in the catacombs.

The Church at Rome

Who founded the church at Rome we do not know. It was not founded by Peter. Peter's ministry was to the Jewish people (Galatians 2:9). Visitors from Rome, in Jerusalem for the Passover and converted at Pentecost, went back to the capital, carrying the seed of the gospel and established this new center in Rome. During the twenty-eight intervening years, many Christians from all parts of the East had migrated to Rome, some of them Paul's own converts.

Paul was eager to visit this church, and sent them this letter from Corinth, from the home of Gaius, a wealthy Corinthian Christian, while he was on his third missionary journey. It was written in the fourth year of Nero, then Emperor of Rome. In this Epistle, he sets forth his gospel (Romans 1:16-17).

Paul the servant (1:1), writes to the saints at Rome (1:7), concerning the Savior (1:3-4).

Paul the servant is:

Set apart for the gospel—1:1
Serving in the gospel—1:9
Saved by the gospel—1:16.

Is the gospel of Christ gripping you this way? Are you saved by it, set apart for it, and serving in it?

After Paul's greeting to the church, he thanks God for their faith (v. 8). Notice Paul's expression of obligation to this church (vv. 14-15):

"I am debtor" *(KJV)*—1:14

"I am eager" to fulfill my obligation—1:15

"I am not ashamed" of the message—1:16.

Why was Paul not ashamed of the gospel of Christ? Because it reveals what the sinner needs and what he may have on the ground of simple faith. "A righteousness of God"—the righteousness of Jesus Christ.

The gospel has dynamic power. It is the power of God unto salvation. Do you realize that nothing short of the power of God could make one Christian?

Paul was not ashamed of the gospel of Christ even in Rome. The terrible sinfulness of humans, as pictured in 1:18-32, had reached its climax in Rome.

Paul spoke from the white-hot conviction that is born of experience. On the road to Damascus, at one blow, he had all the props of works, of race and of character knocked out from under him. He caught a full glimpse of the glorified Christ. Thenceforth he had but one message—faith in the crucified and risen Lord. He would hear nothing else; he spoke nothing else; he lived nothing less. He proclaimed that henceforth "the just shall live by faith" *(KJV)*. One must simply believe. There is only one salvation, and that is by the acceptance of the gospel of Christ. For therein is a righteousness God gives or "imparts" to us when we believe in Christ. He does not say we are "made" righteous, but "declared" righteous. God gives to us the righteousness He demands of us. Why is God's righteousness necessary? Because we have none of our own.

After Paul states the subject of the book of Romans, in 1:16-17, he then reveals people's need of this righteousness. *For all have sinned, and all the world may become guilty before God.* From his elevated pulpit, Paul looks around and sees zealous Jews, proud Greeks, boastful Romans and a multitude of ordinary, common sinners like ourselves. What a terrible picture he presents in 1:18-32! First the unrighteousness of the Gentiles is portrayed; then that of the Jews.

The book of Romans tells us of God's method of making guilty people good. The key of this great thesis is found in Romans 1:16-17.

The Person of the gospel—Christ
The Power of the gospel—"power of God"
The Purpose of the gospel—"for salvation"
The People to whom sent—"to everyone"
The Plan of acceptance—"to everyone who believes"
The Particular result—"the righteous will live by faith."

Paul was proud of the gospel because he had proved its power in his own life and in the lives of all who would believe.

Good news! These words will command the attention of anyone. Say, "I have good news for you!" and one can always secure a listener. The real value of good news depends on the source—who said it. That is why the gospel Paul presents is so welcome. The news comes from God. Romans is Paul's shout of joy to a lost world.

The first three chapters describe the hell of sin. The last five chapters describe the heaven of holiness. Intervening chapters describe Christ, the Way.

In Romans, Paul shows us God's method of making a guilty person good. He reveals a sinner's needs and then presents what the person may have by faith: a righteousness from God—Christ, our righteousness. The righteousness of God is a Person. The righteousness God demands is in a Person, Jesus Christ. No one will ever get into heaven with any less righteousness than Christ's righteousness. When you look at Jesus, you see the righteousness God requires.

What We Are by Nature (Romans 1:1—3:20)

Why do we need salvation? Because we are sinners. God has x-rayed the human heart and has given us the picture. He shows us what He finds in us all. But remember, this is the picture of us that God sees. I know your picture is there because it says, "There is no one who does good, not even one" (3:12). This fact Paul proves conclusively in the first three chapters of this book of

Romans. This is the picture of a person without God. Read every word of Romans 3. You will believe then that the natural heart is desperately wicked. Have you ever asked the Holy Spirit to throw a searchlight on your own heart? If you have, you know today that you need a Savior.

The book of Romans presents a courtroom scene. God, the Judge of all the earth, summons Jew and Gentile before the bar of justice. Prisoner after prisoner is brought up.

The general charge is stated—"all under sin" (Romans 3:9). Both the Gentile (2:1-16) and Jew (2:17—3:8) are given the opportunity for a hearing. Their special pleas of "not guilty" are carefully considered and answered, clearing the way for the final verdict from the Judge.

Finally the Judge pronounces the verdict: the "whole world held accountable to God" (3:19). If this were today, newspapers everywhere would blaze this headline. All the television reporters would be announcing it. Can't you hear them? "ALL - THE - WORLD - FOUND - GUILTY!"

Against all this there is no defense. The Judge says, "Is there anyone to plead the cause of the prisoners?" And there is no answering voice. Every mouth is stopped (3:19). There is no room for excuse.

The condemnation of the world is settled. The next step in order will be to reveal the plan of God to save a lost world. Remember, the book of Romans tells us God's method of making people good.

Do not say, "God is love. He will not condemn me." Listen to God's words here: "The wrath of God is being revealed from heaven against all the godlessness" (1:18). He has already passed sentence on everyone. "All...guilty." There is no chance of appeal. It is the decision of the Supreme Court of the universe. Sin is universal—"All have sinned!" Hence we need a world's Savior. Because God is a God of love, He has provided just this One! Repeat aloud John 3:16. The Judge on the bench says, "Is there anyone to appear for the prisoners?" Then the Son of God says, "Yes, I am here to represent these. It is true that they committed these sins. It is true that they are guilty, but I bore their guilt on the cross. I died in their place that they might go free. I am their righteousness." And the Judge sets them free.

We get an awful picture of sin in these first three chapters of Romans. Remember, "sin" is a marksman's word. It means "missing the mark"—the standard God has set for us. God's Word says, "For all have sinned and fall short of the glory of God" (3:23). Fall short in our good deeds? No—of the glory of God. Do not measure your life by any other standard but this. Do not compare yourselves among yourselves. Of course you may not have fallen as short as some others you know, but you are "short" as far as God is concerned.

We are all sinners because we were born into a sinful race. We are all "children of Adam." But we were not only born into sin; we have also sinned ourselves, for "all have sinned." Remember this—we sin because we are sinners. This is our nature. A plum tree bears plums because it is a plum tree. The fruit is the result of its nature. Sin is the fruit of a sinful heart. "The heart is deceitful above all things" (Jeremiah 17:9).

Christ not only saves us from the penalty of sin, but He is also able to free us from the consciousness of guilt and the power of sin. The result of sin is a sense of guilt. A person who has broken the law feels guilty and seeks to hide. This is what the first man, Adam, did. The guilty conscience brings a fear of punishment. The sinner is always trying to flee from the consequences of the broken law. The person fears the judge. This is why a person's sins and consciousness of guilt banish him or her from the presence of God. God does not need to banish the sinner. The person flees of his or her own accord. This is what will happen in the day when the wrath of God shall be revealed (Revelation 6:15-16).

The first thing that is necessary for the freedom of a sinner is that the dreadful consequences of the person's guilt be taken away. The sinner needs more than pardon, for that would leave the person with his or her guilt. Any president or governor or king can pardon a criminal, but not one has the power to remove the guilt. Proper punishment for the deed must be given. This is what Christ has done. "The wages of sin is death" (6:23) and because all of us "have sinned," Christ came to die and bear the penalty for the sins committed against a holy God.

How to Become a Christian
(Romans 3:21—5:21)

Question: How does God save sinners? Answer: "Through the redemption that came by Christ Jesus" (Romans 3:24).

God's plan of salvation runs through the entire Scriptures. It is like the cordage of the British Navy with a scarlet line interwoven through it that you cannot take out without destroying the cord. A scarlet line of salvation runs through Scripture. You can see it very plainly in certain portions of the Bible. Romans 3 is one of them.

When God looks at us, He sees no righteousness (3:10). When God looks at us "in Christ," He sees not only an improvement, but also perfection, for God sees only His own Righteousness, Jesus Christ.

You have become acquainted with one great word of Scripture, "salvation." Here is another—"justification," "just-as-if-I'd...." Everything Christ has done has been credited to my account. His righteousness is mine!

When Christ's righteousness is reckoned as ours, this is called "justification"—we are counted just (righteous) before God. "The just shall live by faith." No one is counted just because of works, but rather by believing on Christ (3:28). This great truth gave birth to the great Reformation of the sixteenth century. It freed the believer from the idea that people were saved by works to a life of faith and liberty in Christ. Not only are we saved by faith, but we must also live by faith, trusting in Christ.

Paul gives us illustrations of justification by faith from the Old Testament. Especially does he tell us of how Abraham's faith was counted for righteousness (chap. 4). Abraham received three things by faith: righteousness, inheritance and posterity (4:3,13,17).

We, too, have great benefits when we are justified by His grace. Grace is unmerited favor. In this life, we find that faith is followed by peace, pardon and promise (5:1-5) and more than all, an assurance of salvation (5:6-11).

How can a person be justified by God? Read Romans 3:24-28. God imparts His righteousness to people in the following ways:

1. By grace—3:24, the source of it. "Grace" means "unmerited favor"
2. By God—He is the giver of it—3:26; 8:33
3. By blood—the reason for it—3:24; 5:9
4. By faith—the means by which it is received—3:22
5. By works—the way it is shown—James 2:21-23
6. By experience—the blessings we enjoy from it—Romans 5:1-4.

When I look into heaven and remember that God who sits on His throne has condemned me, I am in despair. But I see One sitting at His right, holding up a wounded hand, and presenting His pierced feet and side. With these wounds Christ pleads for me, and I have His own assurance that they are efficacious, sufficient to meet my needs.

Salvation

You will find the stream of sin and the river of salvation running along together from Romans 1 through 16. "Where sin increased, grace increased all the more" (Romans 5:20). Paul shows sin in all its squalor and salvation in all its splendor. Some simple steps in these next paragraphs will show you how to become a Christian!

One does not have to be a sinner in the sight of people to be lost. Of course there is a difference in the degree of sin, but not in the fact of sin and its results, "for the wages of sin is death." We may be drowned in seven feet of water and be as dead as if we had been submerged in seventy feet of water. In our inability to save ourselves, we are all on the same level—"There is no difference" (Romans 3:22).

We are saved by Christ's righteousness. He has made it available for us by His death. We are "justified freely by his grace through the redemption that came by Christ Jesus. God presented him as a sacrifice of atonement, through faith in his blood" (3:24-25).

I am a person condemned to die because of my sin, "for the wages of sin is death." But I can look on the cross and see that Christ has already died for me. I believe that He died for my sin.

And so in exchange for my poor, sinful, condemned life, I can accept His righteousness and His life (1 Peter 2:24).

"Whoever believes in the Son has eternal life" (John 3:36). "But now a righteousness from God, apart from law, has been made known,...This righteousness from God comes through faith in Jesus Christ to all who believe" (Romans 3:21-22). Apart from a person's effort to be good, God has provided His righteousness, the Lord Jesus Christ. Our righteousness is as filthy rags (Isaiah 64:6).

Your sin is on Christ. He has borne it for you. Have you accepted Him as your Savior and passed from death unto life (John 5:24)? If you have decided to let Christ be your sin bearer, you now have His salvation (Romans 3:24).

Justified by Faith

A murderer may stand at the bottom of a mine and you on the highest peak of the highest mountain, but you are as little able to touch the stars as he. You cannot attain unto the righteousness that God demands, no matter how far you climb.

Forgiveness is the removal of our unrighteousness, an unclothing or putting away of sin.

Justification is the act of being clothed with the righteousness of God's own providing. It is perfect.

The person who put faith in Christ an hour ago is just as much justified as the oldest Christian living. We never become any more justified than the minute we received Christ. Justification depends upon something done outside of us, something done on the cross of Calvary.

Justification takes care of all the sin and guilt upon us, buries all this sin and guilt in the grave of Jesus Christ, and then sets us in heavenly places with Christ our Savior.

A question many ask is this: "How could one man die for the whole world?" One man might take another man's place and be his substitute. That is all right, you say, but for one to die for the whole world—that is nonsense! Let us see if this is true!

None of us like the idea of being called a "sinner," but we must face what we are. Listen to what Paul says in Romans 5:12-21. We were born sinners. We were not asked if we wished to come into this world. We woke up to the fact one day that we were subject to a sinful nature. Adam, the head of our race, was not created that way (Genesis 1:26). He deliberately sinned and his sinful nature was passed on to us all. We sin because we are sinners.

But over against Adam, the head of the natural race, we find Christ, the Head of a spiritual race—"a new creation." When I was born in this body, I was born a descendant of Adam. I have his nature, which is sinful. When I am born into the family of God, by Christ Jesus, I have Christ's nature, which is holy. In the words of Scripture, "For as in Adam all die, so in Christ all will be made alive" (1 Corinthians 15:22). I did not choose to be a descendant of Adam. I may choose to be a child of God. If one man's sin made it possible for all the race to die, one Man's righteousness made it possible for all the race to get out of this condition (Romans 5:15).

Have you received "eternal life by Jesus Christ our Lord"? Are you a sinner "in Adam," or are you a son "in Christ"?

How to Live a Christian Life (Romans 6—8)

We have learned how to become a Christian. Now we must find out how to live like a Christian. It is one thing to accept what Christ has done for you. It is another thing to experience it as personal and real.

In Romans 6, there are three important words. Mark them:

"Know" that Christ died for you (6:3-5,10); know that you died with Christ (6:8).

"Reckon" *(KJV)* on this! "In the same way, count yourselves dead to sin but alive to God in Christ Jesus" (6:11). If a trustworthy relative told you he had put $1,000 in the bank for you for a trip and you could withdraw it any time you needed it, you would count on it, I am sure, though you never saw the money. If you should question it, and not withdraw it, the money would never be yours. If you reckon it yours by signing a check and passing it through the bank window, that which you have never seen becomes a reality. Reckoning makes things real! Because we are dead to sin and alive unto God, how shall we live? (See 6:13.)

"Yield" *(KJV)*—"Do not offer the parts of your body to sin, as instruments of wickedness, but rather offer yourselves to God, as those who have been brought from death to life; and offer the parts of your body to him as instruments of righteousness" (6:13).

This means "let go" of your life and "let God" live through you. This is the surrendered life. This is the right way to live a life of victory and blessing. Let Him work His will in you and through you.

Christians soon find a new standard for life. They do not try to live up to the Law, for they are no longer under it. They strive to please the One who dwells within them. "For to me to live is Christ," and I "do all to the glory of God."

Romans 6 reveals the secret of a life of victory. I am living in Christ! Dead to sin but alive to God! It tells me how I can lead a Christian life. Self, we have learned, was a condemned thing, unable to be good, never righteous (chap. 3). Now when self becomes a Christian and tries to live a Christian life, it finds this to be impossible. We are saved by faith, and we cannot live by our own efforts.

This sad truth is revealed in Romans 7. It tells us why we cannot live a victorious life. Mark the little *I* and you will find it is used thirty-eight times in the twenty-five verses of this chapter (in the *KJV*). The Holy Spirit is never mentioned. Although *I* tries, it finds only defeat.

Dr. W. H. Griffith Thomas, the famous New Testament scholar, said, "It is not hard to live a Christian life; it is impossible."

Paul said, "I have been crucified with Christ and I no longer live, but Christ lives in me" (Galatians 2:20).

Listen to the words of the man who tries to live by his own effort. "What a wretched man I am! Who will rescue me from this body of death? Thanks be to God—through Jesus Christ our Lord! So then, I myself in my mind am a slave to God's law, but in the sinful nature a slave to the law of sin" (Romans 7:24-25).

Finally, *I* finds that there is One who is sufficient. Struggling yields to power, defeat is changed to victory, misery is transformed into joy. When *I* goes out, Christ comes in.

The life "in Christ" is a wonderful thing. Paul says, "Because through Jesus Christ the law of the Spirit of life set me free from the law of sin and death" (8:2). This is what happens. When I am in an airplane I am free from the law of gravity. The higher law operates in the plane to lift it above the clouds, although the law of gravity a few minutes before held me fast to the earth. The law of gravity is not destroyed, but rendered inoperative. This is what happens in my life when I am "in Christ." The law that operates by the Spirit in my life lifts me above the world and sin, and sin no longer has dominion over me. I am free. I am without condemnation. Have you stepped into Christ? Are you living on a plane far above evil principalities and powers?

Have you come to the end of "self"? Remember, *I* never brings anything but failure. It is the *I* in "s-I-n" that must be removed. Put *O* in its place and you have "SON." He will give you victory!

Step out of the self life into the Spirit-filled life. In Romans 8, instead of the word *I* we find the word "Spirit" used twenty-one times. We must yield our lives to Him. This is our part. Then He will fill us with His Spirit. That is Christ's part.

This glorious chapter opens with "no condemnation," and ends with "no separation." This is a picture of our life "in Christ." Christians are safe: Christ is around them; the Spirit is within them; and God is for them.

Why Israel Is Set Aside (Romans 9—11)

The story of the Jewish people being set aside and scattered throughout the world without a homeland, without a king is a warning for us (Romans 9—11). God is a sovereign God, and He will do what He will. He has a perfect right to turn to the Gentiles, because most Jewish people would not seek the righteousness of God, which is by faith (9:32). They tried to set up their own righteousness. But people do not build up righteousness. They only receive it. If God will put aside His chosen people, will He not put us aside if we are disobedient?

Let us be careful lest we become self-willed and disobedient, not heeding God's commandments.

Ask Christ to take control of your life and guide you in His path. There are wrecks outside His divine course. The Old Testament story of the Hebrew people is a solemn lesson to us. Read the wonderful description of God's mercy in Romans 11:32-36.

How to Serve God (Romans 12—16)

"Therefore, I urge you, brothers, in view of God's mercy, to offer your bodies as living sacrifices, holy and pleasing to God—this is your spiritual act of worship" (Romans 12:1).

In this appeal, Paul urges us to have our lives measure up to our beliefs. He shows that the doctrine of justification by faith will not allow laxity in life or conduct. We are saved to serve. The Christian life must be lived in its relation to God, self and others.

It may surprise you to find out that up to this point we have not had to do a thing but believe on Christ and yield ourselves to Him to use as He will. Now we are to serve!

Until we have been saved by His grace and transformed by His love, we can do little for God. Read 1 Corinthians 13. But when we present ourselves to Christ and become filled with His love we can find much to be done. Christ wants a "living sacrifice," not a dead one (Romans 12:1). Many will die for Christ. Few will live for Him. Many of you might rather be burned at a stake than stand the ridicule of your associates. One definition of a modern Christian is "a person who will die for the church he or she will not attend." How many of us say nothing when Christ's name is brought into question or is used in vain!

Let others see Jesus in you! Live for Him, then you will be ready to die for Him.

The first part of Romans is what God did for us. The last part of Romans is what we may do for God.

We find our Christian service in:

Church—12:3-8
Government—13:1-14
Disputed things—14:1—15:3
The whole world—15:4-13.

Chapter 34

Understanding First Corinthians

First Corinthians Portrays Jesus Christ, Our Lord

Selected Bible Readings

Sunday:	Division in the Church (1 Corinthians 1:10-31)
Monday:	Human Wisdom (1 Corinthians 2:1-16)
Tuesday:	Worldliness in the Church (1 Corinthians 3:1-23)
Wednesday:	Immorality in the Church (1 Corinthians 5:1-13)
Thursday:	The Lord's Supper (1 Corinthians 11:1-34)
Friday:	Hymn of Love (1 Corinthians 13:1-13)
Saturday:	The Resurrection (1 Corinthians 15:1-58)

The name "Lord" is very prominent in this book (1 Corinthians 1:31; 2:8,16; 3:20; 4:4; 5:4-5; 6:13, etc.). This is full of meaning because much of the confusion that had crept into the church at Corinth had come because the believers failed to recognize Jesus Christ as Lord.

The archaeologist's spade is making Corinth live again! Corinth was the most important city of all Greece in Paul's day. Its wealth was fabulous. Men spent their days in tournaments and speeches. Luxury, dissipation and public immorality were rampant among this great industrial and seafaring population. Corinth attracted great crowds of foreigners from the East and West. Their gods were gods of pleasure and lust. There was, besides, much culture and art. The city abounded in studios of language and schools of philosophy.

As in most cities, there was a large colony of Jews who had kept a strong moral standard and held to their religious beliefs. But the city itself was the center of a debased form of the worship of Venus.

If we read Acts 18, we find how the gospel reached this wicked city. The apostle Paul, then a man about fifty years of age, in the garb of a working man, entered the busy metropolis and went through its streets in search of a workshop where he might earn his own living. No billboards advertised the coming of a world-renowned evangelist. This tradesman came into town and began his tentmaking. This was a leading industry in that day, as building is today. He went into business with the well-to-do tentmakers Aquila and Priscilla. He was always able to support himself, making enough to carry on his missionary work. A wonderful work was done in Corinth during the year and a half Paul was there. He began by speaking in the synagogues to mixed congregations of Jews and Greeks.

First Corinthians is a difficult book to outline, for it takes up many wonderful subjects. "In him you have been enriched with everything" (1 Corinthians 1:5, *Weymouth*). In Romans, Paul told us that it was by Christ that "we have gained access by faith into this grace in which we now stand" (Romans 5:2). Then follow these riches of grace in Christ Jesus, our All in all. First Corinthians deals with Christian conduct.

Corrections in Christian Conduct (1 Corinthians 1—11)

The wonderful church at Corinth, the brilliant jewel in the crown of Paul's labor, was failing. The worldliness (carnality) of the city had infected the fellowship of believers. It was all right for the church to be in Corinth, but it was fatal when Corinth got into the church. It is a glorious sight to see a ship launched into the sea, but it is a tragic sight when the sea gets into the ship. The Church of Christ should be set as a light in a dark place, but woe unto the Church when the wickedness of the world invades.

Practices common to this wicked city soon crept into the church. There were divisions among them; Christians were going to law with Christians before heathen judges; behavior at the communion table was disgraceful; the women of the church no longer observed standards of modesty; the church membership was arguing over marriage and even spiritual gifts. Finally, the church wrote Paul about these things and asked his advice on the matter. These two letters to the Corinthians were written in answer to their requests.

After the usual greeting (1 Corinthians 1:1-3), Paul refers to the coming again of our Lord Jesus Christ (1:7-8). Then he plunges right into the question of the failure of the church about which he had been told. The source of his information he gives us in 1 Corinthians 1:11.

People had lost sight of God. Three kinds of selfishness had blinded them:

Self-admiration, their intellect had been perverted.

Self-will, their conscience had been darkened.

Self-indulgence, their passions had been given full rein.

The greatest danger to the Corinthian church was from within.

Paul speaks first of the divisions and cliques about which he had learned from friends and travelers. Nothing eats out the heart and life of the Church like party politics.

The Greek spirit of party politics had entered into the church, dividing it into four parties, each trying to get the mastery. Their names are given in 1 Corinthians 1:12. Paul, Apollos and Peter (Cephas) were parties named for their favorite teachers. The Christ Party held to that name as if it did not belong to everyone in the church.

This dissension about religious leaders meant that the Christians at Corinth had slipped off center. There is only one Leader in every church. That Leader and center is Christ. If the Church gets off center here, it goes off all down the line. A great flywheel on center moves quietly; off center it shakes the building to pieces. Christianity must be Christ-centered. If it is Christ-centered, it is powerful. Christ Himself is the "good news." He not only brought God's message, he was also God's message. The Corinthians had slipped off center. Paul, Peter, Apollos were all good men, but not God-men. How many are following religious leaders today rather than Christ Himself! "For to me, to live is Christ" (Philippians 1:21).

Jesus Christ is the only cure for division (1 Corinthians 1:13). Every eye, every heart, every spirit must be turned to one object—Jesus Christ, our personal Savior. Paul said, in effect, "Your factional spirit is a sin. Can you follow a mere man, hoping that he can give you life? Was that man crucified for you? Trusting in what people have to say is foolish. People see nothing in the cross of Christ. Christ alone has all the power and wisdom of God."

Youth and old age alike follow Christ to the cross and then stumble at the blood of the sacrifice. This is what the Jews and Greeks of Paul's day did. Shall we remove the Cross from the gospel because people do not like it? If we do, we remove the world's only way of salvation. We must preach "Christ crucified."

The Cross

"A stumbling block to Jews," an obstacle they could not get over (1:23). They could not understand how such a display of weakness could be a source of power. A man dying on a cross did not look much like a world Savior to them. The scribes and Pharisees scornfully turned from the Cross. To them, the Cross meant failure. The Jews needed signs of power. They demanded something they could see and grasp. The Messiah must be a world prince, a miracle worker. A multitude of Christians are like this today. They worship success as much as did the Jews. They despise weakness and admire force. These people tell us that scientists are apt to stumble at the Cross because they cannot explain how the blood of one Man could wash away the stain of sin.

"And foolishness to Gentiles." The Greek-influenced Gentiles regarded with contempt the unscientific religion first taught in an unschooled corner of the world like Nazareth, by the son of a carpenter who never studied in Athens or Rome. The Greeks idolized brains. But God has never despised the humble things.

Either the Cross is the "power of God" or it is "foolishness." If "foolishness," then you think it is unfit to do any good in your life. But listen! That condemns you, not the Cross.

No one ever leaves the Cross in exactly the same condition as they came to it. You must receive it or reject it. If you receive it, you become a child of God (John 1:12); if you reject it, you are lost (John 3:36). If you neglect it, you are in effect rejecting it.

Paul did not preach Christ the conqueror or Christ the philosopher, but Christ crucified, Christ the humble. Read his words in 1 Corinthians 2:2. Paul remembers that his words will be tried by fire (3:13). To know Christ crucified is the maximum of knowledge.

The Minister

One objection to Paul was that his preaching was too simple. He answered that he could not preach any differently because they were mere babes in Christ. They could not stand anything but a milk diet. The proof of their childish state (carnality) was in this division among them (3:1-4).

Paul points out that the Christian minister is not the head of a school or a rival sect, as the Greek philosophers. He is the servant of God, not a master of people. Paul always called himself a servant of the Lord Jesus Christ. Christian service is only acceptable to God when done in the spirit of Christ, for His glory.

Everyone has four faces—one the world knows, one our friends know, one we know ourselves, one God knows. Paul describes this in 1 Corinthians 4. There are three courts before which we stand:

People—(4:3)
Our own conscience—(4:3)
Jesus Christ—(4:4).

Do not depend on human judgment. The world judges our character upon a single act. The voices of criticism may be loud, but if you go high up on the hilltop with God, you will see the bustle of the crowd, but you won't hear it.

Beware of your friends' judgment because they may be too favorable in their opinion of you. We like to believe all the good things said about us and resent unfavorable criticism.

Paul says, "I do not even judge myself" (1 Corinthians 4:3). Beware when you stand at the bar of your own conscience. When your conscience says to you, "You may do it," it is always well to go to Jesus Christ and say, "May I?" It is hard to be fair with ourselves. No one, no matter how honest, is permitted to judge in his or her own cause.

Paul says there is one judgment to which he will submit—one that is always right. "It is the Lord who judges me" (4:4). I am Christ's steward and to Him am I ultimately responsible. From His judgment there is no escape. His calm eyes are upon me.

Seek praise from Him, which is praise indeed. If He says, "Well done, good and faithful servant," what else matters!

Vice in the Church

In Paul's letter to the Romans, we find his theme to be the righteousness of God. In Corinthians, he enlarges it into the life of righteousness in the Christian. We, as Christians, must act out in our lives what we believe in our hearts. It is a serious thing to profess to live the life of a Christian. If we lower the standard Christ has set, we give the wrong testimony to the world. You are an epistle open and read of all people. What kind of a gospel is "The Gospel According to You"?

Do not let your life be so near the edge of questionable things that some day you will slide off. If you fall, others will fall with you. Watch your testimony.

Righteousness comes from God, but it must be shown in our daily walk. The Corinthians, living in the Hollywood of their day, needed admonition just as we do. Righteousness is from Christ and for Christ. "What would Jesus do?" should be the query to every questionable thing of life. Christ in you is the secret and the way of life.

In the church at Corinth, a member actually was having an incestuous affair with his own stepmother, which was socially immoral among the pagans to say nothing of Christians. Paul reproves them for being puffed up with pride while this scandal existed in the church. He urges them not to tolerate evil among them while calling themselves Christians. Just as leaven spreads through all the dough, so a bad person's spirit spreads through all the Church. The Church should exclude the wrongdoer so as to prove that it does not condone sin (5:13). Discipline in the Church should always commence with mourning and sympathy, not anger or pride or revenge (5:2).

Paul then makes a personal application, useful in our own lives. "Therefore let us keep the Festival...with bread without yeast, the bread of sincerity and truth" (5:8). Self-examination is often the most difficult thing we do, but it is one of the most important.

"Do you not know" ("Know ye," *KJV*) is one of Paul's expressions. His faith was built on facts. He wanted to know things. Underline the "know ye's" in chapter 6. What are we supposed to know?

First, Paul makes the statement, that although it might be necessary at times for Christians to go to law, Christians never should quarrel with each other and then drag this quarrel before a worldly court. What a terrible impression of Christianity this gives to the world! We say when we do it, "We, as Christians, are just as bad as other folk. We want our way. We are covetous and just as ambitious for our own rights as you are." Paul says, "Dare you do such a thing?"

Paul then gives us a picture of the Corinthians as he found them, in 6:9. When we finish verse 11, we find what grace has done!

Christ has paid a great price to purchase us, and it is His purpose to make us like Himself (6:19-20).

If our bodies have been redeemed by the Lord Jesus Christ, then they no longer belong to us, but to the One who purchased us with His precious blood. "You were bought at a price."

God used to have a temple for His people; now He has a people for a temple. When a man steps into the church, off comes his hat, for he realizes he has stepped into the sanctuary. But has he forgotten that the real sanctuary in which Christ dwells is his body? We are taught as boys and girls not to be noisy or boisterous in the church, for it is the house in which we meet God. How much more important that we remember that our body is His dwelling place and that we should do nothing to grieve Him (see Ephesians 4:30).

Liberty Not Recklessness

The Scripture does not lay down little rules for our conduct, and tell us just the things we ought to do or not do, but rather states principles that should guide the Christian's actions. Someone has well said that Christian liberty does not mean the right to do as we like, but rather to do as we ought. Paul puts it, "'Everything is permissible for me'—but not everything is beneficial. 'Everything is permissible for me'—but I will not be mastered by anything" (1 Corinthians 6:12).

A man was walking down the street swinging his arms out from his chest and, by mistake, struck a passerby in the face. The man struck was furious and started to strike the man back. "Hey, isn't this a free country? Can't a fellow do his exercises on the street if he wishes?"

"Yes," was the answer, "but remember where my nose begins, your liberty ends."

Let this be in your mind constantly as far as your conduct is concerned. If your liberty harms another, then your liberty has gone too far.

Yes, I can do anything I want to, but I must be sure my desires are to please Christ. What I do is an example to others and may harm or bless them. I should not only answer the question, "Does my action harm weaker Christians?" but also, "Does it glorify God?"

Marriage

Paul discusses the subject of marriage for the Christian. Controversy had arisen between the Jewish and Greek philosophers about the importance of marriage. Paul would keep the church from scandal, hence his words in 1 Corinthians 7:2. Society is pure and virtuous in proportion as marriage is deemed honorable. Some of the church had tried to discourage marriage, and others thought that when one becoming a Christian should divorce a heathen mate. But Paul was wise. He knew the evil condition in Corinth and advised every man to have his own wife and every woman to have her own husband. He did not believe in a Christian divorcing a pagan partner. He told them that perhaps the Christian would lead an unbelieving mate to Christ (7:16).

Mark 1 Corinthians 7:9,13 in your Bible. Think over these verses. They will tell us much of our Christian responsibility to those who are not Christians.

The Lord's Supper

Paul gives a careful account of the beginning of the Lord's Supper and then tells of its value.

It was established on the night in which Christ was betrayed.

It is celebrated in remembrance of His undying love for His followers.

It was a symbol of His body, which was broken for them (10:16).

It was a new covenant in His blood.

It was a pledge of His coming again (11:26).

We should be careful not to eat or drink in an unworthy manner. "A man ought to examine himself" (11:28) and never eat without self-critique and thankful love.

And "For whenever you eat," do it "in remembrance of me" (see 11:26). Christ wants us to remember Him! Think on Christ when you go to His table. He longs for your love!

It was the custom of the Corinthian church to eat a meal in connection with the Lord's Supper. They all brought food for themselves. Often this led to excesses among the rich, while the poor had nothing. What an unworthy observance of the supper itself this led to! Paul reminds them of the deep spiritual significance of this supper, and of the scandal of their behavior.

Paul closes this scene with these words: "And when I come I will give further directions" (11:34). Other things needed to be straightened out, but he would leave his corrections and go on with his instructions.

Instructions in Christian Conduct (1 Corinthians 12—16)

In 1 Corinthians 12, we see the gifts the Spirit gives to believers. In verses 1-3, he tells of the change that had come into the lives of these Corinthian Christians when they turned from worshiping dead idols to the living Christ. So they might develop in their Christian lives, Christ gave them the gifts of the Spirit (12:4-7). The Holy Spirit is the Giver of spiritual gifts (12:8-11). One cannot teach the Scriptures unless the Spirit gives wisdom. One must pray "in the Spirit" and to sing acceptably to God "in the Spirit." Sometimes we say when we look at a successful Christian man, "My, he is a man of natural abilities," when really he has received many gifts from the Spirit.

Many people in Paul's day were making much of the spiritual gifts Paul mentions. They were coveting the more showy gifts, such as speaking with tongues.

The Corinthian Christians were using these gifts as ends in themselves. Many people today, like the Corinthians of old, pray constantly for the power of the Spirit. They forget that all the gifts God gives were given that Christ might be exalted and others blessed. If God gives me any little gift at all, He gives it not that I may gather people about myself, but that it may through me be a blessing for others. God gave these nine gifts mentioned in 1 Corinthians 12 to assist in the founding of the new church, but they were being used by people to gratify their pride. Paul shows that the purpose of the gifts is for building the church (chap. 12); that they should be used in love (chap. 13); and that their value was to be measured by their usefulness to the church.

God gave gifts such as healing, miracles and tongues, we believe, for "sign" gifts (12:12), to prove to the world that Jesus was the true Messiah and that the apostles were divinely appointed. These miracles, tongues, visions and signs were given to put the stamp of authority upon the apostles and their preaching. Today we are also to believe and walk by faith. If it is God's will for us to have any of these gifts, He will give them to us; otherwise He will not. The Holy Spirit "gives them to each one, just as he determines" (12:11).

The way to use these gifts the Spirit gives is beautifully told in 1 Corinthians 13. This chapter is called the Hymn of Love. Gifts without love are poor things. People talk of love, but they do not live it. Until the love of Christ is in a heart, it is impossible for people to love one another with any degree of permanency. People seem to worship force. But history shows us that the victories of force do not last.

The Pillars of the Gospel

No doubt there was a group in the Corinthian church who did not believe in the resurrection of the dead. Paul in answering this starts out by giving a wonderful statement in 1 Corinthians 15:1-11 of what the gospel is. Paul did not give a new gospel. It was the old gospel, given in Genesis, Exodus and Leviticus.

1. Christ died for our sins according to the Scriptures (15:3).
2. He was buried (15:4).
3. He rose again the third day according to the Scriptures (15:4).
4. He was seen by many witnesses (15:5-6).

If we deny the Resurrection, we deny one of the greatest of all truths of the gospel. Preaching is vain; faith and hope are all vain. But more than all that, no resurrection would mean no gospel at all, for we would be worshiping a dead Christ. There would be no "good news," for there would be no proof that God had accepted Christ's death as an atonement for our sins. If a sailor on jumping overboard to rescue a drowning man were drowned himself, then we would know that he did not save the man after whom he went. If Christ did not come out from the grave, then He could not bring anyone with Him from the grave. Christ's body died, and it was His body that was raised again. His soul was committed into the hands of the Father.

Because Christ lives, we shall live also. "Where, O death, is your victory? Where, O death, is your sting?" (15:55).

Paul gives the many proofs of Christ's resurrection in 1 Corinthians 15:

1. Christ's resurrection
2. His coming again
3. Resurrection of believers
4. Overthrow of Christ's enemies
5. His glorious reign
6. Our mortal bodies shall be changed to immortal.

Chapter 35

Understanding Second Corinthians

Second Corinthians Portrays Jesus Christ, Our Sufficiency

Selected Bible Readings

Sunday: Christ Our Comfort (2 Corinthians 1:1—2:17)
Monday: Living Epistles (2 Corinthians 3:1—4:18)
Tuesday: Ambassadors for Christ (2 Corinthians 5:1—6:18)
Wednesday: The Heart of Paul (2 Corinthians 7:1—8:15)
Thursday: Christian Giving (2 Corinthians 8:16—9:15)
Friday: Paul's Apostleship (2 Corinthians 10:1—11:33)
Saturday: God's Strength (2 Corinthians 12:1—13:14)

Paul was somewhat worried about how the church at Corinth would receive his first letter. He wondered how they had accepted his rebukes, so he sent Titus, and perhaps Timothy, to Corinth to find out the effect of his Epistle. During Paul's third missionary journey, while he was in Philippi, Titus reported that the majority of the church had received the letter in the proper spirit. But there were those who doubted his motives and even denied his apostleship, saying that he did not have the proper credentials for an apostle. Perhaps they questioned this because he was not one of the original Twelve.

Under these circumstances he wrote his second Epistle, to express his joy over the encouraging news of how his first Epistle had been received, and to defend his apostleship.

Paul gives more of his personal history in this letter than in any of his other Epistles. He reveals his courage and his self-sacrificing love. He speaks of glorying or boasting thirty-one times because he was compelled to. Read 2 Corinthians 12:11.

Paul tells us of some things that happened in his life that are revealed only in this letter.

His escape from Damascus in a basket (11:32,33)

His experience of being caught up to the third heaven (12:1-4)

His thorn in the flesh (12:7)

His unusual suffering (11:23-27).

He told none of these until he was compelled to, to prove that if we wanted to boast, he had good reason.

The epistle begins with "Comfort": "Praise be to the God and Father of our Lord Jesus Christ, the Father of compassion and the God of all comfort" (1:3).

It closes with "Comfort": "Finally, brothers, good-by. Aim for perfection, listen to my appeal, be of one mind, live in peace. And the God of love and peace will be with you" (13:11).

In the middle we find the reason for comfort: "And God is able to make all grace abound to you, so that in all things at all times, having all that you need, you will abound in every good work" (9:8).

The Source of this comfort is: "'My grace is sufficient for you'" (12:9).

Paul's Ministry (2 Corinthians 1—7)

Paul opens this second Epistle with his usual greeting and thanksgiving (2 Corinthians 1:1-3). Everyone loves a true story. Paul tells so many personal experiences of his life in this letter that it makes everyone love to read it. He begins by telling of the great trouble through which he had been passing. Through all of his trials he had learned to know God better. God is always made more real to us in times of sorrow. We find that God never fails.

Paul's sufferings in Asia were of a very serious nature. Very likely he went through a dangerous sickness in which they despaired of his life (1:4-11). He appreciated their prayers and now he was appealing to their love and sympathy. He wanted them to be ready for much that he was to write about concerning the defense of his apostleship.

Paul had a clear conscience about his sincerity and faithfulness while he labored among them. He explained that he sent his first letter instead of coming himself, that when he did come he might be able to praise and not scold them (1:23—2:4). To this statement he calls God to witness.

The teachers of Jewish law of Paul's day carried letters of introduction with them. They were Paul's chief troublemakers. They tried in every way to fight him. We hear them asking, "Who is this Paul?" "What letters of recommendation from Jerusalem does he have?" How foolish this question was to Paul! Did he need a letter of recommendation to a church he himself had established? He answers, "You yourselves are our letter, written on our hearts, known and read by everybody" (3:2).

The lives of true Christians at Corinth served as letters to recommend both Paul the servant and Christ the Lord. Living epistles are read when Bible Epistles are not. Remember your life is an open letter. Christian lives are about the only religious books the world reads. They do not study God's Word, but they do study God's people. This gives us a great opportunity for good, for we may lead people to Christ.

Paul's gospel was a triumphant and transforming gospel (3:18).

Paul's ministry was a triumphant one, but it was filled with suffering. Warfare always is full of illustrations of triumph through suffering. Victory costs! Paul tells us much about his tribulations (chaps. 4; 6; 11). When Paul was so gloriously converted, the Lord said, "I will show him how much he must suffer for my name" (Acts 9:16). It seems as though the trials began immediately and followed his pathway for thirty years. But Paul was always optimistic because he knew that afflictions here would increase glory beyond (2 Corinthians 4:17-18).

"The pessimist sees a difficulty in every opportunity.

The optimist sees an opportunity in every difficulty."

Paul could sing as he suffered for he knew the wonderful grace of God. He was always conscious of the presence of the Lord

Jesus Christ. He knew that the greater the suffering in this present world, the greater the glory of eternity (4:8-18). Paul lived with his eye on the future!

Christ nowhere promises that a Christian will be free from suffering or sorrow. Rather do we hear that "In this world you will have trouble" (John 16:33). Christ allows us to get into trouble that He may deliver us. He allowed Daniel to be put into the den of lions that He might pull him out. He allowed Shadrach, Meshach and Abednego to go into the fiery furnace that He might deliver them. He allowed Paul to be shipwrecked that He might save him. Our God is able to deliver!

Paul finds his comfort through all his troubles in the fact of the resurrection that Christ promised. He lived under the inspiration of the fact that one day he was to have a changed, glorified body. Our suffering bodies will soon be exchanged for painless glorified bodies. Whether we live or die, we must keep this reward in view (2 Corinthians 5:10).

The aim of Paul's ministry is that people may be reconciled to God (5:20). People are God's greatest concern. As Christ's ambassador, he makes his appeal to people of the world.

He follows this with an appeal to holy living (6:11—7:16). Holy living means wholly unto God. Read these verses, every one! He appeals to his fellow workers not to receive God's loving kindness in vain, but to open their hearts to Him. God demands a clean and separated life. He wants Christians to separate themselves from unbelievers.

Liberal Giving (2 Corinthians 8—9)

Paul tells the church at Corinth of the generosity of the churches of Macedonia to the Jerusalem Famine Fund. Although poor themselves, they begged for an opportunity to give, and they gave liberally because first they gave themselves to the Lord. The fund was gathered from all the churches of Asia Minor and Greece. It had been started a year before (1 Corinthians 8:10). Paul was in Macedonia at the time he wrote this. He had accepted no pay for his work from any of the churches except Philippi. Christ was the example for these early Christians (8:9). The Lord knows that if He gets us, He will get our gifts and our service.

How should we give?

Give out of your poverty—(8:2)

Give generously—(8:3)

Give willingly—(9:7)

Give proportionately—(8:12-14)

Give cheerfully—(9:7)

Give bountifully—(9:6).

God has ever promised to reward the generous giver (9:6). He enriches us with spiritual graces as well as with material things. These gifts strengthened the ties of brotherhood between the Jewish and Gentile Christians. "Thanks be to God for his indescribable gift!" (9:15).

This is the reason for our giving, "'For God so loved the world that he gave his one and only Son'" (John 3:16). God Himself delights to give.

Paul's Apostleship (2 Corinthians 10—13)

The charge against Paul by some in the church was that he was a coward. He was bold in his writings, but was weak in personality. The New Testament gives us no suggestion about what Paul looked like. To imagine that this man, who turned city after city upside down, was weak is absurd. He was a powerful and dominating person. He was a man of outstanding gifts and had a keen and inquiring mind. Beside this, Christ lived in him and worked through him.

His enemies said that no apostle would work with his own hands and support himself; they pointed to the other apostles. But Paul explained that he had the right to receive pay, yet refused it lest his example be abused by these false teachers who would commercialize the ministry. He declared that at least he founded his own churches and did not go around troubling churches founded by others, as they were doing.

Paul stated also that if these false teachers could boast of their power and authority, then he would boast, too. In a dramatic manner, he challenged these critics to compare themselves with him in every way. He was a loyal Hebrew; he had worked more than all the rest of them put together; as a martyr he had suffered more than they all, on land and sea. He realized the poor taste of boasting about oneself, and he disliked to do it, but they had forced him to it. When Paul boasted, it was for the glory of God.

"When they measure themselves by themselves and compare themselves with themselves, they are not wise" (2 Corinthians 10:12). We all have a tendency to take a wrong standard for measuring character. We compare ourselves among ourselves. We conclude we are as good as the average. But average Christians are not what the Bible requires. Let us pray Wesley's (John Wesley, 1703-1791, British, founder of the Methodists) prayer, "Lord, make me an extraordinary Christian."

Paul was caught up into "paradise," even to the third heaven. Recall that Jesus went into paradise at His death (Luke 23:43). There Paul had been given marvelous visions and revelations, and heard things that could not be put into speech (2 Corinthians 12:4). No doubt no human language could describe the glory. It would have been like trying to picture a sunset to a person born blind. Paul had nothing to compare it with that we could understand.

It seemed as though because of these heavenly experiences, God allowed Paul to suffer "a thorn in [his] flesh." The Lord knows the danger of pride of heart after such an experience, and so He permitted a "a messenger of Satan, to torment [him]." Paul himself called his affliction "a thorn in my flesh" (12:7). There have been many speculations about what this "thorn" really was. It would appear that God has not told us what it was so that all might know that the grace that was sufficient for Paul in his trouble would be enough for any thorn given to any of us.

Purpose of Testing
Many wonder why God does not remove "thorns" from the flesh when we pray to Him. We must learn that God always answers prayer, but sometimes the answer is no. He knows it will be better for us to bear the thorn than be without it. "Thorns" in the flesh have made many to lean on Christ.

Sometimes a "thorn" is a warning to keep us from sin and failure. God proved to Paul that no matter what his weakness was, His strength was sufficient.

A minister one day buried his only child. He went into his study the next day to prepare his message for Sunday, but he could not. His grief was too great. Through his tears, which would insist upon coursing down his cheeks, his eyes fell on these words: "My grace is sufficient." It seemed to read this way: "My grace IS sufficient." He wrote it that way on a card and hung it in front of his desk. He learned to know a God who is always present. Every word is important.

My—means God.

Grace—unmerited favor. I bring Christ what I have, my sin. He brings me what He has—His righteousness. The exchange is made. He takes my sin and gives me His righteousness. This is grace, wonderful grace!

Is—the present, always.

Sufficient—enough and to spare. "Our sufficiency is of God" (3:5, *KJV*). Here is where Charles Haddon Spurgeon laughed out loud. "To think," said he, "that our little cups could exhaust the ocean of His grace."

We are satisfied with Jesus. Is He your personal comfort? God gives us unusual strength for unusual tasks. Paul says, "For when I am weak, then I am strong" (12:10). There is strength and courage in the heart in which Christ is dwelling.

The Duty of Self-Testing

"Examine yourselves to see whether you are in the faith; test yourselves" (2 Corinthians 13:5). In this second letter, Paul emphasizes that the Corinthians might know themselves—test themselves to make sure of their faith. He was anxious that none of them should be deceived. Use every means to know where you really stand spiritually.

Do not depend on a mere profession of religion. Do not rely on church membership. Joining the church saves no one. Joining Christ saves us. Examine your standing.

Do not trust a past experience. Live only for today. Trust only in a present love, a present faith, and a present service. This gives you the test of your spiritual life in Him.

Do not rest upon mere approved methods of conduct. One may go through the forms of religious worship and not be religious. Wax museum figures wink and blink and seem to breathe, but there is no particle of life in them. Some people go through the motions of religion. Examine yourself about the motives that move your life. Is it to please God or people? What do you love? The adversary always tells us we are "good enough," but Christ says we must be perfect. Here are some tests to use:

Do I love to think of Christ?

Do I love to pray?

Do I love to study God's Word?

Do I love Christian friends?

Do I love the Church?

Do I love to serve Christ?

Second Corinthians closes with the benediction that today brings to a close many a church service (13:14).

Chapter 36

Understanding Galatians

Galatians Portrays Jesus Christ, Our Liberty

Selected Bible Readings

Sunday:	Only One Gospel (Galatians 1:1-24)
Monday:	Justified by Faith (Galatians 2:1-21)
Tuesday:	The Law Points to Christ (Galatians 3:1-29)
Wednesday:	Law and Grace (Galatians 4:1-31)
Thursday:	Stand Fast in Christian Liberty (Galatians 5:1-16)
Friday:	Flesh Versus Spirit (Galatians 5:17-26)
Saturday:	Sowing and Reaping (Galatians 6:1-18)

Galatians shows that the believer is no longer under the law but is saved by faith alone. "It is for freedom that Christ has set us free. Stand firm, then" (Galatians 5:1). The "law" is that portion of God's Word found in the first five books of Moses (Genesis— Deuteronomy) by which every phase of Israel's life was to be guided.

During Paul's second missionary journey (Acts 16:6), he was delayed in Galatia by sickness (4:13). Though ill, this tireless servant of the Lord could not remain silent, but kept on preaching the gospel. The theme of his sermon was "Christ crucified" (3:1). It was at this time that he succeeded in founding the Christian churches in Galatia (1:6). They were scattered over a rural district and the people were country folk. Teachers of the law had followed Paul, teaching salvation by works, claiming that even if Christianity were true, Christians should be circumcised and do all the works of the law. These teachers explained that the reason Paul had not taught the Galatians this was that he was not a true apostle and had learned his doctrines from others. This had upset the new converts.

Circumcision was the initial rite of the Jewish religion. If people born Gentile wished to become Jewish, they had to observe this ceremonial law. It was much like foreigners in our country taking out citizenship papers. If they actually take out papers, although born on foreign soil, they are just as much a citizen as those born here.

False teachers had begun to "bewitch" the people by telling them they must keep all kinds of ceremonies. Paul wanted them to know that nothing, no fetishes or works or ceremonies could bring them to Christ. Salvation comes by believing on Christ—nothing else.

Being very fickle and loving something new and a change, the Galatians were on the verge of accepting the views of these false teachers. When Paul heard it, so urgent did the matter seem that, because no one was with him to write it, he wrote the letter himself (6:11).

It has been said that Judaism was the cradle of Christianity and very nearly its grave. God raised up Paul as the Moses of the Christian Church to deliver it from this bondage. This Epistle has done more than any other book in the New Testament to free our Christian faith from Judaism, and from the burden of salvation by works, taught by so many false cults, which has threatened the simple gospel of the Lord Jesus Christ. Many people want to do something to be saved. The question of the Philippian jailer, "What must I do to be saved?" is the question multitudes ask. The answer is always the same. "Believe in the Lord Jesus, and you will be saved" (Acts 16:31).

A religion without the cross is not Christ's religion. Christ did not come merely to blaze a trail through a tangled forest or to set us an example of true living. He came to be a Savior. The power of the Cross is:

To deliver from sin—1:4; 2:21; 3:22

To deliver from the curse of the law—3:13

To deliver from the self-life—2:20; 5:24
To deliver from the world—6:14
In the new birth—4:4-7
In receiving the Holy Spirit—3:14
In bringing forth the Spirit's fruit—5:22-25.

This Epistle of Galatians is the Christian's Declaration of Independence. Our battle hymn is "Christus Liberator." "So if the Son sets you free, you will be free indeed" (John 8:36). Folks imagine that restrictions destroy liberty. The opposite is true. On entering a free public park, the first thing we see is, "Don't walk on the grass," "No dogs allowed," "Don't pick the flowers." And yet this is a free park! We do not complain. These laws preserve the park. Were they not enacted it would be no more a park than any vacant lot in the neighborhood. Thus it is with society at large. If we revolt against God and His order, civilization will lapse into barbarism. This is what is happening in the world today. Liberty is not freedom from law—that is recklessness. Liberty is freedom from the Mosaic law system, but subjection to "Christ's law" (1 Corinthians 9:20-21). Paul speaks of the liberty we have "in Christ" (2:4). "Where the Spirit of the Lord is, there is freedom" (2 Corinthians 3:17). This is the one great secret of liberty.

This is the liberty that is told of in this book, so get hold of Galatians and let Galatians get hold of you. In Galatians we are not servants working for a living, but sons working in our living. Learn what it is to be free in Christ! Christ said, "I no longer call you servants,...Instead, I have called you friends" (John 15:15).

Galatians contrasts Law and Grace:

In Romans we find our *standing*.

In Galatians we take our *stand*.

Paul tells us:

In Romans to use our *heads* to grasp the great facts of Christianity.

In 1 Corinthians to put out the *hand* to grasp our privileges in Christ.

In 2 Corinthians to lift our *hearts* to receive the comforts that are ours.

In Galatians to stand on our *feet* in the liberty that Christ gives.

Introduction (Galatians 1:1-11)

This is the only time in all of Paul's writings in which he does not express his thankfulness. Rather he says, "I am astonished" (1:6). This is the only church of whom he does not ask prayers. How could he, seeing they were bringing dishonor upon the Lord (Galatians 1:6-9)?

Paul marvels that these new Christians could give up the gospel of liberty so quickly and accept a legalistic message that was no gospel at all. Twice he pronounced a curse upon those causing the trouble. He says if an angel from heaven were to preach any other gospel than the one he preached "let him be eternally condemned ("accursed," *KJV*)!" (1:8-9).

What was this gospel Paul preached? Paul's gospel shuts out all works. "Know that a man is not justified by observing the law, but by faith in Jesus Christ...because by observing the law no one will be justified" (2:16). The difficulty about salvation is not that we should be good enough to be saved, but that we should see that we are bad enough to need salvation. Christ can save only sinners. Grace cannot begin until the law has proven that we are guilty, as the book of Romans shows each of us to be. Then Christ offers us His righteousness.

A gospel of mixed law and grace has no power. The false teachers of this kind of gospel were "accursed" because they pervert (not deny) the gospel. They admitted that Christ must die upon the cross, but denied that faith alone in His sacrifice was sufficient for salvation. They taught that to be saved one must keep some part of the law at least. They thought that simple faith according to the gospel Paul preached was not sufficient for salvation. People still like this kind of preaching because they believe they can do something to obtain merit before God.

Paul shows us the seriousness of our condition outside Christ. When a medical specialist says, "Your only hope is this or that," you know you must be in a critical and serious condition. Here are the words of a great gospel expert. Paul declares that our position is so serious that the gospel of the grace of God is our only hope. There is no other.

Paul introduced the atonement (1:4), a truth once so dear to them, but now practically rejected. Christ gave himself for our sins.

Paul Defends His Apostleship (Galatians 1:12—2:21)

Paul's teaching was authorized by God Himself (Galatians 1:11-24). He proves that he received his gospel directly from the Lord. Only God could have changed him from a murderer to a preacher.

We can learn many things by experience, but that is not so with the things of God. To know them they must be revealed to us. "I did not receive it from any man, nor was I taught it; rather, I received it by revelation from Jesus Christ" (1:12).

Paul did not consult with anyone about what he should preach, but retired to the wilds of Arabia for three years and there listened to God. He was taught by the Spirit. He had been with Peter and James only fifteen days after the three years in Arabia so he couldn't have learned much from them.

The authority behind Paul's gospel is shown by his rebuke of Peter (2:11-21). To prove that Peter was not a greater apostle than he, he points out in Galatians 2:11-21 how he had openly rebuked Peter for being two-faced about Jewish customs when he was in Antioch. He made no secret attempt to undermine Peter's authority. Paul was not dominated by this strong apostle to the Jewish people. Verse 11 is an unanswerable argument against the supremacy of Peter. "I want you to know, brothers, that the gospel I preached is not something that man made up" (1:11). It is good to know that the friendship between Peter and Paul was so real that it stood this severe test. (See 2 Peter 3:15.)

What does "justified" mean? God credits to my account what Christ has done—just-as-if-I'd done it. A criminal is pardoned though the person cannot be regarded as righteous. But justification is that act of God whereby He not only forgives us, but also puts Christ's righteousness to our account. God justifies sinners without justifying our sin. He gives us a righteousness not our own, but Christ's.

How are we justified? "Not by works" (Galatians 2:16-17, *KJV*). Works are excluded! We are not justified by the works of the law, but by the faith of Jesus Christ.

There are no degrees of justification. The moment we believe on Christ we are made just. Justification is:

By God—Romans 3:26; 8:33

By grace—3:24

By blood—3:25; 5:9

By faith—3:21-28.

Paul ended his great apology by a personal word of testimony, which gives us a complete picture of the Christian life both positively and negatively. "I have been crucified with Christ and I no longer live, but Christ lives in me. The life I live in the body, I live by faith in the Son of God, who loved me and gave himself for me" (Galatians 2:20). It is a paradox.

This verse is true of every believer. We do not need to be crucified with Christ. We have been crucified with Him. He died in our place. Now we live not by law but by faith. Christ was our sacrifice for sin and now is our sufficiency for the new life. The Christian life is a dying life—dying daily to self and sin. The crucified Savior lives in those who have shared His crucifixion.

Paul Defends the Gospel (Galatians 3:1—4:31)

"I've tried religion for the past five years and it hasn't worked. I gave it up," were the words of a young man when a preacher asked him to accept Christ.

"Why, I tried religion for fifteen years and it did nothing for me. I gave it up too," the preacher said.

A pause followed. "Then why are you a minister?" the youth asked.

"Then I tried Christ, and He fully met my needs. It is not religion I am recommending to you, but a living, loving Savior."

"Religion," a word once so commonly used among Christians, is fast becoming out of vogue because it has been twisted and misapplied. A religious person now means one who has accepted a creed or observes certain ceremonies or attends certain places of public worship. But all this is not sufficient. There must be a living faith in a living Savior. It is possible to have a religion without the gospel. This was the peril that faced the Galatian Christians. Many people count on their sincerity in believing some creed they have worked out to save themselves. They say, "The golden rule is my religion." But there is no salvation in that for "without the shedding of blood there is no forgiveness" of sin (Hebrews 9:22).

People who do not believe in foreign missions say that non-Christians have their own religions and so why disturb them? Yes, they have so much religion that they are bowed down under the weight of the load, but no good news of the gospel. But we are commanded to preach the gospel to every creature.

Religion is the best people can do. Christianity is the best God can do. See the results of people's best: "by observing the law no one will be justified" (Galatians 2:16). How can a person be made just? "By faith in Christ and not by observing the law" (2:16). Christianity is God's best. Christ is no sheriff. He is "the Lamb of God, who takes away the sin of the world" (John 1:29). We are pronounced righteous not by works of the law, but by faith in Him.

Paul is defending the gospel of Christ. He describes his own preaching as having so fully set forth the cross that it was as if they had seen Christ crucified in their midst (Galatians 3:1). He shows what the law could not do, but what grace had done.

Paul puts a challenging question to these "foolish Galatians." He cries, "O foolish Galatians, I have brought you the true gospel, and you received it with eagerness and gratitude. Now suddenly you drop the gospel. What has got into you?

"Come on now, my smart Galatians, you who all of a sudden have become professors while I seem to be your pupil, did you receive the Holy Spirit by the works of the law or by the preaching of the gospel?" (author's paraphrase). This question was a challenge to them because their own experience proved the truth of Paul's preaching to them.

"You cannot say you received the Holy Spirit because you kept the law. Nobody ever heard of such a thing. But as soon as the gospel came, you receive the Holy Spirit by the simple hearing of faith," Paul adds (author's paraphrase).

It is hard for us to believe that the priceless gift of forgiveness of sins and the gift of the Holy Spirit are not gained by real effort, but God offers them to us free of charge. Why not take them? Why worry about our own unworthiness? Why not accept them with thankfulness?

Immediately foolish reason says, If people don't have to do a thing for their salvation or for an atonement for their wrongdoings, then they will become shiftless and will not even try to do good. But we have found that when we have accepted the gospel with a thankful heart, then we get busy on good works. We want to please God. Those who think we ought to be saved by our works think faith is an easy thing, but we know from personal experience how hard it is to simply believe. Martin Luther tells us that Christians are not sinless, but God no longer chalks sin against them because of their faith in Christ.

"Consider Abraham: 'He believed God, and it was credited to him as righteousness'" (3:6). Abraham may have had a good standing with others for his upright life, but not with God. In God's sight, Abraham was a condemned sinner. You see righteousness had been given to Abraham on the ground of his faith, not his works. If faith without works was sufficient for Abraham, why should we turn from faith to law? "Abraham believed." That is faith. Faith says to God, "I believe what you say."

It must have startled the proud and troublesome legalists when Paul told them that not those born of Abraham's flesh and blood, but those who believe in Christ Jesus are the true children of Abraham (3:26-29). Though born in obscurity, through the new birth, all can sit down with Abraham as a child of the father of the faithful (3:14,29). Abraham believed God and it was accounted to him for righteousness (3:6-7).

The Curse of the Law

The curse of God is like a flood that swallows everything that is not of faith. Remember, the law Paul is talking about is not civil law. Civil law has its place, but civil righteousness will never deliver a person from the condemnation of God's Law. Just because I am a law-abiding citizen does not mean I am a Christian. Governmental laws are blessings for this life only, but not for the life hereafter. Otherwise many unbelievers would be nearer heaven than some Christians are, for unbelievers often excel in civil righteousness.

A guilty man would never come before a court and plead innocent because he is a good church member, a fine giver or a member of a Sunday School class. Neither can a sinner come before the court of heaven and plead that because he is in public office or a good citizen or a moral man that God should accept him. The civil courts require that you keep the law. The court of heaven requires that you have faith in Jesus Christ.

The law cannot give righteousness but it does bring death upon all those who do not keep it (Galatians 3:10). Law demands perfect obedience. Many think they should get something for keeping the law. Really they should get nothing. People ought to keep the law and get nothing for doing so. You live in a city all your life and during your lifetime you keep the laws of that city. Will the city council present you with a gift because you have not broken the laws? Of course not. You ought to keep the law. But suppose after twenty years of law keeping you then commit a crime. The authorities will then give you something—a jail sentence for breaking the law. The Bible tells us that a curse (a sentence) is upon all who break the law, while a blessing is upon all those who live by faith.

"Christ redeemed us from the curse of the law by becoming a curse for us" (3:13). As all had broken the law, all had come under its curse. But Christ has redeemed us. "Don't turn back to the law from which Christ redeemed us. O foolish Galatians, who hath bewitched you, that ye should turn from the blessing of faith to the curse of law?" (author's paraphrase of several verses).

The law deals with what we are and do, while grace deals with what Christ is and does. What good is the law? We find the answer in Galatians 3:19-20. Everything has its purpose. Let us see the purpose of the law. The law is given to restrain the wicked by giving punishment for crime, just as civil laws keep people from murder and theft because of the fear of jail or the electric chair. These restraints do not make people righteous, but they do restrain them from crime.

Another purpose of the law is spiritual. The law reveals to us our sin, and blindness and contempt of God. As long as we are not murderers or thieves, we would swear we are righteous. How does God show us what we really are? By the hammer of the law. As long as we think we are right, we are proud and despise God's grace. This monster of self-righteousness needs a big ax, and the law is just that. When people see by the law that they are under God's wrath, they begin to rebel and complain against God. The law inspires hatred of God. What does this beating by the hand of the law accomplish? It helps us to find the way of grace. When the conscience has been thoroughly frightened by the law, it welcomes the gospel.

Law reveals sin, but does not remove it. The law proves that we are all sinners by nature and directs us to Christ! We so often think that we become sinners when we commit some sinful acts. But it is because we are already sinners that we commit the act. We lie because we are liars. We steal because we are thieves. We do not become liars when we utter the lie. The law only proves we are liars.

The law too was given to drive us to Christ by showing us our need. The gospel tells us that Christ is the only One who can meet that need (3:23—4:11). Paul says the law was our "schoolmaster" *(KJV)* to shock us into a sense of our need of Christ that we might be justified by faith in Him (3:24). God's law is not like the cruel schoolmaster of former times, a regular tyrant. His law is not to torment us always. God's law is like the good schoolmaster who trains children to find pleasure in doing the things they formerly detested.

The law really has a place in leading us into a Christian experience. Did you ever see a woman trying to sew without a needle? She would make poor speed if she sewed with only a thread. This is like God's dealing with us. He puts the needle of the law first, for we sleep so soundly in our own sins that we need to be aroused by something sharp. Then when He has the needle of the law fairly in our hearts, He draws a lifelong thread of gospel love and peace and joy.

Sons of God

Paul tells us that all are not the children of God. We find that it is faith in Christ, not works of the law or the Fatherhood of God or the brotherhood of people, that makes us children of God. "You are all sons of God through faith in Christ Jesus" (Galatians 3:26). Faith, not works, puts us into the family of God.

As long as an heir is underage there is no difference between that person and a slave, for the heir is under the control of a guardian. So Paul shows us in Galatians 4:5-6 that all believers are children of God, yet all children are not "sons"—grown-up ones. "Adoption" is a Roman legal word and means "the placing of a son" in a son's legal position. It might be receiving into a family one who does not belong to it by birth or the legal act of acknowledging the person coming of age. Christ came to ransom us so that we would be no longer slaves under the law, but possess all the privileges of full-grown sons and daughters and heirs.

As another illustration of their state of freedom in Christ, Paul reminds them that Abraham had two sons—Ishmael, the child of Hagar the bondwoman, and Isaac, the child of Sarai the free woman. Ishmael did not enjoy the blessings of a son in Abraham's house, but was left out in the cold, although he was the firstborn; Isaac was called. This is what happens to those who seek to be saved by keeping the law. But Isaac, the child of promise and faith, was the heir of all things. So we are heirs of a spiritual promise.

Paul Desires the Gospel Be Applied (Galatians 5—6)

The first application of the gospel pertains to one's own personal freedom from the law. Paul wants the Galatians to hold fast to their personal liberty. The gospel of God's grace gives true liberty (Galatians 5:1-12). "It is for freedom that Christ has set us free. Stand firm, then, and do not let yourselves be burdened again by a yoke of slavery" (5:1). If the Galatians seek to be saved by keeping the law, they are bound by the law. Their liberty should be prized because it cost so much, the blood of Christ.

"Stand firm." This is one of Paul's favorite expressions. Maintain your position of erectness!

1. In the faith—1 Corinthians 16:13
2. In the liberty—Galatians 5:1
3. In the Spirit—Philippians 1:27
4. In the Lord—Philippians 4:1.

The gospel of grace guards against recklessness (Galatians 5:13-15). Many people are afraid to live under grace instead of law for fear it will lead others to "live as they please and do as they like." Grace will always lead a person to live as God pleases and like what He likes.

We abuse our liberty:

By lack of love—Galatians 5:13-14. "Serve one another in love. The entire law is summed up in a single command: 'Love your neighbour as yourself.'" Use love!

By unclean living—Galatians 5:16-26. See how the flesh "acts up." Read this list of its seventeen evil works, 5:19-21. These are sins of the mind as well as the body. This is what we are by nature and these are the things we do. Christ has given the Holy Spirit to make us free from these. "Live by the Spirit, and you will not gratify the desires of the sinful nature" (v. 16). Let the Holy Spirit rule your life.

Children begin to walk by someone holding on to their hand. We begin our walk by the Spirit holding on to us. But He is not only a help outside as in the case of a child, but He helps within. Think of walking arm in arm with the Holy Spirit! This means no running ahead or lagging behind (5:16).

The nine graces are:

1. Toward God (a) love (b) joy (c) peace.
2. Toward others: (d) patience (e) kindness (f) goodness.
3. Toward myself: (g) faithfulness (h) gentleness (i) self-control.

In contrast to the work of the sinful nature, we see the nine-fold fruit of the Spirit (5:22-23). If we abide in Christ (John 15) we shall be free to bear fruit with God. Are we showing this cluster of fruit in our lives?

Sowing and Reaping (Galatians 6:7-9)

"A man reaps what he sows" (Galatians 6:7).

If we sow to the Spirit, we shall reap a spiritual harvest. If we sow to the flesh (the lower appetites), we will reap moral weakness (6:7-8).

The harvest will not be according to how much we know, but how much we sow. We may have a large supply of seed in the barn of the mind, but unless it is planted in suitable soil it will bear no harvest. Sow the seed of thoughts in word and deeds. God's Word always brings forth seed after its kind.

Sow the seeds of your life in the soil of the Spirit, not the soil of the flesh. In the Spirit it will honor God, but in the flesh the seed will rot and bring forth corruption. The Spirit brings forth only good fruit, the flesh only evil.

Many deceive themselves by saying, "It doesn't matter what I sow if I am sincere." Would that be good advice for a farmer? Self-life will never produce the fruit of the Spirit. "Sowing" and "reaping" are agricultural terms. The Christian worker is not likened to a salesman or mechanic, but to a farmer. Christian work is not buying and selling, but sowing and reaping. When dealing with souls, we are not mechanics. We are not just to fix over "run-down" lives, but we are to plant the living Word.

Paul bore in his body the slave marks of Jesus. These were marks of:

Ownership—I belong to another. The Greek word *stigma* means a brand, a mark, sometimes burnt into the face, body or arm of a slave or criminal. What were Paul's stigma? They were scars he had received by persecution and hardship he had endured for Christ (2 Corinthians 6:4; 11:23). The rough hands of a laborer tell that he is the slave of hard toil; the weather-beaten face of a sea captain, the wounds of a soldier, the lines in a mother's brow are all honorable. The slave marks of Christ speak, first, of a changed character and, second, of a labor of love for Him.

Devotion—What scars had the false teachers received for Christ? None. They saved themselves. But behold me!

Commission—The false teachers came armed with letters of authority. I am without letters of recommendation. But behold my scars! They constitute my commission.

In Christ we are free to know the boundless life that is in Him. In Him we are "a new creation" (Galatians 6:15). We are a new creation; we have a new life in Christ. No wonder Paul cries out, "May I never boast except in the cross of our Lord Jesus Christ, through which the world has been crucified to me, and I to the world" (6:14). "Let the world go by! I have Christ, and having Him, I have all things," Paul is saying. Oh, the joy of a free, full life in Christ Jesus.

Contrasts in the Book of Galatians

Grace and Law

The one thing that distinguishes our Christian faith from all others is the grace of God. Grace is unmerited favor of God to us when we are undeserving.

Law shows us our need.

Grace shows God's provision to meet that need.

Law says we must work for our salvation—"Do."

Grace says salvation is free, a gift—"Done."

Faith and Works

Faith makes us receive salvation by believing.

Works keep us striving to earn it.

Fruit of the Spirit and Works of the Flesh

The Spirit gives us daily victory over sin.

The flesh makes us prone to sin.

Cross and the World

The Cross means love and sacrifice.

The world suggests force and selfishness.

Chapter 37

Understanding Ephesians

Ephesians Portrays Jesus Christ, Our All in All

Selected Bible Readings

Sunday: The Believer's Position (Ephesians 1:1-23)

Monday: Saved by Grace (Ephesians 2:1-22)

Tuesday: A Mystery Revealed (Ephesians 3:1-21)

Wednesday: A Christian's Walk (Ephesians 4:1-32)

Thursday: Following Christ (Ephesians 5:1-20)

Friday: Living with Others (Ephesians 5:21—6:9)

Saturday: Christian Warfare (Ephesians 6:10-24)

In this Epistle, we enter the holy of holies in Paul's writings. Paul speaks in 2 Corinthians 12:2 of being "caught up to the third heaven." Here, as it were, he gives his report. He seems to be carried away as he tells of it. It is the greatest revelation of truth that God has given to us. It is the mystery that has been hidden from before the foundation of the world.

This book shows us the great mystery of the Church. The real Church is the Body of Christ, and believers are members of that sacred Body of which Christ is the head. The Father not only prepared a body in which Jesus Christ would suffer, but He also prepared a Body for Him in which He should be glorified. The Greek word for church is *ecclesia*, which means an assembly of called-out ones. Christ is taking out a people for His name (Acts 15:14). The Church is an organism. It is the Body of Christ. Every believer is a member of Christ's Body, and He is the head of the Church.

Imagine for a moment that the Body is like a great building. The "stones" are redeemed human beings. Christ, the Head, occupies the great throne room. All the parts are like "rooms" in the building. With this picture in mind, it is easy to see the whole story of the mystery of the Church. The suffering of Christ in an earthly body is now to be made up for by erecting a spiritual body or "building." Come with Paul through this glorious structure as he outlines it in Ephesians:

The believer's position—chapters 1—3: (1) in Christ, and (2) in "heavenly places."

The believer's walk—chapters 4—6: (1) ecclesiastically, chapter 4; (2) morally, chapter 5; (3) socially, 5:21—6:9; (4) martially, 6:10-24.

Paul seems to present a picture of "Christ's Temple of Ephesus," which the Christian may enter. It is "a holy temple in the Lord" (2:21). We approach in these chapters, one after another, six magnificent rooms in this great temple. They are all "in Christ." Let the scenes of this book be laid in each of these rooms successively.

The Anteroom (Ephesians 1)

Let us enter this sacred temple with hushed voices and bared heads. Christ is going to allow us to go into His holy presence. The door opens into the spacious anteroom, where we read upon the walls our standing with God through Jesus Christ. "Blessed...with all spiritual blessings. Chosen...in him before the foundation of the world...holy and without blame before him in love....Accepted in the beloved" (Ephesians 1:3-6, *KJV*). These are some great wall mottoes for Christians. It will tax every spiritual energy to live up to them.

Our Blessings
The blessings of the Christian are not only "heavenly," but also "in the heavenly realms." Go through this first chapter and mark all you find "in Christ."

We are saints in Christ Jesus—(1:1)
Blessed in Christ—(1:3)
Chosen in Him—(1:4)
Adopted by Christ—(1:5)

Lavished with love in Christ, the One God loves—(1:6)
Redeemed and forgiven in Christ—(1:7)
Revealed His will in Himself—(1:9)
Everything centered in Christ—(1:10)
Participants in God's good plan in Christ—(1:11)
Glorified in Christ, sealed with the Holy Spirit—(1:12-13)
Inheritance in Christ (1:14)
Faith in Christ—(1:15)
Wisdom in Him—(1:17)
Hope in Christ—(1:18)
Power in Christ—(1:19-20)
Made alive in Christ—(2:5-6)
Created in Christ—(2:10)
Brought near to God in Christ—(2:13)
Growing in Christ—(2:21)
Built in Christ—(2:22)
Sharers in His promise in Christ—(3:6)
Wisdom of God manifested in Christ—(3:10-11)
Freedom and confidence through Christ—(3:12).

Was this always our position? (2:11-13). We learn on entering this temple that our calling and position have been planned and worked out by God the Father, the Son and the Holy Spirit before the foundation of the world (1:4). All Christians should know their calling above everything else (1:18). The true knowledge of it will govern their lives.

Our Redemption

The Father planned it—1:4-6
The Son paid for it—1:7-12
The Spirit applied it—1:13-14.

"In him we have redemption through his blood, the forgiveness of sins, in accordance with the riches of God's grace" (Ephesians 1:7).

Redemption is the most glorious work of God. It is greater far than His work of creation. He spoke a word and worlds were formed, but it cost Him the life of His beloved Son to redeem the world. Paul delighted to dwell on this theme. The reason was that he had experienced Christ's redeeming love. He had been redeemed from sin, from the curse and bondage of the law. He had been washed clean in the blood of Christ, and anointed by the Holy Spirit. Well might he glory in his Redeemer.

To redeem means to buy back, to pay the ransom price. This is what Christ did for us when we were captive under sin. Let us consider: the sinner is a captive:

1. *To sin*—"Jesus answered them, 'Verily, verily, I say unto you, Whosoever committeth sin is the servant of sin'" (John 8:34, *KJV*). We feel that bondage. We know sin rules our lives.

2. *To Satan*—Paul speaks of sinners, recovering "from the trap of the devil, who has taken them captive to do his will" (2 Timothy 2:26).

3. *Under law*—We have broken the law and for this reason "the whole world is a prisoner of sin" (Galatians 3:22). The literal meaning is "shut up in prison." We have been put under arrest for violating the law.

The captive is in a miserable state and needs to be redeemed.

The provision for our redemption is: Christ is our Redeemer! "In whom we have redemption."

The means of redemption—"In whom we have redemption through his blood..." "Not with perishable things such as silver or gold...but with the precious blood of Christ" (1 Peter 1:18-19). Christ voluntarily took our place. He stood charged with our sins and paid the penalty with His blood.

The fruits of redemption—Even "the forgiveness of sins" is the result of redeeming love and this is "according to the riches of his grace." Grace is unmerited favor. His forgiveness is according to His abounding favor, without limiting it by our demerit.

He casts our sins behind His back. He blots them out of His book of remembrance. He sinks them into the depths of the sea. He removes them as far as the east is from the west. Yes, He forgives "according to the riches of his grace."

We hear a great prayer in this anteroom. Think of hearing Paul pray (Ephesians 1:15-23)! Paul wants every one of us who are believers to realize fully our privileges in Christ. He wants the eyes of our understanding to be enlightened that we might behold the glory of Christ. There is no use of showing a gorgeous sunset to a blind person. So we cannot understand the greatness of God until the Great Physician has healed our spiritual eyes.

Each believer should know the three "whats" in this prayer. Do you know the answers?

What is the hope of His calling?

What are the riches of the glory of His inheritance in the saints? Think of Christ's inheritance in us. He has suns and stars, but He wants sons and saints.

What is the exceeding greatness of His power? What the Church needs today is power. She is shorn of her real strength.

The Audience Chamber of the King (Ephesians 2)

Next we are conducted into the glorious audience chamber of the King, into the divine Presence. We "have access to the Father by one Spirit" (Ephesians 2:18). We would tremble as we entered if we did not hear the gracious words sound out, "You were dead in your transgressions and sins,...But because of his great love for us...made us alive with Christ...and seated us with him in the heavenly realms" (2:1-6). But best of all, there is a sweet Voice sounding through the corridors, Welcome here! "Consequently, you are no longer foreigners and aliens, but fellow citizens with God's people and members of God's household" (2:19). All of this is in sharpest contrast to what we were "formerly" (2:11-13). We once were "far off." Now we are "near."

In this audience chamber, we find that God has made both believing Jews and Gentiles "one" in Christ. We can better understand this by an illustration from our day. Dr. Keller (Frank A. Keller, medical evangelist and educator; in 1924 he had already spent twenty-seven years in China), on loan from the China Inland Mission to the Hunan Bible Institute, tells of a barber who was marvelously converted. He had been an opium addict and a moral degenerate. In desperation, he came to the missionaries, and prayer was answered for him. His appetite for opium left and he became a living witness for Christ.

During the barber's stay in the mission, a young man of "the student class" came as an inquirer, but, seeing the barber, he refused to go in. (A barber's occupation was held in contempt in China.) One day, thinking the barber had gone, he entered the mission and met the barber. Being too polite not to speak to him, he engaged in conversation. The barber told of the wonderful change that had come into his life through Christ. Class barriers melted away. The barber soon was a guest in the student's home, surrounded with wealth and culture. Christ had "made both one." This is what Christ will do with both Jew and Gentile, slave and free. Christ makes each one of us a new person and gives us access and approach into the very audience chamber of the King.

This new person has access to God through the blood of His Son (2:13). He is our Mediator, and He says, "No one comes to the Father except through me" (John 14:6). Then when we have been redeemed, the Holy Spirit introduces the new person at the court of heaven. He does not ask Peter for the privilege, nor does He consult the saints, nor does He invoke the "Mother of Jesus." There is only one Mediator and that is the Lord Jesus Christ. The Father rejoices in the new person and welcomes us into His very presence.

The Masterpiece Planned

God is producing a masterpiece, His Church. Paul says, "For we are God's workmanship" (2:10). This comes from the Greek word *poiema*—poem or masterpiece.

In Ephesians 1, we find how God planned and worked in the production of this Masterpiece. We were "chosen in Christ" to be holy and blameless (1:4). In the ages of past eternity, God was thinking about us, loving us and planning to bless us. Know this, before Satan ever appeared to spoil the happiness of people upon this earth, God made plans to make all who would believe on Him to be blameless.

Then in Ephesians 2:1-10 we find how it was produced. Look at the material He used. Read these verses. How does God take us up and produce a masterpiece out of such material? We see:

What the nature of a person is—2:1-3

What the walk of a natural person is—2:2.

"But God"—see God act! He changes all by His touch! This "But

God" is the bridge that leads us out of our dark and hopeless condition (2:4). When all human strength is at an end—"But God." Remember Christ comes to give life to the dead.

A quaint old legend tells of a piece of marble crying out from a pile of material that was left as rubbish after a great building had been erected. It was saying, "Glory, glory!" A passerby, hearing the cry, stopped. He learned from the marble, half-covered with dust and rubbish, that Michelangelo had just passed by and said, "I see an angel in that stone." Now he had gone to get his mallet and chisel.

Humanity was like that stone in the heap, broken and useless, but the great Sculptor saw it and began His masterpiece. As Michelangelo Buonarroti (1475-1564) saw the angel in the old stone, so God sees the image of His Son in wretched humanity. The grace of God carved a George Müeller (1805-98, famous philanthropist and preacher) out of a wayward family member, a John B. Gough (1817-1886, British temperance orator, active in London, England and Scotland) out of a barroom wreck.

The greatest proof of Christianity is that it has produced a new person who is approved unto God. Only God could make a Paul out of Saul.

Destiny of the Masterpiece

What a destiny it is (2:7)! What is a little suffering with a few trials here in comparison to the glory in the "ages to come" *(KJV)*. He will show the "exceeding riches of His grace" *(KJV)*. He will tell the universe what He has accomplished.

Salvation is the gift of God. "For it is by grace you have been saved, through faith—and this not from yourselves, it is the gift of God" (2:8). Faith is a gift, too. "Faith comes from hearing the message" (Romans 10:17). Faith is the channel of salvation. It is the hand that receives the gift. It connects us with God.

The Throne Room (Ephesians 3)

Standing at the doors of the throne room are the stalwart guards of Law. They demand: "Who goes there? Why do you come? What are your credentials?"

I answer feebly, "A sinner; I come to see the Lamb. I have nothing to recommend me for admittance."

Then I hear the voice of the Lamb from within, the call of the Son of Grace. "It is one of my sheep. Invite her in. My blood covers all. She needs no credentials." And Grace brings me past the stern guards of Law unto the throne of His mercy.

"In him and through faith in him we may approach God with freedom and confidence" (Ephesians 3:12). What a piling up of words to persuade us of our privilege and position as Christian believers! We are "accepted in the beloved" (1:6, *KJV*).

Here we behold the King! With Paul we bow our knee "before the Father, from whom his whole family in heaven and on earth derives its name" (3:14-15). Is posture a small thing? Kneeling is the attitude of humility, confession and entreaty. Remember the holiest men in the Bible have approached God this way. David, Solomon and Daniel knelt upon their knees. These men stooped to conquer, knelt to prevail.

Paul tells how God had held back from the Gentiles the secret that they should be heirs and shareholders of the gospel and have admission into the Church (His Body) on the same terms as the Jewish people (3:8-10). To "bring all things in heaven and on earth together under one head, even Christ" (1:10) was God's plan.

The word "mystery," which occurs three times here, does not mean something mysterious. It merely means it is hidden until the appropriate time comes for God to reveal it.

The mystery of the Church is that the Gentiles are to be equal partakers with the Jewish people of God's promises (Ephesians 3:6). All this was "by faith" (Romans 15:9-10; Galatians 3:8-9). This is a radical thing that God would make the Gentiles with the Jews coheirs of Christ and comembers of His Church.

Paul prays again and his prayer is recorded in Ephesians 3:13-21. The first prayer recorded in chapter 1 gave us three "whats." This prayer gives us four "thats" and is steeped in the love of Christ.

That they should be strengthened by His Spirit.

That they might have Christ dwelling in their hearts.

That they might understand what is the breadth, length, depth and height of the love of Christ.

That they might be filled with the fullness of God.

Paul enjoys the "riches" of the gospel. It is bountiful in its gifts and inexhaustible in its resources.

If we are to enjoy this life in the Temple of God, we must be yielded in obedience to Him. If we yield to His plan for our lives as willing subjects, we will find that in His hand our lives will be filled with joy and beauty.

The Jewel Room (Ephesians 4)

Here amid the flash of the jewel room we will get our decorations and our garments of holiness—"Be completely humble and gentle; be patient, bearing with one another in love" (4:2). Here are our banners and emblems—"one Lord, one faith, one baptism" (4:5). Here are the brilliant gems of the graces as we will take them—"But to each one of us grace has been given as Christ apportioned it" (Ephesians 4:7). We must "put off," or lay aside, the old life as we would lay aside a garment, and "put on" the new life as a new garment (4:22-25).

We must be different, but how? In what respect? What are the things we should be very careful about? We must put away lying. Our speech shows our spirit. We must put away all bitterness and anger and harsh words. Be kind to each other. We must not have anything to do with deeds of darkness for we are children of light. Read all of Ephesians 4:31-32.

We must go into God's robing room not to make the garments, but to put them on. God is the Tailor and He makes our dress to conform to our position and purpose in life. God wants His sons and daughters to wear suitable garments.

We have discovered as we have come into this temple what our riches are in the heavenlies (1:18-21). Now we must "live a life worthy of the calling you have received" (4:1). The way we live must correspond to our creed. A heavenly calling demands a heavenly conduct.

What is a "walk"? It is not a path or a way of moving about over the earth or even a sphere of work. A Christian's walk includes conduct, attitudes and consecration; it is, in short, "a way of living before men."

We are to walk (Ephesians 4:1-3):

Humbly—"Be completely humble and gentle"

Lovingly—"Be patient, bearing with one another in love"

Peacefully—"Make every effort to keep the unity of the Spirit through the bond of peace."

We know that our spiritual lives affect our social lives. But many turn it around and attempt to create a social life that will create a spiritual life. This cannot be. When we are in right relation to God, we will be in proper relation to people.

When God puts upon us His jewels of grace, He seals us by His Spirit (4:30). It is like a young man putting a diamond upon the engagement finger of one whom he has promised to marry. The Lord knows them that are His and we are sealed unto the day of redemption. The seal is the mark of ownership. "They are mine." A seal is set for security. We are sealed unto the day of redemption. Have you the seal? Show it then!

The Choir and Oratory Room (Ephesians 5)

In the jewel room, we were bedecked as children of God and enjoined to walk worthy of our calling. We were sealed with the seal of ownership. Now we are to go out and be followers of God as dear children. A Christian is *I* following Christ—Christ-*I*-an. The walk of a Christian:

Walk in love—Ephesians 5:1-2

Walk in light—5:8

Walk carefully—5:15-16.

"Do not get drunk on wine, which leads to debauchery. Instead, be filled with the Spirit" (5:18). The body, mind and spirit cannot function without outside stimulants. No one will think clearly or feel deeply unless something without excites him or her. But this is where the tragedy comes. The world has plenty of powerful stimulants that give quick and joyous reactions. But the results are devastating. Our bodies and minds are not made for such ruinous flames and are destroyed. Our bodies are for God's altars. "Therefore, I urge you, brothers...to offer your bodies as living sacrifices, holy and pleasing to God—this is your spiritual act of worship" (Romans 12:1) is God's plea. The Holy Spirit fires our bodies and spirits and sets them aglow, but never destroys. Therefore God commands, "Be not drunk with wine...but be filled [set aflame] with the Spirit" *(KJV)*. We can burn and never be consumed. We may live dangerously for God and never be in danger.

It is just as great a sin not to be filled with the Spirit of God as it is to be drunk with wine. Don't think that only ministers and missionaries need to be filled with His blessed Presence, but all! God's Spirit is waiting that He might fill His temples (5:19-20).

"Speak to one another with psalms, hymns and spiritual songs. Sing and make music in your heart to the Lord" (5:19). Sing, Christian, sing! Christ wants it so. A singing heart guarantees a transformed life. When the Spirit fills the heart, the lips overflow with praise. We will walk the Christian life as we sing and talk about Christ.

This joyful praise of Christian meetings is in contrast to the noisy drunken revelings of Ephesus. Singing is the most natural joyous expression of the Christian life. Have much of it in your church groups. There is music in God's house. God does not delight in sighing and groaning or weeping, but in songs of praise and adoration, in rejoicing and thanksgiving. He is the One who inspires the poet, the hymn writer, the artist in the world. The devil is the author of distress and discord.

There is social life in this great music room of God's temple. We find it in relationship to everyone.

The Lord not only tells us to walk carefully in the spiritual sphere of our lives, but also in every other field. How is your walk as a Christian before your family, your friends and your acquaintances? God demands a walk worthy of Him every place and everywhere. How practical all of this is! How simple yet how spiritual! Only men and women who believe that the Christian life "is not I but Christ" could fulfill such demands. Christ is the key to a life of victory in the Son of God. He teaches that a child of God can and must, under all circumstances, be a living witness to the power of Christ in his or her life.

The Armory (Ephesians 6)

Now we stand in a room hung with the whole armor of God. The armor is His, not ours! But He tells us to put it on. We must put on the whole of it if we will be safe. The armor is not for a museum where we can go and look over its strength, but it is for the battlefield. Polished armor hanging up in the hall of our creed will not save us in the day of battle. What a relief to know that we do not have to provide the armor! How ignorant we are of the strength and stratagem of the enemy! How inadequately we judge our own ability and weakness!

Paul says, "Finally, be strong in the Lord and in his mighty power" (Ephesians 6:10). You can be strong! You must be strong! But remember this! "Be strong in the Lord, and in the power of his might!" As soon as we are brought into communion with God, we need to be fitted for the fight of faith. All who belong to the kingdom of God's dear Son have the forces of the kingdom of Satan against them, so they need to be covered with the whole armor of God.

The Christian's walk includes a warfare. Let us know the wiles of the forces marshaled against us! We have been raised to the heavenly places of fellowship with Christ. Let us maintain the honor of our calling and the wealth of our high estate. As good soldiers, let us stand and defend our interests. The crying need of our day is for strong people. In Ephesians 5, we were asked to put on clothing suited to the new person moving in society. Here we are to put on armor necessary to the soldier.

You must come to Calvary for each piece of this wonderful armor. When we come and take it for ourselves, we can see that our whole body is covered. We are to "be able to stand against" the enemy. Stand, Christian, in the victory Christ wrought on Calvary. But you notice there is no armor for the back. The Christian is never supposed to run from enemies, but fight the good fight of faith, praying always!

"The full armor of God":

Girdle of truth
Breastplate of righteousness
Shoes of readiness to bear the gospel
Shield of faith
Helmet of salvation
Sword of the Word
Prayer.

Chapter 38

Understanding Philippians

Philippians Portrays Jesus Christ, Our Joy

Selected Bible Readings

Sunday: Joy Triumphs over Suffering (Philippians 1:1-30)
Monday: Joy in Christ (Philippians 2:1-11)
Tuesday: Joy in Salvation (Philippians 2:12-30)
Wednesday: Joy in Christ's Righteousness (Philippians 3:1-9)
Thursday: Joy in Christ's Will (Philippians 3:10-21)
Friday: Joy in Christ's Strength (Philippians 4:1-7)
Saturday: Joy in Christ's Provision (Philippians 4:8-23)

The Epistle to the Philippians was written to the first church founded in Europe. Paul was called there by the vision and the cry, "Come over to Macedonia and help us" (Acts 16:9).

Paul urges the Church to have Christian unity and joy. This letter shows how unity among Christians can be broken. Christ is the secret of joy. "Finally, my brothers, rejoice in the Lord!" (Philippians 3:1). Then there is a pause. Paul is trying to think of some better last word to speak, but he can't find it. Presently he cried out, "Rejoice in the Lord always. I will say it again: Rejoice!" (4:4). This is joy in the midst of trouble and problems.

Paul and Silas, you remember, sang in the jail there at Philippi at midnight when their backs were bleeding and sore! He is rejoicing now as he writes this letter, chained to a Roman soldier, for he knows that his very chains are helping him to spread the gospel. He could reach some in Caesar's household that he never otherwise could have brought to Christ. He urged his Philippian converts to rejoice because they were allowed to suffer for Christ (1:29).

"The joy of the Lord is your strength" (Nehemiah 8:10). The word "joy," or "rejoice," occurs in this Epistle sixteen times. Paul seems to laugh out loud for sheer joy in this letter. He is the rejoicing apostle. "Joy" and "rejoice" and "all" are the words to underline. "Be glad" is Paul's exhortation. We are commanded to rejoice. We break a commandment if we rejoice not, for joy drives out discord. It helps in the midst of trials. "Joy is a bird; let it fly in the open heavens, and let its music be heard of all men." Sinners, like Augustine, are attracted to Jesus by the joy of Christians.

It hardly seems possible that Paul is writing from prison with chains holding him. His words seem to come from a light heart. It is evident that the soul of this great apostle is free! There is an atmosphere of joy even from prison.

This letter has no definite plan, but it is the sweetest of all Paul's letters. There is no scolding. It is more of a love letter.

Paul mentions the Savior's name forty times in this short Epistle. Some of the most wonderful things concerning Christ and the Christian life are here. So that your life may be purified, dangers avoided and progress made, Christ must be your joy, your trust and your aim in life. Paul tells us of his joyful triumph over trying circumstances because of his trust in Christ.

Joy in Living (Philippians 1)

Paul loved to call himself the servant (really "bond servant") of Jesus Christ. He had been made free by Christ and now he wants to serve Him as long as he should live. He starts his Epistle, "Paul and Timothy, servants of Jesus Christ." That is the reason he says, "For to me to live is Christ" (1:21).

Notice when Paul writes his letters he puts his name first. How sensible this is, for the first thing you do in opening a letter is to turn to the end and find out who wrote it.

Although in prison, Paul could pray for his friends. "I thank my

God every time I remember you. In all my prayers for all of you, I always pray with joy" (Philippians 1:3-4).

Paul lived to intercede for others. So should every true Sunday School teacher, Christian friend, father, mother, brother or sister remember others in their prayers without ceasing. Have you a prayer list? Do you talk with the Lord about your friends? "Making request with joy"? Why can we rejoice in prayer? What is your answer?

Although Paul was in prison, chained to a soldier, people came to hear him preach. The Roman guards were so interested in the gospel that they spread it around. This encouraged others to be bold in preaching, and many found Paul's Christ.

There is great power in the witness of a consistent life. You may be bound to unsympathetic companions, but by your life you may win them for God. Your obstacle may become your pulpit. Christians who work for Christ when everything is against them stir up others.

"For to me, to live is Christ" (1:21). Can you say this? Is Christ everything to you? Do you live for Him? Is your one aim and purpose to glorify Him?

Listen to the cries of the people of this world. What are they? To the successful businessperson it is, "To me to live is wealth." To the scholar it is, "To me to live is knowledge." To the soldier it is, "To me to live is victory." To the young man, "To me to live is pleasure." To the man desirous of recognition, "To me to live is fame." To the high school student, "To me to live is recognition." So we could go on and listen to all the voices of the world, but one is heard over them all—"To me to live is not wealth nor knowledge not fame nor glory but Christ. Christ first, last, midst all, and always Christ."

Christ is the *giver of life*—"I have come that they may have life, and have it to the full" (John 10:10).

Christ is *life itself*—"I no longer live, but Christ lives in me" (Galatians 2:20).

Christ is the *model of my life*—"Be perfect, therefore, as your heavenly Father is perfect" (Matthew 5:48).

Christ is the *aim of my life*—I desire to make known "the

power and coming of our Lord Jesus Christ" (2 Peter 1:16).

Christ is the *reward of my life*—"Thanks be to God for his indescribable gift!" (2 Corinthians 9:15).

Paul says:

When I travel, it is on Christ's errands.

When I suffer, it is in Christ's service.

When I speak, the theme is Christ.

When I write, Christ fills my letters.

Joy in Service (Philippians 2)

Paul gives us the wonderful Example of the Christian life that we may follow in His steps. We must imitate Christ for although He is Lord of all, He became servant to all! Paul urges the Church to complete his happiness by living together in love and unity. Is there anything more Christlike for Christians to do? "Make my joy complete by being like-minded" (Philippians 2:2). This is not an easy thing to do. It means love without compromise.

What is the most important social grace? Elegance of manners? The gift of saying agreeable things? No, it is courtesy of heart and not mere fashion. D. L. Moody says, "Strife is knocking others down; vainglory is setting oneself up." "In humility consider others better than yourselves" (2:3) is an astonishing phrase; in other words, "I am willing to be third."

We must always bear in our thoughts the example of Jesus Christ (2:5-11). Paul says, "Your attitude should be the same as that of Christ Jesus," which is self-forgetting love. Although He was God, He humbled Himself. Not only did Christ take on Himself the form of man, but also the form of a servant. Then He humbled Himself more. He who was author of life became obedient unto death. But even more than this, He faced an ignominious death, "even the death of a cross." This must be our spirit (See Matthew 16:25.)

Paul is practical as well as profound. He never leaves us in the clouds. He never separates knowledge from action. Christianity is both life and creed. The creed without the life amounts to little. After Paul has scaled the heights in Christ's exaltation, he has no idea of leaving us there. "Therefore, my dear friends...continue to work out your salvation with fear and trembling" (Philippians 2:12). "Work out" means live out—not working for salvation, but showing the works of salvation. God has a plan for each of our lives as He had for Jesus. We must live it out. It is an absolutely personal matter. No one can do it for you. God plants in our hearts salvation in Christ, great, divine and wonderful to be lived out. Can you go about it without "fear and trembling"? Happy is the person who finds God's plan for life and falls in with it.

Christian experience is not something that is going on around you, but in you. "Christ liveth in me"!

"Do everything without complaining or arguing" (2:14), Paul is saying, "Don't be grouchy! You can't glow if you are!"

Having committed our lives to the control of the Lord, we are under orders. Don't murmur or complain! "If God is supreme, why did He allow this thing to happen?" should never pass your lips. You cannot ask your Commander in chief the "why" of anything He asks you to do.

Paul shows us, too, that there is a sacrificial side of the Christian life. That which costs nothing amounts to nothing. Paul feared his work might be "in vain." So much in life is done "in vain." Are we running "in vain," or working "in vain"? So many days are spent in vain! So many books are written in vain! So many sermons are printed in vain! So many gifts are given in vain! The Christian life should be a sacrifice if we are to follow Christ. Does your faith cost anything?

But if Christ is our Example, then we see that there is no cross without a crown. If we suffer with Him, we shall also reign with Him. We are God's luminaries in a dark age. No flame can shine brightly when it is filthy. The Christian who brings honor to the Lord must be faultless, innocent and unblamable.

Joy in Fellowship (Philippians 3)

Paul tells the Philippians that the duty of all Christians is that they be joyful. A long-faced Christian is the worst advertisement against Christianity. The world doesn't want a greater burden; it wants a light heart. How can a Christian be joyful in a world so full of sorrow? Paul tells us in the first verse—"Rejoice in the Lord"!

Saul of Tarsus, a man rich in religious background, seeking for the best, had gone from one religion to another. He was an earnest searcher after truth and blameless as far as the law was concerned, but he had found nothing that satisfied him. One day Christ found him, and in this marvelous paragraph we see he gladly sacrificed everything and counted the treasures of this world as nothing in comparison with Christ. He set a new standard of values. He had a new reason for life. Christ had stepped in between Paul and his old ideals and made him change the headings at the top of his ledger. He erased "gains" (credits) and wrote "loss" (debits). This was his choice in life.

Paul weighed both the world and Christ and remembered the words of the Lord Jesus, "What good will it be for a man if he gains the whole world, yet forfeits his soul?" (Matthew 16:26).

In Philippians 3:12-14, Paul tells us that every person's life is a plan of God! The one thing I do should be to carry out this plan. Neither the successes nor failures of the past must keep me from "pressing on" today. "I am ready for anything and equal to anything through Him Who infuses inner strength into me; I am self-sufficient in Christ's sufficiency" (4:13, *AMP*).

When Paul met the Lord on the way to Damascus (Acts 9), his whole being was changed. His eyes were opened. He discovered in Christ a store of spiritual wealth that made him count all that he had as trash (Philippians 3:7). He had boasted of lineage and pedigree; he was blameless in the law; he had every honor and privilege, but now he was willing to lose everything to gain Christ.

Here are some of the ambitions of Paul's heart. Mark these in your Bible.

"That I may gain Christ" (3:8). Christ had won him. Now he wished to win Him as a daily prize.

"I want to know Christ" (3:10). There are degrees of knowing Him.

"And be found in him" (3:9). To be found in Christ means we are blameless and complete.

"I want to know Christ and the power of his resurrection" (3:10). The power of the gospel is in a risen Christ.

"I want to know...the fellowship of sharing in his sufferings" (3:10). This means a life consecrated to Him, conformable unto His death.

"I press on to take hold of that for which Christ Jesus took hold of me" (3:12). He wanted to know Christ's purpose for seizing him on that road to Damascus.

"I press on toward the goal to win the prize" (3:14). The higher the calling, the greater the prize.

Do you know that your citizenship is in heaven, that you have been born from above? (3:20-21). Therefore we should live as citizens of a better country, a heavenly Kingdom. Love not the world nor the things of this world, but be loyal to Him who rules in the "heavenly Jerusalem." When Christ comes, He will change these bodies of ours into bodies like unto His own fit for His heavenly kingdom.

Christ's residence was for thirty-three years here on earth, but it did not naturalize Him as a citizen of earth. Let us not forget where our citizenship is. Remember Paul's advice in Romans 12:2: "Do not conform any longer to the pattern of this world, but be transformed by the renewing of your mind."

Joy in Rewards (Philippians 4)

"Rejoice in the Lord always. I will say it again: Rejoice! Let your gentleness be evident to all. The Lord is near" (Philippians 4:4-5). This blessed hope of Christ's coming again casts its gracious influence over all of life. Paul prays that the Christian may have joy at all times and not be worried by cares.

D. L. Moody says of verse six:
"Be careful for nothing;
Be prayerful for everything;
Be thankful for anything!"

Yes, the way to be anxious about nothing is to be prayerful about everything. The prayer of faith must be a prayer of thanksgiving because faith knows how much it owes to God. Put your prayers into God's hands and go off and leave them there. Do not worry about them. Give them completely as the farmer gives the wheat to the soil after the soil has been properly plowed. If you do this, then the peace of God will stand guard over your heart and mind.

Guard your thoughts! Paul tells us what to think about and remember. "As [a man] thinketh in his heart, so is he" (Proverbs 23:7, *KJV*). Thoughts determine your life! Therefore whatsoever things are true, honest, just, pure, lovely, of good report, virtuous, praiseworthy, think on these things!

Paul expressed his gratitude for the loving thought that had promoted the church at Philippi to send him gifts. He was especially happy about their gifts, not because he was in want, for he had learned to be content in any circumstance with Christ (Philippians 4:11). He could do all things through Christ who strengthened him. But their gifts meant "fruit that may abound to your account" (4:17, *KJV*). He opened God's bank account to them. "And my God will meet all your needs according to his glorious riches in Christ Jesus" (4:19).

Chapter 39

A Quick Look at the New Testament

Matthew Through Philippians

Information Please

1. Which of the Gospels portrays the manhood of Jesus?
   (a) Matthew, (b) Mark, (c) Luke, (d) John.
2. In which Gospel is the plan of salvation best presented?
   (a) Matthew, (b) Mark, (c) Luke, (d) John.
3. The Sermon on the Mount is stated at greatest length in:
   (a) Matthew, (b) Mark, (c) Luke, (d) John.
4. The genealogy of Jesus is given in:
   (a) Matthew, (b) Mark, (c) Luke, (d) John.

What's the Answer?

1. Name five outstanding miracles of Jesus.

2. Name three persons with whom Jesus had a personal interview.

3. In which one of Paul's letters is the "Love Chapter" found?

4. How is Jesus portrayed in each of the four Gospels?

5. How is Jesus portrayed in each of the six of Paul's Epistles we have studied so far?

    Romans:

    1 Corinthians:

    2 Corinthians:

    Galatians:

    Ephesians:

    Philippians:

6. Why did Paul call the Galatians "foolish"?
    a. Because they followed other leaders
    b. Because they turned back from their liberty in Christ to the bondage of the law
    c. Because they formed a new church.

7. A Christian's "works" count before God:
    a. For his or her salvation
    b. For rewards
    c. For escape of punishment.

8. Name the Epistles of Paul in their order from Romans to Philippians.

9. Trace the spread of Christianity from Jerusalem to Rome as given in the book of Acts.

Completion Test

1. Matthew was written especially for the _____
2. The only Gospel that tells the story of the wise men is

    _____
3. The two greatest preachers in the book of Acts whose
    names begin with *P* are _____ and _____ .
4. The greatest event in the book of Acts begins with *P* also.
    What is it? _____

Chapter 40

Understanding Colossians

Colossians Portrays Jesus Christ, Our Life

Selected Bible Readings

Sunday:	Paul's Greeting and Prayer (Colossians 1:1-14)
Monday:	Seven Superiorities of Christ (Colossians 1:15-29)
Tuesday:	Christ Exalted (Philippians 2:1-16)
Wednesday:	Complete in Christ (Colossians 2:1-19)
Thursday:	Old and New Man (Colossians 2:20—3:11)
Friday:	Christian Living (Colossians 3:12-25)
Saturday:	Christian Graces (Colossians 4:1-18)

Ephesians and Colossians were written about the same time, while Paul was a prisoner in Rome. They both contain great doctrines of the gospel, and were to be read aloud in the churches. They are very similar in style, yet very different in emphasis.

Ephesians talks about all believers, calling them the "body of Christ." Colossians talks about the Head of the body, Jesus Christ.

In Ephesians, the Church of Christ is the important item. In Colossians, the Christ of the Church is emphasized.

Both are needed. There cannot be a body without a head, nor a head without a body. Notice this all the way through Colossians—"Christ," "Christ," "Christ."

Heresy had broken out in the church at Colosse, misleading the young believers, calling for the worship of angels (Colossians 2:18) and a strict observance of Jewish ceremonies (2:16,21). This heresy was a mixture of Jewish, Greek and Oriental religions, and all this called forth this statement of the truth of the Supreme Lordship of Christ. This Epistle draws a faithful portrait of Christ in all His glory and dignity.

Christ Our Head

Christ is all in all. The failure of the Colossians was at this very point, not holding fast to the Lord. The place Christ holds in any religious teaching determines whether it is true or false. Some thought in Paul's day, as now, that Jesus was but a man, and Christ was the divine Spirit that came at His baptism and left Him at the cross. This meant that Christ did not die, but simply that Jesus died. You can see that this is the root error of many cults today. Every modern cult is based on just the same old heresy and misrepresents the truth in regard to Christ and His Person and work. It is good for us, in reading the Colossian letter, to examine our own belief and see that we always put the Head, Christ Jesus, in His rightful place in our thinking and glorify this wonderful One.

Have you noticed that many of the Epistles were used to answer the heresies that crept into the early churches everywhere?

This letter begins, like twelve others, with the name of Paul, and is addressed to Gentile believers.

The church was likely founded by Epaphras (1:7) in the town of Colosse, about 100 miles east of Ephesus. It consisted of Gentile Christians. Philemon was a member. Paul kept in close touch with the people and was greatly beloved.

Epaphras went to Rome to tell Paul of the heresies that were creeping into the church. These false teachings took Christ off the throne and denied His headship of the Church. To help answer them, Paul sent this letter back by Epaphras. He writes especially on the preeminence and deity of Christ, for Christ is very God.

The gospel, by this time, had been brought to "all over the world" (1:6) and had been "has been proclaimed to every creature" (1:23). Thirty-two years after Christ's death, the gospel had reached the whole Roman world. It needed only one generation to establish the Church as a worldwide fact.

The Church's position "in Christ":

United in Christ—Colossians 2:2
Complete in Christ—2:10
Dead in Christ—2:20
Buried with Christ—Romans 6:4
Risen with Christ—Colossians 3:1.

Christ Our Life

"And your life is now hidden with Christ in God" (Colossians 3:3).
This Epistle tells us that Christ is our life and we are complete in
Him (2:10).

The Christian life is not a creed or a system of doctrine or a
certain kind of worship, but a life that is Christ's very own within you. Christ is all in all:

In His deity—The image of the invisible God (1:15)

In creation—Sovereign Creator of the universe (1:15-16)

In preeminence—Before all things (1:18)

In redemption—Reconciling the universe through His blood
(1:20-22)

In headship—Over all principalities and powers (1:18; 2:14)

In His Church—The Head of the body (1:18; 2:19)

In His indwelling presence—The Christian's hope (1:27).

God has given Christ preeminence in all things (1:18). We dare
not give Him a lower place!

In Romans we are justified in Christ; in 1 Corinthians we are
enriched in Christ; in 2 Corinthians we are comforted in Christ;
in Galatians we are free in Christ; in Ephesians we are made alive
in Christ; in Philippians we are joyful in Christ; in Colossians we
are complete in Christ.

Colossians presents the glorious culmination of it all. We are
"complete in him." We are "rooted and built up"; we are
"grounded and settled." We discover the facts of this building
process in the four chapters of this book.

Building "downward," rooted in Jesus, *established and firm* (1:23)

Building "upward," *built up in him* (2:7)

Building "inward," *hidden with Christ* (3:3)

Building "outward," *be wise in the way you act towards out-
siders* (4:5).

"The deeper life" is rooted in eternity. It begins in Him Who was "in the beginning with God." God gives eternal life.

The "higher life" is the life Jesus is living for us at the right hand of God, and living in us, for "I have been crucified with Christ and I no longer live, but Christ lives in me" (Galatians 2:20).

The "inner life" is all the life we have as Christians. It is the life "hid with Christ" in God. It is life real and sufficient, for we are "complete in him" (Colossians 3:3; 2:10).

The "outer life" is that expression of life that makes Christ known to others. "What you are speaks so loudly, people cannot hear what you say."

The Deeper Life (Colossians 1)

Paul opens this letter as he opens so many: "We always thank God" (Colossians 1:3). He rejoices in the good news from the brethren scattered abroad in the various churches he founded.

Notice Paul's favorite words, "faith," "love" and "hope" (vv. 4-5), which he so often uses. He wants everyone to have faith in Christ, love toward others and hope of heaven.

Paul tells us the secret of the deeper life that we as Christians should have in Christ. Dig downward first and become "established and firm" ("grounded and settled," *KJV*) in Christ (1:23). Send the taproot of your Christian faith down deep into His life, as the great oak sends its root into the heart of the earth. We find that storms may beat against the solid oak, but it stands fast, for it is rooted deep. In sharp contrast is the California redwood. It may have acres of roots, but they are spread close to the surface of the earth. The giant redwood lifts its head several hundred feet into the air, but it has no taproot. Its roots cannot hold. When the storm beats against it, it topples.

Send your roots down into Christ. The source of your life is in Him. The Japanese have a way of cutting the taproot of the trees of the forest and confining them in miniature gardens and flower pots. The tree gains its life from the little surface roots and only grows to a few feet in height. Every soul is stunted until it puts its taproot into God and begins to draw on Him.

Next Paul presents a glowing description of the mighty Christ, the Superior One. He is "all in all."

We find in this first scene that not only are we in Christ, but also that Christ is in us. "Christ in you, the hope of glory" (1:27). This is what it is to be a Christian: living in Him—this glorious, wonderful Person, the Creator of this universe, in whom we have redemption through His blood—and having Him live in us.

In closing this scene, notice Paul's beautiful prayer for the Church in Colossians 1:9-14. He expresses his desire for all Christian believers.

That they might be filled with a knowledge of Christ's will. He wants us to know how to live a Christlike life, for the fullness of Christ's wisdom will keep us from error.

That they might walk worthy of the Lord, fruitful in work, increasing in knowledge.

That they might be strengthened with might so as to be able to withstand all temptations.

That they might be thankful.

The Higher Life (Colossians 2)

"So then, just as you received Christ Jesus as Lord, continue to live in him, rooted and built up in him" (Colossians 2:6-7). Paul is always practical. Again he says, "Act out what you believe. You commenced well. Go on as you have begun! We have received Christ, and have been grounded and settled in Him Let us therefore walk in Him" (see 1:23). Paul always wants our walk and life to correspond with our belief. It is sad when a Christian believes in Christ and acts like the devil. No one will accept our profession as sincere. If we have received Christ, let us walk as He would have us. If we have been rooted in Him, let us grow up in Him. If we have been founded on Him, let us be builded up on Him. All of these are outward evidences of a changed heart. "Walking" expresses life. "Growing" exhibits an inner power. "Building up" shows progress of character until the structure is complete.

We have to do a great deal more than just believe "truths about Christ." We must "receive Christ" if we are to have life. We cannot earn it or purchase it. It is a free gift (2:6). We are rooted in Christ. That means we draw our nourishment from Him. A plant cannot grow unless it is in touch with the life-giving soil. We are built up in Him. We have our foundation in Him. Every structure needs a foundation. All this must be our experience if we would be built up. The Christian life is starting in Christ and then growing in His grace and gifts. We must be as dependent on Christ for steadfastness of walk as we were for our assurance of salvation.

All the life we have as Christians is the life "in Him."

Walking in Him—2:6

Rooted in Him—2:7

Built up in Him—2:7

Brought to perfection in Him—2:10

Dead with Him—2:20

Risen with Him—3:1

Hidden with Him—3:3.

This is the life—real and satisfying eternal life. We find in this chapter that Christ is all-sufficient, "For in Christ all the fullness of the Deity lives in bodily form" (2:9). This is a tremendous truth for us to grasp. In this Jesus, who walked on the earth, dwelt the whole Godhead. But more than this—in Him was the fulness of the Godhead.

Let us look again. "For in Christ all the fullness of the Deity lives in bodily form." This Jesus was very God in all of His fulness. Neither angels, nor prophets, nor saints rank with Him—for He is the very embodiment of the divine fulness!

Our lives must first be built downward, "rooted in Christ." Next we must build upward, "rooted and built up in him, strengthened in the faith" (2:7), rearing a stately structure to His praise, and of course, wholly by His grace. This is the higher life.

The higher you go with the Lord, the steadier is your disposition, the less disturbing are temptations and the smoother is your everyday life.

We see Paul's personal concern for the Church at Colosse. He longs for the Christians to be established and kept firm in their convictions so that the shrewd philosophers and legalists of their day would not deceive them. The best way to be protected from the snares of the world and its philosophy is an understanding of the perfection of Christ, for He is all and in all. Be rooted and grounded in the Word lest you be swept away by false teachers.

Some of the popular street-corner philosophers of the day were teaching that people are unworthy to approach Christ directly. They needed to approach Him by means of angels (2:18). Some in our day teach that we need to approach God through the virgin Mary or through some other person. Christ says He is the only mediator between God and people. He adds, "I am the way...No one comes to the Father except through me" (John 14:6). Paul rebukes the Colossians for their failure to recognize the supreme Headship of Christ and the only Mediator between God and people.

Paul reminds the Christian that when Jesus died on the cross, He freed us from the law. Therefore we need not let others judge us regarding food or drink or severe treatment of the body (see Colossians 2:16-23). The sacrifice God asks is a broken spirit, not a beaten body. A sinful heart can dwell in a fasting body. Self-imposed hardships are of no value in offsetting the thoughts of a sinful heart. We like to think that when we have done something bad we can erase our record by doing something we think is good. But we must remember that only what Christ does is good, for "there is no one who does good, not even one" (Romans 3:12). If *God* is taken out of *good*, nothing—o—is left.

The Inner Life (Colossians 3)

Building our life cannot be only downward, "rooted in Christ," but upward, "built up in him," but our building must also be inward. Let us know that Christ is the believer's life. Many believe that Christ gave us life as one would put a living seed into a flower pot. The pot would hold a detached thing—life. But Christ is more than that. He Himself is in the believer. The life that is in Christ is in the believer. The illustration He gives, "I am the vine; you are the branches" (John 15:5).

We find that our new life in Christ makes us less interested in the things the world offers. We become "dead to the world." We find ourselves "hid with Christ," and as we know Him we discover, one by one, the beauties of the Lord Jesus. "Compassion, kindness, humility, gentleness and patience" (Colossians 3:12). "Let the word of Christ dwell in you richly" (3:16). It will make a difference.

The Brown family lived in a house that was an eyesore in the neighborhood. Weeds grew over the porch; the shades were always torn; the curtains were sagging and soiled. One day in passing by the house we saw the grass cut; fresh white curtains were hung at the windows. The broken steps were mended. "When did the Browns move?" we asked.

"Why, they haven't moved," answered our neighbor.

"Oh, yes, they have. The Browns don't live in that house anymore. A new family has moved in. I haven't seen the people yet, but I know by the appearance that a new owner occupies the house."

Yes, our outward life will be different. Others will see Christ living in us.

Because we are rooted in Christ and our life is in Him, we are not only identified with Him in His death, but we are also in union with Him in His resurrection. In Christ's death we died to sin, and in His resurrection we rose to walk in a new life. Because we are "risen with Christ," we should seek those things that are above, and show to the best of our ability the goal of our lives.

For example, the submarine is made to travel under the water. Yet, every submarine is equipped with a periscope by which it seeks those things that are above. It travels in the water, but the well-being of those in it depends on a knowledge of what is above.

We live in the world, but we must set our minds (affections) on things above, for we are citizens of a heavenly country. Look upon Christ and He will draw you upward.

The Christian's Wardrobe

First we must "put off" the old nature. Paul tells us to put it to death (3:5-9). After we receive our new life in Christ Jesus, then we must "put to death, therefore, whatever belongs to your earthly nature." It should not be necessary to tell Christians they must put off things that are more like the devil than the Savior!

Any self-denial or asceticism not built on our union with Christ, whether practiced by the priests of India or the Buddhists of Thailand or the monks of Catholicism or a Protestant layperson, is condemned at the start.

Christianity is not a series of giving-ups; it is a new life. Children do not give up playing jacks; they outgrow it. As we come to know Christ better we find that some things no longer interest us. Christ adds so much to our lives that there is no room for the old things. The first thing we know, we have lost interest in the old and are busy with the new life in Christ.

Paul admonishes us to destroy our old nature and "put off" all its vices. Read over Paul's black catalogue. There is immorality, impurity, passion and greed. Then there are passionate anger and wrath and the many sins of speech. Let us forever give up these sins. It is possible in Christ.

Can you imagine how ridiculous you would look if when you went to buy a new suit you refused to take off the one you had on, but rather insisted that the new one should be tried on without "putting off" the old one! This is what many Christians do. They try to put the garment of a new life on over their old nature. It just doesn't fit. We must lay aside sin first, then "put on the new man."

A Christian's conduct is what people see you do. As clothes indicate what kind of a person you are—they tell whether you are careful or careless; they tell whether you are a soldier or civilian, a king or a commoner—so outward expression will show "whose [you are] and whom [you] serve" (Acts 27:23).

Now Paul thinks of our new nature in Christ. "Put on the new self" (3:10). This new nature we receive from Christ is ever being renewed as we grow in the knowledge of our Lord and Savior. But we must not become so absorbed in our great privileges in Christ that we neglect our duty to our fellow humans. Our knowing Christ should make us much more thoughtful of others. The new Christian not only puts away, but also puts on or adds to his or her life. Let us "put on" the excellences of this new life, such as tenderness, kindness, humility, patience, forgiveness and love (Colossians 3:12-14). Yes, these are the things with which we are to adorn ourselves. If we lived like this we would find perfection on earth. Paul says all these virtues are like pieces of clothing, all held in place by a belt of love. This fills our lives with the peace of God.

Do you remember how Luther Burbank (1849-1926, American horticulturist, botanist and pioneer plant breeder) took the little wild daisy and developed it into a bloom of five to seven inches in diameter, and the little poppy developed into a blossom ten inches across? So our Christian graces must be cultivated and enlarged. Too often they perish for want of care. Too often the fruit of our lives looks only like the ordinary fruit of the world. We must grow into the full stature of the fullness of Christ. As long as we live, there is something new for us to learn. We should never stop growing.

Set down all the commands given to you in this chapter.

Christ Is Our All or Nothing

Yes, "Christ is all, and is in all" (3:11). If Christ is not all in your life, He is nothing. No surer test can be given to any false teaching of today than this: Where does it put Jesus Christ? The Bible says: "Every spirit that acknowledges that Jesus Christ has come in the flesh is from God" (1 John 4:2). This is the test of every creed. Does it proclaim that "we have redemption, the forgiveness of sins" (1:14)? If so, it is true; if not, it is false (1 John 4:1-3).

A Christian heart is a singing heart (Colossians 3:16). Christ wants us to be taught in His Word, and then He wants us to express our joy in Him by singing hymns.

The Outward Life (Colossians 4)

This chapter introduces another phase of our life in Christ, the outward life. We found we must build within, cultivating the virtues of the new life in Christ. But there is something more. We want our new life to be seen and felt among others (Colossians 4:5). This is the way we present Christ to the world. Remember, "Christians" mean "little Christs." The life of Christ is not written only by great authors such as Farrar (Frederic William Farrar, 1831-1903, British, Dean of Canterbury, prolific and influential author) or Edersheim (Alfred Edersheim, 1825-89, Austrian biblical scholar and author). It was not ended when the Gospels were completed. Christ is living in us. His life is told today in living Epistles that are known and read by all people.

Chapter 41

Understanding First Thessalonians

First Thessalonians Portrays Jesus Christ, the Coming One

Selected Bible Readings

Sunday:	Christ's Coming an Inspiration to Young Christians (1 Thessalonians 1)
Monday:	Christ's Coming an Encouragement to the Faithful Servant (1 Thessalonians 2)
Tuesday:	Christ's Coming an Incentive to Love Among Christians (1 Thessalonians 3:1—4:12)
Wednesday:	Christ's Coming a Comfort to the Bereaved (1 Thessalonians 4:13-18)
Thursday:	Christ's Coming a Challenge to Holy Living (1 Thessalonians 5)
Friday:	Christ's Sudden Coming (Matthew 24:1-27)
Saturday:	Tribulation Days (Matthew 24:29-51)

The second coming of the Lord Jesus Christ is the truth Paul is presenting in these two letters to the Thessalonians, and it would be missing the mark not to recognize it. The two Epistles contain twenty different references to the coming of the Lord. This is the hope of the Church. It is mentioned in the closing of every chapter of 1 Thessalonians: "To wait for his Son from heaven" (1:10); "in the presence of our Lord Jesus Christ when he comes" (2:19); "in the presence of our God and Father when our Lord Jesus comes with all his holy ones" (3:13); "caught up together with them in the clouds to meet the Lord in the air" (4:17); and in the last chapter, "May your whole spirit, soul and body be kept blameless at the coming of our Lord Jesus Christ" (5:23). In view of all this, should anyone raise the question: Will Christ come again?

Christ's first coming was sudden and a surprise to the philosophers of His time. We learn that His second coming will be no less surprising.

Paul, accompanied by Timothy and Silas, had spent only three Sundays at Thessalonica on his second missionary journey, but during that time he not only founded a church, but he also grounded it firmly in the faith. In the short time he was there, Paul created a great stir. His enemies accused him of having "turned the world upside down" (Acts 17:6, *KJV*). On account of this great stir, the brethren sent the apostle away. He went on to Berea and Athens and Corinth. It was from here he wrote this first letter to the Thessalonians and sent it by Timothy. We know he had only been gone a short time, for he said he was "torn away from you for a short time" (1 Thessalonians 2:17).

It is an unprecedented thing even in the ministry of Paul, this establishment of a flourishing church in less than a month. He preached to them for three Sabbath days, although no doubt he continued his meetings during these weeks. Paul's success in Thessalonica has not been the usual experience of missionaries among the non-Christian peoples. Carey (William Carey, 1761-1834, British missionary and author) in India, Judson (Adoniram Judson, 1788-1850, American pioneer missionary) in Burma, Morrison (Robert Morrision, 1782-1834, British pioneer missionary) in China, Moffatt (Robert Moffatt, 1795-1883, Scottish missionary, translator and father-in-law to David Livingstone) in Africa each waited seven years for their first converts. But here, the Holy Spirit allowed Paul to reap a sudden harvest.

During this short stay in Thessalonica, a great number of Greeks and women believed (Acts 17:4). Paul began at once to feed this church with the meat of the Word. He talked of the Holy Spirit (1 Thessalonians 1:6), of the Trinity (1:6) and of the second coming of Christ (1:10). The church was composed mostly of Gentiles rather than Jewish believers.

Being greatly concerned about the young converts, Paul sent

Timothy from Athens to strengthen their faith and to bring him news of how they were getting along. Timothy brought back a favorable report that was a great comfort to the apostle-founder of the church. However, Timothy had discovered that there were some faults to be corrected. The church held some false views concerning the Lord's coming. They were worried about some who had died, fearing that they would not have any part in the rapture and glory of the Lord's return. Others were so overwhelmed by the truth of Christ's return that they were neglecting their daily tasks (4:10-12). Wishing to correct these wrong views and to inspire and comfort these new converts, Paul wrote this Epistle.

This is an intimate Epistle. The letter is a heart-to-heart talk. Paul gets very close to his "brothers" (i.e., brothers and sisters in the church). This word occurs fourteen times. It is a message of comfort and instruction to those who are in the midst of persecution.

There should be nothing doubtful or divisive about this "blessed hope" of our Lord's return. No one can read the Word without finding the teaching. Let us not quarrel with one another about so sweet a message as our Lord's "I will come again." This is the Christian's hope. Let us rather be watchful, for we know not the day nor the hour when the Son of man comes.

Christ's Coming (1 Thessalonians 1)

If you wish to know how to get on with other folks in Christian work, just go over the things Paul said under the guidance of the Spirit. This is the kind of service the Lord Jesus would have us render in His name.

Paul did not try to please others in ways that displeased God.

Paul did not try to capture others by flattery.

Paul was not covetous of what they had.

Paul was not seeking glory for himself out of his work.

Paul kept at his task day and night.

Paul always encouraged others.

In Paul's greeting he includes his fellow-workers, Silas and Timothy. Silas had been with him when he founded the church at

Thessalonica, and Timothy had been his special messenger to them, carrying the good news of their progress and reporting their needs back at Corinth. We can learn much from Paul. He knew the secret of friendship so many would like to possess. He loved people. The Bible tells us how to have friends. "There is a friend who sticks closer than a brother" (Proverbs 18:24). This is just what Paul did. He always acknowledged others in his service and expressed appreciation for their part in every work done.

Praying as Paul Prayed

"We always thank God for all of you, mentioning you in our prayers" (1:2). Do we follow up our new converts as Paul did? Teacher, do you? Paul's converts were in more than a score of different cities, yet he carried them "all" in his heart and kept in touch with them.

Do you have a prayer list? Do you pray for others by name? Do you "make mention" of your friends before God? If you find it difficult to speak to others about Christ, try speaking to Christ about others, and soon you will be speaking to others about Him. All of us can do this, even the most timid.

Are we realizing as Christians why we are in the world? How seriously are we taking our task? Have we any evidence that we have been "approved by God" (1 Thessalonians 2:4) to be entrusted with the gospel? Paul sets forth in this letter the intensity of his ministry; his willingness to die for his new converts; and his dealing with each one.

Paul thanks God for this church. The beauty of this church did not consist of a gorgeous building of mortar and stone, but a people who are in God the Father and in the Lord Jesus Christ (1:1). He is very pleased about the wonderful growth these young converts have made. He holds them up as an example everywhere he goes (1:7). Already their zeal has made a profound impression all over Macedonia and Achaia (Greece), and everyone is talking about the wonderful way God is working in this young, vigorous church at Thessalonica.

"You became a model to all the believers in Macedonia and Achaia" (1:7). This is what everyone in the world is looking for—

Christians who live the Christian life, who act what they believe. This is just what the Thessalonians did. Nothing was mentioned of the financial condition of their "annual budget." But their faith in God was known everywhere (1:8). Their missionary enthusiasm in sounding forth the Word of God had been felt all through Greece. They were what every church should be.

Life in Three Tenses (1 Thessalonians 1:9-10)

Past tense—"turned to God": The believers at Thessalonica "turned to God from idols." There must be a personal turning to God from sin and unbelief if one is to become a child of God. The idols of our lives are numerous and varied. To turn to God is to forsake everything that would divide our affections or hinder us in following Him with our whole heart.

Present tense—"to serve the living God": They "turned to God from idols to serve the living and true God" (1:9). What a change! Serving a living God instead of going through a dead ritual that only mocked their needs by a dead silence!

Future tense—"to wait for His Son from heaven": They were serving and waiting! These early Christians believed that Christ would come again, as He had promised. This was called "that blessed hope." The prophets of old waited for the coming of the Messiah long ages before He came, but "in the fulness of time" Christ did come. The Church may have to wait long for His promised coming again the second time. Many have lost the vision and hope. But in the fullness of time He will come as He said. Mark in your Bible these blessed promises: John 14:3; Acts 1:11; 1 Thessalonians 4:16; Revelation 1:7.

Paul believes that his one reward for all his toil and pain and suffering will consist in presenting to Christ these converts of his ministry when He comes again.

Christ's Coming (1 Thessalonians 2)

Paul gives us these descriptions of his services at Thessalonica:
"Not a failure"—2:1
"We dared to tell you his gospel" in spite of contention—2:2

Not from "error" or "impure motives," nor trickery—2:3
"Not trying to please men but God"—2:4
"Never used flattery"—2:5
For God's glory, not "for praise from men"—2:6
"Gentle"—2:7
Affectionate—2:8
"Worked night and day"—2:9
Backed by holy living—2:10-12
Successful in its results—2:13-18.

What a man was Paul! He preached to please God, and lived to convince people of the truth of his preaching. His conduct commended his preaching. The Thessalonians became an eager missionary church. He was not a flatterer, neither did he seek wealth. He came as simple as a child and as gentle as a nurse caring for little children. He was never idle, but toiled night and day. Giving them this example of his own life, he pleaded with them to make their daily lives worthy of the name "Christian."

Paul urged the Thessalonians "to live lives worthy of God" (2:12). A Christian's walk is a Christian's life. An Indian pastor who was worried about the inconsistent lives among some of his flock said to a missionary, "There is much crooked walk by those who make good talk." Our walk and our talk should be twins going along on the same trail.

It is so true for young people that this life holds such strong interests, such demanding problems, such vital experiences, that even this most blessed hope for the future is not the only teaching we must help them find in God's Word. Paul's letter to the Thessalonians proves how well Paul knew this, for it abounds in plenty to do right now while we wait for that day of Christ's appearing. All the way through, Paul enjoins us to "work" and "labor" while we "hope."

Paul looked forward during these trying days to the "Lord Jesus Christ at his coming." His greatest reward, after he has seen his wonderful Savior's face, will be to present to Christ the young converts of his ministry, letting them share in the glory of His advent. They will be his "crown of rejoicing" (2:19-20, KJV).

Christ's Coming (1 Thessalonians 3:1—4:12)

This scene describes Paul's "labor of love" among the brethren. Paul was aware of the strain under which the members of the church at Thessalonica were living. He sent Timothy from Athens to encourage them under their bitter persecution.

Timothy had brought back the good news of their "faith" and "love." This report filled Paul with unbounded joy. How glad Paul was to hear of their firm stand in the faith and to know that they thought kindly of him and his fellow workers and longed to see them! In the midst of their persecution and suffering, Paul flashed the light of that wonderful day when they would be made "blameless and holy," when they shall be changed in a moment at the return of Christ and His holy ones (1 Thessalonians 3:13).

The test of any hope a person holds is what it does for him *now*. Paul told them that the coming of the Lord should be an incentive to:

Right living—3:13
Consistent walk—4:1
Purity—4:3-7
Love—4:9-10.

Paul urges personal purity and a life that is consistent with their testimony (4:1). This is the place where most Christians fail. Let us strive to have our ideals beyond reproach. Our attitude toward each other should be one of love. Remember the two commandments Jesus gave. First, "You shall love the Lord your God," and second, "your neighbor as yourself." Paul charges us to "make your love increase and overflow for each other" (3:12; see also 4:9-10).

We discover that looking for His glorious appearing does not mean living a life of idleness (4:11-12). Looking for Christ never makes idle hands. If we were expecting a loved one to return home after a long absence, we would not just sit down as the day of his return approached. Rather, we would be busy getting everything ready, doing the things the loved one wanted done. Can you imagine a mother waiting for her son to come home from the service, just sitting down and letting everything go! She would be fixing up her son's room, making his favorite cake and preparing his favorite food as she listened for his footsteps. This is the true Christian's attitude concerning our blessed Lord's return.

Christ's Coming (1 Thessalonians 4:13-18)

A little band of Indian converts in Canada came to a missionary with a strange request. "We are always hearing what God has done," they said. "Now tell us what He is going to do."

Where would you find an answer to that wise request? We have it in our Bibles. He shall come again (1 Thessalonians 4:16)! If one of your best friends said he was coming to see you, you would not rest until you found out when he was coming and how. But our wonderful Lord and Savior says He is coming and He will transform the whole world and glorify all humanity. Can it be possible that we would be less curious about His coming than we would be about the fleeting visit of an earthly friend?

There is so much in these few verses that end with, "Therefore encourage each other with these words" (4:18). There is comfort because of His sure return.

The Christians at Thessalonica were disturbed because of their mistaken ideas about Christ's coming. They were under the impression that Christ's coming was soon and they were worried about what would happen to those who had died. What part would they have in His glorious coming and kingdom?

When Christ returns to earth, He will not come alone. Our loved ones who have fallen asleep in Christ "will God bring with him." What a meeting that will be! Death does not end all. Parents and children, husbands and wives, loved ones and friends will be united. How anxious we are to know that "ours" will be in that happy throng.

"The Lord himself will come down from heaven" (4:16). Christ does not say He is going to send the messenger of death to bring His bride (the Church) home. He is coming Himself for her! "This same Jesus...will come back in the same way you have seen him go into heaven" (Acts 1:11). And "they will see the Son of Man coming on the clouds of the sky, with power and great glory" (Matthew 24:30). What a marvelous hope this is!

The Dead Shall Rise

Those who have Christian loved ones who have died should not give way to undue sorrow when they lay them in the grave, for they have a double assurance from Christ's Word. There is the hope that one day all the dead in Christ shall rise and the additional assurance that He may come again at any time. When Christ comes, He will greet the believers who are dead first and bring them with Him (see 1 Thessalonians 4:13-14). When the archangel shall sound the trumpet call of God, announcing the Lord's coming, then "the dead in Christ will rise first" to meet Him (4:16). Then those that are alive and remain shall be caught up in the clouds to share with them the glory of His coming, and to be forever with the Lord (4:17-18).

The second coming of Christ was the bright hope of the Early Church. The greatest fact of the past is that Christ came the first time, as a man, and died on the cross to free us from the penalty of sin. The greatest fact of the future is that He is coming again, as a King, to free us from the presence of sin (Matthew 24:42).

The Living Shall Meet Him

"After that, we who are still alive and are left will be caught up together with them in the clouds to meet the Lord in the air" (4:17). Paul assures us that all shall not die before He comes. "We will not all sleep, but we will all be changed—in a flash, in the twinkling of an eye, at the last trumpet. For the trumpet will sound, the dead will be raised imperishable, and we will be changed" (1 Corinthians 15:51-52).

"And so we will be with the Lord forever" (1 Thessalonians 4:17). Made like Him, we shall ever be with Him. He has gone to prepare a place for you. "I will come back and take you to be with me that you also may be where I am" (John 14:3). Heaven is where Christ is now. There we will be. This is heaven's greatest honor conferred on mortals.

This is the order of these great events:

The Lord's descent from heaven

The dead in Christ raised

The living believers changed

The whole company caught up to meet the Lord in the air.

The truth of Christ's coming again thrills us. He went away in the clouds (Acts 1:9). He will come back in triumphal glory (Revelation 1:7). The angels will be with Him (Matthew 25:31). The believers of the past ages will be raised; those that are alive will be changed, and as Enoch and Elijah were translated into heaven, so will the whole Church be caught up, to give a joyful welcome to the returning Savior!

Christ's Coming (1 Thessalonians 5)

Christ's second coming will be like the coming of a thief in the night or like the flood in Noah's time. The world will know nothing of His return. They scoff at the idea. But Jesus said there would be "signs" before His coming so that watchful believers may know when the time is drawing near. Over and over again Jesus told them that His coming would be as a thief in the night (Matthew 24:36,42; 25:13; Mark 13:32-37; Luke 12:40; 21:25-35). He warned His disciples to be ever on the watch. This should be their duty and their attitude. Christians need have no fear of that glorious day.

Don't fix dates! We should live watchful lives. We should not live lives of sleepy indulgence, but "be alert and self-controlled" (1 Thessalonians 5:6). The hope of Christ's coming does not mean a life of idleness. Activity should be the theme of our lives, as we find it in this chapter.

While you wait, Paul gives you a grand octave upon which to play great melodies of hope. Strike every note on this wonderful octave. If you do, your life will be rich.

"Be joyful always"—5:16

"Pray continually"—5:17

"Give thanks in all circumstances"—5:18

"Do not put out the Spirit's fire"—5:19

"Do not treat prophecies with contempt"—5:20

"Test everything"—5:21

"Hold on to the good"—5:21

"Avoid every kind of evil"—5:22.

Have you ever thought of Paul as a human example of what it means to follow Christ? Paul was "as straight as an arrow" and "as clean as a hound's tooth." Paul could challenge a critical examination of his record as a Christian. Paul had a brilliant mind, and a highly cultured one. We are apt to say, "How hard it is for a brainy man to remain loyal to his Maker!" But Paul humbly prostrated his wonderful intellect at the feet of his Master. The only explanation of such a life is that it was entirely yielded to Christ. You can't be perfect in this life, young people. But there is one thing you can do 100 percent. It is what Paul did. You can give yourselves totally and without reserve to the Master.

Discuss the thoughts and habits we must cultivate in ourselves to make our lives count for Christ—physical, mental and spiritual. Discuss methods of cultivation.

"You also must be ready, because the Son of Man will come at an hour when you do not expect him" (Luke 12:40). Every morning when we rise we should say to ourselves, "Be ready for your Lord's return for He may come today." Every night our closing question should be, "Would I be ready for my Lord if He should come before I wake?" (1 Thessalonians 3:12-13). Don't live to be ready to die, but live that you may be ready for Christ's coming (5:4-8)!

Chapter 42

Understanding Second Thessalonians

Second Thessalonians Portrays Jesus Christ, Our Returning Lord

Selected Bible Readings

Sunday:	Paul's Salutations (Ephesians 1:1-2; Philippians 1:1-4; Colossians 1:1-3; 1 Thessalonians 1:1-3; 2 Thessalonians 1:1-4)
Monday:	Christ's Coming Our Comfort (2 Thessalonians 1:5-12)
Tuesday:	Events Preceding Christ's Coming (2 Thessalonians 2:1-12)
Wednesday:	An Appeal to Sound Doctrine (2 Thessalonians 2:13-17)
Thursday:	The Close of the Age (Matthew 24:13-31)
Friday:	Warnings to the Wicked Concerning His Coming (Matthew 24:30-31; Mark 8:38; 2 Thessalonians 1:7-8; Jude 14-15; Revelation 1:7)
Saturday:	Consistent Christian Conduct (2 Thessalonians 3:1-18)

This is the second Epistle about the "blessed hope," or the coming again of our Lord Jesus Christ. These Thessalonians were forward-looking people. Paul talks to them about what is uppermost in their minds and thoughts. The first Epistle says, "He is surely coming again." The second Epistle says, "But work and wait till He comes."

The second coming of Christ is mentioned 318 times in 260 chapters of the New Testament. From this, we see how important this subject is. We read the prophecies of the Old Testament with deepest interest, to find out about our Lord's first advent upon this earth. We should be just as interested to discover what the New Testament teaches regarding His second coming "in power and

great glory." He said He was coming again. Here are His words:
"And if I go and prepare a place for you, I will come back" (John
14:3). He intended that His disciples should understand that His second coming would be in as literal a sense as His going away.

First Thessalonians tells about Christ coming for His Church.
The coming of Christ should be cleared up a bit in our minds.
One day Christ will come to take away His bride, the Church. He
will not be seen of the world at that time, but those who are His,
including the dead in Christ, shall be "caught up" to meet Him.
This is the teaching of 1 Thessalonians. After a period of seven
years of tribulation for those left on the earth, Christ will appear
to the world with His Church to establish His throne upon the
earth. Then He will be seen by all people. His "coming," then,
includes both of these two events, seven years apart. We as
Christians are looking for the first event. The world will not see
Him until the end of the seven years (2 Thessalonians).

Second Thessalonians tells about Christ coming with His
mighty angels. The two events, Christ coming for His Church and
His coming with His mighty angels, are really two aspects of but
one occurrence. Between these two aspects, the Jewish people
reoccupy their own land; the gathering of the Gentile nations
against them takes place; the Antichrist becomes the world ruler;
he makes a covenant with the Jewish people and breaks it.
Following this is the great tribulation. (See Matthew 24:21-22.)
Then Christ will come with His saints and set up His kingdom on
this earth with Jerusalem as the center. Christ will come first and
receive His own unto Himself before that great and terrible day
"of His revelation" in judgment upon His enemies.

This second letter was written almost immediately after
1 Thessalonians. In addition to their trials and persecutions,
the Thessalonian Christians were "unsettled" and "alarmed"
(2 Thessalonians 2:2) by deceivers who made some believe that
they were already passing through the great tribulation and that
the day of the Lord was already here. Paul tries to clear up the difficulty. Always, when war is threatening and sorrow seems to
cover the earth, people wonder if they are in the end "tribulation" time. This second epistle to the Thessalonians is good for

all to read so that these errors in our thinking shall be cleared up.

The church at Thessalonica was carried away with the expectation of Christ's glorious return. Who can help but be thrilled when thinking about His triumphant coming? But we must keep our feet on the ground. We must work while we wait, and pray as we watch, for there is much to do while Christ tarries.

The message here is something like our Lord's word to His disciples in Acts 1:6. You remember their eager question, "Lord, are you at this time going to restore the kingdom?"

"Leave that with the Father," Jesus in effect replied. "Do your day's work and wait. The kingdom is coming."

Christ's Coming (2 Thessalonians 1)

We find that Silas and Timothy are mentioned again in the salutation of this letter. From this we judge that this letter followed the first rather quickly. These two aides were still with Paul. Paul commends the young Christians at Thessalonica warmly before he rebukes them. Let us always look and see if we can find something to commend in those we would criticize. Paul did this so often. He noticed that the promise of the Lord's coming again had inspired them to a growth in faith (2 Thessalonians 1:3) and "perseverance" (1:4). They knew that when Christ came, wrongs would be righted and the Lord would deal with those who had oppressed them, for this was a much persecuted church (1:5-7).

How does Paul describe this event of the coming of Christ? It is sudden and startling. "This will happen when the Lord Jesus is revealed from heaven in blazing fire with his powerful angels." This is no mild appearing for "those who do not know God." It will be very different for His own. We read that unbelievers "will be punished with everlasting destruction and shut out from the presence of the Lord and from the majesty of his power on the day he comes" but that Jesus will "be glorified in his holy people and to be marveled at among all those who have believed" (1:7-10). What a wonderful day this will be for them! Yes, He is coming. Remember the promise of the two as Jesus went into heaven. Read Acts 1:11. What a sharp contrast is shown between the

glorious destiny of believers when Christ comes and the punishment of the wicked (2 Thessalonians 1:7-12)!

Many believe that Christ will not come to set up His kingdom
till all the world is converted, but verses 7-12 of this first chapter
seem to destroy this view. Read them carefully and you will find
that the thing emphasized is that the coming of the Lord will be
a terror for the disobedient, and Christ says, "When the Son of
Man comes, will he find faith on the earth?" (Luke 18:8).

The world has never seen our Lord Jesus since it crucified Him.
He has been hidden from its view. But one day He will appear to
the whole world. In 1 Thessalonians 4, Paul says that at first Christ
will descend from heaven and, with the shout of the archangel, the
Church will be caught away to be forever with the Lord. At that
time He will be seen only by His own. He is coming for His
Church. Paul says, "For the Lord himself will come down from
heaven, with a loud command, with the voice of the archangel and
with the trumpet call of God, and the dead in Christ will rise first.
After that, we who are still alive and are left will be caught up
together with them in the clouds to meet the Lord in the air. And
so we will be with the Lord forever" (1 Thessalonians 4:16-17).

Here in 2 Thessalonians Paul says He will appear to the world with
the angels of His power "in blazing fire with his powerful angels. He
will punish those who do not know God" (1:7-8). First He comes to
take His own out of this world. They will be caught up to meet Him
in the air (1 Thessalonians 4:17). Then He appears for judgment (Jude
15). "Whoever does not have, even what he has will be taken from
him. And throw that worthless servant outside, into the darkness,
where there will be weeping and gnashing of teeth" (Matthew 25:29-
30). Christ is coming in the air for His saints, and later He is coming
to the earth with His saints to set up His kingdom. "When the Son
of Man comes in his glory, and all the angels with him, he will sit on
his throne in heavenly glory" (Matthew 25:31).

Christ's Coming (2 Thessalonians 2)

The Thessalonian Christians were suffering great persecution, and
some of them had begun to think they were passing through the

great tribulation of which Christ spoke as the terrible time that should precede His coming, and that the day of the Lord was already present. They were disturbed about the time of the Lord's coming and were entertaining wrong views about the nearness of His return. The reason for this was that a forged letter and report, both supposed to have come from the apostle Paul, had confused the church and added fuel to the fire (2 Thessalonians 2:2). Jesus had told the disciples, "See to it that no one misleads you" (Matthew 24:4, *NASB*).

The coming again of Christ to the earth is the great future event the Church has looked forward to since Christ ascended from the Mount of Olives and the two men in white apparel said that this same Jesus would so come in like manner as He went into heaven (Acts 1:11). Because of its greatness, it has overshadowed all other events.

One day we traveled up the western highway to Mount Rainier. The morning of the day we arrived the air was clear. The vision was perfect. There was the majestic snow-covered mountain. It seemed so near that it would only be a few minutes until we would be climbing up its side. We ate our breakfast and started off in anticipation. We rode on and there it was, but we hadn't reached it. Every once in a while a low hill and a turn in the road would cut it off from our vision, but though it would reappear in all its glory, we weren't there yet. For three hours we traveled. There it was, the greatest thing on our horizon. Other things fell into insignificance in proportion to its grandeur and importance. Lunchtime came and still we had not arrived, but it kept beckoning us on. Finally it was upon us. We were there! This is a picture of Christ's coming again in glory. It has loomed big on the horizon of every Christian's life since the Early Church. It is the "blessed hope" of the Church. His coming is "at hand" because it is the greatest future event, but it may not be immediate because God must finish His plan before Christ comes. Do not be anxious. God will take care of His own program of the ages. But know this—the "man of lawlessness" (2 Thessalonians 2:3) must be revealed first, and the "secret power of lawlessness" (v. 7) work itself out.

The "man of lawlessness" ("man of sin" in the *KJV*) is the same as the Antichrist spoken of by Daniel the prophet, and by the Lord in Matthew 24:23-24. In Revelation 13:1-8, John tells about him.

The Antichrist is a counterfeit Christ. Satan in a last desperate effort will try to imitate Christ. The world would not have God's Man; now they must have Satan's man.

Before the Day of the Lord's Judgment

The Lord's coming will be "sudden," but sudden does not necessarily mean "immediate." They were to wait expectantly for this time when the Lord would gather His children to Himself. Christ tells us always to be ready. The "day of the Lord" is "at hand" but it will not come until certain things take place. God always follows a program. Paul warns the people against confusing the hope of Christ's coming for His Church with the day of the Lord's judgment. Before this "day of the Lord's judgment," the following things must happen:

A great "falling away" from the faith (2 Thessalonians 2:3, *KJV*). How true this is, in the day in which we are living! People are leaving "the faith that was once for all entrusted to the saints" (Jude 3), and "denying the sovereign Lord who bought them" with His own precious blood (2 Peter 2:1), and "crucifying the Son of God all over again and subjecting him to public disgrace" (Hebrews 6:6). The world acknowledges Christ to be a teacher, but not the Savior. "Because of the increase of wickedness, the love of most will grow cold" (Matthew 24:12). These are perilous times. Scoffers will arise and ridicule the idea of Christ's coming.

The "lawless one" must be revealed. He will be revealed before Christ appears to the world. But not until the Lord has caught up His own will the lawless one come into public view (2 Thessalonians 2:8). This "lawless one" is described in 2:4. He will oppose God; he has the title "Antichrist."

The "man of lawlessness" will open his awful campaign against the Lord. When Christ comes, He will find the Antichrist ruling with all power and signs and lying wonders. It will be a time marked with strong delusions. This is Paul's prediction of the Antichrist. "The sin of man has its final outcome in the man of sin." Read Matthew 24:24. He will be destroyed by Christ.

The Antichrist—"Christ's counterfeit":

Will establish himself in Jerusalem—Matthew 24:15

Will make war with the saints—Revelation 13:7

Will be worshiped as God—2 Thessalonians 2:4

Will do signs and lying wonders—2 Thessalonians 2:9

Will work for only three and a half years—Revelation 13:5-6

Will be cast into the lake of fire at Christ's coming—Revelation 19:20.

Is the World Getting Better?

Does Paul teach that the world is getting better? Is it true that the preaching of the gospel is going to win the whole world for Christ? If so, has the gospel failed? What is God's plan for this present age?

The gospel has not failed. It is accomplishing just what Christ intended it should accomplish—the gathering out from the world of a people for His name, the Church. On the other hand, there is this "mystery of lawlessness" working (2:7, *NASB*), a development of anarchy among all classes of society. Don't be disheartened. Paul gives us a picture of the state of the world at the close of this age when Christ shall come again. There will be a great departure from the faith. In fact, Christ asks, "When the Son of Man comes, will he find faith on the earth?" (Luke 18:8). This is the picture of the Church preceding Christ's return—a falling away, a great apostasy. Does Christ really mean this? We should judge so from His description of the end days in Matthew 24:1-14,36-42.

When Christ returns, He will find Antichrist (the man of lawlessness) carrying out his satanic plans. From the description of the man of lawlessness in the Scriptures and his diabolical role of "counterfeit miracles, signs and wonders" (2 Thessalonians 2:9), we do not see how that and the millennial glory could exist together. It is just as God said it would be. Indeed, the darkest clouds that are gathering are but harbingers of the golden day that is surely coming when our Lord Himself shall return to take up the reins of government.

Christ's Coming (2 Thessalonians 3)

The time of this glorious event is to be left with God. The delay in the Lord's coming gives us real opportunities for service. We might have two wrong views of the Lord's coming. Either we become restless and troubled because of having to wait so long, or grow idle because we know that when He comes He will right every wrong and overthrow iniquity. But both of these attitudes are wrong. We are not just to stand and wait, but rather have "our loins girded" for service, making ready for the glorious day when He shall come. Let us not abandon the work Christ has given us to do.

Paul gives some instructions to the Thessalonians:

Stand firm—don't be influenced by false teaching (2:15).

Hold to the teachings we passed on to you—don't lose any of your foundation truth (2:15).

Encourage your hearts (2:17).

Strengthen you in every good deed and word (2:17).

Then Paul asks for their prayers (2 Thessalonians 3:1). His heart was burdened and he needed their fellowship. He had great confidence in their faith.

The hope of Christ's coming stimulates without exciting; sobers without depressing. It is a balancing doctrine. We find in this Epistle that our Lord's delay gives us opportunities to:

Be loyal to Him—2:15

Evangelize the world—3:1

Pray for His servants—3:1-2

Patiently wait for Him—3:5

Live a holy life—3:6-14.

Some thought that because Christ was coming they would just withdraw from business and not work, claiming the right to be supported by the brethren who had money. Paul was very drastic in his dealing with these lazy fellows. The attitude on the part of these men was absolutely wrong, and he asked them to look to him for an example. He never ceased to labor while he was preaching to them. He laid down a great principle of life that "if a man will not work, he shall not eat" (2 Thessalonians 3:10). Any view of Christianity that makes a man neglect working for his livelihood is not of God. Although Paul always advocated charity toward those in need, and spent much time in taking up offerings for the poor, yet he was very severe in condemning the able-bodied fellow who could but would not work. He forbade the Church to support these folks, and even urged them to withdraw fellowship from them.

Chapter 43

Understanding First Timothy

First Timothy Portrays Jesus Christ, Our Teacher

Selected Bible Readings

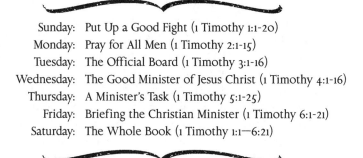

Sunday: Put Up a Good Fight (1 Timothy 1:1-20)
Monday: Pray for All Men (1 Timothy 2:1-15)
Tuesday: The Official Board (1 Timothy 3:1-16)
Wednesday: The Good Minister of Jesus Christ (1 Timothy 4:1-16)
Thursday: A Minister's Task (1 Timothy 5:1-25)
Friday: Briefing the Christian Minister (1 Timothy 6:1-21)
Saturday: The Whole Book (1 Timothy 1:1—6:21)

The key verse to 1 Timothy is 3:15, that "you will know how people ought to conduct themselves in God's household, which is the church of the living God." Realizing that behavior is based upon belief, Paul stresses sound doctrine.

First and 2 Timothy and Titus are the three pastoral Epistles, written to ministers in charge of important churches instead of to the churches themselves. Both Timothy and Titus were given explicit directions for shepherding the sheep, for guarding the churches after Paul should be called "home," as he knew he soon would be (2 Timothy 4:7-8). Timothy had been entrusted with the government and supervision of Ephesus, and Titus of the church at Crete. How inadequate both of these young men felt!

Because Timothy was a young man, we may expect to find in Paul's writings to him valuable suggestions for other young men who are living the Christian life, and we are not disappointed in this expectation; but we also find helpful suggestions for those who are older in years. It would be interesting for your class to select from the two letters to Timothy the admonitions that are up to date. It would be helpful for those who think the Bible is out of date.

In this day of modern education, it is well to offer to young people a commendation of the faith of their fathers, and to warn them against what is falsely called "knowledge" (6:20). It is well to enjoin them to "fight the good fight, holding on to faith and a good conscience" (1:18-19). And when athletic contests threaten to consume the major portion of interest and time in scholastic circles, it is good for young Christians to remind themselves that though "physical training is of some value, but godliness has value for all things, holding promise for both the present life and the life to come" (4:8). And who can hear Paul's words to his young associate without hearing him say across the years to our own young people. Whatever it costs, "keep yourself pure" (5:22).

It was a real honor for the young Timothy to enjoy the friendship of the apostle Paul. He was one of Paul's own converts, and Paul calls him "my son whom I love, who is faithful in the Lord" (1 Corinthians 4:17). During the impressionable days of Timothy's boyhood, while Paul was visiting Lystra, the people first tried to worship the apostle, then sought to take his life. How Timothy had listened to the gospel preached by Paul! He saw him heal the cripple, heard him as he appealed to the multitude and then saw him stoned and left for dead. But the next day Paul rose and came again into the city. Among the most enthusiastic converts of that city were Eunice and her son Timothy.

When Paul came back to Lystra on his second missionary journey, he took Timothy along as his companion. What a wonderful thing for so young a man! After long years of training under this mighty man of God, Timothy was left in charge of the important church at Ephesus. This brought the timid young man face-to-face with serious problems. Think of this inexperienced young fellow being left in that big church to take the place of a man like its founder Paul! How unworthy he must have felt! How he leaned on the apostle for advice and direction!

While Timothy was acting as pastor in Ephesus Paul wrote his two letters to Timothy, as letters of instruction and guidance indeed to Timothy, but also as a handbook for Christian pastors through the centuries. Paul instructed Timothy to deal severely with false teachers, to direct public worship, choose church officers and to work with all classes found in the church. But most important of all, he must lead a life that would be an example to all. Timothy had a hard task.

Paul had won a vast multitude to Christ during his stay in Ephesus. In the succeeding years, the number of converts increased tremendously. Within the next fifty years, so many of the non-Christians turned to Christ that their idolatrous temples were almost forsaken.

One of the things to remember about this time of the Early Church is that there were no church buildings. Groups of Christians met in homes. No churches were built until about 200 years after Paul's day, and not until Constantine (Constantine the Great, d. 337, Roman emperor) put an end to the persecution of Christians. This meant that there would be hundreds of small congregations, each with its own pastor. These pastors were called "elders" (Acts 20:17). In these letters to Timothy they are called "overseers" (1 Timothy 3:1; "bishops" in the *KJV*). Timothy's work was with these various pastors. Remember, there were no seminaries to prepare leaders. Paul had to train his own men. But in spite of no buildings and no theological seminaries, and also in spite of continued persecution, the Church grew by leaps and bounds.

Warning Against False Teaching (1 Timothy 1)

Paul calls Timothy his "true son in the faith" (1:2). It is clear that the boy was led to Christ by Paul. He was an example of one accepting Christ as a child because he had been brought up in a home in which the Scriptures were taught. This is the kind of Christian experience we need to emphasize today as not only possible, but also as that which should be the normal experience.

There has never been a day when the Church has been free from false teachers who present new and strange doctrines. They are hard to combat because they base their teachings on parts of God's Word, and do not "correctly handle the word of truth" (2 Timothy 2:15) and interpret it as a whole. What the Church needs today is instruction in the vital truths. In contrast with the teaching of the Law and "myths and endless genealogies" (1 Timothy 1:4), Paul puts "the glorious gospel of the blessed God" (1:11). Therefore Timothy must safeguard against any other doctrine. Don't mix fables and legends with the gospel!

Paul warns Timothy to hold "faith and a good conscience" (1:19) because these save people from spiritual shipwreck. It is a thrilling sight to see a ship loosened from her moorings and plunging into the ocean. But it is a solemn sight, too, considering the many storms she is likely to meet. If this is true of a ship, how much more so of a Christian starting out on the voyage of life.

Paul speaks plainly of some who, having put away faith and a good conscience, have caused spiritual shipwreck and are wrecked for two worlds. Let us pay heed to his warnings.

Even in that first-century Church, Paul was called upon to warn his young coworker Timothy against the false teaching that is much like the false doctrine of the twentieth century. Paul had warned them when he left Ephesus seven years before, that savage wolves would ravage the flock (Acts 20:29-30). Now they were there in full force and presented young Timothy with his worst problem.

Paul's charge to Timothy included more than soundness in doctrine. He wanted soundness in life. Paul realized that a person can believe the Word of God completely and yet live a life far from its truth. It is sad when one's life and one's belief are poles apart!

In this letter, Paul says that the best way of fighting error is with a life that measures up to the standards set down in God's Word. Remember, many of us are the only Bibles others ever read. Christians have to live better than other people in this world if their testimony is to count. We either commend Christ to others by our lives or we drive them away from Him. How often have we heard, "Well, if that's what Christianity does for a person, I don't want any of it!"

Paul wants Timothy to live a life that will vindicate the truth he preaches. He challenges him to be a good soldier of Jesus Christ. Let us remember that we will not fight very hard for a truth we do not live. As with Timothy, so with us. "What Timothy will preach will be empowered and made mighty by what Timothy is." Timothy is charged to fight the good warfare (1 Timothy 1:18). This presents the thought of a campaign and all the responsibilities of the officer in command.

Paul humbly declares: "Here is a trustworthy saying that deserves full acceptance: Christ Jesus came into the world to save sinners— of whom I am the worst" (1:15).

Here we catch a glimpse of the man, who probably did more for Christ than any other throughout the ages since the world began, bowed to his knees with the feeling of his own unworthiness. Although Paul was once a blasphemer, now God in His grace had appointed him an apostle; and although he had persecuted Him, now he could proclaim His love. The closer we get to the heart of Christ, the more we realize our own unworthiness. A singer may think he has a very good voice, but let him compare himself with a Caruso (Enrico Caruso, 1873-1921, the great Italian operatic tenor) and he feels as if he could never sing again. The reason many people today do not have a sense of sin is that they are not near to Christ. Just to stand in Christ's presence is enough to make us feel condemned. Paul did not realize how sinful he was until he was brought face-to-face with his Lord and Savior. He felt his miraculous conversion was intended to be an example of how God can save and use the chief of sinners. Read 1:2-15.

Directions for the Church (1 Timothy 2—3)

The Church has a great calling. We are not only called upon to plead with people to turn to God, but also to plead with God the cause of people. Read what Paul says: "I urge, then, first of all, that requests, prayers, intercession and thanksgiving be made for everyone—for kings and all those in authority" (1 Timothy 2:1-2). Yes, he tells us to pray for rulers. It is well to remember that Nero was the emperor of Rome at this time! Under this wicked despot, Paul was imprisoned and soon would be beheaded. This proves to us that we must pray for bad rulers as well as good, "that we may live peaceful and quiet lives in all godliness and holiness" (2:2).

Remember when we pray that God "wants all men to be saved and to come to a knowledge of the truth. For there is one God and one mediator between God and men, the man Christ Jesus" (2:4-5). Paul makes it clear that when we pray for someone we can go straight to God for that person. We need no saint or virgin to approach near to God, only the One who gave Himself a ransom for all. Our blessed

Lord Himself stands in God's presence pleading for us.

Do you remember the legend of Aeschylus who was condemned by the Athenians and was just about to be executed? His brother Amyntas, the brave warrior who had just gained a victory for Athens, came into the court. Without a word he held up the bleeding stub of the arm that had been severed in the battle. As the judges looked upon the wound, they said, "For the sake of Amyntas, Aeschylus is counted innocent and set free!"

When we look to heaven and remember that God has condemned us because of our sin, we would despair. But we see Jesus sitting at the right hand of the throne on high, holding up His nail-printed hands, and presenting His pierced feet and wounded side, pleading for you and me.

Finally, let all who pray be clean in conduct and pure in character (2:8-10). Let us lift up "holy hands" when we pray. That means that we should not fill our lives with worthless pleasures or needless things that absorb, but come to the Lord with a heart that is cleansed (1 John 1:9).

Church Leadership

When we think of church officers, we immediately think of the "official church board." Paul tells us the kind of people that really ought to be on the church board. If the Church shall fulfill her mission of proclaiming the gospel and praying for all, then she must be governed properly and know the real reason for her existence. Two officers are described who shall direct the church: bishops and deacons. Paul outlines the requirement for both groups.

We find as we look at this that the pastor must be a man of blameless character, "husband of but one wife," not quarrelsome, not greedy for money. He must be a skillful teacher, and one who makes his own children obey. He must not be a new convert lest his head be turned with pride. He must have a good reputation in his community (3:2-7). It is important that the Church have the right leadership. Good pastors lead a church forward. How we need good and faithful shepherds today!

Deacons must have the same moral qualifications as elders or pastors. This office is not inferior, but different. The two offices were to be complementary to each other. A deacon must be as carefully chosen. Sometimes it may be necessary to appoint women to this office.

Paul shows us the need of Christian conduct. Church manners are a lost art in most places today. It makes a great deal of difference how we behave, for behavior reveals character. It is not "dohavior" but "be-havior" that counts. What we are speaks so loudly that people cannot hear what we say.

The Church
Paul gives us a beautiful description of the Church and states her purpose. He tells you how Christians "ought to conduct themselves in God's household, which is the church of the living God, the pillar and foundation of the truth" (3:15). The Church upholds all truth in the sight of people. She is the only earthly institution to which Christ committed the preaching of the gospel.

Directions for the Pastor (1 Timothy 4—6)

Picture the young pastor Timothy awed by his instructor, the fifty-year-old apostle Paul, as he says, "in later times some will abandon the faith" giving themselves up to spiritualism and all of its teachings. They will tell you if you would be holy, you must not marry, neither should you eat certain kinds of food. But let us not put a ban on that which God has given for our good. Turn a deaf ear to foolish "isms" filled with "do this" and "don't do that." People are always trying to find what they can "do" to inherit eternal life (see 4:2-5). But Paul goes on to say, "If you point these things out to the brothers, you will be a good minister of Christ Jesus" (4:6).

Lead a godly life. "Godliness has value" (4:8). True religion is an appeal to common sense. God says it pays. In one way, Christianity is a business. It asks us to get out our account books, to study the current prices, to consider the possibilities of profit and loss, and decide, "What good is it for a man to gain the whole world, yet forfeit his soul?" (Mark 8:36). Paul, after taking account, found that what he had counted as "gain" was "loss."

Does it pay to invest in the Christian life? Does it pay from the standpoint of life right now? God says it does. Christ says, "Seek first his kingdom and his righteousness, and all these things will be given to you as well" (Matthew 6:33).

A noted Puritan once said that God had only one Son, and He made Him a minister.

Paul says to the young minister and to those of you who may be ministers, "Don't think entirely in terms of the physical, how you can please your body." Everyone is thinking in terms of "having fun," of "doing things." The body must be fed, clothed, entertained and pleased! "Physical training is of some value," says Paul, "but godliness has value for all things, holding promise for both the present life and the life to come" (1 Timothy 4:8). Start living for eternity!

"Set an example for the believers in speech, in life, in love, in faith and in purity" (4:12). Carry conviction and command respect. In order to do this, give much attention to your reading and preaching and teaching. The best way to combat any error is by reiterating the simple gospel truth. The Bible itself will do the job, if only you give it a chance. "Give yourself wholly to" the Scriptures (1 Timothy 4:15). If a man is to succeed in the ministry, he must pour all his strength into it. It demands the whole person, the whole time. Godliness does not starve real living. You will not become a sissy if you are good. Godliness is not "goody-ness."

The way a minister treats his flock is of vital importance. He must deal wisely and fairly with each one. The widows must be cared for. Elders must be honored and supported, but they must also be reproved, even in public, if they are found guilty, that others may be warned. In other words, sin can never get by in the Church, no matter who is guilty of that sin.

Paul even remembers the Christian slaves. They must be taught. Those who serve unbelieving masters are to let their service be a testimony to these unbelievers. Those who serve Christians should not take advantage because of their spiritual relation. Love should make us serve the better.

"Fight the good fight of the faith" (6:12). Christ makes His appeal to the heroic in a man or woman. The Christian life is not a thing to be entered into lightly. We will not be carried into heaven on flowery beds of ease. We must fight if we would be conquerors. But it is a "good fight."

Chapter 44

Understanding Second Timothy

Second Timothy Portrays Jesus Christ, Our Example

Selected Bible Readings

Sunday:	Stir Up Thy Gift (2 Timothy 1:1-9)
Monday:	Hold Fast to the Truth (2 Timothy 1:10-18)
Tuesday:	Endure Hardness as a Soldier (2 Timothy 2:1-15)
Wednesday:	Follow Righteousness (2 Timothy 2:16-26)
Thursday:	Know the Scriptures (2 Timothy 3:1-17)
Friday:	Be Faithful to the End (2 Timothy 4:1-22)
Saturday:	Receive a Crown (1 Corinthians 9:25; 2 Timothy 4:8; James 1:12; 1 Peter 5:4; Revelation 2:10; 3:11)

"Endure hardship with us like a good soldier of Christ Jesus" (2 Timothy 2:3). Be loyal to Christ and His Word!

In 1 Timothy, Paul enjoins a straight gospel; in 2 Timothy, a straight life.

In 1 Timothy, Paul is saying, "Guard the doctrine which is our message from God." In 2 Timothy, Paul is saying, "Guard the testimony which is our life from God."

First Timothy seems to say, "Shoulder arms! Polish the metal! Ammunition ready!" Second Timothy says, "Attention! Onward march! Face front, shoulders square, keep step with our Leader, who is Christ!"

The walk is as necessary as the weapon. The sons of Wilberforce (Samuel Wilberforce, 1805-73, British pastor and church planter) said of their father, "After a while father gave up preparing his discourses and simply prepared himself." Guard the witness diligently.

We are reading a letter of Paul's, written from his last imprisonment in Rome, in which he himself says his course is "finished" here on this earth. What ground had he covered? Note every city or province and island in answering this question. To how many thousands had he preached his Christ, do you suppose, in those at least thirty different localities? In how many languages had he testified for Christ? How many of his letters have found a place in the Christian Bible? Are these letters still being read?

After writing his first Epistle to Timothy, Paul was arrested again, in Greece or Asia Minor, and hurried back to Rome, this time as a criminal (2:9). While waiting in the Roman dungeon for "the time for his departure" (4:6) he wrote this last letter to his beloved son in the gospel, Timothy. His arrest had been so sudden and unexpected that he had had no time to collect his valuable books and parchments, or even to take his warm cloak with him (4:13).

This second imprisonment was very different from the first. Then he had his own rented house; now he was kept in close confinement. Before, he was the center of a large circle of friends, accessible to all, but now he was alone (4:10-12). Before, he had hoped for freedom; now he was expecting to die (4:6). Paul had already appeared before the wicked Nero, but his case had been postponed (4:16-17). He expected to appear again in the winter and wrote urging Timothy to come immediately and bring Mark with him. He asked him to bring the things that were left (4:9,11,13,21). Being uncertain whether Timothy could get there before his death (and he did not, for his trial probably took place in June rather than the next winter), he wanted to give him his last words of warning and encouragement.

It is well to remember that this is Paul's last writing! His pen was to be dried forever. This Epistle is very personal. He mentions twenty-three individuals. Although alone and facing death, yet he forgot himself in thinking of others. The Bishop of Durham (the Right Reverend Arthur Michael Ramsey, 1904-1988, Bishop of Durham from 1952-1956; later he became the Archbishop of Canterbury) said, "I have often found it difficult deliberately to read these short chapters through, without finding something like a mist gathering in my eyes. The writer's heart beats in the writing."

Endure in the Camp—The Home (2 Timothy 1)

Parental example is the greatest answer to the problem of juvenile delinquency. We must first guard our testimony in the home, which is the training center of the Christian life. This is the hardest place to begin. Many young people today do not have a strong Christian influence in their homes. The problem of youth today is often the problem of parents. Parents are never found in church; they never hear the Word preached or taught and the family altar is unheard of. This kind of a home produces spiritual and social illiterates.

Timothy had been reared in a Christian home with his mother, Eunice, and his grandmother Lois. Paul mentions these wonderful Christian women and commends Timothy for having had early training at a consecrated hearth (2 Timothy 3:15).

Paul remembers Timothy's pure faith that "first lived in your grandmother Lois and in your mother Eunice and, I am persuaded, now lives in you also" (1:5). Someone said, "When you want to make a great person, start with his grandmother." Whatever may be the value of that observation, one thing is sure—when you want to build a Timothy, you must begin in the Primary department.

Paul calls Timothy "my true son" (1 Timothy 1:2). It seems clear that the youth was led to confess Christ by Paul during his first missionary journey. He was a Christian from childhood. It is no surprise that Paul saw in Timothy a lad of promise as a minister in the Early Church. He became Paul's understudy, and at the end of the apostle's life, he was the best man to whom Paul could turn over his work.

Timothy possessed fine qualities, but he had excellent training as well. He was a thoroughly Christian young man. He had a splendid reputation in his own church. He was the constant companion of the great apostle Paul. He knew the Word of God and made use of it in his life and teachings (3:14-16). He demonstrated a splendid spirit of unselfishness in his service. He was given great responsibilities by Paul. All this was instrumental in a large degree in his training (1:3; 3:15; 4:6-12).

Man of God

Timothy is addressed as "man of God" (1 Timothy 6:11). What does that mean? Godliness comes from the Word and prayer, God speaking to us and our speaking to God. Manliness includes truth in the mind, love in the heart and righteousness in the life. Manliness is due to godliness. The grace of God makes a man godly and then proceeds to make him manly.

No man ever lived a life of such constant abiding in Christ as Paul. Now that he was about to leave the Church he had established, he is concerned about its future. He is warning the youthful and timid Timothy that henceforth he must stand alone in comforting and directing the Church. Paul's son in the gospel, now perhaps thirty-five years of age, must emphasize above all things a doctrine that is true and sound, for "savage wolves" had already begun to play havoc with the Church (Acts 20:29-30).

The key verse is 2 Timothy 1:13: "What you heard from me, keep as the pattern of sound teaching, with faith and love in Christ Jesus." Paul's life was characterized by an unceasing effort to guard in its purity the priceless treasure of the Christian faith. He wanted it kept untarnished. We live in a day when it is being said that it is deeds not doctrine that count, but Paul's teaching was that conduct must be based on creed. "As a man thinketh...so is he" (Proverbs 23:7, *KJV*). Wrong thinking makes for wrong acting. World War II was brought about by men possessed with wrong creeds. These creeds soon became conduct, and millions died to correct it.

Stir the Gift

How easy it is for us not to make use of our gifts and natural endowments! How many lose all initiative! How few people think! Timothy had one of the gifts of the Spirit (1 Corinthians 12). He seems to have been neglecting to use it. In the first letter (4:14) Paul says, "Do not neglect your gift" and in the second letter (1:6), Paul writes, "Fan into flame the gift of God." How about our gift? Have we ever let God tell us what it is? Cultivate whatever God has given. Remember, everyone has some talent. To be sure, some have five talents, others two and others only one. But stir up the gift you have.

Two men had been discussing the possibility of permanently destroying weeds in the garden, and failed to agree. A third person who had been listening said, "You differ, my friends, concerning the possibility of utterly destroying the weeds in the garden plot. One thinks fire will permanently destroy the weeds, while the other is sure fire will only increase their next growth. But in one thing you will agree with me. We must all agree that no weeds will spring up in that garden as long as the fire is kept burning." Young people, stir up the fire in your heart. It is easy to let it die down. This will keep down the weeds in your life. Keep your love constantly burning for Christ by serving Him.

We find in this first chapter one of the apostle's "I know's." It is a verse that gives us great assurance. "I know whom I have believed, and am convinced that he is able to guard what I have entrusted to him for that day" (1:12).

What is your persuasion? Will your answer come swift and strong as Paul's, "I am convinced that he is able to guard what I have entrusted to him for that day"? Make it very personal. Don't say, "I know IN whom," as the verse is so often quoted, but "I know WHOM I have believed."

I know One who is able to keep. Put your life in His hands. He will hold you fast. The psalmist said, "Commit your way to the Lord; trust in him and he will do this" (Psalm 37:5). Second Timothy 1:12 is the sequel.

Endure in the Field (2 Timothy 2)

We must "endure hardship...like a good soldier" (2 Timothy 2:3) away from home, in the school, in the office and in the place of business. This is our field of service and discipline. Here we are to stand the test as one who "needeth not to be ashamed."

Paul says, as a faithful steward "entrust to reliable men who will also be qualified to teach others" (2:2). As a brave soldier, endure hardships. A soldier does not become entangled with ordinary affairs, but is under the authority of a superior officer. He leaves his business and friends to serve in the army. Let that be our attitude. The athlete, too, must observe this to gain the wreath of victory. Just as the farmer is the first to enjoy the fruit of the harvest, so will it be with you. Avoid business entanglements that will keep you from rendering the best service. Watch, too, lest the comforts of life and the common enjoyments make us love ease too well (2:3-7).

Endure your hardships courageously and with the spirit of a hero. Don't just endure!

For one who was a good man, Paul was enduring the cruelest of suffering. He was charged as a criminal and was being put in chains. But he was glad to suffer anything, just so the gospel would not be chained. He reminds Timothy that he is worshiping a living Christ. "Remember Jesus Christ, raised from the dead, descended from David. This is my gospel," he said (2:8). Even though his body was bound, his mind was on "eternal glory."

Paul urged the people to keep away from foolish discussion, for these only breed quarrels and a Christian should not quarrel (2:24). Do not argue about the Christian life. Live it! Outlive the world— live better than they do—and they will soon listen to what you have to say. The best argument for Christ is a victorious life.

God gives us a sure foundation upon which to build our lives— the foundation laid by God (2:19). It "stands firm," for that Rock is Christ. All who build on it are sealed for Him. This is the inscription: "The Lord knows those who are his." It is wonderful to know that we are known personally by Him. This is not true of any other religion under heaven. In Christianity we are God's children and He knows every one of us. "And even the very hairs of your head are all numbered" (Matthew 10:30). He calls us by name.

God's work needs real gentility. It was said of the Messiah, "You stoop down to make me great" (Psalm 18:35). Gentleness and conviction in the ministry will break down hatred for the Church and give the Church its rightful place. Study to be gentle. Don't send people away by your cruel criticism, but draw them to Christ by love.

Endure in the Fight (2 Timothy 3)

When the battle is on and our faith is assailed, stand firm and strong. Fight effectively with a life that is lived "godly in Christ

Jesus" (3:12). During every engagement, let us wield the Word that is the sword of the Spirit. Let us be soldiers "thoroughly equipped for every good work" (3:17).

There is but one way to be strengthened against all these vices today. We find it in verses 14 through 17. The Scriptures will make us wise unto salvation (3:15). Jesus met His temptations by the Word of God. We can do no better.

Have you ever heard anyone say, "I was a drunkard, a disgrace to my family, a nuisance to the world, until I began to study mathematics and learned the multiplication table, but since then I have been happy as the day is long. I feel like singing all the time, for my heart is at peace!" Have you ever heard a man ascribing his salvation from drunkenness and sin to the multiplication table or to science? Of course you haven't. But thousands have said, "I was unhappy and heartbroken. I had no reason for living until I heard God speak to me through His Word, and now I know the living Savior."

The Word of God is the only thing that will keep the Church in this terrible day. The church of Rome put aside the Word and the Dark Ages was the result. The Protestants brought it back into circulation, but Christians everywhere are neglecting it. The ignorance of the Word today is appalling.

Paul's catalog of first-century vices sounds like a list of twentieth-century vices (3:1-5):

Lovers of themselves more than lovers of God.

Lovers of money—those who will do anything to gain possession of what they want.

Proud and boastful—pride fills the natural heart.

Blasphemers *(KJV)*—taking God's name in vain.

Disobedient to parents—there seems to be no respect today in the home.

Unthankful—no gratitude, taking everything for granted.

Unholy—those who care for neither God nor people.

Without natural affection *(KJV)*—mothers taking the lives of their own children; divorce courts full; pornography and homosexuality rampant.

"Truce-breakers" *(KJV)*—promises mean nothing.

Lovers of pleasure—this age has gone pleasure-mad.

Having a form of godliness but denying its power—there is only one source of power and that is the gospel of Christ Jesus.

Endure to the Death (2 Timothy 4)

To endure to the end and look back over a hard and bitter fight and say, "I have won!"—that is enduring as a good soldier. Life's last hours for Paul were full of glory. He forgot that the lions in the arena or the flames at the stake or a cruel cross might end his earthly life at any moment. His good fight was ended, his long hard race was run, and now only the memories of a noble life gave him great peace.

He closes this letter with a solemn farewell charge to Timothy before God and Christ who will judge him and who soon will appear to spread the gospel everywhere. "Preach the Word; be prepared in season and out of season...For the time will come when men will not put up with sound doctrine" (vv. 2-3).

Paul's Valedictory

This is the grandest utterance of the grandest mortal who ever lived. Where can we match Paul's words that he wrote from his dungeon to Timothy, his own true son in the faith? Let us picture the old battle-scarred hero of the Cross, standing in the gloomy dungeon, bound with chains and looking up through the one opening in the roof of his cell through which only a tiny shaft of light could enter, but which reveals his countenance with the expression of perfect peace. His lips are moving, and we hear him say, "I have fought the good fight, I have finished the race, I have kept the faith. Now there is in store for me the crown of righteousness, which the Lord, the righteous Judge, will award to me on that day—and not only to me, but also to all who have longed for his appearing" (2 Timothy 4:7-8).

Ever since Jesus had laid His hand upon him, Paul seemed to have been contending in the arena and running in the stadium. There had been scarcely a moment of rest. It was an intense training and a strenuous wrestling all the way through. But within, peace reigned. His questions were answered. His sins were forgiven. His wants were supplied. Peace within but the athlete's contest without. This is the true Christian life.

Coming with Crowns

The crown is for Paul but it is also for us—"to all who have longed for his appearing." You and I, whose achievements are so much less than Paul's, may yet be partakers of Paul's heaven.

Surely the "crown" that gleams before us should spur us on to a new diligence in service. Do we love His appearing?

The last verses of this letter give us a glimpse of the loneliness of this great wrestler and runner. Many were leaving him under the stress of persecution. "But the Lord stood at my side and gave me strength, so that through me the message might be fully proclaimed" (4:17). This is the secret of Paul's success. This is why he could fight a good fight and finish the course. His greatest opportunity seemed to be reserved for the end. He stood in Nero's courthouse, face-to-face with the "lion," as he designated him. He was alone as far as human help was concerned. The great basilica was crowded and every eye was fastened on the forsaken old man at the bar. Did he lose heart? Was he afraid? No, indeed! He leaped to the height of the momentous occasion. He was not content in defending himself. That he did, but much more. To the multitude, curious and hostile, he told clearly the gospel of Christ, and all the Gentiles heard.

Chapter 45

Understanding Titus and Philemon

Titus and Philemon Portray Jesus Christ,
Our Pattern; Our Lord and Master

Selected Bible Readings

Sunday: Church Officers (Titus 1:1-9)
Monday: Church Enemies (Titus 1:10-16)
Tuesday: Church Influence (Titus 2:1-8)
Wednesday: Church Rule (Titus 2:9-15)
Thursday: Church Works (Titus 3:1-15)
Friday: A Christian Gentleman (Philemon 1-7)
Saturday: A Prisoner's Plea (Philemon 8-25)

Understanding Titus

The importance of good works is stressed in this Epistle. Not that we are saved by good works, but we are saved for good works. God presents His ideal for the Church and its officers and members.

The Epistle to Titus was written by Paul. Titus was bishop of Crete, a hard post (1:12-13). Paul had given Titus the difficult task before of settling the differences at Corinth and tactfully persuading the Church to do the right thing in the matter of divisions. Paul's second letter to the Corinthians shows how successful Titus was in this mission. Titus was a Gentile. No doubt he was one of Paul's converts during the early years of the apostle's ministry. He accompanied Paul and Barnabas to Jerusalem seventeen years after Paul's conversion.

When Paul heard that Apollos was about to go to Crete, he took the opportunity to send this letter to Titus (3:13). It is full of practical advice to the young pastor and directed him in his administration, and warned him against the heretics of his day. He asks Titus to come to him and to report about the condition of the church in the island. Although this is a personal letter, it undoubtedly was to be read to the church also.

The letter is very much like Paul's first letter to Timothy, being written about the same time, and dealing with the same subjects.

Works for Church Officers (Titus 1)

Paul presents himself in this scene as the "servant" of the Lord Jesus Christ, then as His apostle. Paul loves to call himself a bond-slave of Christ. Another time he says of Christ, "whose I am and whom I serve." It is terrible to be a slave to most anyone or anything, but to be a slave of Jesus Christ—to be bought by Him, that is wonderful! It is a slavery of love.

"In grace," Charles H. Spurgeon once said, "you can be under bonds yet not in bondage. I am in bonds of wedlock but I feel no bondage. On the contrary it is joy to be so bound."

Paul kept his eyes steadfastly on heaven as he neared the end of his earthly life. Read what he says of his apostleship: "for the faith of God's elect and the knowledge of the truth...resting on the hope of eternal life" (1:1-2).

Paul left Titus in Crete to superintend the work of the church organization there. It was a hard situation, but Paul had given him a difficult task before at Corinth and he had worked out the problem. In Crete he was to set things in order and ordain elders in every city (1:5).

What kind of officers the church should have was well described. These qualifications are stated carefully. Only a man of character should even be considered. He must be blameless in his home life (1:6), blameless in his personal life (1:7-8) and true to the Word (1:9).

How do you act at home? What kind of a Christian are you there? This is so often the test of your Christianity. It is the home life that counts. The Christian household is the main evangelizing agency everywhere. When the home is Christian, the community is Christian. For this reason, the "bishop" ("overseer" or "elder") and pastor are enjoined to set a good example before the people. He must have but one living wife, but he is not compelled to be married. On the other hand, he is not to be prohibited from marriage, as the Roman Catholic church normally decrees. Because a minister is judged by his family life, he must rule his own children well, for he who cannot rule his own household well cannot rule the church of God (1 Timothy 3:5). He must be a man of moral courage and sympathy. He must be a good teacher and encourage others by his teaching.

The Cretan churches were being upset by outside teachers who, for the sake of making money, were working havoc in "whole households" (Titus 1:11). This probably meant whole congregations, for the Early Church met in private homes. Paul calls these fellows "detestable, disobedient and unfit" (1:16) and said they must be stopped in their teaching. He demands severity in dealing with them. How much false teaching there is today everywhere! More cults and sects are being started by men and women by which they make themselves rich.

During the 1906 California earthquake, an old saint in San Francisco remained in her room, joyously rocking back and forth in her chair, singing, while all around her people were running in dread of death. After all was over, someone asked her how she could have had such a feeling of joy. "Oh," replied the old saint, "I was so happy in the thought that my God was mighty enough to rock the world like that, while He held me securely in His hand. I did not have time to be frightened."

So in this day in which we are living, when all is being shaken in confusion about us, and "there are many rebellious people, mere talkers and deceivers,...They must be silenced, because they are ruining whole households by teaching things they ought not to teach—and that for the sake of dishonest gain" (1:10-11), who "claim to know God, but by their actions they deny him" (1:16), so let us, I say, rest our faith not on the reasonings and opinions of people, but on the infallible Word of God. By this Word alone judge new and strange doctrines, and stop the mouths of those who handle the Word of God deceitfully (1:9-11).

Works for Church Members (Titus 2—3)

Paul believed that doctrine must be expressed in life, and so he had a word to Titus about the aged (Titus 2:2-3), the youth (2:4-6) and the slaves (2:9-10).

The Aged:

Older Men—"temperate, worthy of respect, self-controlled, and sound in faith, in love and in endurance.

Older Women—"be reverent in the way they live" and "not to be slanderers or addicted to much wine, but to teach what is good" (2:3); and to train younger women to become good wives and mothers.

Youth:

Exercise self-control, be examples of a noble life.

Servants:

Obey masters, be diligent and faithful, give satisfaction; don't contradict, don't steal.

Life with a Capital *L*

Leave the old life.

Live the new life.

Look for that blessed hope and glorious appearing of Christ (2:11-13).

How essential that this be our foundation! Then we can "make the teaching about God our Savior attractive" (2:10). To think that we in any way can adorn the wonderful gospel by our lives! Just as we put a frame on a beautiful picture to enhance its beauty and make it more conspicuous, so we must adorn and make more beautiful the gospel of Christ. A king in his royal robes is more easily recognized as such than one in ordinary clothing. How we can either make or mar the gospel! What is the "gospel according to you"? In all things show thyself a pattern of good works

(2:7). The test of fellowship is not warmth of devotion, but holiness of life. One cannot live on strong "feelings." Some mistake religious feeling for holiness and good thoughts for good conduct. There is use and abuse in religious emotion.

Be so faithful in your attitudes and obligations of life that critics of your religion will be silenced (2:8). Make others say, "If this is what Christ can do for you, there must be something to your religion."

Not that we are saved by good works, but we are saved unto good works. Paul says we are saved by His mercy (3:5), and justified by His grace (3:7). But because we have been saved at such a cost, we should show it by "good works."

Good Works

"God our Savior" did not save us as a result of our good works, but through His kindness and according to His mercy. He cleansed us by His blood and gave us a new life by His Holy Spirit. But we are to show forth good works:

"An example by doing what is good"—2:7
"Eager to do what is good"—2:14
"Ready to do whatever is good"—3:1
"Careful to devote themselves to doing what is good"—3:8
"Doing what is good...for daily necessities"—3:14.

Paul urges citizens of the heavenly kingdom to be good citizens of the country under whose flag they live. Every Christian should be submissive to rulers and authority (3:1-2; Romans 13:1-7; 1 Peter 2:13-17).

Don't say anything of a person if you can't say something good, is a wonderful admonition to follow. Paul said it long ago. "Slander no one" (3:2). Don't be quarrelsome. Show a gentle spirit in your dealing with others. It is well for us to remember that "we too were foolish, disobedient, deceived and enslaved" (3:3). Yes, we had all the faults we hate in others. It is well to remember that the things we criticize in others are very apt to be our own weaknesses. We like to call attention to these faults in others to take eyes off ourselves. Try this test on yourself.

Avoid controversies and foolish discussions. They are always useless and futile. Often an argument only strengthens a person in what was believed before. Do all you can to correct someone, but if the person persists in causing divisions among you, after being warned once or twice, have nothing more to say to that person. Reject the person (3:10). Devote your time in doing good.

Understanding Philemon

Christian love and forgiveness are given prominence in this book. It shows the power of the gospel in winning a runaway thief and slave, and in changing a master's mind. This is a book in applied Christianity, a textbook of social service.

The Reverend Sir W. Robertson Nicoll (1851-1923, American journalist and man of letters and editor of the *Expositor's Bible*) once said: "If I were to covet any honor of authorship, it would be this: That some letters of mine might be found in the desks of my friends when their life struggle is ended."

We don't know whether Paul coveted this honor or not, but tucked away in your New Testament, between Titus and Hebrews, you will find a model letter written by a master of letter writing. It is a personal letter from Paul to Philemon. Only one chapter, of twenty-five verses, but containing such strong and beautiful statements and so well expressed that it stands out as a gem, even in the Book of books.

Notice the courtesy and tactfulness of Paul's letter. Our letter writing can be a ministry for God, if we make it so. Some who find it hard to speak to anyone about Christ can write about Him. Then, too, a letter is good for the one who receives it, for the person has a chance to read and reread and think it over. Use the pen in witnessing to your friends. Remember all that has been preserved to us of Paul's ministry has come mainly through his Epistles. What a heritage his letters are for all Christians today! In order to appreciate what God thought of correspondence, see how many letters He kept for us in Holy Scripture.

In this letter, Paul intercedes with Philemon (who was an out-standing member of the church at Colosse) for a runaway slave by the name of Onesimus who had stolen from his master and made his way to Rome. There he had been providentially brought face-to-face with Paul and had found Christ as his Savior. He became endeared to the apostle by his devoted service. But Paul knew he was Philemon's lawful slave and so he could not think of keeping him permanently. So Paul sends him home and pleads with Philemon to take him back. He makes himself personally responsible for the debts that Onesimus owes, asking that they be charged to his (Paul's) account. He wished to save the runaway slave from the severe and cruel punishment he deserved according to Roman law. Paul believes the slave must not encounter his outraged master alone.

This letter deals with the question of slavery. Paul does not demand the abolition of slavery, but he shows that slavery can never be the fruit of Christianity. This beautiful letter from God's aged servant, in bonds for the gospel, foreshadows the time when the bonds of Christ's love should break the bands of slavery.

Onesimus was merely one of a world of slaves belonging to a handful of masters. In 300 B.C., 21,000 citizens of Athens owned 400,000 slaves. It was not so different proportionately in the days of the Roman Empire, at the time of the writing of this Epistle. Roman masters owned from ten to two hundred, even a thousand or more slaves, who had no rights of life or liberty!

Paul's Plea for Onesimus (Philemon 1-25)

Here is a letter from Paul, the aged (Philemon 9). It is not always the passing of years that brings old age. The apostle had become prematurely old through work, anxiety and eagerness of spirit. He was only about sixty, but he was a prisoner, and as such he appealed to his friend Philemon.

Paul speaks of himself as a prisoner, not, as in the letter to the Colossians, with the authority of an apostle. He writes as a friend to a friend. He says of Philemon that he is "our dear friend and fellow worker" (v. 1). He does not say these kind things just to flatter his friend, but because he always looked for the good in others.

This letter is addressed to a man and his wife, and presumably a son, in Colosse. A little meeting of Christians was held at their home. Paul gives us a beautiful picture of a Christian home in the time of the Early Church. This family was the nucleus of that home-church and doubtless other believers in Colosse gathered there for worship. One of the causes for the spiritual decline today is the lack of "the church in thy house." Is there one in your house? It begins around the family altar.

Paul always begins his letters with commendations unless there is a reason for not doing it, as in Galatians. He speaks of love and faith, and tells of the joy he finds in fellowship. Even though he was separated by a great distance from his friend Philemon, nevertheless this man's loving helpfulness to others had done Paul good in that far-off prison in Rome. He prays that Philemon's faith may ever grow.

Paul was a wonderful student of human nature. The picture he portrays of himself as the bent and battered "prisoner of Christ Jesus" (v. 9) opens a well of sympathy in the heart of Philemon as he reads his friend's letter. Onesimus, whose name means "profitable," had robbed his master and run away to the big city of Rome. In some way, he fell in with the little band of Christians surrounding Paul and was converted. Paul sends the boy back to his master with this friendly personal note. He takes pleasure in playing with the fellow's name. The "unprofitable" servant now will be "profitable." Christ makes a person profitable to others.

In approaching the main purpose of the letter, Paul does not blurt it out at once. He anticipates anger, and so he uses the finest tact. He admits that Onesimus had been good for nothing in the past, but playfully alludes to his name, hoping to put the reader into a favorable mood.

While Philemon's voice trembles, Mother Apphia is wiping her eyes on her apron, and son Archippus is clearing his throat. All three read on into the letter. Paul has his little joke and pun, and the faces of the trio break into smiles. Onesimus, meanwhile, nervously fumbles with his cap in back of the door, then breaks into a broad grin, and the tension is over.

Paul's action with regard to Onesimus is an illustration of the Lord's work on behalf of the sinner. Paul does not minimize the sin, but he pleads for forgiveness for the sinner on the ground of his own merit in the eyes of Philemon, his friend. More than that, he makes himself personally responsible for the debts of

Onesimus. "Charge it to me" (1:18). This is the message of the gospel. For Christ bore our sins in His own body on the tree. This is what Christ does—takes the sinner's place.

Social Management

The secret of the solution of the capital-labor problem lies in the love of Christ, such as undoubtedly existed between Philemon and Onesimus after the slave returned home.

This Epistle gives a clear idea of the attitude of Christianity to the social organization of the world. The subject of the Epistle is slavery, which was widespread in that day. If slavery is wrong, why did not Paul say so instead of apparently condoning it in this letter to the owner of a runaway slave? If Paul had made slavery an issue, he would have torn society to shreds. Instead he presents principles that would surely undermine slavery and in time actually did so. Brotherhood in Christ is more than emancipation. Christianity does not merely free the slaves, but teaches them that they and their masters are one in Christ.

Has Christianity yet driven slavery from the world? Here in this Epistle began the abolition of slavery. This terrible menace has been vanquished wherever brotherly love of Christ has been shed abroad. But there are still portions of the world in which slavery is practiced. Sometimes it is disguised by other names, but wherever human life is sold, wherever forced labor is carried on, it exists. It takes changes in people's thinking to destroy slavery. Christ came to change people; He frees us from sin's slavery and sends us forth to abolish slavery of every kind.

If Timothy or Tychicus took Paul's dictation of this letter, Paul took the stylus or quill and wrote in his big, nearsighted scrawl: "I, Paul, write it with my own hand, I promise to repay it [in full]—and that is to say nothing [of the fact] that you owe me your very self" (v. 19, *AMP*).

General Letters

of The New Testament

**Hebrews • James • 1 Peter • 2 Peter
1, 2 and 3 John • Jude**

Key Events of General Letters

Jesus is the pinnacle of God's revelation. True citizenship not in the world but heaven.

Hebrews 1; 11

God uses persecution to purify our faith. Following Jesus may bring hardship.

1 Peter

We can trust God to do right. Evil will be punished and faith rewarded.

2 Peter

General Letters: Our True Citizenship

The General Letters are letters of encouragement to believers, many of whom have suffered persecution for their faith. The General Letters remind us that Jesus Christ is the pinnacle of God's revelation to us; that our true citizenship is not in this world, but in heaven; that God uses persecution to purify our faith; that following Jesus may very well bring hardship upon us; and that we can trust God to do what is right because the day is coming when evil will be punished and faith rewarded.

Chapter 46

Understanding Hebrews

Hebrews Portrays Jesus Christ, Our Intercessor at the Throne

Selected Bible Readings

Sunday: Christ Superior to Prophets and Angels
(Hebrews 1:1-14)
Monday: Christ Superior to Moses (Hebrews 3:1-19)
Tuesday: Christ Superior to Aaron (Hebrews 5:1-14)
Wednesday: Christ's Superior Covenants (Hebrews 8:1-13)
Thursday: Christ's Superior Atonement (Hebrews 10:1-25)
Friday: Christ's Superior Faith Life (Hebrews 11:1-40)
Saturday: Christ's Superior Privileges (Hebrews 12:1—13:25)

We as Christians have that which is better—better in every way. The key word to the book of Hebrews is "better." It occurs thirteen times (in the *KJV*).

Some words in this book help us in understanding it. Trace the words "eternal," "perfect," "once," "blood" (mark this in red), "without," "better (superior, greater)," and the expression "we have... therefore let us," "sat down" and "heavenly."

The author of this Epistle is unknown. Many have speculated, but there is no certainty. Hebrews is attributed to Paul, and although many question his authorship, there is abundance of evidence in his favor.

This book has been called the fifth Gospel. The four describe Christ's ministry on earth; this one describes His ministry in heaven at God's right hand.

The glories of our Savior are exhibited in this Epistle. Our eye is fixed upon Jesus, the "the author and perfecter of our faith" (Hebrews 12:2). He is set before us "crowned with glory and honor" in the heavens (2:9).

This book was written, first of all, to Jewish believers in Jesus, probably of Jerusalem, who were wavering in their faith. Because of the taunts and jeers of their persecutors, the Jewish believers in Jesus were beginning to think they had lost everything—altar, priests, sacrifices—by accepting Christ. The apostle proves that they had only lost the shadow to be given the substance (Jesus Christ). They were undervaluing their privileges in Christ and were engaged in self-pity and discouragement. They were in danger of even giving up their faith (5:11-12). They had started well (6:10), but had not made progress (6:11). The Christian life is like riding a bicycle—if you do not go on, you go off. The writer is trying to lead them from an elementary knowledge to a mature grasp. He exhorts them to be loyal to Christ. He shows them the superiority of Christ over all previous revelation. The writer wanted to keep them from drifting back into their traditional rites and ceremonies. They were urged to let go of everything else in order to hold fast the faith and hope of the gospel.

The book is also a timely warning and a word of comfort to all, especially in this day when many have little instruction in the things of Christ and are inclined to be led astray by many fads and cults.

Hebrews shows skill in dealing with the discouraged Jewish believers in Jesus. The writer tells all that we have in Christ.

How often when you take a trip for the first time over a new road, you drive straight along anticipating where it will lead, and what difficulties you may encounter. It seems to be the thing to do. Coming back over the same road, you look around and notice things. Do this in studying the book of Hebrews. Read it through, and do not be overanxious about the things you cannot understand. Then you can go back over the road in your reading and take notice of the many things along the way. You could spend months in Hebrews. It presents so many wonderful truths. At the first reading, you will be impressed by one fact above all others: that Jesus Christ is prominent on every page. This is not true in all the other books of the New Testament. In Acts, the apostles, disciples, Jews and pagans are predominant. In Romans, a great doctrine attracts our attention. In the other letters, the Church and its problems are considered, but here it is our Lord Himself. He is:

Greater than prophets—1:1-3
Greater than angels—1:4—2:18
Greater than Moses—3:1-19
Greater than Joshua—4:1-16
Greater than Aaron—5:1—10:18.

The reason the writer uses these comparisons stated above is that each of these held a place of great importance in rabbinical Judaism. They were the framework of Jewish worship, and it must be proved that something or some One "better" had come to take their place if their followers are to transfer allegiance.

This book was written to strengthen the faith of wavering believers. Paul's great argument is the superiority of Christ over all others.

Do we know the real difference between having Christ as a Savior and as a Priest? Well, this book answers the question.

The book of Hebrews proves that we can never understand the Old Testament without the New, or the New without the Old.

The Superiority of the Person of Christ (Hebrews 1:1—4:13)

Nowhere is our Lord's deity and humanity so emphasized as in Hebrews 1 and 2. As our great High Priest, Christ is able to understand all our need because He is perfect Man. He is able "to sympathise with our weaknesses" because He "has been tempted in every way, just as we are—yet was without sin" (4:15). He is able to meet all our needs because He is perfect God. He is able.

The opening sentence of the book of Hebrews (1:1-4) is one of the grandest in the Bible. It ranks with the opening words of Genesis and of John. We find Jesus there: His deity, His glory, a Creator, Heir of all things, superior to all things and Savior.

Write down all you find about Christ in Hebrews 1 and 2. If you knew nothing more about Him than you found in these two chapters, you would know much.

Two great truths are taken for granted—the existence of God, and that He reveals Himself to us. He revealed Himself before, "in the past...to our forefathers through the prophets...but in these last days he has spoken to us by his Son." The Bible records a series of stories of how God speaks to people and reveals His will and His plan to them. How marvelous to hear His only begotten Son speak!

Remember, this letter is written to correct the erroneous idea that the Jewish believers in Jesus had lost some things because they had taken up Christianity. The letter is written to remove this misconception. Christianity is not "giving up," but "receiving," receiving the greatest gifts of life, in fact Life itself, for Christ is Life.

Superiority of the Person of Christ

The Lord Jesus Christ is greater than any human leader (prophets) (1:1-3):

He is God's Son.

He is Heir of all things.

He created the universe.

He is Himself very God.

He sustains all things by His word.

He cleansed us from sin.

He sat down at the right hand of God.

The Lord Jesus Christ is greater than angels (1:4-2:18):

He has the more excellent name of Son (1:4-5).

Angels worship Him (1:6).

He is the eternal God (1:7-12).

His throne is forever (1:8).

He is the ruler of the coming age (1:11-13).

The Lord Jesus Christ is greater than Moses (3:1-19):

Moses was a faithful servant.

Christ is the Son over His own house.

The Lord Jesus Christ is greater than Joshua (4:1-16):

Joshua was a great leader. He led the Hebrews into the Promised Land, but he did not lead the people into rest. What he failed to do, the Son accomplished. Jesus is greater, for He alone gives real rest.

It is well to notice that angels and human spirits (of those who die) are not the same. Human life is a different order of creation than angels. We do not become angels when we die. Angels are a separate creation of God. They are now and will be in heaven, our servants (1:14). Angels worship Christ just as we do.

When God wanted to save us from our sin, He did not send an angel, but His Son. God came not in the form of an angel, but in the form of a man. He became Man to redeem man. He suffered as a man and died as a man that He might be our Redeemer (2:10). Jesus tasted the bitterness of death for us, in order that He might render the devil powerless who has the power of death. He came up from the grave with the keys of hell and of death; no longer can the devil lock any of us in death.

Consider Jesus

This is our weakness. We look at ourselves and our own weakness. Consider Him (3:1). This is the astronomer's word. Set your telescope to the heavens and gaze upon Him.

Many Jewish believers in Jesus were confused about Christ's ministry on earth. They thought He came to enforce the laws Moses had given. Moses was the lawgiver and Christ must enforce them. This was their interpretation. But Christ is His own Lawgiver. The old Mosaic system was imperfect and weak (7:11,18). It had served its purpose. Now Christ has a "better way." Christ is over Moses. Moses was only a servant; Christ is a Son, the Master in His own house. He is the Heir (3:6).

Canaan, the land that flowed with milk and honey, was the Promised Land into which Joshua led the children of Israel. But this is only a picture of the rest of faith in God Himself that every Christian should enjoy. Saint Augustine said that no soul found rest until it found its rest in God. Joshua could not lead the children of Israel into this perfect rest and trust in God, but Jesus did. Cease from self-effort and yield yourself to Christ (4:10). Trust Jesus as your Joshua and "enter in" to His land of promise. Cease struggling and place all in His hand. (Read Psalm 37:5.)

Two Great Warnings

Warning 1: Give heed not to neglect so great salvation as is offered to us not by angels, but by the Lord Himself. Take heed to what the Son speaks (2:1-4).

Warning 2: Take heed not to depart from the living God (3:12).

Hebrews 4:12 shows the power of God's Word. Let the Word search and try you! Let God's Word have its proper place in your life. It searches out every motive and desire and purpose of your life, and helps you in evaluating them. Christ is the living Word of God. He is alive (quick) and powerful and all wise and all knowing.

The Superiority of the Priesthood of Christ (Hebrews 4:14—10:18)

Here begins the main theme. "Now the main point of what we have to say is this: We have such a High Priest" (Hebrews 8:1, *AMP*). Christ has been compared with all others, the prophets, angels, Moses and Joshua, but the most important comparison is with Aaron, the high priest. The writer shows that the priesthood of Christ is greater than the priesthood of the Levitical law.

The central point in the book is Christ's eternal priesthood and His sacrifice that availed for the sin of the world. The Epistle dwells upon the supreme importance and power of the blood of Christ in obtaining redemption for us. He has purged us from our sins and opened the way into the heavenly sanctuary and to the very throne of God.

Christ is Himself a priest. Listen to the Word: "Therefore, since we have a great high priest who has gone through the heavens, Jesus the Son of God, let us hold firmly to the faith we profess. For we do not have a high priest who is unable to sympathize with our weaknesses, but we have one who has been tempted in every way, just as we are—yet was without sin. Let us then approach the throne of grace with confidence, so that we may receive mercy and find grace to help us in our time of need" (4:14-16).

Jesus Christ not only had the qualifications of a priest like Aaron, the earthly high priest, but He also is a High Priest forever after the order of the eternal Melchizedek priesthood because this priesthood is continuous and will never end. The Aaronic priests could not make people perfect because they themselves were sinful, but Christ is eternal and sinless.

Christ's Priesthood Is Like Melchizedek (Genesis 14)

A royal priesthood—Both were kings of peace and righteousness.

Was universal—Not only for Jewish people.

Had no human ancestry—"Without father or mother."

Had no successor—When Melchizedek passed away, no one stepped into his place. So Christ is a priest forever.

Let us find an important fact here. Christian ministers are nowhere called "priests" in the New Testament except as all Christians are called "priests" (1 Peter 2:9). We have learned from Paul's letters that Christian ministers are called "teachers" and "pastors."

The glories of our Savior are exhibited in this Epistle. Three great "betters" are connected with our High Priest.

Christ—A Better Priest

Of a better covenant (Hebrews 8:13): A better covenant because it is based on better promises. These promises are written on the heart, not on tablets of stone (8:10).

Of a better tabernacle (9:1-12): Christ officiates in heaven. The Tabernacle was of this world. The high priest entered into the holy of holies once a year, but Christ has entered into the heavenly sanctuary "once for all."

Of a better sacrifice (10:18): He Himself is the sacrifice. He offered Himself as a lamb without blemish to cleanse us. The sacrifices of the Old Testament were calves and goats. They could not take away sin. They were but the shadow. This Sacrifice needed to be offered only once.

Christ is called our High Priest. What does that mean? We are taught very plainly in the Word that sin has cut people off from God. No sinner can approach God. The way has been closed. In the Old Testament, a representative, the high priest whom God appointed, could come into God's presence only once a year after sacrifice for the sins of the people had been made. He must offer the blood of calves and goats not only for the sins of the people, but also for his own sins, for he, too, was a sinner. He then would go into the holy place, then on beyond the veil into the holy of holies where the Ark of the Covenant rested. Here was the mercy seat, and here God met people through the mediator, the high priest.

How can we approach God today? Christ has made that possible. He is our High Priest, our representative before the Father. He entered into the heavenly sanctuary, God's presence, bearing the blood of His own sacrifice to cleanse us from our sins and to give to us eternal salvation. His blood had to be shed, for "without the shedding of blood there is no forgiveness" (9:22). "But when this priest had offered for all time one sacrifice for sins, he sat down at the right hand of God" (10:12). "It is finished," He said on the cross (John 19:30). All His work of redemption had been completed, hence we see Him sitting. We find this picture of Christ often in Hebrews.

Our High Priest is at the right hand of the Father at this minute, making intercession for you and for me (7:25; 8:1; 10:12). He has gone "now to appear for us in God's presence" (9:24). This is why we can have boldness to enter into the holiest by the blood of Jesus, by a new and living way (10:19-20). Avail yourself of this glorious privilege.

In Hebrews 9, our Lord's three great appearings stand out:

Past—On the cross—"But now he has appeared once for all at the end of the ages to do away with sin by the sacrifice of himself" (9:26).

Present—At the right hand of the throne—"now to appear for us in God's presence" (9:24).

Future—In the clouds of glory—"and he will appear a second time, not to bear sin, but to bring salvation to those who are waiting for him" (9:28).

Christ, a Better Sacrifice
Christ offered Himself as the sacrifice, a Lamb without blemish or

spot. The priest offered the lives of calves and goats, but these sacrifices could not take away sin. This better Sacrifice had only to be offered once and for all (10:10-18).

Because Christ has made this new and living way into the presence of the Father, let us come boldly to the throne of grace. The sin question is settled forever.

Let us not only approach the throne of grace, but let us also not neglect "meeting together, as some are in the habit of doing" (10:25). There is nothing like Christian fellowship to make us grow. D. L. Moody visited a woman who had grown cold in her Christian life. She said she had not been able to come to church, but otherwise she could not understand what had happened to make her feel as she did about spiritual things. Without saying a word, Mr. Moody arose and lifted out a live coal from the grate and placed it on the hearth. In a few moments the glow was gone and the coal was black. "I see it," she said. You cannot continue to glow in your Christian life alone. You need the warmth of fellowship with other Christians. This is a command to us.

The Superiority of the Life in Christ (Hebrews 10:19—13:25)

From now on, the writer tells us the kind of life we should live because of Christ's work as High Priest for us. We know He is at the right hand of God and that He ever liveth to make intercession for us.

After one has accepted Christ, there are levels of Christian living. Some Christians live in the basement of Christian experience, merely inside the building, but where it is dark, dismal and gloomy. Others live on the ground floor. They leave the first foundations and go on. Some sunlight enters, but their outlook is upon the circumstances about them. They live very close to the world. Still others live up higher. Sunlight and warmth flood the rooms. The noise and attractions of the worldly street do not disturb them. The air is pure. The outlook is toward the blue skies and distant mountains. These live above the world, hid with

Christ in God. God wishes us all to live continuously in this high realm.

Let us study a few men and women of God whose names are given in Hebrews 11 who were living a high look. The Holy Spirit tells us the secret of each life is faith, yet it is not so much his or her faith as their reliance upon our faithful God.

A Working Faith

The secret of Christian living is simply allowing Christ to meet our needs. Some say, "I have no faith; I can't believe." Yet we constantly place faith in our fellow humans. You want to go to New York from San Francisco. You buy your ticket and get on the airplane. In the course of your journey, a pilot will guide your plane. Without seeing him or knowing a thing about his ability, you trust your life to him. Faith is just trusting God, believing Him. There is nothing mysterious about faith. It is a simple act of the will. Either we will believe God or we won't. We decide. It is as simple as turning on an electric light switch. This is not a difficult or baffling or mysterious thing to do. But the result? Light and power. When we decide to believe God absolutely, then supernatural life and power enter our lives. A miracle is wrought within us. One of the practical results of faith is that it makes weak people strong (11:34).

To live in the Hall of Faith forever we need to do two things. First, like anyone entering a race, "let us throw off everything that hinders" (12:1). Yield everything to Christ. Second, we are really to believe that Jesus is trustworthy. When we do, we have given up the sin that so easily besets us—for that is the sin of unbelief. We give up that sin when we "fix our eyes on Jesus" (12:2).

Only one kind of human being in the world can please God. Who is it? (11:6). It is not what we do for God, but what God does for us that makes a life of power and strength. Our great God, rather than our great faith, is the thing to think most about. It is fashionable to be doubtful rather than sure about the great facts of God and Christ and salvation. But this cannot please God. To please God:

Forsaking
All
I
Take
Him

Christ is the belief that brings salvation.

Because of the great company of witnesses on the bleachers watching from heaven, let us run the race of life God has set before us. As any athlete does when preparing for a race, let us lay aside every sinful habit and anything that would hinder us (12:1-2).

Let us have patience—12:1

Endure chastening—12:11

Follow peace and purity of heart—12:14

Always looking to Jesus, the author and finisher of our faith.

A life well pleasing in His sight will be made possible by the Lord Himself.

"May the God of peace, who through the blood of the eternal covenant brought back from the dead our Lord Jesus, that great Shepherd of the sheep, equip you with everything good for doing his will, and may he work in us what is pleasing to him, through Jesus Christ, to whom be glory for ever and ever. Amen" (Hebrews 13:20-21).

Chapter 47

Understanding James

James Portrays Jesus Christ, Our Pattern

Selected Bible Readings

Sunday: Faith Tested (James 1:1-21)
Monday: Faith Lived Out (James 1:22-27)
Tuesday: Faith and Brotherhood (James 2:1-13)
Wednesday: Faith Dead Without Works (James 2:14-26)
Thursday: Faith and Tongue Control (James 3:1-18)
Friday: Faith Rebukes Worldliness (James 4:1-17)
Saturday: Faith in Prayer (James 5:1-20)

The law of Christ for daily life is found in the word "doers." "But be ye doers of the word, and not hearers only" (James 1:22, *KJV*).

The author of the book is no doubt James, the brother of our Lord. He may well be called the practical apostle. He stands for efficiency and consistency in life and conduct.

Three men by the name of James are mentioned in the New Testament—the son of Zebedee, the son of Alphaeus, and James the Great, our Lord's brother. Although James refers to his own brother Jesus only twice, he does it in a most reverent manner. Though he knew Him so well, there was no familiarity, for he called Him Lord and Christ. He associates his brother with God so as to imply an equality with the Almighty. If Jesus were not deity, this would be blasphemous.

Guidebook for Everyday Religion

The book of James is the most practical of all the Epistles, and has been called "A Practical Guide to Christian Life and Conduct." This book is the Proverbs of the New Testament. It is filled with moral precepts. It states the ethics of Christian faith. It is full of figures and metaphors. It is often quite dramatic in style. It compels real thought. Hebrews presents doctrine; James presents deeds. They go together in vital Christian faith.

Neither is there conflict between Paul and James. Only superficial reading of both would bring that indictment. Paul says, "Take the gospel in." James says, "Take it out." Paul saw Christ in the heavens establishing our righteousness. James saw Him on the earth telling us to be perfect even as His Father in heaven is perfect.

Paul dwells on the source of our faith. James tells of the fruit of our faith. One lays the foundations in Christ; the other builds the superstructure. Christ is both "author and finisher" (Hebrews 12:2) of our faith. Not only believe it, but live it! Although Paul lays great stress upon justification by faith, we have noticed in his Epistles, especially in Titus, that he lays great stress on good works. It is an astounding fact that while Paul uses the expression "rich in good deeds" (1 Timothy 6:18), James uses "rich in faith" (2:5). It is well to notice, too, that when James seems to speak in a slighting way of faith, he means a mere intellectual belief and not a "saving faith" that is so essential. James exalts faith. He says its trial worketh patience. His Epistle opens and closes with a strong encouragement to pray (1:6; 5:14-18). He only denounces the spurious faith that does not produce works.

James calls himself a "servant of Jesus Christ." He proudly accepts this title as a description of what his relationship was to Jesus. This speaks of real humility because James nowhere refers to the fact of his earthly relationship to the Lord Jesus Christ, a brother.

James mentions the name of God seventeen times, but he repeats the name of Jesus only twice. James was bitterly opposed to Jesus and His claims up to the time of His death, but after the Resurrection he was converted by a special and private interview with the risen Lord (1 Corinthians 15:7). This adds value to James's testimony about the deity of our Lord. Immediately he became a man of prayer and was made bishop of the church at Jerusalem

(Acts 15:13-21). His life work was to win the Jewish people and to help them believe in Jesus their Messiah. At the end, he was slain by the religious leaders in A.D. 62. Tradition says he was probably forced to the roof of the Temple by the high priest and rulers and commanded to blaspheme the name of Christ. He, rather, boldly proclaimed the fact that Jesus is the Son of God. James was hurled from the roof to instant death.

James says his Epistle is written "to the twelve tribes scattered among the nations" (1:1), to those who lived outside the holy land. Then there were no lost tribes for he addressed his letter to the twelve whose location was well known at the time. Like Hebrews, it is addressed to the Jewish believers in Jesus. The Jewish people to whom he wrote had not ceased to practice their religion, although they had embraced Jesus as Messiah. Many of them had believed on the Day of Pentecost, and had carried home only a partial understanding of the gospel. In their enthusiasm at having found the true Messiah, they neglected the graces and virtues that should accompany faith in Christ. They taught that all that was necessary to have salvation was to believe that Jesus was the true Messiah and Savior. They were in great danger of being discouraged in their faith by the persecution of their own unbelieving country people.

Faith Victor over Temptation (James 1:1-21)

After the briefest of greetings, James plunges straight into his subject. Realizing that these scattered Jewish believers were undergoing severe testing of their faith, he begins by telling them how they must meet temptation and tries to encourage and comfort them.

Spiritual arithmetic is of value. The arithmetic of the Bible is important and none of us can afford to ignore it. James invites Christians to "count." "Count it all joy when ye fall into divers temptations" (1:2, *KJV*). We usually count it joy when we escape temptation and sorrow. Instead, we should count testing as a glorious opportunity of proving our faith, just as the automobile manufacturer knows that the best proof of the car's worth is the road test. Why we must count it joy is not because of the trial itself, but what it will work out. In other words, use your trials. What is the purpose of testing? God makes our trials the instrument of blessing (1:3). Too often our trials work impatience, but God will give grace that His real purpose may be accomplished. Patience is more necessary than anything else in our faith life. We forget that time is nothing with God, for with Him a thousand years is as one day, and one day as a thousand years. Christ's purpose in our lives is that we shall be perfect and entire, wanting nothing.

Let us be careful where we lay the blame of temptation. Read James 1:14 carefully. Testings of character come from God (Genesis 22:1), but temptations to evil never come from Him, but from the adversary through our own corrupt nature (James 1:13), and the appeal is made to meet a proper desire in an improper way (1:14). Instead of wrong things coming from God, we find that only good and perfect gifts come from above, from the Father of lights, who never changes (1:17). Our God is a God who loves to give. Alexander the Great said to one overwhelmed with his generosity. "I give as a king!" Our Father in heaven gives to us as the infinite God.

It is hard to behave wisely, but God's wisdom will help you to do it. Put together the teaching on wisdom in this short letter. Pray for wisdom to behave wisely in time of trial. When you are wronged and insulted, ask God how you shall act. "If any of you lacks wisdom, he should ask God, who gives generously to all without finding fault, and it will be given to him" (1:5). What a sad lack! What a mess such a lack can lead us into. Does James say, "If you lack wisdom, sit down and think or study"? No, he says the wisdom we need is from above.

Did it ever occur to you to thank God for temptations? Do you think of your temptations as blessings? Yet James says, "Consider it pure joy, my brothers, whenever you face trials of many kinds" (1:2). Do you count it so? Then he adds, "Blessed is the man who perseveres under trial" (1:12). How spineless and weak you would become without temptation. Valueless is the character that knows no testing. There is a joy of overcoming. There is no greater satisfaction than to know we have resisted temptation victoriously.

James begins and ends with prayer (1:5-8; 5:13-18). Prayer is one of the easiest subjects to talk upon, but one of the hardest to practice. Find all you can about this subject in this Epistle. What about his practice? Tradition tells us that on his death they discovered that his knees were worn hard as a camel's through constant habit of prayer.

Faith Shows in Our Actions (James 1:22—2:26)

Don't be merely listeners to God's Word, but put the gospel into practice. What is the good of people saying they have faith if they do not prove it by actions? We must not be satisfied with only "hearing." We must go on "doing" (James 1:22). People who are hearers and not doers are like those looking at themselves in a mirror and then going away and forgetting how they looked (1:24).

James says we must keep looking into the mirror of God's Word to remember how we look, to find out the sin in our lives. Those who look carefully into the Scriptures and practice them will be blessed in what they do. Those who think they are religious and don't control their tongues, these people's religion is vain. The religion that does not influence the tongue is not a true or vital one. An uncontrolled tongue in a Christian is a terrible thing— guard it. Control your temper. It is dangerous. Under trial, be slow to speak. Keep the draft closed and the fire will go out (1:26).

What shall we do with the Word?

Receive it—1:21
Hear it—1:23
Do it—1:22
Examine it—1:25.

Works Are Results

Works do not save us, but they are a pretty good evidence that we are saved. "whatever you did for one of the least of these brothers of mine, you did for me" (Matthew 25:40) is not a "saving" text, but a "sign" text. What He has done is our salvation; what "you have done" is the proof of it. Keep faith and works in their proper place.

Because of all this, James says in effect, "The faith you have is the faith you show." "Religion that God our Father accepts as pure and faultless is this: to look after orphans and widows in their distress and to keep oneself from being polluted by the world" (1:27).

Christianity is a brotherhood that has no "respect of persons" (2:1-4, *KJV*).

How the world today ignores James's command not to show favoritism! The world worships the successful, strong and wealthy, and despises the person who is poor. A Christian must not show partiality to the person of wealth and position, James tells us, but it seems that money and honor are the only things that people worship today. Showing favoritism is not only a breach of good manners and discourtesy to the poor, but it also is a sin to worship rank and insult the poor. By doing this, we break the law of God. "Love your neighbor as yourself" (Leviticus 19:18). This law of love is a royal law (2:8). It comes from heaven's Royalty. We are not only to admire and respect others, but also to love them as we do our own selves (2:1-13).

What Is Sin?

To disobey God's law is sin. It is human to gloss over sin. A little girl said when excusing herself for something she had done, "I haven't broken the commandment, I only cracked it." James says that whosoever obeys the whole law and only makes a single slip is guilty of everything (2:10-11). That person is a lawbreaker. If brought into court for violating a traffic ordinance, he or she does not plead that all the other laws have been kept. The judge is interested only in the fact of whether this person has broken this particular law. If so, this person is classified as a lawbreaker. We may have a fine chain, but of what use is it if all the links are good except one? That broken link renders the entire chain useless.

It is clear that the one sin thought of here is mentioned in 2:9—showing favoritism to the wealthy.

Faith that does not express itself in works is of no value. Faith is revealed by what we do. What is the use of us saying we have faith if we do not prove it by our actions? Just as a body without a spirit is dead, so faith is dead without actions (2:17).

Has the phrase "friend of God" ever gripped you? God evidently needed a friend, and He found in Abraham the friendship He desired. What is essential to become a friend of God (see 2:23)?

Faith Shown in Our Words (James 3:1-18)

Our speech reveals what and whose we are. It expresses our personality more than anything else. Anyone who controls his or her tongue, James says, is a perfect person (3:2). If a person has mastery over that difficult member, the tongue, the rest is easy. A person is able to curb the whole nature. Just as we control a spirited horse by a firm hand on the bridle, so the hand of the Man, Christ Jesus, can grip and firmly use the bit and bridle on our tongues. Just as a great ship is controlled by a very small rudder and turned in any direction the captain determines, so the pierced hands of Jesus can firmly control and wisely use the helm of our lives—our tongue. The tongue, though small, is very powerful. It can determine the course of human life.

Remember, this same tongue can be used to testify for Christ and praise His holy name. It is the instrument the Holy Spirit uses to magnify the Lord (3:9-10). We should not praise God and curse people who are made in His likeness! Cruel words have wrecked homes, broken friendships, divided churches and sent untold millions to ruin and despair. Many people who call themselves Christians seem not to make the slightest effort to control the tongue.

Faith Shown in Our Purity of Character (James 4:1-17)

The devil has organized this world system upon principles opposed to God in every way. They are principles of force, greed, ambition, selfishness and pleasure. The believer should be crucified to this world (Galatians 6:14). We should count its passing pleasures, its honors, its treasures as of little value, and remain unmoved by its attractions. The world is that system of things about us or that spirit within us that is blind and deaf to the value of spiritual things and cares nothing about doing the will of God. Because we live in the world, surrounded by all its attractions and the things needful to our daily living, we must be very watchful to keep our affections above the border line of the world (James 4:4).

People keep asking, "How can we end war?" But James goes back farther and tells us what causes war. A cause of most of the wars that have devastated the earth has been some nation's desire to get what does not belong to it. This has always been the cause of quarrels between individuals. Selfishness is the root of it all. Next, people fail to pray, or if they do it is with a wrong motive, to spend what they get upon themselves instead of having their lives glorify God (4:1-3). God promises to answer prayer, but He will not give to those who would consume it on their own pleasures.

It is common to see worldly minded Christians praying for purely selfish reasons. Often you hear people say, "I don't believe in prayer. I prayed for a new car, and God didn't give it to me," or "My husband was sick and I prayed that God would heal him, and he died." In either case, the answer might easily have led the person farther away from God. The car would have been driven to the beach and not to church. The family circle restored could make the wife find her joy in her husband rather than in her Lord.

Four times the word "lust" is found in the first five verses of James 4 (in the *KJV*). Dr. Jowett (Benjamin Jowett, 1817-1893, British educator and theologian) defines it as "anything that steams the windows of the soul and blurs our vision." This word "lust" can be translated "pleasures." This helps give meaning to these verses and furnishes the clue to the teaching they contain.

Overindulgence in pleasure is sinful:

First, there are "fights and quarrels among you" (4:1). The newspapers are filled with horrible pictures of this every day.

Second, your desires "battle within you" (4:2). If pleasure is allowed to have its own way in us, a war is on and we are mastered by it.

Third, "When you ask, you do not receive, because you ask with wrong motives, that you may spend what you get on your pleasures" (4:3). Overindulgence in pleasure always affects the prayer life. We stagnate in our Christian life.

Fourth, "You adulterous people"—how a pleasure lover degenerates in the Christian walk! He or she becomes a friend of the world, an enemy of God (4:4).

What is the cure for all this? Examine 4:6-10.

Submit to God (4:7). We have made a mess of our lives because of a lack of surrender to God.

"Come near to God and he will come near to you" (4:8). Come with clean hands and a pure heart.

"Humble yourselves before the Lord" (4:10). Remember yourself as a sinner and take the lowly place. Then God will lift you up.

To be friends with the world means to be at enmity with God (4:4). Jesus said, "You cannot serve both God and Money" (Matthew 6:24). Therefore surrender yourself to God and be not subject to the devil. When the devil is resisted by those who have surrendered themselves to God, he flees.

How easy it is for us to plan without God, yet how futile! Let us submit all our plans to the Lord and see what His will is in the matter. "If it is the Lord's will" (James 4:15). One of the most amazing things in all of God's Word is that though He holds the whole universe in His hands, He has a definite plan for each one of our lives. Our lives are a series of surprises. We live just one day at a time. We know not what shall be on the morrow (1 John 3:1-2). What a wonderful God we have!

Faith Shown by Our Prayer Lives (James 5:1-20)

Evidently, many of the humble folk among the Jewish believers were being oppressed by the rich and their hard earnings were being "kept back by fraud" (James 5:4, KJV). James warns the rich! "You have hoarded wealth in the last days" (5:3). How true this is today—heaped up millions, yes, billions. The coffers of the rich are full indeed. They are charged with fraud and injustice. How much goes on today under the cloak of Christianity! It is true there are some great Christian souls among the rich, but for the most part, James's picture of wealth holds good. You remember that Jesus said it was easier for a camel to go through the eye of a needle than for a rich man to enter heaven.

Here again the tongue is brought in. It is amazing how many Christians take the name of the Lord in vain in ordinary conversation (5:12). God says, "The Lord will not hold anyone guiltless who misuses his name" (Exodus 20:7; Deuteronomy 5:11). This is a serious indictment.

Prayer is a golden key that, kept bright by constant use, will unlock the treasures of earth and heaven.

James gives us a series of short phrases of advice. If anyone is in trouble, he should pray. If anyone is merry, he should sing. If anyone is sick, he should send for the elders of the church and let them anoint him with oil and pray for him (5:13-14). The Bible says, "And the prayer offered in faith will make the sick person well; the Lord will raise him up. If he has sinned, he will be forgiven" (5:15). If anyone has wronged another, he should confess his fault to that one (5:16). The prayer of faith demands confession of sin, and a will surrendered to God. Elijah's mighty prayer that opened and closed the heavens is an example to us, for "the prayer of a righteous man is powerful and effective" (5:16).

This Epistle closes abruptly on a high plane. It is with the gracious act of a Christian who finds someone erring from the truth and converts that person. Although only God can save a soul, He uses human instruments to accomplish it. "Whoever turns a sinner from the error of his way will save him from death and cover over a multitude of sins."

Chapter 48

Understanding First Peter

First Peter Portrays Jesus Christ, Precious Cornerstone of Our Faith

Selected Bible Readings

Sunday: Precious Faith (1 Peter 1:1-12)
Monday: Precious Blood (1 Peter 1:13-25)
Tuesday: Precious Cornerstone (1 Peter 2:1-10)
Wednesday: Precious Saviour (1 Peter 2:11-25)
Thursday: Precious Is a Meek and Quiet Spirit (1 Peter 3:1-22)
Friday: Precious Suffering of Christ (1 Peter 4:1-19)
Saturday: Precious Crowns (1 Peter 5:1-14)

Jesus lived the kind of life described in this letter of Peter's and in 1 John: "Whoever claims to live in him must walk as Jesus did" (1 John 2:6). To "abide in Christ" is to rest quietly where we are. We who have received Christ as Savior are "in him" (Colossians 3:3). The secret of walking "in newness of life" (Romans 6:4, *KJV*) or victorious Christian living is simply to "remember Jesus Christ" (2 Timothy 2:8) and to rest on the blessed eternal fact of His sufficiency.

"Now to you who believe, this stone is precious" (1 Peter 2:7). Peter talks about seven precious things. Mark these in your Bible:

Precious trial of faith—1:7
Precious blood—1:19
Precious Cornerstone—2:4-6
Precious Christ—2:7
Precious spirit—3:4

Precious faith—2 Peter 1:1

Precious promises—2 Peter 1:4.

Peter has been called the "apostle of hope," as John was the "apostle of love" and Paul the "apostle of faith." The word "hope" is found in 1 Peter 1:3,13,21; 3:15.

Another word (or its equivalent) is used fourteen times in this short Epistle (in the *KJV*), and that is "suffering," the suffering of Christ and of Christians in following Him.

Try a complete reading at one sitting of this short four-page letter, preferably in *Phillips* or *New International Version* or another modern translation. Mark in two colors each mention of *joy* and *grace* and *glory* (in red perhaps), and of *suffering* (in black). At least twenty-six times Peter dwells on the joy and glory that are ours who have received God's grace against the fourteen times he mentions the suffering of Christ and the Christian following Him.

Try to see that Peter was enlarging on the statement, "Let us fix our eyes on Jesus, the author and perfecter of our faith, who for the joy set before him endured the cross, scorning its shame, and sat down at the right hand of the throne of God" (Hebrews 12:2). He knew the connection between suffering and joy and glory.

This book was written by Peter toward the close of his busy life (around A.D. 67) and was delivered by Silas (5:12), one of Paul's companions. Peter had become a leader of the apostles. He was the spokesman. He belonged to the inner circle of the three friends of Christ. He was the preacher at Pentecost. The first twelve chapters of Acts are centered around this apostle and his ministry. He went about preaching to the Jewish people. At last he died a martyr's death, being crucified under the Roman emperor Nero. According to tradition, at his own request, he was crucified with his head downward, considering himself unworthy to even resemble his Master in death.

The picture of Peter in the Gospels is amazingly different from that found in his own writings. In the Gospels we see Peter, the impulsive, restless soul, sometimes fearless but again a coward, even going as far as to deny his Lord with a curse! In his own Epistles we see him patient, restful and loving, and having a courage purified and strengthened by the indwelling Spirit. This is a wonderful illustration of the transforming work of God in a human life.

The Christians to whom Peter is writing were suffering "fiery trials" from people who did not believe in Jesus. The Christians would not join their pagan neighbors in idolatry and drinking and lust, so they were called haters of the human race and were classed with thieves and murderers. Lives today are on the auction block, sold to the highest bidder. The world is bidding high. Let Christ have a chance. (See 1 Peter 1:18-19.)

This letter was evidently written at a time when general dislike of Christians was threatening to pass into active persecution (2:15; 3:13-17; 4:12). It was about the time of Nero's persecutions. Peter himself suffered under this cruel emperor not later than A.D. 67. Read 1:1-3,6-9; 2:13-17; 4:12-19.

A subject repeatedly mentioned is the "reappearing" of our Lord and Savior. Mark this as the letter is read. The influence of this "blessed hope" on the Christian's way of life cannot be escaped. This short Epistle is full of golden nuggets of truth, which can be marked and memorized. Try it!

Let us discover what this letter has for our own lives as we read it. We are not enduring persecutions of hostile emperors, but we are meeting on every side the alluring temptations of that same adversary, the devil, who is seeking those whom he may win away from Christ, who endured all for us. Although we are not witnesses of the suffering of Christ as was Peter, we may be taught by the same Holy Spirit. Ask the Holy Spirit to teach you today!

This book gives us good plain advice from Peter about how we ought to live. Read it and take heed! We find here how Peter has been growing in his experience. This letter shows him some twelve or more years after the last record of him in Acts 15. He wishes to encourage the believers and so he gives his own personal testimony. He adds assurance because he could prove from his own experience all he was saying. There is power in personal testimony. This personal note sounds through all the letter. The Christians were experiencing a time of trial (1:6). They needed encouragement from one who knew what trial meant. Peter points away from the trials to the future glory that awaited them (1:7), to the example of Christ (2:21) and the reward that would follow (4:13).

Privileges of the Christian (1 Peter 1:1—2:10)

Peter, who is an apostle of jubilant hope, addresses this Epistle to the "strangers" scattered everywhere. It is a letter to homesick Christians. He tells these persecuted and discouraged ones of a near and precious Savior. Let it lift you up and fill you with joy! This is the purpose of the book.

What are our privileges as Christians? First, we are redeemed by the precious blood of Christ. This is our position in Christ (1:18-19). Because of this relationship to Christ, we have everything in Him that God desires us to possess. If God has given us His Son, will He not freely with Him give us all things? (Romans 8:32.)

The life of faith is described at the beginning. We are born of God (begotten) (1:3). At the end there is an inheritance for us (1:4), and to assure us of it we are "kept" by the power of God (1:5). What a life this is!

We have been begotten by Jesus Christ into a lively hope—1:3

We have in reserve an imperishable inheritance—1:4,5,10

We are kept by the power of God—1:5

We are being purified to fit us to stand with Christ—1:7

We have salvation for our souls—1:9

We have a gospel that angels desire to look into—1:12

We have a great hope—1:13

We have redemption through His blood—1:18-19

We shall not be put to shame—2:6

We are born again by His Word—1:23

We are built up a spiritual house—2:5

We are a chosen people—2:9

We shall have a crown of glory—5:4.

Peter gives good plain advice about how we ought to live (1:13-16). Here he says, "Therefore, prepare your minds for action; be self-controlled; set your hope fully on the grace to be given you when Jesus Christ is revealed" (1:13). Fashion your life after the Lord Jesus Christ. Don't live your life after the old pattern. "Be holy, because I am holy" (1:16). "Love one another" (1:22). Seeing you are "born again" (1:23), live like it. You are a new creature in Christ Jesus.

How can anyone put away all wickedness as Peter commands (chap. 2)? Not by effort! Not by trying! Not by practice! Not by setting our willpower against sin! But by trusting that God by His grace can do it. The only people who can "put away" sin are the ones who, having received Christ as Savior, know that Christ has "put away" their sin.

First, we must "rid ourselves." Peter summons us to abandon some ugly things—wickedness, guile, hypocrisy, envies and evil speaking (2:1). From the root of wickedness all these noxious weeds spring. These must go from our hearts if we would grow. Weeds always choke out the plant if we allow them to spread. All that challenges the supremacy of the Lord Jesus Christ must go, whether it be our sin or our righteousness. Sometimes even good things keep us from God's best. "But seek first his kingdom and his righteousness, and all these things will be given to you as well" (Matthew 6:33). We must be careful of this. The choices you must make are not always between bad and good, right and wrong, but between the good and the best. As for God, "his way is perfect" (Psalm 18:30).

Christian Infants

We are called "newborn babies" (2:2). Newborn babies have no treasury of supplies in themselves. They are helpless and dependent from morning till night. They need food, clothing, shelter, the tireless care of a mother and protection of a father. It is a parable of Christian men and women. Christians have nothing in themselves, but they have access to the unsearchable riches of Christ and are filled with all the fullness of God. As new Christians, we have a new longing in our hearts, a new hunger. We are not self-sustained; we are God-sustained. We are newborn babes the whole way through. Peter describes the attitude as desiring the spiritual milk, "the sincere milk of the word" *(KJV)*. Food makes a difference. Spiritual milk makes us grow unto salvation. So that's the thing we live on. The Word as "milk" suggests that it is a perfect food for children, containing all the elements for building up the body. So the Word is perfect for building up the soul.

"Word" in 2:2 could very well mean Christ as well as His Word, for in the third verse we read that if you have once tasted of the Lord you will find He is gracious. He is the nourishment of our souls.

Peter says that when we become "children of God" (John 1:12), we are like newborn babies (1 Peter 2:2,3). We need food to make us grow. This is just what God has provided in His Word. Desire the Word as newborn babes, and eating it, grow thereby. You will find that it tastes good (Jeremiah 15:16; Ezekiel 3:1-3). Christ will become real and gracious to you (1 Peter 1:23; 2:2-3).

A Study in Stones

Right here Peter turned to another figure and called Christ a "stone," rejected by men, but precious in God's sight (2:4). Everyone in this world has to do something with this "Stone," Christ Jesus. He is in every person's path. We can lift Him up and put Him in as the chief Cornerstone of our lives, which is God's will. But if we do not, we must stumble headlong over Him, trag-ically, to our death. To many people in the first century, He was a stumbling block and a rock of offense. To many today, He is just that. What have you done with this precious "Cornerstone"? Is He in His rightful place in your life?

And we are stones, too, laid up on Christ as the foundation and cornerstone to make a spiritual temple to God. This makes it very important for each one of us to find our right place in God's plan and stay in it. The "spiritual house" (2:5), built up of believers, is the corporate temple of the Holy Spirit, as the individual Christian is the individual temple of the Holy Spirit (1 Corinthians 6:19).

We are not only "living stones" in a spiritual temple, but each of us is also a priest in this temple. Priests represent God to peo-ple, and people to God. Christians are a "holy priesthood" (1 Peter 2:5). Are you representing God to others by your life, and others to God by your intercessory prayer? As priests, we cannot offer lambs and goats today, but Paul tells us to offer ourselves a living sacrifice (Romans 12:1).

A Precious Savior

"Now to you who believe, this stone is precious" (1 Peter 2:7). Charles Spurgeon's wonderful preaching started here. When only a youth in his teens, he was walking out with a friend to an appointment in the country.

"I hope the Lord will bless you," said his companion.

"Me!" exclaimed the young fellow, "I never preached."

"Well, if you don't preach this time there will be no preaching."

Right there the young man, appointed of God, all unaware of the fact that he was to be the greatest preacher of his age, bowed his head. In a few minutes he rose and addressed the crowd in the words of this text in 1 Peter. God was there. It was his first text and the theme of all his gracious ministry. Christ was ever precious to him and his sermons were precious to the people.

Duties of the Christian (1 Peter 2:11—4:11)

Peter is giving us wise counsel by telling us how to behave in the game of life. Up to this point, he has been exhorting the Christians to walk worthy of their new calling. Now he urges them to glorify God before an ungodly and persecuting world. A greenhouse religion is of very little value to others. It is good for us to be compelled to justify our faith before our fellow humans.

Peter offers a simple program. Anyone can follow it. Any earnest seeker can find the way Peter commends. His first suggestion is that we remember we are "pilgrims" *(KJV)*. We are not settled here, but we are on our way to an eternal city. It is important that we keep this in mind, otherwise we will be tying our lives to stakes that will be shaken loose some day.

But for Christians who have followed Peter's plan, all is different. They have invested time and thought and money in the pursuit of Christ's plan for their lives. Christians find life "sweeter as the years go by," and the end is the best of all!

The greatest satisfaction that can come to Christians is to please the Lord and Savior. In the power of the Lord, live for Christ in all phases of your life. Do not shut Him out of even the most insignificant parts. It will not be easy; the devil will see to that. He will use every weapon against you. But Christ has already won the victory over him and that victory may be yours for the asking. Read again 1 Corinthians 15:57.

Christians are not at home in this world. They are away from home, "as aliens and strangers in the world" (1 Peter 2:11; "as strangers and pilgrims," *KJV*), for "our citizenship is in heaven" (Philippians 3:20). We are in the world, but not of it (John 17:11,14).

Peter makes an earnest appeal in this scene. First there is a call to purity of life. Christians are warned against all fleshly appetites, for they are like an infection in our blood. If we once let them have a place in our lives, they will contaminate our souls and pollute our characters worse than any disease harms our bodies. There is no health, strength or personhood left in us and all on account of sin. The soul may be dragged down to hell or lifted up to heaven. The body is the main channel through which debasing influences affect the soul. A Christian's life is to be true in the presence of those who are not yet Christian. This will disarm opposition and glorify God. Peter says, "I urge you...to abstain from sinful desires" (2:11).

The Power of Influence

We are to influence others by what we say and do. "Keep your behavior excellent among the Gentiles" (1 Peter 2:12, *NASB*). People are not reading much religious literature on paper, but they are doing a lot of reading in religious (or antireligious) works by those professing Christ. It seems trite to say, but it is true that more are won to Christ by the true Christian life of the believer than by any other means. If it is true that what you are speaks so loudly I cannot hear what you say, then it is equally true that your deeds speak so loudly that I cannot help but believe what you say.

This subject of the way a Christian lives is discussed from 2:12—4:11. It was the all-important topic in Peter's mind for those

Christians who were the only "Bible" known or read of the world in their day.

"Though [the pagans] accuse you of doing wrong" (2:12). The Christians were accused of horrible crimes. They were called atheists because they denied the Roman gods. They were regarded as unpatriotic because emperor worship was the official religion. To reject the state religion was considered an outrage against the state itself. The Christians would often be obliged to depart from social customs and often bore the stigma of evildoers. The answer to all this must be in the superior moral life of every Christian. They must live beyond reproach.

Today some of you are subjected to severe tests. Your companions do many things, both in business and recreation, that you as a Christian cannot do. Your action will be misunderstood and misrepresented. You will be called "narrow" or a "killjoy" or a "wet blanket." The best way to meet all such criticism is not to assume an air of superiority or holier-than-thou attitude. Don't regard yourself as a martyr, but accept the position by smiling and trying to be helpful to those who are finding fault with you. Nothing cools opposition like a gentle laugh of love.

Freedom Defined

"Live as free men, but do not use your freedom as a cover-up for evil" (2:16). I heard an amusing story of the early days of the Russian Revolution. After the Czar had abdicated, a stout old woman was seen walking leisurely down the middle of one of the busiest streets in Saint Petersburg, at no small peril to herself and to the great confusion of traffic. A policeman pointed out to her that there was a walk for pedestrians and that the street was for wagons, automobiles and horsemen. But she was not to be convinced. "I am going to walk just where I like," she said. "We've got liberty now." When we assert to do as we like, we are as thoughtless and foolish as the old woman. Freedom is not a question of doing as we like. It is rather a question of doing as we should.

Peter tells his readers how to live their lives (2:17, *KJV*).

"Honour all men!" Show respect for others.

"Love the brotherhood." Every social problem could be solved.

"Fear God." The fear of the Lord is the beginning of wisdom. "Honour the king." Show respect for your government.

One of the most convincing and powerful demonstrations Christians can give that they have a newborn life is the enduring of wrong and injustice patiently (2:19-20). That is when we show forth the grace of God. That is what Christ did while He was on earth and in submitting to His crucifixion and death. This is what His followers are to do as we "follow in his steps" (2:21).

Patience in undeserved punishment is one way of testifying for Christ. A wicked crowd in his regiment took a violent dislike to one Christian soldier because he wouldn't swear or gamble or travel a loose life with them. His days were made miserable. But he never lost his temper or gave in or tried to pay them back, and in the end he led one of the worst of the fellows to Christ.

Such suffering by Christians from injustice, without retaliation or defense, is a reflection of the vicarious atonement of Christ (2:24). "With man this is impossible, but with God all things are possible" (Matthew 19:26). We are to suffer "patiently." Patience is noble because it is Christlike (1 Peter 3:17-18; 4:12-16). Peter points to the example of his Master. The secret of patience is always found in divine grace (James 1:3-4).

The Man Who Suffered for Me

"Christ suffered for you" (2:21). A lady was visiting in a hospital. She went up to a bed on which lay a wounded soldier and said gently, "Thank you for being wounded for me." The young man's face brightened. That was a new thought to him. It made the pain more bearable to look upon it in that light. Do you realize that many years ago One was wounded for you? And that One was the Son of God Himself? Yes, He was wounded for my transgressions, by His stripes I am healed (2:24).

Charles H. Spurgeon puts it this way: "The remedy for your sins and mine is found in the substitutionary suffering of the Lord Jesus Christ, and in this only. But if I say of a certain ointment that it heals, I do not deny that you need a bandage with which to apply it to the wound. Faith is the linen which binds the plaster of Christ's reconciliation to the sore of my sin. The linen does not heal; that is the work of the ointment. So faith does not heal; that is the work of the atonement of Christ."

We find in chapters 2 and 3 some instructions for the various relationships of our lives. First, there are some personal instructions (2:1-12). Next we find our social relationships. Servants should obey their masters with respect, not only those masters who are good and considerate, but also those who are arbitrary. In 3:1-7, our home relationships are mentioned. Naturally the home begins with the marriage relationship. "Wives, in the same way be submissive to your husbands." This means unselfish devotion so as to win his love and admiration. This might sound unreasonable if we did not hear the injunction to husbands (3:7) that they "be considerate as [they] live with [their] wives, and treat them with respect." This makes a wife subject to love that acts in knowledge and not according to selfish desires. It is manly for a husband to be tender toward his wife. God's plan is that the love of husband and wife should be a mutual thing. Each one shall consider the other. The result of all this will be a marriage relationship in which prayers are not hindered (3:7). Prayer is the surest secret of success in any married life.

Peter says that the Christian is a:

"Baby" (2:2), desiring the milk of the Word.

"Living stone" (2:5), built into the temple of life.

"Priest"—offering spiritual sacrifices.

"Stranger"—to keep himself unspotted from the world.

"Alien" ("Pilgrim," *KJV*)—good deeds along the way.

"Citizen"—render obedience to rulers.

"Man"—honor all people in the fear of God.

"Servant"—subject unto Christ.

"Sufferer"—to be patient, committing all to Christ.

"Steward" (4:10).

"One speaking the very words of God" (4:11).

Peter gives the way to be happy in a world that is wretched. "For, 'Whoever would love life and see good days must keep his tongue from evil and his lips from deceitful speech. He must turn from evil and do good; he must seek peace and pursue it. For the eyes of the Lord are on the righteous and his ears are attentive to their prayer, but the face of the Lord is against those who do evil'" (3:10-12). He quotes Psalm 34:12-14. This is a remedy that works today as well as it worked in David's time. The best way of making this life happy and prosperous is to keep from speaking evil and from slander and to be always ready to overcome evil with good.

A Ready Answer

Another important command is given in 1 Peter 3:15. This is for every one of us. "Always be prepared to give an answer to everyone who asks you to give the reason for the hope that you have." Have you an intelligent answer to give to others of your trust in Christ? If not, stop right here and get one ready. What does Christ mean to you?

Christ's sufferings in the flesh were physical and literal. "He himself bore our sins in his body on the tree" (2:24). Christians' sufferings, spoken of in 4:1, are spiritual. Christ suffered when He was put to death on the cross. "For Christ died for sins once for all, the righteous for the unrighteous, to bring you to God" (3:18). Christians take up their cross and follow Christ, denying themselves (Matthew 16:24). The phrase "Arm yourselves also with the same attitude" (1 Pet. 4:1) means the same as the words, "If anyone would come after me, he must deny himself and take up his cross and follow me" (Matthew 16:24). Such a high resolve will involve a measure of actual suffering, for God's will may cut across our desire to gratify some bodily craving. Very few in this world escape suffering, either mental, physical or spiritual. We cannot choose the way we shall suffer.

Often God allows us to go through life denied the one thing we wish more than anything else. But we should be comforted in this that whom God loves, He chastens. If He grinds down the surface of our lives, it is that the stone may shine the more brilliantly. The many facets of the diamond are what make it dazzling. Know that the greater the suffering in this world, the greater the glory in heaven. This is what Peter means in 4:2.

The Christian sometimes has to forego the gratification of even right desires. The natural cravings of the body for food and drink, for example, are not to be considered merely as ends in themselves. They come to have a spiritual meaning that whether we eat or drink, or whatever we do, we do all to the glory of God (1 Corinthians 10:31). "Therefore, if what I eat causes my brother to fall into sin, I will never eat meat again, so that I will not cause him to fall" (1 Corinthians 8:13). Sometimes we must refuse for the sake of others. This is "the mind of Christ."

Be careful not to follow the world, "doing what pagans choose to do" (1 Peter 4:3). What the heathen world wanted the Jewish believers in Jesus to do Peter names here. "Debauchery" is mentioned. The Greek word means "that which disgusts"; the English word, "anything which excites impure desire."

Trials of the Christian (1 Peter 4:12—5:14)

Nero was subjecting the Church to awful persecutions. Trials resulting from loyalty to Christ are inevitable. Christ sits as a refiner before the fire. The assayer takes the most pains with the most precious metals as he subjects them to the heat. Such fires melt the metal and only the molten mass releases the alloy or takes its new form in the mold. Christ allows us to be subjected to the heat until all the dross is burned out, and just as the assayer sees his face in the molten mass and knows it is pure, so Christ can see His own face reflected in our lives.

Christians were burned every night in Nero's gardens. It looked as if the devil were about to devour the Church (1 Peter 5:8). It was a "fiery trial," but God would use its very heat to burn out the dross and leave the pure gold (1:7). History is replete with the record of the many persecutions of Christians. Some have been even more brutal than Nero's. Millions of Christians through the centuries have been subjected to every conceivable kind of torture. These words have been for them, too. How ashamed we should be even to mention our little troubles in light of these!

Don't be surprised when you are tried in the fire, as if some strange thing were happening to you (4:12). Don't think that Christ has promised that we, as Christians, shall be spared from pain or misfortunes or death. In fact Christ says, "In this world ye shall suffer persecution." This means no doubt that people will persecute the real Christian, because the world hates Christ and anything called by His name.

Peter exhorts the leaders of the Church to care for the flock. "not lording it over those entrusted to you" (5:3), but to serve them. Jesus had told Peter to "feed my sheep" (John 21). Undershepherds are to receive their rewards from the Chief Shepherd when He shall appear (1 Peter 5:4). His crown of glory shall be fadeless.

The Christian life is like a jungle battle. Peter tells us who our enemy is. He is the devil. His work is opposed to all that is good in this world. He is pictured as a roaring lion, seeking his prey (5:8). This adversary is cagey, appearing sometimes as an angel of light, at another time as a serpent, coiled for the strike. He always "prowls around like a roaring lion looking for someone to devour." He is watching for the vulnerable spot, for the unguarded door to our hearts. Paul tells us what armor we should wear in Ephesians 6. But we need not be afraid, for "the God of all grace, who called you to his eternal glory in Christ, after you have suffered a little while, will himself restore you and make you strong, firm and steadfast" (5:10).

Chapter 49

Understanding Second Peter

Second Peter Portrays Jesus Christ, Our Strength

Selected Bible Readings

Sunday: Christian Virtues (2 Peter 1:1-14)
Monday: Christ's Word Exalted (2 Peter 1:15-21)
Tuesday: Christless Teachers (2 Peter 2:1-14)
Wednesday: Christ Against the Backslider (2 Peter 2:15-22)
Thursday: Christ's Coming Scoffed (2 Peter 3:1-9)
Friday: Christ's Coming Assured (2 Peter 3:10-18)
Saturday: Christ Our Hope (2 Peter 1:1—3:18)

The first letter was to console; the second to warn.

In his first letter, Peter was trying to encourage Christians who were suffering terrible persecutions from without. In his second letter, he is warning them of danger within the Church.

Christians need moral courage even more than physical courage. It is our duty to do right under all circumstances, with no qualification and no hesitation. "A Christian is never off duty." To stand up for truth is often more difficult than to go into battle. Illustrations from the Bible are found in Joseph (Genesis 39:9), Nehemiah (5:7; 6:1-16), Daniel (1:8) and Paul. History is full of instances, too: Polycarp (Saint Polycarp, c. 69-c. 155, bishop of Smyrna, leading Christian figure in Roman Asia in the middle of the second century), Martin Luther, Latimer (Hugh Latimer, c. 1485-1555, British bishop of Worcester and Reformer), John Wesley, Joan of Arc (Saint Joan of Arc, 1412-1431, a French national heroine and a beloved saint of the

Roman Catholic Church). They were never ashamed of Christ, because they knew Him.

Peter, in warning against the dangers from within, urges them to grow strong in "the grace and knowledge" of Christ (2 Peter 3:18). Christian knowledge is the best way to overcome the false teaching that was creeping within the walls. We obtain knowledge of Christ through His Word. Don't neglect the Word of God! It is indeed "a lamp to our feet, and a light to our path" (Psalm 119:105). In 1 Peter, we hear much about suffering. In 2 Peter, we hear much about knowledge. Shallow knowledge makes superficial Christians. Paul said, "I know whom I have believed" (2 Timothy 1:12). It is not what you believe that gives you strength, but WHOM you believe. Peter knew that heresy often leads to immoral living. Christianity must have a creed if right conduct is to be assured. Leaders were using the church for money-making schemes. Leaders in the church were permitting wrongdoing of every sort. The false teachers were laughing at the Lord's coming, and the Church could easily cease from looking for that "blessed hope."

Simon Peter, a servant and an apostle of Jesus Christ, is the writer. The first name, Simon, suggests his old, unstable nature. The name Peter (meaning a "rock") suggests the new nature Christ had given him, strong and true. He calls himself a bondslave (servant). Slavery is the happiest life in the world when the slave has the right master. There is only one right Master, and He is Jesus Christ. His slaves know the only true meaning of freedom.

Peter, the apostle of hope, speaks again to the younger Christians in the faith. He urges them to look toward heaven while dwelling for only a season in a very bad world. He stirs up their pure minds "as reminders to stimulate you to wholesome thinking" (3:1). He talks about the readers as those who have obtained "a faith as precious as ours" (1:1). We remember how Peter's faith was kept through Christ's prayer for him. "But I have prayed for you, Simon, that your faith may not fail. And when you have turned back, strengthen your brothers" (Luke 22:32). This is how our faith can be preserved also.

Christian Virtues (2 Peter 1:1-21)

Do the days seem dark to you and does sin seem to abound everywhere? That is the way the world looked to the young Christians of Peter's day. So they would not be discouraged by this outlook, he showed them how to escape "the corruption in the world caused by evil desires" (2 Peter 1:4). Here it is. God has "given us everything we need for life and godliness" (1:3).

Look at a criminal condemned to be hanged. Suppose a messenger comes to him and says: "The governor has taken your case into consideration, and I have brought you a purse of a thousand dollars."

The criminal will say, "What good will it do me? I am to be hanged tomorrow."

"Well, I have another message. He has considered your case and sent you the deed to a million-dollar estate."

The condemned man despairingly shakes his head and says, "What can I do with that? I must be hanged tomorrow."

But the messenger goes on. "Stop! I have another offer to make. I have brought you the governor's own inauguration robe for you to wear with special favor."

The condemned man bursts into tears as he says, "Do you intend to mock me? How would I appear ascending the steps of the gallows, wearing the governor's own robe?"

Then the messenger says, "Wait, I have one more message. The governor has sent you a pardon. What do you say to that?"

The poor man looks at him and says he doesn't believe it. But the messenger hands him the pardon, signed by the governor, bearing the official stamp upon it. Then the man leaps for joy while tears of gratitude run down his face.

Then the messenger says. "I am not through yet. I have brought you the pardon, the purse of gold, the deed, and the royal robe which are yours in addition." These are the "all things" God has given us in Christ, His Son. When we have these, nothing can defeat the young Christian.

The way I can escape the awful sins in this world every day and all the day is by partaking of His nature and letting Him live through me. Lay hold of the "very great and precious promises, so that through them you may participate in the divine nature" (1:4). I am a sharer in the very nature of God. Everyone does not have the nature of God. The divine is not within human hearts. His image remains in us, though marred (1 Corinthians 11:7), but not an atom of His life. We are dead and lifeless apart from Christ. The "divine nature" of God becomes ours only when the divine Savior becomes ours. This is a wonderful truth. We ought to take courage when we remember that with Christ in us, "the divine nature" also is within us. The "very great and precious promises" are before us. We ought to go straight ahead, fearing nothing (2 Peter 1:4).

The "divine nature" God has given us should be shown in the everyday practices of the Christian life. That is all Christian character is. It is no more or less than the practice of Christian virtues. If we turn to Galatians 5, we will find that Christian virtues are only the fruit of the Spirit.

Do others know you are a Christian by the way you look and act? You remember that night by the fire, when a smart young girl recalled that Peter had been with Jesus, Peter gave her some of the choice language of the Galilee fishing trade to try to prove otherwise. The crowd picked him out by his accent (Mark 14:66-71). He gave himself away by a word. Later, the rulers picked him out as a companion of Jesus by his appearance and talk. The world recognizes us in exactly the same way. Something about a person's whole bearing proclaims him or her as a companion of Jesus Christ. As soon as we hear someone speak about Christ, we can tell what that person is.

Although God gives us a changed, divine nature, He wants us to do our part in developing this priceless gift (1:5-11). We are sharers in the very life of God, therefore we should press on to possess more. God says, "Add one grace to another."

Multiplication—"Grace and peace be yours in abundance" (1:2)

Addition—"Add to your faith" (1:5)

Subtraction—"Cleansed from his past sins" (1:9).

Steps to Heaven

Seven steps go up from faith, and the last one is love. These steps are the Christian virtues every Christian should have. Let's climb slowly and thoughtfully up this flight of stairs and see how far we have gone. To your faith add goodness, knowledge, self-control, perseverance, godliness, brotherly kindness and love. This is the result of our precious faith.

The fuller the measure of these virtues, the greater will be our knowledge of Jesus Christ our Lord. Know Christ, for to know Him is life eternal, and in none other is there salvation. (See Acts 4:12.)

Someone has said this is a seven-story-and-basement building. Add story to story, but be sure to put faith at the foundation. If you try to build without the proper base, the building will become top-heavy. To be sure, faith is the foundation grace. But a foundation is of little use if no building follows. During the days of the depression it was a common sight to see the framework of a great building standing stark and gaunt, weeds growing around it, abandoned by the men who had begun a good work, but because of the depression had ceased before it was finished. The foundation was substantial and adequate, but for years was entirely useless because nothing was added to make it habitable.

Peter, like Paul, warns Christians from standing still. Don't remain babes in Christ, tripping over every teaching, but grow strong.

"But if anyone does not have them, he is nearsighted and blind" (2 Peter 1:9). Nearsighted Christians we will be, unfit for enlistment in God's army, if we do not have these virtues. Be sure of your position in Christ. Don't ever doubt your calling in Him. Spare no effort to put God's call and choice beyond all doubt. Spare no effort in prayer, in study and in talking with older Christians. Life is full of so much uncertainty, but you do not have to be uncertain in spiritual things. A spiritual certainty produces a stability in life, and "you will never fall" (1:10).

A Christian's ambition should be to have a full life. Peter wants you to have an abundant entrance into the haven of rest, Christ's eternal kingdom (1:11).

Folding Our Tents

Peter, like Paul, was conscious of his approaching death. He has a beautiful name for death, "I will soon put [this tent of my body] aside" (1:13,14). *Moffatt* says, "The folding up of my tent." Because he knew he was about to leave them, he wanted to stir them up by putting them in remembrance of what he so well knew. His memory pictured before him the great transfiguration scene. There he had witnessed the glory of Christ. Any doubt about His reality or of His coming again in power was forever banished from his mind. God Himself had borne testimony of His glory and honor, and a voice said, "This is my Son, whom I love; with him I am well pleased" (1:17). He heard the voice from above. This is the testimony of deity. Now Peter knew. He was sure. He wanted them to know that he was not telling them fairy stories when he told them of the power and coming of the Lord Jesus Christ, but he was an eyewitness of His majesty.

Remember, Peter suffered and died for this truth he was telling. At one time he said, "We cannot help speaking about what we have seen and heard" (Acts 4:20).

People depend too much on feeling instead of knowledge based on facts. Peter didn't want these Christians to rest on feelings. When the devil sees a poor soul in agony on the waves of sin getting close to the Rock of Ages, he just holds out the plank of feeling to him and says, "There, get on that. You feel more comfortable now, don't you?" And while the man stands there getting his breath again, out goes the plank from under him and he is worse off than ever.

Added to the evidence of the transfiguration is the "word of the prophets made more certain" (1:19), rather, prophecy made sure. This does not put Christian experience (the vision on the mount) over against prophecy, but it says the word of prophecy is confirmed by experience. They go together. Peter throws much light on the inspiration of the Scriptures. See 1 Peter 1:10-12; 2 Peter 1:4,16-21; 3:15.

Remember the divine origin of the Scriptures. Dr. Gray (James M. Gray, 1851-1935, teacher and expositor-evangelist, president of Moody Bible Institute 1903-23; consulting editor for *The Scofield Reference Bible*) says, "Private interpretation means private origin. God is the One who has spoken" (referring to 1:21).

A native in India, writing to a friend about a great revival they were having, said, "We are having a great 'rebible' here." Not a bad idea. The Church needs to be re-Bibled!

Christless Teachers (2 Peter 2:1-22)

Are the times in which we live hard, temptations strong and opposition powerful? Expect it and rise above it. We are warned that it shall be so. The world always has been and always will be full of antagonism to the truth and to those who speak it. But God will bring it to naught. In the meantime, "the Lord knows how to rescue godly men from trials" (2 Peter 2:9).

Peter tells of the coming, the influence and the doom of the false teachers in this dark and appalling chapter. We need not be surprised at their coming, for Christ warned us of that in Matthew 7:15; 24:11,24, and we have listened to Paul's words about them to Timothy (1 Timothy 4:1-3; 2 Timothy 3:1-9).

What a black list is this account in Peter's second Epistle of the false teachers' deeds! There is no softening of the shade from one end to the other. It is a black picture indeed. Read it! No wonder Peter warned the Church of false prophets!

"Secretly introduce destructive heresies"—2:1

"Denying the sovereign Lord who bought them"—2:1

"Bring the way of truth into disrepute"—2:2

"Exploit you with stories they have made up"—2:3

"Follow the corrupt desire of the sinful nature"—2:10

"Despise authority"—2:10

"Bold and arrogant"—2:10

"Not afraid to slander celestial beings"—2:10

"Like brute beasts"—2:12

"Blaspheme in matters they do not understand"—2:12

"Pleasure is to carouse in broad daylight"—2:13

"Blots and blemishes" in society—2:13

Revel in "their pleasures while they feast with you"—2:13

"Eyes full of adultery, they never stop sinning"—2:14

"Seduce the unstable"—2:14

"Experts in greed"—2:14

"An accursed brood"—2:14

"Left the straight way and wandered off"—2:15

"Springs without water"—2:17

"Mists driven by a storm"—2:17

"Mouth empty, boastful words"—2:18
"Appealing to the lustful desires of sinful human nature"—2:18
"Slaves of depravity"—2:19.

The false teachers of today do just what is told here. First, they "secretly introduce destructive heresies" (2:1). They do it subtly. They don't believe in the deity of Christ—that Jesus, who was born of a virgin, was actually God. Peter describes the "damnable heresy" *(KJV)* they bring in. This is it—"denying the sovereign Lord who bought them." It does not say that they deny the Lord that "taught" them. Practically every false religion acknowledges Christ as a great teacher, but will not accept Him as Savior, the One who "bought" us with His own precious blood. They deny the blood atonement.

Blood test—This is the mark by which to test and reject the false teacher. Ask for credentials of teachers who are abroad today. When any teacher does not put the Cross at the center of his or her teaching, beware! Turn from that teacher. Our redemption is in the blood. Jesus bought us with His blood.

Popularity test—These teachers are popular. "Many will follow their shameful ways" (2:2). Don't think it strange that false religions, of which there are many varieties, are able to procure a large following. Peter told us they would. People do not want to be told they need a Savior. That makes them admit they are sinners. They only want to be taught, not "bought." They "will bring the way of truth into disrepute" (2:2). All these false teachings talk about "truth," but they forget that Christ said, "I am the way and the truth and the life. No one comes to the Father except through me" (John 14:6). He is not just a part of truth—He IS TRUTH. He is not a way-shower—He is THE WAY. He does not come to show us how to live. He is LIFE.

Vocabulary test—"In their greed these teachers will exploit you with stories they have made up" (2 Peter 2:3). Words mean little in many of these false religions. A new meaning is given to many words. They say they believe in everything; but when we ask them what they mean by it, it is far from what the Scripture says. They keep the form of words, but the meaning is pumped out. It is like an egg with holes in either end and the inside blown out. The form of the egg is there, but the real substance is gone. Christ said that people would even say, "Lord, Lord," but He would say, "I never knew you. Away from me, you evildoers!" (Matthew 7:21-23). Words mean nothing unless there is heart in their meaning. How these false religions prey upon the people for money! You cannot have healing unless you pay. A "practitioner" demands a price. God says we may come to Him "without money and without cost" (Isaiah 55:1).

God can only do one thing with these kinds of teachers, and that is to destroy them. "Light that is trifled with becomes lightning." Peter declares with no uncertain sound that that shall be the end of false teachers who cover themselves with the cloak of the Church (2:3-9). They shall certainly be punished. God did not even spare the angels who sinned! He sent a flood upon a godless world in Noah's day. Sodom and Gomorrah were reduced to ashes. All these were as a warning to the godless of every generation of what God has in store for them. One thing we can be sure of, no matter how severe the judgment for the false teacher may be, the deliverance of God's people is promised. Leave the punishment of the wicked with God.

As we read on, we find much else that these wicked teachers will do. They will malign Christ's apostles; they will ensnare weak people, promising them freedom, while as a matter of fact they are enslaving them in corrupt habits (2:2-22).

Christ's Coming (2 Peter 3:1-18)

False teaching about Christ that denies His deity and power results in false thinking. The first question it raises is about the coming of Christ. To help the Church in this, Peter reminds them of the things Jesus had said. People misunderstood Him and thought His return might be in that generation. Peter tells them that time is nothing with God—"With the Lord a day is like a thousand years, and a thousand years are like a day" (2 Peter 3:8). He will keep this promise as He has kept all His promises, but according to His own time.

"The Lord is not slow in keeping his promise,....He is patient with you, not wanting anyone to perish, but everyone to come to repentance" (3:9). The last days are to be sad days, for scoffers shall make fun and say, "Ha, ha, where is the promise of Christ's coming? As far as we can see, everything is going on just as it has from the beginning of creation. Nature goes along in the even tenor of her way. There have been no signs of any radical change. The promise of His coming has failed." These scoffers were evil, but the sad truth today is that good people scoff at the promise of His coming. They make sport of the great hope of the Church. How illogical was their reasoning about Christ's not coming! Here they are! He had not come, hence He was not coming. Nothing different had happened, hence nothing unusual was going to happen. Because our Lord has not come as yet, shall we give up hope? No, indeed. Rather, rejoice in the fact that His return comes nearer every day.

Floods and Fires

Peter reminds these skeptics that a mighty flood did drown the world once, and Christ likened His coming to the flood in Matthew 24:37-38. No doubt Peter heard Him say it. But next time God will destroy the earth by fire. Will it be literal fire? Was the flood literal? Stored within the earth are oils and gases and fire enough to burn it up. Volcanoes are the release of these elements. Scientists now tell us we are sitting on a crust of earth only thirty miles in depth. Beneath this is a mass of molten matter. At a word, God could release a spout that would bury the earth in literal fire. The devastation caused by the atomic bomb has proved the possibility of such catastrophe. Or our earth may collide with some other heavenly body.

We know that when God's clock strikes the hour, the earth will melt with a fervent heat. The earth shall be burned up and in the great explosion the heavens will pass away. Then "new heavens and a new earth" will emerge (3:13).

Today people are heady and high-minded. They think they know everything. But all this is to be expected. Satan will not give up his hold on this earth without protest. But his days of liberty are numbered and Jesus shall reign. "First of all, you must understand that in the last days scoffers will come, scoffing and following their own evil desires. They will say, 'Where is this "coming" he promised? Ever since our fathers died, everything goes on as it has since the beginning of creation.' But the day of the Lord will come like a thief" (2 Peter 3:3,4,10). Scorn and scoffing did not hold back the flood when it was unloosed. The angel's mighty trumpet will make short work of the foolish "I don't believe it" and "I don't think it is true" and "I don't see it." Nevertheless, we, according to His promise, look for new heavens and a new earth wherein dwells righteousness. It will not be entirely a destruction, but a new earth will be constructed. Look toward the East, for the "Sun of righteousness will rise with healing in its wings" (Malachi 4:2).

What effect should all this have on our lives? Peter answers in verse 14. We will be diligent in our service, striving always to be peaceable, spotless and blameless in character. Don't grow careless because He is delaying, for one day the Lord will come suddenly. Be patient while He delays, knowing that He does it because He is long-suffering and would give the last man, woman and child a chance to accept Him.

What lives we ought to live while we wait for His coming! We may hasten it by our holy living. Faith in the return of our Lord must lead to this. Then we may hasten it by a holy conversation. Watch your speech. Don't forget to look forward with an eager gaze. Then be diligent that you be "found spotless, blameless and at peace with him" (3:14). Are you looking forward to His coming? What effect has this hope had upon your life and conversation?

Peter's last word of warning is "Beware!" This is a note of caution. "Be on your guard so that you may not be carried away by the error of lawless men and fall from your secure position" (3:17).

Know and Grow

The remedy against falling back is to "grow"—make progress. "Grow in grace and in the knowledge of our Lord and Savior Jesus Christ." Are you growing in your knowledge? Christian knowledge is an effective weapon against heresy. Christianity without a creed cannot stand against the attacks of the critics. If you are not growing, beware lest you fall by the way, for we are living in a wicked world where people are enemies of God and His truth. A living thing ought to grow. When there is no growth, there is no life. The foundation of growth is the knowledge of Christ. As we grow in this, we grow in likeness to Him.

Chapter 50

Understanding First, Second, Third John and Jude

Jesus Christ, Our Life; the Truth; the Way; Our Keeper

Selected Bible Readings

Sunday:	Walking in Fellowship (1 John 1:1—2:14)
Monday:	Walking as Children of God (1 John 2:15—3:24)
Tuesday:	Walking in Love (1 John 4:1-21)
Wednesday:	Walking in Knowledge (1 John 5:1-21)
Thursday:	Walking in Truth (2 John 1-13)
Friday:	Walking in the Way (3 John 1-14)
Saturday:	Walking Without Falling (Jude 1-25)

Understanding First John

First John was written by the aged apostle John in the year A.D. 90, probably in Ephesus. Unlike the other apostles, he does not address his letter to any church or any particular person. He writes to all Christians, old and young (2:12-14). He calls Christians by a tender word *teknia*—which means "born ones" or "bairns." God is dealing with His very own born-again children.

John told us why he wrote his Gospel—that "you may believe that Jesus is the Christ, the Son of God, and that by believing you may have life in his name" (John 20:31).

He wrote his Epistle that those who believe in Christ might KNOW that they have eternal life (5:13).

Turn to the Gospel of John 20:31 and read it along with 1 John

5:13. The Gospel was written to show us how we might receive eternal life. The Epistle of 1 John was written to assure those who have believed that they have eternal life by believing "that Jesus is the Christ." The Epistle of 1 John appears to have been intended as a companion to the Gospel of John. Thus we find the word "believe" running all through the Gospel of John, and the word "know" running through the Epistle. The word "know" is used more than thirty times in this short letter. Underline it each time you discover it.

John wrote for four reasons:

1. That they might be happy—1:4
2. That they might not sin—2:1
3. That they might be on guard against error—2:26
4. That they might KNOW—5:13.

Someone has well named this the "Really and truly Epistle." It has a confident, exultant tone all the way through. John was the disciple whom Jesus loved. He stood close to Him on the cross at Calvary. He looked into the empty tomb on that morning of the Resurrection. On Patmos, he was lifted up by the Spirit and saw a door opened into heaven. This one gives us his witness of these facts. "We know," he says, "There is no possibility of doubt about it." "That which was from the beginning, which we have heard, which we have seen with our eyes, which we have looked at and our hands have touched—this we proclaim concerning the Word of life"—JESUS (1 John 1:1)! John gives us evidence for his knowledge. He has heard and seen and handled the Word of life. He longs to bring his hearers into intimate fellowship with the Father and His Son, that their joy might be full (1 John 1:3-4,7; 2:13-14).

Christ, who was God, took on flesh and dwelt with people so they could hear His voice, see His face and feel the touch of His loving hand. This brought God down to people that we "may have fellowship." To walk in fellowship is to live in agreement.

God wants us to have fellowship with Him, and in Him to have fellowship with one another (1:3).

John says we not only must believe like Christians, but we also must act like Christians. In chapters 1-3, we find out whether we are living like Christians. In chapters 4 and 5, we discover whether we are believing like Christians. Striking lightning is accompanied by thunder. So "striking" faith is accompanied by life and testimony (2:3). Some people say they believe God, but act more like the devil. This cannot be. We must be as orthodox in our behavior as we are in our belief. Do the truth and believe the truth. "If we claim to have fellowship with him yet walk in the darkness, we lie and do not live by the truth" (1:6).

John exalts God in his Epistles:

God is Light—1:5
God is Love—4:8,16
God is Righteous—2:29
God is Life—5:11-12
God is Truth—2 John
God is Good—3 John.

Right Behavior (1 John 1:1—3:24)

John gives us seven tests of Christian behavior. Read these and find what your rating is as a Christian. They are easy to find because each of these tests is introduced by "if we say" or "the one who says." The test is this—"if we say" one thing and do another, we are not living as Christ would want us to, in full fellowship with Himself. How much easier it is to talk than it is to do! As Dwight Moody said, "We talk cream and live skim milk." For "our fellowship is with the Father and with his Son, Jesus Christ" (1 John 1:3). We are to walk together, talk together and live together. We are to eat at the same table (Revelation 3:20). We are one family (Ephesians 3:15). God is my Father because Jesus Christ my elder Brother has made me a child of the King. Therefore I must behave that way. Fellowship brings joy (1:4). There is no joy greater than fellowship with a friend.

I walk with a God of light. "God is light; in him there is no darkness at all" (1:5). If my walk is with Him, I will walk in the light of His love and grace. There are seven tests of our walk with God.

First Test—Walk in the Light

"If we claim to have fellowship with him [the God of light] yet walk in darkness, we lie and do not live by the truth" (1:6).

Is there known sin in your life? If there is, you are not walking with Christ. His presence throws light on your conscience and heart and shows the presence of sin in your life (Ephesians 5:13). A Christian who is walking in fellowship with God will enjoy fellowship with other Christians (1 John 1:7). Have you ever picked up a stone that has been lying on the ground for a long time? The minute you lift it, loathsome things move in every direction to flee from the light. Light reveals sin. Known sin will keep you from fellowship with Christ, but fellowship with Christ will keep you from sin. Do you ask Him to throw His searchlight upon your heart?

Second Test—Admit You Are a Sinner

"If we claim to be without sin, we deceive ourselves and the truth is not in us" (1:8). You cannot walk with God and practice sin in your life at the same time. God keeps showing us the sin in our lives. On the cross He redeemed us from the penalty of sin once and for all. But let us know, too, that if we confess our sins, He keeps cleansing us from the sins that creep into our lives by our contact with this world.

When a farmer plows his field, he throws out every stone he finds. But the next year as the plow goes deep into the furrow, he finds other stones that had remained hidden the year before. He throws these aside as they turn up. Then the next year the same thing occurs. So in our lives! God will reveal by the plow of His Spirit the sins that are hidden in our lives we did not know were there. Don't be discouraged, but use His remedy.

"If we confess our sins, he is faithful and just and will forgive us our sins and purify us from all unrighteousness" (1:9). Don't pray in an indefinite way. Name it before God. Is it pride, lack of trust, anger, love of pleasure more than God? Well, whatever it is, lay it out before God and tell Him what it is. Call it by name. Then claim God's promise. "He is faithful and just" not only to "forgive us our sins," but also to "purify us from all unrighteousness." A human parent can forgive our misbehavings, but only God can cleanse us from sin.

Third Test—Obey God's Will

"The man who says, 'I know him,' but does not do what he commands is a liar, and the truth is not in him" (2:4). Obedience is a real test. God makes a very strong statement. If you say you are a Christian and do not obey Him, you are a liar. The one who is a Christian keeps God's commandments.

What are Christ's commandments? "Love the Lord your God with all your heart and with all your soul and with all your mind and with all your strength" (Mark 12:30; Luke 10:27). Do you love God that way? Put yourself to a few tests. Do you spend more time watching television than you do with God? Then you don't love Him with all your heart. Are you ambitious to carry out some plan in your life that you hope will bring you fame or wealth or just enjoyment? Don't say you know God when you won't keep His commandments. Do you know His will for your life? Do you want to? This is a test of your Christian life. Are you obedient to His Word? His still small voice? Many times we do not want to let God talk to us. We will not listen to Him because we are afraid of His will for us. Youth looks for a career. God has a career for each one of us. He has a plan for every step of our lives, for "a man's steps are directed by the Lord" (Proverbs 20:24). We must obey in everything for "everything that does not come from faith is sin" (Romans 14:23).

You will begin to know what God wishes as you grow to know Him better. A group of fellows were going to a nightclub of bad reputation. They stopped to ask a young chap to go along. "I can't go," he said.

"Why not?" his associates asked.

"Well, because my mother wouldn't want me to."

"How do you know she wouldn't? She doesn't even know we are going."

"Because I know my mother," was his very wise reply. This is true when you learn to know God—you will know what His desires are (3:24).

Christ says, "You are my friends if you do what I command" (John 15:14). His command is in that very chapter: "This is my command: Love each other" (John 15:17).

Fourth Test—Imitate Christ

"Whoever claims to live in him must walk as Jesus did" (1 John 2:6).

We should be Christlike in all our life. Christ says, "You are the salt of the earth" (Matthew 5:13). Salt preserves food from spoiling. Are you the preservative of your crowd? Do you keep the language clean? Do you refrain from using God's name in vain? Does your presence keep them from doing questionable things?

A little Chinese girl said, "I know why Christ said, 'You are the salt of the earth.' Because salt makes folks thirsty and Christians should make others thirsty for Christ." Are you making folks thirsty?

People are too lazy to look up. Few try to find Christ. So Christ wants others to see Him reflected in us. In the famous Sistine Chapel in Rome, the beauty of the art is in the ceiling. As you enter, you are given a mirror. It seems strange to see people walking around looking down when the paintings are above. But they see all the glory reflected in the mirrors before them, without breaking their necks. Be a reflector. Let the beauty of Jesus be seen in you.

Fifth Test—Love Others

"Anyone who claims to be in the light but hates his brother is still in the darkness" (2:9).

Another acid test of the Christian life is love (2:7-11). Love changes a person. Love makes us have a concern for the welfare of others.

God speaks of love to others, personal attitudes. There are three chief attitudes toward others: hatred, which is murder (3:15); indifference—a feeling akin to hate—no concern (4:20-21); love. Love shows itself in different ways (2:9-11; 3:14); physically—concern for welfare (3:16-18); spiritually—concern for another's soul.

Sixth Test—Relationship to the World

"If anyone loves the world, the love of the Father is not in him" (2:15).

We live in a present evil world (Galatians 1:4). The scheme of things as they exist today is not the standard for the Christian. Whenever you find Christians obeying them, they are walking on forbidden ground.

All sins may be put into three categories: (1) lust of the flesh (2) lust of the eyes; (3) pride of life (see 2:16-17, *KJV*).

1. *Lust of the flesh.* Temptations come through the body and its appetites and passions, what the *NIV* calls the "cravings of sinful man." The devil tempted Jesus in this way first. Jesus had been fasting forty days, and every atom of His being cried for bread. How plausible was Satan's temptation! It was the same appeal to appetite Satan made to Eve. In all those thousands of years, the devil has invented no new weapons of attack. "Tell this stone to become bread" (Luke 4:3). The temptation for self-gratification is one of the strongest that can assail us. Appetite is still one of the most vulnerable points when Satan attacks us. The necessity for bread and pleasure is supposed by some to justify any means to get them. It is not necessary that we should live at all! There is only one moral necessity—to trust God and keep His commandments.

2. *Lust of the eyes.* Foiled with one weapon, Satan quickly drops it and tries another. Taking Jesus into a high mountain, he showed Him *(lust of the eyes)* all the kingdoms of the world in a moment of time. "So if you worship me, it will all be yours" (Luke 4:7). Satan was working his second trick.

How people worship at the altar of riches and honor because they long for what their eyes see of this world!

Your eyes can blacken your soul! Be careful what you see. If you throw a white tennis ball against a sooty wall, a black mark will be left upon it. If your eye is thrown against impure objects, be sure a mark will be left upon your mind and heart. Be careful what you see!

3. *Pride of life.* Everyone wants spectacular success, and to be able to boast "of what he has and does." The devil took Jesus to the pinnacle of the Temple and told Him to cast Himself down, and if He was the Son of God, He would be kept by angels. It was a pro-

posal to leap from the pinnacle of the Temple into immediate popularity. It is a temptation for any person to be popular. We all have human ambitions. How many people of genius have been led astray because the glittering prize of ambition has been held up before them! We want to win it at a single stroke. How strong is the temptation to take a shortcut to our ambition, whether of education or wealth or position and power! We are in danger of selling our very souls to gain our end! Even Jesus saw the world spread before Him and saw how short and alluring was the step that was promised Him, but to become the subject of the prince of this world would have ended His mission as the Savior of the world.

Seventh Test—Prove Christ Is Righteous by Your Life

Do we acknowledge Christ by our life (2:22)? "If you know that he is righteous, you know that everyone who does what is right has been born of him" (2:29). Others watch us to see if we "do righteousness." Those who abide in Christ will bear the same fruit in their lives that Christ bears and that is righteousness.

A few verses in chapter 3:1-10 are difficult to understand unless we know what the original text means.

"Everyone who commits (practices) sin is guilty of lawlessness; for [that is what] sin is, lawlessness." This is *The Amplified Bible* translation of 3:4. If we know Christ as God dwelling in our lives, we will not "practice sin." "No one who continues to sin has either seen him or known him" (3:6), and in verse 9, "No one who is born of God will continue to sin, because God's seed remains in him; he cannot go on sinning, because he has been born of God." It is possible for Christians under strong temptation to fall into sin for the time, but they will not keep practicing it. If people continually practice sin, they may well doubt their conversion! We should consider sin as God does. Sin cost God His Son!

Right Belief *(1 John 4:1—5:11)*

We need a creed by which to live. The word "creed" comes from the Latin word *credo*—"I believe." There are sins of the body that we all commit, but there are sins of the heart and disposition as well. God is as interested in what you believe as in how you act.

You cannot believe things that are not true about Christ and at the same time have fellowship with Him. It is absurd to say that it doesn't make any difference what you believe as long as you are in earnest. This statement is unsound. We cannot believe what is false and have it affect our lives and then go out and live a life that is true. This is not any more possible than that we can believe that an eight o'clock train leaves at nine o'clock and not miss the train. Neither can we sincerely believe a bottle contains a healing medicine when really it is a deadly poison and, taking it, find anything but death.

The unsound teachers of John's day were denying the fact that Christ truly suffered and truly rose again. They said He was only a mystery man who appeared and vanished, but He was not God.

You cannot deny the death of Christ on the cross and find a pardon for your sin. You cannot deny the resurrection of Christ and enjoy the privileges of Christianity that are found in a living Christ. You cannot deny that Christ is God and find any access to the Father.

Your sin can start in your intellect. What do you believe? Christ wants to be our only Teacher. What we believe determines how we act.

Is a creed necessary? Read John 3:16 and see if you think it is. It says, "Whoever believes in him shall not perish but have eternal life." Christianity is Christ-centered. Christ out of Christianity leaves nothing. This means death. If we believe not, we shall die, but if we believe, we shall live (Romans 10:9-10).

Many Christians are spiritual babes in Christ. They are led astray with every new "wind of doctrine." They are susceptible to all about them. When doubt fills their minds, they sink in despair. Hence, everyone ought to be given a way whereby to test every religion to see if it be true. Especially is this true in this day of so many religious beliefs. John states the test very clearly in 4:1-3: "Dear friends, do not believe every spirit, but test the spirits to see whether they are from God, because many false prophets have gone out into the world. This is how you can recognize the Spirit of God: Every spirit that acknowledges that Jesus

Christ has come in the flesh is from God, but every spirit that does not acknowledge Jesus is not from God. This is the spirit of the antichrist, which you have heard is coming and even now is already in the world."

What Shall We Believe?

John makes some plain statements in 1 John 4:1-3:

1. We must believe "that Jesus Christ has come in the flesh"— in "carnis" (4:1-2; 5:20-21). He is the incarnate Lord. This is the first thing we must be sure of. We must believe that when Jesus walked this earth He was God clothed in human flesh. "Veiled in flesh the Godhead see; Hail th'incarnate Deity," wrote Charles Wesley (1707-1788, hymn writer and brother of John Wesley). He took upon Himself the form of a man that He might die in our place, and bare our sins in His own body on the tree.

John records, "The Word became flesh and made his dwelling among us. We have seen his glory, the glory of the One and Only, who came from the Father, full of grace and truth" (John 1:14). Christ's earthly life was thirty-three years, but that is not His whole existence. Christ was with the Father from the beginning. More than 2,000 years ago, this Man of the ages came to this earth at His first advent. He did not begin life at the manger. He merely took upon Himself the form of a man. Then He remained on this earth thirty-three years. He died and was buried and rose again. Then He went back to where He came from.

Think how Christ was received on the earth the first time He came! "He came to that which was his own, but his own did not receive him" (John 1:11). They did not think that this One "in the flesh" before their eyes was God. They called Him a blasphemer when He claimed to be equal with God, "I and the Father are one" (John 10:30). For this they put Him to death. They would not believe that Jesus Christ was God come in the flesh!

2. We must believe in the deity of Christ (4:15; 5:5), that He is the Son of God, the only begotten Son. The liar is the one who denies that Jesus is the Christ, the promised Messiah (2:22). The Old Testament prophets told us the Messiah was coming. The angel chorus said that the Babe born in Bethlehem was this Messiah who was

prophesied. Simeon saw Christ in the Babe (Luke 2:25-35).

3. We must believe that "God is love" (4:8). There is no force in the world to compare with Christian love. Its power is seen in the great fact that "God is love." All through this chapter, it isn't our love that is the definition of love at its best, but God's love that is the measure. Listen! "Love comes from God....God is love....This is love: not that we loved God, but that he loved us and sent his Son as an atoning sacrifice for our sins. Dear friends, since God so loved us, we also ought to love one another" (4:7-11). Love turns our hearts away from ourselves. We cannot really love God without loving others. So we become channels of blessing to others around us because of what God is in us.

Nothing could influence our lives as much as the love of God, for "God lives in us" (4:12).

A man went to a pastor and said, "Sir, I want to enter into your religion."

"My friend," said the pastor, "our religion must enter into you."

God's love was shown in the gift of His Son to be a sacrifice for our sins (John 3:16; 1 John 4:9-10). When we look at the cross, we catch a glimpse into God's heart of love. The cross was the only way God had of showing us His heart. It is a picture of infinite love poured out in all its fullness. Christ did not die *to make* God love people. He died *because* God had loved people always with an everlasting love. "For God so loved..." Our salvation does not depend upon what we are, but upon what God is, and God is love!

God's love is first directed toward the individual. Then the individual must affect society. God is unseen and there are many who need God's love. So we will show it to others when we love. And when we love, we are like God. We ought also to love one another.

4. We must believe that Christ is our Savior (5:10-12). Christ was sent to be "the atoning sacrifice [or, propitiation] for our sins" (2:2; 4:10; Romans 3:25) because sin barred people from God's love, for "the wages of sin is death" (Romans 6:23). So Christ took the judgment of sin upon His own body on the cross and made it possible for God to show mercy righteously. Propitiation is the satisfaction by Christ's death of the whole demand of the law

upon the sinner. Propitiation is the cause of life, for through the sacrifice of Christ we have everlasting life (4:10).

"Anyone who believes in the Son of God has this testimony in his heart. Anyone who does not believe God has made him out to be a liar, because he has not believed the testimony God has given about his Son. And this is the testimony: God has given us eternal life, and this life is in his Son. He who has the Son has life; he who does not have the Son of God does not have life" (1 John 5:10-12).

God and Love

Love is the supreme test of our Christian faith. "We know that we have passed from death to life, because we love our brothers. Anyone who does not love remains in death" (3:14). The word "love" occurs forty-eight times in this first Epistle of John (in the *KJV*). We find out how love acts in 1 Corinthians 13.

"Whoever does not love does not know God, because God is love" (4:8). Love is the first instinct of the renewed heart. Where do we get our love? From within? No, from above. "We love because he first loved us" (4:19). What if we do not love? God says, we "do not know God."

We should show our love to Him by loving one another (1 John 4:7). Those who have love in their hearts have fellowship with God (4:16). But where there is no love, there is no fellowship (4:19-21).

Rich Rewards (1 John 5:12-21)

The rewards of life in Christ are stated in the last verses:

Assurance of eternal life—5:13

Power of prayer—5:14-15

Power of intercession—5:16

Victory—5:18 and 5:4-5.

Underline the word "know" in verses 12-20. We can have confidence when we know Christ. John uses the word "know" more than forty times in his Epistles. True Christianity is more than a creed—it is something that can be known and felt. We *know* that Christ was manifested to take away our sins. We *know* that we have passed from death unto life. We *know* that whatsoever we ask we shall receive. John assures us of these truths.

Understanding Second John

Second John is a good example of John's private correspondence to an individual. This letter was addressed to an unknown Christian woman. This is the only book in the Bible addressed to a woman.

The word "truth" is found five times in this short letter of thirteen verses. It is the key word. "Love" also occurs five times. Truth and love are inseparable.

We must test all the teachings in the world by the Scriptures "for the truth's sake" (v. 2, *KJV*). This is the final test. Test your experience by the Word of God, but never test the Word of God by your experience!

The truth John speaks of is from above, the Truth as it is in Christ Jesus. We are to walk in the truth, not just admire it. Then we will love one another (v. 5). This love is genuine and not subject to change. "Christ's love compels us" (2 Corinthians 5:14). The proof of our love is in our walk. "And this is love: that we walk in obedience to his commands" (2 John 6).

John speaks of the teaching, or doctrine of Christ: "Anyone who runs ahead and does not continue in the teaching of Christ does not have God" (v. 9). This is the test of the gospel. Not what I think or what someone else has thought or said or done, but what has Christ said? What is He to you? Is He the Son of God?

Many false teachers were traveling among the churches (vv. 7-11) who would not confess that Jesus Christ was here in the flesh. This is "the deceiver and the antichrist" (v. 7). See also 1 John 4:1-2. They did not believe in the humanity of Christ. They denied His incarnation. If you call Him "Lord" and deny His deity, you are a liar and an antichrist. John says this.

Apply this test to some of the popular religious movements of our day—Christian Science, Spiritualism, Unity, Jehovah's Witnesses, the Unification Church, Scientology, Transcendental Meditation and other similar movements. They deny the "Christ doctrine" mentioned here.

Don't be friendly with these false teachers, John commands, or entertain them, for thus you share in their wicked work.

Understanding Third John

Do you remember what Christ said of Himself in John 14:6? "I am the way and the truth and the life." We find Him portrayed in 1, 2 and 3 John as:

    1 John—Jesus the Life
    2 John—Jesus the Truth
    3 John—Jesus the Way.

Third John was written to his generous and warmhearted friend called Gaius. This man was the type of the true Christian layman who has dedicated his wealth and talent to the Lord. His purse strings are loose and his latchstring is out. All he has belongs to Christ. He is the picture of the man who has found Christ to be the "Way," and in his everyday life, he tries to show that gracious Way to others. Such people, scattered here and there, have through the years kept not only the Church alive in an unfriendly world, but have also kept Christ's love burning brightly in the midst of God's people when all seemed dark.

Gaius was noted for his loving hospitality. John urges him to continue entertaining the traveling preachers in spite of bitter opposition of an autocratic and blustering church official named Diotrephes. Hospitality is a manifestation of Christian love.

You can be either a Gaius, helping in the kingdom, or a Diotrephes, hindering the cause.

What a splendid thing to be rich and powerful and to choose to lay all your gifts and talents at Jesus' feet, like Gaius and Demetrius!

Understanding Jude

Jude was a brother of the Lord. He knew Peter. They walked with the Master and no doubt talked together after His departure. They evidently thought much alike about the great issues of the day.

Second Peter and Jude are very similar in thought and language. Both men were dealing with the dangers confronting the doctrines of the Church.

No doubt certain persons who denied "the only Lord God, and our Lord Jesus Christ" had joined the church. They were not outside, but inside the church. They had crept in unawares.

Alas! What church is without them today? They are with us, but not of us. Christ will judge these evil people as He did the fallen angels.

These intruders had begun to teach error in the church (vv. 3-4,8,16,19). A leaven of evil was at work among the readers. These intruders were:

"Godless men"—worldly

"Change the grace of our God into a license for immorality"—carnal

"Deny Jesus Christ our only Sovereign and Lord"—skeptical

"Reject authority and slander celestial beings"—lawless

"Grumblers and faultfinders"—critical

"Flatter others for their own advantage"—flatterers

"Follow mere natural instincts and do not have the Spirit"—immoral.

In contrast to these evil fellows we find the true followers of the faith, lifting high the cross of Christ (vv. 20-23). They were building on the foundation of Christ:

"Praying in the Holy Spirit" (v. 20)

"Keeping" in God's love (v. 21)

"Waiting" for God's mercy (v. 21)

"Winning" souls for Him (vv. 22-23)

"Resting" on His keeping power (v. 24).

Thank God for this noble army of faithful ones! Of these God says that their reward shall be that there He will "keep you from falling and...present you before his glorious presence without fault and with great joy" (v. 24).

Prophecy
of The New Testament

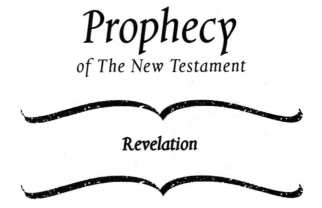

Revelation

Key Events of Prophecy

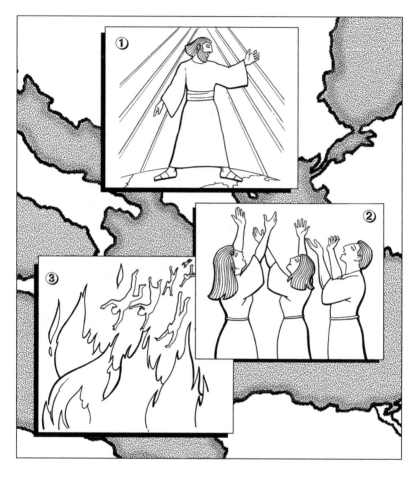

Prophecy: Jesus Christ Will Certainly Return!

The book of Revelation describes the end of human history. There will be severe trials and tribulations; Satan will deceive nations; he will viciously persecute believers. But those who believe will overcome Satan by the blood of the Lamb ①, the word of their testimony and the sacrifice of their lives (Rev. 12:11). God will bring those who believe Him ② into His heavenly kingdom. Satan and all his demons and those who followed him will be thrown into the lake of fire ③ forever. But believers from among every people, tribe and tongue and language will worship the Lamb forever.

Chapter 51

Understanding Revelation

Revelation Portrays Jesus Christ, Our Triumphant King

Selected Bible Readings

Sunday: Christ and the Churches (Revelation 1:1—3:22)
Monday: Christ's Throne and the Seven Sealed Book
            (Revelation 4:1—6:17)
Tuesday: Christ's Trumpets Sounded (Revelation 7:1—9:21)
Wednesday: Christ and the Woes (Revelation 10:1—12:17)
Thursday: Christ and Antichrist (Revelation 13:1—15:8)
Friday: Christ's Final Triumph (Revelation 16:1—18:24)
Saturday: Christ the Lord of All (Revelation 19:1—22:21)

Revelation is the only book of prophecy in the New Testament. It is the only book in the divine library that especially promises a blessing to those who read and hear. "Blessed" is a strong word. "Blessed is the one who reads the words of this prophecy" is what the book of Revelation says of itself (Revelation 1:3), but after reading the first chapters about the churches, and the last chapters describing heaven, not many of us read much in this book.

Revelation presents a glorious, reigning Christ. The Gospels present Him as a Savior, One who came to take the curse of sin, but in this last book we see no humiliation. In one way Revelation is the most remarkable book in the whole sacred canon. Revelation tells us about the reign of Christ on this earth that Satan wants to control. It tells of Christ's complete and eternal victory over Satan. It describes Satan's defeat and punishment, first for a thousand years, then eternally. It tells more about Satan's final doom than any other book. No wonder Satan doesn't want people to read it!

Does "revelation" mean a riddle? Most people, when speaking of this book, seem to think it does. No, it means just the opposite—"unveiling." It is written in symbols. It was sent and signified by the angel to John. The hard of hearing have a sign language. Each gesture is filled with meaning. So is every sign in Revelation. There are 300 symbols in this book and each has a definite meaning. Symbols are wonderful and speak great truths.

The content of the book seems to indicate that most of its events are yet to be fulfilled.

This book is the Revelation of Jesus Christ, not the revelation of John. It is not the revelation of the growth of the Church and the gradual conversion of the world, but it is the Revelation of Jesus Christ! It was given by Christ Himself to John (Revelation 1:1-2). The book deals with the return of the Lord to this earth. It describes the readiness or unreadiness of the Church for this great happening (3:20). There are descriptions of the tremendous events on earth and in heaven just before, during and after His coming.

What is meant by "the time is near" (1:3)? Almost 2,000 years have passed since these words were spoken, but the idea is "the next on the program." No matter how much time may intervene, the next thing after the day of grace is the kingdom age to be ushered in by our Lord's coming.

Few people who have any imagination have not sat down and thought, *I wonder how it would feel to be a king.* But Christ says when He comes He will make us reign as kings (1:6)!

Then "those who pierced him" shall see Him (1:7). Although that refers especially to the Jewish people, who at Christ's coming will turn to Him as a united people and be saved (Romans 11:25-26), at the same time it means many others who have pierced Christ will see Him. Have YOU pierced Him?

Christ is the theme of this wonderful book. It gives an authentic portrait of the Lord Jesus as the triumphant One. No less than twenty-six times do we find in it Christ's sacrificial title "Lamb" (Revelation 5:6). In addition, we see a vision of the future of the Church and the world in relation to Him.

It has been said that the saving blood of Christ runs through the entire Bible like a red cord. It has also been said that the second coming of Christ runs through the Bible like a golden cord. We are saved and washed clean in His blood in order that we may be ready and eager for His return.

A to Z

Revelation is a wonderful way to finish the story that began in Genesis. All that was begun in the book of beginnings (Genesis) is consummated in Revelation. In Genesis the heaven and earth were created. In Revelation we see a new heaven and a new earth. In Genesis the sun and moon appear; in Revelation we read that there is no need of the sun or moon, for Christ is the light of the new heaven. In Genesis there is a garden; in Revelation there is a holy city. In Genesis there is the marriage of the first Adam; in Revelation the marriage supper of the second Adam, Jesus Christ. In Genesis we see the beginning of sin; in Revelation sin is done away. So we can follow the appearance of the great adversary, Satan, and sorrow and pain and tears in Genesis, and see their doom and destruction in Revelation.

Things are very dismal in the world today. No one living has ever known such uncertainty about the future of human events. But things were dismal when the apostle John, an old, old man, was exiled to the Isle of Patmos. He had been banished for his testimony of Jesus (1:9). While on the island, John was forced to labor hard in the mines and quarries. But His Commander-in-Chief appeared to him and delivered a ringing message and ultimate glory.

God had determined from the beginning that His Son would be the Ruler of this universe (Isaiah 9:6-7).

Revelation is the greatest drama of all time. The plot is tense throughout; the final scene is glorious, for Christ comes unto His own. The Hero is our Lord Himself; the villain is the devil. The actors are the seven churches. The characters unloosed by the seals of chapters 6 and 7 are introduced by the "four horsemen." Then those summoned by the trumpets in turn leave the center of the scene of action, and we see the Antichrist, the world ruler, stalking across the stage (chap. 13). This incarnation of the devil himself is determined to set up his own kingdom and be worshiped by people. But Christ brings all to naught. This majestic Actor, bringing His hosts with Him, comes forth the long-looked-for King of kings and Lord of lords. He drives His enemies from the stage in utter defeat (chap. 19).

After all the struggle has ended and the beasts have been destroyed and the devil bound and "the old order of things has passed away. He who was seated on the throne said, 'I am making everything new'" (Revelation 21:4-5). This book brings to a climax the great story commenced in Genesis, and as all good stories should, it ends "And they lived happily ever after."

Notice the sevens in this book:
- Seven churches
- Seven seals
- Seven trumpets
- Seven signs
- Seven last plagues
- Seven dooms
- Seven new things.

Past—The Things Which Thou Hast Seen (Revelation 1:1-18)

Here is the last picture of Jesus Christ given in the New Testament. Many artists have tried to portray Him, but they have failed. Here is an authentic portrait (1:13-16). He is standing in the midst of the seven golden lampstands, representing the churches (v. 20). Lampstands prove that the Church is to be a light bearer. "You are the light of the world" (Matthew 5:14). How many churches today—electronic or otherwise—are for entertainment, bazaars and to promote money-making schemes, instead of lights to shine in a dark place!

Christ is likened to a "son of man," but it is clear from the vision that the One whom John saw was more than human. He was the Son of Man. Everything symbolizes majesty and judgment, and this thought of judgment strikes the keynote of the book. Christ is presented to the whole world as Judge:

"Dressed in a robe reaching down to his feet"—flowing robes a token of dignity and honor

"Head and hair were white like wool"—He is the Ancient of Days

"Eyes were like blazing fire"—intelligence; bringing hidden things to light

"Feet were like bronze glowing in a furnace"—brass symbolizes judgment

"Voice was like the sound of rushing waters"—power and majesty

"Right hand"—in these are kept the seven stars

"Mouth"—out of it came sharp double-edged sword of judgment

"His face was like the sun shining in all its brilliance" (1:12-18).

John's vision was not of this age in which we are living, but of a future day when people shall appear before Christ to be judged (John 5:27-29). Now, we may have all of God's grace, mercy and forgiveness for the taking. Now, Christ is before us to be judged. We can reject Him if we choose. In Revelation, John is picturing Christ in judgment. The day of mercy is past, now we stand before the Judge.

When John saw this glorious One, he fell at His feet as dead, so overpowering was the vision (Revelation 1:17). But Christ's words were reassuring. He said He was the living One, and though He had been dead, He was alive forevermore, and held the keys of death and Hades. Then follows the command to write what is found in this book (1:19). We do not have the usual picture of Christ starting in Bethlehem and ending at the Mount of Olives, but here we have His life in heaven, as the crown and culmination of all.

Have you ever seen the Lord? When Moses saw Him, his face shone. Job abhorred himself and repented in ashes. Isaiah saw himself unclean. Thomas said, "My Lord and my God." Saul (Paul) fell down and worshiped Him as Savior. What would happen to us if we really saw the Lord?

Present—The Things Which Are (Revelation 1:30—3:22)

In the second and third chapters, we find Christ's love letters to His churches. These letters are alike in pattern. Christ dictated them to the angels of the seven churches to whom He addressed these letters. In each, look for the speaker, praise, reproof, exhortation and promise.

The churches named were churches that actually existed in John's day. In dealing with them, He seems to give us a brief church history from the first-century Church to the Church of today, in seven periods:

Ephesus—the Church of the first love, the apostolic Church (2:1-7)

Smyrna—the persecuted Church—Diocletian to Constantine (2:8-11)

Pergamos—The Church under imperial favor—under Constantine (2:12-17)

Thyatira—the papal Church—the Dark Ages (2:18-29)

Sardis—the Reformation Church—protestantism, sixteenth and seventeenth centuries (3:1-6)

Philadelphia—the missionary Church—period ushered in by the Puritan movement (3:7-13)

Laodicea—the rejected Church—Church of the final apostasy (3:14-19).

Discover where you find Christ at the end of this Church age. "Here I am! I stand at the door and knock. If anyone hears my voice and opens the door, I will come in and eat with him, and he with me" (3:20). He is outside, knocking to get in. The Church will not let Him in, but He pleads with the individual: "If anyone...opens the door, I will come in." Have you opened your heart's door to Christ?

Let us take heed to words such as those found in this letter: "Yet I hold this against you:...Nevertheless, I have a few things against you:...Nevertheless, I have this against you" (2:4,14,20). These are the warnings of a faithful Savior.

Discover how Christ is set forth in these two chapters. Remember, this book is the Revelation of Jesus Christ. What are the promises to the overcomers? See if you can find seven.

Future—The Things Which Shall Be (Revelation 4:1—22:21)

The great revelation proper unfolds with the sound of trumpets and "a door standing open in heaven. And the voice...said, 'Come up here, and I will show you what must take place after this.'"

First the throne of God comes into view (4:1-3). Revelation becomes the "book of the throne." This is the great central fact that pervades the book. This throne speaks of judgment. The throne of grace is no longer seen. The scene is a courtroom. The Judge of all the earth is on the bench; the twenty-four elders, representing the twelve patriarchs of the Old Testament and the twelve apostles of the New, are the jury (4:4). The seven spirits of God (4:5; 5:6) are the prosecutor, and the four living creatures are court attendants, ready to carry out the will of the Judge.

Next in importance to the Lamb Himself is the sealed book (5:1). Who can possibly open the book? None, save One. He "has triumphed. He is able to open the scroll and its seven seals" (v. 5). Christ prevailed in the wilderness after forty days. He prevailed in Gethsemane. On Calvary He prevailed when He dropped His divine head on His pulseless breast and said, "It is finished" (John 19:30). On the third day He arose from the dead and conquered death, sin, hell and Satan. This same Christ now claims the kingdom of the world by right of conquest.

The day of tribulation begins with the opening of the seven seals (chap. 6). This describes the Great Tribulation period spoken of by the prophet Jeremiah in Jeremiah 30 as the "time of Israel's sorrow." Christ also referred to it as a great tribulation such as has never happened upon the earth (Matthew 24:21). During the Great Tribulation, God will allow sin to work out its tragic results. God's hand will be lifted from humans and beasts. The earth will be filled with war, hunger, famine and pestilence. Judgment must come on those who have rejected the Son of God and put Him to an open shame. We as Christians can look for Christ, not for calamity, because our Savior is coming to receive us to Himself and free us from this day.

Four Horsemen

In the sixth chapter we see the famous "four horsemen" (Revelation 6:1-8). Restraint is removed as the seals are broken. The forces of evil have been held in check. When the seals are torn away, war and destruction are set loose. People will reap what they have sown. The anguish and horror of the period will be the result of human ambition, hatred and cruelty.

First, we see the white horse of religious witness come before the final catastrophe upon the earth. Then comes the red horse, and universal war breaks upon the world when peace will be taken from the earth. The black horse of famine and scarcity follows upon universal war. Lastly, the pale horse of pestilence and death comes forth with merciless tread.

The sixth seal (6:12-17) brings social chaos, the complete breaking up of society and a boasted civilization. Darkness, falling stars, heavens rolled up as a scroll, islands moving, is the picture presented. Then the most tragic prayer meeting on earth with kings and priests, rich and poor, fleeing from God in a general stampede, praying for death, for "For the great day of their wrath has come, and who can stand?"

There is a momentary pause (chap. 7) while the saved of the tribulation period are presented. These are "a great multitude" (7:9) with their garments washed and made white in the blood of the Lamb. The "sealed" are all Israelites—whom God will gather unto Himself (Hosea 1:9-10; Romans 11:25-26). The "great multitude" is from all nations. This proves that the gospel preached in the tribulation period will be most effective.

The Seven Trumpets

Silence in heaven for thirty minutes! Orchestras cease! Seraphim and cherubim fold their wings! All is still! It is as though all heaven was waiting in breathless expectation. This is the calm before the storm (chap. 8). War, famine and pestilence have devastated the earth. Now His judgments have come upon the earth and Satan, knowing his time is short, is exceedingly wrathful. We find unprecedented activity of demons, 200 million demons sweeping across the earth. Hell is let loose! Sin is allowed its full sway, and death is preferable to life (9:1-21). Satan does his last work upon the earth.

Finally we see Satan incarnating himself in the Antichrist. His portrait is given in Revelation 13. See also Daniel 12:11; Matthew 24:15; 2 Thessalonians 2:3. This Antichrist will be a world ruler. He demands the honors due to Christ Himself. He will be the political ruler of this world. He is the embodiment of wickedness. He will be shrewd and clever and a real leader of people. The Antichrist will be a Caesar, an Alexander, a Nero, a Hitler, a Stalin, a Mao Tse-Tung all in one. A person can neither "buy or sell unless he had the mark." Mergers and trusts were unheard of a few years ago. The "mark of the beast" is like the brand mark of ownership or the token of allegiance such as the swastika. It will be impossible for people to buy or sell without permission. The number 666 is "the number of a man." Six is the number of evil, so three sixes express a trinity of wickedness.

The final doom of the Antichrist will be the lake of fire at Christ's coming (Revelation 19:20). There will be plagues such as those of Egypt—blood, hail, fire, locusts, darkness, famine, sores, earthquakes, war and death. In these plagues is summed up the wrath of God upon a Christ-rejecting world.

The Seven Golden Bowls

In the trumpets, Satan is releasing his power to accomplish his objectives. The bowls are God's power released against Satan. The bowls are God's answer to the devil. The bowls blast the dominion of Satan. Satan has dared to challenge God's power. God is now answering the challenge. Satan is forced into action. His kingdom is shaken to its foundations and he is undone. This event ends in the battle of Armageddon (16:13-16). This battle is described in chapter 19. In the closing scene of the war, Christ takes the leadership of His armies and brings His foes to their doom.

The Dooms

The seventh bowl announced the "dooms" that were to follow. Civilization has come to utter collapse. Even though God has revealed its utter evil, nevertheless people blaspheme God and do not repent (16:9,11). Today, amid the luxuries of invention, people are dissatisfied and far from God. Hatred has turned into wars of colossal dimension. God pronounces seven "dooms" (chaps. 17-20). First the doom of great systems—ecclesiastical (chap. 17), commercial (chap. 18), political (19:11-19); then the beast and the false prophet (19:20-21), followed by the nations

(20:7-9), and the devil (20:10), and finally, the doom of the lost is pronounced (20:11-15).

The Marriage of the Lamb

The "Hallelujah Chorus" (by George Frideric Handel, 1685-1759) announces the coming of the long-promised King, our Lord Jesus Christ, the heir of David's throne, to catch away His bride (1 Thessalonians 4:17). Hell has been let loose on earth. Satan and his cohorts have done their worst and Christ has finally triumphed. Righteousness, long on the scaffold, is now to mount the throne. The marriage of the Lamb is come (Revelation 19:7). The marriage supper of Christ will take place in the air. The saints will be rewarded in the air according to their works. This time of rejoicing will continue until Christ returns to the earth with His bride, to set up His millennial kingdom.

After the Battle of Armageddon (19:17-19), Christ, having subdued all His enemies, will take alive Antichrist (19:20) and the false prophet and cast them with a strong arm into the lake of fire. This is a name for Gehenna, the place where torment never ceases and from which none return. Christ will make an end of Satan's entire system.

The Millennium

This is the time when Christ, the Prince of Peace, will establish His kingdom upon the earth for a thousand years. The devil is to be bound for a thousand years (20:3); the saints Christ brings with Him will reign with Him for a thousand years (20:4,6); the wicked dead will not rise until the end of the thousand years (20:5).

There will be a thousand years of peace and joy upon the earth, when "the earth will be filled with the knowledge of the glory of the Lord, as the waters cover the sea" (Habakkuk 2:14). It will be a glorious time to live. No wars, no weeds, no wild animals, no taxes, no heartache of death! When this period has come to an end, then the devil will be released again. He will come to test the nations (Revelation 20:7-9). We discover their real attitude and learn that they prefer Satan to Christ. We can hardly believe it, but read 20:7-8: "When the thousand years are over, Satan will be released from his prison and will go out to deceive the nations in the four corners of the earth—Gog and Magog—to gather them for battle. In number they are like the sand on the seashore."

Satan is the author and instigator of war. After a thousand years of peace, Satan gathers them to "the war." Not a few gather, but a countless number, like "the sand on the seashore." But "fire came down from heaven and devoured them" (20:9). Human rebellion against God seems almost unbelievable, but "The heart is deceitful above all things and beyond cure. Who can understand it?" (Jeremiah 17:9).

Satan's Doom

Satan is treated too lightly by the average person. He is mighty! He is the deceiver of the whole world. He fell from the highest place, next to God Himself, to the lowest depths—"the lake of fire." Christ described it as "the eternal fire prepared for the devil and his angels" (Matthew 25:41). The devil is given a life sentence (Revelation 20:10).

The blazing white throne of the final judgment is set. The One sitting upon it shall judge all people. Read Revelation 20:11-15. The "dead" are brought before Him. The sea gives up its dead. The grave gives up its dead. Hades gives up the dead. The dead are judged according to their works (20:12-13). Final doom is pronounced. The Savior is now the Judge. "If anyone's name was not found written in the book of life, he was thrown into the lake of fire" (20:15). Judgment must come before the golden age of glory can be ushered in. Someone has called hell the penitentiary of the universe, and the universal cemetery of the spiritually dead.

John names seven new things:
A new heaven and earth—21:1
A new people—21:2-8
A new bride—21:9
A new home—21:10-21
A new temple—21:22
A new light—21:23-27
A new Paradise—22:1-5.

Happily Ever After

Yes, God's story ends "and they lived happily ever after." Read the triumph of God in Revelation 21 and 22. Satan has not been victorious in his attempt to separate people from fellowship with God by sin ever since his meeting with the first man and woman in the garden of Eden. He has utterly failed and we will be with Christ forever and ever!

Don't try to analyze or interpret these chapters. Rather, meditate upon them. This is heaven! How limited words are in explaining its glory! The fellowship between God and people is restored. God "dwells with his people." Every purpose is realized and every promise is fulfilled. Heaven is the opposite of what we experience here. All is beautiful!

The last words of Christ in His Revelation are, "Yes, I am coming soon." Our response should ever be, "Amen. Come, Lord Jesus" (22:20).

Chapter 52

A Quick Look at the New Testament

Colossians Through Revelation

Outstanding Truths

Christ's Second Coming
Twentieth Century False Religions
Christ the Head of the Church
The Power of a Christian Life
The Word "Better" in Hebrews
Power of the Tongue

What's the Answer?

1. Which Epistles are suggested by the following words?
   Righteousness
   The unruly tongue
   Christ's coming again
   Christian love
   The good fight (the wrestler)
2. What was the occasion for each of the following statements and in which book is it found?
   a. "I have fought the good fight, I have finished the race, I have kept the faith. Now there is in store for me the crown of righteousness, which the Lord, the righteous Judge, will award to me."
   b. "For the Lord himself will come down from heaven, with a loud command, with the voice of the archangel and with the trumpet call of God, and the dead in Christ will rise first."

    c.   "I am not ashamed of the gospel, because it is the power of God for the salvation of everyone who believes."

    d.   "And we know that in all things God works for the good of those who love him."

    e.   "Approach the throne of grace with confidence."

    f.   "Blessed is the one who reads the words of this prophecy, and blessed are those who hear it and take to heart what is written in it, because the time is near."

3. This gives a study of the most notable sentences in the Epistles. Pick out the ones that seem most important to you. (Use concordance if necessary.)

"All Scripture is God-breathed."

"Now faith is being sure of what we hope for and certain of what we do not see."

"Faith without deeds is useless."

"Now to you who believe, this stone is precious."

"Add to your faith goodness; and to goodness, knowledge."

"If we confess our sins, He is faithful and just and will forgive us our sins and purify us from all unrighteousness."

4. What were the last words of:

Christ?	Luke 24:46-53
Paul?	2 Timothy 4:1-9
Peter?	2 Peter 3:10-18
James?	James 5:10-20
Jude?	Jude 17-25
The Bible?	Revelation 22:8-21

5. Check the correct answer:

Thessalonians tells:

❑ the sin of the tongue; ❑ of Christ's second coming; ❑ of Christ, the High Priest.

The heroes of the faith are found in:

❑ Timothy; ❑ Hebrews; ❑ Revelation.

Timothy was:

❑ Paul's son; ❑ an early missionary; ❑ Paul's convert.

God's future plans are revealed in:

❑ Hebrews; ❑ Titus; ❑ Revelation.

Part Three
Appendices

Teaching Suggestions

"Do your best to present yourself to God as one approved,
a workman who does not need to be ashamed and who
correctly handles the word of truth"
(2 Timothy 2:15).

The primary purpose of this book is to give the Bible student a panoramic view of the Bible so that it is seen as a cohesive whole instead of a series of unrelated stories set down in archaic English. The Bible is the story of what God is doing in history. Like any good story, it has a beginning and an ending. It starts with the Creation; conflict is introduced with the workings of Satan and the fall of humanity, introducing the dilemma. The rest of the story is solving that great dilemma by God and the final triumph of His purpose at the second coming of Christ. All the events in between fit into that story and contribute to the unfolding of the "plot."

The Bible has one main theme—redemption—and many subthemes that run through the entire book. Redemption is hinted at in the beginning—Genesis 3:15—and developed as the main theme, coming to a climax with the advent of Christ. The subthemes, interwoven into the narrative, and all dependent upon the main theme of redemption, are all defined and illustrated in the events of the Bible. For instance, the innate rebelliousness of sinful humanity is played up and becomes a major chord in the story of the wandering in the wilderness and in Judges, as well as in other minor episodes. The mercy of God is portrayed in Hosea; the victory He gives, in Joshua.

Class Teaching Methods

Fortunately, twenty-first-century thirst for knowledge includes a wholesome curiosity about what the Bible teaches. In accompaniment to churches' expanding Sunday School enrollments, home Bible-study groups are springing up and churches gladly respond to desires for weekday classes.

For the use of students in such classes, *What the Bible Is All About 101, 102, 201, 202* are available. Available also are *What the Bible Is All About Group Study Guide* and *What the Bible Is All About Video Seminar Package*. These are study guides to be used with this parent volume, *What the Bible Is All About.* They may be secured from your church supplier.

If you are teaching the Bible, remember two things about your class or home study group:

1. Chances are they *do not* have any systematic knowledge of the Bible. Most of your students will not have attended Sunday School consistently enough to be really well informed. They see the Bible as a collection of unrelated stories with morals, interspersed with long, dull passages they have never bothered to read; some beautiful poetry; some outstanding verses. The *pattern* of the Bible will be new to them. The history will certainly be a hazy impression of dignified characters in flowing garments either wandering in the wilderness or tending sheep somewhere in the Middle East.
2. You can get across one main idea each lesson—and only one.

Now, keeping those two facts firmly in mind each time you teach, you want to do these things: give your class a picture of the whole of God's pattern, emphasizing how the particular book you are teaching fits into that whole, and drive home the major lesson of that book.

Ample material is provided for you to use any of several different approaches, but a few very broad principles apply, whatever method you pursue.

First, always keep the whole scope of the Bible in mind. To begin with, read through this book for main impressions and emphases—quickly, just picking out the main points. Details will come later, as you work on each chapter.

Second, begin preparing each lesson a week in advance. You may have had some issues raised during the last class session that need to be clarified. Write those down. It's better to work on the lesson a little bit each day and then put the final touches on it at the end of the preparation period. You will find that preparing a lesson this way is a little bit like making a pot of stew—the longer it simmers the better it gets.

Third, though by no means third in importance, do as much reading as you can in the book of the Bible you are teaching. This book has the most important passages listed. For instance, in the chapter on Genesis is a list of the beginnings that are noted in that book, along with the Scriptures. In each chapter the outline covers the major events of the book.

Fourth, constantly bring your thinking back to the central theme of each book. This is the thing you want to get across to your students! Other lessons may be drawn—other themes you will mention—but keep referring back to this *main* theme. Cohesiveness ought to be the watchword of the teacher using this material.

Fifth, bear in mind the character and needs of the students you are teaching—they are not all alike. You may have a class of young adults, all wearing that brittle mask of self-sufficiency that cracks so easily to show the uncertainty underneath. They need absolutes, and they will respond to the absolutes of the Bible. They also need love and understanding, and they will open up like flowers to the understanding grace of God. Teach to those needs. A middle-aged group is another thing entirely. They may still have many of the same needs as the young adults, but added to this is the new dimension of attainment and power. It is up to the teacher to present the Bible in a manner suited to its importance. This age group especially needs to be buttressed against the persuasively presented false philosophy that security is to be found in "things." We ought to stress that God's kingdom must always have priority.

Finally, do remember that you are teaching, primarily, and not giving a devotional. Because we are all aware, as we ought to be, of the need to know Christ better and to love Him more, we tend to forget that one of the major means to achieve these ends is to teach what the Bible says. There is no substitute for real teaching. All kinds of inspirational meetings are designed to impel Christians to action, to move them to decision, help them with their devotional lives—but the Bible study is to give knowledge and directive to their faith. Anything that makes your teaching clear and explicit, that clarifies and explains, is good. If you use stories and illustrations to bring out your point, be sure they *do* just that. If they have an emotional punch, well and good; but beware of mere sentimentality. You may move a class to the edge of tears with a touching little story of a dying child, but if there isn't a real solid Bible truth in that story the effect is not so lasting.

Now, three basic methods might be used with this material:

1. Student preparation method
2. Class discussion method
3. Lecture method.

Each method has some advantages and certain disadvantages; consider them, and see which one will best suit your class and its needs.

Student Preparation

Preparing for the lesson requires real work by the students. For instance, on the week preceding the study of the chapter on Genesis you might assign sections to the students. Tell each one to read the section assigned, study the Scriptures, and then give in his or her own words at the next session the lesson to be drawn from that story. Give each one a specified time to speak, allowing yourself at least ten minutes to sum it all up and bring out the main theme of the book.

The advantages are obvious—this encourages interest and Bible study on the part of the students. Most of them love to have a part, and unless you have an entire class of introverts you should be able to find enough each week to participate. There are some drawbacks to this. Unless your people are dependable, they may either prepare poorly or be absent from the class when they are supposed to shine. This may be avoided by a telephone check during the week. Occasionally you'll get the original thinker who becomes so entranced with an obscure passage that he or she dwells on it to the exclusion of the main part of the story, sometimes drawing some very odd conclusions from the Scripture! The time can also get away from the speakers and you may be left with one minute for summing up. Experiment with this way of teaching—perhaps you will want to modify it a bit or use it once in a while. It requires just as much preparation on the part of the teacher, for you must be on your toes to see that the lesson is rightly presented.

Class Discussion

Class discussion can be done in one of several ways. You might hand out discussion topics for the following week. These topics should be worked out from the lesson material, not simply using the questions at the end of the chapter. For example, in the lesson on Genesis you might find the following topics: What is God's answer to man's disobedience? How did sin enter the world? How does the Abrahamic Covenant illustrate the grace of God?

It is amazing how many people are seriously concerned about a question such as the origin of sin; they may ask some searching questions and want to go far beyond pointing out Satan as the tempter. They may well ask you, "Yes, but if Satan was originally created by God, how could he be evil? How can a good God create something evil?" Be prepared to treat such a question with respect. A quick answer is not always the best answer, and such a profound issue demands more than a facile reply. Sometimes it may be a good thing to tell the class you will bring the answer next week, rather than hurry through.

In using this class discussion method, the teacher must be sure to keep the talk from wandering far afield. Remember, you have a point to put across and you can't do justice to more than one major lesson. If the discussion dribbles off into pointlessness, keep pulling the class back to the main theme. One great secret in teaching is to know when an issue raised by the class is vital to their faith—something they've wondered about, puzzled over and need an answer to—or when it is merely an oddity to quibble over. If, in the course of the lesson, your students seem concerned about a point you are making, don't be hesitant about taking more time to clarify that point. You may have to skim lightly over the rest of the lesson because of it; but you remember the fifth basic principle—that you are *teaching to their needs.* As you can see, this kind of classroom work requires a nice balance between adherence to the main purpose of your lesson and flexibility within that framework. Such a method is very demanding on the teacher, but the rewards are great.

Another way of using the discussion method is to ask the students to hand in the questions they would like to have answered and then guide the discussion. This assumes a great deal of interest and intelligence on the part of your students, and there is one caution: you may have two or three very precocious and uninhibited students; they are all too willing to speak at length on their ideas about the lesson. They may be getting a great deal out of being so verbose, but the rest of the class is not. Regardless of the brilliance of the few vocal ones, the others don't want to listen to them; they want to hear from someone "in the know"—someone with more authority behind his statements than simply "Joe, who always talks too much anyway." Frequently these extroverted pupils are the ones who linger after class with special questions, or problems. They do need attention, but not to the exclusion of the rest of the class, and some of the quieter students who need to be gently coaxed into sharing their ideas.

Lecture

Lecture does not mean a rigid, formal presentation. It can be as flexible as either of the other methods or used in combination with one of them. After you have established a good rapport with your class, they'll feel free to interrupt the lesson when they have questions.

Let's take the chapter on Genesis, again, as our example. Read over this chapter carefully. Read through the book of Genesis, not stopping for details, but simply reading to get the broad outline of the book. This can be done, remember, at the first of the week. Let the lesson build slowly in your thinking.

Now you are ready to begin thinking about the emphasis you want to give the chapter. There is enough written material in the book so that if you merely read through it, your class time would be consumed. But what you have been provided with is the raw material of the lesson; it is up to you to shape it and give it emphasis.

First, think of the whole scope of the Bible as you want to present it. Beginnings are vitally important, and Genesis contains the plot, in germ, of the whole story of the gospel. Read over the first portion of the chapter carefully until it becomes your own.

Second, go over the rest of the material and decide where you want to stress a point, where you can cover lightly. Because all the stories are referred to again and again in the Bible as examples, they need to be well told. You may wish to dwell longer on one than on the others in order to make a point. These should be related not as different stories but as parts of the whole. You have a double purpose in each lesson—to present the book in its proper relation to the entire scope of the Bible; and to bring out one grand truth, one practical lesson, from each book. Of course, you may cover several subthemes, but keep coming back to the main lesson.

Third, go over your lesson, tie up any loose ends and decide how you are going to sum it all up. The closing portion of your lesson is of prime importance. Here is where many a good speaker goes wrong. There is, as you know, a kind of timing that is the one main source of effective speaking or teaching. Some fortunate people have a built-in sense of timing—they know just how to build interest, when to hesitate the merest fraction of a second before uttering the punch line of a funny story, just when to move in fast for a climax, and, most important of all, when to stop. There is a Spirit-chosen time to stop—when you have made your point, *don't embellish it.* After you have said, in the most effective way you can, what you want them to remember, *that's all.* Resist the temptation to add just one more effective little sentence; it will not be at all effective if it's said after the psychological stopping time. Your audience has already mentally left; you might as well close.

Now, here are some reminders—little tips to tuck away in the back of your mind. It would be ideal if your students remembered everything you gave them each week, but be realistic—they will not. Recapitulate a little—not in detail, which would bore them terribly, but *briefly* go over the material covered. Do this in a positive way so you won't make them conscious of their failure to remember. Say, "Of course you recall..." and then tell them what of course they did not recall. Because none of us assimilates knowledge in wholesale gulps, the teaching process consists largely of telling and retelling the same truths in different ways, so that gradually—very, very gradually—those truths become a part of the lives of those who are learning them.

Because this is a discussion of methods, we have not mentioned the very obvious things that underlie successful teaching—your desire to present Christ in a winning way, your constant dependence on prayer and your utter reliance on the guidance of the Holy Spirit.

Beyond and above all the timeworn and timeless truths about teaching—our duty to do it, the satisfaction it affords, and all the reasons for devoting the time and the work and the energy to it—lies the deep and abiding pleasure of handling the Word of God, to which we are all committed.

Guiding the Prayer Time

Begin each class session with prayer.

Prayer is the keynote of success. Neither a class nor an individual can succeed in Christ without it. Prayer is the breath of the Christian. We are commanded to "pray continually" (1 Thessalonians 5:17). As natural as breathing is to a natural person, so natural should prayer be to a spiritual person. Does all this describe you? Does the time of prayer in class have meaning or is it just a part of the normal procedure? It is a true statement that the class will go no further spiritually than you as teacher lead them.

What does prayer mean to you? To guide the time of prayer in class you must be completely sold on its necessity yourself. You might make it a standard practice to ask the Lord daily for His guidance as you lead your students. Ask Him to give you a love and understanding of them that is like unto His love and understanding of you. Pray for the individuals by name if possible. Prepare your lesson, prayer receiving an important part in your consideration.

As you come to class, have an attitude that shows your complete dependence upon the Holy Spirit to guide your thoughts and words. Before you teach, ask that God will lead you. Do not rush through the opening prayer time, but do not prolong it to the place of boredom. Give opportunity for the students to take part if they desire. Encourage, but do not force participation. Be careful that neither you nor any other more mature Christian monopolize the prayer time. This is a time to talk to God, not the time to preach a sermon. When you pray, *really pray.*

Visual Teaching Aids

Visual aids for adults may be divided into four main types: projected, chalkboard, diagrams and charts, and maps. Use the aid (or combination of aids) that best illustrates a particular lesson.

Projected Aids

Preview the videocassette or film before class. In this way you can prepare for the discussion that will follow the presentation and foresee any difficulties the film may create. Projected aids should not be

looked upon as "teaching crutches," but should be used either to introduce the lesson or to summarize that which has been taught.

Set up the VCR or slide projector well in advance of the presentation. Be sure that all is in good working order. The projector should
have a 500-watt bulb and a cooling fan. If the room is small, a 300-watt
bulb may be adequate, but test first to be sure. The projector should be
placed on a rigid stand at the back of the room and high enough to
avoid head shadows on the screen.

Place the screen in line with the projector and high enough to allow
clear view by the class. Where it is not feasible to use the screen and
darken the room, the projector may be placed at the front of the room
and a sheet of white paper suspended between projector and class. The
film should be turned around so the class can read the titles.

If you are using a sound system, it should be placed near the projector. If at all possible, use an auxiliary speaker at the front of the
room. Ideally the operator should adjust the sound level and synchro-
nize the sound and the picture as the showing progresses.

Chalkboard

A chalkboard may be purchased or you can make it yourself. Use a
piece of Masonite, the size appropriate to your class, and paint it with
chalkboard paint. Or you can put a piece of clear plastic over a piece
of cardboard (covered with white paper) and write with a grease pen-
cil. If you would like to keep the outlines so you can refer back to them
in later lessons, use a flip chart. Fasten several pieces of paper or cardboard together at the top and then turn each piece as you complete the
writing on it. Suit the size of the board to the size of your class. Often
a portable board is sufficient.

The chalkboard is an indispensable part of teaching equipment. It
provides an economical aid because it can be reused repeatedly. It
serves to center the student's interest on the point under discussion.
But, needless to say, if the chalkboard is to be used successfully it must
be wisely and efficiently used. All representations placed upon it
should be definite and immediately purposeful; meaningless doodlings
are confusing and distracting and are evidences of the teacher's lack of
skill. To be easily readable, the material should be clearly and accu-
rately reproduced with a minimum degree of artistry. Not too much

material should be used at any one time because this clutters up the board and gives it a messy appearance. It also tends to reduce the space left for writing and makes it less intelligible.

Generally speaking, it is a good idea to erase material that is not needed to avoid distraction.

When outlines, summaries or similar materials are to be used by the group immediately, they should be placed on the board before the class convenes. If the teacher writes on the board while the class waits, valuable time is lost and the interest wanes. Do not be afraid, however, to use the chalkboard as the lesson develops. Put certain points on the board. List ideas that discussion brings forth. Write the reference for some Scripture that you are using. Let the students do some of the writing.

Use the chalkboard often in your lesson presentation. It will assist in keeping the development clearly in mind.

Diagrams and Charts

A good diagram must maintain two standards. First of all it must be technically correct; it must be correctly and neatly drawn in the proper proportion and completely labeled, and explained. Nothing can be left to the imagination. In the second place, it has to be artistic because it must command the student's respect and thus encourage interest and understanding.

The diagram must be adequately explained or interpreted and have a definite application made from it.

Various types of charts may be used. For example, a chronological chart that lists events in the proper sequence is often a help in getting an overall view of the book or topic under study. The use of titles, labels, columns, lines, arrows, numerals, colors, variations in sizes of charts, light and heavy type, diagrams, illustrations, pictures, maps, appended explanatory notes and other devices help to clarify the material and make it more readable and meaningful.

Charts may be shown to clarify genealogy or to trace historical sequences. A time-line chart will serve to keep specific events within the right general periods. Charts may be used effectively to show the relationship of one main thought to its several component parts.

Charts and diagrams may be prepared on poster board, on flannel boards or on chalkboards. Flip charts may be made in which each event or thought has its own specific representation.

Maps

Maps are indispensable. We are continually making and using maps—either mentally or graphically. When taking a long trip by car, we use a road map until it is thumb worn.

As educational devices, maps help the student to visualize and localize important geographical areas.

Make sure that the student comprehends the purpose of the map—what is intended to be made clear with the use of the map. Is it the distance between two places? Or is it the extent of territory covered? Or is it the type of terrain present in certain sections?

Use maps at the opportune moment. The map should be used when it is most needed to answer questions, solve problems or supply information or data. Studying a map apart from an actual situation makes it a meaningless exercise that lacks purpose and life.

Do some map work. For example, trace the spread of the Church throughout the world. A world map will show the mission work being done on the foreign and home fields. A map of Paul's journeys would be helpful. To show the spread of Christianity throughout the world, shade the area on the map. Areas of non-Christian influence can be indicated also, perhaps with overlays of plastic. You may want to show the mission areas to which your own church has contributed.

Visual teaching need not be elaborate to be effective. A simple statement of what is being taught is all that is required. Use a variety of methods to impress these great truths upon the minds of your students.

Appendix 2

Becoming a Member of God's Family

This appendix has a threefold purpose. First, it can be used by a teen to read about becoming a member of God's family. Second, it can be used by parents, in the home, to help their children become members of God's family. Third, it can be used by a teacher to help a student become a member of God's family. Any person who wishes to lead another person to Christ should become familiar with the explanation given in this appendix.

In the Old Testament, God promised to send a Messiah or Savior to His people. The Messiah would save God's people from their sin, from the wrong things everyone has done. The people in the Old Testament times knew about the promise of a Savior and looked for Him.

In the New Testament, God's promise came true! The Savior was born in Bethlehem, just where God promised! (see Micah 5:2). Jesus Christ was born, grew up and died for our sins.

God's Word always comes true. You can trust God's faithfulness, for He made it possible for you to become a member of His family. Here's how:

Step One: God Loves You

The Bible says in 1 John 4:8 that "God is love." He loves you very much. He loves you because He made you and He is concerned about you and your life today.

Step Two: You Have Sinned

The Bible also says that you and all other people have sinned. In Romans 3:23 we read, "For all have sinned and fall short of the glory of God."

We have all done wrong and our sins keep us from being friends with God. As you read in the books of the Old Testament, sin always leads to trouble. Because you are a sinner, your sin will cause much trouble in your life. Romans 6:23 tells us how bad this trouble will ultimately be. "For the wages of sin is death."

God does not want people to ruin their lives with sin. It makes Him sad when you sin and spoil your happiness and the happiness of other people. Because of sin, people cannot enjoy God's loving presence in their lives, nor can they live with God in heaven. Not one of us is able to remove sin from our lives or to earn God's forgiveness by even our very best efforts.

In the beginning of the Bible is the story of Adam and Eve, the first two people. Adam and Eve lived happily with God until they disobeyed Him. That was the first sin. One of the results of the sin was that Adam and Eve were separated from God, thereby robbing life of its greatest joy and ultimately bringing the penalty of death upon themselves. All of us sin, so someday each of us will die, too.

However, the Bible is clear that there is another life after we die. The Bible is also clear that sin will continue to separate people from God's love forever. Because everybody has sinned, how does anybody get to go to heaven?

Step Three: God Paid the Price

The Bible says in Romans 6:23, "For the wages of sin is death, but the gift of God is eternal life in Christ Jesus our Lord." We have seen that the result of sin is death. However, because God loves you so much, He offers eternal life as a free gift. You cannot work hard enough to earn eternal life. All you can do is accept it as a gift.

God gave His only Son to die for you on the cross. The Bible says in 1 Corinthians 15:3, "Christ died for our sins according to the Scriptures." Because Jesus was the perfect Man—without sin—He accepted the results of sin—death—in your place. The Bible says in 1 John 4:14, "The Father has sent his Son to be the Savior of the world."

Step Four: Ask God for His Forgiveness

If you admit that you have sinned and believe that God gave His only

Son to die in your place, God will forgive you and make you clean from all sin.

Tell God that you know you are a sinner.

Tell God you believe Jesus Christ is your only way to have your sins forgiven.

Tell God you want to learn to love and follow Christ in every area of your life.

Tell Him that He is great and wonderful.

It is easy to talk to God. Jesus taught us to talk to Him as we would to a loving Father. He is ready to listen. What you are going to tell Him is something He has been waiting to hear.

If you believe and have told God you believe, you are now a child of God! God has forgiven all your sin. You are a Christian. And that makes you a member of His family.

God has made everything right between you and Him. He has forgiven you and He looks upon you as if you had never sinned!

Step Five: Live as God's Child

The Bible says in John 1:12, "Yet to all who received him, to those who believed in his name, he gave the right to become children of God." As a child of God, you receive God's gift of everlasting life. God is with you now and forever.

Now that you are a member of God's family, God wants you to live as His child.

You Can Talk to God

Because God is your heavenly Father, He wants you to talk to Him in prayer. You can tell God how you feel, thank Him for His gifts to you and ask Him to help you obey and follow Him.

You can also talk to God when you sin. Ask God to forgive you and He will. The Bible says in 1 John 1:9, "If we confess our sins, he is faithful and just and will forgive us our sins and purify us from all unrighteousness." God will forgive you and help you do what He says.

You Can Read God's Word

God gave His Word so that everyone can read about Him and His great love. Find out more about God by reading about Him in your Bible. The Bible says, "I have hidden your word in my heart that I might not sin against you" (Psalm 119:11). As you read God's Word, you will stay close to Him. It's just like reading a letter again and again. You can do the same thing with your Bible.

You Can Obey God

Your heavenly Father wants you to obey Him. He tells you in His Word how you should live. Jesus summed up God's law with two command-ments (see Matthew 22:37-40):

1. Love God with all that you are.
2. Love your neighbor as yourself.

God wants you to be an expression of His love in the world.

You Can Tell Others About Jesus

Jesus said in Acts 1:8, "you will be my witnesses." Jesus was talking to His disciples before He went back to His Father. Even though Jesus was talking to His disciples, He was saying these words to you, too. You can be a witness when you tell others about Jesus and how His love has helped you. Ask God to give you opportunities each day to tell about—and to show—God's love.

Appendix 3

A Glossary of Bible Words

Abba (Ab-uh)
An Aramaic word that means "Daddy." Aramaic was the language spoken by Jesus and other Jews living in Judea and Samaria.

admonition
Teaching, instruction, usually with the idea of a warning.

adultery
Sexual union between a man and a woman when either or both of them are married to someone else. Adultery is a sin.

adversary
An enemy or someone who is against you. Can refer directly to Satan (1 Peter 5:8).

advocate
Someone who supports, comforts, gives help to or speaks up for another person. Jesus and the Holy Spirit are *advocates* for members of God's family (John 14:16,26; 1 John 2:1).

affliction
Great trouble or pain.

alien
A person from another country; a foreigner.

altar
A place where sacrifices were made to worship God. An *altar* could be a pile of dirt or stones, a raised platform of wood, marble, metal or other materials. The *bronze* or *brazen altar* was used for burnt offerings in the Tabernacle's courtyard. It was a large box, eight feet square and four-and-a-half feet high, made of wood covered with bronze. A much larger altar replaced it when Solomon built the Temple. The *altar of incense* (also called the *golden altar*) was smaller, covered with gold, and placed just in front of the veil to the holy of holies. Every day, both morning and evening, incense was burned here,

symbolizing the prayers of the people.

Amalekites (uh-MAL-uh-kites)
Nomadic, warlike people inhabiting the region southwest of the Dead Sea. Because of their vicious attack against the Israelites after the Exodus from Egypt, God pronounced judgment on them. Battles against the Amalekites were fought by Joshua, several of the judges, by Saul and by David, and were finally destroyed in the days of Hezekiah.

amen
"Let it be so!" or "This is the truth!" *Amen* is often said after a prayer to show that people agree with what has been said and believe that it will happen.

Ammonites
Descendants of Ben-Ammi, grandson of Abraham's nephew, Lot. They lived east of the Dead Sea, and were nomadic, idolatrous and vicious. The Ammonites often opposed Israel.

Amorites
Descendants of Canaan, a son of Ham, and grandson of Noah. Because of their wickedness, God told Abraham of future destruction He would bring. This punishment occurred under Moses and Joshua, and their land was given to the tribe of Reuben.

Ancient of Days
A name for God that describes Him as the ever-lasting ruler of heaven and earth (Daniel 7:13-14).

angels
Heavenly beings created by God before He created Adam and Eve. *Angels* act as God's messengers to men and women. They also worship God.

anoint
To pour oil on a person or thing. A person was *anointed* to show that God had chosen him or

her to do a special job. Samuel *anointed* David to show God had chosen him to be king.

antediluvian (ANT-ay-da-LOO-vee-un)
Before the Flood. The term is from the Latin, and is used in reference to the period and people before Genesis 7—9.

antichrist (AN-tih-christ)
A great enemy of Christ Jesus who pretends to be the Messiah. The Bible tells us that before the second coming of Christ, an *antichrist* will rule over the world.

Antioch (AN-tee-ock)
1. The capital of Syria, site of the first Gentile church, which sent Paul and Barnabas on their first missionary journey. 2. A town in Asia Minor that Paul visited on his travels.

apostle
A person chosen and sent out as a messenger. In the New Testament, *apostle* usually refers to one of the twelve men Jesus chose to be His special disciples. Paul and some other leaders in the Early Church were also called *apostles.*

appeal to Caesar (SEE-zer)
If a Roman citizen accused of a crime thought that the trial or verdict was unfair, he could request that the emperor hear the case. Paul, a Roman citizen, once did this.

Arabia
The large area between the Persian Gulf to the East, the Indian Ocean to the south, the Red Sea to the west, and Israel, Syria, and Mesopotamia to the north.

Aram (AIR-um)
A son of Shem, grandson of Noah. The name is sometimes applied to all the land and people of the Fertile Crescent, but usually is focused on the region that became known as Syria. The Aramaens were a Semitic people, and their history often intersects that of the Hebrews.

Aramaic (air-uh-MAY-ik)
The main language spoken by Jesus and other people who lived in Judea and Samaria when Jesus was alive. At least some parts of the books of Daniel and Ezra were written in Aramaic, as was most of the Talmud, a compilation of Jewish laws and traditions.

Ararat (AIR-uh-rat)
A mountainous region of Armenia, between the Black Sea and the Caspian Sea where Noah's ark ran aground.

archangel
Chief angel. The term in the New Testament refers to Michael.

ark of God ark of the covenant
A special wooden chest that was covered with gold. God told Moses exactly how to make the ark because it was to show the people of Israel that God was with them. The ark was about 4 feet long, 2 feet tall and 2 feet wide. On top, two golden figures of angels faced each other. The two tables of stone on which the Ten Commandments were written, a pot of manna and Aaron's rod that budded were kept inside the ark. The ark was placed in the most holy place in the Tabernacle.

Armenia (arr-MEEN-ee-uh)
The area north of Assyria, containing the Ararat mountain region.

armor bearer
A person who carried the large shield and necessary weapons for a king or army officer.

Artemis (AR-tuh-mis)
A Greek goddess whose Roman name was Diana. Her most beautiful and influential temple was built in Ephesus.

ascend
To go up. Jesus *ascended* to heaven to return to God the Father.

Assyria (uh-SEER-ee-uh)
Powerful and aggressive nation, the most powerful middle eastern empire from the tenth century B.C. through most of the seventh century. Nineveh was the capital city. Assyria conquered Israel and took its inhabitants captive.

Athens
A major Greek city, center of its art, science and learning. *Athens* was visited by Paul on his second missionary journey.

atonement
To make up for a wrong act; to become friends again. In the Bible, *atonement* usually means to become friends with God after sin has separated us from Him. In the Old Testament, the Israelites brought sacrifices to *atone* for their sins. The New Testament teaches that Jesus Christ made *atonement* for our sins when He died on the cross. Because Jesus died to "make up" for our sins, we can have peace with God.

Baal (bale), **Baalim** (BALE-um)
The name *Baal* means "master." *Baal* (plural,

Baalim) was the name of many false gods worshiped by the people of Canaan. They thought the *Baalim* ruled their land, crops and animals. When the Israelites came to the Promised Land, each area of the land had its own *Baal* god. Names of places were often combined with the name *Baal*, such as Baal-Hermon, to show that Hermon belonged to *Baal*. Eventually, *Baal* became the name for the chief male god of the Canaanites. They believed that *Baal* brought the sun and the rain and made the crops grow. The Israelites were often tempted to worship *Baal*—something God had told them they were never to do.

Babel (BAB-ul)
The name popularly given to the tower built in a vain attempt by people to reach "the heavens" (Genesis ll:1-9). God blocked their effort by confusing their languages.

Babylon (BAB-u-lun), **Babylonia**
Refers to both the capital city and country, among the major political and cultural centers of the ancient world. The city of Babylon was located at the junction of the Euphrates river and major east-west caravan routes. For nearly a thousand years, until the rise of Assyria in the ninth century B.C., Babylon dominated much of the Middle East. Near the end of the seventh century B.C., Babylon regained its independence and for nearly 100 years asserted its influence throughout the region and was a constant threat to the Kingdom of Judah, finally resulting in the destruction of Jerusalem and the captivity of Judah's leading citizens. Babylon was captured by the Persians in 539 B.C., and then continued to decline until destroyed by the Greek army under Alexander the Great.

balm
A sticky, sweet-smelling sap that was used as a medicine to heal sores or relieve pain. The plant or tree from which the sap was taken is unknown today.

balsam trees
Trees that grow in the Jericho Plain. The sweet-smelling sap of the trees and the oil from their fruit were used as medicine.

baptize
In the Old Testament, to *baptize* meant to wash with water. But in the New Testament, when John the Baptist called the people to be *bap-*

tized, he was using water to show that people were truly sorry for the wrong things they had done and that they were asking God to forgive their sins. Today, a person is baptized to show that he or she is a member of God's family.

barren
A woman who could not have children was called *barren*. Fields that did not produce crops or fruit trees that did not grow fruit were also called *barren*.

Beelzebub (bee-EL-zee-bub)
A god the Philistines worshiped. In the New Testament, *Beelzebub* (or Beelzebul) is another name for Satan—the prince of the demons.

believe
To have faith or to trust that something is true. The Bible tells us that we can *believe* that Jesus Christ is God's Son and trust Him to keep His promise to forgive sins. We show that we *believe* that God loves us and wants what is best for us by obeying His commands.

Bethel
A site, a few miles directly north of Jerusalem, where God confirmed to Jacob the covenant He had made with Abraham. Jacob named the place *Bethel*, meaning "House of God." It figures prominently in many biblical events, and for a time the ark of the covenant was kept there. After the division of Israel from Judah, Jereboam made Bethel one of two centers of idolatrous worship, which continued until Josiah's reforms.

betroth (be-TROTHE)
Engaged to be married.

Bible
The word *Bible* comes from the Greek word *biblos*, meaning book.

bier
A stretcher or platform on which a dead body was carried to the place where it would be buried.

birthright
The special rights the oldest son in a Hebrew family enjoyed. When his father died, the oldest son received a double share of all that his father owned. He also received the right to make decisions for the entire family. Esau sold his *birthright* to Jacob for a bowl of soup.

bishop
Overseer, a leader in the Early Church.

bitter herbs (urbs)

A bitter green salad eaten at Passover to remind the Israelites of the sorrow, pain and bitter hardships they suffered as slaves in Egypt.

blaspheme

To say bad things against God, to swear using God's name, or to do actions that show disrespect to God. The Bible says that *blasphemy* is a sin. The Jews punished *blasphemers* by stoning them to death. Jesus and Stephen were falsely accused of *blasphemy*.

blemish

A spot or mark that makes something not perfect.

bless

The word *bless* is used in different ways in the Bible: 1. When God blesses, He brings salvation and prosperity and shows mercy and kindness to people. 2. When people bless, they (a) bring salvation and prosperity to other persons or groups; (b) they praise and worship and thank God; (c) they give good things or show kindness to others.

bondage

Being in slavery. In the Old Testament, the Israelites were in *bondage* to the Egyptians for many years. In the New Testament, *bondage* means slavery to sin. Jesus died and rose again to set people free from sin. Christians are no longer slaves to sin, but are free to love and obey God and His Son, Jesus.

breastpiece

A square of colored linen cloth worn by the high priest when he entered the Holy Place. The *breastpiece* was decorated with twelve precious stones. Each stone represented one of the twelve tribes of Israel. The *breastpiece* reminded the priest to pray for each of the tribes of Israel.

breastplate

A piece of metal armor that protected a soldier's throat and chest.

burnt offering

A sacrifice, or gift, to God that was burned upon an altar. The offering was a perfect animal, such as a goat, sheep, lamb or ram. *Burnt offerings* were always given for cleansing, or atonement, for sin.

Caesar (SEE-zer)

The family name of Julius Caesar, a famous Roman leader. Later the name *Caesar* was added to the name of each Roman ruler, so it became a title that meant the same as "emperor" or "king."

Calvary

A rugged bluff outside ancient Jerusalem. *Calvary* is from the Latin word for "skull," either because the hill resembled a skull, and/or because it was the site of executions.

Canaan (KAY-nun), **Canaanites**

Canaan was a son of Ham and a grandson of Noah. His descendants settled in and gave his name to the areas God promised to Abraham and which were later known as Judah (Judea) and Israel.

canon of Scripture (KAN-un)

Measuring rod or standard. For Protestants, the sixty-six books of the Old and New Testaments have been widely and historically accepted because they have met the standard of being true and authoritative. (Catholics and Orthodox Christians also revere the Apocrypha.)

capstone

The stone that holds two walls together; the final most important stone that finishes a wall. When the Bible calls Jesus a *capstone*, it reminds us that He is the head of the Church and that He holds all Christians together.

captivity

The seventy-year period when Jews were in exile in Babylon.

caravan

A group of people and their belongings, who traveled together for protection from robbers and wild animals. When families moved, they often traveled in a *caravan*. Traders also traveled in *caravans*.

Carmel (KAR-mel)

A high ridge that juts into the Mediterranean Sea. Mount Carmel was the site of Elijah's contest with the prophets of Baal.

census

Counting the number of people living in an area or country.

centurion (sen-TOUR-ee-un)

An officer in the Roman army who was the leader of 100 men.

chaff

The worthless husks removed from grain. Farmers in Bible times got rid of *chaff* by throwing grain in the air on windy days. The light *chaff* blew away on the wind; the heavier grain fell to the ground. In the Bible, the word *chaff* often means something bad or worthless.

Chaldea (kal-DEE-uh)

The country of Babylon. The term is also used of the southern region of Babylonia. The Chaldeans overthrew the Assyrians in the late seventh century B.C. and established the regime that brought Babylon to its greatest power.

chariot

An open, two-wheeled cart pulled by horses.

chief priest

See *high priest.*

cherub, cherubim

Heavenly beings, described as having multiple wings and both human and animal form. They are presented in Scripture as directly serving God. Carved representations of *cherubim* were placed on the Ark of the Covenant, and they were embroidered on the tabernacle's curtains. Solomon's Temple contained huge figures of *cherubim.*

chosen people

The Jews, as descendants of Abraham, were selected by God to be "a great and powerful nation, and all nations on earth will be blessed through him" (Genesis 18:18). The New Testament declares that the Church has become the spiritual recipient of this blessing and responsibility (1 Peter 2:9).

Christ

The Greek word that means God's Chosen One. Messiah is the Hebrew word meaning the same thing. Jesus was the Christ.

Christian (KRIS-chun)

In the Bible, the word meant "little Christ." Today people who believe Jesus Christ is God's Son and follow His teachings are called *Christians.*

church

An assembly or gathering. The word *church* is used to refer to both local groups of believers in Christ as well as all believers.

circumcise

To cut an unneeded flap of skin, called the foreskin, from the penis. For the Israelites, *circumcision* was a sign of the special agreement (or covenant) they had with God: If they worshiped and obeyed Him, He would be their God and they would be His people. Abraham was the first Hebrew to be *circumcised.* After Abraham, Hebrew baby boys were *circumcised* when they were eight days old. Leaders in the Early Church said that it was not necessary for men or boys to be *circumcised* to become part of God's family.

cistern

A hole dug in the earth or a rock to collect and store water. Empty *cisterns* were sometimes used to store grain or as prisons.

City of David

City of David has three meanings: 1. It is another name for the town of Bethlehem where David was born; 2. Part of the city of Jerusalem was known as the *City of David;* 3. The entire walled city of Jerusalem was sometimes called the *City of David.*

city of refuge

One of six cities set aside by Moses where a person who had accidentally killed someone could stay until a fair trial could be held. While the person was in a *city of refuge,* he would be safe from family or friends of the dead person who might want to kill him.

cloak

A long, loose fitting robe people in Bible times wore over their other clothing.

commandment

A rule or teaching people are to follow. Moses received the Ten Commandments from God. The Bible gives commandments for Christians to follow because they love Him and want to obey His Word.

conceive

1. To become pregnant; 2. To think up or imagine something.

concubine

A slave woman in Bible times who lived with an Israelite family and had children by the father of the family. She was considered an extra or second-class wife.

condemn

1. To find someone guilty of doing something wrong and to declare or pronounce a punishment. 2. To be against or disapprove of something because it is wrong.

confess

To *confess* means to tell or agree about what is true. *Confess* sometimes means telling God your sins. *Confess* can also mean to say in front of other people that you believe that Jesus is God's Son and that He died and rose again to forgive you of your sins.

conscience

A feeling about what is right and what is wrong;

a sense of knowing what is good and what is bad.

consecrate

To set apart something or someone to serve God in a special way.

convert

A person who has changed from one belief or way of thinking to another. A person who decides to follow God's way instead of his or her own way has become a *convert.*

Corinth

A city in Greece. Always a commercial center, the Roman conquerors made Corinth the capital city of the province. Paul taught in Corinth for a year and a half.

cornerstone

A large stone in the foundation of a building at the corner of two walls. It holds the two walls together. The *cornerstone* is the first and most important stone laid when a building is started. Jesus is called the *cornerstone* of our faith in God because He is the most important part of our knowing who God is.

counselor

One who gives advice or help. Sometimes the Bible uses the word *Counselor* as another name for Jesus. In the New Testament, the Holy Spirit is also called the *Counselor* of Christians.

covenant

An agreement. In the ancient Near East, sometimes covenants were made between two people or groups of people. Both sides decided what the agreement would be. However, in the Bible, the word usually refers to agreements between God and people. In a *covenant* between God and people, God decides what shall be done and the people agree to live by the *covenant.* The *Old Covenant* of law set standards of behavior in order to please God. The *New Covenant* of grace presents God's forgiveness based on faith in Jesus' death and resurrection.

covenant fathers

Abraham, Isaac and Jacob, (father, son and grandson) often mentioned together in Scripture in reference to God's promises to His people.

covet (KUV-et)

Wanting very much to have something that belongs to someone else.

create

To cause something new to exist or to happen.

God *created* everything that exists.

crucify

To nail or tie a person to a cross until he or she is dead. *Crucifixion* was a slow, painful punishment the Romans used for their enemies and the worst criminals.

cuneiform

Wedge-shaped form of writing used in ancient Sumeria, Babylon and Persia.

curse

In the Bible, to *curse* does not mean to swear or to use bad language. When a person *cursed* something, he or she wished evil or harm to come to it. When God *cursed* something, He declared judgment on something.

Dan

One of the twelve tribes of Israel, whose territory was directly north of Judah and west of Benjamin and Ephraim. Also the northernmost city in Israel.

deacon

Helpers or servants in the church. In the New Testament, men and women deacons were chosen to take care of the needs of people in the church. Today churches give their deacons many different jobs to do.

debt

Something a person owes someone else—usually money. In the Lord's Prayer, the word *debt* means sins or wrongdoing. The word *debtor* means those who sin against us.

decree

An order or law given by a king or ruler. A *decree* was often read in a public place so that many people would hear the new law.

dedicate

To set apart for a special purpose. In the Bible, the word usually means that a person or thing is given to God to serve Him in a special way.

demon

An evil spirit working for Satan (the devil). People can be tempted, harassed or "possessed" (controlled) by demons. Jesus has authority over all demons and in his earthly ministry ordered evil spirits to come out of many people.

denarius (duh-NAIR-ee-us)

Roman money. A *denarius,* which was a small silver coin, was the payment for about one day's work.

detest
To hate.

devote
To set apart for a special purpose or reason.

disciple
Someone who follows the teachings and example of another. In the New Testament, *disciple* usually refers to a person who believed that Jesus is God's Son and loved and obeyed Him. Sometimes *disciples* means the twelve men Jesus chose to be His special friends and helpers. At other times, it refers to all people who love Jesus and obey His teachings.

dispersion
Refers to the deportation of and emigration of Jews from the Promised Land. The term usually focuses on the Assyrians' forced relocation of people from the Northern Kingdom of Israel to distant locations throughout the Assyrian Empire. While large numbers of people from Judah who were exiled in Babylon did return, there was no similar restoration for the people of Israel.

doctrine
Teaching, instruction, usually referring to the content of what is taught.

Eden
The perfect garden God created, between the Tigris and Euphrates rivers, in which Adam and Eve lived before they sinned.

edict (EE-dikt)
A written law or order given by a king or ruler.

elder
In the Bible, the word *elder* has several meanings: 1. In the Old Testament, an older man in a family, tribe or town was called an *elder*. 2. Also in the Old Testament, each town had a group of older men known as *elders*. They made major decisions for the town. 3. The first four books of the New Testament usually refer to the Sanhedrin—the group of men who governed the Jewish people in Jesus' time—as elders. 4. In the Early Church, the church leaders were often called *elders*.

enmity
Hatred or bad feelings that make two people or groups enemies.

envy
A strong feeling of jealousy caused by something someone else has or does well. *Envy* can cause a person to try to make him- or herself better than the other person. The Bible says *envy* is sin.

Ephesus (EFF-uh-suss)
A city on the eastern coast of the Aegean Sea. *Ephesus* at one time was a commercial center, but had fallen into decline by the first century A.D. The city was the site of a large temple to the goddess Diana. Paul visited Ephesus on his missionary travels.

Epistles
Letters sent to individuals or groups. Twenty-one New Testament books were letters, most of which were sent to specific churches or church leaders.

eternal
Lasting forever; without end. God is *eternal* and members of God's family have *eternal* life.

eunuch (YOU-nuk)
1. Men who could not have children because their sex organs were damaged, altered or defective were called *eunuchs*. 2. The title *eunuch* was sometimes given to the man who was the most important helper or advisor to a king or queen.

evangelism
Evangelism is the act of telling the good news of the gospel of Jesus Christ to others.

evangelist
Someone who tells the good news about Christ. The term is from the Greek work meaning "a messenger of good."

everlasting
Never ending; forever.

exile (EG-zyl)
To make someone leave his or her country and live somewhere else. The Jews were in *exile* in Babylon for seventy years.

faith
Faith has two meanings in the Bible: 1. To be certain about the things we cannot see or to trust someone because of who he or she is. For example, a Christian has faith that Jesus is God's Son. 2. "The faith" means the whole message about Jesus Christ—that He is God's Son and that He came to take the punishment for our sin so that we may become members of God's family.

faithful
Always loyal and trustworthy. God is *faithful*. We can always trust Him to do whatever He has promised. We are also to be *faithful* in doing what is right.

Fall

The original sin of Adam and Eve that broke the perfect relationship between people and God.

famine (FAM-in)

A time when there is not enough food to keep people and animals alive. *Famines* can be caused by lack of rain, wars, insects that eat crops and bad storms.

fear

Today, *fear* most often means being afraid of something or someone. However, the Bible often uses the word *fear* to describe the sense of respect or awe that sinful people (and we are all sinful, according to Romans 3:23) should have for God because of His perfection, sovereignty and holiness.

feasts

1. Dinners, celebrations and banquets are often called feasts in the Bible. 2. Jewish religious holidays and celebrations are also called feasts.

fellowship

A time when friends who are interested in the same things come together. In the Bible, *fellowship* often means the friendship Christians share because they love God and His Son, Jesus.

fig

A brownish, pear-shaped fruit that grows on trees. *Figs* are plentiful in Israel. They can be eaten raw, cooked or dried.

firstborn

The first child born into a family. A *firstborn* son received special rights and power. He became head of the family after his father died and he received twice as much money and property as his brothers.

firstfruits

An offering to God of the first vegetables, fruits and grains the Israelites picked from their fields. The people offered their *firstfruits* to God to thank Him for supplying their food.

flax

A useful plant grown in Palestine. The seeds of the plant were used to make linseed oil and the fibers of the plant were woven into linen cloth.

flint

A very hard stone that can be sharpened to a fine cutting edge.

flog

To beat with a whip or stick.

forefather

A person from whom one is descended—an ancestor. Your father, your grandfather, your great-grandfather and your great-great-grandfather are some of your *forefathers*.

foreigner

A person who is from another country.

forgive

A decision of the will to stop feeling angry and to stop blaming a person for something wrong he or she has done; to be friends again. God *forgives* everyone who repents of sin and believes that Jesus died to take the punishment for his or her sins. When God *forgives* a person, God forgets the person's sins forever. God instructs Christians to *forgive* each other in the same way He has *forgiven* them.

forsake

To leave, to go away from, to leave completely alone.

frankincense (FRANK-in-sense)

A very expensive, hard gum made from the sap of a terebith tree. *Frankincense* was used to make sweet-smelling perfume. The Israelites used *frankincense* in religious ceremonies. One of the special gifts the wise men brought to Jesus was *frankincense*.

fruit

Evidence, outcomes, results. Although *fruit* is sometimes used in Scripture to refer to foods, it is commonly used to refer to the actions produced by good or evil in people's lives. The *fruit* of the Spirit (Galatians 5) refers to virtues produced in a Christian's life by the Holy Spirit.

Galilee (GAL-uh-lee)

The area around the Sea of Galilee. Jesus grew up, preached and did most of His miracles in *Galilee*.

gall

A bitter poisonous plant. The juice from the plant may have been used to make a painkiller. Jesus refused a drink of *gall* mixed with wine when He was dying on the cross.

Gaza (GAH-zuh)

A major Philistine city. From the time of the judges until its destruction by Alexander the Great, Gaza was at times under the control of Israel or Egypt.

generation

The length of time from birth till procreation.

Grandparents, parents and children are three different *generations.*

Gentiles
All people who are not Jewish.

Gibeon (GIB-ee-un)
The only Canaanite city to make peace with Joshua, although done deceptively. The town, located a few miles northwest of Jerusalem, became an important place of worship, and Solomon had come to offer sacrifices at Gibeon when God spoke to him in a dream.

gifts
Abilities provided by God to believers that allow the accomplishment of good works.

Gilead (GILL-ee-ad)
The region of Israel west of the Jordan river.

Gilboa (gill-BO-uh)
A mountainous area south of Lake Galilee, was the site of King Saul's final battle against the Philistines. Both Saul and his son Jonathan died in this battle.

Gilgal (GILL-gal)
A town near Jericho, site of the Israelites first camp after crossing the Jordan river. Gilgal was the site of Saul's confirmation as king, and the place where he disobeyed Samuel's instructions, resulting in his being rejected by God as king.

glean
To pick fruits or grain that the harvesters missed. The Bible told farmers to leave some crops in the field for hungry people to *glean.*

genealogy
A listing of ancestors. Various such lists are included in Scripture to show lines of family descent.

glorification, glorify
The act of being made perfect, as God is perfect. Also to honor, praise and magnify God for His perfection.

glory
Great beauty, splendor, honor or magnificence that can be seen or sensed. The Israelites saw the *glory* of the Lord in the cloud that filled the Tabernacle. The shepherds saw the *glory* of the Lord when the angels told them Jesus had been born. *Glory* can also mean to praise; to be proud or happy; to boast.

Golgotha (GAHL-gah-thah)
The place outside Jerusalem where Jesus was hung on a cross. In Aramaic, *Golgotha* means "the place of the skull."

Gomorrah (gah-MORE-uh)
A city near the Dead Sea in the time of Abraham. Gomorrah and its neighbor Sodom were destroyed by fire from heaven because of the great wickedness of the people.

Goshen
The area of the Nile River delta where Jacob and his family settled under the protection of Joseph, Egypt's prime minister.

gospel
Gospel means "good news." The good news of the Bible is that God sent His son Jesus to take the punishment for sin and then raised Him from the dead so that any person who believes may have new life. The story of the life, death and resurrection of Jesus Christ told in the first four books of the New Testament is also called the *gospel.* The books are also called the four *Gospels.*

grace
Love and kindness shown to someone who does not deserve it—especially the forgiveness God shows to us. We don't deserve God's *grace* because we sin against Him. God showed *grace* to all people by sending His Son, Jesus, to be our Savior. God's *grace* allows us to become members of His family (see Ephesians 2:8). God's *grace* also keeps on helping us live as God wants us to (see Acts 20:32). A person cannot earn God's *grace* by trying to be good; it is God's free gift.

Greece
A leading cultural, political and commercial center of the ancient world. In the fourth century B.C., under Alexander the Great, Greece conquered much of the Mediterranean and Middle East, resulting in the spread of Greek culture throughout the region, even after Alexander's successors were defeated by the Romans.

Greek
The international language of the Mediterranean world in the time of Jesus. Most of the New Testament was originally written in "common" Greek, not in the classical language of ancient Greece.

guilty
Having done wrong or broken a law. A person who is *guilty* deserves to be blamed or punished.

Hades (HAY-dees)
A Greek word that means "the place of the

dead." Another word used in the Bible that means the same as *Hades* is "Sheol." *Hades* was thought to be a dark, shadowy place. Hell, or Gehenna, was a much more fearful place—it is not the same as *Hades*. If a person has asked Jesus to forgive his or her sins, that person does not need to fear either of these places because he or she will live forever with Jesus.

Hallelujah
A Hebrew word that means "praise the Lord!"

harlot
A prostitute; a woman who gets paid for having sexual relations with another person. The Bible says *harlotry* is a sin, but like other sins, it can be forgiven. Sometimes the Bible uses the word *harlot* to describe people who turn away from God to worship idols.

harvest
To gather ripe fruits, vegetables, grain and other crops from fields, vineyards and orchards.

heaven
1. The sky or universe beyond earth. 2. The dwelling of God, the angels and those granted salvation.

Hebrew
A name derived from Eber, a descendant of Noah's son Shem, and used to refer to the nation God chose to be His special people—the Israelites, later in history known as the Jewish people. *Hebrew* is also the name of any member of that nation, as well as the language they speak. Most of the Old Testament was originally written in the *Hebrew* language.

Hebron (HEE-brun)
An ancient city less than twenty miles southwest of Jerusalem. Abraham lived there for a time, and David made it his capital during the seven and a half years he was king of Judah, before moving the capital to Jerusalem when he had been accepted also as king of Israel.

heir
Someone who has the right to receive the property or position of another person when that person dies. In Bible times, the *heir* was usually a son. The Bible says that anyone who is a member of God's family is His *heir*. God will never die, but because we are His children, God keeps on giving us great love, care and kindness.

herbs (urbs)
Plants or parts of plants used to make teas, med-

icines and to flavor food.

Herod (HAIR-ud)
The family name of five kings appointed by the Roman Emperor to rule Judea in New Testament times. Jesus was born during the rule of *Herod* the Great. The names of the other four kings are *Herod* Archelaus, *Herod* Antipas, *Herod* Agrippa I and *Herod* Agrippa II.

high place
Altars and places of worship built on the tops of hills or mountains. Sometimes altars to God were built at *high places*. However, the *high places* were usually for the worship of idols. The Israelites were told to destroy the *high places* in their land where idols were worshiped.

high priest
The most important priest of all the priests who served God in the Tabernacle and later in the Temple. In the Old Testament, he offered the most important sacrifices to God for the people. In New Testament times, he was also a powerful political leader. He was the head of the Sanhedrin—the group of men who governed the Jewish people. He even had a small army. The *high priest* wore special clothing described in Exodus 28:1-39. Aaron was the first *high priest*. All other high priests were his descendants.

Hivites (HIGH-vight)
One of the Canaanite tribes defeated by Joshua.

holy
Pure; set apart; belonging to God. God is *holy*. He is perfect and without sin. Jesus is *holy*, too. He is without sin and dedicated to doing what God wants. Because Jesus died to take the punishment for sin and then rose again, people who believe in Him have the power to be *holy*, too. God helps them to become more and more pure and loving, like Jesus.

holy place, holy of holies
The Tabernacle and the Temple were divided into two main areas. The larger area, known as the *holy place*, could only be entered by the priests who were carrying out their sacred duties. The smaller area, known as the *holy of holies*, was separated by a large curtain (veil), and could only be entered once a year by the High Priest on the Day of Atonement.

Holy Spirit
The personal but unseen power and presence of

God in the world. The book of Acts tells us that the *Holy Spirit* came to followers of Jesus in a special way after Jesus had gone back to heaven. The *Holy Spirit* lives within each one whose sins have been forgiven. Jesus said that the *Holy Spirit* is our helper and comforter. The *Holy Spirit* teaches us truth about God. He helps us understand the Bible and helps us pray in the right way. He gives us the power and strength to do what Jesus wants.

Hosanna

A Hebrew word that means "Save now!" The Hebrews shouted the word to praise someone important.

hypocrite

A person who pretends to be something different from what he or she really is. In the Old Testament, *hypocrite* means a godless person. In the New Testament, it means a phony. Jesus called the Pharisees *hypocrites* because they did many things to make themselves seem very religious, but they would not listen to God.

idol

A statue or other image of a god that is made by people and then worshiped as if it had the power of God. Idols are often made of wood, stone or metal. Sometimes the Bible calls anything that takes the place of God in a person's life an *idol.* God tells us not to worship *idols,* but rather, to worship only Him.

Immanuel

A name for Jesus that means "God with us."

incense

A mixture of spices held together with thick, sticky juice that comes from trees and plants. *Incense* is burned to make a sweet smell. In the Tabernacle and Temple, *incense* was burned on a small golden altar to worship God.

inheritance

Money, property or traditions received from another person. Often a person receives an *inheritance* after another person's death. The Bible tells us that everything that is God's belongs to Jesus Christ. By His death on the cross, Jesus made it possible for us to share His *inheritance* with Him.

inspiration

The process by which God communicated His word to the human writers of Scripture. *Inspiration* is from the Hebrew and Greek words

meaning *breathed,* conveying a vivid image of God imparting His truth to His people.

Israel

In the Bible, the word *Israel* has several meanings: 1. It is the special name God gave Jacob (meaning "Prince with God"). 2. It is another name for the Hebrew nation—God's chosen people. 3. It is the name of the nation ruled by the judges and the first three Hebrew kings—Saul, David and Solomon. 4. It is the name given to the Northern Kingdom after Jeroboam led ten tribes to separate from Rehoboam and the two southern tribes. (The Southern Kingdom was called Judah.) 5. After the Northern Kingdom of *Israel* was captured by the Assyrians, the word *Israel* was sometimes used to mean the Southern Kingdom. 6. It is also a name used for the people of God. The Bible often uses the term "children of *Israel,*" meaning they were descendants of Jacob.

Israelite

A citizen of the country of Israel; a descendant of Jacob (Israel).

jealous

Jealous has several different meanings: 1. It can mean being careful to guard or keep what one has. This is the kind of *jealousy* the Bible is talking about when it says that God is a *jealous* God. He loves His people and wants them to turn away from sin and to love and worship Him. 2. Another kind of *jealousy* is to be angry and unhappy when someone else has something you want. The Bible calls this kind of *jealousy* a sin. 3. Another kind of *jealousy* is being afraid of losing someone's love or affection.

Jebusites (JEB-yoo-sight)

A Canaanite tribe that controlled the hilly terrain of Jerusalem until defeated by David.

Jehovah

This is an English translation of one of the Hebrew names for God. A more accurate translation is Yahweh. This name was considered to be very holy, and religious Jews would not take this name on their lips.

Jericho (JERR-ih-koh)

A city several miles north of where the Jordan River enters the Dead Sea. *Jericho* was the first city conquered by the Israelites under Joshua's leadership. The city's walls and gates were rebuilt in the time of Ahab. *Jericho* was the home of

Zacchaeus, the infamous tax collector who reformed upon meeting Jesus.

Jerusalem
The most important city of Bible times. It was the capital of the united kingdom of Israel and the kingdom of Judah. The Temple was built in *Jerusalem,* so many people traveled to the city to worship God. In 587 B.C., *Jerusalem* was captured and mostly destroyed by Babylonian armies. The city was rebuilt when the Jews returned after seventy years of exile in Babylon. Jesus taught in the city of *Jerusalem,* was crucified outside the city wall, was buried near the city and then rose again. The first Christian church began in *Jerusalem* after the Holy Spirit came to the believers there.

Jews
At first, *Jew* referred to anyone who was a member of the tribe of Judah. By the return from exile in Babylon, it meant anyone who was a descendant of Abraham or who was a follower of the Jewish religion.

Jordan River
The main part of the Jordan River from the Sea of Galilee, winding southward into the Dead Sea. Numerous biblical events involved this famous waterway, including Jesus' baptism.

Josephus (joh-SEE-fuss)
A Jewish historian. Written near the end of the first century A.D., his *Antiquities* contains the first non-Christian reference to Jesus.

Judah
1. One of the sons of Jacob and Leah. 2. The descendants of *Judah,* who became the tribe of *Judah.* 3. The Southern Kingdom when the Israelites divided into two separate countries after the death of King Solomon. (The Northern Kingdom was called Israel.)

Judaism (JOO-day-izm)
The faith, laws, traditions and teachings of the Jewish religion. Judaism is based on worshiping the one true God, circumcision as a sign of being one of God's chosen people, worship on the Sabbath (Saturday), obeying God's laws and following the traditions given from one generation to another.

Judaizers (JOO-day-ize-urs)
People who claimed that a person must keep the Jewish laws in order to become a true believer in Jesus.

judge
In the time of Moses, a *judge* helped people settle their disagreements. When the Israelites were settling the Promised Land after the death of Joshua, God chose leaders called *judges* to rule the people. Often these *judges* led the people in battle against their enemies. Some of the *judges* were Deborah, Gideon and Samuel. After kings began to rule Israel, *judges* once again settled disagreements and took care of official business.

judgment
1. In the Old Testament, *judgment* can mean God's laws of instructions. 2. *Judgment* can also mean God's punishment of a person or nation for disobeying Him. 3. In the New Testament, *judgment* can mean to criticize or disapprove of someone. The Bible says Christians are not to *judge* each other. 4. *Judgment* can also mean the end of the world as we know it when God will *judge* sin, and reward those people who have lived for Him.

justice
That which is right and fair. Most of the prophets in the Bible emphasized that God is *just,* and that He wants His people to act *justly.* Many of the warnings given by the prophets were done so because the leaders and people were guilty of *injustice,* cheating others, especially the poor.

justification, justify
God's action of declaring that sinners are made righteous by faith in Jesus Christ. God forgives their sin and becomes their friend. God also gives them the power to live right. *Justification* is possible because Jesus Christ died to take the punishment for sin.

Kadesh (KAY-desh)
A location between the Sinai desert and the southern boundary of Canaan. From here, Moses sent twelve spies into Canaan, but the people rebelled, resulting in the Israelites spending an entire generation in the desert.

kingdom of heaven
The *kingdom of heaven* is also called the "kingdom of God." It means God's rule in the lives of His chosen people and His creation. In the Old Testament, the people in God's kingdom were the Israelites. In the New Testament and now, the people in God's kingdom are those who believe in and follow the Lord Jesus Christ. When Jesus comes again, then God's kingdom will become

visible to all people.

kinsman

A relative.

Lamb of God

A name for Jesus that tells us that He died to take away our sins. When a Jewish person had sinned, he or she offered a lamb as a sacrifice to God. Jesus became like one of those lambs when He gave Himself as a sacrifice to die so that our sins can be forgiven.

lampstand

The Tabernacle was furnished with one large, seven-branched *golden lampstand* (menorah), placed opposite the golden table. In the Temple, ten golden lampstands were placed along the interior walls, five on a side.

law

The word has several meanings in the Bible: 1. It can mean all the rules God gave to help people to know and love Him and to live happily with each other. The Ten Commandments are part of God's *law*. 2. The first five books of the Bible are called the *Law*. 3. The entire Old Testament is sometimes called the *Law*. 4. Any rule that must be obeyed, whether it was decided by God or by people, is a *law*. 5. God's rules in the Old Testament plus other rules added by Jewish religious leaders are sometimes called the *Law*. 6. In Romans 2:14-16, the conscience of an unbeliever who knows he or she has not followed his or her own moral code.

leprosy (LEP-ruh-see)

A name used for several serious skin diseases. People with *leprosy* were called *lepers*. The Jewish law said that *lepers* had to stay away from people who did not have the disease. *Lepers* lived outside their cities and towns, either by themselves or with other *lepers,* until the disease showed signs of healing.

Levites (LEE-vites)

Descendants of Levi, one of the sons of Jacob and Leah. Some of the *Levites* were religious teachers. Others took care of the Tabernacle, and later, the Temple. Only *Levites* who were descendants of Moses' brother Aaron could become priests.

Lord's Supper

The Passover meal Jesus celebrated with his disciples the night of his arrest. Also the continuing observance in which Christ's followers gather to eat and drink in order to "proclaim the Lord's death until he comes" (1 Corinthians 11:26).

locusts

A *locust* is a large insect like a grasshopper. Sometimes *locusts* travel in huge swarms, eating all the plants they can find. In Bible times, *locusts* were sometimes eaten as food.

lute

A stringed musical instrument. It has a pear-shaped body and a neck. It is played by plucking the strings.

lyre (lier)

A small harp with three to twelve strings. A *lyre* was held on the lap when it was played.

Magi (MAY-ji)

Men who lived in the countries of Arabia and Persia and who studied the stars. People thought the *Magi* had the power to tell the meaning of dreams. Several of the *Magi* followed a star to Bethlehem and brought Jesus expensive gifts. The *Magi* honored Him as a newborn king.

manger

A box in a stable where food was placed for cattle, donkeys or other animals. When Jesus was born, His first bed was a *manger*.

manna

The special food God gave the Israelites for the forty years they traveled in the desert. The Bible says that *manna* looked like white seeds or flakes and tasted sweet.

mantle

A loose fitting outer robe or coat.

master

1. A name for Jesus. It means "teacher." 2. An overseer, boss or owner of a slave.

mediator

A person who settles differences or arguments between two or more people. Jonathan was a *mediator* between David and Saul. Moses was a *mediator* between God and Israel. By paying the punishment for sin, Jesus became the *mediator* who makes it possible for us to have peace with God.

mercy

Showing more love or kindness to a person than he or she expects or deserves.

Mesopotamia (MESS-oh-poh-TAME-ee-uh)

The region between the Tigris and Euphrates rivers. The term derives from two Greek words meaning "middle" and "river." The Assyrian nation developed in northern Mesopotamia, Babylon in the central region, and Sumer (including Ur) was in the south.

Messiah
The Savior whom God promised to send. Jesus is the *Messiah*. In Hebrew, *Messiah* means "the Anointed One." In Greek, the word for "the Anointed One" is "Christos." Christ is the name used in the New Testament to show Jesus is the Savior.

millennium
Thousand years. The term is used in reference to Revelation 20:1-15, which mentions a thousand-year period in which Satan is bound and Christ rules.

millstone
One of a pair of large stones used to grind grain into flour.

miracle
Some event or wonderful happening done by the power of God.

Moabite (MOE-uh-bite)
A person from the country of Moab, located just east of the Dead Sea. Moab often fought against Israel and at times was under the control of Israel's kings. Ruth, an ancestor of David and of Jesus, was a Moabite.

Moriah (MO-rye-uh)
The hill in Jerusalem on which Solomon built the Temple. Jewish tradition claims this is the same Mount Moriah on which Abraham began to sacrifice Isaac.

mortal
An ability to die. All people, plants and animals are *mortal*. God is not *mortal;* He lives forever and will never die.

Mount of Olives, Mount Olivet
A hill just outside Jerusalem, the site of many biblical events.

myrrh
The sap of the *myrrh* bush. *Myrrh* was used to make anointing oil smell good, as a perfume, as a pain killer and to prepare a body for burial. The Magi brought Jesus a gift of *myrrh*.

mystery
A truth that is understood because of God's revelation. The term appears only in the New Testament, mostly in the letters of Paul, and refers to God's plan to redeem the world through Christ.

nard
A pleasant-smelling oil made from the roots and stems of spikenard plant. This plant grew in India. Because the oil had to be brought all the way from India, it was very expensive. Mary poured *nard* over Jesus' feet.

Nazarene (NAZ-uh-reen)
A person who lived in the town of Nazareth. Because Jesus lived in Nazareth for almost 30 years, He was often called a *Nazarene*. Later, Christians were sometimes called *Nazarenes* because they were followers of Jesus.

Nazirite (NAZ-uh-rite)
A Hebrew person who promised to serve God in a special way for a certain length of time. The time could be anywhere from 30 days to a lifetime. To show dedication to God, a *Nazirite* would not cut his or her hair, eat or drink anything made from grapes, or touch a dead body. At the end of the time, the person lived like other people. Samuel and Samson were *Nazirites* all their lives. Some scholars believe John the Baptist was also a *Nazirite*.

Nebo
A mountain, adjacent to Mount Pisgah, overlooking the Dead Sea. Moses viewed the Promised Land from these peaks.

New Covenant See **Covenant**.

New Testament See **Testament**.

nomad (NO-mad)
A person who lives in a tent and moves from place to place. *Nomads* usually move when seasons change or when they need to find grass for feeding their animals. Abraham was a *nomad* for much of his life.

Northern Kingdom
Refers to Israel, formed when Jereboam led the northern tribes in rebellion against Rehoboam. From the beginning, Israel's kings led the people in idolatrous practices, resulting in God's judgment in the form of Assyrian conquest. A series of massive relocations dispersed the Israelites throughout the Assyrian Empire, and replaced them with people who became known as Samaritans.

oath
A serious promise that what a person says is true. In Bible times, people often made an *oath* by saying, "God is my witness." The *oath* often asked for God's punishment if what was said was

not true. Jesus taught that people who love and obey Him do not need to make *oaths* because they should be known for saying only what is true.

offering

A gift of money, time or other possessions a person gives to God because he or she loves Him. In Old Testament times, people brought food and animals to the Tabernacle or Temple as *offerings* to God. The *offerings* were often burned on the altar. Animal *offerings* were always killed. Their blood symbolized sins being forgiven by death. Christians believe that we no longer need to offer sacrifices for the forgiveness of sins because Jesus' death is the once-for-all sacrifice through which our sins can be forgiven. (See **Sacrifice**)

offspring

For humans, *offspring* are sons and daughters. For animals, *offspring* are their young.

oil

In the Bible, *oil* almost always means olive *oil*. Oil was squeezed from the olives and used in food, as a fuel for lamps, as a medicine for wounds and as a hair dressing and skin softener. Olive *oil* was used to anoint priests and kings. It was also used in religious ceremonies in the Tabernacle and later in the Temple.

ordain

The word *ordain* has several meanings in the Bible: 1. It can mean to cause to happen. Psalm 65:9 says that the streams are filled with water to provide people with food because God has *ordained*—or caused—it. 2. To appoint or set apart a person to do special work. Paul was *ordained* to be a missionary to the Gentiles. 3. *Ordain* can also mean to decide or command.

overseer

A person who watches over and takes care of others. Joseph was an *overseer;* he watched over and directed other people who worked for Potiphar. In the New Testament, leaders in the Early Church were sometimes called *overseers.* Paul told these leaders to take care of the people in the church in the same way a good shepherd cares for his sheep.

ox, oxen

Strong male cattle. They were used for pulling plows, wagons and other heavy loads.

pagan

A person who does not worship the true God, especially a person who worships idols.

Palestine

A name given by the Greeks to the land of the Philistines who, until 604 B.C., occupied the southeastern coast of the Mediterranean Sea between Egypt and Syria. Throughout history the term "Palestine" often has been used to describe the Holy Land.

parable

A story that teaches a special lesson or truth. Jesus often told *parables* to teach important lessons.

paradise

Heaven.

paralytic (pair-uh-LIH-tic)

A person who has lost the ability to move one or more arms and/or legs.

Passover

One of the Jews' most important feasts. The Jews celebrate *Passover* every spring as a reminder that God freed them from slavery in Egypt.

The word *Passover* comes from the way the angel of death "passed over" the homes of Israelites on whose doorposts the blood of a lamb was sprinkled. In Egyptian homes, where there was no blood on the door posts, all the firstborn sons died. This terrible disaster convinced the Egyptian Pharaoh to let the Israelites leave Egypt. At the *Passover* feast, the Jews eat bread made without yeast (unleavened bread), bitter herbs and lamb. The unleavened bread reminds them that the Israelites left Egypt in a hurry. There was no time to let bread rise. The bitter herbs remind them of their suffering in Egypt. The lamb reminds them of the lamb they killed for the first *Passover.* The *Passover* feast was the last meal Jesus ate with His disciples before He was crucified.

Passover Lamb

The lamb killed at Passover as a sacrifice. The Bible says that Jesus is our *Passover Lamb.* He was sacrificed to deliver us from sin, just as the first *Passover Lamb* was sacrificed to deliver the firstborn sons of the Israelites from death and to provide them with escape from Egypt. (See **Passover**)

patriarch

A father, either of a family or a nation. The word usually refers to either Abraham, Isaac or Jacob—

the founders of the Hebrew nation. Jacob's sons and David are also called *patriarchs.*

patriarchal period

The term refers to the time before Moses when the oldest male in a family or clan was the undisputed head In both temporal and spiritual matters.

penitence

Repentance, expression of remorse for sins.

Pentateuch (PEN-ta-tuke)

The first five books of the Old Testament. The term is from the Greek word meaning "five scrolls." These five books are also referred to as the Books of the Law, the Books of Moses and the Torah (Hebrew).

Pentecost

A Jewish feast celebrated 50 days after Passover. Today the Christian Church remembers *Pentecost* because on the first *Pentecost* after Jesus' resurrection, the Lord sent the Holy Spirit to His followers as He had promised (see Acts 2).

Perizzites (PEAR-ih-zite)

One of the Canaanite tribes defeated by Joshua.

persecute

To continually treat someone cruelly or unfairly, even though the person has done nothing wrong. The early Christians were *persecuted* for teaching that Jesus is God's Son.

Persia

The territory between the Persian Gulf and the Caspian Sea, and the last of the Middle Eastern powers before the conquest by Alexander the Great. Until the mid-sixth century B.C., the Persians were controlled by their northern neighbors, the Medes. Under Cyrus, the Persians became the dominant partners, then led in the conquest of Babylon to the west. Cyrus then released the foreigners, including the Jews, who had been held captive by Babylon. Esther, as queen to one of Cyrus's successors, foiled an attempt to destroy the Jews remaining in Persia.

Pisgah (PIZZ-guh)

A mountain, adjacent to Mount Nebo, at the northeastern end of the Dead Sea, which Moses climbed to view the Promised Land.

Pharaoh

A title of the rulers of ancient Egypt, just as "president" or "king" or "prime minister" are titles of top officials in countries today.

Pharisee

A Jew in the time of Jesus who tried very hard to obey every part of the Jewish law. Many sincerely tried to please God and to be holy. Some of the *Pharisees* worried more about keeping every little rule than about caring for people. Jesus commended the *Pharisees* for what they taught, but often scolded them because of what they did. Speaking of those *Pharisees* and Scribes who opposed Him, Jesus said on the outside they seemed very holy, but on the inside they were full of lies and hate (see Matthew 23). Saul of Tarsus (later called Paul) was a *Pharisee.* Many other *Pharisees* also ended up following Jesus.

Philippi

A city in Macedonia (northern Greece). The first European city visited by Paul on his missionary journeys.

Philistines

The people of Philistia, a region along the southeastern coast of the Mediterranean Sea. During most of Old Testament history, the Philistines were major competitors with Israel for territory and power. The Philistines, whose origins may be traced to Crete or Greece, were far ahead of the Hebrews in technology, having mastered skills in working with metal. They adopted at least some of the Canaanite gods and often controlled much of ancient Israel until a series of decisive defeats at the hands of David. Still, battles with Judah and Israel continued for centuries.

plague

l. A very serious disease that spreads quickly among people in an area. It often causes death. 2. Anything that causes great harm or suffering. For example, sometimes crops were destroyed by a *plague* of locusts. 3. The ten great disasters God sent to the Egyptians to convince their king to free the Israelites. Read about these *plagues* in Exodus 4—12.

plunder

l. To loot or rob, especially during a war. 2. The property taken by *plundering.*

pomegranate (PAHM-uh-GRAN-ut)

A fruit about the size of an apple. The *pomegranate* fruit is encased in a tough, reddish skin. The fruit is ruby red, very juicy—and filled with edible seeds. *Pomegranates* grow on small, bushy trees.

precepts
Commands, rules or laws.

predestined
Decided or chosen beforehand. In the Bible, the term refers to God's choice.

priest
Among the Jews, a *priest* was a man who offered prayers and sacrifices to God for the people. They led the public worship services at the Tabernacle, and later at the Temple. Often the *priests* also taught the Law of God to the people. The *priests* of Israel were all descendants of Aaron's family. The New Testament says that Jesus Christ is now our High Priest, the One who offered Himself as the perfect sacrifice for our sins (see Hebrews 8—9). All Christians are also *priests* (see 1 Peter 2:9). We are to help others learn about and worship God.

proconsul (PRO-kon-sul)
A ruler in the Roman government. The Roman Empire was divided into provinces or states. The highest Roman official in each province was called the *proconsul.*

prophecy
The message from God that a prophet spoke or wrote to people. Some prophecies told about what God would do in the future.

prophets
Men and women in the Old and New Testaments chosen by God to tell His messages to people. Also refers to the 17 Old Testament books written by prophets.

prostitute
(See **harlot**)

proverb
A short, wise saying. The Bible book of *Proverbs* is made up of many wise sayings.

provoke
To make angry; to cause trouble on purpose.

psalm
A Hebrew song or poem. A *psalm* usually praises God or tells the deep feelings of God's people. The Bible book of *Psalms* is made up of many Hebrew poems and songs.

publican
A tax collector. In the New Testament, the tax collectors secured revenue for the Romans, earning bitter condemnation as traitors.

purge
To make clean and pure.

Purim (POOR-im)
A Jewish holiday to celebrate the victory of Queen Esther and the Jews over wicked Haman.

rams
Mature male sheep. *Rams* were used for sacrifices and food. Their wool was used to make warm cloth and their horns were often used to make musical instruments called rams' horn trumpets.

ransom
The price paid to buy the freedom of a captive or slave. The New Testament says that all people are held captives to sin and death. When Jesus died on the cross, He paid the price—the *ransom*—to rescue us from the powers of sin and death. (See **redeem**)

raven
A large, black bird.

reap
To gather ripe grain and fruit. The Bible also uses the word *reap* to describe the reward or punishment people receive for their actions (see Galatians 6:9).

rebuke
To correct someone sternly; to scold someone.

reconcile
To help people who have been enemies become friends. In the New Testament, the word usually refers to bringing God and people together again through Jesus' life, death and resurrection. Sin separates people from God, but by dying, Jesus took the punishment for sin. When a person comes to know and love Jesus, he or she learns to love God instead of being His enemy. When this happens, the person is *reconciled* to God.

Red Sea
The Hebrew name for the body of water crossed by Moses and the Israelites when escaping from Egypt means literally "Sea of Reeds." Various bodies of water between the northern tip of the Red Sea's Gulf of Suez and the southern marshes of Lake Menzaleh in the Nile Delta have been suggested as possible sites for that miraculous crossing.

redeem, redemption
To buy freedom. In Bible times, a person could buy a slave and then set the slave free. The slave had been *redeemed* by the person who had paid the price and then given freedom. The New Testament tells us that by dying, Jesus paid the price to "buy us back" and set us free from our

slavery to sin. (See **ransom**)

redeemer
A person who redeems someone else. The term is used in the Old Testament to refer to God and to the Messiah who was promised to come.

reeds
Different plants growing in swamps or along the edges of water.

refuge
A place where one is safe from danger; a shelter. (Also see **city of refuge**)

remnant
A small part that is left over. In the Old Testament, *remnant* usually refers to the few Israelite people who remained faithful worshipers of God after their exile in Babylon.

repent
Repent means to turn around and go in the opposite direction. In the Bible, to *repent* means sorrow for wrongdoing, but must include that you stop doing wrong action and start doing what God says is right. *Repentance* always involves making a change away from sin and toward God.

restore, restoration
1. To bring back; to establish again. 2. To bring back to a former or original condition. 3. To return something lost, stolen or taken. The return of the Jews from being captives in Babylon is referred to as their *restoration*.

resurrection
1. To come back to life after being dead. Jesus died, and was buried. After three days He rose from the dead. That event is called the *Resurrection*. It shows Jesus' power over sin and death. 2. A future time when everyone who has ever lived will live again in new, spiritual bodies that will never die. Those who do not love God will be separated from Him forever.

retribution (re-truh-BYOU-shun)
A payment that is deserved, revenge. The punishment that comes to a person because he or she has broken God's law is called *retribution*.

revelation
To make known something that was hidden or unknown. In Old Testament times, God *revealed* Himself through His mighty acts and through His words to the prophets and to other people such as Abraham, Moses and David. In the New Testament, God made Himself known by sending

Jesus Christ. As Jesus lived on earth, He *revealed* God's love, His holiness and His power, helping us know what God is like. One of the ways God *reveals* Himself to us is through His Word, the Bible. The last book of the Bible is called the *Revelation* of Jesus Christ because it shows how Jesus will triumph over evil.

revenge
Punishment, injury or harm done to pay back a wrong.

reverence
A feeling of deep love and respect. *Reverence* should be our feeling about God and His holiness, power and love.

righteous
Thinking and doing what is *right* and holy. The word is used in three ways in the Bible: 1. To tell what God is like: He does only what is *right* and holy. 2. A person who has accepted Jesus as Savior is looked at by God as being free from the guilt of sin. God sees the person as being *righteous*. 3. People who are members of God's family show their love for Him by living in *righteous* ways. They do what is *right* and holy.

Roman
1. A person who lived in the city of *Rome*. 2. A person who was a citizen of the *Roman* Empire. A *Roman* citizen enjoyed special rights and protection. For example, he or she could not be punished without a fair trial, nor could a citizen be crucified.

Rome
A city in Italy, capital of the Roman Republic and Empire. The Romans defeated the remnants of Alexander the Great's Empire and established control over most of the Mediterranean world in the first century B.C. The spread of Christianity in the first centuries A.D. in spite of widespread, official persecution, was certainly aided by the ability to travel freely through the Empire.

Sabbath
The weekly day of rest and worship God set apart for all people. In the Old Testament, it is the seventh day of the week (Saturday). For the Jew, *Sabbath* starts at sundown on Friday and lasts until sunset on Saturday. Many Jews and some Christians observe the *Sabbath* on Saturday. Because Jesus rose from the dead on a Sunday, most Christians set aside Sunday as the day of

rest and worship (see Acts 20:7).

Sabeans (Suh-BEE-uhn)

People of Sheba on the southern Arabian peninsula. They are mentioned occasionally in the Old Testament in connection with their commercial activities, including slave trading.

sackcloth

A rough, dark cloth usually woven from goats' hair. When someone died, the person's friends and family wore clothes made of *sackcloth* to show that they were very sad. A person would also wear *sackcloth* to show that he or she was sorry for sinning.

sacred

Holy; belonging to God; set apart for God.

sacrifice

A gift or offering given to God. A *sacrifice* usually involved killing an animal to pay for sin. The New Testament tells us that Jesus died as the once-for-all *sacrifice* for sinners and that no further *sacrifices* for sin are necessary.

Sadducees (SAD-you-seez)

A sect of Jewish religious leaders in New Testament times, to be distinguished from the Pharisees (see **Pharisees**). They said that only the laws in the first five books of the Old Testament had to be obeyed. They did not believe in the Resurrection or in angels or spirits. When the New Testament speaks of the "chief priests," it is referring to the *Sadducees.*

saints

The word means "God's people." The New Testament says that all Christians are *saints.* Paul often addressed his letters "to the *saints.*"

salvation

Sometimes *salvation* (or deliverance) means to be rescued from evil. Sometimes it means to be kept from danger or death. In the New Testament, *salvation* usually means to be rescued from the guilt and power of sin. By His death and resurrection, Jesus brings *salvation* to people who believe in Him.

Samaritan (suh-MARE-uh-tun)

A person who lived in or came from the area north of Judea/Judah known as Samaria. The *Samaritans* were only partly Jewish. They worshiped God differently than the other Jews did. The Jews and *Samaritans* hated each other—perhaps because of the differences in the ways they worshiped. Jesus showed that He loved the *Samaritans* as much as any other people by traveling through Samaria, teaching the *Samaritans* about God. Jesus told the story of the *Good Samaritan.* Most Jews traveled around Samaria. Jesus traveled through Samaria.

sanctification, sanctify

To be set apart for God's use. A Christian's *sanctification* is an ongoing process. When a person becomes a Christian, he or she is *sanctified.* The Holy Spirit continues helping him or her become more and more like Jesus, which is the process of *sanctification.*

sanctuary

A holy place; a place where God is worshiped. In the Bible, *sanctuary* usually refers to the Tabernacle or to the Temple.

Sanhedrin (san-HEE-drun)

The highest Jewish political and religious court. In New Testament times, the *Sanhedrin* was made up of 71 men who were experts in Jewish laws. The *Sanhedrin* included the high priest, members of wealthy or prominent Jewish families and members of the Pharisee and Sadducee religious groups.

Satan

The most powerful enemy of God and all people. Other names for *Satan* include the devil, the evil one, the prince of this world, the father of lies, the enemy, the adversary, Lucifer. *Satan* is the ruler of a kingdom made up of demons. He hates God and tries to destroy God's work. The Bible tells us that in the end, God will destroy *Satan* and the demons.

Savior

A word that means "he who saves." The Old Testament almost always speaks of God as the *Savior* of His people. Sometimes God sent someone to help His people, and that person was called a *savior.* In the New Testament, *Savior* refers to Jesus. He died and rose again to rescue or save us from our sin.

scepter (SEP-tur)

A short rod held by a king or queen to show that he or she was the person who had the most authority and power.

scorpion

A small animal, something like a spider. It has a long tail with a poisonous stinger on the end. Its sting can kill a small animal and is very painful to humans.

scribe

1. An expert in understanding the Jewish law. Scribes taught the people God's laws. They also copied the Old Testament writings onto scrolls. Ezra was a *scribe*. By New Testament times, the *scribes* often served as judges in Jewish courts because they knew so much about the law. 2. A writer or secretary who earned his living writing letters or important papers for other people.

Scripture

The Bible. Before the New Testament was written down, *Scripture* meant the Old Testament. After the New Testament was written down, Christians began calling both the Old and New Testaments *Scripture*. The word *Scripture* means "writing."

scroll

A long strip of papyrus or parchment that has writing on it. A stick was attached to each end of the strip so that it could be rolled up to make it easier to read, store and carry.

seal

A small tool or ring that had a design cut into one side. The owner of each seal had his or her own special design. When the owner wanted to put his or her own special mark or brand on something, the person would press the seal into hot wax or soft clay. As the wax or clay hardened, it kept the design in it. Seals were used in many ways. Some of them were to show that two people had reached an agreement, to seal a letter, to show who owned something. Also called a signet.

Second Coming

The promised return of Jesus Christ to rule the earth at the end of this present age.

seer (SEE-uhr)

A prophet; a person who, with God's help, could see what would happen in the future. (See **prophet**)

Semite

Descendants of Shem, one of Noah's three sons. The term also refers to people who know languages belonging to the "Semitic Family" of languages. In ancient times the Semites included the Canaanites, Hebrews, Arabs, Assyrians, Babylonians, Arameans (Syrians) and Ethiopians.

sensual (SEN-shoo-uhl)

1. Appealing to the body's senses. 2. Caring too much for physical pleasures.

seraph, seraphim

Heavenly beings, mentioned only in Isaiah's vision of God (Isaiah 6). *Seraphim* are evidently similar to, or possibly the same as, the cherubim mentioned elsewhere in the Bible.

servant

A person who works for the comfort or protection of others. Jesus said He is a servant. He instructed His followers to be servants to each other instead of trying to have authority over each other. In the Bible, the word *servant* sometimes means slave.

sexual immorality

To use *sex* in ways that God says are wrong; *sexual* union between two people who are not married to each other is a sin.

sheaf, sheaves

A bundle or bundles of cut grain stalks.

Shechem (SHEEK-um)

An area and a city, west of the Jordan river, near Samaria. It is mentioned frequently in the Old Testament, and Jereboam made it the first capital of Israel when the Northern Kingdom split from Judah in the south.

sheep pen, sheepfold

A protected place for sheep to stay.

shekel (SHEK-uhl)

A small weight of silver or gold that was used as money.

shepherd

A person who took care of sheep. *Shepherds* found grass and water for their sheep, protected them from bad weather and wild animals, brought them safely into a sheepfold at night, and cared for sick or hurt sheep.

Shiloh

A town in the hill country west of the Jordan river, between Bethel and Shechem. For about 400 years, from the time of Joshua until the building of Solomon's Temple, Shiloh was home to the Tabernacle. However, when the ark of the covenant was captured by the Philistines in the days of Samuel, Shiloh gradually faded in importance.

sickle

A tool having a sharp curved blade that is attached to a short handle. A *sickle* is used to cut stalks of grain.

siege (seej)

Surrounding a city or town by an army so that nothing can go in or out. The purpose of a *siege* is to make the city or town surrender.

signet

See **seal**.

sin

Any act or thought that is against the way God wants us to act or think. The Bible says that all people have *sinned*. *Sin* separates us from God. God sent Jesus to die to take the punishment for *sin*. Because Jesus died, our *sins* can be forgiven and the separation between God and us can be removed.

Sinai (SIE-nie)

A desert peninsula between Israel and Egypt at the northern tip of the Red Sea; also a mountain on the peninsula where Moses received the Ten Commandments. Thus, Sinai is also used in reference to the Old Testament's covenant of law.

slander

To say untrue things about a person in order to hurt his or her reputation. The Bible says that *slander* is sin.

slave

A servant who is owned by his or her master and could be bought or sold like property. People became *slaves* if they were defeated in battle by an enemy or if they were unable to pay their debts. A *slave* had to do whatever the master ordered.

Sodom (SOD-um)

A city near the Dead Sea in the time of Abraham. Fire from heaven destroyed Sodom along with its neighbor, Gomorrah, because of its great wickedness.

Son of Man

A name for Jesus. Jesus called Himself the *Son of Man* many times. The name means that Jesus is a real man and that He is the One God promised to send in Daniel 7:13. *Son of Man* is also the title by which God called the prophet Ezekiel.

soothsayer

A person who said he or she could tell what would happen in the future—a fortune-teller. Both the Old and New Testaments say that *soothsaying* is wrong.

sorcerer

A person who claimed to be able to make spirits work for him or her. The Bible says that *sorcery* is a sin.

soul

In the Bible, the word *soul* usually refers to the part of a person that cannot be seen, but controls what a person thinks, feels and does. Sometimes *soul* means the whole living person. The words *soul* and "spirit" can mean about the same thing, but sometimes are distinguished from one another.

Southern Kingdom

Refers to the kingdom of Judah after Jereboam led the northern tribes to rebel against Rehoboam and form the Northern Kingdom of Israel. For more than two centuries, until the destruction of Israel by the Assyrians, the two kingdoms were contentious neighbors. The longer existence of Judah is attributed to the occasional godly kings who led the people in spiritual reforms.

sovereign

Having authority and power over everything. God is *sovereign*.

sow

To plant seeds. In Bible times, a farmer *sowed* seeds by scattering them by hand over a plowed field.

spirit

The unseen part of a person that controls what he or she thinks, feels and does; soul. The Bible says that God is a spirit, showing that He does not have a physical body. (See **soul**)

staff

1. A strong stick used for support when walking or climbing. 2. A strong wooden rod that has a hook on the end used by a shepherd as he cared for sheep.

statute

A law or command. In the Bible, *statutes* usually refers to God's laws.

stiff-necked

Stubborn, rebellious and unwilling to learn.

stone

To throw large stones and rocks at a person until he or she is dead. *Stoning* was the way people were punished for disobeying certain parts of the Jewish law. Stephen was *stoned* for teaching that Jesus is God's Son (see Acts 7).

submission

To choose to work with or to obey another person in a thoughtful, gentle way. The Bible says that Christians are to *submit* to each other in the same way Jesus *submitted* to God when Jesus came to earth.

Sumer (SOO-mur), **Sumerians**
The region and people of southern Mesopotamia, one of the oldest cultural centers in the ancient Middle East. Ur, one of the major cities of Sumer, was the original home of Abraham.

synagogue
A place where Jews meet together to read and study the Old Testament and to worship God.

Syria
The region directly north of Israel, called Aram in the Hebrew Bible and some modern English translations. The name *Syria* was not widely used until after Alexander the Great.

Tabernacle
The portable tent where the Israelites worshiped God. They used it while they wandered in the desert after they left Egypt and for many years after they entered the Promised Land. Moses and the people built the Tabernacle by following God's instructions. The *Tabernacle* was used until it was replaced by a permanent place of worship called the Temple. The *Tabernacle* is described in detail in Exodus 26.

table
The Tabernacle and Temple were furnished with a golden *table* on which twelve loaves of bread, one for each tribe of Israel, were placed each week, symbolizing the presence of God among His people.

talent
A large amount of silver or gold worth a huge amount of money. One *talent* was considered to be the amount of money a working man would earn in about ten years.

Temple
The permanent place in Jerusalem where the Jews worshiped God. The first *Temple* was built by King Solomon and the people by following the instructions God had given Solomon's father, King David. The *Temple* was a very beautiful place. It was destroyed and rebuilt twice. In A.D. 64, the *Temple* was destroyed again. It has not been rebuilt.

tempt
In the Bible, the word *tempt* has two meanings: 1. To test a person to improve his or her spiritual strength. 2. To try to get someone to do something wrong.

testament
An agreement, covenant. The 39 books of the Hebrew Bible are called the Old *Testament*, referring to God's original covenant of law. The 27 books of the New *Testament* present the covenant of grace that came through Jesus Christ.

testimony
In the Bible, *testimony* has more than one meaning: 1. In the Old Testament, it often refers to the Law of God. 2. In the New Testament, *testimony* usually means giving proof that something is true.

tetrarch (TET-rarck)
When a country in the Roman Empire was divided into sections, the head of each part was called a *tetrarch*. In the New Testament, Herod Antipas is sometimes called a *tetrarch* and sometimes a king. He was the ruler of Galilee in the time of Jesus.

threshing floor
The place where grain was trampled by oxen or beaten with a stick to separate the heads of grain from the stalk. A *threshing floor* was usually a large, flat rack or a large area of clay that was packed hard. *Threshing floors* were usually built where wind would blow away the chaff and leave the heavier grain. (See **winnow**)

Tishbite
A person, such as Elijah, from Tishbe, a town somewhere in Gilead, the West Bank region, between the Jordan River and the desert.

tithe
To give God one-tenth of what you earn. For example, if you had ten dimes, you would *tithe* by giving one dime to God.

tomb
A place where dead people were buried. In Bible times, *tombs* were often natural caves or caves dug into stone cliffs.

tongues
Languages. The New Testament records miraculous speaking in *tongues*, indicating the Holy Spirit enabling believers to speak in languages they had never learned.

trance
In the Bible, a *trance* is the deep, dreamlike state in which a person received a message from God. Peter was in a *trance* when God showed him the vision of the animals in a sheet (see Acts 10:10).

transfigured
To have been changed in appearance or form. The Bible tells us that Jesus' physical appearance

was changed—*transfigured*—as three of His disciples watched. His face glowed and his clothes became shining white. Moses and Elijah appeared and Jesus talked with them about His coming death.

transgression

A sin; disobeying the law of God.

treaty

A formal agreement between people, or groups or countries.

trespass

To go against the rights of someone else. We *trespass* against people when we do something unfair to them or when we break laws made to protect people. We *trespass* against God when we break His laws. In the Bible, another word for *trespass* is "sin."

tribe

The twelve tribes (clans, families) of Israel. Each of the tribes was descended from one of the twelve sons of Jacob. The descendants of Levi were assigned the honor of caring for the Tabernacle and were not given a territory as were the other eleven tribes. (They were given 48 townsites in which to live.) The descendants of Joseph were divided into two "half tribes," Manasseh and Ephraim, Joseph's two sons.

tribulation

Trouble, affliction, sometimes as punishment for wrongdoing. The *Great Tribulation* refers to a period of extraordinary, worldwide suffering when the anti-Christ is allowed temporary control of human affairs.

tribute

In the Bible, *tribute* usually means money or services a weaker nation was made to pay to a stronger nation.

trumpet

A straight tube that was bell shaped at one end. *Trumpets* were played at every Temple service. (Also see **trumpet of rams' horns**)

trumpet of rams' horns

A curved ram's horn, blown as a signal. *Trumpets of rams' horns* were used in religious ceremonies and in battle.

tunic

A loose shirt reaching to the knees. A *tunic* was usually worn as an undergarment.

turban

A head covering made by twisting cloth and wrapping it around the head.

unclean

Unclean does not mean dirty. It means any action, thought, food, person or place God had said is displeasing to Him. One of the ways a Jewish person could become *unclean* was by eating food God had said not to eat. Other ways a person could become *unclean* were by touching a dead body or by getting a skin disease called leprosy. A person could become clean again by going through certain ceremonies.

unleavened bread

Bread made without yeast. *Unleavened bread* is usually flat, like a pancake or cracker.

Ur of the Chaldees

A major cultural and commercial city in ancient Mesopotamia. Ur was the original home of Abraham.

vengeance

Punishment for wrongdoing. In the Old Testament, a person was told exactly how much he or she could do to punish someone for a wrong he or she had done. But the New Testament tells people not to punish those who have wronged them. Instead, they are told to trust God to take care of the punishment because He is the only one who is completely fair and just.

vile

Disgusting or evil.

violate

1. To break the law. 2. To force someone to have sex; to rape. 3. To make something unholy.

viper

A poisonous snake.

virgin

A person who has never had sexual intercourse.

vision

A *vision* was a way God showed someone a truth that would otherwise not be known. God used *visions* to show a message of truth in pictures. Sometimes people were asleep when God gave them *visions* (see Ezekiel 8:1-4 and Acts 10:9-29).

vow

A promise made to God.

wail

A long, loud cry to show sorrow.

widow

A woman whose husband has died.

wilderness

A large area of land where few people lived.

Depending on the amount of rainfall, the land might be a barren desert or it might grow grass and other vegetation on which sheep and other herds of animals could graze.

will

Purpose, intention, plan.

wineskin

A bag made from an animal skin. Wine, milk, water and grape juice were stored in *wineskins.*

winnow

To separate the kernels of grain from the worthless husks removed from the grain. This was done by tossing the grain into the air during a strong breeze. The breeze would blow away the light husks and the heavier kernels of grain would fall to the ground.

wisdom

Knowledge, understanding, applying knowledge and insights to life situations. *Wisdom* in the Bible usually refers to a God-given ability, rather than human common sense.

witness

1. In the Bible, a *witness* was a person who told what he or she had seen. 2. To tell others what you have seen. Jesus told His followers to be *witnesses.* We are to tell what we have seen Jesus Christ do in our own lives.

woe

Misery, sorrow or great suffering.

womb

The part of a woman's body where a baby grows until it is born.

wonder

A miracle. A thing or event that causes surprise and awe. God did many *wonders* to convince Pharaoh to let the Israelites leave Egypt.

works

Actions, deeds. Although the Bible encourages us to do good *works,* it clearly teaches that no *works* can earn enough merit to secure salvation.

world

1. The planet Earth. 2. People who follow Satan. 3. Anything that belongs to life on earth instead of eternal life with God.

worldly

Attached and attracted to values and commitments that go against God rather than being attracted to the values and commitments of the eternal kingdom of God. The Bible warns against loving the things of the *world* more than the things of God.

worship

Anything a person does to show love and respect. Some people worship idols. Some people worship the one true God.

wrath

Very great anger.

Yahweh

An English equivalent of the Hebrew word for God; also translated "Jehovah."

yoke

1. A wooden bar that goes over the necks of two animals, usually oxen. The *yoke* holds the animals together when they are pulling something such as a cart or plow. 2. Two oxen *yoked* together. 3. The word *yoke* is sometimes used as a word picture for any burden or demand. Slavery, imprisonment, taxes or unfair laws were called *yokes.* 4. A partnership.

Zealot (Zel-ut)

A member of a Jewish group in the time of Jesus who wanted to fight against and overthrow the Roman rulers in Judea. Jesus' disciple Simon (not Peter) was a Zealot.

Zion (Zie-un)

Zion has several meanings: 1. One of the hills upon which the city of Jerusalem was built was called Mount *Zion.* 2. The entire city of Jerusalem was sometimes called *Zion.* 3. *Zion* is another name for the nation of Israel. 4. *Zion* is another name for heaven.

Appendix 4

Maps

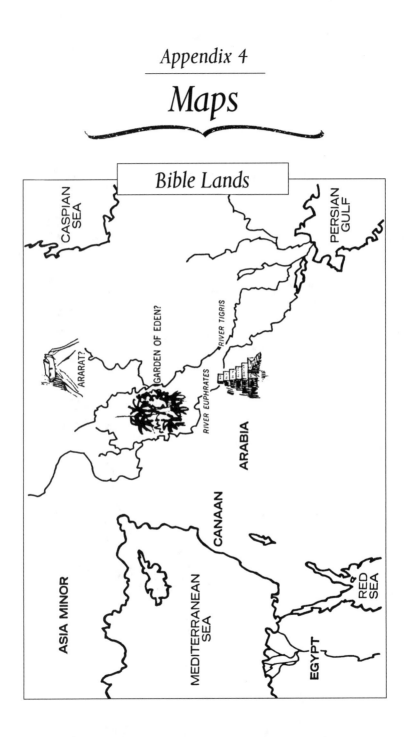

Bible Lands

CASPIAN SEA

PERSIAN GULF

GARDEN OF EDEN?

RIVER TIGRIS

ARARAT?

RIVER EUPHRATES

ARABIA

CANAAN

ASIA MINOR

MEDITERRANEAN SEA

RED SEA

EGYPT

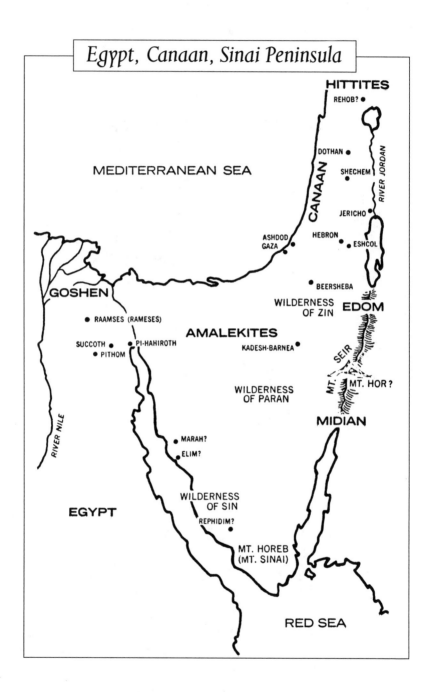

Egypt, Canaan, Sinai Peninsula

HITTITES

REHOB? ●

MEDITERRANEAN SEA

DOTHAN ●

SHECHEM ●

CANAAN

RIVER JORDAN

JERICHO ●

ASHDOD
GAZA ●

HEBRON ●

ESHCOL ●

GOSHEN

BEERSHEBA ●

WILDERNESS
OF ZIN

EDOM

RAAMSES (RAMESES) ●

AMALEKITES

SUCCOTH ●
● PITHOM

● PI-HAHIROTH

KADESH-BARNEA ●

SEIR

MT. ● MT. HOR?

WILDERNESS
OF PARAN

MIDIAN

RIVER NILE

MARAH? ●

ELIM? ●

WILDERNESS
OF SIN

EGYPT

REPHIDIM? ●

MT. HOREB
(MT. SINAI)

RED SEA

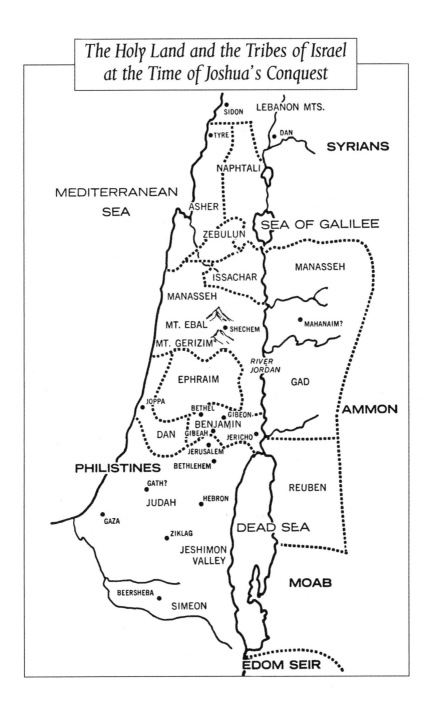

The Holy Land and the Tribes of Israel at the Time of Joshua's Conquest

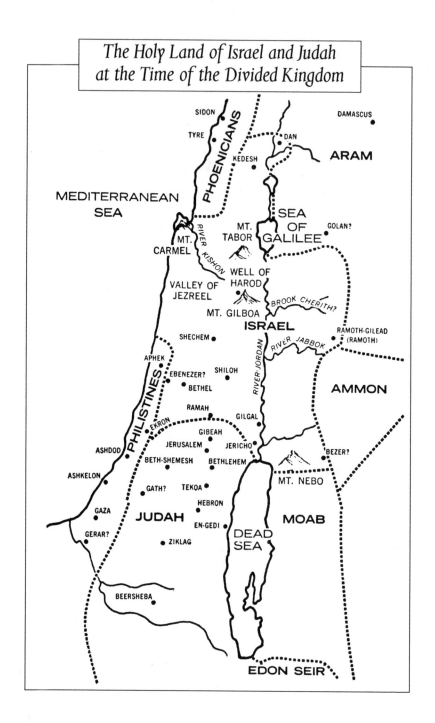

The Holy Land of Israel and Judah at the Time of the Divided Kingdom

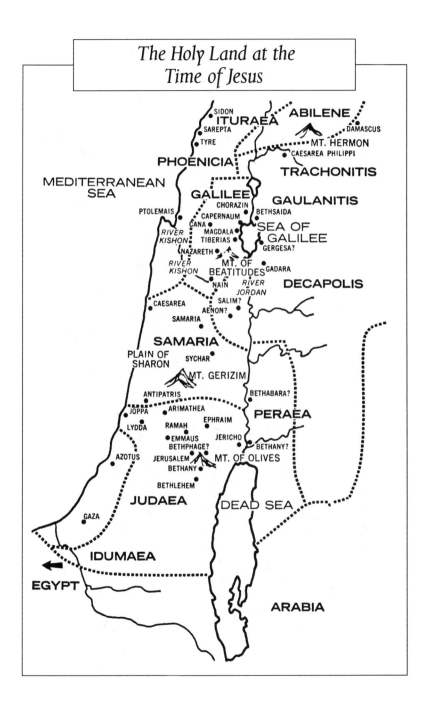

The Holy Land at the Time of Jesus

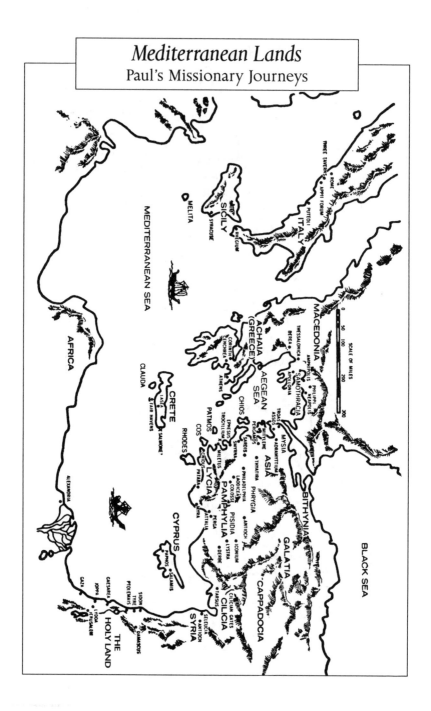

Bible Reading Plans—One Year

ONE-YEAR PLAN
O.T. Books of Law and History

By the end of	Read Through	No. Pgs.
1st mo. ⎯	Genesis 37	⎯
2nd mo. ⎯	Exodus 25	⎯
3rd mo. ⎯	Leviticus 23	⎯
4th mo. ⎯	Numbers 28	⎯
5th mo. ⎯	Deuteronomy 30	⎯
6th mo. ⎯	Judges 8	⎯
7th mo. ⎯	1 Samuel 21	⎯
8th mo. ⎯	1 Kings 2	⎯
9th mo. ⎯	2 Kings 10	⎯
10th mo. ⎯	1 Chronicles 17	⎯
11th mo. ⎯	2 Chronicles 31	⎯
12th mo. ⎯	Esther 10	⎯

ONE-YEAR PLAN
O.T. Books of Poetry and Prophecy

By the end of	Read Through	No. Pgs.
1st mo. ⎯	Job 41	⎯
2nd mo. ⎯	Psalm 62	⎯
3rd mo. ⎯	Psalm 117	⎯
4th mo. ⎯	Proverbs 18	⎯
5th mo. ⎯	Isaiah 8	⎯
6th mo. ⎯	Isaiah 43	⎯
7th mo. ⎯	Jeremiah 6	⎯
8th mo. ⎯	Jeremiah 38	⎯
9th mo. ⎯	Ezekiel 15	⎯
10th mo. ⎯	Ezekiel 45	⎯
11th mo. ⎯	Amos 6	⎯
12th mo. ⎯	Malachi 4	⎯

ONE-YEAR PLAN
New Testament Books

By the end of	Read Through	No. Pgs.
1st mo. ⎯	Matthew 20	⎯
2nd mo. ⎯	Mark 8	⎯
3rd mo. ⎯	Luke 6	⎯
4th mo. ⎯	Luke 23	⎯
5th mo. ⎯	John 13	⎯
6th mo. ⎯	Acts 11	⎯
7th mo. ⎯	Romans 1	⎯
8th mo. ⎯	1 Corinthians 11	⎯
9th mo. ⎯	Ephesians 6	⎯
10th mo. ⎯	Philemon	⎯
11th mo. ⎯	2 Peter 3	⎯
12th mo. ⎯	Revelation 22	⎯

Bible Reading Plans—Two Year

TWO-YEAR PLAN
New Testament Books

By the end of	Read Through	No. Pgs.
1st mo.	Matthew 11	
2nd mo.	Matthew 20	
3rd mo.	Matthew 27	
4th mo.	Mark 8	
5th mo.	Mark 16	
6th mo.	Luke 6	
7th mo.	Luke 13	
8th mo.	Luke 23	
9th mo.	John 6	
10th mo.	John 13	
11th mo.	Acts 2	
12th mo.	Acts 11	
13th mo.	Acts 20	
14th mo.	Romans 1	
15th mo.	Romans 14	
16th mo.	1 Corinthians 11	
17th mo.	2 Corinthians 10	
18th mo.	Ephesians 6	
19th mo.	1 Thessalonians 5	
20th mo.	Philemon	
21st mo.	Hebrews 13	
22nd mo.	2 Peter 3	
23rd mo.	Revelation 8	
24th mo.	Revelation 22	

TWO-YEAR PLAN
O.T. Books of Poetry and Prophecy

By the end of	Read Through	No. Pgs.
1st mo.	Job 20	
2nd mo.	Job 41	
3rd mo.	Psalm 33	
4th mo.	Psalm 62	
5th mo.	Psalm 88	
6th mo.	Psalm 117	
7th mo.	Psalm 150	
8th mo.	Proverbs 18	
9th mo.	Ecclesiastes 7	
10th mo.	Isaiah 8	
11th mo.	Isaiah 27	
12th mo.	Isaiah 43	
13th mo.	Isaiah 59	
14th mo.	Jeremiah 6	
15th mo.	Jeremiah 23	
16th mo.	Jeremiah 38	
17th mo.	Jeremiah 52	
18th mo.	Ezekiel 15	
19th mo.	Ezekiel 29	
20th mo.	Ezekiel 45	
21st mo.	Daniel 12	
22nd mo.	Amos 6	
23rd mo.	Habakkuk 2	
24th mo.	Malachi 4	

TWO-YEAR PLAN
O.T. Books of Law and History

By the end of	Read Through	No. Pgs.
1st mo.	Genesis 21	
2nd mo.	Genesis 37	
3rd mo.	Exodus 6	
4th mo.	Exodus 25	
5th mo.	Leviticus 5	
6th mo.	Leviticus 23	
7th mo.	Numbers 11	
8th mo.	Numbers 28	
9th mo.	Deuteronomy 9	
10th mo.	Deuteronomy 30	
11th mo.	Joshua 14	
12th mo.	Judges 8	
13th mo.	1 Samuel 2	
14th mo.	1 Samuel 21	
15th mo.	2 Samuel 12	
16th mo.	1 Kings 2	
17th mo.	1 Kings 16	
18th mo.	2 Kings 10	
19th mo.	1 Chronicles 1	
20th mo.	1 Chronicles 17	
21st mo.	2 Chronicles 8	
22nd mo.	2 Chronicles 31	
23rd mo.	Nehemiah 3	
24th mo.	Esther 10	

Answers to Biblical Questions
for Everyone in Your Life

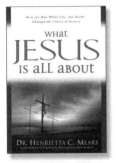

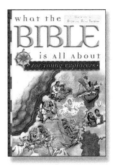
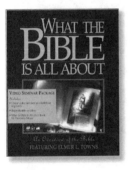
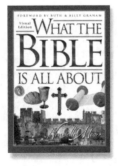
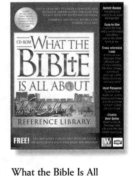

Gospel Light Is
God's Word for a Kid's World

At Gospel Light, we remember what it's like to see the world through a child's eyes. That's why our Sunday School curriculum is designed to **reach kids right where they are**. We help them learn about God and His Word through **hands-on activities** that engage their intense curiosity and openness to learning new things.

For **over 70 years**—since Dr. Henrietta Mears wrote the first lesson in 1933—Gospel Light has equipped teachers with the best tools for reaching children with God's love.

Find out for yourself why Gospel Light Sunday School curriculum is God's Word for a kid's world!

ISBN 08307.26578

Gospel Light
God's Word for a Kid's World!™

www.gospellight.com